Strategic Human
Management

...fore the last date shown below.

Strategic Human Resource Management

Christopher Mabey and
Graeme Salaman

BLACKWELL
Business

First published 1995
Reprinted 1996

Blackwell Publishers Ltd
108 Cowley Road
Oxford OX4 1JF
UK

Blackwell Publishers Inc.
238 Main Street
Cambridge, Massachusetts 02142
USA

British Library Cataloguing in Publication Data

A CIP catalogue record for this book is available from the British Library.

Library of Congress Cataloging-in-Pubication Data

Mabey, Christopher, 1951–
    Strategic human resource management / Christopher Mabey and Graeme Salaman.
        p.   cm.
    Includes bibliographical references and index.
    ISBN 0–631–18504–6 (hbk. : alk. paper). – ISBN 0–631–18505–4 (pbk. : alk. paper)
    1. Personnel management. 2. Industrial management. 3. Human capital. I. Salaman,
Graeme. II. Title.
HF5549.M215 1995
658.3–dc20   95-14674
                                                                                                      CIP

Commissioning Editor: Richard Burton
Desk Editor: Sarah McNamee/Cameron Laux
Production Controller: Pam Park
Text Designer: Pam Park

Typeset in 11 on 13pt Baskerville by Keyword Typesetting Services Ltd
Printed in Great Britain by T J Press Ltd, Padstow, Cornwall.

This book is printed on acid-free paper.

Contents

List of figures

List of tables

Preface

We wish to acknowledge, and express our gratitude to numerous colleagues who have been involved in the production of this text. While we must take responsibility for the final product, it has been significantly enriched by the work and contribution of a number of people. Most important of these is our colleague here at the Open University Business School, Greg Clark, who contributed chapter 4 to this volume; as well as Ed Rose and Paul Iles, both at Liverpool John Moores University, who contributed chapters 5 and 8 respectively.

We also wish to thank all those reviewers who commented on earlier drafts of these chapters, and whose comments have helped enormously in showing us how to hone the texts to ensure that they combine practical relevance with logical and conceptual rigour.

For the last few years the authors have been researching and teaching on HRS issues. Within the Open University, such work has the attraction and benefit of being a collective activity. Six years ago our interest in and knowledge of strategic approaches to HRM matters was initiated and developed within the context of a team of colleagues within the university. The result was an Open University Business School course for MBA students called 'Human Resource Strategies', since studied by more than 1,500 middle to senior managers in the UK and wider Europe. We wish now to record our debt to the collective work of the course team and to the lively and stimulating discussions that occurred during the genesis of this course. Our thanks for colleagueship and a community of shared interests, and for lively debate and critique, to: Sheila Cameron, Heather Hamblin, Eric Cassells, Andrew Thomson, Geoff Mallory, Tim Clark, Rosie Thomson, Carolyn Hooker, June Payne, Karen Legge, David Guest, Phil Beaumont, Chris Brewster, Peter Anthony, Paul Dobson, Paul Bate, Charles Bethnell-Fox, Arthur Francis, Angela Bowey, Bryn Jones, Roland Pearson, John Roberts, Mike Smith, John Storey, Paul Topham, Peter Fell, David Lloyd, Andrew Pettigrew, John Richards, Stephen Rick, Shaun Tyson, John Smith, Judith Walker.

The world needs 'completer-finishers' and since the authors of this volume probably have strengths elsewhere, we are indebted to Barbara Sinclair and Amanda Killick at the Open University Business School for their progress-chasing and secretarial stamina. Finally, our thanks to the Blackwell team, and to Richard Burton and Cameron Laux in particular.

Christopher Mabey
Graeme Salaman

Introduction

Over twenty years ago Cohen and March wrote: 'we do not believe that any major new cleverness that would conspicuously alter the prevailing limits in our ability to change the course of history (in organizational theory and practice) will be discovered.' Yet Argyris, who quotes this remark, points out that these same authors are prepared to concede that a major tenet of Western ideas is faith in the notion of choice – 'which assumes pre-existence of purpose, the necessity of consistency, and the primacy of rationality' (Argyris, 1976, p. 363) values which, if capable of being realized, would represent a major break from the inertia of history.

But is history changeable? Can those who manage organizations escape from the iron cage of their own intellectual, cultural and institutional limitations? Is recognizing the constraints of history, and a willingness to break free from these constraints, sufficient to initiate change? How much choice do we really have? How much choice are we prepared to exercise?

The Promise of HRS

These questions haunt this book, as they haunt the theory and practice of 'human resource strategies' (HRS). HRS – which is described at length in this volume, along with its antecedents and its implications, claims to offer ways out of the perennial characteristic dysfunctions of organizations – dysfunctions and limitations which are all too apparent to us as employees, consumers, citizens, shareholders, human beings. These are seductive promises, beguiling offers. They must be taken very seriously. But the magnitude of a promise should not discourage assessment of the likelihood of it being delivered.

Yet there is an increasing number of books and articles about HRS which, with titles including such expressions as myth, rhetoric and metaphor, focus on HRS as a sort of story, a fable about what might be done which is then contrasted with the realities of what is done – the realities of organization, of power, of market. These priorities and politics which lie behind HRS are disguised by the language of HRS but by being disguised, are also served by this language. This book reflects this concern with rhetoric and reality, and tries to describe both and to explain the discrepancies between them.

On the one hand nothing could be more reasonable than to seek to design an organization to ensure that it was capable of achieving the strategies designed for it. And few things could be more important, particularly at a time when the self-confidence of the West, and even of the once all-powerful USA, has been badly shaken by the extraordinary success of Japanese and more recently other south-east Asian economies and organizations. Hence the attractiveness of HRS; hence indeed its very existence. For at its simplest and best, HRS means (or offers) a powerful promise: the achievement of appropriate organizational capability.

However, as this book will demonstrate, while this dream is important enough to merit very serious attention indeed, we must not blind ourselves to some inherent problems that arise when designing and implementing organizational change. The best literature on HRS reflects this tension: excitement about the promise of HRS and HRS initiatives, coupled with concern about the limitations of HRS. The tension is also apparent in this volume. Indeed, tension represents its organizing principle.

We try to offer advice, to show how HRS change can be done and done well; we try to describe best practice, and if we don't recommend solutions at least we will map options. But we also take very seriously the need to warn – to warn against glib, superficial promises; and the ahistorical, atheoretical, uncritical nature of much HRS.

HRS is big business; it promises a great deal, and these promises are seductive. But while it is true that 'huge resources have been committed in the last four decades or so to managerial activities often designed by consultants, or academics with consulting aspirations, aimed at improving managerial effectiveness, all too often this has a transitory nature which seems to proceed from deep disillusionment with one panacea that has run its course to high enthusiasm for the next' (Gill and Whittle, 1992, p. 282). There is a noticeable and striking pattern apparent in the history of approaches to organization change and improvement: first, there is high enthusiasm, extravagant promises, followed by failure, deep disillusionment and rejection. And then silence, as if it had never happened. Until the next time; for oddly, despite the frequency of this pattern – this triumph of hope over experience – it doesn't seem to disturb or reduce enthusiasm for the next solution, the next panacea.

HRS places great emphasis on the capacity, indeed the possibility, of organizations learning about the environment, about their performance, their objectives, their capability; and in the light of this learning, to change, and to learn from the change, and so on. Capability in HRS is not simply capability to achieve a given strategy, important as this is; it is also, and primarily, capability to develop, and redevelop, strategy in the first place, and thus to design and oversee the necessary systemic change. But there may be a paradox here, one spotted long ago by Argyris: 'One might say that participants in organisations are encouraged to learn to perform as long as the learning does not question the fundamental design, goals and activities of their organisations . . . The . . . high degree of consonance between learning acculturation and the kind of limitations placed on learning within groups and organisations result in processes that limit exploration and information and so help provide stability but also inhibit learning in fundamental organisational issues' (Argyris, 1976, p. 367).

How far does HRS really intend what it often promises: an emphasis on valuing and developing the organization's 'human resources'; and how far does its focus on new structures, systems, cultures, mask a concern to retain certain fundamental priorities and values such as short-termism, and boardroom privilege?

Can we who need these HRS solutions, and who are disturbed by the failure of our organizations and the principles on which they are built (principles to which we are or have been committed), recognize the need for new principles of organization? Can we, who are part of the problem, escape the assumptions and habits we wish to reject? How can we think anew? Is HRS actually possible?

The Distinctiveness of this Text

These are not the only potential limitations to the possibility of HRS – there are many others, discussed within this volume. How far does HRS *really* question the basic (and possibly limiting and damaging) assumptions of senior, Western management? How far are the objectives actually pursued by HRS initiatives sensible and productive, in the long term? Is HRS essentially a guide to corporate cost-cutting, in another guise? Or does it really represent, at least potentially, a way out of the habits and mind-sets and values that very clearly are hampering the full flowering of organizational, and indeed national potential?

This book will steer a middle path between these extremes: we believe that there is a great deal that is exciting and interesting in HRS, and we will describe these developments and try to excite and enthuse you with the possibilities they offer. We also believe that HRS is important and powerful and therefore needs to be taken very seriously, and understood – and we will show how and why HRS is having such a dramatic effect on the way senior managers think and talk about, and act on, issues of organizational change. But we also believe that some features of HRS need serious and radical critical attention because they are based on unacceptable and flawed assumptions, they are contradictory and ill-considered; and these weaknesses too need airing. So the book is a mixture of description, analysis and critique; of excitement, moderation and concern. This is a difficult mixture, but we hope an interesting and stimulating one, and we believe that to offer anything less than this would be to do the reader a disservice.

We also believe that this combination of elements makes this textbook distinctive. There are already books that offer critiques – but that is all they do. And there are many books that offer HRS recommendations and prescriptions; but that again is all they do. This book not only tries to do both, it tries to assess the implications of critique for prescription, and to draw out of an assessment of strengths and weaknesses some suggestions that are of use to the practitioner. We see our duty in this volume not simply to warn but also to be of real practical assistance to someone who needs advice on what to do and how to do it.

There is another distinctive strength of this volume: its origins in an MBA programme for mature students of management. A consequence of this provenance is that the book is designed not simply as an adjunct to teaching – although we think that it will play this role admirably – but as the centrepiece of a course on HRS. To support the book in playing this role, we have added learning objectives, key point summaries, discussion questions and so on, as you will see. And those who use this volume as a basis for teaching will have access to a tutor's guide which will offer some suggestions for the structure and content of teaching activities and inputs based on the book. Another major benefit, we feel, is that these materials and this book's structure have been developed over a number of years in the course of teaching and research, and endless discussions between the authors, colleagues and students. As teaching materials, at least, they have been developed through and from experience – sometimes painfully.

The book not only contains a variety of approaches and angles (descriptive, analytic, evaluative); it also contains a mixture of levels of analysis and presentation. We believe that a major and proper purpose of a book like this is to describe what is happening and to describe the literature that is known as HRS, and its constituent debates and themes: training, performance, culture, the learning organization, and so on. So one objective of the book is to map the field.

But another purpose is to identify, to make explicit and to engage with the theory underpinning HRS. Very frequently this theory is implicit and submerged. We will try to bring it to the surface. If we are to assess the value of an argument or prescription it is crucial to know and assess the theoretical underpinnings on which it is based. This is one major way in which we may escape the sad cycle, mentioned earlier, of fashionable panacea being greeted with (unjustified) rapture and being followed by disappointment and rejection. Theory is important in any attempt to think about or plan organizational change, for such activities are inevitably based on theoretical assumptions about what organizations are, how they work, and how they can be changed.

When characterized stereotypically it is not difficult to establish qualitative differences between personnel management and human resource strategies (see for instance Guest, 1987; Storey, 1992). But, as these authors point out, this is not comparing like with like. Rather it is distinguishing personnel management practice from the normative ideals of human resource management gleaned primarily from the 'excellence' literature. One of the themes of this book is *choice* between human resource strategies: the selection of appropriate cultural, structural and behavioural strategies to redress organizational inertia and facilitate competitive success, and chapter 1 examines the nature of these contingencies by differentiating open and closed approaches to HRS.

By tracing some of the historical antecedents to the HRS approach and resisting the notion of a standard set of pre-packaged human resource strategy solutions, we attempt to distil the conceptual and practical essence of HRS. At a planning level human resource policies will be integrated with the strategic objectives of an organization. Human resources will be viewed as vital to the achievement of these objectives, so investments will be made in the appropriate knowledge, competences and attitudes of the workforce. The psychological contract between employer and employee is thus based on commitment rather than on compliance. There will be a coherence between the various human resource policies and practices chosen to bring about this commitment, with a heavy reliance on the involvement of the line manager and his or her ownership of the process. Typical hallmarks would be devolved responsibility and decision-making, and flexibility leading to organizational adaptability. Nevertheless, while such attractive features of HRS can be described in some detail, they remain normative and over-simplified.

Firstly, such descriptions tend to assume a reasonably rational conception and implementation of the organization's overall strategy; that this can be readily interpreted without distortion or political connivance; that suitable HR interventions can be found to 'fit' the strategy; that a 'package' of HR strategies can be pursued without internal contradiction, and that varying interest groups within the organization will subscribe implicitly to the goals and values advocated. Secondly, such descriptions seem to imply that – given its 'self-evident' benefits – there is widespread adoption of strategic HR policy and practice. But what indication is there that organizations are implementing human resource strategies? Focusing on large, diversified, multi-national companies in Britain, Purcell (1989) points to the structural and attitudinal constraints put on the development of integrated human resource initiatives. He argues that the pressure of 'second-order' strategies on unit managers to achieve short-run rates of return on investment and to maintain improvements to profit margins inhibits any attempt to build long-term, socially responsible human resource policies.

Looking further afield, cross-national research (Brewster et al., 1991) seems to indicate a slow and undramatic uptake of human resource strategies in the companies they surveyed in ten European countries. Despite this pessimistic picture case studies and case extracts are cited which suggest that organizations are at least attempting to reorientate their human resource planning processes and to choose human resource policies in a strategic manner in an effort to achieve the organizational outcomes they promise. And this brings us to the final and perhaps clinching set of questions. When organizations endeavour to manage their human resources strategically in this way, are they then successful? Do they perform better than those who do not? Do the benefits of adopting human resource strategies outweigh their inherent costs? Having critically assessed the theory and the practice, the claims and the reality, the cogency and the contradictions of HRS, we leave it to subsequent chapters to take up the crucial questions raised by this opening chapter.

Managing Change, Development and Performance

The first area we turn to is that of Managing Change (chapter 2), partly because most HRS initiatives imply significant systemic change within – and sometimes beyond – the boundaries of an organization, and partly because focusing on the process of policy-formulation, decision-making, influencing and negotiation of outcomes provides an appropriate context for the analysis in subsequent chapters. Of course, change is endemic to even the most stable and traditional of industries. The question is, to what extent can the opportunities which arise and the conflicts of change be managed in a purposeful manner? Incremental change is constant but largely calculable and undisruptive. However, change associated with HRS is typically transitional and in some cases transformational for the company concerned. People at all levels and with as many agendas are involved, the resources required are less determinate, the repercussions less easy to control, and the outcomes – possibly many months, even years hence – almost impossible to predict with any kind of precision. In these circumstances, how can HR interventions be meaningfully planned, how can support be won from those holding the budget, and how can the fine line between organizational control and individual creativity be maintained? Some of the options are discussed. Whether to cultivate the change process through grass-roots support, via a successful pilot project nurtured quietly but credibly in some corner of the organization, or whether to rely on a top-down 'cascade'; whether to use the HRS to primarily target skills and behaviours, or the way jobs are configured, and the way roles and responsibilities are assigned, or – most ambitious of all – to attempt to shift the cultural centre of gravity in the organization. Each implies a very different mix of HR measures, some more broad in their scope and desired effects than others. Other choices concern the style of the change management process (indeed some would argue that this 'gameplan' is almost as important as the content of the HR package itself), the degree to which broad ownership of the HR schemes is sought prior to their implementation (which is frequently dictated by commercial urgency and/or top-team predisposition), and the type of change agency called upon to steer the HRS through the organization. The chapter considers organization development as one approach to managing change but draws upon other models too, noting that in crisis and turnaround situations, relatively 'aggressive' actions and symbols are often employed to break the mould and discredit past, cherished paradigms, to be followed by more participative initiatives that rely on trust and loyalty! This brings us to the dissonant gap between the intention and the perception of given change scenarios. Here we note that all sorts of factors – psychological, institutional, idealogical, structural, occupational – will lead to divergent interpretations of the motives, appropriateness and ultimate usefulness of the change process as it is experienced and observed. Some of this is manageable, but much is not.

Training has always been a favoured human resource response to individual and organizational performance issues, and is an essential, arguably a central, tool of strategic HR which we examine in chapter 3. Certainly, the way development activities are conducted and co-ordinated is a telling index of how an organization views and values its staff: as commodities to be maximized at minimum cost, at one extreme, to resources to be developed to potential, at the other. The chapter takes the rational model of training provision to address skill performance gaps as its starting point. For instance, it is suggested that successful training is grounded in a careful diagnosis of not just present but future strategic requirements which takes account of the current and projected skills which are trainable within the company and/or available in the external labour market. We examine the assumptions frequently made by HR and line managers about what different types of training can realistically achieve and suggest a model which facilitates an informed match between the learning theories which underlie different training methods and the developmental activities chosen to address them. This focus on individual learning is broadened to encompass cultural and infrastructural factors which can either obstruct or reinforce the internalization of new ideas, attitudes and ways of working. Again, training and development activities that are mutually supported by other HR policies and that can be seen to integrate vertically with the overall organizational objectives are more likely to be seen as successful than those which are *ad hoc*, fragmented and unhinged from the performance reviews, target setting and reward strategies of the organization. However, the chapter also questions the undeniable logic of such propositions, noting that the aims, design, delivery and evaluation of training and development is very much contested territory in organizations, with clients, sponsors, providers and participants in training each having their own stakes and agendas in the training process. Many of these issues are taken up in the later chapter on learning organizations.

To pick out performance management in order to examine its particular role in HRS – as we do in chapter 4 – is arguably unnecessary. After all, managing performance is an intrinsic ingredient in all human resource strategies. Indeed, the very notion of firstly segmenting activities such as formal performance review, appraisal, staff development, team building and reward strategies from each other, and secondly, isolating them from the all-pervasive, ongoing aspects of the management role is indicative of piecemeal personnel practice rather than inherent human resource strategy. However, it is because performance management is such an essential thread running through so many other strategically oriented HR activities that we believe it deserves special attention. There are assumptions underlying the way performance is managed in organizations that unless surfaced and tested may introduce incipient weakness into every other HR policy and practice.

The conventional textbook view of performance management sees it as a strategy for enhancing individual, team and organizational performance through an agreed framework of goals, objectives and standards. It attempts to incorporate and integrate performance appraisal, coaching, counselling, rewards and recognition; and this is achieved by focusing on the setting of goals, their measurement, feedback on performance, and recognition of high performance in order to add value and enhance both current and future organizational performance. In order to test the adequacy and appropriateness of this approach, we assess the practical value of one particular performance management model that has widespread – though usually tacit – currency in organizations today: expectancy theory. While the internal logic of the theory has much to commend it, some of the more rational and deterministic premises on which it is based are questioned, particularly in the context of implementing human resource strategies. By way of pursuing these questions, we focus on one aspect of performance management currently characteristic of HRS in public and private sectors alike, namely, performance-related pay (PRP). We ask to what extent PRP is a genuinely new approach to enhancing commitment and output, how successful it is in aligning personal performance with corporate objectives, and the degree to which this potentially divisive motivational device is compatible with other HR strategies adopted by a specific organization, and with the emancipatory claims of 'soft' HRS generally.

Industrial Relations

Chapter 5 assesses the vexed question of whether strategic HRM heralds a 'new' era of industrial and work-place relations. Traditionally, industrial relations in the UK specifically, and the West generally, has been characterized by collective representation of employees, inspired by solidaristic ideologies, fuelled by class divisions, orchestrated/supported by national agreements and focused upon rule-making and procedural arrangements at plant level. In such an environment the aspirations of HRS would seem to have little chance of realization. However, as the chapter carefully documents, political, legislative and attitudinal changes through the 1980s and 1990s have led to a radically different industrial context. The rapid erosion of the West's traditional manufacturing base, the eclipse of class politics, the decline of the manual, core working class due to the de-industrialization of Western economies, the reduction in the number of employees affected by collective bargaining and the decentralization of pay determination are among the socio-political factors discussed as giving rise to a sea-change in IR. Taken together with the growing evidence of individualistic employment relationships, non-unionized greenfield sites or perhaps single union representation, and an espousal – on the part of senior management impressed by the Japanese model – of co-operation rather than conflict, the convergence of the new style IR and HRS looks to be both possible and opportune. Drawing upon surveys and case studies of what is actually happening rather than what might be prescribed, this potential compatibility and convergence is analysed. In particular, we examine whether HRS does or should incorporate new IR approaches, whether HRS fails to recognize or effectively bypasses unions, and whether HRS can in fact coexist with more collectivist values and practices.

Culture and Learning

A text on human resource strategy would not be complete without some analysis of the claims made that organizational culture has a determining influence on corporate performance and individual commitment. This is a view that gathered pace and appeal in the 1980s and continues unabated today. In chapter 6 we link the origins of this appeal to the 'excellence' approach which attributes organizational success and motivated staff to the cultivation of a 'strong' culture, and puts the responsibility for this largely in the hands of senior management, as leaders and role models of the organizations they run. We go on to explore the ideological, conceptual and empirical limitations of such a view, and the fact that the 'dark' side of high performance and commitment-generating cultures usually comprises instrumental goals, controlling norms and exploitative processes and procedures. Conceptually, the notion of a unified and malleable culture seriously underestimates the systemic conflict inherent in most organizations, the unequal power structures and the heterogeneity of employee groupings. It also seriously overestimates the capacity and wit of managers to influence differentiated cultures and subcultures in anything approaching a predetermined manner. This is not to say cultures cannot change, or be changed. However, caution needs to be exercised about the level of change that is being attempted and for whose ends. At a time when the devolving of decision-making to autonomous groups of employees and the empowering of staff are much in vogue as HR strategies, it is important to distinguish consensus from control, commitment from compliance, behavioural changes from attitudinal – or even value – change and the genuine migration of cultural norms from the superficial manipulation of meanings and symbols, mission statements and corporate logos.

In many ways chapter 7 is the reverse side of the earlier 'training and development strategies' coin. Rather than focusing on the way training activities are diagnosed, designed and delivered – albeit in a contested arena of competing objectives, incomplete understanding and scarce resources – this chapter asks how it is that some organizations, and the individuals within them, seem to learn faster and more astutely than others.

The importance of learning is linked to the current pressures for change facing most if not all organizations. Within a stable, unpressured environment, the need for organizational learning on a major scale is seen as unnecessary. In fact, of course, there were never stable, unpressured environments; just environments which were *perceived* as unthreatening, where organizations failed to detect the small signs of emerging change and threat, or reacted to them confidently in terms of established ways of doing things which required no change or replacement. In chapter 7 we argue that it is precisely the capacity of organizations to be so structured and organized that they are able to perceive accurately and to react appropriately to internal and external signals (*even when it seems to be unnecessary*) that facilitates organizational learning. But what is it that distinguishes this kind of natural, incremental and necessary learning from the so-called 'learning organization'? Part of the answer lies in the ability of all members of the organization to question established habits and methods, to think the unthought or unthinkable and to discuss the undiscussable. Challenging their own and others' assumptions in this way paves the way to double-loop, even triple-loop learning at times when not to take such creative leaps is commercially suicidal: here the object of enquiry is error in the learning process itself. Despite the evident virtue in this kind of approach, it is perhaps surprising to find so few firms getting beyond short-term problem-solving. In this chapter we explore why it is that development activities often fail to 'deliver' the knowledge, skills and attitudes intended, why the fruits of learning at an individual level – when this does occur – are so infrequently garnered corporately, and why it is that organizations have an inbuilt defensiveness against new insights. We also discuss the central paradox of whether learning can be managed. This is a key issue for strategic HRM, because by definition the term implies focused, integrated and organizationally productive outcomes, and yet learning theory tells us that learning is most likely to occur when unfettered from external controls and undistorted by interfering agendas. Once again, in our consideration of HRS, we find ourselves in ethical territory: learning is not a neutral, apolitical activity. Learning is constantly taking place, whether deliberately constructed and reflected upon or not. The motives may be enthusiastic but 'suspect', the outcomes may be valid but 'negative', the lessons may be real but 'mistakes', the applications may be well-intentioned but 'wrong'. It all depends, of course, on who is asking the questions, for what reason and the degree to which yardsticks of learning are consensually derived. In short, the learning organization is probably more to do with a shared culture than procedural contrivance.

International and Critical Perspectives on HRS

The field of international HRS is relatively immature. It is characterized by models which remain largely untested in practice, with broad perceptions based on the idiosyncrasies of one – or a few – specific case organizations, and with confusion often reigning as to the level of analysis under discussion: world system, international view, country/culture perspective or firm-level outlook. For all this, indeed because of these uncertainties, we include a chapter on international HRS in this volume. Undoubtedly it is a dimension of HRS which few organizations can afford to ignore legislatively, demographically, culturally and politically, even if – competitively – they do not inhabit a global or international market-place themselves. We consider the impact of the world system on, for example, the international division of labour, and we draw upon cross-cultural research to better understand the implications upon country-level HRS. However, for the most part, and consistent with the rest of this volume, we take an organizational perspective in order to analyse what might be learnt about recruiting, training, teamworking and rewarding across international boundaries, and how HRD initiatives might be used to heighten awareness of national diversity and optimize the advantages of employing an increasingly multicultural workforce.

While there is some evidence to suggest that organizations are achieving success in these areas, however, the effort and investment needed to support such strategic change – both structural and attitudinal – is high and not without instances of ethnocentric insensitivity.

Having made a detailed examination of several key ingredients of, and themes within, HRS (chapters 2–8), we return in the final chapter to a more searching analysis of the propositions that underlie the concept of strategic human resource management itself. Many of these issues were raised in chapter 1, others have become apparent in our discussion of specific HR strategies; collectively they comprise a set of highly pertinent and provocative questions. How, for instance, at a conceptual level, can contradictions within HRS be reconciled? The need for greater central control at the same time as devolved decision-making and greater autonomy for staff groups; the exhortation to align HR policies with strategic objectives in a financial context that urges short-term profitability; the delayering, downsizing and redundancies of competitive restructuring associated with 'hard' HRS alongside the empowering, commitment-generating, developmental policies typical of 'soft' HRS; the encouragement of teamworking and collective responsibility for quality in a context of individualistic performance-related reward strategies and personal contracts? At an implementation level there are further inherent difficulties with HR strategies as advocated: even if issues of vertical, horizontal and sub-unit integration can be overcome, do managers actually have the capacity to discern and design HR initiatives which 'fit' the external demands and internal capabilities of the organization? And, even if such matching were achieved, how long would the chosen strategies be appropriate before market exigencies rendered them outmoded or redundant? The harsh competitive climate of the early 1990s led to many European enterprises adopting HR measures which overruled the previously favoured soft HRS approach.

Having considered difficulties with HRS from conceptual and implementation perspectives, the chapter goes on to examine two further and possibly more fundamental flaws in the more celebratory claims of HRS. The first concerns the way decisions are made and enacted in organizations. Too often it is assumed that strategies – including HR strategies – are conceived and delivered in a political vacuum, where the correctness of proposal policies will be self-evident, where consensus is both achievable and sustainable and where appropriate cultural and structural levers can be pulled in concert to bring about the desired outcomes. A number of inhibiting factors are discussed which interfere with the rationality of these processes: including the inbuilt inefficiencies, indifference, ignorance, defensiveness and learned helplessness of managers and senior management teams. The final concern we raise takes us from the inevitability of delusion in organizational strategy-making to the possibility of knowing deceit on the part of those arguing the HRS case. We suggest that, for all the personal and corporate benefits arising from the renewed interest in the more enlightened management of human resources, there is a real risk that the rhetoric of HRS has been and will be used to usher in old forms of managerial control: that the changes proposed in the name of HRS, with their developmental appeal and espoused valuing of the individual – resonating as this does with wider cultural and political agendas of free markets, personal performance and corporate excellence – actually serve the agendas of organizational leaders most conveniently; and that the language of HRS has more to do with defining the meaning of work and securing commitment from a workforce who are no less oppressed and no more emancipated than they traditionally have been.

REFERENCES

Argyris, C. (1976) Single-loop and double-loop models in research on decision-making. *Administrative Science Quarterly*, 21, pp. 363–75.

Brewster, C. and Hegewisch, A. (eds) (1994) Policy and practice in European HRM: The evidence and analysis from the Price Waterhouse Cranfield Study. London, Routledge.

Cohen, M. and March, J. (1974) *Leadership and Ambiguity*. New York, McGraw Hill.

Gill, J. and Whittle, S. (1992) Management by panacea. *Journal of Management Studies*, 30, no. 2, pp. 281–95.

Guest, D. (1987) Human resource management and industrial relations. *Journal of Management Studies*, 24, no. 5, pp. 503–21.

Purcell, J. (1989) The impact of corporate strategy on human resource management. In Storey, J. (ed.), *New Perspectives on Human Resource Management*. London, Routledge.

Storey, J. (1992) *Developments in the Management of Human Resources*. Oxford, Blackwell.

1 HRS: An Overview

> ## Learning Objectives
>
> - *to become generally more aware of what HRS is, why it is distinctive and the extent to which HRS is actually happening.*
> - *to understand where HRS came from and be able to make informed, critical and questioning analyses of HRS ideas and recommendations.*
> - *to recognize the types of current organizational changes that are widely seen as indicative of HRS.*
> - *to be aware of the debate about the extent to which these changes do or do not constitute HRS-type change.*
> - *to know what HRS is, in its various forms. There are various definitions of HRS, and a number of issues and problems arise from these different definitions.*

Introduction

This book is intended to be both descriptive of HRS and its key constituent ideas and analytical of the approach and its ideas. It is intended that the reader leaves the volume not only better informed about what HRS is, but better able to evaluate different human resource strategies. These goals require us to consider the concept or approach of HRS carefully and critically; not to tear it apart for the sake of it, but to see how robust and impressive it is in terms of its constituent ideas and assumptions. This activity however, which starts in this chapter, is not easy, mainly because HRS is an 'elusive target, characterised by a diversity of meanings and ambiguous conceptual status' (Hales, 1994 p. 51).

From the chapters in this volume it will be apparent that HRS is defined in different terms. There is no single entity 'HRS', but a variety of different definitions and approaches. Furthermore, HRS as an approach has much in common with other approaches to organizational restructuring, such as a focus on internal marketing (see Hales, 1994). Because of the variety and complexity of approaches to HRS, it is important to have some understanding of how HRS is defined and used. It might seem that a discussion of the nature and merits, and the provenance of the ideas and assumptions inherent in approaches to organizational restructuring such as HRS is simply academic and unnecessary. After all, if it works, why worry? But, as we shall see, it isn't easy to know whether or not it *is* working; and what do we mean by *working* anyway? Working for whom, over what time-scale? And even if HRS is working (by whatever measure), what costs are involved, and what costs are we prepared to pay, or to suffer? Thorough discussion of HRS, even from the most hard-nosed, practical point of view, requires some analysis of the ideas and assumptions inherent in the approach. It may be, for example, that one of the reasons for the lack of take-up of HRS, or its lack of success, is that the approach is flawed by some fundamental contradictions and confusions: that it doesn't make sense as a collection of ideas. For example (and this is discussed at different points in the text) does HRS assume a conception of group relations within the organization – that all groups and parties share the same goals, values and objectives? If there is such a unitarist assumption, how realistic and secure is it? And does HRS thinking and practice in some cases move from assumptions (however precarious) to facts? Does HRS: 'drift from proclaiming the idea of organizations as harmonious teams, in which there is a congruence of values and interests among members as a *desideratum* to asserting such congruence as fact. According to this view, conflict is simply the contingent outcome of a failure by management, adequately to cognise employee "needs" or to find the points at which these needs can be made to converge with the "goals of the organisation". The possibility of a fundamental plurality of interests or inevitability of conflict is never entertained' (Hales, 1994, p. 62).

HRS ideas are attractive and powerful; they largely define the agenda of organizational change and restructuring. But for some commentators their attractiveness does not necessarily reflect their practical value: in fact their appeal may owe as much to their resonance with larger, social values as to their practical realism. Like the ideas of Reagan and Thatcher (under whose auspices HRS developed) HRS presents as inevitable and necessary organizational strategies which may be simply political choices aimed at displacing the costs of organizational decline to the less advantaged members of the organization. The magic of HRS is that it does this by trying to induce a sort of hypnotic trance wherein all members of the organization become convinced of the unassailability and neutrality of ideas and policies which serve political purposes while denying their possible origin in interests, faddishness and power. Indeed, is HRS essentially a formula for managing decline, down-sizing and retrenchment, or genuinely, as it claims, a formula for unleashing, focusing and enhancing organizational creativity and capability?

After all, as chapter 9 discusses in detail, while HRS has become the major approach to organizational restructuring, and is clearly extremely attractive to senior managers – so much so that this approach dominates current thinking on organizations and change – it has also been criticised on a number of fundamental fronts, most of them concerned with the status and value of HRS thinking and HRS ideas. It has for example been accused of offering (or assuming) a naïvely optimistic view of internal organizational relations which is either ill-informed, or cynically manipulative, trying to advance control, exploitation and manipulation under the guise of a rhetoric of consensus, mutuality and empowerment. It has also been held to consist of contradictory ideas – individualism (in pay schemes, for example) *and* co-operation; commitment *and* flexibility (through flexible employment practices); strong cultures *and* changeability and adaptability (Hales, 1994, p. 60). Clearly the ideas and assumptions of the approach require thorough inspection.

This chapter provides an overview of HRS. It addresses three interrelated issues:

- Some organizational changes of the types which are widely seen as indicative of HRS.
- A consideration of what HRS is, in its various forms. This section focuses on definitions, and the issues and problems that arise from different definitions. HRS is a term used in various ways to focus on a variety of practices, and to advance a variety of policies and priorities.
- The background to HRS – where it came from. Few of the ideas in HRS are new, as this section shows. Yet there *is* something important and distinctive about HRS, not simply as a set of practices, but as a body of powerful ideas and associations, powerfully packaged, and influential in its implications.

What's Going On?

It is now a cliché of those who work in and write about organizations that something new is happening with respect to the nature and speed of change in and around organizations. This is a time when employees are increasingly exhorted to change, to learn new skills, develop new values. For many people this change is a personal reality: jobs change, markets change, organizational systems change, work technologies, products, relevant legal frameworks change. Change is in the air . . . It's exhorted; it may even be happening . . .

Let's start with some typical and key views. In box 1.1 are three descriptions of HRS projects. The descriptions differ markedly in what they describe and in the implied evaluation of what is described. Clearly HRS involves not only inherent differences in what it purports to be but also differences in how the impact of these change projects are evaluated.

Box 1.1   Differing conceptions of HRS

First, the Personnel Director of Nissan UK:

In the United States Pratt and Whitney has examined its 60-year-old culture. The company concluded that it was product-orientated, achieved quality through inspection, saw its people as an expendable resource, believed in management by control and used one-way communication. Now the value system has changed to one where the customer is the centre of the universe, quality is built in and people are regarded as the single most important part of the organisation and its only appreciable asset. The purpose of management is to facilitate and thus recognise that the largest single repository of ideas is the workforce, so 'two-way communications' is of paramount importance.

(Wickens, 1987, p. 183)

Or consider these remarks, about the then chairman of BP – Robert Horton's – efforts to change the company in the late 1980s:

Horton wants to reinforce its [BP's] strengths as a corporation while allowing its constituent businesses much greater flexibility and speed of response in the market place; achieving this 'tight-loose' balancing act . . . is one of the most difficult tasks facing multinationals today. In a phrase, Horton's task is the complete stream-lining of BP: not just of its complex, costly, committee-ridden and over controlled formal organisation but also of the way managers behave within it . . . In place of the existing culture of bureaucracy, constant second-guessing and extreme distrust, Horton wants to create what last autumn he called 'the corporate equivalent of perestroika and glasnost' . . . a structure with the minimum of controls and the maximum of delegation of responsibility, plus a supporting culture of openness, informal communication and verve. In other words rather than establish a shallower, flatter, more efficient pyramid, he wants to develop an organisation that works, thinks and feels entirely differently.

(Lorenz, 1992, p. 6)

Or this:

the litany of innovative HRM social practices . . . should be regarded as cultural constructions fabricated through Government policy and corporate administrative fiat. They are self-conscious attempts not merely to change social behaviour but to transform the norms and values guiding social behaviour. As such, in the majority of cases, their introduction and implementation has been based on a fairly simplistic set of psychologistic behavioural assumptions: the structural context of social interaction is changed while, at the same time, attempts are made to engineer change in the interpretative frameworks of social action. We have seen the techniques of advertising, marketing and proselytising enlisted to propagate new images of organisational 'reality'. The imposition of this new social order has been mediated by the 'market' and massaged with management exhortation to induce not merely the acceptance of a negotiated order but, ultimately, individual normative commitment. . . . The HRM 'movement', a self-seeking cultural product, has been installed to manufacture, mediate and administer cultural transformation in an environment softened up by recession and unemployment. Fear is a great catalyst; but what is being constructed to replace it?

(Keenoy and Anthony, 1992, pp. 235–6)

So what *is* going on? On the one hand we have people extolling the need for change, and change of a particular sort, or insisting that these changes are occurring. On the other there are people claiming that all these changes represent a glib attempt to exploit current weaknesses and manipulate employees' ways of thinking, even their values. It is precisely this complex, messy and contentious terrain that this chapter attempts to clarify and map.

We can start with some broad areas of agreement. It is undeniably the case that recently, as companies and organizations in the UK and USA have been 'confronted by Japanese competition and employment stereotypes, struggled with recession and searched for excellence, so the vocabulary for managing their workforces has tended to change. "Personnel management" is giving way to "human resource management", or better still to "strategic human resource management"' (Legge, 1989, p. 19).

In this passage Legge draws attention to both environmental pressures of a business nature (Japanese competition), and to pressure of a moral, or ideological sort (Japanese employment stereotypes, 'excellence'). It is exactly this mix of identified business challenges and the seductive offer of ways of meeting these challenges that constitutes the attraction of the HRS approach. And it is this relationship between 'environmental challenges' and organizational responses, which constitutes the central plank of the HRS argument. For example, Hendry and Pettigrew argue that in the mid 1980s: 'changes in the political, economic and business environment over the past few years have cued many organisations to rethink their business strategy and at the same time the content and style of their human resource policies' (Hendry and Pettigrew, 1986, p. 3).

But is there any reality to all of this? Is anyone actually taking these claims and exhortations seriously? Is it actually *possible* to achieve all these goals, however desirable they may be?

Severance and Passino noted that 'recent studies of Fortune 1000 CEOs [Chief Executive Officers] document strategic planning and implementation to be the area of greatest concern to chief executive officers. It is also the area to which they currently allocate the greatest amount of their time and the one to which they feel that even more of their attention should go'

(1986, p. 1). This US survey concludes that the dominant manufacturing strategy of the 1980s has been one of dramatic quality improvements coupled with significant cost reduction achieved through the elimination of inventories and the slashing of direct labour content. The most obvious marketing strategy has been the attempt to increase current market share while offering new products into the market. Strategy implementation has been punctuated by a replacement of the management team and characterized by substantial investments in plant, equipment, R & D, and manufacturing control systems (Pettigrew, 1988, p. 2).

Surveys in the UK context by Thomson, Pettigrew and Rubashow (1985) and in the United States by Severance and Passino (1986) have begun to unravel the anatomy of strategic change in commercial companies. The 1984 Thomson et al. survey of 1,000 middle and senior executives and directors in 190 companies enquired about changes made since 1979. Thirty-three per cent of the managers reported 'radical changes', with 56 per cent acknowledging 'some change' and 10 per cent indicating little or no change. Factors influencing changes in strategy most notably included the general recession and changing markets (Pettigrew, 1988, pp. 1–2). However, do these developments add up to HRS?

Storey (1992, p. 82) has distinguished some key differences between HRS and traditional industrial relations. Storey and Sisson assess the extent to which these 25 key dimensions of HRS have been implemented in a number of UK firms. The results of their survey are presented in figure 1.1.

The ticks represent the researchers' own assessment of what was going on, based on 'multiple sources of information'. This evidence would seem to suggest that HRS is occurring, and that there is 'extensive take-up of HRM-style approaches in the British mainstream organizations. Two-thirds of the companies recorded a definite tick scoring on a least 11 of the dimensions' (Storey and Sisson, 1993, p. 19). Clearly then there is a lot going on – there is considerable evidence of pervasive organizational change of a sort which can legitimately be regarded as typical of HRS.

However, the authors also sound an important warning. If a critical test of HRS is an explicit and deliberate connection between HR strategy and corporate strategy, or evidence of a clear, people-focused strategy, then these results do *not* support pervasive HRS: 'apart from an insistence on a customer orientation, most cases failed to show much in the way of an integrated approach to employment management, and still less was there evidence of strategic integration with the corporate plan. This finding lends some support to the view that the HRM model is not itself a coherent, integrated phenomenon. Many of the initiatives . . . arose for diverse reasons, . . . [this] might indicate the true nature of the HRM phenomenon – i.e. that it is in reality a symbolic label behind which lurk multifarious practices' (Storey and Sisson, 1993, pp. 22–3).

Similar results are reported by Guest, who, summarizing a 1985 study by Bureau of National Affairs in the USA notes that this research found that 44 per cent of employers had installed some sort of employee-involvement programme to improve productivity; 24 per cent had installed quality circles, and 44 per cent flexitime. Job enrichment and job enlargement had been introduced by 27 per cent and 28 per cent respectively (Guest, 1990, p. 385). However, as Guest points out, evidence of take-up of these measures in itself is not enough to indicate commitment to HRS.

What's going on? Environmental change

Within HRS thinking these processes and programmes of organizational change are attributed to challenges and pressures in organizations' environments which make such change necessary.

Organizational environments are certainly changing. And they are changing in new ways. The key environmental changes are characterized as: the decline of the traditional industries of mature capitalism (steel, coal, shipbuilding etc.); the drastic increase in competitive pressures, particularly from the newer industrialized economies; and the increase in environmental pressures from deregulation and from political, consumer and environmental lobbies. Within the UK, the decline of manufacturing industry and the transformation of what remains has been accompanied by the imposition, in the still very considerable public sector (over 25 per cent of the workforce employed), of politically derived pressures for performance measurements and improvement. Changes in energy costs, resources, inflation, employment legislation, and new technology are also important challenges.

As discussed further in chapter 8, the rise of highly competitive economies in south-east Asia using new technology, relatively cheap labour and new organizational principles poses a major threat to established Western and European businesses; as does the emergence of a genuinely international market – a world economy – through computer-based communications and the emergence of multinationals operating at a global level. Yet also crucial is the changed nature of international competition, the decline and fragmentation of hitherto mass markets, resulting in the need for customized products: 'there are no non-niche markets any more' (Peters, 1989, p. 28).

Economic environmental changes include changes in markets, or market segments, changes in competition (new entries, takeovers, decline), changes in the national or local economy in terms of inflation rates, unemployment, interest rates and balance of trade. Political changes include the single European market in 1992, legal and political deregulation, the European Social Charter, levels of UK government or local authority spending, privatization/public ownership, the end of the Cold War, the Green

	Austin Rover	British Rail	Bradford Council	Eaton Ltd	Ford	ICI	Jaguar	Lucas	Massey Ferguson	NHS	Peugeot-Talbot	Plessey	Rolls-Royce	Smith & Nephew	Whitbread	Total ✓
Beliefs and assumptions																
'Business need' is prime guide to action	✓	✓	✓	•	✓	✓	✓	✓	✓	•	✓	✓	✓	✓	✓	13
Aim to go 'beyond contract'	✓	•	✓	✓	✓	✓	✓	✓	✓	✓	•	✓	•	✓	✓	11
Values/mission	✓	•	✓	✓	•	✓	✓	✓	✓	✓	✓	•	•	•	✓	11
Impatience with rules	✓	✓	✓	✓	•	✓	✓	✓	✓	•	✓	✓	•	•	✓	10
Standardization/parity not emphasized	✓	•	✓	✓	•	✓	•	✓	✓	✗	•	✓	✗	✗	✓	8
Conflict de-emphasized rather than institutionalized	✓	•	✓	•	•	✓	•	✗	•	•	•	✓	✗	•	✓	5
Unitarist relations	•	•	✗	✗	✗	•	•	✗	•	✗	✗	✓	✗	✗	✓	2
Nurturing orientation	•	✗	•	•	•	•	•	•	•	•	•	•	•	•	•	0
Strategic aspects																
Customer-orientation to fore	✓	✓	✓	✗	•	✓	•	✓	✓	•	•	✓	✓	✓	✓	11
Integrated initiatives	✓	✗	✓	✗	•	•	•	•	•	•	•	✗	✗	✗	✓	3
Corporate plan central	✓	•	✓	✗	•	•	•	•	•	✗	•	✗	•	•	✓	3
Speedy decision-making	✓	✗	•	✗	•	•	•	•	•	✗	✗	•	✗	✗	✓	2
Line managers																
General/business/line managers to fore	✓	✓	✓	✓	✓	✓	✓	✓	✓	✓	✓	✓	✓	✓	✓	15
Facilitation is prized skill	✓	✓	✓	•	✓	✓	✓	•	✓	•	•	•	✗	•	✓	9
Transformational leadership	✓	✗	•	•	•	•	✓	✓	✓	✓	•	•	•	•	•	4

Key levers

	Austin Rover	British Rail	Bradford Council	Eaton Ltd	Ford	ICI	Jaguar	Lucas	Massey Ferguson	NHS	Peugeot-Talbot	Plessey	Rolls-Royce	Smith & Nephew	Whitbread	Total ✓
Increased flow of communication	✓	✓	✓	✓	✓	✓	✓	✓	✓	✓	✓	✓	✓	✓	✓	15
Selection is integrated key task	✓	✓	✓	✓	✓	✓	✓	✓	✓	●	✓	✓	●	x	✓	12
Wide-ranging cultural, structural and personnel strategies	✓	✓	✓	●	✓	✓	✓	✓	✓	✓	✓	✓	●	●	✓	12
Teamworking	●	●	✓	✓	✓	✓	✓	✓	✓	✓	●	✓	✓	●	✓	11
Conflict reduction through culture change	✓	●	✓	✓	✓	✓	✓	✓	✓	✓	●	✓	●	●	✓	11
Marginalization of stewards	✓	●	●	●	x	●	✓	✓	✓	✓	✓	✓	●	●	✓	8
Learning companies/heavy emphasis on training	✓	●	✓	x	●	●	✓	✓	✓	●	●	●	✓	●	✓	6
Move to individual contracts	●	✓	●	x	x	x	●	●	●	●	●	✓	●	x	✓	3
Performance-related pay, few grades	✓	●	●	●	x	x	x	●	●	●	●	●	x	●	●	1
Harmonization	✓	●	x	x	x	x	●	x	x	x	●	●	x	x	●	1

Key: ✓ = yes (existed or were significant moves towards); x = no; ● = in parts

Figure 1.1 Key HRM characteristics
Source: Storey and Sisson, 1993, pp. 20–1.

movement and energy issues. Technological changes include the likely or current form of technological developments and the costs and implications of such developments. Social changes refer to factors which affect people as consumers/users of an organization's goods or services via the influencing of attitudes, life-styles, values, expectations; or which affect people as employees. Of obvious importance here are demographic trends which bring about staff and skill shortages.

However, the argument that these changes *require* or *cause* organizational change, and organizational change of a certain sort, with definite implications for all aspects of organizational structures, systems and skills, is a crucial element in HRS approaches, albeit a contentious one. This view has some obvious advantages, one of which is that it attributes responsibility for organizational change, with all its implications for skills, careers, jobs, to forces outside the organization itself. Senior managers, according to this approach, are not responsible for initiating organizational change; rather they are *irresponsible* if they do not change it in line with the requirements of the environment. One common consequence of such thinking is the imposition of internal market structures which are presented as necessary responses to environmental pressures. However, this notion of the market as a distributive mechanism has become an ideological shibboleth in contemporary politics and as such conceals and serves real political structures.

The BP example, discussed below (box 1.2), shows that the pressure for change within BP came from the chairman and processes he initiated, such as the surveying of 4,000 members of staff. While in theory HRS starts with an analysis of the organization's environments, in practice, existing organizational arrangements and senior managers' mind-sets may well obstruct this process. This is also shown by the BP case and is discussed further in chapter 9.

What's going on? Strategic 'responses': the link between environments and strategies

These environmental pressures are typically seen as associated with a series of strategic responses. In this section a variety of key strategic, HR responses are identified and considered. Child's (1987) analysis is typical of many commentators who have attempted to identify classified developments in the environment with classified responses from the organization. The attempt to track relationships between environments and organization, and the argument that the environment is the ultimate source of organizational changes, are fundamental to HRS thinking.

Child argues that environmental and competitive pressures produce three types of strategic challenge.

- The first is *demand risk*, that is, a reduction in the market and/or an increase in levels of competition. This brings the risk of sharply fluctuating demand or demand collapse. It follows recession, increased global competition, entry of new competitors to the market and is compounded by variations in product specifications. It leads to a need for flexibility and responsiveness and improved quality.
- The second strategic challenge derives from *innovation risk* – the failure to match competitors' technological innovations. To counter this, organizations need to retrieve or develop the capacity to innovate.
- The third is the strategic risk of inefficiency, the *inability to match competitors' costs*. This leads to a drive to cut costs. These three strategies: innovation, quality and cost may all occur within one multi-product/service organization.

Each of these environmental challenges, it is argued, is *met* by an organizational response, and Child proposes that the complexity of current forms of organization, with particular reference to the nature of relationships (or transactions) between elements of the organization (departments, sub-units, suppliers, agents, head office), has implications for such responses. For example, a common response to the need for flexibility in the face of demand risk is to move to looser internal organizational relationships in order to encourage innovative capacity, in the shape of new ideas and concepts, within a context of commercial and production support. 'The organisational contribution here turns on the integration of inputs to innovation from a range of sources (some external to the enterprise) and the facilitation of speedy implementation attuned to commercial needs' (Child, 1987, p. 34). On the other hand, pulling in the opposite direction is the need to counter inefficiency risk, which requires increased control over operations, inventories and so on. It also requires tight control and co-ordination of outside suppliers. A number of commentators have noted this classic HRS contradiction, in various forms: on the one hand HRS highlights the importance and benefits of being able to ensure staff comply rigorously with managerial intentions and requirements (quality programmes, JIT (just-in-time) systems, customer-care programmes, and the like), yet at the same time HRS frequently advocates the importance of empowerment, staff 'ownership' and involvement which are aimed to achieve staff commitment and participation. The only solution to this contradiction is if HRS managers ensure that staff commit themselves freely and energetically to precisely those behaviours and standards management wish them to support. This is clearly unlikely. However, some commentators have claimed that this is precisely what HRM achieves – that it creates a situation 'which motivates the employee to respond favourably to management's demands' (Gronroos, 1990, p. 43; quoted in Hales, 1994, p. 65). Less optimistically the tension between control and commitment may account for the charge that HRS is 'employee manipulation dressed up as mutuality' (Fowler, 1987). It may also explain the focus on symbols as much as substance in many HRS initiatives.

Box 1.2   HRS change in BP

In 1989 BP went through a fundamental and radical process of organizational restructuring called Project 1990. This project and the thinking and negotiations that lay behind it, are described by Lorenz in a series of articles (Lorenz, 1992). Work on the change proposals was carried out by a team hand-picked by the chairman of the time – Robert Horton. This group regarded no aspect of the company as sacred and was apparently guided by an upswell of concern at all levels of the company. BP had recently gone through a massive divestment programme, withdrawing to core businesses. Lorenz describes Horton's ambitions in the language of Peters and Waterman. He notes that Horton wanted to reinforce BP's strengths. While allowing BP's businesses much greater flexibility and speed of response in the market place, his goal being complete streamlining of BP: not only of its complex, costly, committee-ridden and over-controlled formal organization but also of the way managers behaved. He wished to replace the existing culture of bureaucracy, constant second-guessing and extreme distrust with a structure with the minimum of controls and the maximum delegation of responsibility and with an atmosphere of openness and informality. Horton and his team wanted: clear vision, continuous innovation, open communication, empowered people, deep trust, team accountability – when the current reality was the opposite of these qualities.

Lorenz describes a 'burning impatience for change on all fronts – structure, process and culture', which was evident right across the company. Evidence for this was gathered through 4,000 questionnaires distributed to staff, yet despite the claims of the change champions that change was necessary and that the proposed changes would successfully impact on BP's performance, there were still a number of senior managers who found it hard to fully comprehend the proposals, or who doubted their efficacy, indeed even their practical possibility. Of these people, Horton himself remarked that he was not prepared 'to let the long shadows of conservatism loom around to foul up the process'.

Central to the changes were changes in organizational structures: regional structures were redefined on a regional and business mix; businesses, wherever they were located, now reported to their respective international business heads, with consequent implications for reductions in numbers of regional co-ordinators' jobs. In the head office staff would no longer work in large, formal hierarchies but in small, flexible cross-functional teams. But these changes were seen as inextricably associated with changes in management style and culture (away from centralization, control and authoritarianism towards greater trust and delegation), and with changes in personnel systems and procedures – especially appraisal systems which focused unhelpfully on individual rather than team performance.

Fundamental to the success of the change was the behaviour of Horton himself, the chairman. Senior managers noted that Horton would himself have to model the new style and overcome his naturally autocratic style. His position was also closely associated with the success and survival of the change programme.

Horton is no longer with BP.

It is interesting to note that Child not only uses a classification of strategic pressures, thus asserting an hypothesised close connection between environmental and organizational structures, but also argues that these threats require different sorts of organizational solutions. Child is here offering a classic HRS model: i.e. that organizational structures change (are changed/ should change) in line with environmental challenges and demands, an argument which is fundamental to HRS. However, the BP case suggests that the HRS 'response' to change pressures may be influenced as much by fashions of organizational change as by the identification of HRS appropriate to business strategies. We shall return to this relationship in the discussion of strategy/HRS interconnections, below.

But Child also makes another key point. He notes how organizational responses to one threat (flexibility, delegation) might conflict with other responses (the increased control necessary for reduced costs). In other words, HRS in practice (and indeed in theory) might involve irreconcilable contradictions. This too will be discussed later.

Like a number of other writers, Child offers a map of the relationship between a set of strategic risks and a number of organizational 'responses' However, what is crucial in this form of analysis is the processes whereby environmental 'challenges/threats' are perceived, defined, recognized – and the processes whereby *suitable* strategic responses are discussed, selected, implemented. Also crucial is the nature of the relationship between strategic response and the design and implementation of a human resource strategy. These are all social and human processes, so they can go wrong. They will not be neutral. And being organizational processes they will be influenced by existing structures of power, interests and values. These issues are explored in subsequent chapters, where we argue that one of a number of fundamental weaknesses of the HRS approach is its simplistic approach to processes of organizational decision-making about HRS matters.

Change champions within organizations always justify the change in terms of its positive impact on some desired outcome, and explain it in terms of the pressures and threats of the environment. And it is a funda-mental feature of HRS as a body of ideas that it asserts a critical relation-ship between 'environment', strategy and human resource strategies. But no environmental development can have any effect within an organization, can produce any 'response' at all, unless it is identified and interpreted by managers, who then seek to change the organization in terms of their theory of what needs to be done. It is precisely one of the critical features of HRS that it offers a conception of the necessity for and nature of the connections between environment, business strategy and HRS. Since such ideas are powerful in their consequences it is important to assess where this appeal lies. In other words, HRS thinking and writing play a significant role in the definition and construction of the very 'forces' which it claims to handle.

This is not to deny that distinctive relationships between environments, strategies and HRS *are* apparent. Cappelli and McKersie (1987), for exam-ple, argue on the basis of their research that management may initiate a programme of what Sisson calls 'asset management': 'Shifting the firm's capital away from the high-cost/low-profit businesses to those that are more profitable: in the extreme case it means selling all or part of the business and transferring the assets to an alternative line of business in the same or another country' (Sisson, 1989, p. 23). This may well result in divestment or acquisition, organic growth along established policy parameters or joint ventures.

An alternative approach involves the attempt to improve the 'value added' by each employee. Here, efforts are made to change employees' behaviour through modifying systems, structures, training, and so on, in the areas of activity where that value is added.

There is evidence that UK companies have pursued both these strategies. With respect to the second, organizations have frequently attempted to cut costs, to reduce payroll numbers, to reduce stocks and inventories. Frequently staff reductions have necessarily been accompanied by the intro-duction of new production methods, new forms of work organization and new technology, particularly information technology. Elsewhere Hendry et al. have described a set of 'generic strategic responses' to environmental challenge and change: competitive restructuring; decentralization; internationalization; acquisition and merger; quality improvement; technological change; and new concepts of service provision and distribution (Hendry et al., 1988). These strategic responses to environmental change may themselves occasion further change: for instance, diversification will require internal change, new structures, systems and cultures.

What's going on? Strategic responses: flexibility

It has also been forcibly argued that during the 1980s management has increasingly reacted to the environmental developments described earlier by attempting to cope with variations in the nature and quantity of consumer demand by achieving greater internal organizational flexibility: by becoming 'the flexible firm'. This is a common element in HRS thinking, and possibly in HRS practice. It offers a good example of the key elements (and weaknesses) of HRS thinking.

A number of different characteristics are covered by the expression flexibility: numerical flexibility, which is the ability to adjust the number of employees in response to varying demand; functional flexibility, which is the ability to use the skills of the workforce in varying ways in response to demand; and financial flexibility, which means adjusting wages to demand and to performance. The notion of the 'flexible firm', developed by Atkinson (1985) at the Institute of Manpower Studies, describes the elements seen as necessary to be able to adjust quickly and readily to market changes. The flexible firm, which exhibits the three sorts of flexibility described above, may also operate flexible employment practices whereby workers are divided into 'core' or full-time, reasonably secure workers, and 'peripheral' or part-time workers with less advantageous conditions.

However, a major problem with the flexibility thesis (which characterizes much HRS thinking) concerns the *status* of the argument. Is Atkinson describing actual practices or supplying a framework for analysis of change (without making any assumptions about the extent of such changes)? Is he talking about what management wants and is trying to do, or what it should do? That is, is he describing management thinking or management practice? In fact, in the case of the flexibility debate, Atkinson argues that while 'flexibility has become an important theme in emerging corporate thinking' (1985, p. 26), in reality, 'relatively few UK firms have explicitly and comprehensively reorganized their labour force on this basis' (p. 28). Certainly there have been significant examples of numerical, functional and financial flexibility, yet the scope and significance of these changes remains unclear.

Part of the problem of the nature and implications of organizational efforts to achieve flexibility, when these have taken place, arises because of confusion about the meaning of the term and ambiguity about the reasons for flexibility initiatives. Pollert's remarks about flexibility could apply equally to a great deal of HRS writing and prescription. She notes: 'The concept of flexibility is highly amorphous; it obscures changes in the management of labour, such as job enlargement, effort intensification and cost controls, by conflating them into flexibility . . . the use of the new orthodoxy of "flexibility" in descriptions of changing employment and work organisation has caused enormous confusion by imposing a single typology on a diversity of social realities' (Pollert, 1988, p. 1). Pollert notes that the importance of flexibility is less as a useful way of classifying a large variety of changes in the organization and employment of labour over the last decade (for these changes are more varied than similar), and more as an extraordinarily powerful idea which is used to describe the 'emergence of a new era' of work and organization. The real question, as Pollert notes, and to which we will return in the final chapter, is why this idea is so powerful and attractive.

Nevertheless, there is no doubt that over the last decade there has been very considerable interest in flexibility. For some HRS writers it is an inherent and defining feature of HRS itself. Much of this interest derives from the Japanese model of organization and from other environmental pressures (Blyton and Morris, 1992, pp. 117–18). Also there is evidence that a number of companies report efforts to increase flexibility of one sort or another. Yet this evidence is inconclusive.

Lane notes that many UK firms claim to be seeking to improve functional flexibility, yet surveys also show that progress had been slow: 'for the vast majority of companies flexible working consists of slow change over a number of years' (Lane, 1989, p. 182). Studies show evidence of continuity of employment practices, as well as some change towards flexibility. And with respect to task flexibility, Elger summarizes the evidence thus: 'The most striking feature of the findings on functional flexibility . . . is actually the modesty of rather than the radicalism of the changes involved, and the centrality of reduced manning levels rather than upskilling' (Elger, 1991, p. 50). There is evidence of 'mundane' change, but little sign of a serious move towards multi-skilling.

This is important, because, the issue with flexibility, and so much HRS-type change, is not simply *what* is happening, but the *meaning* of what is happening – the motives and intentions of management; the consequences for workers' skills and commitment. Are these apparent flexibility initiatives truly strategic? A number of writers have offered classifications of different approaches to flexibility. Blyton and Morris (1992) distinguish between *strategic* and *ad hoc* approaches – the former seeking to use flexibility initiatives to further long-term business purpose; the latter being limited, piecemeal, opportunistic and aimed at increasing control. Elger's review of current research on flexibility suggests that these initiatives typically represent the reassertion of managerial control over job mobility allied to work intensification (Elger, 1991, p. 56). Not surprisingly, such moves have been related to the increase in productivity during recent years. But this should be seen not as indicating a radical shift to a new-style human resource approach to the management of labour, nor as revealing the benefits of the new approach. It simply shows the efficacy of the old patterns of management, at least in the short term: 'recent productivity gains do not step from a fundamental reorganisation of the forces of production in Britain but . . . are the product of a series of step-by-step changes' premised upon a 'new and intrinsically fragile, power shift arising from the exceptionally brutal crisis conditions of the early 1990s' (Nolan, 1989, p. 101, quoted in Elger, 1991, p. 58).

What's going on? Other strategic responses

Teamworking is another major element of the claimed new approach to the management of labour (and of human resources). And great claims have been made for the pervasiveness, and beneficial consequences, of team work (see Buchanan, 1992). Allied to this are work changes which, again borrowing from the Japanese, attempt to overcome the classic disadvantage of the traditional, scientific management forms of work organization: low levels of worker motivation and commitment resulting in poor-quality work, insignificant creativity, and a poor balance of the flow of work through the assembly process. The Japanese shop-floor system of work organization, through quality circle programmes, 'empowers' workers so that, in groups, they become involved in aspects of management decision-making such as quality and problem-solving, and in management decisions on tools, materials handling layout and improvements. This system seeks to make every worker a quality inspector, to be responsible for continuous change and improvement, and through 'just-in-time' production methods and improved supplier–end-user relations seeks to balance the assembly process. These methods, particularly just-in-time material flow systems, quality circles and teamworking, have been applied in Europe and hailed as a revolutionary break with previous practice and a crucial stage in the achievement of competitive levels of quality and efficiency.

Another significant area of change, which also reflects the pursuit of flexibility but on an organizational level rather than at the level of work design, is the move among many organizations towards types of structure which achieve the twin goals of accountability of management decision-making and sufficient management control over delegated decision-making. This is attempted by decentralization, reduction of bureaucracy, reduction of layers of management and thus the separation of parts of the business into separate, accountable business units, autonomous within a structure of financial controls and corporate policy. These developments have not only occurred within the private sector. British Rail and the National Health Service have also been exposed to decentralization and division into profit-responsible divisions. These developments represent an effort to achieve an optimum relationship between the corporate centre and operating companies. Goold and Campbell (1986) in a study of 17 multi-divisional UK firms, identify three types of centre-operating company relationship, each of which is empirically apparent and each of which solves some problems and raises others (see Storey and Sisson, 1993, pp. 80–6).

A similar sort of development is the move towards formal and explicit service-level agreements between service departments and their internal customers. For example, within local authorities discrete divisions may now be required to install service agreements formally specifying what each division agrees to supply to its internal customers. For external services they are required to arrange for competitive tendering as usual. Interestingly, one result of this move is to increase the quantity of bureaucratic paperwork, with the details of each interdepartmental relationship being formally specified.

For some years it has been widely maintained that an important element in organizational change – possibly the most important element – is an organization's culture. This refers to the symbolic, normative aspect of organizational life which, culture proponents argue, is a fundamental determinant of employees' behaviour and attitudes, and specifically of their sense of commitment and enthusiasm. Culture can be defined as: 'the taken for granted assumptions, beliefs, meanings and values enacted and shared by organisational members' (Gowler and Legge, 1986, p. 9). The concept of culture is used to draw attention to the role and importance of the irrational within organizations, seeing the organization as a source of primary social relations and as a significant shaper of fundamental social values (see chapter 6).

Changes have also occurred in the traditional areas of personnel: selection, assessment, payments systems and training. A study by the Institute of Personnel Management reported that nearly 20 per cent of the organizations studied had a formal performance management programme, three quarters said they had performance-related pay, and a third Total Quality programmes (Bevan and Thompson, 1992, p. 15; quoted in Storey and Sisson, 1993, p. 135). Yet here too the evidence is inconclusive. Follow-up studies suggested that many of the performance management claims were unjustified. Studies have, however, confirmed the growth of performance-related pay schemes (Storey and Sisson, 1993, p. 136). (For a useful overview of HRS-type developments on many personnel dimensions see Storey and Sisson, 1993.)

There is evidence of a revitalized interest in assessment centres and in the design of reward systems and their relationship to performance, often defined in terms of the growing interest in management competencies. Performance-related payment allied to measured performance is not only to be found among the major private-sector companies within the UK: it is also characteristic of the once traditional financial sector, local authorities and even the National Health Service (see chapter 4).

With all these changes debate continues on two fronts: their empirical pervasiveness and their significance. Is there a major and qualitative change in the design of work and the structuring of work organizations, and the design of key personnel processes signifying a comprehensive programme of *strategically driven* change? Or are these undeniable developments either so piecemeal, uneven and variable in their implementation or so driven by opportunism and a traditional concern for tightened management control that they cannot possibly be seen as indicating any major strategic transformation?

What Is HRS?

HRS is indeed an elusive target: a set of exhortations, a metaphor, a set of substantive propositions, a mass of contradictions. HRS is not any single thing but a variety of differently conceptualized approaches. In what follows, an attempt will be made to try to make some sense of the different senses of the term by offering some maps to the rather confused terrain. It is important and useful to have a general understanding of how the approaches to HRS differ, because this allows one to evaluate the approaches on offer, and to understand the prescriptions and assumptions that are inherent in each approach.

Some useful definitions

We start with some issues of definition. What is HRS? What do people mean by the term? The issues here are not trivial. Different definitions carry different assumptions, assert different causal relationships, even seek different goals. However, if we are to be able to explore the differences between views and definitions of HRS, we first need to identify the general characteristics of the field. Sisson argues that there are four features associated with HRM:

1 a stress on the integration of personnel policies both with one another and with business planning more generally;
2 the locus of responsibility for personnel managers no longer resides with

(or is 'relegated to') specialist managers, but is now assumed by senior line management;

3   the focus shifts from management–trade union relations to management–employee relations, from collectivism to individualism;
4   there is stress on commitment and the exercise of initiative, with managers now donning the role of 'enabler', 'empowerer' and 'facilitator' (Sisson, 1990, p. 5, quoted in Blyton and Turnbull, 1992, p. 3).

Hendry and Pettigrew argue that the strategic aspect of HRM consists of four key elements:

1   the use of planning;
2   a coherent approach to the design and management of personnel systems based on an employment policy and manpower strategy, and often underpinned by a 'philosophy';
3   matching HRM activities and policies to some explicit strategy;
4   seeing the people of the organization as a 'strategic resource' for achieving 'competitive advantage' (Hendry and Pettigrew, 1986).

The authors point to a minimal specification of HRM as a degree of dual integration: coherence of HR practices with each other, and of all HR practices with the organization's strategy (see box 1.3).

Clearly these various summaries have themselves some common themes. At its simplest, the overlap has been described by Beaumont in these terms: 'the key message of the HRM literature is the need to establish a close, two-way relationship between business strategy or planning and HRM strategy or planning' (Beaumont, 1992, p. 40). First, the stress on strategic integration – organizational and personnel structures and systems should be designed to support, or 'fit', the strategy of the organization; secondly, staff should be managed and treated so that they are committed to the organization and its goals; and thirdly, by achieving the first of these, there will be real tangible benefits for the organization in terms of critical outputs like quality and performance. Thus the second of these (which will rely on a variety of organizational measures and changes) 'is seen as a method of releasing untapped reserves of "human resourcefulness" by increasing employee commitment, participation and involvement' (Blyton and Turnbull, 1992, p. 4). While the third feature ensures the value of these achievements: 'maximising the economic return from the labour resource by integrating HRM into business strategy' (ibid.). The clearest and most explicit statement of this causal relationship has been offered by Guest (see below), who has argued that only when organizations pursue a clear and coherent policy aimed at achieving four specific goals will the identified performance benefits be achieved.

However, while there are common elements there are also some crucial differences in approaches to HRS. In order to explore these it is necessary to look at some approaches in more detail.

Box 1.3   HRS change in Fiat

Cressey and Jones have studied programmes of HRS-type change in Fiat. They note that while aspects of HRS are being introduced quite widely, this is not necessarily associated with the management explicitly espousing or claiming a commitment to HRS principles.

Reorganization within Fiat has involved recruitment, retraining and changes in jobs – skills, authority and specialisms. Efforts have been made to engage the ordinary worker in the quality upgrading of the product which is, as the authors note, a typical HRS initiative, and for some writers a fundamental tenet of HRS. Work roles have been redesigned and operating systems changed to further this goal.

Job changes were associated with efforts to change workers' attitudes and values – the organizational culture – in order to enhance employee commitment. The Fiat programme involved a series of interconnected changes: integrating personnel, industrial relations and business policies; culture change and employee commitment programmes; individualized reward and appraisal schemes; downgrading the role of unions and enhanced consultation.

The authors also note that the specific human resource policies evident in the case of Fiat occurred 'downstream' of major strategic and investment decision making: 'human resources are the last link in the chain of policy development and implementation. Often policies from HRM will not be adopted as the most desirable foundations in the architecture of the business but as solutions to glaring inadequacies in existing programmes by specific transplants of HRM-style practices' (1992, p. 62). The main focus of the change programme at Fiat is summarized by a quotation from an official Fiat publication: 'The cornerstone of all Fiat's plans and operations is the maximization of the vital resource constituted by the ideas, experience and team spirit possessed by its employees at all levels' (Fiat *Facts and Figures*, 1988).

Gianni Agnelli took over as chairman of Fiat in 1966, and worked to decentralize the group, which had previously been highly centralized. By the late 1960s Fiat was being squeezed by falling demand and increasing worker unrest. By the 1970s Fiat was a loss maker. Management adopted a policy of concession towards the highly unionized and militant workforce with a significant degree of shop-floor control, allied to an inflation-linked bargaining system.

Performance suffered, and by the end of the 1970s leftist activity involved violence and arson. In 1980 Agnelli left to be replaced by Cesare Romiti as sole managing director. Faced with what amounted to the imminent collapse of managerial authority, Romiti reacted by announcing several thousand redundancies. This resulted in factory occupation and strikes, but in response to these, middle managers and clerical workers mounted an enormous demonstration which ended the strike.

With militancy reversed, Romiti mounted a programme of investment focused on robotics and new technology allied to a centralized system of business administration and the elimination of many union negotiating processes. The change programme reduced labour costs significantly: possibly by as much as 47 per cent over seven years through technology and rationalization. By the end of the 1980s Fiat was at the top of the European sale league with Volkswagen.

However, Fiat had also to improve flexibility of product and productivity through employee commitment to a number of corporate goals and quality of organization, services and product. Although automation and new technology are central to the achievement of these goals, it became clear that use of technology was inadequate without the redesign of some key jobs, since minor disruptions or failures now placed a great burden on workers' initiative and commitment. Cressey and Jones note that 'by the mid-1980s individual managers were already aware that the basic quantitative gains from computer-programmed automation would need complementing by an expansion of production workers' responsibilities to cover both quality enhancement and the optimisation of machine time' (1992, pp. 65–6).

The solution to this was the identification and creation of a key new job and therefore a new worker: the *conduttore* or line controller. This work role was designed to enable individuals to interface between three system elements of the new computerized production process: materials, supply of units and control of operations on the units. 'The advantages of this new work role are that the *conduttore* has his or her own video terminal for making operating changes to the control systems, can undertake simple maintenance tasks that might otherwise involve the complex re-allocation of maintenance specialists' (1992, p. 66).

This new role required a significant change of culture, a process which also aimed to 'sell' the new role to middle managers and union officials. *Conduttore* also required training – a total of twelve months, ten months of which was formal classroom format. The new role is justifiably regarded as a fundamental change. Workers below the *conduttore* and managers above it may well see the new role as a threat to identity and authority, and as a source of resentment. The *conduttore* is a sign of a larger process of organizational change. Romiti has stressed the importance of a move towards greater co-operation, and the importance of achieving employee participation in the business and in change, on a wider front. (Source: Cressey and Jones, 1992, pp. 61–74.)

Two classic approaches

It is common to distinguish two influential American schools of HRS. These are represented by two key texts from two institutions (Michigan and Harvard): *Strategic Human Resource Management* (Fombrun et al., 1984) and *Human Resources Management: A General Manager's Perspective* (Beer et al., 1985). The first, as Hendry and Pettigrew remark, focuses on strategic management, the other on human relations (see also Blyton and Turnbull, 1992, p. 4).

The Michigan group developed the notion of strategic HRM which entailed the interconnection of business strategies, organizational structures and HRM (which meant, in this context, key personnel systems: selection, appraisal, rewards and development). HRM systems were best designed to support the implementation of corporate strategy. The key contributors argued in a classic statement that 'just as firms will be faced with inefficiencies when they try to implement new strategies with outmoded structures, so they will also face problems of implementation when they attempt to effect new strategies with inappropriate HR systems. The critical management task is to align the formal structure and the HR systems so that they drive the strategic objective of the organisation' (Fombrun et al., 1984, p. 37).

At the heart of the Harvard approach (Beer et al., 1985) was the responsibility and capacity of managers to make decisions about the relationship between the organization and its employees such as to maximize the organizational outcomes for key stakeholders. This approach tends to adopt a particular approach to work-place relations: emphasizing unitary, integrative, individualistic systems, undermining workforce organization or collectivist values as outcomes of management choices about the key HRM levers affecting workforce–organization relations. This approach focuses on managers' responsibility to manage four key HRM policy areas: employee influence (participation); human resource flow; reward systems and work systems (work organization). Beer and Spector define this approach as follows:

> A business enterprise has an external strategy: a chosen way of competing in the market place. It also needs an internal strategy: a strategy for how its internal resources are to be developed, deployed, motivated and con-trolled . . . external and internal strategies must be linked.
>
> (Beer and Spector, 1985, p. 6)

The concept of strategy in these definitions draws on that of the Harvard Business School in the 1950s. Corporate strategy is the establishment of a company's long-term goals, policies and plans and the adoption of courses of action to achieve these goals. The notion of strategy, as its military origins suggest, means choosing means and resources to achieve selected objectives. But business strategy involves two key elements: formulating strategies and implementing them. However, establishing the proper link between HR strategy and corporate strategy may prove difficult, as we shall see.

One important issue that is raised and to which we shall return is the excessively rationalist notion of strategy. Experience suggests that strategic decision-making, either corporate or HR, is incremental, piecemeal, *ad hoc*, incomplete, and negotiated and only partly rational. Both cases discussed so far – BP and Fiat (above) – demonstrate this. In the case of BP, the pressure for change was based on a formal survey of employees initiated by those who were convinced of the need for change; the HRS change programme itself was clearly derived from the classic consultancy texts of the period – especially the 'excellence' literature. The Fiat case suggests that the pressure for HRS-type change came from a business strategy (flexibility, productivity and quality) and from the recognized need to establish a new interface role to handle the requirements of new technology systems which were them-selves key elements of the business strategy and the restructuring process. The Harvard notion of strategy tends to focus on the role of external, market pressures. These can clearly be very important, yet internal issues and resources are also important in establishing the need for, and the form of, successful HR strategies.

Overviews of the relationship between strategy and HRS

Useful overviews of the relationship between strategy and human resource strategies have been offered by Beaumont (1992), Hendry and Pettigrew (1990) and Storey and Sisson (1993). Beaumont traces a broadly similar development of the HRS approach to that offered by Hendry and Pettigrew. His analysis focuses on various conceptualizations of the relationship between types of corporate strategy and types of human resource strategy. Like other authors, he notes that three bases of classification have been employed: stages in the business or product cycle; different types of business strategy as identified by Porter; and connections between strategy and structure in terms of types and numbers of products.

These studies, most of which are American, tend to use a limited sense of HRS, which they call human resource management (HRM), and which refers broadly to elements of conventional personnel policies and activity: selection, assessment, training, appraisal, and so on. That is, HRM does not refer to cultural or structural dimensions. Nevertheless, a number of studies have attempted to plot the connections between aspects of HRS (or HRM) and aspects of organizational strategy. This requires the classification of such business strategies. Some researchers, following Chandler's (1962) emphasis on growth strategies that lead to structural modifications in organizations, have used a classification of types of strategy based on variations in product focus and have related this to aspects of HRM. Consider by way of illustration table 1.1, which is drawn from such analysis and which correlates aspects of personnel strategy (HRM) with organizational characteristics as defined by numbers and types of products.

From within another tradition, Beer and Spector have noted when discussing their Harvard approach, that, for example, 'a competitive strategy based on becoming the low-cost producer may indicate different approaches to compensation and employment security than a competitive strategy that depends on product innovation. The very idea of an internal Human Resource strategy implies there is consistency among all the specific tactics or activities that affect human resources' (Beer and Spector, 1985, pp. 5–6).

The work of Schuler and Jackson (1987) also argues that three discrete business strategies – innovation, quality enhancement and cost reduction – are associated with distinctive variations in key aspects of HRM as defined by the Harvard approach.

In table 1.2 variations in four key human resource functions are related to variations in the life-cycle stages of businesses – growth, maturity and decline.

Table 1.2 argues that there is – or should be – a temporal dimension of HRM and business development. It suggests that different aspects or dimensions of an organization's HRM system (what we would call the personnel systems dimension of HRS) are of particular salience at different stages of the product life cycle.

There are two immediate problems or limitations with all this. The first is that it is rather obvious and simplistic to translate, on paper, business strategies into their obvious HRS or HRM elements. We also need to consider to what extent these logical connections are apparent, or possible,

Table 1.1 Human resource management links to strategy and structure

Strategy	Structure	Human resource management			
		Selection	Appraisal	Rewards	Development
1 Single product	Functional	Functionally oriented: subjective criteria used	Subjective: measure via personal contact	Unsystematic and allocated in a paternalistic manner	Unsystematic, largely through job experiences: single function focus
2 Single product (vertically integrated)	Functional	Functionally oriented: standardized criteria used	Impersonal: based on cost and productivity data	Related to performance and productivity	Functional specialists with some generalists: largely through job rotation
3 Growth by acquisition (holding company) of unrelated businesses	Separate, self-contained businesses	Functionally oriented, but varies from business to business in terms of how systematic	Impersonal: based on return on investment and profitability	Formula-based and includes return on investment and profitability	Cross-functional but not cross-business
4 Related diversification of product lines through internal growth and acquisition	Multi-divisional	Functionally and generalist oriented: systematic criteria used	Impersonal: based on return on investment, productivity, and subjective assessment of contribution to overall company	Large bonuses: based on profitability and subjective assessment of contribution to overall company	Cross-functional, cross-divisional, and cross-corporate/divisional: formal
5 Multiple products in multiple countries	Global organization (geographic centre and world-wide)	Functionally and generalist oriented: systematic criteria used	Impersonal: based on multiple goals such as return on investment, profit tailored to product and country	Bonuses: based on multiple planned goals with moderate top management discretion	Cross-divisional and cross-subsidiary to corporate: formal and systematic

Source: Fombrun et al., 1984, p. 53, adapted from Galbraith and Nathanson, 1978.

Table 1.2: Critical human resource activities at different organizational or business unit stages

Human resource functions	Introduction	Life-cycle stages		
		Growth	Maturity	Decline
Recruitment, selection and staffing	Attract best technical/ professional talent	Recruit adequate numbers and mix of qualified workers; management succession planning; manage rapid internal labour market movements	Encourage sufficient turnover to minimize lay-offs and provide new openings; encourage mobility as reorganizations shift jobs around	Plan and implement workforce reductions and re-allocation
Compensation and benefits	Meet or exceed labour market rates to attract needed talent	Meet external market but consider internal equity effects; establish formal compensation structures	Control compensation	Tighter cost control
Employee training and development	Define future skill requirements and begin establishing career ladders	Mould effective management team through management development and organizational development	Maintain flexibility and skills of an ageing workforce	Implement retraining and career consulting services
Labour–employee relations	Set basic employee relations philosophy and organization	Maintain labour peace and employee motivation and morale	Control labour costs and maintain labour peace; improve productivity	Improve productivity and achieve flexibility in work rules; negotiate job security and employment adjustment policies

Source: Kochan and Barocci, 1985.

in reality. Secondly, these elegant frameworks may seem rather confusing and muddled because their definitions of different dimensions do not always tally. In order to make sense of, or to be able to make sensible judgements about HRS proposals, it is important to be aware of these differences and to recognize their implications. This we do in the next section.

Open and closed approaches to HRS

We need to distinguish two different approaches to HRS. The models described above, for example, share one important feature, which distinguishes them from other approaches: they all assert that the suitable form of HRS will vary with the type of business strategy. There is no one best way. These approaches are *open* or *contingent* with respect to the characteristics of the 'appropriate' HR strategy, and do not seek to impose one particular package of measures in every case. These approaches do not say what a particular HR strategy should be like; for this is a matter that can only be solved with reference to particular circumstances and particular strategies. The view of Hendry and Pettigrew, for example, is entirely open: it says nothing about what a coherent, planned, contingent strategy would be like in any particular case. It would simply be 'appropriate'.

This is also what Fombrun et al. and Schuler and Jackson and others try to do. Their definitions argue that for a particular business strategy there is a single, or very limited range of, HR strategy options. They simply attempt to describe what a particular HR strategy would be like for a particular business strategy – it would be contingent.

Thus a cost-reduction strategy would have different implications for HRM than an innovation strategy. This is important because for many HRS writers, the essence of HRS lies in the application of a specific and limited range of policies in every situation which might be termed a closed view. For example, Peters and Waterman (1982) imply that *regardless of the nature of the business, or the business strategy of stage in the product life cycle, one HR strategy is appropriate.* In a similar vein, others define HRS not in terms of achieving a suitable human resource strategy, but in terms of installing certain fixed elements, or in terms of certain fixed goals, regardless of business strategy. For example, Guest has argued that the key elements of HRS are:

- Integration of relevant employee activities into general organizational strategies and policies;
- Fluid and adaptive organizational structure;
- High-quality staff and internal practices to achieve high-quality products;
- Optimal employee commitment to enterprise goals and practices (Guest, 1987).

Presumably the argument here is that these goals are necessary and valuable in every case, for every strategy and every set of conditions.

Obviously these open and closed views cannot live happily together. There will be difficulties in reconciling the proposition that HRS strategies should be integrated with, and supportive of, the business strategy (whatever this is), with the proposition that all HR strategies should consist of the same elements (see Peters and Waterman, 1982) regardless of the business strategy pursued.

There are then two broadly different types of HRS. They share some features, notably that there should be a close, supportive and mutual relationship between organizational strategy and HR strategy. But one school then leaves the content of this relationship open, arguing that the only test of any HR strategy is its *appropriateness* or *fit* to the strategy. This is the open or contingent approach. The other approach is more closed. It too asserts the importance of the organization strategy–HRS connection, but sees the essential *HRS* as consisting of the implementation of some or all of the policy goals listed by Guest and others, such as participation, quality and flexibility.

Some writers try to have it both ways. Beaumont, for example, argues that 'The key messages . . . in the human resource management literature are a strategic focus, the need for human resource policies and practices to be consistent with overall business strategy, and the need for individual components of a human resource management package to reinforce each other, *while the individual components of the package should particularly emphasise teamwork, flexibility, employee involvement and organisational commitment*' (Beaumont, 1993, p. 25; our emphasis).

Poole takes a similar view but adds a moral (or moralistic element). He defines HRS as follows:

> Human resource management is viewed as strategic; it involves all managerial personnel . . . it regards people as the most important single asset of the organisation; it is proactive in its relationship with people; and it seeks to enhance company performance, employee 'needs' and societal well being.
>
> (Poole, 1990, p. 3)

On the other hand the open, general sense of HRS is presented diagrammatically in figure 1.2.

The model in figure 1.2 starts with an analysis of the environment within which organizations exist, and which they seek to control or survive in through certain strategies. These strategies, once defined, in turn require certain sorts of desired behaviours if they are to be achieved. If, for example, a bank is planning to move to a more customer-focused, sales-driven approach, and away from an emphasis on regulations and procedures and central bureaucratic control, then the attitudes, skills and behaviour of staff will have to change. These desired behaviours will be produced by certain sorts of human resource strategies (and not by others). People have to know what to do, want to do it, and be able to do it. To stick with our bank example, this change will probably require changes in training (for customer-care skills and others), in job descriptions (which will now specify

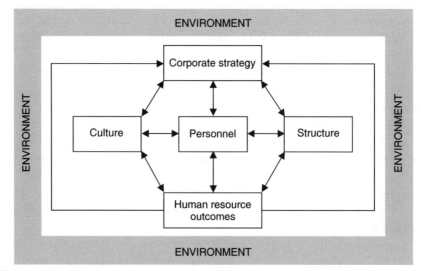

Figure 1.2   The 'open' approach to HRS

business and performance targets), in management style (greater discretion) and direction (towards new business), in internal assessment procedures (possibly the use of assessment centres), in organizational structures (more decentralized structures), in culture (away from rule compliance, towards a more commercial, entrepreneurial approach), and so on.

As can be seen from figure 1.2, this open approach to HRS has three key HRS components. These three constituent strategies are intended to sub-sume all aspects of organization which have an impact on employees' behaviour (structural, cultural and personnel) and one fundamental con-ceptual assumption – that of 'integration', or appropriateness. If these are 'appropriate', they will produce the desired behaviours, at least to some degree. This proviso is important because a possible human resource strat-egy would be to accept that a given strategy might be somewhat beyond the current capacities of systems, structures and staff, and that therefore they have to 'stretch' to achieve it. Ultimately, however, if integration of HRS and strategy is not seen as necessary to the achievement of strategy, the effort to achieve integration is seen as a necessary dynamic behind organ-izational pursuit of strategic objectives.

The degree of fit achieved will affect the relationship between behaviour and strategy, and will affect the level of achievement of organizational goals. The degree of success of the HRS components in supporting the achievement of corporate strategies must be monitored and evaluated. This is a fantastically idealized picture: in reality achieving it is extremely rare, and the risk in these rarified discussions of the abstract principles of HRS is that people begin to believe that the world is actually like this. It is not; and it is crucial that we recognize the many ways in which reality differs from these models.

At the same time, the objectives of HRS are sound. Ensuring that the organizational system (with all its constituent elements) supports the achievement of the overall strategy, that staff are clear about, willing, able and motivated to do what is necessary to achieve the organization's goals, is obvious good sense. But numerous factors will interrupt these processes: every stage is complex and subject to pressures which will discourage cool, detached, systematic analysis and implementation. The possibility of rational analysis within organizations is limited by political phenomena, and where proposed change will affect existing interests and established values and power bases, the interplay between these interests will have an impact on HRS decision-making. As we see in chapter 2, achieving change within organizations is difficult, particularly when change occurs within a context of rapid and urgent environmental challenges. Also the world in which organizations actually exist is highly unstable and dynamic; the normality of constant change means that the situation will change even during the change process, requiring adjustment to some ongoing processes, delay in others, acceleration to others, and so on.

The open, contingent HRS model is in principle dynamic (and idealized): it involves a series of active relationships, many of which are reciprocal. Senior managers define the business the organization is in. This then frames a particular organizational environment, including a market or market segment. Within this environment, the organization's managers develop a strategy. This strategy reflects an understanding of the environment, and a knowledge of the organization's human resource strengths. The achievement of the strategy requires certain sorts of behaviours. These will be produced by the appropriate choice of structural, cultural and personnel strategies. And these must in turn be integrated so that they mutually support each other. Once in place these strategies will produce human resource outcomes, and will thus support or influence the achievement of the organizational strategy. But their effect will only be known through constant evaluation and monitoring, which very likely will result in modification to the HRS plans, or to how they are implemented, or to the organizational strategy itself.

The basic argument is that competitive advantage will accrue to those organizations best able to exploit environmental opportunities and avoid or survive threats; and that the strategic management of human resources will assist organizations in this by encouraging and generating the appropriate sorts of behaviours, attitudes and competencies from employees.

As noted, human resource strategies involve an attempt to produce a match between key strategic priorities and the organizational processes which will produce the behaviours necessary for their achievement. This 'integration' has two aspects.

First, human resource strategies must be integrated with organizational strategy in the sense that they must be mutually supportive. The usual view of this is that HRS must be designed to achieve organizational strategies; but it is also possible that organizational strategies might be chosen in the light of existing human resource strengths and experience.

> HRM [has] a role in creating competitive advantage, in which the skills and motivation of a company's people and the way they are deployed can be a major source of competitive advantage. A company can methodically identify wherein its HR strengths lie and gear its HRM policies and business strategies towards utilizing and developing these advantages. The HR skills that will be crucial for the future in its industry can be identified, and it can take steps to acquire these.
>
> (Hendry and Pettigrew, 1986, p. 7)

Secondly, the separate constituent elements of HRS must be integrated such that they mutually support each other. There must be internal consistency. There is no point in recruiting qualified, ambitious, enthusiastic staff to fill repetitive, dead-end jobs, or in starting graduate selection without a graduate/management development scheme, or in 'empowering' supervisors without first ensuring that they are capable of taking on the increased responsibilities. Similarly, there is little value in launching a culture change programme emphasizing customer-care values when reward systems and management systems fail to incent, and possibly even demoralize, key staff. You can probably think of your own examples here – occasions when one aspect of organizational structure or policies seems to work against other priorities.

Schein, for example, argues that 'the major problem with existing HRPD [human resource planning and development] systems is that they are fragmented, incomplete, and sometimes built upon faulty assumptions about human or organisational growth' (Schein, 1987, p. 29). He argues that successful organizations are those which are able to match organizational needs with individual needs, thus achieving organizational growth along with individual development, commitment and creativity. For Schein HRS (or HRPD) involves the fulfilment of *both* individual and organizational needs. This is a 'soft' view of HRS and one which is typified by ideas not only about how organizations and individuals learn – they learn and develop together – but also about how they should interrelate. Like many writers in this field, Schein's view of HRS is not only highly prescriptive, it is highly normative and value laden. It describes how he would prefer people and organizations to interact.

Note then that the development of this idealized model of HRS involves four discrete stages. These are cyclical and continuous. They are also highly demanding.

- the formulation of an organizational strategy;
- the identification of the key behaviours necessary to achieve strategic objectives;
- the identification and implementation of the organizational processes required to generate these behaviours;
- the monitoring of the effectiveness and success of the change programme.

For example, if a major strategic objective is the achievement of competitive advantage through greater responsiveness to customers and reduced lead time, then this objective requires staff to be willing and able to identify and respond to customer requirements, and able to control the production process. This in turn may require delegation of authority, change in job skills, more 'flexible' working practices, a change of attitude, new staff in key positions, etc. But this process also assumes that senior management have been able to scan the organization's environment thoroughly; have picked up the key signals in time, analysed these sensibly and thoroughly and understood their implications for the fortunes of the organization; have developed an appropriate strategy to handle and exploit these developments, and have in turn been able and willing to restructure the organization to ensure its capability to support the new strategy. This is a daunting and demanding list of prerequisite steps for any group of senior managers.

Figure 1.3, which describes HRS developments in the computer industry, illustrates these relationships. The figure depicts, in the cases of the companies studied, the HRM (human resource management) factors developed in response to business strategies which in turn were responses to business pressures. The details of each column need not concern us here; the interesting point is the clear establishment, by the researchers, of connections *across* the various levels, between HRM elements, business strategies and business pressures.

Another important issue that emerges from these studies concerns the nature and direction of the links between the two sorts of strategy (business strategy and HR strategy). This is the point made persuasively by Lengnick-Hall and Lengnick-Hall that the effective matching of HRS and organizational strategies need not only mean manipulating personnel activities, organizational culture, etc., to match and support corporate strategy. The relationship could well work the other way around. They write: 'Firms that engage in a strategy formulation process that system-

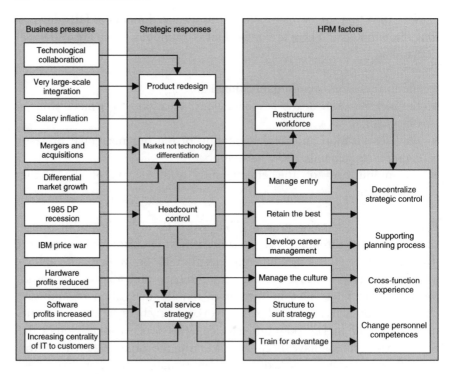

Figure 1.3   HRM responses to a changing environment
Source: Sparrow and Pettigrew, 1988, p. 42.

atically and reciprocally considers human resources and competitive strategy will perform better over the long term than firms that manage human resources primarily as a means to solve competitive strategy issues' (1988, p. 468).

Achieving 'fit' between HRS and business strategy

These models may allow the impression that the achievement of an appropriate 'fit' between business strategy and HR strategy is relatively uncomplicated. Yet it will already be clear that both formulating and implementing strategic human resource strategies is complex and difficult. We have seen, for example, that many writers have argued that little HRS is occurring at all, and that while much change is occurring, little can be called true HRS change. Furthermore much of this change is found to be unsuccessful (Storey and Sisson, 1993).

Beaumont notes that there 'has been relatively little systematic empirical research designed to identify the nature and determinants of the human resource management policy mix of individual organizations. Some potentially useful conceptual discussions of the issue have put forward a number of general and specific hypotheses but these have rarely been taken up and tested' (Beaumont, 1993, p. 19). Similarly, Storey and Sisson (1993) argue that much of the work attempting to match business to HR strategies is vulnerable for two reasons: because of a simplistic notion of strategy, and of the connections between the two types of strategy; and because of limitations on managers' willingness and ability to formulate appropriate HR strategies. Much work on the relationship between HR and corporate strategies assumes a rational, consensual, explicit and unilinear process of strategic decision-making. The reality, however, is not like this. This means that strategies may not always be easy to discern, that the processes of deci-sion-making may be implicit, incremental, negotiated, compromised.

In Europe, a study by researchers at Cranfield of HRS developments in France, the UK, Germany, Spain and Sweden defined HRS in terms of three key variables:

- Coherent, planned and evaluated policies on all aspects of personnel management that are developed with respect to corporate strategies;
- A move from collective to individual employee relations;
- An increase in line management responsibility for personnel manage-ment and a corresponding change in the role of the personnel function.

Now this definition of HRS, which is concerned with personnel activities and the location of the personnel function, may seem a little odd, and this may be due to the need to define HRS in terms that were relatively easily measurable. But the application of these criteria to a number of European organizations produces an interesting and familiar conclusion: 'there appears to be a relatively high level of acceptance of certain tenets of HRM policies across all countries (although to varying degrees), with far less evidence that this formal acceptance is carried through into coherent planned and evaluated policies' (Brewster et al., 1990).

Hendry and Pettigrew also note that efforts to match these frameworks to identify HRS requirements have not proved very illuminating, although this exercise is valuable in principle. The lack of empirical data has led to 'prescriptive theorizing and the armchair exercise of matching strategy to HR practices – a game easy to indulge in since there was little empirical backing for these formulations' (1990, p. 34). The authors point out the need for empirical analysis of the connections between HRS and corporate strategies, and the need to employ a conception of strategy as an incre-mental process (1990, p. 35).

These authors identify a number of key points with respect to the rela-tionship between strategies and structures which are important because they identify some of the key areas where the idealized stages of the HRS can, and will, be seriously influenced by the realities of organizational decision-making, negotiation, bounded rationality and the application of historic and probably out-dated ways of thinking. They are:

1 That strategy should not be seen as a ready-formed output to which human resource strategies are moulded.
2 That structure and culture change can precede strategy.
3 That human resource strategy developments need not be simply reactive to strategy but 'can contribute to it through the development of culture, as well as by the frames of reference of these managers who make strategy'.
4 The rationality of strategic and HRS thinking is inevitably, within an organizational context, limited (Hendry and Pettigrew, 1990, p. 35).

The elements – and values – of HRS are not new. But their combination, and the power of their combination, which arises from its capacity to manipulate the meanings attached to programmes of organizational change, as much as to achieve performance outputs, is new. The power of HRS resides in the *combination* of old elements in a new package, which resonates with key extra-organizational values and frames of reference. This is discussed more fully in chapter 9. In this section we will identify some major contributions to the core ideas of HRS.

Hendry and Pettigrew note that many of the academics who supported the value of radical organizational change were highly prescriptive and normative, stressing: 'commitment' (Walton and Lawrence, 1985), 'mutuality' (Beer et al., 1985) and 'communitarianism' (Lodge, 1985). Essentially these authors were offering an indictment of American organizations, as structures that destroy commitment, that produce deskilled and oppressed staff and therefore destroy any chance of developing the qualities that were then seen as fundamental to corporate success (most borrowed from Japan): loyalty, commitment, responsibility, intelligence. In his review of critics of the American HRM literature Beaumont (1992) notes some important points. First, that many of the key messages of the HRM movement (and indeed of HR) are not new: the Human Relations school had long preached the relationship between job satisfaction and productivity; socio-technical systems theory had emphasized the need to integrate technology and human systems; and Burns and Stalker (1961) had long asserted the importance of flexible organizational and work forms in organizations facing competitive, uncertain and unstable competitive environments. But this misses the point: these ideas may have been around before, but they were never so powerful. The important point about HRM and HRS is not the quality of the ideas but their *power* - that senior managers are now taking these issues seriously.

Hendry and Pettigrew note the origin of HRS in the crisis of confidence in American economic performance initiated by the perceived failure of

American manufacturers in the face of Japanese competition, and most obviously propounded in work of Abernathy et al. (1981). This crisis produced a widespread concern to address many aspects of organizational functioning, including organizational cultures, and thus moved beyond the traditional focus of Organizational Development (OD) or Quality of Working Life (QWL) programmes. The British emergence of a human resources approach was also centred around a concern for declining competitiveness, but was additionally associated with the organizational implications of Thatcherism, with particular reference to entrepreneurism and client focus (see Du Gay and Salaman, 1992). The decline of trade-union power allowed an opportunity for drastic organizational change, not least in work design. The personnel management function itself increasingly saw a chance to integrate its function with corporate objectives: 'What HRM did . . . was to provide a label to wrap around some of the observable changes while providing a focus for challenging deficiencies – in attitudes, scope, coherence and direction – of existing personnel management' (1992, p. 19).

As a body of ideas HRS did not arrive fully formed: many of the values, assumptions and arguments of HRS have been around for some time, although they have not previously been fused together as they are now. Hendry and Pettigrew (1990) in their review of the origins and history of HRS argue that a concern with the organizational benefits of an emphasis on the development of 'human resources' goes back, at least in management writing, to Drucker (1954), and has been evident in the argument that a well-trained and co-operative workforce is likely to contribute positively to organizational and economic development. Some writers have applied this argument to organizational structures, others to employment policies, or to job-design principles.

By the 1970s British writers were beginning to make a distinction between hard and soft versions of HRS: between what Morris calls 'human resources' and 'resourceful humans' (Morris, 1974, p. 110), the former meaning the strategy of treating staff as a resource like any other, to be exploited and controlled; the latter, representing attempts to develop and utilize the creativity and resourcefulness of staff for benefit to employer and individual. The importance of both these objectives – and the inherent 'contradiction' between organizational attempts simultaneously to achieve both control and commitment, obedience and innovation – has long been a central focus in research and writing within industrial sociology.

What is new about HRS, however, is the amalgamation of a number of ideas, the strength of the essential argument about the relationship between structures and strategy, and the widespread awareness that organizational change is necessary to achieve the required degree of fit. The work of organization theorists known as the Aston School, for example, suggested that organizational structures or profiles on a number of measured dimensions varied with the sort of work the organization was doing. Other writers have argued a relationship between structures and aspects of the production process. If structures vary with activities connected to organizational purposes, it is a small step to argue that structures fit, or are more or less appropriate to, these purposes.

The argument that different structures are likely to encourage or suppress creativity and flexibility has a number of sociological antecedents. One major constituent was the idea that bureaucracy may have limitations, and that different ways of structuring work might be more appropriate for different forms of organization and/or for different tasks or environments. Burns and Stalker, for example, argued that organization structures differed in their capacity to produce innovation, and that innovative structures were less controlling and allowed more autonomy (Burns and Stalker, 1961).

Some Key Sources: Theories of Work Design

A major source of HRS ideas and assumptions is the long tradition of analysis of job-design principles and their implications. It has four elements, all of which are fundamental to much HRS thinking.

First is the notion that shop-floor staff would produce better quality work and be more committed to their employer if their jobs were designed to allow greater skill and autonomy. This has a long pedigree, for example, in the 'quality of working life' movement (QWLM) and in job enrichment programmes. Even during the period when bureaucracy and Taylorism were widely regarded as the twin pillars of industrial organization – principles which had much in common in their emphasis on regulation, specification, control – there were those who argued against them, sometimes on moral grounds, sometimes on the basis of efficiency. Henry Ford himself noted that the principles of work design implemented by, and made notorious through, the Ford plants achieved high levels of control over the process of production but totally failed to achieve a similar level of control over the workforce. Indeed, the approach actively undermines such control by subjecting employees to a regime which is so insufferable that they become alienated from the work process, the product and the employer. It thus achieves some types of control, over work speeds and output, for example; but sacrifices others, such as that over quality and employees' attitudes and commitment. Ford wrote: 'Machines do not give us mass production. Mass production is achieved by both machines and man. And while we have gone a long way toward perfecting our mechanical operations, we have not successfully written into our equations whatever complex factors represent Man, the human element' (Ford, quoted in Littler and Salaman, 1986, p. 91).

The costs of this approach were quickly appreciated. But employers, noting such costs and attempting to develop solutions, were unable to escape from the limited thinking which produced the initial problem. Davis et al. (1972), on the basis of a survey of job design, found practices were consistent with the principles of scientific management – minimizing the dependence of the organization on the individual and minimizing the contribution of the individual to the organization. By adhering to the very narrow and limited criteria of minimizing immediate cost or maximizing immediate productivity, scientific management designs jobs based entirely on the principles of specialization, repetitiveness, low skill content and minimum impact of the worker on the production process. Management then frequently spend large sums of money and prodigious effort on many programmes that attempt to:

1 counteract the effects of job designs;
2 provide satisfaction, necessarily outside the job, which the job cannot provide;
3 and build on the satisfaction and importance of the individual which the job has diminished (Davis et al., 1972, p. 81).

But others saw that a better solution was to design jobs in ways which allowed inherent satisfaction, and which thus encouraged creativity and commitment (the QWLM). This approach is a major forerunner of the principles of current HRS. Those who argued against bureaucracy and against Taylorism/Fordism proposed that both were wrong, not because they were stifling and inhumane (although many thought this), but because they were inefficient, either absolutely, or at least under conditions where quality, responsiveness, flexibility and innovation were important.

The HRS movement – at least the 'soft', humanistic approach – includes values and assumptions derived from writers who questioned the efficacy and morality of Taylorist work forms. But, as Guest has noted, the use of these 'psychological growth theories' underpinning HRM tend to 'sit comfortably' with the 'individualist, anti-union stance of employers, combining to provide a coherent anti-union or at least non-union strategy' (Guest, 1990, p. 388).

The second theme of work-design analysis concerns the importance of relationships at work. Within HRS, work and employment are frequently seen as a major focus of social relationships and personal identification. This is particularly obvious in the emphasis on teamworking and on organizations as sources of meaningful work-based cultures. This emphasis on the social and relational aspect of work derives largely from the 'human relations' movement. This approach is based on the famous studies undertaken by the Western Electric Company at the Hawthorne Works in Chicago from the 1920s to the early 1940s, which concluded that work attitudes (satisfaction, frustration, tolerance of supervision, etc.) were strongly influenced by social relationships at work, particularly by the existence, membership and culture of the work group. This 'social man' was discovered to supplant the 'economic man' of Taylorism. Human relations proponents argued that within work-based social relationships or groups, worker behaviour, particularly productivity or co-operativeness with management, was thought to be shaped and constrained by the worker's role and status in a group. Other informal sets of relationships might spring up within the formal organization as a whole, modifying or overriding the official structure of the factory, which was based on purely technical criteria such as the division of labour (Rose, 1988, p. 104).

Thus the human relations movement bequeathed to HRS the suggestion that workers had significant social needs that could be satisfied at work, and the idea that if satisfied, these needs could be used to influence the workers' attitudes and behaviour.

The third element concerns the role and possibility of choice of work and organizational structures – a key HRS idea. HRS and the QWLM, on which it draws, have both been influenced by the work of the Tavistock Institute. The researchers there identified the advantages, in terms of output and morale, of self-managing groups with a degree of autonomy. The Tavistock studies have been used to argue that work-design principles are not determined, but can be chosen, and that achieving the right form of work design (enhanced work-group autonomy and responsibility) increases benefits for the organization and the employees.

This leads us to the fourth element of job-design studies that is influential in HRS: the conceptualization of the nature of the relationship between organizations and their employees. Taylorism, and to a lesser degree bureaucracy, define the relationship between employee and organization explicitly in terms of a clear contract of wages paid in return for measured effort or output. Taylorism thus represents the managerial equivalent of the instrumental worker who defines work entirely in terms of financial rewards. An obvious outcome of this approach is that both parties have an interest in minimizing their part of the exchange and maximizing the contribution of the other side. This view thus leads to, or reflects, a notion of the employment relationship as inherently competitive or conflictive. However, approaches to work design that argue the importance of allowing employees discretion and responsibility, and insist that staff will react to greater trust by increased commitment, and will react positively to enriched jobs and empowered roles, assume, at least implicitly, a high degree of shared interest between employer and employee. They argue that what is good for the employee is good for the organization; that conflict, if it occurs, is pathological and deviant; that there is little if any need for trade unions to mediate between staff and employer. Furthermore, they not only assume this, they assert it.

The distinction between the consensus and conflict views of employee/organization relations is important because clearly the work place is a place of co-operation and commitment, of conflict and consensus. And while the HRS movement on the whole, if not exclusively, argues that organizations and their staff share interests (so that to benefit staff is to benefit the organization and vice versa), it is obvious that major grounds for conflict between employers and employees exist and are inherent in the fact that organizations are hierarchical and inegalitarian. This has a number of implications. HRS may offer more effective ways of organizing staff and structuring jobs but it will not eliminate conflicts within employing organizations, which may surface in ways that disrupt HRS initiatives. Also, if HRS is based upon a consensus view of essential harmony it will be vulnerable when competitive pressures force decisions on wage increases, redundancies or increased output which run counter to this message. Another possibility is that within a conflict scenario some staff may regard typical HRS pronouncements as manipulative and ideological rather than as signalling a real change of approach.

Some key sources: The Japanese example

The Japanese threat is important in understanding the origins and development of HRS because senior managers in the West are faced not only by vigorous Japanese competition; they are also faced by what they see as a management approach which threatens what they do and how they do it. Of course lessons can be drawn from aspects of the Japanese model, and the 'excellence' literature draws selectively from the Japanese exemplar. The HRS approach is heavily influenced by some key elements drawn from Western perceptions of the Japanese model: for example, the 'high-context,' culture of Japanese corporations (see box 1.4).

Box 1.4   High-context corporate culture

The nature and role of Japanese corporate cultures, which have been seen as contributing to the performance of Japanese organizations, have been described as 'high-context' cultures, in contrast to 'low-context' corporate cultures (Hall, 1977). 'Context' refers to the framework within which communications make sense.

   To communicate properly and meaningfully, it is necessary to understand the context of communications, to pay attention to the right things. According to Hall, Japan, unlike the US, is a high-context culture (Hall, 1977, p. 45). In this sense, Japanese socialize meaning and experience into a deep value structure which can form the context of particular events or situations. Social relationships and communications in Japan reflect the way Japanese use uncertainty and interdependence in subtle ways and in what appear to be ambiguous communication signals. What this reflects in reality, however, is the high-context culture wherein contextual factors provide meaning and value to social relations (McMillan, 1985, p. 35).

The two culture types differ with respect to four dimensions: characteristics of business; characteristics of communication within the organization; characteristics of rules within the organization; and a category of general distinguishing characteristics.

With respect to business, high-context cultures are characterized by low-pressure sales, long sales cycles, high customer and employee involvement, the avoidance of protagonist/antagonist relations and acceptance of ambiguity. Whereas the low-context culture features the reverse of these: high-pressure sales, us and them attitudes, and so on. Within the high-context culture communications are indirect, economical, expect a great deal of interpretation from the listener, depend very much on the form of the communication and are difficult to change. Within the low-context culture, on the other hand, communications are once again characterized by the reverse of these features and are to the point, explanative and content-focused. Rules within high-context cultures are holistic and integrated and cannot be manipulated. Generally the two types of culture differ with respect to the way in which the high-context focuses on covert knowledge, rather than on legalistic and specified relationships and data, and emphasizes responsibility for organizational employees.

As McMillan notes, the important point of Hall's argument is the suggestion that the key features of the Japanese management system lie not so much in the uniquely Japanese elements of Japanese social culture, but in the broad characteristic of these elements – characteristics which could occur outside Japan. McMillan himself argues that a number of non-Japanese organizations display high-context cultures: for example, the Jesuits, IBM, Michelin.

The value of Hall's analysis is that it argues the superiority, in human resource terms, of the 'high-context' type cultures over 'low-context' ones, because in the former, organizational meanings and values are transmitted not only through direct forms of communication but also through symbols and values. Furthermore, high-context cultures' relationships, both external (with customers, banks and suppliers) and internal (with employees), are long-term and supportive, in contrast to the view of these relationships in low-context cultures, which defines them in oppositional, contractual terms. Hall does not argue that there is anything necessarily or essentially Japanese about high-context cultures. Nevertheless, interest in Japanese-type corporate cultures has contributed significantly to the emphasis on culture in HRS writings and consultancy.

Of obvious importance to Western approaches to HRS is the Japanese attitude towards staff. Employees of large Japanese organizations are clearly seen as a resource which must be cherished and made best use of. The pattern of employment relations in large firms means effectively that staff will not be laid off: they are a fixed cost, not a variable one. The system of lifetime employment, allied to the Nenko system of wages tied to age and length of service, creates a major opportunity and a major need for large-scale staff development. In this context it is possible to describe employees as a corporate resource to be developed and used. HRS borrows this language. It may not always borrow the institutional framework within which it is located in Japan.

Finally, HRS borrows many ideas from Japanese production methods. There are three main elements. The first is 'just-in-time' (JIT) production, which aims to produce the right materials or products in the necessary quantities and quality at the appropriate time. It reduces stocks, reduces scrap, and highlights inefficiencies and forces them to be addressed. It also reduces lead times. Cellular working and total quality control (TQC) are associated with JIT. Cellular working groups combine processes and machines with a multi-skilled workforce to enhance flexibility. TQC attempts to locate responsibility for quality in the manufacturing process by making it the responsibility of the operator. HRS schemes borrow many of these ideas – some of which, it has been suggested, originated in the West anyhow, and were recognized early on by Japanese industrialists as ways of avoiding some of the inefficiencies and pathologies of Western methods (Dore, 1973).

But there is need for caution when borrowing from Japan. Thompson and McHugh (1990) note the power of the Japanese model for Western business leaders concerned about declining competitiveness. These authors note the importance of JIT, flexibility, quality programmes, and so on, but argue that the main focus has been on management skills, attitudes and values, including a commitment to the management of human resources. However, these authors argue that this 'culturalist' emphasis (advocated by many seminal writers like Ouchi, 1981; Pascale and Athos, 1992) underestimates the importance of other Japanese elements, notably the nature of industrial organization and production expertise. They note, for example, how the JIT system, with all its advantages, depends upon 'flexible labour utilisation and harmonising of tacit skills, close managerial involvement in production, multi-purpose machinery and reductions in set-up times . . . Such a system also frequently depends on a set of relations between large corporations and suppliers' (Thompson and McHugh, 1990, p. 202).

The 'culturalist' explanations also seriously underestimate the role and importance of state intervention and support in Japan, with the Japanese state historically playing an active part in shaping domestic markets, overseeing the supply of long-term cheap credit and supporting technological development. The role of culture as a determinant of organizational performance is discussed in chapter 6.

Some key sources: The consultancy and 'excellence' literature

This prescriptive management literature variously claims to have identified the necessary structural/behavioural features of the organization of the future, or of the successful ('excellent') organization. Thus Handy describes three future types of organization: the federal organization with marked decentralization; the contractual organization in which there is a substitution of fees for wages; and the professional organization where the number of experts and professionals is increased (Handy, 1984, pp. 78–89). The Prospect Centre, a management consultancy, argues: 'Turning outwards to face an increasingly turbulent environment, successful companies have developed strategies based on quality, innovation and responsiveness to their customers' (Prospect Centre, 1988, p. 1). Wickens, on the basis of his study of a Nissan plant in the UK, talks of the three key elements of corporate success: teamworking, quality and flexibility (Wickens, 1987). Peters, whose contributions to this literature are highly significant, stresses the importance of 'new products, new markets, new competition and new thinking' (Peters, 1989, p. 27). Against new environmental demands, he argues, organizations must achieve quality design and service, and must be flexible in responding to customer requirements; large corporations must learn to behave in new ways; new organizational configurations other than the traditional (but inflexible) hierarchical bureaucracy must be developed; big may no longer be best; single organizations will be replaced by co-operative networks, and the ordinary member of staff will necessarily be committed to improvement and retraining (Peters, 1989, pp. 28–9).

Wood (1989) points out that many of these 'excellence' texts focus on the need for continuous change, for achieving a form of organizational structure which is consistently capable of responding to changing circumstances: 'learning to love change', as Peters puts it. The need for change follows the fact that environmental change – changes in markets, producers, competitors – is now constant and endemic. Structural responses are not adequate:

they over-complicate and produce rigidity. Organizational responsiveness and opportunism arise from unleashing the creativity and enthusiasm of staff. Peters and Waterman have urged companies to adopt the eight claimed attributes of 'excellence' companies: a bias for action; close to the customer; autonomy and entrepreneurship; productivity through people; hands-on, value driven; stick to the knitting; simple form, lean staff; simultaneous loose–tight properties. Central to the 'excellence' literature, Wood notes, is not just that environments are changing and that organizations must change in line with the broadly anti-bureaucratic direction described, but that these changes must be produced by changes in culture: 'Culture is paramount as it structures the way people think, make decisions and act in organisations' (Wood, 1989, p. 385).

The shared message of these writers moves beyond their anti-bureaucracy, pro-flexibility stance and coheres around a strongly culturalist perspective: change, it is argued, can only come from changed attitudes and outlook, not from systems and structures. One reason for this is that the process of decision-making is seen as excessively rational, logical and systematic, not as it is: fumbling, gradual and messy. For this reason, a strong culture of innovation and risk-taking is more likely to produce appropriate outcomes than mere structure or systems. The excellence/consultancy literature differs from more analytical writing not only in its preference for broad-ranging prescription, but also in its neglect of issues of power, authority and conflict, and the political processes to which these give rise (Wood, 1989, p. 381). Organizations, of whatever sort, are houses of power. Power is the blood that supports the system: it is a reward and a resource, and is inherent in any structure having co-ordination and direction. Because power is inherent it will affect the potential of a human resource strategy and its direction. These issues are considered further in chapter 9.

Conclusion

Something is certainly going on. Organizations are changing and they are changing in new ways and with new intensity. Many of these changes seem dramatic and certainly attract much attention. Whether or not these changes add up to HRS-type change is another matter. It partly depends on the view you take of what HRS is; and we have noted that definitions of HRS differ markedly. But it also depends upon the extent to which current programmes of organizational change are, behind all the claims, actually concerned with enhancing and focusing organizational capability for growth and performance; or façades which disguise and justify cost cutting, downsizing, attacks on unions, increased control and surveillance of 'flexible' and frequently deskilled staff.

Parallel with these changes, and inspiring or legitimating them, exists a body of ideas, of a various and complex nature, known as HRS. These ideas promise much, and the management dream-makers and purveyors of promises, ensure that the promises are publicized and amplified. But closer analysis suggests some conceptual, logical problems with these dreams. The issue is not simply their efficiency – that managers may be disappointed with HRS in practice. It is whether anyone really believed them in the first place. Is HRS a promise that is not yet completely fulfilled, a disturbed dream (a failed promise that could never work), or a dream that is most powerful in disguising and distorting the realities it advocates? These issues are pursued further throughout this text and revisited in the final chapter.

The ideas in HRS thinking are not new. But their combination is new, and their resonance with extra-organizational socio-political values is new, and is crucial to their power and appeal. In this chapter we have plotted some of the major sources of HRS ideas. The importance of HRS lies as much in the management of meaning as in the management of staff: indeed it collapses this distinction itself. HRS signifies the attempt to manage staff by managing meanings as much as by managing systems and structures, for not only does it involve the redefinition of why and how these are being changed, but in many cases it also entails systematic attempts to manipulate employees' values and attitudes.

Key points

- *Organizations are currently changing, sometimes fundamentally and drastically. These changes are often described – and justified – as HRS changes. It is therefore important to know what HRS is, and if these changes are genuinely examples of this ambitious approach to organizational change which seeks to align organizational systems, structures and skills with organizational strategies in order to improve organizational effectiveness.*
- *These changes are usually associated with changes in organizations' environments. The changes themselves occur on a number of levels: structures, cultures, job design (flexibility) and elsewhere.*
- *However, it is far from clear that these changes are always examples of genuine HRS – i.e., that they are systematically integrated with each other and related to the organization's overall strategy.*
- *Part of the difficulty is due to the various ways in which HRS is defined. Some key differences are identified and discussed.*

> • *HRS is not new but it consists of a powerful combination of new ideas, which carry their own historic assumptions and purposes. These constituent ideas and their intellectual origins are important in accounting for the appeal of HRS. That is why they need to be thoroughly identified and dismantled.*

Discussion questions

1　What current changes occurring within organizations are typically claimed to be examples of HRS?
2　In the light of current definitions of HRS, can these developments be seen as genuine examples of HRS-type change?
3　What are the key sources of HRS ideas and themes, and what are their implications for the HRS approach and its assumptions?

REFERENCES

Abernathy, W., Clark, K. B. and Kantrow, A. M. (1981) The new industrial competition. *Harvard Business Review,* Oct., pp. 69–77.

Atkinson, J. (1985) Flexibility: planning for an uncertain future. *Manpower Policy and Practice,* 1, summer.

Beaumont, P. B. (1992) The US human resource management literature. In Salaman, G. et al. (eds), *Human Resource Strategies,* London, Sage.

Beaumont, P. B. (1993) *Human Resource Management.* London, Sage, pp. 20–38.

Beer, M. and Spector, B. (eds) (1985) *Readings in Human Resource Management.* New York, Free Press.

Beer, M., Spector, B., Lawrence, P., Mills, D. and Walton, R. (1985) *Human Resources Management: A General Manager's Perspective.* New York, Free Press.

Bevan, S. and Thompson, M. (1992) An overview of policy and practice. In *Performance Management: An Analysis of the Issues.* London Institute of Personnel Management.

Blyton, P. and Turnbull, P. (eds) (1992) *Reassessing Human Resource Strategies.* London, Sage.

Blyton, P. and Turnbull, P. (1992) HRM: debates, dilemmas and contradiction. In Blyton, P. and Turnbull, P. (eds) *Reassessing Human Resource Management.* London, Sage, pp. 1–15.

Blyton, P. and Morris, J. (1992) HRM and the limits of flexibility. In Blyton, P. and Turnbull, P. (eds) *Reassessing Human Resource Management.* London, Sage, pp. 116–30.

Brewster, C. J., Hegewisch, A., Holden, L. and Lockhart, T. (1990) Trends in human resource management in Europe 1990. Cranfield, Bedfordshire, Price Waterhouse Cranfield Project working paper.

Buchanan, D. A. (1992) High performance: New boundaries of acceptability in worker control. In Salaman, G. et al. (eds), *Human Resource Strategies*. London, Sage, pp. 138–55.

Burns, T. and Stalker, G. M. (1961) *The Management of Innovation*. London, Tavistock.

Cappelli, P. and McKersie, R. B. (1987) Management strategy and the redesign of work rules. *Journal of Management Studies*, 24, no. 24, pp. 441–62.

Chandler, A. D. (1962) *Strategy and Structure*. Cambridge, Mass., MIT Press.

Child, J. (1972) Organisational structure, environment and performance: The role of strategic choice. *Sociology*, 6, no. 1, pp. 1–22.

Child, J. (1987) Information technology, organization and response to strategic challenges. *California Management Review*, 30, no. 1, fall, pp. 33–50.

Cressey, Peter and Jones, B. (1992) Business strategy and human resource. In *B884 Human Resource Strategies, Supplementary Readings 1*. Milton Keynes, Open University, pp. 61–74.

Davis, L., Canter, R. and Hoffman, J. (1972) Current work design criteria. In Davis, L. and Taylor, J. (eds), *Design of Jobs*. Harmondsworth, Penguin.

Dore, R. (1973), *British Factory – Japanese Factory*. London, Allen and Unwin.

Drucker, P. F. (1954) *The Practice of Management*. New York, Harper.

du Gay, P. and Salaman, G. (1992) The cult(ure) of the customer. *Journal of Management Studies*, 29, no. 5, pp. 615–33.

Elger, T. (1991) Task flexibility and the intensification of labour in UK manufacturing. In Pollert, A. (ed.) *Farewell to Flexibility?* Oxford, Blackwell, pp. 46–66.

Fiat (1988) *Facts and Figures*.

Fombrun, C. J. (1983) Strategic management: Integrating the human resource systems into strategic planning. *Advances in Strategic Management*, vol. 2. Greenwich, Conn., JAI Press.

Fombrun, C. J., Tichy, N. M. and Devanna, M. A. (1984) *Strategic Human Resource Management*. New York, John Wiley.

Fowler, A. (1987) When chief executives discover HRM. *Personnel Management*, Jan., p. 3.

Galbraith, J. R. and Nathanson, D. A. (1978) *Strategy Implementation: The Role of Structure and Process*. St Paul, Minn., West Publishing.

Goold, M. and Campbell, A. (1986) S*trategies and Styles: The Role of the Centre in Managing Diversified Corporations*. Oxford, Blackwell.

Gowler, D. and Legge, K. (1986) Images of employees in company reports – Do company chairmen view their most valuable asset as valuable? *Personnel Review*, 15, no. 5, pp. 9–18.

Gronroos, C. (1985) *Service Management and Marketing*. Lexington, Mass., D. C. Heath.

Gronroos, C. (1990) Internal marketing – theory and practice. In Bloch, T., Upa, G. and Zeithaml, V. (eds), *Services Marketing in a Changing Environment*. Chicago, American Marketing Association.

Guest, D. E. (1987) Human resource management and industrial relations. *Journal of Management Studies*, 24, no. 5, pp. 503–21.

Guest, D. E. (1989) Human resource management: Its implications for industrial relations and trade unions. In Storey, J. (ed.), *New Perspectives on Human Resource Management*. London, Routledge, pp. 41–55.

Guest, D. E. (1990) Human resource management and the American dream. *Journal of Management Studies*, 27, no. 4, pp. 377–97.

Hall, E. T. (1977) *Beyond Culture*. New York, Doubleday.

Hales, Colin (1994) Internal marketing as an approach to human resource management. *Journal of Management Studies*, 5, no. 1, pp. 50–71.

Handy, C. (1984) *The Future of Work*. Oxford, Basil Blackwell.

Hendry, C. and Pettigrew, A. (1986) The practice of strategic human resource management. *Personnel Review*, 15, no. 5, pp. 3–8.

Hendry, C. and Pettigrew, A. (1990) Human resource management: An agenda for the 1990s. *International Journal of Human Resource Management*, 1, no. 1, pp. 17–43.

Hendry, C., Pettigrew, A. and Sparrow, P. (1988) Changing patterns of human resource management. *Personnel Management*, Nov., pp. 37–41.

Keenoy, T. and Anthony, P. (1992) HRM: Metaphor, meaning and morality. In Blyton, P. and Turnbull, P. (eds), *Reassessing Human Resource Management*. London, Sage, pp. 233–55.

Kochan, T. A. and Barocci, T. A. (1985) *Human Resource Management and Industrial Relations*. Boston, Little Brown.

Lane, C. (1989) New technology and changes in work organisation. In Lane, C., *Management and Labour in Europe*. Aldershot, Edward Elgar, pp. 163–95.

Legge, K. (1988) Personnel management in recession and recovery. *Personnel Review*, 17, no. 2.

Legge, K. (1989) Human resource management: A critical analysis. In Storey, J. (ed.), *New Perspectives on Human Resource Management*. London, Routledge, pp. 19–40.

Lengnick-Hall, C. and Lengnick-Hall, M. (1988) Strategic human resources management: A review of the literature and a proposed typology. *Academy of Management Review*, 13, no. 3, pp. 454–70.

Littler, C. and Salaman, G. (1986) *Class at Work*. London, Batsford.

Lodge, G. C. (1985) Ideological implications of changes in human resource management. In Walton, R. E. and Lawrence, P. R. (eds), *HRM Trends and Challenges*. Boston, Harvard Business School Press.

Lorenz, C. (1992) A drama behind closed doors that paved the way for a corporate metamorphosis. *B884 Human Resource Strategies*. Milton Keynes, Open University, pp. 5–7.

Lorenz, C. (1992) Countdown to a consultative revolution. *B884 Human Resource Strategies*. Milton Keynes, Open University, p. 8.

Lorenz, C. (1992) Re-appraising the power of regional barons. *B884 Human Resource Strategies*. Milton Keynes, Open University, pp. 9–10.

Lorenz, C. (1992) A cultural revolution that sets out to supplant hierarchy with informality. *B884 Human Resource Strategies*. Milton Keynes, Open University, pp. 11–12.

McMillan, C. J. (1985) *The Japanese Industrial System*. New York, de Gruyter.

Morris, J. (1974) Developing resourceful managers. In Taylor, B. and Lippitt, G.

L. (eds), *Management Development and Training Handbook*. New York, McGraw-Hill.

Nolan, P. (1989) The productivity miracle? In Green, F. (ed.), *The Restructuring of the UK Economy*. Hemel Hempstead, Harvester.

Ouchi, W. (1981) *Theory Z*. Reading, Mass., Addison-Wesley.

Pascale, R. T. and Athos, A. G. (1992) *The Art of Japanese Management*. New York, Simon and Schuster.

Peters, T. (1987) *Thriving on Chaos*. Basingstoke, Macmillan.

Peters, T. (1989) New products, new markets, new competition, new thinking. *The Economist*, 4 Mar.

Peters, T. J. and Waterman, R. H. (1982) *In Search of Excellence: Lessons from America's Best-run Companies*. New York, Harper & Row.

Pettigrew, A. (1988) Introduction: Researching strategic change. In Pettigrew, A. (ed.), *The Management of Strategic Change*. Oxford, Blackwell, pp. 1–14.

Pollert, A. (1988) The 'flexible firm': Fixation or fact? *Work Employment and Society*, 2, no. 3, pp. 281–316.Poole, M. (1990) Editorial: Human resource management in an international perspective. *International Journal of Human Resource Management*, 1, no. 1, pp.   1–15.

Prospect Centre (1988) *Strategies and People*. Kingston, UK, Prospect Centre.

Rose, M. (1988) *Industrial Behaviour*. Harmondsworth, Penguin.

Salaman, G., Cameron, S., Hamblin, H., Iles, P., Mabey C. and Thompson K. (eds) (1992) *Human Resource Strategies*. London, Sage.

Schein, E. (1987) Increasing organizational effectiveness through better human resource planning and development. In Schein, E. (ed.) *The Art of Managing Human Resources*. New York, Oxford University Press, pp. 25–45.

Schuler, R. S. and Jackson S. E. (1987) Linking competitive strategies with human resource management practices. *Academy of Management Executive*, 1, no. 3, pp. 207–19.

Severance, D. G. and Passino, J. H. (1986) *Senior Management Attitudes toward Strategic Change in US Manufacturing Companies*. Ann Arbor, Mich., University of Michigan Press.

Sisson, K. (1989) Personnel management in transition. In Sisson, K. (ed.), *Personnel Management in Britain*. Oxford, Blackwell, pp. 23–54.

Sisson, K. (1990) Introducing the *Human Resource Management Journal*. *Human Resource Management Journal*, 1, no. 1, pp. 1–11.

Sparrow, P. and Pettigrew, A. (1988) Contrasting HRM responses in the changing world of computing. *Personnel Management*, Feb., pp. 40–5.

Storey, J. (1992) *Developments in the Management of Human Resources*. Oxford, Blackwell.

Storey, J., and Sisson, K. (1993) *Managing Human Resources and Industrial Relations*. Buckingham, Open University Press.

Thompson, P. and McHugh, D. (1990) *Work Organisations: A Critical Introduction*. Basingstoke and London, Macmillan Education Ltd.

Thomson, A., Pettigrew, A. M. and Rubashow, N. (1985) British management and strategic change. *European Management Journal*, 3, no. 3, pp. 165–73.

Tichy, N., Fombrun, C. and Devanna, M. A. (1982) Strategic human resource management. *Sloan Management Review*, winter, pp. 47–61.

Walton, R. E. and Lawrence, P. R. (eds) (1985) *HRM Trends and Challenges*. Boston, Harvard Business School Press.

Wickens, P. (1987) *The Road to Nissan: Flexibility, Quality, Teamwork*. London, Macmillan.

Wood, S. (1989) New wave management? *Work, Employment and Society*, 3, no. 3, pp. 379–402.

2 Managing Change

Learning Objectives

- *to examine a range of assumptions that govern attempts to bring about strategic change in organizations and note the influence such assumptions have upon the change pathways chosen.*
- *to understand why many well-conceived and well-planned change interventions fail or result in unpredictable and unhelpful outcomes.*
- *to review a range of change management strategies, what premises they are built upon and what – potentially – they can achieve.*
- *to decide upon the most appropriate strategic approach in terms of scope, speed and style, for a given human resource initiative.*
- *to anticipate the likely sources of personal and institutional reaction and resistance to strategic change, and take this into account in the way the change process is managed.*

Introduction

There will be occasions when business strategy, and by implication human resource strategies, will be aimed at steady-state scenarios. For example, the intention may be to reinforce existing priorities within the organization: this may require modifying the reward system so it reflects a greater performance-related element, or perhaps extending an appraisal system which is working well at management grades to include supervisory staff and their teams as well. Such human resource initiatives will undoubtedly promote significant changes for certain groups of individuals but are unlikely to cause shock waves throughout the organization (although even minor revisions of policy like these can be delicate and their introduction requires sensitive handling!). However, in this text we have been dealing typically with human resource interventions which are advocated by, designed at and launched from a strategic level. While not *all* human resource initiatives necessarily imply change, most do, and this is especially the case where they are linked to wider strategic intentions.

It is not unreasonable, then, to start a text on human resource strategies with an examination of change management. This apparently simple task takes us immediately to the heart of some very fraught questions. To what extent is it possible for organizations to initiate change in a proactive and purposeful manner? Can change be broken down into discrete chunks of activity? If it is possible to define a particular change strategy, how realistic is it to talk of that strategy being managed? Why do the 'simplest' of change interventions so quickly become problematical and unworkable? Why within the same organization do individuals often hold such emotively and radically different assessments of the same change initiative? Before enlisting the support of various change management approaches in our quest for strategically managed human resources we need to address some of the assumptions and paradigms that underlie them.

As table 2.1 shows, each aspect of change management (intention, implementation and interpretation) is governed by a set of assumptions which will – by implication – significantly alter the way organizational change is conceived and construed by those involved. Generally speaking, the left of each pair of assumptions (in italics) represents the received wisdom on the subject of change management, particularly in the US literature (e.g. French and Bell, 1984; Beckhard and Harris, 1987; Buller, 1988; Porras and Silvers, 1991; Schuler, 1992). Even if and when change comes to be seen as positive and pervasive, implementation can still be shaped by deterministic thinking. And, even if and when the less predictable, relational and multi-faceted dimensions of change implementation have been recognized, it is still possible to interpret the outcomes in a way that downplays or ignores the differing versions, meanings and ideologies with which they are invested.

In this chapter we take a closer look at each set of assumptions in table 2.1 and discuss the implications of these for the way human resources are directed and developed in organizations.

Change Management Assumptions

Assumptions about intention

It is by now well understood that the destiny of an organization is very much dependent on how well it attunes to and successfully confronts pressures to change. These may be either internally generated, such as attempts to innovate, task and technological demands, resource scarcities, the expression of focused discontents and the like, or come externally from the environment in the form of demographic, economic, political, cultural, scientific, legislative or competitive influences. 'Within the literature, contingency theory has been widely adopted to explain organizational performance as a function of the fit between an organization's internal arrangements and environmental characteristics (Lawrence and Lorsch, 1967). Volatile and uncertain environments require "organic" management systems, threatening environments require centralized control, diverse environments require decentralized organizational forms, and stable, predictable contexts make bureaucratic forms effective' (Nicholson, 1993, p. 208). However, as the author points out, knowing the need for contingent relations does not necessarily mean an organization *can* adapt its design characteristics accordingly, nor integrate its subsystems to consistently and collectively

Table 2.1 Change management assumptions

Assumptions about intentions of change: is change	Implications
Exceptional or endemic?	• Arrangements made for scanning, filtering and responding to signals for change
Threatening or desirable?	• Behavioural and structural readiness to do things differently
Deviant or normal?	• Cultural responsiveness to do things differently
Assumptions about implementing change: is change	**Implications**
Controllable or controlling?	• Perceptions about the rightness, speed, scope and pace of change strategy
Rational or relational?	• Attention given to historical, cultural and political (internal/external) contexts
Discrete or multi-faceted?	• Arrangements made to cater for systemic repercussions
Assumptions about interpretation of change: is change	**Implications**
Directional or reciprocal?	• Allowances made for differing versions of change process
Managing people or managing meaning?	• Credence given to differing choice and evaluation of change outcomes
Problem-solving or pattern-seeking?	• Extent to which differing views, predispositions, ideologies explored, understood, tolerated

fit new or revised organizational goals. Furthermore, the contingency approach tends to emphasize the need to adapt when change comes, rather than to assume change as a given. It also tends to treat change as exceptional rather than endemic. Notice how this predisposition has important implications for the way boundaries are scanned, external/internal signals are interpreted, and how flexibly internal systems and structures are configured.

Another commonly held view is that individuals generally find change more threatening than desirable. Research by Dopson and Stewart (1993) found middle managers in the UK more resistant to change in the public than in the private sector. They linked this more negative stance to: seeing change as caused by a political decision rather than competitive threat; seeing change as abnormal; receiving little help to adapt to change; and seeing oneself as primarily a 'professional' rather than a manager. The inevitability of resistance to change through denial, inaction, or action which is a retreat to the familiar has been challenged when it comes to managers:

> We propose an alternative interpretation, that managers respond to unfamiliarity by acting and therefore adding to it. They act in ways that convert

exogenous into endogenous change. Ways of creating alternatives will perhaps be those that have produced previous success. Action in the face of
unfamiliar change may be an attempt to recreate previous success or mastery; however, it is not a defensive denial of change, but rather a bid to better
it. If action is the more common response to change among managers, then
this implies a whole set of new problems and issues which are not anticipated
in current change management models. . . . Our research lends support to
this view of change as a political process, in which managers obtain power by
acting. By acting, seizing the initiative, the individual retrieves power over
events.

(Crouch, Sinclair and Hintz, 1992, pp. 42–4)

A related, implicit assumption about change is to regard it as something
which happens to or is perpetrated upon, a relatively passive organization.
The usually unquestioned belief is that 'change is manageable, its outcomes
predictable and capable of being directed by those possessing organizational authority' (Hosking and Anderson, 1992, p. 7). Of course it is probably more realistic to see individuals and the people who constitute the
organization they work in, as 'co-constructing' each other; both acting,
understanding and making sense of change as joint and dynamic players
in the process. 'This perspective places the process of co-construction at the
centre of person–organization relationships. This means that change is also
centred, rather than being treated as a deviation from the stable norm'
(Hosking and Anderson, 1992, p. 11). Once again this placing of change at
centre stage rather than as an aberration from the 'normal' smooth running
of the system, makes a crucial difference to the way an organization operates, and in particular, the way change implementation is construed.

Assumptions about implementation

Based on their study which examined the successful and the less effective
management of strategic and organizational change in eight UK companies
over more than 20 years up to 1989, Pettigrew and Whipp (1991) concluded:

> Our research at firm level in four sectors of the UK economy confirms the
> findings of the critical school of writers – that in practice the development of
> an HRM approach within a firm cannot be assumed. In the same way its
> positive contribution to competitive performance cannot be taken for
> granted. The dimensions which the vast majority of writers in the field
> minimize we see as paramount: the process by which human resources are
> developed such that they can contribute to the ability of the organization to
> accomplish strategic change and generate competitive bases. (1991, pp.
> 210, 211)

Consistently, they found the difference between successful and unsuccessful change depended on the extent to which there had been a raising HRM consciousness in the organization, using situationally appropriate features to create a positive force for change, and demonstrating the need for business and people change. In short, successful organizations paid as much attention to the *process* of human resource change and its degree of progressive acceptance outside the HRM department, as they did to the substance of the policies and procedures themselves.

Despite this essential highlighting of both the processual and contextual dimensions alongside the content of strategic change (Whipp, Rosenfeld and Pettigrew, 1989), there is nevertheless a tendency to focus on the outcomes of strategic decision-making whether in performance or quality terms. 'In this way, the underlying model is understood to have normative value for management – helping them to manipulate decision processes so they make "better" strategic decisions' (Hosking and Anderson, 1992, p. 9).

Box 2.1 describes how a medium-sized mutual life insurance company (under the pseudonym of Pensco) embarked on a programme of corporate change. One important plank in the change strategy was the reorganization of clerical work into team-based production groups.

Box 2.1 Which comes first: the policy or the practice?

'The team-building programme can be summarized as an attempt to elicit employee commitment to the corporate objectives of profitability under the rubric of success and efficiency, and maintaining or increasing market share. In so doing, team-building exposes employees to the competitive environment of the financial services market, personalizing company goals and pushing responsibility for achieving corporate targets down to employees. What the team-building programme aimed to achieve therefore, was the incorporation of employees into a managerially-led construction of the company-wide team, high levels of commitment to corporate/commercial objectives, motivation and self-discipline to achieve those objectives, personalizing company goals, and "cascading" responsibility for achieving corporate targets down to employees.

Yet employees did not always accept the hype surrounding these management practices: the idealized notion adopted by Pensco of how "team spirit" would be advanced assumes a passivity on the part of the employees which is often contradicted. The identity of a worker cannot simply be erased and reconstructed at will by management – employees are clearly capable of some degree of distance from, resistance to, and criticism of what they regard as management manipulations. . . .

There is little doubt that senior management in Pensco wanted to create a more self-disciplined clerical operative within an organizational culture transformed to reinforce and reward that discipline. However, in so far as this new form of management control was achieved it could not be directly linked with senior management decision-making. For despite management claims of success with team building, the improved working practices and self-discipline derived much more from slowly evolving and contingent changes in team working occurring in the lower reaches of the organization. Some of these improvements were enhanced as an unintended consequence of resolving recruitment shortages by employing "mature entrant" women; for it emerged almost accidentally that they could be employed as highly competent "matriarchal" leaders of teams. This was a fortuitous rather than planned strategy but once these older women were seen not only to resolve serious staffing problems but also . . . [to have] a positive impact on team working, the "mature entrant scheme" was further institutionalized as a formal personnel policy. Otherwise team working, the publicly displayed league tables and the prizes awarded to departmental managers and section leaders responsible for specific team target success, was a line management issue.' (Kerfoot and Knights, 1992, pp. 660, 663–4.)

The brief glimpse in box 2.1 at the attempts to introduce new working arrangements in one organization illustrates well some of the conundrums and contradictions associated with change management. Invariably such initiatives start with ideal models of good practice and policy intentions in the heads of senior management. However, even if it were possible to tightly control the methods and processes chosen to implement the changes (and this is doubtful), the full range of reactions, responses and countervailing forces is largely unpredictable. New factors emerge, unintended outcomes surface, latent support or opposition arrives from surprising corners of the organization, and external events frequently eclipse original intentions. In the case of Pensco, 'Changes in traditional working arrangements were stimulated by a number of coincidental factors, sustained by managers much lower down the hierarchy, but made possible by the encouragement of a Chief Executive who was routinely circumventing his AGM [Assistant General Manager] of Personnel in seeking to transform organizational practice' (Kerfoot and Knights, 1992, p. 663). Organizational change, then, is inevitably iterative and cyclical in nature and contingent upon a diverse range of often unconnected and unco-ordinated processes. It is also entirely possible for an organization to be experiencing discontinuous reorientations in different parts or all of its subsystems. Such changes may be incremental, continuous and contra-dictory, yet when accumulated their net effect may result in radical change for the organization (Van de Ven, 1988). Rarely can change be viewed as an isolated and bounded activity, without important systemic repercussions on other parts of the organizations.

Assumptions about interpretation

This, in turn, makes the assessment of outcomes an equally imprecise art. It really depends on who you ask, what stake they have in the change process, the extent to which they have been consulted and involved, and whether they perceive their interests to have been furthered or damaged as a result. Such diverse interpretations and retrospective sense-making (Weick, 1979) are not unimportant, because it is this 'history' which predisposes indi-viduals to future change initiatives within the organization. Research by Crouch et al. (1992):

> suggests that how managers interpret change is likely to be determined by a complex interplay of organizational and personal characteristics, such as perceived performance and perceived scope to influence outcomes, which may be partially a function of organizational seniority. Our embryonic understanding of these factors should provide an important qualification to our willingness to prescribe change management strategies, since a man-ager's capacity to 'manage meaning' for others is clearly dependent on her or his own interpretations. Neither the perceptions, nor management, of change is free of a manager's interpretative framework, along with its biases and roots in past experience.
>
> (1992, p. 42)

At the very least this implies that the outcomes of change processes are influenceable but ultimately beyond the control of any one actor or group of actors, and certainly not as easily orchestrated by management as some writers have led us to believe (e.g. Peters and Waterman, 1982; Kanter, 1983).

In some ways the managing of change in organizations mirrors at a macro-level the dynamics of interpersonal communication. Just as there is potential distortion between the intent of the original message, the way it is 'heard' by its target group (and onlookers), the manner in which it is then interpreted, and finally the way any outcomes are invested with mean-ing by all participants, so the rhetoric of HR change initiatives is frequently quite different from the interpretations by those on the 'receiving end' (typically under-researched in the literature – see for instance Storey,

1989, p. 181; Keenoy, 1990, p. 7; Mabey and Iles, 1991). And these short-term interpretations may, again, be quite different from the ultimate rationalization of the 'new order'. Such perceptual interference is, of course, magnified within an organizational context since change management resembles a cacophony of conversations rather than single monologue or dialogue.

This chapter is organized around these layers of 'communication'. Although the implementation of human resource strategies is rarely as rational, purposeful and cohesive as depicted, it is helpful to at least start with the conscious intentions of such change efforts and then to track the iterative, trial and error activities that ensue.

In some cases, human resource initiatives are applied to a 'steady-state' scenario or they are relatively small scale; however, for our purposes here, we are assuming that the design and launch of new or revised human resource policies represents a fairly major strategic thrust for the organization, implying changes to personnel practices at least, and potentially having an impact on internal structures and cultures as well. In such cases the implementation of human resource strategies will resemble a change management process.

Finally, this 'inability to communicate' or capacity to bring about change in a predetermined manner, may be more to do with the underlying logics of change than the more tangible tactics of change being employed. Change is often presented as a matter of ideological or political choice, but the 'detailed consequences and inner logic of the alternative systems are rarely subjected to critical analysis' (Morgan 1986, p. 270). See box 2.2.

Box 2.2   Uncovering the logics of change

'The way one formulates basic problems is critical in determining the way they will be solved. To the extent that we focus on problems as clashes of interests we can only find solutions where there are winners and losers. Thus the firm closes its plant, leaving the community and government to deal with the unemployment. The drive for efficiency in health and legal services produces crises and anomalies in health-care and the administration of justice that are passed on to the community rather than solved by the services concerned. An understanding of a problem in terms of the logics of change that produce it, on the other hand, opens many different scenarios, often involving possible change in the logic of the system itself. Often this will lead to a new understanding of the interests represented in the problem, and a reformulation of the relations between those involved.

Typically such reformulation has to begin locally, through an examination of specific problems that may then be found to be connected with wider systemic issues. These wider issues may need to be addressed on a broader front with others sharing the same concerns. Thus local labour–management committees, established to find innovative responses to the decline of local industries, may eventually link up with other similar groups interested in effecting some kind of structural change in the industrial system through broad-based community and political action. Similarly, local legal groups dealing with local problems may combine to influence the funding and structure of the services with which they are concerned.' (Morgan, 1986, pp. 269–70.)

The Intentions of Change Management

Typical change responses

In this section we assess some of the triggers which lead an organization to re-examine its utilization of human resources and some of the motives underlying the development of human resource strategies. Sometimes these are portrayed as calculated and well considered (e.g. Tichy, Fombrun and Devanna, 1982), but in reality they are the product of iterative experimentation, trial and error, and shifting business priorities. Drawing on evidence gathered from a range of sectors in the UK (Pettigrew, Hendry and Sparrow, 1988) and mainland Europe (Barham, Fraser and Heath, 1988), a number of strategic human resource responses have been reported which organizations choose or are forced to take.

Some of these strategies were structural in emphasis, some were cultural and some focused on behavioural initiatives. Occasionally the human resource strategy encompassed all three and was an example of enlightened anticipation. At other times it was more piecemeal than coherent, more tactical than strategic, and came as a reluctant afterthought.

Invariably, however, the starting point for strategic human resource change is the impact of competitive forces which expose some kind of business performance gap. In response an organization reassesses its product market or makes technical changes to its operation. This may involve new concepts of service provision, different channels of distribution, restructuring and/or decentralizing business units (sometimes as part of a policy of internationalization as in box 2.3 and developed more fully in chapter 8), acquiring new business or engaging in cost-reduction activities. Each constitutes a strategic shift and usually implies the need for new competencies or skills, and in some cases, values, amongst its staff.

Box 2.3 The Norsk Data Spirit

Norsk Data is an American computer company, located in Europe and managed with Japanese management methods, with some Scandinavian personal value systems. From the Americans, we have learned to focus on marketing and on profit. We have developed an internal measurement system so that we measure ourselves always on financial criteria. Like Japan, we use the consensus method, where the idea is to make the decisions at the most appropriate level, which is not always at the top, nor at the bottom, but at the level where the most knowledge is available and where the people are most effective. It means that we must have managers who accept that they cannot force their opinions upon their subordinates. They have to fight like everybody else with their ideas and the best ideas will win, and not necessarily the ones which come from the top or the bottom. Where we differ enormously from Japan and America is in our value system. We are much softer in Europe than in America and Japan. We try to use that to our advantage. We comprise people from all over the world: with varied backgrounds, priorities and contributions to make. Underneath the differences, however, are some values binding us together. To varying degrees, our people:

- are co-operating individuals;
- have a strong personal need to make a contribution;
- have a rich dose of initiative;
- are willing to take on responsibility; and
- are honest to themselves and others.

There is no strict 'Norsk Data Norm'. If there was such a norm, we would be just like any other faceless organization. Norsk Data is made up of individuals like yourself. We have the 'Norsk Data Spirit'. If you'll be yourself, and use your whole personality in your job, the rest of the team will stand behind you and your efforts. The computer industry used to be about computer companies selling to other computer people. They all spoke the same language. That died in 1979. We are now changing from being a computer industry to being a service industry and this requires a change in profile of the company. Today, 60 per cent of our people are close to the customer – 40 per cent in customer support, including customer training and documentation, and 20 per cent in marketing and sales. Twice as many staff are involved with the customer after the sale of the computer than before. (Rolf Skar, Chief Executive, Norsk Data; from Barham et al., 1988, pp. 10, 29–30.)

In the short term, temporary advantage on costs, for example, can be achieved by the imposition of what some writers (Legge, 1989) have termed 'hard' HR policies such as compulsory redundancy delayering, 'rightsizing' or other restructuring methods. However, to sustain a cost-reduction/ leadership strategy requires a deeper and significant change in the attitude and behaviour of the employees that remain. Similarly, commitment to quality, another key competitive nostrum of the 1980s and 1990s, requires a long-term perspective. This linkage between business strategy and employee attitudes and behaviour has led to the notion of a 'soft' HR approach in which the employee is regarded as a valued asset to be developed and not just exploited as an expensive factor of production. But how can human resource policy priorities be formulated and matched appropriately to the stage of an organization's strategic development? In a paper which makes this linkage more explicit Schuler and Jackson (1989) use analysis of employee role behaviours and a typology of HRM practices in six key areas which are linked to notions of competitive strategy (table 2.2).

Claimed causal patterns of change

This kind of analysis helps to demonstrate the likely linkage between an organization's product–market strategy and the desired, relevant human resource practices most likely to assist in 'delivering' that strategy. Such sensitivity to the demands of customers and the nature of competition is, after all, one of the key elements that differentiates human resource strategy from the traditional conception of personnel management. Another value of this contingency approach is that it highlights the possibility of multiple human resource strategies, for example, in different business units or functional areas of the same organization and/or the ability to change human resource policies over time to complement the changing requirements of evolving product or service life-cycles and business priorities. In short, the idea that there is 'one best way' to design and implement human resource strategies is scotched.

However, as noted in chapter 1, this attempt to 'fit' human resource strategy and business strategy has come to be viewed as somewhat prescriptive and not reflective of reality (Boxall, 1991). An empirical study by Jackson (1992) cited by Boxall suggests, for example, that while there is partial support for 'the proposition that organizations pursuing an innovation strategy seek to develop personnel practices for hourly paid workers broadly consistent with that thrust, it also demonstrated that personnel practices vary with manufacturing technology, industry sector, organizational structure and size and union presence. Most significantly, the research demonstrated that personnel practices were substantially different

Table 2.2 Employee role behaviour and HRM policies associated with particular business strategies

Strategy	Employee role behaviour	HRM policies
1. *Innovation*	A high degree of creative behaviour	Jobs that require close interaction and co-ordination among groups of individuals.
	Longer-term focus	Performance appraisals that are more likely to reflect longer-term and group-based achievements.
	A relatively high level of co-operative, interdependent behaviour	Jobs that allow employees to develop skills that can be used in other positions in the firm; compensation systems that emphasize internal equity rather than external or market-based equity.
	A moderate degree of concern for quality	Pay rates that tend to be low, but that allow employees to be stockholders and have more freedom to choose the mix of components that make up their pay package.
	A moderate concern for quantity. An equal degree of concern for process and results. A greater degree of risk taking. A high tolerance of ambiguity and unpredictability.	Broad career paths to reinforce the development of a broad range of skills.
2. *Quality enhancement*	Relative repetitive and predictable behaviours. A more long-term or intermediate focus	Relatively fixed and explicit job descriptions. High levels of employee participation in decisions relevant to immediate work conditions and the job itself.
	A moderate amount of co-operative, interdependent behaviour	A mix of individual and group criteria for performance appraisal that is mostly short term and results oriented.
	A high concern for quality	A relatively egalitarian treatment of employees and some guarantees of employment security.
	A modest concern for quantity of output. High concern for process. Low risk-taking activity. Commitment to the goals of the organization	Extensive and continuous training and development of employees.

Table 2.2 Cont'd

Strategy	Employee role behaviour	HRM policies
3. *Cost reduction*	Relatively repetitive and predictable behaviour	Relatively fixed and explicit job descriptions that allow little room for ambiguity.
	A rather short-term focus	Narrowly designed jobs and narrowly defined career paths that encourage specialization, expertise and efficiency.
	Primarily autonomous or individual activity. Moderate concern for quality	Short-term results-oriented performance appraisals. Close monitoring of market pay levels for use in making compensation decisions.
	High concern for quantity of output. Primary concern for results. Low risk-taking activity. Relatively high degree of comfort with stability	Minimal levels of employee training and development.

Source: Schuler and Jackson, 1987, p. 213.

for managerial and hourly employees across the whole sample' (Boxall, 1991, p. 67). The 'fit' model is also underpinned, Boxall argues, by an overly rationalistic conception of how strategy is formed, suggesting that strategy is always deliberate or formulated rather than emergent (Mintzberg and Waters, 1985). Furthermore, the empirical validity of simplistically mapping HRM practices to strategy has been questioned in a recent review by Ogbonna (1994). He notes that 'although researchers have articulated the links between strategy and culture on the one hand, and between strategy and human resource management on the other, there has been very little attempt to either develop the link between culture and human resource management or indeed link the three concepts' (1994, p. 1).

Another weakness of contingency conceptualizations is that they tend to underestimate the *way* change is introduced (see box 2.4). Human resource decisions, like any other area of strategic policy-making, may appear to have objective soundness, but in fact they are inevitably influenced by the cultural context of the organization and interpreted by those involved according to their personal frames of reference, their subjective motivations and the incomplete information they possess at the time. For example, one important interest group omitted from table 2.2 above is that of the unions and their view of what constitutes a safe, equitable and motivational working environment. Fundamental and strategic change is only likely to occur when the prevailing paradigm of the organization has been challenged, discredited or devalued (Johnson, 1987). A number of factors can contribute to this erosion: the arrival of an 'outsider', the exposure of deficiencies in the current paradigm via divergent views, the reconfiguration of power, the activating and legitimizing of dissent and the overt advocacy of a new paradigm by those with power. It is noticeable, for instance, how many human resource interventions are ushered in by newly appointed chief executives enjoying a brief honeymoon period in which to assert their particular brand of people management.

Box 2.4   Strategy formation: Rational or rationalized?

'In our view it is the limits to managerial action which are as telling in understanding the outcome of strategic changes rather than the assumed width of their discretion. Many views of strategy and competition emphasize the complexity of the firm's environment. We give equal emphasis to the intricacy not only of the environment but also of the firm itself. The processes by which strategic changes are made seldom move directly through neat, successive stages of analysis, choice and implementation. Given the powerful internal characteristics of the firm it would be unusual if they did not affect the process: more often they transform it – seldom is there an easily isolated logic to strategic change. Instead, that process may derive its motive force from an amalgam of economic, personal and political imperatives. Their interaction through time requires that those responsible for managing that process make continual assessments, repeated choices and multiple adjustments.' (Pettigrew and Whipp, 1991, pp. 30–1.)

Change Management Strategies

So far we have examined the intentions behind attempts to manage change in organizations: the knee-jerk reactions and the more considered strategies, the explicit 'game plans' and the covert agendas, the public rationalizations and the private motives. To distinguish between intention and implementation is, of course, artificial for two reasons. First, how change strategies unfold depends very much on the mental maps inside the heads of decision-makers. Whether they are articulated or not, each of us possess different assumptions not only about *what* changes are required (in the work place and out) but – even more crucially – about *how* they are to be enacted. Much of the conflict associated with change derives 'from the differences in the ways each of us constructs reality' (McWhinney, 1992, p. 21); in other words, it is as much about personal values as the substance of the change itself. Second, intention does not precede implementation in quite the sequential way more linear, deterministic models of change would have us believe. With these important qualifications in mind, this section assesses the choices available as an organization embarks upon change. Invariably, the intent of a change strategy is to alter the way organizational members think, behave, interact, communicate, make decisions, reward, monitor, praise and coach. In short, the way they perform. Such changes may be sought at an individual or work-group level or across the whole organization; they may require immediate action or be phased in over a period of years; they may be radical or incremental in nature; and the people involved may be receptive, indifferent or intransigent. Each of these conditions influences the unfolding of the change process. Subsequent chapters will explore more fully both the possibilities and difficulties associated with the claimed causality of specific change strategies. Here we note three broad approaches that have received support in the literature. The first argues that until the culture of an organization is reoriented little else will change, except at a cosmetic level and over a limited period of time. An alternative view is that behavioural change and enhanced organizational performance flow – primarily – from the way the organization is structured with regard to its strategy. Finally, a third view points to the importance of the *style* of change management, as against its intrinsic content.

Cultural change

Culture change is often glibly prescribed but is more difficult to achieve in practice. It is relatively straightforward to change what Payne (1991) calls the explicit culture by making changes such as removal of clocking in/out, the phasing out of canteens for different seniority levels, the introduction of development centres, the restructuring of business units and so on. Underlying values or implicit cultures are somewhat harder to shift and usually require a heavy investment in education and training over a sustained period of time. What is significant about several of the cultural-change interventions reported in recent years at organizations like British Telecom (Price and Murphy, 1987), Billiton, Royal Dutch Shell (Benjamin and Mabey, 1990), British Airways (Goodstein and Burke, 1991), and Manchester Airport (Jackson, 1992), is the way multiple leverage points were used to initiate and support the changes and the way organization-wide human resource practices were deliberately aligned to reinforce desired cultural changes.

However, there are few, empirically-based frameworks to guide the implementation of cultural-change strategies. The closest we come to a thoroughly researched model is in the field of organization development (OD), which has been defined as 'an intervention strategy that uses group processes to focus on the whole culture of an organization in order to bring about planned change' (Rowlandson, 1984, p. 90). As can be seen from its history (box 2.5), OD is more a philosophy than a set of techniques, and can be seen as an umbrella term for all kinds of change strategies, especially those that address culture. Here we re-examine some of the basic tenets of the OD approach and then assess the assumptions and applicability of OD for devising and managing strategic human resource interventions.

Box 2.5 The historical roots of organization development in the UK and US

'In the 1980s, in the US, work on organizational change from a human relations perspective continued in the same vein as the previous decade, but with another name: organization development (OD). Douglas McGregor, in the context of his work with Union Carbide in 1957, has been identified as "one of the first behavioural scientists to talk systematically about, and to implement, an organization-development program" (French 1978, p. 540).

According to French and Bell, OD has taken the "ongoing work team, including supervisor and subordinates" as its key units and "puts a primary emphasis on human and social relationships" (1984, pp. 15, 20), thus again demonstrating its continuation in the human relations tradition. The stock in trade of the OD consultant was a series of experimental group exercises which developed within human relations management training: sensitivity, T-groups, encounter groups and laboratory training.

In Britain, OD became a popular topic of discussion in management and personnel publications. Its definitions tended to be wider than in the US, influenced by the more sociological tradition of organizational behaviour in the UK. For example, an article on OD in *Personnel Management* by the head of the organizational effectiveness at Shell was summarised as covering "the whole gamut of techniques – from quality circles to improving the quality of working life" (Pritchard, 1984, p. 30). She includes the open systems and socio-technical approaches, strategic planning and industrial democracy. It would seem that, by 1984, the term OD in Britain was beginning to refer to any techniques of planned organizational change and to acquire some distance from the sensitivity approach. Pritchard and others point out that OD practitioners can have many different titles while performing a similar job: "adviser, consultant, facilitator, change agent, occupational psychologist, third party, behavioural scientist" (Pritchard, 1984, p. 30).' (From Hollway, 1993, pp. 111–3.)

A typical starting point when making an OD intervention is to define the mission or 'cause' of the organization, preferably in a participative manner, so that employees feel some sense of ownership (Beckhard and Harris, 1987; Beckhard and Pritchard, 1992). This mission usually includes a statement of the organization's purpose accompanied by a strategy which spells out the activities, standards and behaviours required to fulfil the mission, as well as some articulation of the values necessary for the mission to be successful. 'The acceptable modes of individual behaviour in pursuit of the company's objective have to be very clear. Values provide a basis for shared understanding of what to do, what choices must be made to achieve the ends and the legitimacy of the means to be employed' (Kleiner and Corrigan, 1989). In other words, there is nothing intrinsically good and legitimate about a well-defined strategy if it is seen as morally redundant or personally irrelevant by members of the organization.

A mission can be described as meaningful and 'strong' when the links between business imperatives (reflecting the organization's outer context) and its internal culture and structure (denoting its inner context and capability to change) are clear and reinforcing (see figure 2.1). Obviously, this figure oversimplifies matters, but it does help to show the interrelationships between a variety of levers in change management. It would be rare for the mission of an organization to be smoothly informing its human resource development and HRM activities in the streamlined way that the figure suggests. Equally it would be unusual for the 'upward thrusts' to be acting in such a concerted and sequential fashion. 'Organizational reality is far more messy and cyclical, with strategy often evolving, rather than being deliberately planned, and culture emerging, rather than being consciously managed' (Thomson and Mabey, 1994, p. 28).

However, if something of the mutual reinforcement depicted in figure 2.1 does occur, the benefits it gives to the formulation and implementation of a human resource strategy are clear. An organization with clear strategic intent and appealing values will find it easier to recruit, select, promote and develop the appropriate kind of people. Certain applicants will be attracted to the organization because of what it stands for; other employees may 'deselect' themselves and leave. A sense of mission may help to build

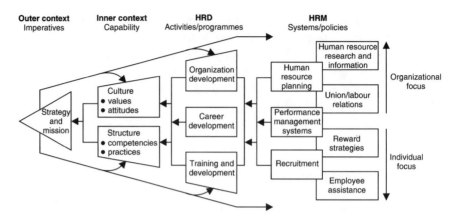

Figure 2.1   The role of HRM in managing strategic change
Source: Thomson and Mabey, 1994.

co-operation and trust as individuals and teams search for solutions that are in the best interests of the organization as a whole rather than certain factions or departments. Again, a clear values framework allows the necessary discretion and judgement to be exercised in decision-making whether it be in matters of strategic direction or at the level of everyday choices (see for instance, Kanter, 1991).

It should be noted, however, that the presence of strong value attachments *can* lead to inflexibility and internal contradictions when striving for organization commitment (Coopey and Hartley, 1989; Iles et al. 1990). Once the mission has been articulated and an audit of its current capabilities and capacities carried out, the change effort becomes a matter of managing the transitional state – all the tasks and activities that will take the organization from its present condition toward the achievement of its strategic goals. Beckhard and Pritchard (1992) emphasize that this transition has to be co-ordinated very actively by top management since it is at this point of implementation that many change efforts die. They must create the enabling structures dedicated to accomplishing these tasks, either by becoming project managers themselves or by appointing project leaders/steering groups for overall change management. Additionally, they need to develop specific strategies for obtaining necessary commitment from key players, they need to establish mechanisms for the internal communication of change, and crucially, they need to assign dedicated resources, experts and consultants to assist in particular aspects of the change process.

There is evidence that this approach has been used as an effective means of preparing for and launching change interventions (e.g. Williams et al., 1989; McCalman and Paton, 1992; Mabey and Mayon-White, 1993). Box

2.6 describes how one organization, Grampian Health Board in Scotland, attempted a wholesale shift in a culture. Given the size, complexity and history of Grampian this looked to be a very ambitious aim. In addition, the readiness of staff to contemplate and undergo change was low (previous attempts at restructuring had been unsuccessful) and Grampian had limited internal resources. Nevertheless, with the help and influence of external consultants, the Board chose to embark on a classic OD exercise to carry through the changes.

Box 2.6 Culture change at Grampian Health Board

The change strategy involved a range of initiatives across its administrative, ancillary, nursing and medical disciplines. It focused on four stages of activity:

1 Where are we now? What are the problems?
2 Where do we need to be? What will it look like?
3 How can we change? What are the techniques?
4 When should we measure results? How can we do it?

The first stage involved gathering, synthesizing and feeding back data about the current issues, grouped under five headings: strategy, structure, people, resources and communications. Significantly, this was not immediately translated into an agenda of change activities.

Being clear about present problems is all very well; being clear about future alternatives is more difficult. Our view was that the five problems were a double-edged sword. On the other hand they may have led down the path of attending to non-critical issues; just because communication is bad now, does not mean that it needs to be better in the future. That all depends on whether good communication is a critical success factor for the organization. Similarly, just because teamwork is not seen as bad enough to be a problem now, does not mean it will not become critical in the future.

(Fullerton, Ironside and Price, 1989)

Many senior management meetings and workgroups were held which eventually defined the 'Where do we need to be?' question. These were published as a 'Vision, a Mission, and a Management Approach'. The gap between this desired future state and the present state (as determined by a culture audit questionnaire and interviews) led to a concerted change programme. This included a range of human resource initiatives such as performance management (personal objectives, appraisal and performance), restructuring geared to consumer groupings, training in customer care, problem solving, planning and leadership as well as measures to control costs, enhance quality and improve internal communications. As part of stage four, the cultural audit (first conducted in 1987) was repeated in May 1989. On each occasion a cross-section of staff was asked to rate eight 'themes' of culture (communication, creativity, structure, systems, strategy, motivation, training and teamwork) as they currently experienced them.

The results of these culture audits were compared, combining all the scores for all themes and dividing the respondents into hierarchical levels. Senior and middle managers show positive trends, basic grade staff show a small improvement while supervisors show a small but worrying negative change in their attitudes. Some of the cascaded processes of the human resources programme had not yet reached the supervisors at this point. As a consequence they were experiencing a rapidly changing environment yet with more expected of them. There was pressure for change from below but insufficient support and development to cope with the new demands. Not surprisingly they viewed the situation as *worse* than it had been previously.

This account of change at Grampian helps to draw together some of the key principles for OD-based change management. First, the effectiveness of any change and development activities will be dependent on how well the individual and organizational problems and issues are diagnosed. Second, OD techniques can be used in isolation (e.g. sensitivity training, team-building exercises), but usually OD change implies a multi-faceted change effort using 'many leverage points to initiate and support the changes' (Goodstein and Burke, 1991, p. 171) at individual, interpersonal and structural levels. Third, the change activities incorporated within an OD intervention anticipate resistance to change and blinkered parochialism: therefore most are designed to – in some way – unfreeze such attitudes, broaden horizons and increase empathy and readiness to think and behave differently.

Early criticisms of OD focused on the inability of experiential groupwork to achieve organizational goals, the over-reliance on personal changes in trust and openness (rather than taking on board the politics of the organization) and its ideological bias against strong management (Hollway, 1993, p. 112). Somewhat ironically, more recent culture change programmes based around shared values have been criticized for being based upon managerialist, top-down assumptions (Beer, Eisenstat and Spector, 1990);

for overlooking the inherent contradictions of an organization striving for a 'strong culture' on the one hand and skills flexibility and devolved responsibility on the other (Legge, 1989; Ogbonna, 1992); and for underestimating the cynicism of professional knowledge workers in the 1990s who are increasingly more resistant to corporate cultural manipulation (Hope and Hendry, 1994). More fundamental still is the presumption that culture can be changed in a deliberate and predetermined manner to implement strategic change. We revisit this issue in chapter 6.

It would be a mistake to regard culture-focused changes as synonymous with OD, however. Bate (1990) has outlined a number of cultural-change approaches, and he argues that each has its appropriate place at different stages in the management of change (table 2.3). So, it is likely that the disruptive style of the aggressive approach would prove useful when used positively as an unfreezing device at the start of a large-scale human resource initiative. This might involve restructuring responsibilities and lines of communication and introducing new performance review and reward systems. The collusive style of the conciliative approach might then be used to facilitate a period of consultation and ownership; more subtle human resource management levers could include career development activities and revised induction procedures. At this point the emerging ideas would need pulling together into a systematic consensus perhaps via the indoctrinative approach, although it would be better for the emphasis to be on learning rather than on teaching – especially where changes in norms and attitudes are being sought. Extensive training would also figure prominently, reinforced by well-defined succession planning and appraisal systems to reward newly acquired skills and competencies. Once the parameters for the change have been established, the networking and alliance building typical of a corrosive approach could be harnessed to translate and implant the normative order. This would best be achieved by on-the-job human resource management in the shape of informal reward and recognition, role modelling and team briefing. At this stage conciliation might work well again to give enduring form and shape to the new order.

Structural change

An alternative, and very different, change strategy is that which addresses the structure of the organization and the design of jobs and working arrangements as the key levers of change.

The linkage between strategy and structure is well established in the literature stemming from Chandler (1962). He argued convincingly that structural change is triggered by an organization's inability to fully realize the strategy it is following due to administrative deficiencies caused by a mismatch between the new strategy and the existing structure. This

Table 2.3   Approaches to cultural change

Approach	Characteristics	It can:	But it usually:
Aggressive	• Rapid change • Dismantles traditional values • New culture is non-complex • Top-down, monitored • Detailed plans/ actions	• lead to a strong, integrated culture • suit a situation where there is a simple source of authority	• mobilizes dissent • is politically naïve • lacks skills, breadth of support leads to crisis or change
Conciliative	• Reasonable, quiet • Slow grafting onto new values • Deals with means, not ends • Collusion, not confrontation • Continuous development • Based on power and control	• lead to a 'common-sense' welcoming of the new culture • disarm opposition	• loses sight of its radical intent • gets seduced back to status quo
Corrosive	• Uses informal networks • Unseen manipulation • High participation • Act first, legitimize later • Planned programmed	• lead to genuine and large-scale change initiated by small-scale network	• is used to defend existing order and oppose change initiators
Indoctrinative	• Explicit learning process • Socializing • Unified, logical framework • Advocates one world view	• lead to wide-scale changes at an informational, technical level	• does not succeed in bringing about fundamental cultural change

Source: Adapted from Bate (1990).

argument that growth strategies result in different types of organizational structure has been taken further by Galbraith and Nathanson (1979), and Miller (1986).

At the work-place level, early organization analysis in the UK (e.g. Rice, 1958; Trist et al. 1963) had an impact on programmes to restructure the work place in the 1970s: specifically autonomous group working and initiatives under the 'Quality of Working Life' banner. More recent evidence (Fortune, 1990) points to a QWL resurgence associated with a productivity breakthrough in the 1990s. Cameron et al. (1992) report that despite some resistance from supervisors and middle managers the team concept is spreading rapidly in industries other than the motor industry, such as aerospace, electronics, food processing, steel and financial services. This has also found expression in the rush by Western managers to attempt the introduction of Japanese work practices into their organizations. Gleave and Oliver (1990) reported that two-thirds of the Times 1000 were using or planning to use just-in-time production, and 95 per cent were using or planning to use total quality control. This they suggest is due to the demonstrated capability of the major Japanese corporations to engineer a good 'fit' between their manufacturing strategy and their human resources strategy (Gleave and Oliver, 1990; see also Oliver et al., 1992).

An example of this strategic approach is given in box 2.7.

Box 2.7   Isuzu: indigenization of imperialism?

By 1987, after 10 years of loss-making, the Bedford Commercial Vehicle part of the Vauxhall plant at Luton was facing closure by its owners General Motors. Poor labour relations and intense foreign competition had plagued the company such that it was now haemorrhaging £500,000 per week, adding up to total losses of £26 million per year (Wille, 1990). Drastic action was called for to avert massive redundancies in Luton.

Such action came. In September 1987 General Motors entered a joint venture with Japan's Isuzu, which took a 40 per cent share in the business and appointed one of its Japanese executives as president of the new business. Together with four Japanese advisers and a British Vice-President he helped the new business, renamed IBC vehicles, return to profit. This took three years. On the face of it the unthinkable has happened. The best elements of Japanese working practices have been indigenized and grafted into the heartland of British car assembly; worker attitudes have shifted radically, and commercially the plant has been turned around. Another, more cynical interpretation is that at a time of economic crisis, foreign systems have been imposed, the unions have been railroaded into guarantees of co-operation, and a small number of employees are working harder to produce more with fewer defects.

The human resource strategy, conceived in order to bring about these radical changes in the company, consisted of four interrelated ingredients. The first three were structural and 'aggressive' (Bate, 1990). A totally new employment agreement was drawn up, a radically revised inventory production system was introduced and the whole work force was reconfigured into teams. Fourthly, in order to facilitate these changes the organization embarked upon comprehensive skills training.

The employee agreement hammered out by unions and management during 1987 was an essential springboard for a return to profitability; without it the joint venture could not and would not have been launched. In many ways it was an example of what Marsden et al. (1985, p. 118) have described as an attempt to minimize the extent to which employees and their representatives could interfere with the production.

In contrast to the change strategy at Grampian described in box 2.6, where there was a concerted and deliberate attempt to orchestrate culture change through a top-down, system-wide educational strategy, at IBC there was a determination to improve output at team level, aided and abetted by appropriate training, job redefinition and a reworked labour agreement. Almost as a byproduct this appears to have resulted in a change of attitudes and possibly even the culture at the plant. It can be seen that the human resource strategies at the two organizations were predicated upon two very different assumptions about change. The leading external consultant at Grampian has articulated his approach elsewhere (Price, 1987), and we have simplified this in figure 2.2. This can be contrasted to the unfolding of events (it would be too formal to describe it as a carefully planned change programme) at IBC, depicted in figure 2.3. At Grampian it was the attitudes and values held by individuals that were initially targeted for change. The assumption was that once the core culture is beginning to shift, then and only then can appropriate systems and procedures be put into place in order to bring about the desired behaviour change. This in turn is believed to translate into enhanced quality of service and produce customer satisfaction and internal co-operation. At IBC the model of change was almost the reverse: the unspoken assumption here was that a radical redefinition of organization roles, systems and procedures would lead to a positive step-change in behaviour at individual and team levels. Apparently not anticipated was the fact that these new employee behaviour patterns would lead, over time, to a wholesale revision of work-place norms, beliefs and possibly even values, which collectively determine culture. The seeming success of targeting the level of relationships, roles and responsibilities as primary levers for renewal lends support to the argument put forward in an influential paper by Beer et al. (1990).

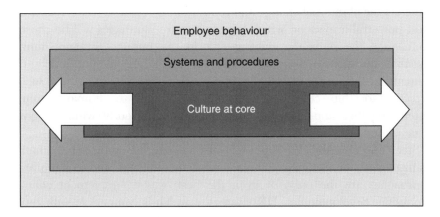

Figure 2.2 Trajectory of change process at Grampian
Source: Mabey and Mallory, 1995, p. 15.

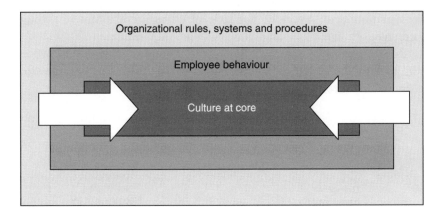

Figure 2.3 Trajectory of change process at IBC
Source: Mabey and Mallory, 1995, p. 15.

Change management style

Attempts to trace a direct correspondence between the strategic intent of an organization and its human resource strategies, whether cultural or structural in their emphasis, can still neglect the vital role of the organizational change programme – or 'game plan' – that is being used to move the organization towards improved performance. According to Stace and Dunphy (1991): 'We can . . . predict more about which human resource strategies should be used from knowing the degree of change and type of change leadership being exercised than we can by knowing the corporate or business strategies being pursued by the management of the organization. It is the degree of internal change and repositioning required which makes the most powerful impact on which human resource strategies will be chosen. So change theory is the missing link in the business strategy/human resource management model' (1991, p. 271). This is not unlike the 'cement' in the model of HRM proposed by Guest (1992b, p. 129) which depicts leadership, culture and strategy as binding the human resource system together and ensuring that it is taken seriously within a given organization.

Stace and Dunphy (1991) put forward a situational approach to change management, challenging the view that incremental and collaborative approaches are the only, or even the best, way to implement change. Alongside 'developmental' HR strategy – which is compatible with much of the relatively recent HRM and cultural-change models, they describe three other HR strategy types and the conditions for their use (see table 2.4). The two important dimensions for choice of change strategy appear to be, firstly, the scale of change (from fine tuning through to corporate transformation) and, secondly, the style of change (collaborative through to coercive).

Based on extensive research Stace and Dunphy related this process model to how each change was managed in 13 Australian organizations (see figure 2.4). From this they discovered that:

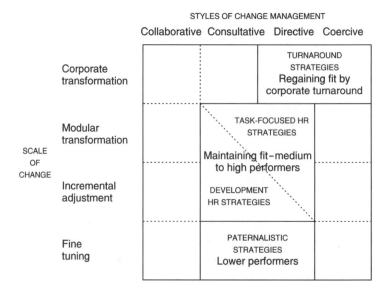

Figure 2.4   The relationship between change strategy, HR strategy and performance
Source: Adapted from Stace and Dunphy, 1991, pp. 277, 281.

Table 2.4 HR strategy types and conditions

Type and features of HR strategy	Conditions for use
Task-focused	
HR strategy is strongly focused on the business unit.	
• Strong bottom line orientation. • Emphasis on workforce planning, job redesign and work-practice reviews. • Focus on tangible reward structures. • Internal or external recruitment. • Functional skills training and formalized multi-skilling. • Formalized industrial relations procedures. • Strong business unit culture.	Use when markets/products/services are undergoing major change and 'niche' strategies are prevalent. HR strategies must deliver the capacity for rapid structural, systems, skill and cultural changes. Strong emphasis on business unit autonomy, maximum devolution, rightsizing (continues redeployment), outsourcing of labour.
Developmental	
HR strategy is jointly actioned by the corporate human resource unit and the business units.	Use when markets are growing and product/market innovation is desired. HR strategies must create cross-organizational synergy, and a 'market leader' culture. Strong emphasis on individual development, corporate-culture management, developing a strong internal labour market (promotions/appointments) and team skills.
• Emphasis on developing the individual, and the team. • Internal recruitment, where possible. • Extensive development programmes. • Use of 'intrinsic' rewards. • Corporate organizational development given high priority. • Strong emphasis on corporate culture.	
Turnaround	
HR strategy is driven for a short period by the executive leadership, characterized by challenging, restructuring or abolishing human resource systems, structures and methodologies.	Use when the business environment changes dramatically: when the organization is not in fit with its environment, and when the business strategy of the organization radically changes. HR strategies must break and abolish redundant HR practices, structures, and redefine a new culture. Strong emphasis on forced downsizing, lateral recruitment, new HR systems and radical work and job restructuring.
• Major structural changes affecting the total organization and career structure. • Downsizing, retrenchments. • Lateral recruitment of key executives from outside. • Executive team building, creating a new 'mindset'. • Breaking with the 'old' culture.	
Paternalistic	
HR practice is centrally administered.	Use only in very limited mass-production situations where the organization has an absolute monopoly on stable markets/products, HR strategies are used as devices for 'control' and uniformity of procedure/operations. Strong emphasis on formal, detailed job descriptions, formalistic employer–employee industrial relationships and industrial 'awards'.
• Centralist personnel orientation. • Emphasis on procedures, precedent and uniformity. • Organization and methods studies. • Inflexible internal appointments policy. • Emphasis on operational and supervisory training. • Industrial awards and agreements set the HR framework.	

Source: Adapted from Stace and Dunphy, 1991, pp. 275, 279.

- the dominant HR strategies were task focused and turnaround, reflecting the relative absence of stable or growth markets and the pressing need to produce greater business flexibility, more work unit autonomy and less centralism via radical change strategies.

- two organizations in the study were pursuing developmental HR strategies, and two were following paternalistic HR strategies due to their highly protected, nearly monopolistic position in their respective sectors.

When the performance of the chosen companies was analysed according to their chosen organizational change strategies and HR strategies, the authors concluded that:

- task-focused and developmental HR strategies are associated with medium- to high-performing organizations;
- turnaround HR strategies are associated with organizations attempting to regain fit due to poor performance or a rapidly changing environment;
- paternalistic HR strategies are associated with lower performing organizations or monopolies.

As a result of his study of the way in which changes were being made in 15 UK organizations, Storey (1992) also rejects the notion of a universal change approach: 'some organizations . . . steered a major new approach to labour management in a step-by-step manner; others launched total programmes. Some of the changes were progressed in a top-down, cascade way, others were bottom-up in character. In some cases the human resource or personnel/IR specialists were intimately involved; in others the process was clearly driven from elsewhere and these specialists were either marginal or even acted in opposition. The overall lesson about managing change was that there is no set formula' (1992, p. 120). Storey also used two dimensions by which to analyse the 'types' of managed-change process: the degree to which change is unilaterally devised by management or negotiated by joint agreement, and the extent to which the path of change conforms to a total package or is characterized by a series of discrete initiatives. Each of the case study organizations was then located on the resulting 'managed-change map' (see figure 2.5). Given the similar typologies, it is interesting to note the resemblance between this map and that generated by Stace and Dunphy (figure 2.4). Storey remarks on a 'significant tendency' for the change process used by the organizations he studied in the UK to move toward the Type 1 (top-down systemic), where there was a greater willingness by management to operate outside the negotiating machinery, a greater degree of careful planning and attempts to integrate different human resource initiatives rather than making changes in an opportunistic fashion. Although in both cases the samples are small, these two studies in

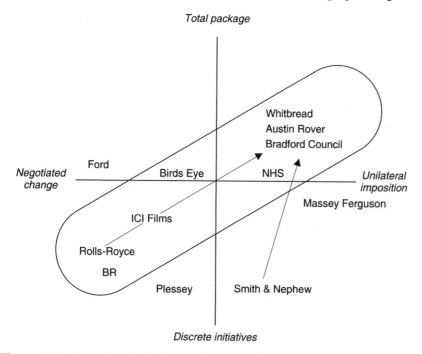

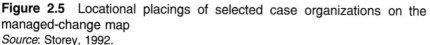

Figure 2.5 Locational placings of selected case organizations on the managed-change map
Source: Storey, 1992.

Australia (Stace and Dunphy, 1991) and UK (Storey, 1992) offer tentative, though consistent, support for the following notions. First, that organizations use a number and mixture of change management styles (with 'hard' and 'soft' approaches not necessarily being irreconcilable); second, that turnaround or task-focused HR strategies and top-down systemic change appears to predominate; third, that there is a discernible shift toward more strategically oriented, total-change approaches; and fourth, that both task-focused and developmental HR strategies are associated with medium- to high-performing organizations.

So how do those initiating organizational change decide which change management strategies are appropriate? According to Harrison (1987) this depends on a number of factors:

- Does the organization need fundamental change, structural reorganization, process or technological innovation, a major overhaul of its internal communication systems and procedures; or does it need more minor system adjustments like tweaking the incentive scheme, adjusting the operating process or shifting the external recruitment target group?

- Is there readiness for change? Is there sufficient unease among members of the organization and external stakeholders (as a result of poor quality, declining sales, labour unrest, missed market opportunities, etc.) to precipitate the adoption of new goals and strategies? If this dissatisfaction does not exist, is there evidence from diagnostic feedback that suggests that it should be?
- How might internal/external stakeholders react to proposed changes? Apart from creditors and shareholders themselves, these might include regulatory bodies (such as the Equal Opportunities Commission), community groups (such as 'green' pressure groups), managers (perhaps threatened by unfamiliar interventions) and unions and employees (perhaps resistant to new work practices and the consolidation of jobs and units).
- Does the organization have the capacity to change? Even if there is no active resistance to change, the organization may lack the resources, the structural capability, the technological expertise or the cultural will-power to facilitate and implement the proposed human resource strategies.
- Will the change strategy bring about undesirable consequences that will outweigh the positive outcomes?

Considering all these factors will lead to the approach most likely to maximize commitment to a successful implementation of a proposed changes strategy, by either eroding, overcoming, or in some instances deliberately arousing, resistance.

The Implementation of Human Resource Strategies

So far we have been discussing the choices, challenges and implications of different change management strategies. In this section we apply this analysis to the implementation of human resource strategies in particular. Subsequent chapters will take up specific areas of human resource policy and practice in more detail; here we briefly sketch out how different change frameworks can inform and guide such interventions, with particular reference to the level, scope and direction of the proposed human resource changes.

Level and degree of intervention

We have seen in the previous discussion that when formulating and implementing change strategies it is important to identify the *level* of analysis (Harrison, 1987): whether the target for change is to be at a task/work-group level, at an intergroup level or at an organizational level. It is also important to identify the *degree* of the HR intervention required, which will depend on the basic nature of the organizational problem being addressed and whether it is concerned with current behavioural symptoms, with structural requirements or with the cultural context of the organization, or indeed a combination of these.

Let us take the first level of analysis. A manufacturing organization might be concerned to radically improve its productivity, reliability and quality. To achieve this it may:

- give assembly-line workers responsibility for minor maintenance (task- and work-group level);
- set up teams to apply a new inventory production system to minimize waste (task- and work-group level);
- give these teams the freedom to collaborate with others in different departments to resolve the occurrence of defects (inter-division level);
- set up new delivery standards for their suppliers in order to cut down on inventory costs (organizational level).

The human resource 'levers' to facilitate these changes differ according to the level of analysis. Thus recruitment, training, job design, involvement in objective setting and incentive schemes, are devised to differentially affect the organizational goals for various categories of staff. Although the very notion of human resource strategy would seem to imply a multi-faceted set of policies and priorities embracing all levels and functions of an organization, it is not the coverage of human resource initiatives that makes them strategic. Rather it is how they are connected: that is, the degree to which they link in with each other and contribute to the achievement of business objectives.

It is important to recognize that by 'level' here we are talking about level of analytical focus, not hierarchical level in the organization. Thus 'poor job definition' at the individual might apply to any level in the organization hierarchy from shop-floor supervisor to main board executive.

Second is the degree of intervention. Behavioural strategies lend themselves to the most direct and least radical human resource initiatives. For example, the sponsorship of managers on MBA and Diploma programmes might be intended to expose selected middle managers to a wider range of rigorous business analysis techniques. As such it could be regarded as an overdue remedy for deficiencies in the current management development system rather than an example of strategic HR change (a behavioural strategy at an individual level). Often, however, this degree of intervention may not be sufficient to achieve the required aims owing to the way jobs are configured, the way roles and responsibilities are assigned and the poor quality of systems support. In these cases the human resource strategy might involve an organization benchmarking their competitors' best human resource practices with a view to overhauling their own human resource planning policies (a behavioural strategy at an organizational level); or it may involve restructuring so that cross-functional groups can operate with greater autonomy and improved communication flows, constituting a structural strategy at a divisional level. Alternatively, attitudes within the organization may prove to be so entrenched and resistant to change that a radical shift in leadership style around a new mission statement might be necessary. This would take the human resource strategy into the cultural arena at an organizational or divisional level.

It can be seen that as the human resource strategies call for a greater degree of intervention they require deeper changes to the infrastructure, information flow and job design, and ultimately the context or culture of an organization. While cultural, and to some extent, structural strategies present possibilities of more deep-seated change, they also present the risk of more widespread systemic disruption if they backfire. Furthermore, this type of human resource change is likely to require considerable time and expenditure.

Speed and scope of HR changes

Consideration of the time it takes to bring about different types of change leads to another dimension of choice when launching human resource initiatives: that is, the required speed and scope of change. Three types of change can be usefully differentiated, each with their own human resource implications.

1   *Incremental* change is an improvement on the old way of doing things, with the aim of doing more things or doing things better. This kind of change, such as the introduction of a new career planning process, does not represent a major change in direction or policy and is therefore unlikely to disrupt the *status quo*. Such a measure could undoubtedly have strategic consequences in terms of preparing for future skill requirements, but if it builds upon an appraisal and developmental process that is already in place, then it could be seen as a fairly minor, refining enhancement which can be implemented quickly.

2   *Transitional* change involves the implementation of new strategies and requires the rearranging or dismantling of old operating methods. A good example comes from the description (see box 2.8) of how three large UK corporations (Pilkington, GKN and IMI) coped with decentralizing from functional structures to divisionalized business units and profit centres.

Box 2.8   The HRM of decentralization

'All three of the companies cited – Pilkington, GKN, IMI – espouse a philosophy of decentralization to varying degrees, with Pilkington least far down this road. However, at some point, all face the question of how far they intend to allow an internal labour market to operate to offset the incipient fragmentation of decentralization. This typically arises over ensuring top succession . . . and doubts over whether the company has adequate "strength in depth" in its management, as it enters a renewed growth phase. In the 1980s, such doubts have been triggered by the combination of decentralization and the demanning that resulted from recession. GKN, for example, lost two-thirds of its UK employees, and more than halved its world-wide complement. IMI and Pilkington both almost halved their UK numbers. Such outflows included a massive haemorrhage of management and technical skills. As a result, as these companies have moved into an era of more confident growth, and additionally as they diversified into new areas, they have been forced to review their whole range of human resource policies. The challenge has been to develop corporately inspired (and, in many cases, corporately managed) solutions which do not negate the benefits of sharper management accountability and employee motivation, which are at the heart of the decentralization philosophy' (Hendry, 1990, p. 98).

The author goes on to describe a range of human resource tactics that were employed to meet this challenge. These include a limited number of 'group contracts' created to retain key managers and produce a pool from which top jobs could be filled.

Difficulties in making appointments in these decentralized organizations also prompted them to review their succession planning and appraisal practices with information on shortfalls and excesses being consolidated into an annual management development register. With the demise of specialist central functions (such as engineering, R & D and management services) the companies used the newly created profit-responsible roles at relatively junior levels as 'seedbeds' of basic learning and broadening experiences for up-and-coming managers. Alongside this the three organizations – particularly Pilkington – assigned people to task-centred action learning teams outside their normal area of operation to help knowledge transfer, promote an organizational perspective and assist cohesion. Each of these shifts in human resource practice and policy represents strategic manoeuvring on the part of the three companies as they adjusted to the 'known new state' of divisionalized business units' (Hendry, 1990, p. 98.)

3   *Transformational* change is usually the most profound and traumatic and is so described because it implies comprehensive change at several levels. The associated features – according to Kleiner and Corrigan (1989) – are:

- reformed mission and core values;
- an altered distribution of power;
- reorganization to support new roles and break the traditional business-as-usual structure;
- revised communication and decision-making patterns;
- fresh leadership bringing the necessary drive, energy and commitment to overcome organizational inertia.

Kleiner and Corrigan also describe transformational change as being implemented rapidly in bursts. We question whether this always holds true. While the initial 'boardroom shuffle' may indeed be swift and mission statements rewritten overnight, the reality of organization change is far more protracted. This is because even transformational change is rarely the simple execution of an elaborate strategic plan. As Quinn (1989) reminds us from his research, strategy formulation and implementation are not separate, sequential processes:

> successful managers in the companies observed acted logically and incremen-tally to improve the quality of information used in key decisions; to overcome the personal and political pressures resisting change; to deal with the varying lead times and sequencing problems in critical decisions; and to build the organizational awareness, understanding, and psychological commitment essential to effective strategies. By the time the strategies began to crystallize, pieces of them were already being implemented. Through the very processes they used to formulate their strategies, these executives had built sufficient organizational momentum and identity with the strategies to make them flow toward flexible and successful implementation.'
>
> (1989, p. 33)

If this is true for business strategy, it is doubly true for the implementation of human resource strategies, which are ideally set in motion to facilitate the information flow, overcome the resistance and build the competences and commitment that Quinn refers to.

Direction of HR changes

A final set of choices confronting those planning and implementing human resource strategies concerns direction. Given that the human resource policies adopted are intended to assist in the delivery of strategic objectives, it might be assumed that the impetus for new or revised human resource strategies will always come from the top of the organization. While the conception of such strategies will usually happen at senior levels, the outworking of the human resource plans and tactics, the harnessing of energy and the mobilization of support can and do emanate from different points in an organization.

Top-down   For a number of reasons, the human resource strategy at Grampian (see box 2.6) attempted to bring about nothing less than a comprehensive change of culture. This was deemed necessary by the Board for the following reasons: (1) in a labour-intensive, service-based organization like the National Health Service, the co-operativeness, internal integration and anxiety-reducing friendliness of staff was reckoned to have a dramatic effect on organizational performance; (2) the previous bureaucratic system of fragmented accountability and indecision needed to be replaced by an attitude of responsible risk taking whereby 'the huge amounts of human talent and energy could be released'; and (3) the introduction of general management principles heralded the need to break down the historical defensiveness between medical and administrative staff. It was recognized that a concerted change programme was needed. This, together with the restructuring into six health-care and three support divisions, made it all but inevitable that the change process would be managerially driven, heavily programmed and organization-wide in scope. The strategic planning process, once devised, had to be fully publicized externally and internally. Senior managers were trained in strategy formulation and the first draft ten-year strategic plan was completed in December 1987 (Fullerton et al., 1989). Although many of the ensuing human resource actions (such as operational planning, team-building workshops and training in creative problem solving) were designed to enhance grassroots participation, the prevailing trajectory of this human resource strategy was top-down. Undoubtedly this has the benefit of providing clear, sustained direction which is well resourced and co-ordinated. It also runs a severe risk of not being owned by large numbers of staff, leading to medium-term indifference, if not sabotage.

Bottom-up   The human resource strategy at IBC (see box 2.7) also had elements that were imposed, planned and administered from the top. Indeed, one interpretation of the events at the Luton plant is to see them as a calculated business move on the part of Isuzu, opportunistically using the ailing assembly plant to enhance their order books in Europe. Likewise, the new contract of employment, the company joint council (with the five trade unions being required to elect a single spokesperson) and the just-in-time working practices were hardly introduced in a participative manner. And yet, having established these non-negotiable elements of the human resource strategy, much of what followed was, perhaps surprisingly, bottom-up. The manufacturing director, George Chalmers, described the change process in the early stages as like 'having a tiger by the tail!'

Assembly-line workers clamoured to become team leaders, not only for the financial incentive, but also for the opportunity to be trained on and off the job (at a local college), for the enhanced career opportunities and for the new sense of kudos that went with the position. The new inventory production system gave teams the expertise and the opportunity to redesign their workstations in an effort to eliminate waste. Even more suggestive of bottom-up change was the obvious sense of pride in their work and work place evident in the IBC plant; teamworking had apparently succeeded in flattening the management pyramid, creating trust in what was previously a highly stratified company (Mabey and Mallory, 1995).

Strictly speaking, bottom-up change would not only be implemented from lower levels of the organization, but initiated from there also. The point about this example is that although the broad business parameters concerning finished vehicle throughput, inventory levels and quality standards were set by senior management, and a new set of human resource 'ground rules' was established in the revised labour agreement, the subsequent human resource *tactics* took place at a grassroots level, and took on a momentum of their own with new cultural norms being established by the work teams themselves at a shop-floor level.

Sideways-in Although the scale of product and capital investment is different, there are parallels between the business strategies adopted for the assembly of light commercial vehicles at Luton and the assembly of aeroplanes at British Aerospace's old Hatfield plant in the late 1980s. At both plants, in an attempt to cut costs, inventories were reduced, there was a move to cellular or team working with corresponding changes to management structure, and comprehensive training was set up to raise awareness of, and transfer skills to, quality working. The interesting feature of the human resource strategy at British Aerospace (BAe) was the use of one cell group (door assembly) as a pilot scheme. The advantages of implementing human resource strategy in this localized manner are clear. It provides a relatively low-risk opportunity to test new layout and operating techniques without widescale disruption (although once running effectively it poses supply and bottleneck problems for neighbouring sections of the assembly process). It facilitates team building and accountability on a small and controllable scale. Equally important is the message projected to the rest of the business: the pilot scheme signals senior management's seriousness about human resource change, provides a demonstration of effective cellular working and is a showcase for the site being innovative. Beer, et al. (1990) give two basic criteria for the selection of so-called 'developmental laboratories':

1　adequate resources (especially skilled managers);
2　a high probability of success, especially if it can be measured in bottom-line terms.

In many ways, BAe's choice of the door assembly conforms to these conditions. It required minimum reorganization and investment costs, the complex mechanical assembly lent credibility to the pilot scheme, but, most importantly, it was a high-profile location with outcomes that could be easily measured. The stunning results appear to support the choice: by 1990, the 30-week assembly cycle had been reduced to 13 weeks; inventory was down by 43 per cent; modification to workflow and layout had resulted in a space reduction of 18 per cent; and a manual saving on labour costs of £9,000 and on transaction costs of £66,000 had been made (Salaman, 1992). Despite these impressive performance figures the Hatfield plant was subsequently closed by BAe for broader political and commercial reasons, which perhaps highlights the vulnerability of sideways-in change, even if it is successful.

Of course, to characterize human resource implementations in these directional terms alone is too simplistic. As we have already noted, there are likely to be elements of all three 'thrusts' in any large-scale organizational intervention and there are many possible subsystems of an organization which could be considered as a starting point for a change effort. Beckhard and Harris (1987) suggest the following:

1 top management;
2 a management group known to be ready for change;
3 'hurting' system (a group where current conditions have created acute discomfort);
4 new teams without a history and whose tasks require a departure from old ways of operating;
5 a staff group that will be required to assist in subsequent implementation of strategy;
6 temporary project teams, specifically set up to carry through a change plan.

The intention in this section has been to discuss where the primary driving force for change is coming from and what human resource strategies are appropriate for the effects being sought. For this reason, we have also considered the level of analysis, the scope of change and the type of change. All of these factors have a bearing on how effective the HR strategy will be for an organization in the longer term.

The implementation of a new or revised human resource strategy will probably need to use a range of change management methods. The higher the level of analysis (intergroup or organizational as opposed to individual) and the wider the scope of the human resource strategy (cultural and structural, as opposed to 'simply' behavioural) the more this assertion holds.

The Interpretation of Change

Up to this point we have been referring to change strategies from a reasonably objective viewpoint and discussing the merits and drawbacks of different change models, styles and methodologies. However, when we begin to explore the way in which such organizational changes are perceived, interpreted and ascribed meaning by those on the receiving end, we are no longer in the realm of single reality.

Perceptions of change

Perceptions of change are inevitably coloured by a host of factors from whim to world view, and everything in between. Some of the more important include the following. *Thinking style*, which has been shown by research to be completely independent of thinking capacity and intelligence (Kirton, 1987; Schroder, 1989; Tefft, 1990), means that two equally capable people could produce very different solutions to the same change scenario. Jung's work on psychological types (1923), operationalized as the Myers–Briggs Type Indicator, reveals two very different *perceiving preferences*: 'The sensing types, by definition, depend on their five senses for perception. Whatever comes directly from the senses is part of the sensing types' own experience and is therefore trustworthy . . . The intuitives are comparatively uninterested in sensory reports of things as they are. Instead, intuitives listen for the intuitions that come up from their unconscious with enticing visions of possibilities' (Myers 1986, p. 57). Research by Crouch et al. (1992) suggests that response to change amongst managers is very much dependent on the *power to act*: 'managers respond to unfamiliarity by acting and therefore adding to it. They act in ways that convert exogenous into endogenous change. Ways of creating alternatives will perhaps be those that have achieved previous success . . . this view of change [is] a political process, in which managers obtain power by acting. By acting, seizing the initiatives, the individual retrieves power over events' (1992, pp. 43–4). We refer, in a moment, to the predicament of those who do not feel themselves to have such room for manœuvre. Such perceptions are closely allied to feelings of *personal worth, power and difference* in the work place – whether this be based on gender, ethnic origin, age, disability and so on. Walker (1994) notes that when 'locked into an either/or approach to life, people become threatened by any deviation from their perceptions of the norm. They fear that others' differences mean they must change. Therefore they close in and join ranks with people whom they believe to be most like themselves. They respond like victims. The difference between feeling and not feeling like a victim is one's sense of personal empowerment – one's ability to accept, move toward and even embrace different ideas and perspectives' (1994, p. 214). Organizations are getting better at acknowledging and valuing *cultural diversity* in the way they introduce change, but insensitivities still persist (Iles and Mabey, 1994).

Then there is something as trivial yet significant as *timing*. Receptivity to change can simply be reaping the rewards from launching the right ideas at the right time. Guest (1992a) attributes the success of the 'excellence' brand of HRM in part to this factor (see box 2.9).

Box 2.9 'Excellent' timing

'Another factor in the success of *In Search of Excellence* was undoubtedly its timing. The book appeared in the early years of the Reagan era when the United States was beginning to rebuild its self-confidence after several years of introspective self-doubt. In industry this had been reflected in uncertainty about how to cope with the increasing threat of Japanese competition. The success of Japan had kindled an interest in Japanese management, and several bestselling business books had appeared either extolling the virtues of Japanese compared with American management [. . .] or extracting elements of Japanese management for the American Market. The most successful illustration of this was Ouchi's (1981) *Theory Z*. The message from *In Search of Excellence* was rather different and fitted in well with Reaganite America. It was that to find the lessons for success in American industry you need to look no further than in your own back yard. The lessons were to be found by exploring the practices of the best American companies and not by looking overseas. Furthermore, what one found by looking at these companies was a return to a number of traditional American beliefs based on keeping things simple, building on what you know best and reinforcing essential values. There is also a careful blend of rugged individualism and reinforcement of the family based on the concept of the organizational family. It is understandable that this optimistic message should strike a chord in American industry.' (Guest, 1992a, pp. 14–15.)

Another powerful determinant of how employees view and respond to change is ideology, or what Morgan (1986) calls *organizational frame of reference*. For instance, the radical view sees the organization as 'the battleground where rival forces (e.g. management and unions) strive for the achievement of largely incompatible ends' (1986, p. 188). This frame of reference is based on very different premises to the unitary perspective which emphasizes common goals and the possibility of achieving them by being a well-integrated team. The pluralist view – somewhere between these two extremes – regards the organization as a loose coalition of diverse individuals and stakeholder groups, which has only passing interest in the goals of the organization. Finally, and more global still, is the *world view* to which individuals subscribe, which influences every area of their lives, including their attitude and response to organizational change: 'we do not have to go beyond differing beliefs about cause to find the sources of unavoidable conflict. We don't have to assume that either party is evil or even that they have opposing goals. Conflicts arise from constructions of their minds, from the beliefs and styles by which an individual or group makes a choice; only incidentally are they in the content of the issue . . . changes take place when boundaries between the logics of alternative realities are transgressed' (McWhinney, 1992, pp. 22–3).

Understanding the sources of these plural and subjective realities is important, because it is upon such rocks of heritage, enfranchisement, ideology and intransigence that organizations' change efforts frequently run aground.

Reactions to change

The implementation of organizational change usually implies personal disruption or discomfort; for example, acquiring new skills, working in a redesigned role or job, being paid and rewarded on a different basis, and having accountability for a larger (or smaller) budget. Sometimes the changes will affect a single department or business unit, but if the human resource initiatives are truly strategic they are more likely to have an impact on everybody in the organization.

Several authors have identified reasons why managers encounter resistance when implementing new ways of doing things, and have offered tactics for dealing with them (e.g. Hirschowitz, 1975; Marris, 1974; Kanter, 1985; Kotter and Schlesinger, 1989). In essence they revolve around three sources of loss: perceived loss of control, loss of security and loss of face.

Change imposed by others feels threatening rather than exciting. The removal of choice leads to a sense of powerlessness resulting in stress and defensive behaviour; as Kanter (1985) notes, 'It is powerlessness that corrupts, not power.' Communicating as much information as possible about the proposed changes can help to alleviate these feelings. This may include creating channels for raising concerns, asking questions and giving feedback.

Commenting on loss of security, Peter Marris makes an insightful comparison between bereavement on a personal level and the collective impact of disruptive organization change (box 2.10).

Box 2.10 Organizational bereavement

'The articulation of this conflict is . . . as crucial to assimilating social changes as mourning is to bereavement. Even if it were possible to foresee how interests might be balanced with the utmost fairness, everyone has still to work out in his or her own terms what it means to their particular attachments, gradually reorientating their essential purposes. No one can resolve the crisis of reintegration on behalf of another, any more than friends can tell the bereaved how to make the best of it. Every attempt to pre-empt conflict, argument, protest by rational planning can only be abortive: however reasonable the proposed changes, the process of implementing them must still allow the impulse of rejection to play itself out. When those who have power to manipulate changes act as if they have only to explain, and, when their explanations are not at once accepted, shrug off opposition as ignorance or prejudice, they express a profound contempt for the meaning of lives other than their own: for the reformers have already assimilated these changes to their purpose, and worked out a reformulation which makes sense to them, perhaps through months or years of analysis and debate. If they deny others the chance to do the same, they treat them as puppets dangling by the threads of their own conceptions. When liberal white people propose reforms on behalf of black, men on behalf of women, rich for poor, even the most honourable intentions can be profoundly alienating, if they assume the identity of those they seek to help and tell them what their lives should mean. The presumption is, I think, more intimately threatening than indifference or hostility, and is bitterly resented. To be told the meaning of your life by others, in terms which are not yours, implies that your existence does not matter to them, except as it is reflected in their own.' (Marris, 1974, p. 155.)

Marris goes on to suggest three principles for the management of change, each of which corresponds to aspects of grief, and represents a crisis of reintegration which cannot be escaped, hurried or resolved on behalf of another.

1 The process of reform should expect and even encourage conflict, because people need to be given the chance to react and voice their ambivalent feelings to help them make sense of what is going on.

2   The process should 'respect the autonomy of different kinds of experience so that groups of people can organize without the intrusion of alien conceptions' (Marris, 1974, p. 156).

3   There must be time and patience, to allow people to digest and accommodate the implications of the proposed changes. In human resource terms this may mean providing a clear timetable of events, sharing the 'big picture' with details about the new state, breaking this down into smaller, more manageable and familiar actions, and letting people take the first step. It will also mean being honest about less palatable aspects of change: explaining the costs at an early stage and face-to-face if possible.

Strategic change initiatives usually imply that the previous procedures, policies or ways of working are inadequate. It is therefore not easy – especially for those who have invested much in these past practices – to suddenly switch allegiance and commitments without feeling *loss of face*. As the sociologist Erving Goffman (1959) has pointed out, people's reactions to events are largely a function of how others define and regard them (their 'social identity') and they will go to great lengths (even engage in actions contrary to their long-term interests) in order to avoid embarrassment. For the initiators of change, the task is one of putting past actions into perspective without unduly discrediting them, and depicting the new circumstances that require fresh strategies. This allows staff to portray flexibility and strength while still retaining a sense of continuity with the healthy aspects of past traditions.

Carnall (1991), building on earlier work by Adams et al. (1976), describes how individuals typically cope with personal life changes (figure 2.6). Self-esteem during the early stage of *denial* may actually increase as the advantages of the present situation are magnified and work-group cohesion solidifies. Unless the change is sudden and traumatic, performance will not necessarily decline as individuals attempt to minimize the impact of changes. The reality of such changes dawns during the *defence* stage – leading to feelings of frustration, depression and defensive behaviours. *Discarding* is the phase when people let go of the past and begin to look forward to the future. From this trough of turmoil and disorientation individuals begin to re-establish their own identity and grow into the new situation. However, they need support and time for this to happen. Self-esteem begins to climb during the period of *adaptation*. As new routines are mastered and early successes are achieved, performance increases. Anger and frustration may still be present, but this is evidence of trying to make the changes work rather than of opposition to them. Finally, *internalization* and a newly established sense of integration occur when those involved have tested, modified and accepted the new system, processes and organization. Carnall (1991)

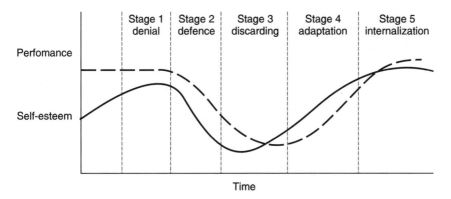

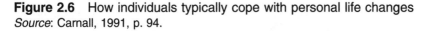

Figure 2.6 How individuals typically cope with personal life changes
Source: Carnall, 1991, p. 94.

notes that the engine for rebuilding performance is the self-esteem of the people involved and suggests four categories of need required during this process: empathy, support, skills and intelligible information.

Barriers to change

Change is not always perceived negatively. Casey (1993) notes that

> People are not by nature resistant to change and neither are organizations; on the contrary, they are open to change and they continually change themselves. It is all a question of where the change comes from: if it comes from within, it feels good; if it is imposed from outside it can feel like a threat, because it is unknown and outside one's own control. It should be no surprise that people (and organizations) are defensive in the face of perceived threat – we are all absolutely right to be defensive when threatened, it is irresponsible not to defend against threat. But it is not the *change* which we resist, it is the *threat* which fills us with fear . . . Organizations are defined as resistant to change, only by those who are trying to change them.
> (Casey, 1993, pp. 89–90)

It is very clear that much depends on the way organizational change is introduced and managed. Box 2.11 shows eight key questions which identify how commitment to a change process might be gained.

Box 2.11   How can change be enjoyed rather than endured?

1   What *personal benefit* will be gained by individuals involved? Active participation in the change process depends on the extent to which the needs, attitudes and beliefs of individual employees are taken into account.

2   What is the view of the official or unofficial leader(s) of the work groups involved? The *expectations and opinions* of those in prestige positions tend to carry more weight than the members of their work groups and/or the influence of staff "trainers".

3   What fresh, *objective information* is available about the need for change? Data centred on one's own organization or group is more meaningful and influential than more generalized information about attitudes and behaviour.

4   To what extent are facts pertinent to the change process generated from *within the work group*? The planning, gathering, analysis and interpretation of diagnostic data by the individuals and groups involved are more likely to be understood and accepted than those presented by outside experts.

5   To what degree can those involved in the change *influence the change process*? Complete participation by all the members of the affected work groups is likely to be most effective. However, participation by representatives of the group and/or the supervisor only can reduce the amount of overt opposition.

6   How *attractive is the work group* to its members? When change is being proposed, group cohesiveness (which will be high if the group satisfies the needs of its members) will operate to reduce resistance to change if the group sees the changes as beneficial. This is because strong group membership tends to lead to greater individual conformity to group norms.

7   Does the change process involve bringing individuals from different groups together, *off the job* in temporary groups? Change programmes that involve individuals within the context of their immediate job situation are likely to be more successful because this group has more psychological meaning to an individual than does a group with only *temporary membership*.

8   How open are the *communication channels* relating to the need for, plans for and consequence of change? Change processes that provide specific knowledge on the progress to date and specify the criteria against which improvement is to be measured are most successful in establishing and maintaining change. (Adapted from Huse, 1980, pp. 120–3.)

Given the formidable array of forces that can get in the way of any change management intervention, how is a critical mass of support mobilized in order to effect lasting change? An early and essential step is the identification of key power groupings wherever they might be situated in the organizational hierarchy and adopting strategies appropriate for each in order to either win their commitment or neutralize their interference. For instance, the unions were cast as 'opposers' to the planned joint venture of General Motors and Isuzu in 1987, and they were systematically 'neutralized'. First they were left out of the final negotiations leading to the formation of the new company. Then they were bound by the newly formulated labour agreement which, among other things, instigated a Company Joint Council which required the five different trade unions to elect a single spokesperson. Finally, the implementation of teamworking and the inventory production system largely circumvented the need for shop-steward representation of worker grievances. In power terms the unions were marginalized. This is not an untypical story of the 1980s. At its most pragmatic, using political power to shape change boils down to appealing to the better interests of key individuals: it is their interpretation of events and whether they perceive gain (ideological or personal) from the proposed changes that will ultimately determine their support or opposition.

Alongside this there are at least four other factors affecting the political terrain of an organization. One is the behaviour of key and powerful leaders whether they be hierarchically senior or leaders of opinion. In order to mobilize change in others, leaders need to be personally open to change themselves (Benjamin and Mabey, 1990).

A second factor is the use of symbols and language to manage the meaning of, and create energy for, change. It could be argued that the effective management of change in organizations requires that explanation be removed beyond doubt and argumentation. 'Other devices for the symbolic construction of reality include the rhetorical construction of oral and written communications so as to outline a general framework, a world view, from which it is difficult to dissent and from which intended consequences flow . . . so as to influence the receiver's framework of reference favourably' (Anthony, 1992, p. 87).

One of the reasons for the occasional success of human resource strategies under the umbrella of Quality is not that the concepts, skills and measurement criteria are revolutionary in themselves (often they are old ideas repackaged), but rather that they have rapidly provided the workforce with a succinct and common language, an incontrovertible logic for describing and attaining high standards and a range of graphic methods for monitoring and improving it. Some manufacturing plants have taken this further by regularly involving staff in 'quality presentations' to customers visiting the plant. This active identification with the finished product provides a powerful cue for employees to attend to detail in their job.

A third factor in the successful implementation of strategy is the formal or informal presence of a change agent, or change management team. Line managers, human resource specialists and external consultants each have unique vantage points when it comes to fulfilling this role. Shipton and McCauley (1993) put forward a strong argument for personal practitioners to take on the role of change consultant. However, each organization is different and the pros and cons of different change agents will vary accordingly (see table 2.5).

Table 2.5   Choosing the change agent

Line manager	Human resource specialist	External human resource consultant
Grassroots knowledge of what will work and what won't	Understand internal human resource systems and how they link	Wide, comparative knowledge of human resource strategies in other organizations
Credibility and successful role model (usually!)	Awareness of business plans and priorities	Can contribute an objective perspective
Vested interests in human resource because judged on people performance	Regular, wide-ranging contact with organization stake-holders	Can use 'expert status' to solicit views widely in the organization
Close relationship with staff promotes concern for their development	Access to human resource networks, internal and external	Knowledge of techniques, frameworks, models to help unlock *impasse* situations
Awareness of (and immersion in) local and organization culture	Author of human resource policies delineating roles and responsibilities; Specialist expertise in diagnosis and delivery of human resource strategies	Fresh insights, ideas can be catalytic
But possibly . . .		
Over-cynical	Limited access to top team	Peddles ready-made solutions
Threatened by change	Lacks credibility with line managers	Objectives coloured by chief client's wishes
Under-resourced	Confused role boundaries with personnel and line management	Poor on follow-through and evaluation
Too immersed to see the need for change		Can leave before implementation and completion
Not being assessed on people performance		

A fourth factor concerns the readiness of the organization to learn from outcomes that were *not* planned. Frequently change initiatives bring about unintended consequences and these can provide valuable learning opportunities (as box 2.12 shows), but only if the organization is alert to such outcomes and capable of consolidating the benefits.

Box 2.12   A French mail-order firm: Planned and unplanned change

'The organization which provided the setting for this case study was a private mail-order firm in the north of France. About two-thirds of the company's 3,500 employees had barely completed primary school, and had clerical and manual jobs such as packing parcels or unloading trucks. Of 649 employees tested by a university educational institute, 52 per cent were found to have language abilities equivalent to that of eight-year-olds in the third year of primary school.

The planned change
Convinced of the potential aptitudes and willingness of its employees and workers, the company decided to introduce general education courses in its training programmes. The objective was to upgrade the low academic levels of volunteer employees and workers, making them eligible for technical or commercial courses which would develop the skills and capacities required to hold jobs in the future.

Traditionally, the company's training programmes were concerned only with job-related matters, and most seminars were reserved for executives and supervisors. In September 1985, however, general education subjects such as spelling and grammar were introduced in the training programmes, and were made available to volunteer clerical employees and workers. Courses were held during working hours in company premises, at no cost to trainees. Eleven courses of four types were offered to volunteer employees. [. . .]

Summary results
The first measure of the project's impact was the number of persons it affected directly. A total of 1,046 persons underwent training in one or more of the eleven courses. That 46 per cent of the target population manifested the expected behaviours in terms of their agreed personal development objectives may be interpreted as the first change in the organization.

The second measure of impact was the actual improvement in the qualifications and skills of the trainees. The upgrading of language and mathematical abilities of the trainees was clearly demonstrated by performance in tests before and after training. [. . .]

Changes in the trainees were not limited to acquisition of the skills and knowledge taught in the eleven courses. There were changes in individual attitudes and receptiveness to learning in general, for example familiarity with test situations and working with groups. Trainees learned about the company structure and practices through their co-trainees; in some cases friendship bonds were created. In 87 per cent of group interviews held at the end of courses, an increase in knowledge about the company's diverse activities and functions was ranked by the trainees as being among the three most important gains from the training. Behaviour modifications which could be categorized as "personality" changes were also reported; such attitudes were transferred to work and non-work situations. In individual interviews of random samples of trainees of the self-assessment courses, 84 per cent cited an increase in assertiveness and self-confidence. [. . .]

The non-anticipated changes
Managers of the company were confronted with the conflict between strict norms of productivity and time "lost in unproductive training". They had to adjust their notions of production to a new notion of training as part of working hours. What was until then a vague notion of "human resources development" became more concrete, and had to be integrated in the existing management practices and rewards system.' (Ernecq, 1992, pp. 279–83.)

In this section we have suggested that change is often resisted not because it lacks visionary value or commercial logic but because of the way it is construed by those on the receiving end. If the change strategy – and almost as important – the way it is delivered, are interpreted negatively or suspiciously by stakeholders, then this collective judgement will impede even the best prepared plans.

Conclusion

We have seen in this chapter that managing change in organization is by no means as straightforward as it seems. All too often the outcomes bear little resemblance to what was originally intended, and the ramifications rumble on – often counter-productively – long beyond intended time-frames.

It is amidst this confusion that those who launched the change intervention invest the organizational impact with new rhetoric – perhaps using selective 'success stories' to shape new ideas and images that will hopefully fuel increased effort, a new phase or a redirection. It is here that assumptions underpinning the change methodology might be revisited and – depending on whether the organization has the capacity for single or double-loop learning (Argyris and Schon, 1981) – new objectives will be fashioned or commitment to traditional ones escalated (Staw, 1980). It is at this stage that an official version of what has actually taken place will emerge: the 'reality' of organization change outcomes will be documented. Of course, this won't prevent other 'versions' from circulating. The extent and degree of diversion or damage caused by such parallel accounts will depend on the extent to which stakeholders on the receiving end feel their access to power and relative status has been enhanced and whether personal and collective goals have been furthered by the changes. In all these ways, then, the objective nature of the change process will be retrospectively reconstructed to form the historical and even, in time, mythological context of successive change interventions. Given that such interventions are never discrete – rather, ebbing and flowing – it can be seen that the cultural context of change is ever complex and potent. Organizational decision-making rarely follows a rational problem-solving pathway: this is more true at the inception of change initiatives than at any other time. Such decisions, about the need to change or revise the way things are done, are frequently an organization's 'garbage can', into which various problems and the solutions of different participants will be dumped (Cohen et al., 1976). Thus the principal participants will be influenced by all sorts of things, such as prior commitments and alliances, the need to justify past actions, the wish to make scapegoats of certain individuals or departments, the desire to cement loyalties and the opportunity for recruiting, socializing and power-broking.

Given that change strategies are often messy rather than well planned, intuitive rather than calculated, cyclical rather than linear, is there any merit in organizations attempting to unravel and analyse the different steps of planning, design and implementation?

We have argued in this chapter that through such analysis valuable lessons can be learned, weaknesses highlighted and cases built for further, more enlightened investment of resources and effort in future change interventions. It is important, for instance, to disentangle the success or failure of the strategy *per se* from the success or failure of its implementation. A change strategy which is both poorly thought through (perhaps owing to inadequate diagnosis) and ineptly implemented (possibly because of poor change management) will obviously achieve nothing. The patient dies during the operation. However, the way an intervention is managed can be a success in its own terms, owing to opportunism and political favour, but still fail to contribute to a successful outcome in terms of organizational strategy. In this case, the operation is a success but the patient still dies. The planning of an intervention may be well timed and incorporate appropriate human resource activities, yet be subverted by widespread resistance because of the way the initiatives are introduced. The patient refuses treatment. The most optimistic – and probably the most ambitious – scenario is where such resistance is anticipated and authentically addressed, and the human resource initiatives have enduring organizational and individual benefits. In this case the patient not only survives the operation but the scars heal as well!

Key points

- *Different change strategies are predicated upon different assumptions about the inevitability, costs, controllability and ultimate value of any 'package' of change proposals. These predispositions will have as much influence on the outcomes as the intrinsic worth of the strategy itself.*
- *Strategic change will be greeted with varying levels of enthusiasm, indifference and intransigence depending on a number of personal, occupational, cultural and political factors as perceived by different interest groups in the organization.*
- *While conventional change strategies have some currency when managing human resource interventions, they typically underestimate the process issues (above) and the game plan necessary to win support for the proposed changes.*
- *Change is constant rather than discrete, and iterative rather than sequential. Hence the meaning invested in current changes and their outcomes will provide the immediate context for any new changes being proposed.*

Discussion Questions

1   Can organizational change be managed?
2   Are individuals passive recipients or co-creators of organizational change?
3   How helpful is OD as an approach to managing strategic HR change?
4   What are some of the options available when planning strategic HR interventions?
5   Why might the same organization change be viewed and evaluated very differently depending on who you ask?

REFERENCES

Adams, J., Hayes, J. and Hopson, B. (1976) *Transitions: Understanding and Managing Personal Change*. London, Martin Robertson.

Anthony, P. (1992) Cultural strategies. Unit 6, *Human Resource Strategies*. Milton Keynes, Open Business School.

Argyris, C. and Schon, D. (1981) *Organizational Learning*. Reading, Mass., Addison-Wesley.

Barham, K., Fraser, J. and Heath, L. (1988) *Management for the Future*. Berkhamstead, Herts, Foundation for Management Education and Ashridge Management College.

Bate, S. P. (1990) A description, evaluation and integration of four approaches to the management of cultural change in organisations. Paper presented to the British Academy of Management Conference, Glasgow, Sept.

Beckhard, R. and Harris, R. (1987) *Organization Transitions: Managing Complex Change*. Reading, Mass., Addison-Wesley.

Beckhard, R. and Pritchard, W. (1992) *Changing the Essence: The Art of Creating and Leading Fundamental Change*. San Francisco, Jossey-Bass.

Beer, M., Eisenstat, R. A. and Spector, B. (1990) Why change programmes don't produce change. *Harvard Business Review*, Nov./Dec., pp. 158–66.

Benjamin, G. and Mabey, C. 1990. A case of organisation transformation. *Management Education and Development* 21, no. 5, pp. 327–34.

Boxall, P. F. (1991) Strategic human resource management: Beginnings of a new theoretical sophistication? *Human Resource Management Journal*, 12, no. 3, pp. 60–79.

Buller, P. F. (1988) For successful strategic change: Blend OD practice with strategic Management. *Organization Dynamics*, 16, pp. 42–55.

Cameron, S., Francis, A. and Storey, J. (1992) Structural strategies. *B884 Human Resource Strategies*. Milton Keynes, Open Business School, Open University.

Carnall, C. (1991) *Managing Change*. London, Routledge.

Casey, D. (1993) *Managing Learning in Organizations*. Buckingham, Open University Press.

Chandler, A. D. (1962) *Strategy and Structure: Chapters in the History of the American Industrial Enterprise*. Cambridge, Mass., MIT Press.

Cohen, M., March, J. and Olsen, J. (1976) People, problems, solutions and the ambiguity of relevance. In March, J. and Olsen, J. (eds), *Ambiguity and Choice in Organisations*. Bergen, Universitetsforlaget.

Coopey, J. and Hartley, J. (1989) Tensions in organisation commitment. Paper presented to the British Psychological Society conference, Windermere, January.

Crouch, A., Sinclair, A. and Hintz, P. (1992) Myths of managing change. In Hosking, D. M. and Anderson, N. (eds), *Organizational Change and Innovation*. London, Routledge.

Dopson, S. and Stewart, R. (1993) What is happening to middle management? In Mabey, C. and Mayon-White, B. (eds), *Managing Change*. London, Paul Chapman.

Ernecq, J. (1992) Planned and unplanned organizational change. In Hosking, D. M. and Anderson, N. (eds), *Organizational Change and Innovation*. London, Routledge.

Fortune (1990) Who needs a boss? *Fortune International*, 7 May.

French, W. (1978) *The Personnel Management Process*. Boston, Houghton Mifflin.

French, W. and Bell, C. (1973) *Organization Development: Behavioural Science Interventions for Organization Improvement*. Englewood Cliffs. NJ, Prentice-Hall.

French, W. and Bell, C. (1984) *Organizational Development: Behavioral Science Interventions for Organization Improvement* (3rd edn). Englewood Cliffs, NJ, Prentice-Hall.

Fullerton, H., Ironside, A. and Price, C. (1989) A picture of health in the 1990s. *Health Service Journal*, June, pp. 73–82.

Fullerton, H. and Price, C. (1991) Culture change in the NHS. *Personnel Management*, Mar., pp. 50–3.

Galbraith, J. R. and Nathanson, D. A. (1978) *Strategy Implementation: The Role of Structure and Process*. St Paul, Minn., West Publishing Co.

Galbraith, J. R. and Nathanson, D. A. (1979) The role of organisational structure and process in strategy implementation. In Schendel, D. E. and Hofer, C. W. (eds), *Strategic Management: A New View of Business Policy and Planning*. Boston, Little Brown.

Gleave, S. and Oliver, N. (1990) Human resource management in Japanese manufacturing companies in the UK: 5 case studies. *Journal of General Management*, 16, no. 1, pp. 54–68.

Goffman, E. (1959) *The Presentation of Self in Everyday Life*. London, Allen Lane/Penguin Press.

Goodstein, L. and Burke, W. (1991) Creating successful organisation change. *Organisation Dynamics*, spring, pp. 5–17.

Goodstein, L. and Burke, W. (1992) Creating successful organization change. In Mabey, C. and Mayon-White, B. (eds), *Managing Change*. London, Paul Chapman.

Greiner, L. E. (1989) Evolution and revolution as organizations grow. In Asch, D. and Bowman, C. (eds), *Readings in Strategic Management*. Basingstoke, Macmillan, pp. 373–87.

Guest, D. (1992a) Right enough to be dangerously wrong: An analysis of the 'In Search of Excellence' phenomenon. In Salaman, G. et al. (eds), *Human Resource Strategy*. London, Sage, pp. 5–19.

Guest, D. (1992b) Employee commitment and control. In Hartley, J. and Stephenson, G. M. (eds), *Employee Relations*. Oxford, Blackwell.

Harrison, M. (1987) *Diagnosing Organizations: Methods, Models and Practices*. Beverly Hills, Calif., Sage.

Hendry, C. (1990) The corporate management of human resources and conditions of decentralization. *British Journal of Management*, 1, pp. 91–103.

Hirschowitz, R. (1975) The human aspects of managing transition. *AMA Personnel*, 51, no. 3, pp. 9–17.

Hollway, W. (1993) *Work Psychology and Organizational Behaviour*. London, Sage.

Hope, V. and Hendry, J. (1994) Corporate cultural change – is it relevant for organisations in the 1990s? Paper presented to the ninth annual workshop for the European Institute for Advanced Studies in Management, St Gallen, Switzerland.

Hosking, D. and Anderson, N. (1992) Organization change and innovation challenges for European work and organization psychology. In Hosking, D. and Anderson, N. (eds), *Organization Change and Innovation Psychological Perspectives and Practices in Europe*. London, Routledge.

Huczynski, A. (1987) Performance through intervention using organisational change methods. *European Management Journal*, 5, no. 1, pp. 49–56.

Huse, E. (1980) *Organization Development and Change* (2nd edn). Minnesota, West Publishing Co.

Iles, P. and Mabey, C. (1994) Developing global capability through management and organizational strategies. Paper presented in the Ninth Workshop on Strategic HRM, St Gallen, Switzerland.

Iles, P., Mabey, C. and Robertson, I. (1990) HRM practices and employee commitment: Possibilities, pitfalls and paradoxes. *British Journal of Management*, 1, no. 3, pp. 147–57.

Jackson, L. (1992) Achieving change in business culture. *Management Decision*, 30, no. 6, pp. 149–55.

Johnson, G. (1987) *Strategic Change and the Management Process*. Oxford, Blackwell.

Jung, C. (1923) *Psychological Types*. New York, Harcourt Brace.

Kamoche, K. (1994) A critique and proposed reformation of strategic human resources. *Human Resource Management Journal*, 4, no. 4.

Kanter, R. M. (1983) *The Change Masters: Corporate Entrepreneurs at Work*. London, Allen & Unwin.

Kanter, R. M. (1991) Championing change: An interview with Bell Atlantic's CEO Raymond Smith. *Harvard Business Review*, Jan.–Feb., pp. 119–30.

Kanter, R. M. (1985) Managing the human side of change. *Management Review*, April, pp. 52–7.

Keenoy, T. (1990) HRM: A case of the wolf in sheep's clothing? *Personnel Review*, 19, no. 2, pp. 3–9.

Kerfoot, D. and Knights, D. (1992) Planning for personnel – human resource management reconsidered. *Journal of Management Studies*, 29, no. 5, pp. 651–68.

Kirton, M. J. (1987) Adaptors and innovators: Cognitive style and personality. In Isaksen, S. G. (ed.), *Frontiers of Creativity Research: Beyond the Basics*. Buffalo, New York, Bearly Limited.

Kleiner, B. H. and Corrigan, W. A. (1989) Understanding organisational change. *Leadership and Organisation Development Journal*, 10, no. 3, pp. 25–31.

Kotter, R. and Schlesinger, L. (1989) Choosing strategies for change. In Asch, D. and Bowman, C. (eds), *Readings in Strategic Management*. Basingstoke, Macmillan, pp. 294–306.

Lawrence, P. R. and Lorsch, J. W. (1967) Differentiation and integration in complex organizations. *Administrative Science Quarterly*, 12, pp. 1–47.

Legge, K. (1989) Human resource management: A critical analysis. In Storey, J. (ed.), *New Perspectives on Human Resource Management*. London, Routledge, pp. 19–40.

Mabey, C. and Iles, P. (1991) HRM from the other side of the fence. *Personnel Management*, Feb., pp. 50–2.

Mabey, C. and Mallory, G. (1995) Structure and culture change in two UK organizations: A comparison of assumptions, approaches and outcomes. *Human Resource Management Journal*, 5, no. 2, pp. 1–18.

Mabey, C. and Mayon-White, W. (1993) *Managing Change*. London, Paul Chapman.

McCalman, J. and Paton, R. (1992) *Change Management*. London, Paul Chapman.

McWhinney, W. (1992) *Paths of Change*. London, Sage.

Marris, P. (1974) *Loss and Change*. London, Routledge and Kegan Paul.

Marsden, D., Morris, T., Willman, P. and Wood, S. (1985) *The Car Industry*. London, Tavistock Publications.

Miles, R. E. and Snow, C. C. (1978) *Organisational Strategy, Structure and Process*. New York, McGraw-Hill.

Miller, D. (1986) Configurations of strategy and structure: Towards a synthesis. *Strategic Management Journal*, 7, pp. 233–49.

Mintzberg, H. N. (1989) The structures of organisations. In Asch, D. and Bowman, C. (eds), *Readings in Strategic Management*. Basingstoke, Macmillan, pp. 322–52.

Mintzberg, H. and Waters, A. (1985) Strategies deliberate and emergent. *Strategic Management Journal*, 6, pp. 257–72.

Morgan, G. (1986) *Images of Organization*. London, Sage.

Myers, I. B. (1986) *Gifts Differing*. Palo Alto, Calif., Consulting Psychologists Press Inc.

Nicholson, N. (1993) Organization change. In Mabey, C. and Mayon-White, B. (eds), *Managing Change*. London, Paul Chapman.

Ogbonna, E. (1992) Organisation culture and human resource management: Dilemmas and contradictions. In Blyton, P. and Turnbull, P. (eds), *Reassessing Human Resource Management*. London, Sage.

Ogbonna, E. (1994) Integrating strategy, culture and human resource management: A case study of the UK food retailing sector. Paper presented to the Ninth Workshop on Strategic Human Resource Management, St Gallen, Switzerland, March.

Oliver, N., Delbridge, R., Jones, D. and Lowe, J. (1992) World class manufacturing: Further evidence in the lean production debate. Proceedings of the British Academy of Management Conference, Milton Keynes, pp. 155–68.

Payne, R. (1991) Taking stock of corporate culture. *Personnel Management*, July, pp. 26–9.

Peters, T. and Waterman, R. (1982) *In Search of Excellence*. New York, Harper and Row.

Pettigrew, A., Hendry, C. and Sparrow, P. (1988) The role of VET in employers' skill supply strategies: Main report. Sheffield, The Training Agency in conjunction with Coopers and Lybrand Associates.

Pettigrew, A. and Whipp, R. (1991) *Managing Change for Competitive Success*. Oxford, Blackwell.

Porras, T. J. and Silvers, R. C. (1991) Organization development and transformation. *Annual Review of Psychology*, 42, pp. 51–78.

Price, C. (1987) Culture change, the tricky bit. *Training and Development*, Oct., pp. 20–4.

Price, C. and Murphy, E. (1987) Organisational Development at British Telecom. *Training & Development*, July, pp. 45–8.

Pritchard, W. (1984) What's new in organization development? *Personnel Management*, July, pp. 30–3.

Quinn, J. B. (1989) Managing strategic change. In Asch, D. and Bowman, C. (eds), *Readings in Strategic Management*. Basingstoke, Macmillan, pp. 20–36.

Rice, A. K. 1958. *Productivity and Social Organisations*. London, Tavistock.

Rowlandson, P. (1984) The oddity of OD. *Management Today*, Nov., pp. 91–3.

Salaman, G. (1992) Media Booklet. *B884 Human Resource Strategies*, Open University, Milton Keynes.

Schroder, H. M. (1989) Managerial competence and style. In Kirton, M. J. (ed.), *Adaptors and Innovators: Styles of Creativity and Problem-Solving*. London, Routledge.

Schuler, R. (1992) Strategic human resources management: Linking the people with the strategic needs of the business. *Organization Dynamics*, summer, pp. 18–32.

Schuler, R. and Jackson, S. (1987) Linking competitive strategies with human resource management practices. *Academy of Management Executive*, 1, no. 3, Aug. pp. 207–19.

Shipton, J. and McCauley, J. (1993) Issues of power and marginality in personnel. *Human Resource Management Journal*, 4, no. 1, pp. 1–13.

Stace, D. and Dunphy, D. (1991) Beyond traditional paternalistic and developmental approaches to organizational change and human resource strategies. *The International Journal of Human Resource Management*, 2, no. 3, Dec., pp. 263–83.

Staw, B. (1980) Rationality and justification in organizational life. In Staw B. and Cummings, L. (eds), *Research in Organizational Behaviour*. Greenwich, Conn., JAI Press Inc.

Storey, J. (1989) *New Perspectives on Human Resource Management*. London, Routledge.

Storey, J. (1992) *Developments in the Management of Human Resources*. Oxford, Blackwell.

Tefft, M. (1990) Creativity through the lenses of the TTCT, MBTI and KAI: The level-style issue examined once again. *Teorie Vedy* (Theory of Science), 1, no. 2, pp. 39–46.

Thomson, R. and Mabey, C. (1994) *Developing Human Resources*. London, Butterworth Heinemann.

Tichy, N. M., Fombrun, C. J. and Devanna, M. A. (1982) Strategic human resource management. *Sloan Management Review*, winter, pp. 47–61.

Trist, E. L., Higgin, G. W., Murray, H. and Pollock, A. B. (1963) *Organisational Choice*. London, Tavistock.

Van de Ven, A. H. (1988) Review essay: Four requirements for processual analysis. In Pettigrew, A. (ed.), *The Management of Strategic Change*. Oxford, Blackwell.

Walker, B. (1994) Valuing differences: The concept and a model. In Mabey, C. and Mayon-White, B. (eds), *Managing Change*. London, Paul Chapman.

Weick, C. (1979) *The Social Psychology of Organizing*. London, Addison-Wesley.

Whipp, R., Rosenfeld, R. and Pettigrew, A. (1989) Managing strategic change in a mature business. *Long Range Planning*, 22, no. 6, pp. 92–9.

Wickens, P. (1987) *The Road to Nissan: Flexibility, Quality, Teamwork*. London, Macmillan.

Wille, E. (1990) Back from the brink. *Ashridge Management Review*, Berkhamstead, summer.

Williams, A., Dobson, P. and Walters, M. (1989) *Changing Culture*. London, Institute of Personnel Management.

3 Training and Development Strategies

Learning Objectives

- *to identify the features that elevate training and development approaches from the tactical and* ad hoc *to the concerted and strategic.*
- *to note some of the ways that an organization's investment in training and development activities can be influenced and triggered by its external environment.*
- *to analyse how strategic business imperatives come to be interpreted and addressed by a range of HR and human resource development interventions.*
- *to explain some of the cultural inhibitors to training and the ways in which organizations can get training and development 'into their bloodstream'.*
- *to explore whether training and development initiatives can be set up so that they are consistent with, and mutually supported by, other HR policies and processes.*
- *to describe a strategic approach to training and development which takes account of the political and sectional realities of organizational decision-making.*

Introduction

The task of this chapter is to formulate a strategic approach to training and development, to attempt to identify the dynamics in an organization which demonstrate that development of self and others is being taken seriously at all levels and that such investment is having a positive impact on individual and corporate performance. Such a quest begs all sorts of questions. Does strategic training only incorporate that which has a quantifiable effect on business objectives, or does it include any development where individual learning is taking place? When we talk of, for instance, management development, who's strategic purpose is actually being served? (See box 3.1.) What activities do we classify under the heading of training and development? Formal training programmes should obviously be included, but what about everyday learning opportunities? Where does learning stop and working begin? And can enhanced expertise, creativity, productivity, even market share be reliably attributed to an organization's investment in training and development?

Box 3.1   The multiple meanings of management development

'If management development is construed as the intersection of three variables – individual career, organizational succession and organizational performance – then much of the ambiguity can be interpreted as the difficulty of trying to manage some kind of accommodation between the variables. In idealized form, management development holds that all three variables can be integrated through compliance with its procedures and activities, offering the promise of a high level of optimization between individual expectations and organizational demands. In practice, each procedure and activity is subject to a range of interpretations and meanings by different parties, resulting in a multitude of assumptions and beliefs in any organization about how the variables are to be integrated. This is the socio-political domain of management – a complex dynamic of hopes and fears, ambitions and the opportunities, threats and disillusionments, conflicts and contradictions.' (Lees, 1992, p. 91.)

Despite the ambiguities that such conflicting agendas throw up and the private misgivings about the purpose and value of much that is done in the name of training and development, organizations continue to commit resources to such activities. The internal contradiction of such policies is well illustrated in the findings of a survey seeking the views of chief executives and personnel managers in 91 UK companies with turnovers greater than £20 million (Parkinson, 1990). Interviews uncovered that:

> Expenditure on the development and training of managers is highest in those companies where management development is part of the corporate plan. Senior managers need to believe that investment will allow them to respond more effectively to a changing environment. Companies in markets which have become increasingly turbulent in the last few years (e.g. retailing, leisure and brewing, and finance and property) demonstrate this, being amongst the largest spenders on management development and training . . . [yet] Few of the companies in the sample were able to quantify the benefits of management development programmes.

(1990, p. 73)

So is it possible to meaningfully map out a strategic approach to training and development? Can learning activities be devised and implemented in such a way that they tangibly impact upon the capacity of a business to deliver its medium- to long-term objectives? Can the various actors, internal levers and political systems be galvanized around a concerted and

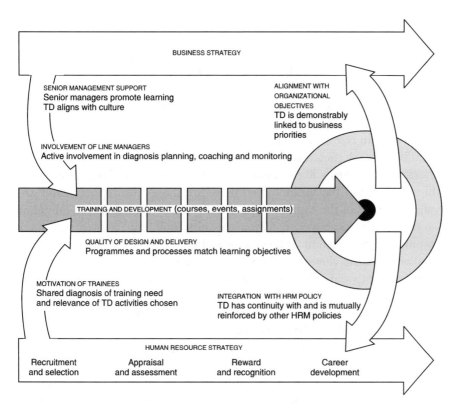

BUSINESS STRATEGY

SENIOR MANAGEMENT SUPPORT
Senior managers promote learning
TD aligns with culture

ALIGNMENT WITH
ORGANIZATIONAL
OBJECTIVES
TD is demonstrably
linked to business
priorities

INVOLVEMENT OF LINE MANAGERS
Active involvement in diagnosis planning, coaching and monitoring

TRAINING AND DEVELOPMENT (courses, events, assignments)

QUALITY OF DESIGN AND DELIVERY
Programmes and processes match learning objectives

MOTIVATION OF TRAINEES
Shared diagnosis of training need
and relevance of TD activities chosen

INTEGRATION WITH HRM POLICY
TD has continuity with and is mutually
reinforced by other HRM policies

HUMAN RESOURCE STRATEGY

| Recruitment and selection | Appraisal and assessment | Reward and recognition | Career development |

Figure 3.1   Strategic training and development (TD)

effective human resource development strategy? Figure 3.1 draws together the key potential ingredients of a rational and strategic approach to training and development.

The logic of the model is that unless attention is paid to all six dimensions shown in the figure, then the quality of training and development will be impaired and their business impact will be flawed.

While the actual training and development activities as experienced by trainees (perhaps a training course or a set of workshops, or on-the-job assignments or other developmental initiatives) are central to the model, they represent only one part of a cyclical process incorporating several other key players in the organization. The target represents the vision, mission or 'cause' of the organization and assumes this is or can be articulated in some shape or form. From this starting point there are two flows: one into business strategy, where the mission will be broken down into medium- and long-term objectives and plans; the other into human resource strategies where the competencies and performance criteria will be defined for the staff employed. This latter flow will hopefully inform each lever of HRM policy and procedure, providing continuity between recruitment and selection practices, appraisal and assessment, reward systems and career development processes. Critically, training and development provision needs to be mutually supported by each of these human resource levers.

Among those who scan the external environment and formulate business strategy for the organization as a whole, it is obviously advantageous to have a human resource specialist. Involvement in this early stage of business planning means that training and development can be set in motion to anticipate and meet likely knowledge, skill and attitude requirements of the workforce in the future. Then there are those who represent the prevailing culture of the organization, usually senior managers and line managers, or some dominant coalition spanning different parts of, and levels within, the organization. While the model makes no assumptions about the *correctness* of their views and the value they jointly attach to training activities, their potential influence upon the nature and outcome of training and development cannot be underestimated. Certain line managers may be part of this dominant coalition, but whether they are or not, they play a separate and important role in the overseeing of training received and the development undertaken by their staff. Through setting up on-the-job development opportunities, pre- and post-course briefings/debriefings and ongoing coaching, their participation in and ownership of training activities for their staff is essential. Next are those participating in the development process. Naturally they need to be motivated and to perceive the training they receive as relevant to their jobs, careers and broader self-development. Finally, the training staff, who may include external consultants and training agencies, are crucial in the way they design and deliver training programmes and development activities. To do this effectively such staff may also assist with initial diagnosis and interpretation of training requirements as well as subsequent evaluation which feeds back into business objectives.

What the overall model highlights is the pivotal link that training and development activities *can* provide between business and human resource strategy. A strategic approach to training and development can be depicted as one where all those involved are engaged in a connected, explicit and developmental purpose which helps to simultaneously fulfil an individual's learning goals and the organization's mission. However, such a conception of training and development is probably both over-mechanistic and idealistic. In the same way that the three variables mentioned in the box above (individual career, organizational succession and organizational performance) will rarely align perfectly, so the agendas and priorities of different interest groups within an organization will inevitably make the rationale for and the content of training activities contested terrain. All the more so, because more than most other HR initiatives, development activities touch upon the core purposes (personal, sectional, professional, cultural, occupational, organizational) and the raw nerves (who is developing whom, why, and to what ends) of the negotiated psychological contract between employee and employer. In the rest of this chapter we explore the role of each of the stakeholders in the training process, in order to understand more fully the possibility and desirability of a truly strategic approach to training and development in organizations.

There are, of course, groups external to the organization with a keen interest in organizational training provision, such as government departments, professional institutes, educational institutions, trade unions and employee associations, political pressure groups and (not least) shareholders and customers. Usually their power bases lie outside or in some cases traverse organization boundaries, but as we saw in the chapter on organization change (chapter 2) their influence upon internal decision-making can be immense. So we start with a consideration of the external environment, and the national training context in particular, within which an organization finds itself.

Do Environmental Factors Determine Investment in Training and Development?

The effectiveness of an organization's training and development practices and policies cannot be divorced from extra-organizational influences, both national and international. These 'situational factors' (Beer et al., 1984), or the so-called 'outer context' (Sparrow and Pettigrew, 1987), include such factors as technological investment, social and political attitudes, institutional practices, external labour markets, demographic pressures and changes in the regulatory context (e.g. privatization, deregulation). Each of these will combine to shape the assumptions and priorities of those responsible for training in a given organization.

Education and training: Some cross-country comparisons

Take, for example, some of the outer context factors which either inhibit or encourage the uptake of training in the UK. Lane's (1989) analysis of flexible specialization shows that the UK compares unfavourably with Germany and France on all five of the indicators chosen (table 3.1).

Attempts to adjust the organization of production to new and changing market demands have been hindered in the UK by traditionally adversarial industrial relations, the need to drastically reorient worker training, and deployment which has a much weaker vocational base to start with (29 per cent of British apprentices, technicians and foremen have formal

Table 3.1   Factors supporting or inhibiting the move towards flexible specialization: a comparative perspective

Factor	Germany	UK	France
Management	Actively committed to continuous technological innovation and competent to initiate and establish new technical systems.	Lack of confidence and, therefore, hesitancy about technological innovation; and a lack of competence to handle the more complex variety.	Technologically innovative management but less successful in adapting designs to the needs of production
Labour-market supply	An ample supply of all-round skilled labour which can be broadly deployed and easily retrained.	A shortage of skilled labour and an absence of flexibility in existing skilled labour.	A shortage of highly skilled and polyvalent labour.
Training system	A well-established training system and a willingness by both management and labour to invest in further retraining.	A haphazard and underdeveloped system and a general reluctance by management to make the long-term investment required.	Recent state intervention to increase the supply of skilled production workers and a management strategy of creating a small, polyvalent worker elite.
Employment relationship	Relatively high degree of employment security and low degree of labour-market segmentation.	Relatively low degrees of employment security. Segmented internal labour market.	Relatively high degree of employment security for the core labour force but a notable increase in labour-market segmentation.
Industrial relations system	A co-operative system aiding worker identification with, and joint responsibility for, the efficient and competitive organization of production. Management no longer actively concerned with achieving domination.	An adversarial system based on a 'minimum interaction' employment relationship. Incompatibility with notion of worker responsibility for production flow and product quality. Management still struggling to re-establish control.	An adversarial system with an emphasis on hierarchy and close management control. Not conducive to the development of general worker responsibility and co-operation.

Source: Adapted from Lane (1989).

qualifications compared with 61 per cent in Germany), and the insufficient development of management technical skill. So it is that the inheritance of skills and capabilities, usually the produce of previous training and recruitment policies at a national and sector level, severely constrains what firms can attempt and how they go about it: 'Frequently underestimated in tracing such change . . . is the way manpower, training and job design policies over a period of time determine the skill structure of an organisation and the scope for adopting and benefiting from new technology' (Hendry and Pettigrew, 1990, p. 28).

Detailed studies of matched industrial plants in Germany and the UK by the National Institute of Economic and Social Research (NIESR) attribute lower productivity, slower adoption and use of new technology, and frequency of downtime in the UK plants to the poorer level of training and technical competence. This and other examples, like the persistent use of subjective and discriminatory recruitment practices, illustrate the slow uptake of improved training and development in the UK (Keep, 1989).

The degree to which the national education and training system supports in-firm training is obviously a key social-political factor and one that is closely linked to skills supply. During the 1980s and early 1990s in the UK the Conservative government was clearly of the belief that: 'the provision, content, finance and level of provision of training is largely the responsibility of employers, and that the role of government institutions is to provide guidance and research, as well as being directly involved in training the unemployed. During the last decade training institutions in Britain have consequently been reorganized to give a greater role to private sector employers' (Brewster et al., 1992, p. 570).

This 'voluntarist' approach can be contrasted with countries where governments legislate and/or regulate the degree to which employers provide vocational and educational training (VET) for their staff. For instance, in Germany employers are obliged to fund two-thirds of VET, but they also enjoy with the trade unions considerable influence over the system, along with central and local government (Beardwell and Holden, 1994). One of the outcomes of this industry-oriented and directed training culture is that Germany has three times more skilled workers than the UK, despite having a labour force of a similar size (Rose and Wignanek, 1991). However, the German functionalist model has been criticized as outmoded, and its export-oriented and ethnocentric emphasis as being ill-suited to the demands of globalization (Evans and Doz, 1989) and openly discriminatory against women and ethnic minorities. Since the introduction of successive legislation in the 1970s and 1980s, France can also be described as adopting a 'directive' training ethos. Laws requiring that employers spend 1.2 per cent of total gross salaries on training employees have had the twin longer-term benefits of encouraging employers to invest beyond the limit as they

Table 3.2   Proportion of salaries and wages spent on training 1990-1

	UK	*France*	*Spain*	*Sweden*	*Germany*
0.01–1.0%	21	4	33	9	20
4% and above	11	27	13	16	11
Don't know	41	2	25	48	47

Source: Price Waterhouse Cranfield Survey (Holden, 1992, p. 120).

discovered the benefits of training and increasing accountability for the training budget. Taken at face value, table 3.2 shows that only 2 per cent of French organizations did not know how much they spent on training, compared to well over 40 per cent in the UK, Sweden and Germany. Interestingly, the training culture in Japan could be described as a mixture of directive and voluntarist. For the core workforce (primarily managerial and professional staff in large-scale companies):

> Lifetime employment allows for the long-term development of employees and enables the creation of a structured succession programme mutually beneficial to both the organization and the individual employee. Decision making is shared at all levels and there is a strong sense of collective responsibility for the success of the organization, and co-operative rather than individual effort is emphasised, although achievement is encouraged. Training and development is part and parcel of company policy in helping to reinforce these working practices, as well as being used to improve skills in technology and other related working practices. Training and development is thus 'embedded' in Japanese companies, rather than extraneous, as in British organizations.
>
> (Beardwell and Holden, 1994, p. 358)

Bournois (1992) notes that France – like the UK – has been less successful in alleviating long-term unemployment especially amongst its young people, possibly due to the poor perception of vocational training initiatives.

Many commentators are doubtful that UK employers can in fact rise to the training challenge posed by the non-interventionist stance of their government, because of a number of underlying structural factors that inhibit organizations investing in their employees, *particularly* in the area of training. In addition to those mentioned above, Keep (1989) refers to four such factors: the shifting of productive capacity and investment overseas by UK companies where they can buy new, pre-trained workforces (and therefore obviate the need to reskill their UK workforces); the trend, among some large UK companies (e.g. food industry), toward takeovers and subsequent divestment which undermine the long-term commitment to their subsidiaries that is a prerequisite to securing a reasonable return on investment in HRD (see also Naulleau and Harper, 1993); the continued dominance of financial management and accounting systems in UK board rooms, which militates against people-centred development over the longer term (see also Tayeb, 1993, p. 61); and the generally low adoption by UK managers of systematic and coherent personnel practices. Actually, this last point is seen as typical of Western Europe as a whole, where according to a survey of 5,450 organizations across ten European countries, 'in most countries and companies selection, appraisal, reward and development of human resources is neither strategically oriented enough nor integrated with each other, nor evaluated in an objective way' (Hilb, 1992, p. 575).

Management development – the state of play in the UK

In relation to management training in the UK, the evidence looks reasonably encouraging. A survey conducted among 2,051 members of the British Institute of Management (BIM) to establish the quality and quantity of training undertaken (of all types, including own-time study) over a calendar year, found that 82 per cent undertook some work-time training activities in 1991, and 49 per cent participated in training in their own time (Warr, 1992). Even allowing for a sample skewed toward larger companies, and a definition of training broader than that of previous surveys, this still represents a significant improvement in the quantity of management training (Handy, 1987; Mangham and Silver, 1986). Another survey of 83 per cent of BIM members found that managers averaged approximately 11 days of training per year, comprising 3.3 days off-the-job training in their own time, 5.3 in their employer's time, plus 2.2 days on-the-job training (Poole and Mansfield, 1992, p. 212). It's worth noting from this survey that 60 per cent of managers report that the training they receive is at their own initiative, and for a further 13 per cent it is also at their own expense. Increasing pressure for professionalism in management is undeniably a spur for such activity and a good goal even though definitions of what this looks like remain problematic. One index of this intent – though not necessarily the most accurate – is the growing number of organizations in public and private sectors which are signing up to support the Management Charter (1,000 employers representing 25 per cent of the UK workforce in 1993: Wills, 1993). Such intentions *could* have a far-reaching impact on the quality of management and business performance in Britain, providing the good practice and infrastructural support proclaimed by the Charter are translated into action.

Nevertheless, a number of questions remain about the growth and health of the UK management training context. One legitimate criticism levelled at many of the glowing reports cited to illustrate advances in management education is that they feature leading-edge companies, typically in the private sector and large enough to be able to afford the luxury of training investment and innovation. While it has always been the policy of the Council for Management Education and Development to foster such success stories, using them as exemplars for other organizations to follow, current progress (at least that which is published) does seem to be at the expense of smaller organizations (see for instance Vickerstaff, 1991), not part of the Management Charter Initiative elite and not based in the South East (61 per cent of providers of management training and 71 per cent of training consultants are located there). Furthermore, little evidence is yet available on the extent to which traditionally disadvantaged groups are benefiting from this apparent growth in development opportunities. The Institute for Employment Research predicts that numbers employed will increase between 1987 and 1995 by 1.75 million and that 90 per cent of this increase will be women workers. The signs so far, however, are that women returners, to take one important source of labour supply, continue to experience downward occupational mobility and appear disproportionately in semi-skilled and unskilled work.

This brief review of the external training climate in a number of countries confirms that certain environmental factors are indeed important in shaping organizational training provisions, but it also highlights that the relationship between them is by no means one of simple manipulation, nor is it free of internal contradiction.

1   Throughout this text we are careful to distinguish the rhetoric of what could and should be done, from the reality of what actually gets done. Drawing this distinction is especially necessary when assessing the influences of outer-context factors upon the training and development plans and practice of individual firms (see box 3.2).

Box 3.2   The role of training in turnaround

'In the period 1985–8, Lucas [a UK-based manufacturer of electrical and mechanical components] has spent around £40 million per annum on training which was equivalent to about 2.5 to 3 per cent of its total sales revenue. This expenditure was viewed as an "investment" in that training and development was being called on to act as a major agent of change. The in-company consciousness of the key role of training was high. It was not seen as a poor-relation, peripheral activity, but as a potent source of change. The highlights of the contribution made by training in this company are:

- its link with the total strategy comprising marketing, product engineering, manufacturing systems engineering and business systems;

- the highly evident top-management commitment to it;
- its role in developing and executing the competitive achievement plans (CAPs) which every business unit is required to have;
- the installation of business and engineering systems into the SBUs [small business units];
- and the underpinning of business task forces through training on an essentially project-requirement basis.

The Lucas case provides an excellent example of a traditional mainstream company which, in seeking to turn itself around from a loss-making situation, has sought a radical strategic response – part of which has clearly involved a drive to enhance the capabilities and commitment of its human resources through the use of training.

And yet the Lucas case is at the same time instructive for another reason. Its training provision – especially its coherent, business-led analysis of the role of that provision – is distinctive for its singularity. Few companies – and this includes the rest of the cases involved in this project – could claim to match the emphasis upon human resource development which has been shown by Lucas. But despite this lead position, it has to be said that only a little digging around is required to reveal that the impact, when viewed from the stance of the intended recipients of such provision, is, even in this lead case, often minimal. The approach looks coherent, sophisticated and integrated when presented by senior exponents, but it is often experienced rather differently by shop-floor workers and indeed by many middle-level managers. Both groups relate how their own recent training experiences have been few and how the investment-in-people theme is countermanded by more visible messages of cost cutting and pressure.' (Storey, 1992, pp. 114, 155.)

It is one thing to launch extensive training plans within an organization, and even to explicitly link these with strategic, business priorities – as was done at Lucas Industries. But, as the author goes on to state, this case illustrates 'the extreme difficulty of formulating and implementing an HRM approach – in part or in whole – in the context of traditional businesses in Britain which not only inherit whole congeries of expectations and past practices but which, at the same time, have also been facing harsh competitive pressures' (Storey, 1992, p. 116).

2   In the last decade, Britain's national training deficit has been exposed in very visible terms. While there is some evidence of gradual improvement, doubts remain about how the shortfall should be addressed and how any

further improvement might be stimulated and measured. The government's approach has been non-interventionist (that of providing support
and infrastructure), but the apparent reluctance or tardiness of employers to
take responsibility for their own training provision poses a dilemma.
Government agencies could become more proactive by stipulating national
targets of training days per year (Warr, 1992), offering financial incentives
to firms to invest in HRD, setting statutory requirements to publish details
of investment in training and development in company annual reports, and
establishing training and development committees based on the model of
health and safety committees (Storey, 1992, p. 175). The problem with all
such enabling and/or penalizing approaches is that they shift the initiative
away from the very place where real development takes place. Yet countries
which have strong directives set by local and central government to enforce
high-quality training standards, like Japan (Dore and Sako, 1989), or the
directed systems of Germany, France and Sweden, appear to be relatively
successful in developing their employees at grassroots level.

3   Another way of stating the internal contradiction of externally
inspired and monitored training activity is that training is not necessarily
equivalent to learning. (It is for this reason that we devote a later chapter to
individual and organizational learning.) Any extra-organizational attempts
to catalyse training and development need to take account of (i) the quality
of training – not simply the amount, (ii) the context of training – whether,
for instance, it is linked to individuals' needs and organizational career
paths, and (iii) the scope of learning – recognizing that learning is a lifetime
activity, fed by all manner of personal experiences and not tethered to the
post of one particular organization. It is encouraging to note that the
framework of National Education and Training Targets in the UK appears
to acknowledge these issues (Warr, 1992).

4   Any organizational training strategy based on prescriptions needs
careful contextualization depending on the sector, product/service and
workforce expectations of the organization concerned. Based on interviews
carried out in sixteen UK companies across several sectors, researchers
reported that 'it was difficult to disentangle types of MTD [management
training and development] from the strategies adopted by sectors and
organizations. In fact, for a number of our larger respondents a major
issue was that of locating a training process within a larger process of
organizational development. That is, the emphasis was as much, if not
more, on the *processual* aspects of implementation as on the content of
MDT' (Brown et al., 1989, p. 80).

This last point leads us on to a detailed consideration of the intra-organizational features that shape the formulation and implementation of HRD at a

firm level. Though undoubtedly influential, the external training climate of any given nation, no matter how favourable, does not automatically translate into effective training and learning for individuals and organizations. There are other sets of factors, historical and political, explicit and implicit, cultural and commercial that will shape and sustain such activity. It is to this 'inner context' (Sparrow and Pettigrew, 1987) that we now turn, in order to discover what choices are available and how they differentiate a strategic from a tactical approach to HRD.

Can Training and Development be Aligned with Organizational Objectives?

Since the early 1980s there has been a growing recognition of the importance of linking training and development – and the practice of HRM generally – to the strategic intent of an organization (e.g. Tichy et al., 1982; Hendry and Pettigrew, 1990; Schuler, 1992). Indeed, it could be argued that: 'Instead of being activities peripheral to the achievement of corporate objects, the human resources of the organization are seen as a vital factor in corporate planning, and training and development as able to make an important contribution to the achievement of business objectives' (Keep, 1989, p. 114). But how realistic is it to have training and development issues on the strategic agenda? What contribution can such discussions have in the process of business planning? If consideration of training *is* a strategic concern, can it be faithfully translated into education, training and development activities which 'deliver' the required knowledge, skills and attitudes in a timely fashion? And, finally, can these business outputs be attributed to training initiatives in demonstrable terms? There is no doubting the internal logic of this classic training 'loop', but in this section we examine available evidence as to whether and how it happens.

Linking training and performance: Some choices

Based on in-depth case study analysis of why companies in the UK invested in training Pettigrew et al. (1988) found that whatever the source of pressure, the common feature of the triggers for strategic change was the highlighting of a skill performance gap. However, the researchers discovered that the particular pathways towards a heightened training and development culture varied from firm to firm. This casts doubt on the simplistic view 'that training leads to improved business performance (and that firms can therefore be expected to train more), or that improved business performance leads to increased (and more effective) training simply because firms can fund it more easily' (1988, p. 41).

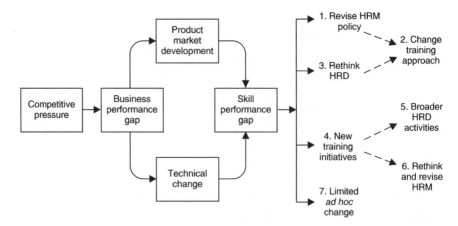

Figure 3.2   Links between business performance and human resource responses
Source: Adapted from Hendry, Pettigrew and Sparrow, 1988, p. 41.

There are in fact a range of possible responses that a firm *can* make, when a skill gap has been identified (see figure 3.2). The exposure may prompt a concerted attempt to revise overall human resource management, and to embracing such things as recruitment criteria, reward schemes, attempts to reduce attrition, enhanced accountability through appraisals, and increased or decreased use of flexible workers (response 1).

A likely but not inevitable outcome of these changes in HRM policy is also a shift in the organization's approach to training (response 2). On the other hand, the skill performance gap may focus specific attention on the organization's human resource development (HRD) (response 3), with higher importance being placed on strategies like graduate recruitment, tiered recruitment or the appraisal process and assessment centres; it is likely that such activities would stimulate demand for off-the-job training as well as secondments, mentoring and self-development. In some cases the response may be direct and straightforward: the setting up of a one-off training course to plug the exposed skills gap (response 4). It is worth noting, however, that such training efforts *can* act as a spur to wider HRD or HRM activity, which in turn begins to shape strategic decisions (responses 5 and 6). A case in point is the management at a car manufacturing plant who, having retrained their production operatives to handle new technology, find this has repercussions on the career expectations and motivation of their newly skilled shop-floor staff; this, in turn, impacts upon the selection criteria when recruiting apprentices and ultimately influences supervisory and management style.

While this figure appears straightforward it should be remembered that the plurality of competing interests in a firm will affect its capacity to respond to external pressures and change itself, whether the change involves products, skills, culture or training systems. Strategic processes of change are multi-level activities which rarely accord with the 'commander' model of strategy management (e.g. Bourgeois and Brodwin, 1984). Under these circumstances it is always possible that an organization's leadership will choose to ignore, will misperceive or will simply fail to detect the skills gap when it arises (response 7), or construct a case for one of the other responses that does not logically follow from the skills gap diagnosis.

The strategic purpose of training: Some possibilities

Many organizations have got to the point of recognizing that training and development is a strategic priority rather than a tactical or knee-jerk response, but choices still remain as to where to direct investment and to what ends. A common conception of strategic training and development – and the one considered as pivotal in figure 3.2 above – is to see it as a means to *assess and address skills deficiencies* in the organization. At shop-floor level recent experience shows that this has frequently meant multi-skilling for craft workers and equipping production operatives with the knowledge and skills necessary to undertake routine maintenance. Upgrading the skills base of *managers* has also been a priority. A report on UK companies (Parkinson, 1990) found improving managers' competencies in core skills such as marketing, finance and production to be highest on the agenda, followed by training in skills and experience necessary to fit individuals for senior management roles. The shortcomings of reducing managerial work to a set of generic competencies have been voiced widely. Such 'narrow vocationalism' can all too easily crowd out any sustained concern with the 'social, moral, political and ideological ingredients of managerial work and the form of educational experience most appropriate to their enhancement and development' (Reed and Anthony, 1992, p. 601). Nevertheless, some pinpointing of the capabilities necessary for staff to perform effectively in their future roles is an essential precursor to investment in training activity. More will be said about methods of diagnosis in the section below entitled 'Who Owns the Training and Development Process?'

Another strategic purpose of training and development is to act as a *catalyst* for change (a purpose which frequently incorporates attempts to enhance skills as discussed above). This approach is frequently associated with organization leaders seeking to orchestrate cultural change amongst their workforce. Using such methods as participative workshops with vertical cross-sections of staff, quality improvement projects, team building, problem-solving groups, and so on, organizations seek to cultivate a fresh way of viewing themselves, their internal 'customers' and the market in which they compete. For instance, the establishment of the National Health Service Training Authority (NHSTA) in the UK was a classic example of using training and development to attempt a reorientation of the total organization so that customer relations became a key target. However, the introduction of catalytic processes in such complex organizations is by no means simple. In this case there were at least three stakeholder groups (the Management Education Division, the National Education Centres and the District General Managers), each having their own definitions of and criteria for successful cultural change (Fox, 1989).

Of course, it is relatively easy to change external *manifestations* of culture; it is far more ambitious to change the ingrained attitudes and cultural norms of staff. Whether such strategies are feasible or even defensible is discussed more fully in chapters 2 and 6; however, what is significant is the way management development, in particular, has been used in a variety of sectors to: 'not only upgrade skills but to structure attitudes. In other words it has become a collective personnel device' (Storey and Sisson, 1993, p. 164). Typically multiple 'levers' of training and development are pulled simultaneously, changes are directed at the whole organization and wider human resource practices are deliberately modified to reinforce the desired cultural changes.

The third and most strategic purpose of training and development is an attempt to give the organization *competitive edge*, both through the content of such activities and the way in which they are delivered. Indeed, it could be argued that this is the tacit intention of the first two purposes. More and more organizations are using human resource strategy, for example, as a way of integrating their business planning processes with organization-wide development and human resource activities, from recruitment through to succession planning. For example, because public enterprises cannot register success simply in terms of profit and market share, the way they acquire resources and deliver services is increasingly becoming a driver for competitive advantage. The crucial issue for such organizations and agencies therefore is the definition of their *raison d'être* in a way that is well understood and owned by their staff. Furthermore, the more an organization comes to have a reputation for progressive training and development, the greater its chances of attracting high-calibre candidates when recruiting.

A fourth strategic purpose of training and development, and one with a different emphasis from the others, is that of encouraging a *learning climate* in the organization. The focus here is on the learning needs of individuals, guided by organizational goals and undergirded by the belief that within each member of staff is a latent talent waiting to be tapped. Accordingly, the trend is away from structured, taught courses and towards enhanced opportunities for self-development through such methods as on-the-job training, strategic secondments and temporary task forces, or computer-based open learning systems where training material is provided which may but not necessarily relate to the individual's job. Chapter 7 explores further the tensions inherent within the concept of the learning organization.

The differing objectives described above are obviously not mutually exclusive; for example, it is not unusual to begin an organization development intervention with a catalytic review of the mission or long-term vision of a given enterprise, and for this to lead to a revised set of roles, responsibilities and departmental goals. Inevitably, this will create demand for a range of training tools (perhaps project management skills, financial awareness workshops and so on). This exposure to a new learning environment may in turn release potential in employees as they become enthusiastic about the unrealized dimensions of their jobs and the possibility of having more control over their own occupational destiny. It may lead them to sign up for job-relevant courses at their local college or to set up self-development groups with colleagues at work. Many organization change interventions in recent years have incorporated widescale downsizing and delayering, with consequent redundancies (not always voluntary) among large tranches of staff. In such cases this search by vulnerable staff for greater control over their occupational destiny takes on a starker and more desperate significance.

The strategic positioning of training: Some difficulties

Despite the intellectual appeal and the positive nature of many case-study accounts which celebrate the integration of training and development with business strategies and competitive performance, the approach is not unproblematic for a number of practical and conceptual reasons. First, we know that the formulation and implementation of strategy at any level is an uncertain and iterative process 'in which [the] additive accumulation of managerial decisions combined with the triggering effects of environmental disturbances can produce major transformations in the firm' (Whipp et al., 1988, p. 16). By implication, the evolution of a training and development strategy is unlikely to be straightforward. At best, those responsible for deriving such strategies will be 'pattern recognisers . . . who manage a process in which strategies (and visions) can emerge as well as be deliberately conceived' (Mintzberg, 1988, p. 85). Given the 'lead times' required for staging most types of training activity, together with the even longer time-scales for organizational benefits to be felt, this poses a real challenge to most training departments reliant on providing institutionalized responses.

Setting in motion training and development activities that enhance collective capability as an instrument of policy, presumes that the organization's strategic intent can be clearly articulated. We know that for many organizations, particularly in the public and non-profit sectors, this is by no means an easy task.

> If agencies are to succeed, they will need a supporting management development strategy which includes techniques for managing careers within agencies for all civil servants. Agencies will also require clearer management objectives. However, given the doubtful utility of the value for money concept, as well as the inseparable link between policy formulation and the delivery of a service, it seems unlikely that the objectives will ever become clearer. An ideology of managerialism based on efficiency is not enough in motivational terms. There must also be a commitment to the public good, because unless there is a moral purpose to public policy, it has no intrinsic worth.
>
> (Tyson, 1990, p. 30)

Secondly, even where organizational objectives are stated, there is often a gap between the espoused intentions and values voiced by those initiating and 'sponsoring' the development and the actual perceptions and motivations of those on the receiving end. Indeed, there may be all sorts of reasons why senior managers fund, and individuals participate in, development activities *other than those publicized*. Some of the differing 'agendas' for investing in management training are given in table 3.3, together with the assumptions underlying and the questions/issues prompted by each one (for further discussion, see Lees, 1992 and chapter 2 above on 'Managing Change'). Take the example of development centres, designed ostensibly to generate individually tailored career development plans (a functional–performance agenda). It becomes apparent that senior management are also using the opportunity provided by 'assessing' at the development centres to informally earmark high fliers (a political reinforcement agenda). Although these are not necessarily incompatible objectives of the one event, they constitute a dangerous tightrope to walk: once the hidden managerial agenda becomes known it is likely that candidates will seek to 'perform' rather than be open to reform.

Thirdly, there is as yet little empirical evidence to demonstrate that UK organizations are actually taking a strategic approach to training and developing their staff, despite all the good reasons for doing so (Keep, 1989; Parkinson, 1990; Storey, 1992). Keep (1989) cites a small number of companies who are leaders in the HRM movement in Britain because they have successfully integrated their training and HRD systems into wider business planning and strategy. Yet a closer look at one of them, Lucas Industries, shows that even here, perceptions differ as to the real impact of training (see box 3.2).

Table 3.3 The many agendas of management development (MD)

Type	Characteristic	Assumptions	Questions and problems
Functional–performance: 'a garage'	Knowledge, skills or attitudes to improve performance, bring about change, increase national 'stock' of trained managers.	• Training needs can be objectively identified and matched against training. • Role performance can be precisely assessed. • There is a tight 'means–end' link between MD and functional performance.	• Overlooks other factors influencing the impact of MD on performance. • Danger of a closed loop: corporate funding will only be given to successful MD interventions, therefore choose MD that can demonstrate success in corporate terms.
Political reinforcement 'a cascade'	MD acts as an extension of the organization's political order. Programmes (e.g. culture change) propagate the skills and attitudes believed by the top team as necessary to turn the company around.	• The top team's perception of how organizational performance is to be improved is correct. • The 'recipe for success' can be translated into an MD programme and cascaded down the organization.	• The MD dogmas are frequently dependent on 1 or 2 key figures – what happens when they go? • The approach leaves little opportunity to be questioned, and the career costs of doing so may be high. Such a climate defies genuine commitment.
Compensation 'a reward'	MD activities are offered as compensation for the deprivations of employment, e.g.: • as a welfare substitute • as an alternative focus to an alienating work place • to promote self-development	• Such activities encourage employees to acquire a habit of learning. • Being sponsored on courses helps motivate managers and engenders commitment to the organization.	• This approach deflects attention from the causes of alienation – offering a palliative instead. • It is deceptive – and morally dubious – to 'use' education in this manner.

Table 3.3   Cont'd

Type	Characteristic	Assumptions	Questions and problems
Psychic defence 'a displacement'	MD provides a safe situation in which to discharge anxieties by giving access to/ participation in more strategic matters.	• Managers need a social system to defend their psyche against persecutory anxiety arising from their competitive career drives. • Apparently fair appraisal systems, target setting and ordered management succession help reduce the fear of disorder and chaos if latent competition were to break out.	• Would greater self-development and self-determination in the work place necessarily lead to unbridled and selfish anarchy? • Only a few MD activities would typically provide an opportunity for such displacement.

Source: Adapted from Lees, 1992, pp. 89–105.

Fourthly it may be that many organizations do not explicitly state the *strategic* intent of their training and development effort, and therefore, while a great deal of such activity is perhaps being carried out, because it has little demonstrable reference to broader organizational goals it is disregarded by onlookers as tactical and non-strategic. However, just because the links with organizational objectives are muffled or unstated it does not necessarily follow that valuable development is not taking place, albeit outside the organization's frame of reference. Herein lies one of the key dilemmas of strategically orientated training and development: the typically unques-tioned assumption that strategic equates to top-down.

Fifthly, there is the difficulty of closing the loop and demonstrating the value to the business of training and development. Attempts have been made to evaluate the cost benefits of training activity ranging from fairly sophisticated utility calculations (Smith, 1992) to more broad-brush deduc-tions: 'making some quite plausible assumptions some 20 years ago, I calculated that if a one-week residential training course increased a man-ager's performance by more than 0.5 per cent, it was more profitable for the company to train than not to train' (Everard, 1991, p. 26). But in a sense such equations miss the point. 'Evaluation is about making value judgements as well as technical ones and it is about power, since action may involve, at the least, persuading others of the rightness of one's values first, through to imposing one's values onto them' (Fox, 1989, p. 205). So it is that different stakeholders will have their own interpretation as to why the training evaluation is being undertaken, have competing views as to which evaluation criteria should be used, hold their own pet preferences as to which methods are best employed to fulfil these assessments, and possibly have opposing opinions as to which methods are valid. Finally and un-avoidably, various stakeholder groups will differ in the weight they place on various evaluation outcomes, depending largely on how they, and the constituent group(s) they represent, are affected by any ensuing changes as compared with other stakeholder groups.

In other words, the way HR interventions are evaluated will be influenced by the perceived fairness of the new normative order (how has my access to rewards, status, authority and power bases been affected?) and social comparison with reference groups (how have reciprocity and exchange relations with significant others been altered?) (Carnall, 1990). Given the complexities associated with such analysis it is perhaps not surprising that so few organizations carry out systematic evaluations of their training and development activities, and even when evaluation research is available it is often ignored (Legge, 1984).

How Influential is Senior Management Support for Training and Development?

Training is a political activity. This is because learning is about discovery of new knowledge (possibly privy to the organization) and concepts (potentially threatening to the uninitiated); it is about access to training courses (who gets selected and who does not); it is about career paths and plans (which secondments are developmental and which signify plateauing); and it is about enlightenment (being inspired by a fresh, corporate approach) or disillusionment (realizing that personal and corporate values do not match). In other words, learning is as much about where the dominant cultural coalition of an organization is located as it is about the acquisition of new skills and techniques. Usually, but not always, this cultural coalition is synonymous with the senior management. In this section we examine the influence of senior managers from two perspectives: as shapers of prevailing culture and as sponsors of training and development initiatives.

Senior managers as shapers of prevailing culture

We deal more fully with culture and its relationship to human resource strategies elsewhere (chapter 6), but the distinctive linking of prevailing culture and the development of human capabilities will be briefly examined here. In many ways culture is a central, all-pervasive reality of organizational life, encompassing the spectrum of attitudes, values, norms, style and cues – verbal, unspoken, visible, subtle, deliberate, unintended – that make up the distinctive feel of an enterprise. Culture has been aptly described as 'the predisposition to behave in a certain way'. Nowhere are people's cultural values more apparent than in the area of training and development. Few managers would argue with the logical implications of declining market share, most department heads would revise their operating plans in the light of budgetary analysis, but when it comes to changing the way others (or more importantly, we) behave the impelling logic seems to melt away! The point is well made by Brooks and Bate (1994). On the basis of an in-depth, ethnographic study of one of the newly formed agencies in the UK civil service, they found any attempt to change from above was neutralized and frustrated by the cultural infrastructure at the local level (1994, p. 177). So when discussing 'prevailing' culture we should be careful not to assume that this is equivalent to the culture of senior management nor neglect the complicating objectives and vested interests of other *non*-prevailing work groups, and the impact these will have on internal development policies. This poses a problem for organizations pursuing HRM policies that are intended to integrate with their business strategies. Particularly for diversified corporations, it is likely that different policies will emerge for different divisions or subsidiaries which mutually reinforce their own business strategy, but possibly contradict HRM policies pursued in other business units or the overall policy priorities of the corporation. On this situation Legge comments:

> strong unit sub-cultures, a claimed ingredient of competitive advantage, might well develop. A problem would only arise if there developed a perceived requirement to integrate two or more sub-units in a manner that required integration at operating level, and hence of personnel. Then not only would the difficulty of merging distinct sub-cultures be likely, but perceptions of potential inequalities and inconsistencies between erstwhile autonomous units' HRM policies might undermine the trust and commitment that is supposed to develop from perceptions of congruence.
>
> (Legge, 1989, p. 31)

Furthermore, cultures are not static; the prevailing culture may appear overbearing and feel relentless, particularly to temporarily disenfranchised groups, but shifting centres of cultural gravity are becoming increasingly commonplace. In some cases this is due to relatively 'aggressive' board-level buy-outs and acquisitions; in other cases it follows decentralizing and/or devolving initiatives where responsibility and empowerment is deliberately pushed out to the further reaches, or down to the lower levels, of the organization.

Training and development is far from being a neutral process where the only resistance trainees have to absorbing new knowledge or acquiring new skills is their individual capacity or learning style. Invariably learning is 'a politicised process where new knowledge, systems and techniques are viewed suspiciously, even rejected because they are seen to represent the priorities of others whose priorities are distinct and possibly opposed, or to result in a re-allocation of organizational resources, or a weakening of a section's traditional power-base' (Salaman and Butler, 1990). The implications of this are discussed further in chapter 7.

Clearly, then, the notion that senior managers can be the shapers of culture, using training interventions to generate and reinforce their particular vision of the business, is too simplistic. Undoubtedly senior individuals can be influential, and as a coherent top team (less common) their collective will can be yet more determining of organizational norms and values, but we have seen that this influence is neither one-way, nor inevitable. A better analogy might be to view senior managers as cultural conductors – giving a pivotal lead to the assembled 'players' while simultaneously being dependent on their assembled creativity and responsiveness; the interplay between conductor and 'orchestra' being a subtle amalgam of motivation, loyalty and expertise, some of which will be won and/or enhanced through training, but much of it attributable to latent talents, predisposition, personal skill portfolio and the fickle chemistry of the moment.

Senior managers as sponsors of training and development

Is the role of senior management more straightforward when it comes to discovering how an organization chooses and sustains its strategy for training and wider development activity? More specifically, how do dominant coalitions influence such decisions?

Again, the best evidence of policy and practice comes from the report produced for the Training Agency (Pettigrew et al., 1988). The researchers uncovered a number of factors present in the twenty companies they investigated that either work towards or against the adoption of fresh and sustained training approaches (figure 3.3). As we have already seen technological or product market changes are driving forces for introducing a training strategy, unless the task skills identified relate to a small number of simple, standardized products or services requiring short learning time. In this instance a dose of 'top-up' training may suffice, and mitigate against a concerted strategy. The non-availability of required skills in the external labour market, and the relative economic stability will also promote training. The items listed in the 'external support for training' box we have

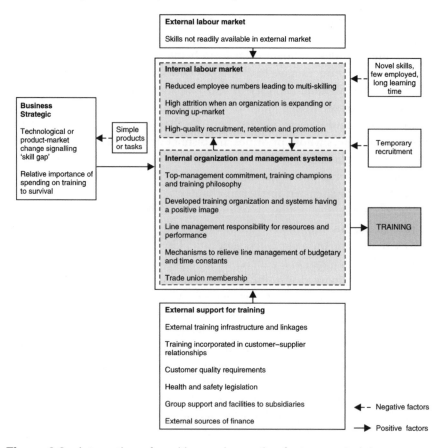

Figure 3.3 Interaction of positive and negative factors on training
Source: Pettigrew, Hendry and Sparrow, 1988.

already discussed – noting, however, that there are many historical, political and cultural factors that threaten to blunt training provision by organization in the UK, especially when compared with other European partners (e.g. Purcell, 1989).

Among the features of the internal labour market that promote training are moves toward multi-skilling of production and maintenance staff typically associated with reducing numbers of employees and expanding the tasks/skills of those that remain. Also, an organization may adopt a positive policy of training and development in order to attract a higher-quality staff, particularly if it has had problems with attrition. Thirdly, when organizations have a tradition of high-quality recruitment, retention and promotion, the training of higher-level skills is a viable option when preparing for and undergoing change because it represents an investment for the future. However, if the need is for specialist skills for a few and the lead time on training skills in-house is long, organizations are likely to opt for external recruitment and/or use contract labour, thus removing the need for HRD investment.

A further crucial set of factors instrumental in the triggering of training activity are those under the category of 'internal organization and management system'. These refer to the key personalities and the political decision-making processes within the organization concerned. A positive culture toward the value of training will be assisted by the following driving forces; first, the presence of 'training champions' especially amongst senior management; second, adequate systems for the diagnosis and delivery of training activities and for these systems to have credibility; third, line managers being encouraged and supported in their training initiatives and being relieved of the budgetary and opportunity costs of releasing staff for development; and fourth, internal pressure for such things as health and safety training (from trade unions) or equal opportunities training (from EO groups).

When Pettigrew et al. (1988) assessed the equivalent organizational triggers for human resource development, as against vocational education and training, the driving forces – apart from top-management commitment to development – were found to be: integrated systems for recruitment, training and placement; awareness of multiple levels to secure effective work performance; the mentoring and monitoring of careers from an early stage; recognizing developmental opportunities within normal management process; and the provision of open learning facilities.

In both cultivating education and training, it can be seen that senior management (or the equivalent dominant coalition) influence a number of these driving forces. Crucially, it is they who define the nature of training and development, and evidence from the National Health Service (see box 3.3) shows how powerful such definitions can be.

Box 3.3   Senior perceptions of training in the NHS

'[G]iven the difficulty of evaluating management development, beliefs about the value of management development are shaped either by a strong organizational culture or by personal experience and . . . chief executives play a key role in shaping culture. Many United Kingdom executives have not been to university, most have not had extensive formal management development and most explain their career progress in terms of person factors rather than management development. They are therefore unlikely to shape a culture which emphasises management development. At best, they will pay lip-service to the idea, but devolve responsibility for implementation to the personnel/management development function.

The managers in question can then be expected to formalise and bureaucratise management development as a means of ensuring control. The resulting formal systems will receive general support but will typically be seen as slightly detached from the mainstream of key organizational activity. Management development will be defined in terms of courses, which will be perceived *as a good thing*, but not the key to organizational and career success. Once such formal activities and beliefs have become established, even sophisticated management developers will find it difficult to change the system.' (Guest et al., 1992, pp. 78–9.)

However, no single factor of those depicted in figure 3.3 is sufficient by itself to create a positive training climate within an organization. It tends to be the case that those investing in training and development for their staff do so because a *number* of the driving forces described above are in place, and because they are relatively uninhibited by particular negative factors.

It goes without saying that organization leaders need to endorse training and development initiatives if only to release the resources and budget necessary to run them. But this is not enough. There needs to be a consistency between the outputs that development programmes teach and cultivate and the observed actions and behaviour of the senior managers who 'sponsor' them. Unless individuals are convinced that senior management value and practise the skills and attitudes being advocated by such activities, they will exhibit instrumental commitment to them at best (Ogbonna and Wilkinson, 1990). In addition, if senior management ignore or misread the cultural centre of gravity themselves, the training initiatives they launch are likely to avail little in the long term and possibly meet with indifference and cynicism in the short term.

Who Owns the Training and Development Process?

In this section we address the question of who is responsible for the process of training and development and its outcomes. This takes us to the core issue of whether training is strategic and if it is, whose strategic purpose is actually being served. A case could be made for each of the interest groups represented in figure 3.1 'owning' training and development. Here we focus on line managers, trainees and developers themselves and – more briefly –

those contracted to design and deliver the training events and learning activities. The individual is well placed to recognize his or her own strengths, weaknesses and development needs in relation to the realities and demands of the job, and given certain circumstances (timeliness, perceived relevance, infrastructural support and reinforcement), is likely to invest a great deal in the training process. Unfortunately, such circumstances cannot be taken as given. In the case of off-the-job and external training, much depends on the quality of the learning activity or training programme, and these will, in turn, be a function of the expertise of the designers, tutors and their support staff. Their motivation is slightly different, however; they will be concerned to construct an effective learning event or set of modules – but from a more detached perspective and with probably less credibility and power to influence outcomes. The respective benefits and drawbacks of relying on specialists, whether internal human resource advisers or external consultants, is summarized elsewhere (table 2.5 in the context of the chapter on Managing Change). Finally, much also depends on the line manager, project manager or supervisor of the individual trainee, since it is they who are uniquely placed to assess both current *and future* skill requirements of the job, and they who can directly facilitate the development of the staff they manage. The linking of training and development to the required performance of the business unit or project for which they are responsible is the obvious advantage here.

Much play has been made in recent years of the difference between the normative models of HRM and personnel management. One purported distinction concerns the role of line managers.

> while both personnel management and HRM highlight the role of line management, the focus is different. In the personnel management models, line's role is very much an expression of the view that all managers manage people, so all managers in a sense carry out 'personnel management'. It also carried the recognition that most specialist personnel work still has to be implemented within line management's departments where the workforce is physically located. In the HRM models, HRM is vested in line management as business managers responsible for co-ordinating and directing *all* resources in the business unit in pursuit of bottom line results. Not only does the bottom line appear to be specified more precisely than in the personnel management models, with much emphasis on quality of product or service, but a clear relationship is drawn between the achievement of these results and the line's appropriate and proactive use of the human resources in the business unit. Personnel policies are not passively integrated with business strategy, in the sense of flowing from it, but are an integral part of strategy in the sense that they underlie and facilitate the pursuit of a desired strategy.
>
> (Legge, 1989, pp. 27, 28)

In order to analyse the respective roles of line manager, trainee and trainer we now look at training and development activity from two perspectives: the degree to which it is in the 'bloodstream' of an organization, and how well it is diagnosed and delivered.

The invisibility and maturity of training and development

The first thing to note is that appearances can be deceptive. A superficial observation of what development activities are taking place in an organization could be very misleading. Take a look at figure 3.4, which is based on an analysis of human resource development in diverse organizations. The first *intermittent* pattern represents a situation where there is little or no genuine commitment to HRD by most line managers. The second pattern could be called *institutionalized*: it occurs where activity and apparent commitment peak, perhaps because there has been a push from above to record training activity, or there is a need to use up surplus development budgets before the financial year-end, or the company compensation plan rewards active involvement by line managers. This may be true of an organization with its own HRD function offering well-established, off-the-job programmes to the rest of the business on a menu basis.

Whereas the activity level in pattern three appears to revert towards that of the first level, it actually depicts the more mature situation where training and development has become a natural and ongoing part of normal work relations: well *internalized* but less visible to the casual observer. This might represent a company where line managers are highly skilled in coaching and developing their staff, able to 'construct' everyday occurrences as

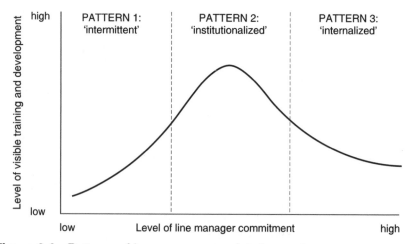

Figure 3.4   Patterns of human resource development
Source: Adapted from Ashton et al., 1975, p. 6.

learning opportunities for themselves and their staff, and where the prevailing ethos of people development militates against departmental talent-hoarding. In their report on how well 144 directors from 41 UK organizations were equipped for their responsibilities, Mumford et al. (1987) conclude that 'most directors have learned through a mixture of relatively accidental and unstructured experiences. Systems of management development have not been widely influential'. From this analysis Mumford puts forward three types of management development (1993, p. 35). The 'informal managerial' comprises reactive training initiatives which are not only unstrategic but also likely to have minimal learning impact. The 'formal management development' type is equivalent to the institutionalized pattern where training opportunities are more purposeful but learning is often limited because it is uncoupled from the trainee's normal activities. The 'integrated managerial' type as with the internalized pattern in figure 3.4, improves the individual and organizational relevance of the training and builds development opportunities around a more self-conscious use of everyday work experience, thus combining the virtues and eliminating the deficiencies of the other two approaches.

Line managers also play a pivotal role in integrating the overarching strategic objectives of their organization with its people development policies and practices. An index of this might be the extent to which all levels of staff are involved in knowledge, skills and self-enhancement in a way that mutually serves organizational purposes and their own growth as individuals. Based on research over many years at the Centre for the Study of Management Learning at Lancaster University, a six-step model describing organizations in ascending degrees of 'maturity' on these dimensions has been devised (Burgoyne, 1988). From this analysis, the author draws three conclusions about strategic mature development activity. First, it has to be conscious and reflective. While a great deal of natural development takes place through the unplanned interpersonal and functional experiences encountered each day, and careers frequently unfold in an uncontrived manner, these cannot be classed as *strategic* processes until they are explicitly linked to the implementation of corporate policy. This, of course, assumes that the corporate strategy has currency! Secondly, the model infers incremental levels of maturity, such that an organization's approach to HRD is likely to grow in sophistication rather than suddenly become Level 5 or 6. It is not inconceivable that different aspects of the training strategy can vary in their connectedness to corporate policy within the same enterprise, and that training and development generally could slip downwards in maturity over time. The third, and perhaps most important, point from Burgoyne's analysis is the linking of training and development with what he calls the 'hard systems' of HRM on the one hand (which we take up in more detail below) and collaborative career planning on the other.

The diagnosis and delivery of training and development

Organizational strategies

From an organizational perspective a training-needs analysis (TNA) is basically a process of collecting data which allows an organization to identify and compare its actual level with its desired level of performance. Performance here could be interpreted as meaning the competencies and attitudes necessary for staff to do the job effectively. Typically the process involves collecting data on current levels of performance and comparing these with the current desired level of performance and the desired level over the long term. The shortfall in these comparisons reveals both immediate and longer-term training needs. However, organizations are not static: their view as to what constitutes effective performance will alter as they move into new business environments.

Sparrow and Bognanno (1993) identify four different categories of competency which help an organization attach a 'shelf-life' to a competency profile for the organization as a whole, or to any given career stream or cluster of jobs: *emerging* competencies are those that will require greater emphasis as the organization pursues its particular strategic path; those that are *maturing* are those that are becoming less relevant – perhaps due to technology or work restructuring. *Transitional* competencies are those required of individuals during any change process (e.g. high tolerance of uncertainty and the ability to manage stress and conflict). Stable or *core* competencies are those that are central to an organization's performance and so have persistent relevance.

The double helix model in figure 3.5 shows how development action undertaken by individuals arising out of an organizationally driven review process can connect to the corporate objectives or mission of the organization (Shepherd, 1991). Each part of the double helix represents a separate circle of demand and supply, but these are typically unconnected. Organizations frequently rely on some mystical process of communication to ensure that managers do the right thing, and where the mission of the organization is well understood and shared, this may just work. Few organizations attempt to connect the systems that actually develop individuals to meet organizational need. They rely on a continuing turnover of people to ensure that individuals match job requirements. In an organization that has little turnover, skills quickly become outdated and the organization becomes less able to meet changing demands. Instant programmes of development are set in motion as solutions and often the training budget is too small to cope.

So how can training and development align with and contribute to the mission of a given organization, assuming such a statement exists and is meaningful (and we know this to be a major assumption)? There are four key elements, all of which rely on the vision and skills of line management. The first is a manpower plan which usually contains a number of people at specific grades and tends to focus on broad requirements. It therefore lacks the refinement of a statement of skill need. The second element is some kind of skills audit. Failure to regularly review skills against need results in emergency recruitment programmes to buy in scarce skills and/or redundancies or redeployment to cut out skills no longer required. A third element is performance appraisal. This usually concentrates on improving performance on the job but rarely reflects development for future needs of the organization. This probably happens because little is known by appraising managers about the strategic needs of the business outside their own areas. Finally, there is development action, frequently seen as something the trainers do. The intention of the double helix in figure 3.5 is to show that the overall process relies on both top-down and bottom-up communication and activity. When operated effectively training and development initiatives will reflect both the strategic priorities of the business as well as the personal aspirations of the individual trainees and developers, although it is usually assumed that the two correspond – at least potentially.

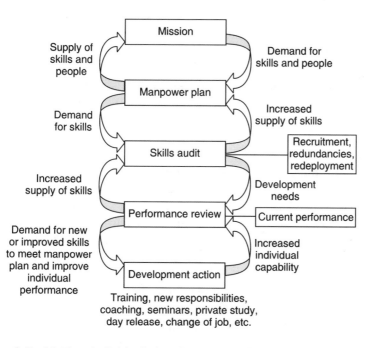

Figure 3.5 Linking individual development action to the organization's mission

Individual strategies

How should training and career development needs, present or future, manifest or latent, be diagnosed? The organizational pros and cons of various methods like questionnaires, interviews, observations and work samples are well established (see for instance Olivas, 1988). Less is known about how participants view such processes, which is strange given that it is their development that is being determined.

Research findings suggest line manager involvement in diagnostic and development activities is valued on two counts: their role in providing feedback on performance and the fact that such feedback and career planning advice is credible because it is coming from someone who is (usually) connected to the organizational power nexus and/or a carrier of important cultural information (Mabey and Iles, 1993; Preston, 1993). The usual forum for diagnosing training and development needs is the performance review or appraisal interview between the manager and his/her subordinate. However, such reviews are by definition evaluative and often linked to remuneration and promotion possibilities. In contrast, training-needs assessment is a process of assessing an employee's mastery of certain skills in his/her present job for the purpose of general self-development rather than for a particular job or set of tasks.

The quality of this diagnostic approach tends to be enhanced when preparatory work is done by both parties; for instance, both could separately rate the skill elements required for the job and the job holder's current performance level against those respective skill areas. A comparison of the congruency or otherwise of these two skills audits will produce a basis for discussion about personal development and assist in the choice of learning opportunities to develop motivational, interpersonal, decision-making, supervisory or other skills. Interpreting the difference in perception of the same job behaviours can be extremely helpful in promoting self-awareness, and there is no reason why peer feedback should not contribute to these insights too. Indeed, many in-house and externally run skills-building programmes incorporate 360-degree feedback (from subordinates, peers, senior colleagues and possibly customers) as a precursor to the training event because such feedback – when sensitively handled – can assist in the 'unfreezing' process, necessary before real learning can take place.

The use of assessment centres for the purposes of selection and internal promotion is well established. A developmental centre or career development workshop uses an assessment centre approach but in a more collaborative manner in order to observe predetermined competencies via multiple assessment techniques in order to arrive at personally tailored development plans for each participant. The intention is to heighten self-awareness of strengths and weaknesses, particularly pertaining to the skill requirement of some future, targeted job, and to construct a plan of learning for the individual which builds on existing potential. However, research has shown that participants in development centres will only be motivated to pursue training plans and apply new learning to their jobs if they perceive the assessment process to be accurate and credible (Iles et al., 1990). In particular, assessors must be perceived to possess appropriate skills in observation, feedback and the facilitation of development recommendations/action plans (Kerr, 1989). Also important are the provision of adequate information before participation, explanation of the role of the centre in the organization's overall career development system and follow-up of development plans (Iles and Robertson, 1989). Centres where there is an incremental sharing of feedback with participants during the event, leading to a jointly agreed diagnosis and development plan at its conclusion, are more likely to be successful (see box 3.4).

Box 3.4   A participant perspective of career development practices

'What these empirical studies show is that some procedures are much better regarded than others by recipients, in terms of their perceived accuracy, validity, fairness, usefulness and value. In particular, development centres, psychometric tests with feedback and career reviews with superiors seem particularly well regarded. Why should this be? What features do such procedures have in common that differentiate them from other procedures much less well regarded, such as biodata, situation interviews, career planning workshops and self-assessment materials? What such procedures seem to share is that they are:

Prospective, not just retrospective – they focus on *future* actions and plans as much as *past* or present activities. The feedback received and the action plans generated can be useful in developing new insights, skills and attitudes.

Catalytic, not just analytic – such procedures do not just present a measurement of personal qualities or skills at a certain point in time, they can also promote personal reflection, greater self-insight, and personal growth.

Collaborative, not just controlling – such procedures do not solely produce a one-way assessment of the person by the organization, with the organization making all the decisions about what happens next. If used appropriately, the participant can also have significant input into what judgements are made and what actions should be undertaken.

> *Overt, not opaque* – such procedures can enable participants to see clearly the connections between the criteria they are being assessed against, the way the various activities undertaken relate to their job, organization and career, and the ways feedback and action planning can be useful to their own personal and career development.
>
> *Anchored, not abstract* – such procedures can be firmly anchored in organizational reality, including the realities of power and influence, by involving line managers as assessors or reviewers, by employing criteria and activities clearly relevant to career progression and organizational effectiveness, and by demonstrably tying feedback and action planning to organizational objectives and strategies.' (Mabey and Iles, 1994, pp. 130–1.)

Whatever approach is used, the diagnosis of training needs is as important for the individuals as it is for the organization. In its crudest sense this diagnosis involves each employee group exploring what they are trying to achieve, the barriers to achieving this and the suitability of training as a means to remove or counteract these barriers. The participation of individuals in this process is essential for two reasons. Firstly, they will have personal strategies, some of which may align with those of the organization, but others which will reflect their career aspirations, their desire for qualifications, their family commitments and their out-of-work interests and commitments. Secondly, they are unlikely to invest much personal effort in training and development activities if they have played no part in identifying their relevance. There is an in-built resistance to development programmes or learning 'opportunities' which are not perceived to be personally, functionally or culturally appropriate. One organization that has worked very hard at participative and culturally sensitive diagnosis is BP (see box 3.5).

Box 3.5　Ensuring cross-culturally valid competencies at BP

'BP chose to create a corporate-wide competency framework. It was appreciated that the process of decentralization and downsizing meant that implementation strategies would vary across businesses and countries. The performance criterion against which competencies were to be established, therefore, was the ability to enable change to happen (whatever that change might prove to be). A competency model was developed with consultants by comparing BP to other multinationals on their database and creating appropriate behavioural indicators that reinforced the culture and would enable Project 1990 to be implemented. It was essentially a desk-top exercise and the labels chosen to group the 67 identified essential behaviours were the same ones that had been used in relation to Project 1990, i.e. Open Thinking, Personal Impact, Empowering and Networking (OPEN).

Over a period of several months, the model was tested and validated internally and was then communicated throughout the business as awareness of the new competency model grew amongst senior managers. It then had to be devolved across all the national businesses. The challenge was that the OPEN competencies (and the 67 behaviours that evidenced them) had been designed to express BP's organizational culture, yet had to be adapted to suit a wide range of national cultures. The cross-cultural validity of the essential behaviours was challenged by non-British or non-American managers. They had been developed by a team of Anglo-Americans. Were they transferable to other countries?

BP conducted its investigation using a two-pronged approach: consultation of experts in the field of cultural diversity and the use of Focus Groups using non-Anglo-American employees. The expert reviews conducted by external academics and consultants sampled twelve countries. It was concluded that the competencies (i.e. the essential behaviours) were capable of cross-cultural implementations and represented a cogent statement of the shift in management behaviours required. However, the behavioural anchors used to describe specific competencies were, in some instances, unnecessarily directive and contained a culturally proactive bias. The greatest challenge came from competencies contained in the Personal Impact (Bias for Action, Knows What Makes Other Tick, Concern for Impact and Self-Confidence) and Empowering (Coaching and Developing, Building Team Success and Motivating) clusters. The recommendation was that BP step back from the behavioural detail of the proposed OPEN competencies and encourage people in different countries to offer their own illustrations of how they might change behaviours and culture. The process demonstrated that the OPEN competencies were capable of crossing cultural barriers in their essential meaning and purpose (reinforcing their use as a 'corporate glue' to integrate human resource policies and practices), but also that their implementation and assessment would require greater effort in order to customize and translate the behavioural indicators to fit the culturally different groups involved. The customization process, however, had to avoid any misinterpretations or fundamental change to the meaning of competencies.

BP ran a series of Focus Groups in France and Germany, in which it presented the intended objective of the behaviour contained within the competency and the intended meaning behind the English words. The Focus Groups each contained 10 to 12 national employees who spoke English as a second language. Meetings were held in the local language and were facilitated by consultants operating in the area of cross-cultural management and fluent in English, French and German. Each group was able to flex the behavioural indicators around each competency so that they were appropriate for their culture and organization. The feared barriers to cross-cultural implementation did not materialize.

Local business trainers and facilitators were then given instruction on how to present the OPEN competencies as part of change programmes being carried out in Europe and Asia-Pacific. It was found that it was better to instruct local trainers on the meaning and purpose behind the competencies, and then let them fashion the actual training process used to introduce the competencies themselves.' (Sparrow and Bognanno, 1993, pp. 54–5.)

Can Training and Development be Integrated with Human Resource Policy?

A strategic approach to training and development would seem to imply the integration of these policies and plans with other, wider HRM strategies being pursued by the organization at the time. By definition such an approach is likely to involve several groups within an organization, including the top team, HRD managers and other personnel specialists apart from those participating in the training and development activities and their line managers. However, is such integration necessarily desirable? And what evidence is there to suggest that organizations are pursuing integrated HRM and that it is having positive outcomes?

Integration: Is it desirable?

A number of different HRM solutions can be detected amongst organizations since the mid-1980s as they grappled with major strategic change. In each case the intention was to 'add value to the organization by identifying, analysing and implementing a set of procedures and activities to solve the various people-related concerns' (Boam and Sparrow, 1992, p. 7). Each of these 'strategic' reactions brought with it a particular focus to human resource activity. Three examples where these HRM policies incorporated particular training and development initiatives are illustrated in table 3.4

The authors go on to advocate a resource development or competency-based approach to HRM. According to this approach organizations generate what they call job models or performance models which define in behavioural terms the criteria of competence at different levels and possibly in different functions of the enterprise. It then makes sense – they argue – to use this model to inform the person specification when recruiting, to provide a reference point for appraisal sessions, to guide the construction of career maps and, possibly, to feed into reward systems. This job or performance models can likewise be the spur for the diagnosis and delivery of training within an organization. Such models identify fairly precisely what a person needs to bring to a given role in order to perform well, and these competencies can be linked directly to business strategy (vertical integration). Once defined in this way, competencies provide the opportunity to create consistency, coherence and mutual reinforcement across and with HRM policies and practices (horizontal integration). If all these levers of HRM are operating in concert there is at least the possibility of tracking their combined impact on the strategic objectives in a way that it is far less likely when HR initiatives are piecemeal and uncoordinated. It also allays the fears of staff, especially those who are career minded, that the corporate goalposts are shifting. However, it is unlikely that even the most thoroughly researched job models will remain static for very long, so human resource specialists need to be vigilant in reviewing the relevance and scarcity of skill mixes in their enterprises.

The emphasis on deriving behavioural repertoires that are organizationally meaningful and specific, rather than arriving at a set of generic knowledge, skills and attitudes for a given sector via functional analysis, is a desirable asset of this approach and would seem – at least, in part – to answer the criticism of competency definition levelled by Reed and Anthony (1992), among others:

All too often, the educational community has retreated into a narrow vocationalism in which the overriding emphasis is given to functional and technical skills which crowd out any sustained concern with the social, moral, political and ideological ingredients of managerial work and the form of educational experience most appropriate to their enhancement and development. . . . This would seem to be doubly inappropriate at a time when the nature of managerial work, and the constantly shifting environment in which it is practised, are likely to undermine and subvert the rigid application of technical skills or 'competencies', which are divorced from the social and organizational context in which they have to be applied.

(1992, p. 60)

Table 3.4   Training and development as part of a wider human resource management response to strategic issues

Reaction	Route	Main focus of attention
'We haven't got the right sort of attitudes or culture round here.'	Cultural/programmatic change	• Creation of a 'vision' for the business • Reliance on charismatic leadership • Large-scale change programmes • Focus on global themes such as quality, customer satisfaction, market awareness • Attention given to internal management processes • Heavy use of internal communications • Investment in training and education • Emphasis on team building at local level
'Better see what we've got and decide what we need before we do anything.'	Strategic/human resource planning	• Proactive data collection about what really happens • Attempts to model what might happen • Measuring the cost and benefits of the way people are recruited, retained and developed • Deciding which areas to invest in • Determining a critical path for the changes • Sequencing and managing the implementation against a plan
'We haven't got the right skills and we don't make the best of what we've got.'	Resource development (competency-based)	• Deciding what type of work needs to be done • Analysing the way effective people do the work • Communicating the model of effectiveness • Making sure recruitment, development and performance management systems mutually reinforce the same behaviours • Providing line managers with tools to assess and develop individual potential

Source: Adapted from Boam and Sparrow, 1992, pp. 8, 9.

Arriving at a recognizable performance model or competency profile for a particular career path in a given organization has the potential for over-coming other problems too. Because behaviours are couched in terms of what people actually do (e.g. 'what differentiates an excellent performer from a mediocre performer in job X?') rather than what they say they do, the model has credibility where culture change programmes based on pre-determined performance models often do not. However, it must be said that involving representative groups of staff (if not all staff as individuals) in the derivation of the competencies concerned is both intellectually taxing and time consuming. Furthermore, resultant lists of competencies are likely to challenge traditional job definitions and promotion criteria as well as encroaching on the even more sacrosanct territory of reward strategies and employment contracts. This is not an argument against pursuing future-orientated, strategic job models, rather a caution concerning the political and cultural consequences of doing so.

Integration: Is it happening?

Given these proposed benefits and associated difficulties, to what extent are organizations adopting an integrated approach to HRM and training and development? Although there may be many more accounts yet to be pub-licized, the number of reported examples is still, as yet, small (see table 3.5).

Further evidence of organizations adopting an integrated HRM approach – not necessarily based on a competency-based model – comes from a study of the UK National Health Service (Guest and Peccei, 1994). Their study aimed to develop and compare four models of HRM (see box 3.6) and to assess their respective effectiveness. Clear support was found for 'organizational integration':

> Where HR policy is 'owned' by top management, in the sense that they have formally agreed a written policy, then senior personnel and line managers give higher ratings of HRM effectiveness. Among personnel managers, this is reinforced if personnel management in the organization is judged to make an important contribution to key (non-personnel) organizational decisions. These results, it could be argued, reinforce the concept of integration in two respects. Firstly they appear to support the importance of an integration of line and personnel policy through a shared contribution to its formulation. Secondly, it implies line management ownership of the policy. Taking the political model a stage further, we might argue that this ownership is an important factor in ensuring the high ratings of effectiveness.
>
> (1994, p. 237)

The research also found positive outcomes arising from the 'process inte-gration' model of HRM:

Table 3.5   Examples of competency-based HRM in the UK

Organization	Key features	Reference
BP	Efforts to link executive competencies to a cultural competency model	Bognanno (1990;1992); Quinn, Mills and Friesen (1992)
Digital Equipment Europe (Ltd)	Creation of a business-oriented human resource strategy around competencies	Smith and Verran (1992)
Bass PLC	Use of competencies to streamline, restructure and recruit in order to build a new company culture	Probert (1992)
Rank Xerox	Definition of boardroom competencies for development Directors, and for first-line management	Coulson-Thomas (1990); Mabey and Iles (1993)
National Westminster Bank plc	Use of competencies to accelerate changes in personnel practices and business performance	Francis (1992)
Medium-sized accountancy organization	Use of competencies to articulate a required performance in a changing business market	Shackleton (1992)
National and Provincial Building Society	Attempts to achieve internal and external integration of HR strategies through a career-focused, competency-based approach	Mabey and Iles (1993)

> The second clear predictor of HRM effectiveness is Process Integration. It appears that how personnel specialists operate matters more than who they are or how well the personnel department is staffed. If they are perceived to operate efficiently, this has an impact on ratings of administrative effectiveness and possibly on measures of labour turnover and absence. If they are perceived to display high quality and responsiveness, this predicts qualitative effectiveness, particularly among line managers.
>
> (1994, p. 238)

Empirical assessment of the effectiveness of HR strategies is, as yet, rare, so it is interesting to note from this study that the combined impact of board-level and day-to-day-level integration are indeed significant, and certainly more so than policy and functional integration. However, the conceptual and practical difficulties of integration are considerable, and these are discussed more fully in chapter 9.

Box 3.6   Four models of HRM integration

1 Organizational Integration: A coherent HR strategy which is owned by the Board and readily accepted by line management. A willingness to incorporate an HR dimension in important strategic decisions.

2 Policy Integration: More concerned with the content of the strategy and the extent to which the resulting policies cohere. A clear and consistent priority for *one* of the following:

- the development and operation of routine, administrative personnel system;
- personnel seen as professionally competent and demonstrate the ability to carry out their mainstream activities very well;
- a coherent set of policies designed to achieve a high quality, committed workforce.

3 Functional Integration: Emphasis upon a high-quality personnel department in terms of professionalism, ratio (of personnel to total staff) and representation on the executive board.

4 Process Integration: Concerned with the efficiency of personnel processes (e.g. value for money, goal achievement) and the quality of personnel processes (e.g. views of internal customers). (From Guest and Peccei, 1994.)

Integration: Is it working?

Another way of assessing the degree to which training and development activities mutually reinforce other HRM initiatives and policies is to look at an organization's human resource development (HRD) plan. A survey of ninety Irish high-technology companies (indigenous and multinational) contains some interesting insights into how organizations operate their strategic HRD (Garavan, 1991). The results highlighted the following:

1   *HRD policy*: 95 per cent of companies had an established HRD function, 81 per cent had a written HRD policy statement. The most important factors cited as shaping this statement were the organization's mission, goals and strategies, although prevailing culture, training needs, current state of technology, top management views and equality of opportunities were also mentioned.

2   *Policy formulation*: it was typically drawn up by the HRD specialist, approved by the Personnel Director and subsequently by other members of

the management team. The recognized benefits of having a written policy statement (published as a policy manual or special brochure) were that it ensured consistency and equality of treatment, helping the managers to make more effective HRD decisions and facilitating the human resource planning process.

3   *Implementation*: three key issues were identified. Publicity of the policy statement (through briefing sessions, induction programmes, etc.) was necessary to ensure it was known, understood and accepted by those implementing it and affected by it. Simple, clear procedures, for instance, and yearly training plans were seen as key mechanisms for driving policy through the organization. Monitoring was seen as a vital safeguard against drift from original intentions and ensured continuous alignment with corporate strategy. In this respect, respondents saw HRD policies as flexible and open to modification, rather than static documents.

4   *Priorities*: the HRD plans of the indigenous high-technology organizations tended to place considerable emphasis on technical training, management development, quality and the management of change. The multinationals gave more prominence to personal development and professional development activities. Garavan suggests this is because they were more likely to have their organization-centred HRD needs met, and could therefore focus more personal/professional development activities (1991, p. 26).

5   *Diagnosis and support*: 85 per cent of respondents had a formalized system for the identification of HRD needs (e.g. questionnaires, performance reviews, discussions with managers and employees, task groups and corporate assessments by the management team), usually done on an annual basis and fed into the HRD plan for that year. Ninety-five per cent of responding organizations had training budgets to support their plan (54 per cent of these were centralized, 20 per cent departmental, the rest a mixture of both), which were up to 5 per cent of annual turnovers for 80 per cent of organizations.

6   *Roles*: 41 per cent of respondents saw it as the sole responsibility of the HRD specialist to implement the HRD plan, 35 per cent indicated that it was the responsibility of the HRD specialist *and* the line manager, 8 per cent the line manager only, and 16 per cent the human resource specialist.

More recent evidence from across ten European countries suggests that the responsibility for training and development by line management is increasing, both in identifying training needs and in making – or contributing to – policy decisions concerning HRD (see table 3.6).

Table 3.6 Training policies across ten European countries

	CH %	D %	DK %	E %	F %	I %	N %	NL %	S %	UK %
Most important method of analysing training needs:										
Analyses of business plans	10	12	27	30	41	39	39	20	36	22
Training audits	19	39	19	8	0	9	1	31	1	16
Line management requests	36	36	44	45	0	35	35	19	18	20
Performance appraisal	21	10	8	8	n/a	13	22	24	38	35
Employee requests	9	3	2	9	31	4	2	7	7	6
Increased responsibility of line management in training and development:	48	31	35	53	60	36	54	56	69	47
Primary responsibility for training and development policies:										
Line management	12	11	23	11	5	2	10	7	14	5
Line management with HR	50	36	41	21	33	12	43	40	52	24
HR with line management	30	37	28	50	53	68	37	44	31	57
HR development	6	17	7	16	6	16	6	91	2	11

Key: CH Switzerland; D Germany; DK Denmark; E Spain; F France; I Italy; N Norway; NL Netherlands; S Sweden; UK United Kingdom.
Source: Adapted from Holden, 1992, pp. 17, 19.

This once again underlines the pivotal role of line managers in the effective integration and implementation of human resource strategies. It is they who interpret and communicate the business plans and attempt to link – at an operational level – the human resource policies to strategic business goals; it is they who operate the procedures and monitor the performance; it is they who devote time and departmental resources to individual and team development; it is they who, in many ways, influence the subculture of their department or business unit. While this greater involvement is to be welcomed 'it puts considerable strain and responsibility on the line manager to perform the role with increasing efficiency, not only in carrying out effective monitoring but ensuring the information is relayed back to the HR central function, which can act as a guide to overall HR policy within the organization in terms of being regionally, nationally and globally strategic in the formulation of HR plans and management succession and other strategic policies' (Holden, 1992, p. 19).

Not all organizations will have or want a dedicated HR function or specialist. However, all but the most skilled line managers will probably need external help when it comes to integrating the diagnosis and delivery of HR with complementary measures aimed at servicing various aspects of the employment relationship. This might involve, among other things:

- using recruitment as a training strategy. Holden (1992) found that in all ten European countries studied, with the exceptions of Germany and Sweden, training for new employees was cited as the most popular means used to aid recruitment out of 11 options;
- more systematic attempts to link training needs analysing training delivery and performance appraisal systems. Brown et al. (1989) found a number of UK organizations were placing more emphasis on processual aspects of training (in this case, management training and development); locating training within the larger context of organization development, although another more extensive UK survey discovered more limited evidence of such perceptions (Parkinson, 1990);
- ensuring that mechanisms are in place to positively reward and reinforce desired attitudes and behaviours (that have been targeted by training courses), recognizing that training typically achieves little more than behavioural compliance among participants while the 'underlying values and assumptions of the actors remain unchanged' (Ogbonna and Wilkinson, 1990, p. 15);
- establishing feedback channels to communicate successes, correct problems and evaluate outcomes against original aims;
- setting up a range of career development systems which are deemed as fair and useful by individuals and tie in with strategic priorities of the organization (Iles and Mabey, 1993). Again, use of on-the-job career development techniques varies from country to country. Hilb (1992) found, across the same ten European countries as in table 3.6, a wide use of planned techniques (formal career planning, succession plans, job rotations and high-flyer schemes) which appear to be strategic, but also a heavy reliance on the performance appraisal, which often is not;
- the attempt to utilize a number of separate HRM policies in concert – including training and development – in order to achieve specific improvement in performance or shifts in mindset within an organiza-tion. Box 3.7 shows how a range of HR policies targeting the need to 'value difference' at BA, were more successful than more general attempts to 'act globally'.

Box 3.7 Valuing difference in British Airways

One of the greatest challenges facing BA's management and staff is: how to act globally but retain their essentially British character. As Lauermann puts it: 'how to generate an understanding and appreciation of cultural differences: how to "Europeanise" manage-ment thinking (especially in a company where American business schools and management consultants have been revered); how to persuade people to learn foreign languages; . . . how to develop our understanding of the industrial relations implications of EC legislation to match that of our Trade Unions' (1992, p. 85). BA initially tackled multiculturalism from a training perspective by putting all senior managers through a training programme which included the Hofstede culture model to understand differences, problems and compatibility between different national groups. However, '18 months later it is quite hard to find people whose thinking was affected by it. A major reason would seem to be that although people understand the general need, they personally had no real hunger for the education or immediate requirement' (Lauermann, 1992, p. 85). A more protracted, but perhaps ultimately more productive, approach is to use the dimension of 'valuing difference', building on gender issues involved in equal opportunity work to include all forms of diversity, with workshops held to explore the business imperatives involved, opening the door to valuing cultural differences. Instead of changing attitudes, the aim has been to encourage exploration of the advantages and risks to BA of equal opportunity and diversity, leading to practical initiatives in recruitment, promotion and training, such as the recruitment of more European graduates, mentoring schemes, the use of European Business schools, the use of flexible employment contracts, and attempting to influence EC legislation.

Summary and Conclusion

We began this chapter with a depiction of the way training and development could be designed and delivered strategically (figure 3.1). This model posed more questions than it answered, however, and these were examined in subsequent sections. We have seen how those determining the strategic direction of an enterprise, those representing the dominant cultural coalition, those in key line management posts, those participating in training and development, the team who actually design and deliver training, and those responsible for integrating the different parts of HR policy each have vested interests in how training and development is conceived, commissioned and how its effects are measured in a given organization.

A stakeholder analysis of strategic training and development

The analysis of this chapter leads us to a reconceptualization of strategic training and development from a stakeholder perspective (see figure 3.6). While the six dimensions of the original model remain broadly intact, it is probably more helpful to represent them as specific stakeholder groups, each with their own predispositions, priorities and degree of proactivity. The model thus intentionally becomes more fluid, and while the underlying sense of business direction remains (represented by the arrow), this is by no means taken as agreed upon or given. Each group of stakeholders will have a different interest in, influence over and ownership of, training and development activities and outcomes. The intersection of boundaries signifies that such sectional agendas will in some cases overlap and align, but broadly speaking the nature of training and development can be seen as central, negotiated territory with the power of the providers of such activities ebbing and flowing between the client, sponsor, manager, participant and facilitator groupings within the organization, each influenced in turn by a host of factors – many of them beyond the boundary of the organization itself.

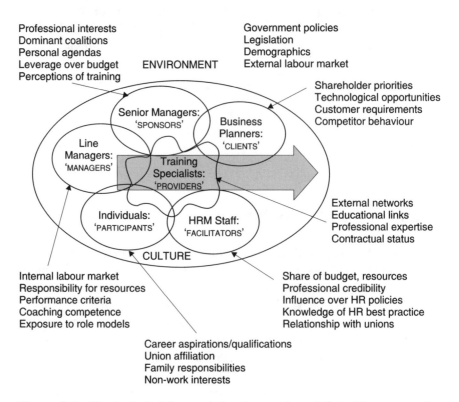

Figure 3.6 Strategic training and development: a stakeholder approach

This interplay of competing and contested views, together with external, environmental forces, will shape the pathway of training implementation in a given organization: whether, for instance, an instrumental approach is taken whereby mass attendance on workshops is advocated, or whether development is seen in the more open-ended context of operational experience where learning is structured, reviewed and internalized without formal intervention.

Take, for example, one company operating in the UK computer supplier sector in the mid- to late 1980s. In chapter 1 we showed some of the competitive and business pressures facing this sector, together with some typical strategic and HRM responses (see figure 1.3). An early trigger in this particular company's concern for and involvement in training activity was the need for new management competencies, or a 'redefinition of the management task'. On the heels of necessary cost reductions there was an urgent requirement to cultivate marketing awareness to support an innovative product strategy instigated by a new top team.

However, all such changes have to be mediated through a firm's internal context. This will include the distinctive structure and culture of the organization, the style and processes of decision-making, the personalities and people, and the tasks and technologies traditionally employed. In this case the move toward a more aggressive marketing mentality in product design and increased profit accountability obviously ran counter to existing culture. The consequent restructuring around business units together with emphasis on customer service operations can thus be seen as internal precursors to investment in training.

Even though management education was used as a primary lever for engendering marketing skills and knowledge in the initial stages, it formed a part of a wider HRM strategy, encapsulated in a five-year plan. This included a range of measures: a new, tiered career structure, a realignment of graduate recruitment, the short-term use of specialist contract staff and the introduction of a performance system linked to appraisals. There were also implications for Vocational Education and Training (VET), notably the project managing of training throughout the company as a means of ensuring that line managers' training needs were properly identified and met, with each new training product having a senior line manager to personally 'sponsor' it.

Given that for this particular company the heavy investment in training and development 'paid off', what made these training activities successful at a strategic level? The answer to this question underlines many of the principles emerging in this chapter. The first and probably the most influential factor contributing to the effectiveness of training and development was the combined impact of a number of separate but connected triggers and levers: competitive necessity, CEO commitment and an HRM strategy that embraced a number of targeted training and career development activities.

Second, there was an explicit and regular attempt to match business plans and people management implications at all levels from business centre manager upwards. Education, training and development activities provided the vital linkage between corporate strategy and HRM policies.

Third, a quality education process was initiated in order to undergird this diagnostic and planning activity and the internal processes required to make it work. Attention was paid to the content of training but also the infrastructure to support it.

Fourth, the capability of the training function was enhanced with highly credible and skilled field managers who could 'internalize and integrate' the knowledge being provided by external trainers.

Fifth, the two-tiered training activity combined top-down cascaded modules with locally driven training initiated by line units. Each training product was 'sponsored' by a senior manager, thus building-in line management ownership and content relevance. An added stimulus for high-quality training was attendance on courses of customers who demanded value for money.

A final small but not insignificant factor was the removal of budgetary constraints from line managers, accompanied by block funding arrangements for departments' training projects a year in advance.

This case serves to illustrate some of the complex connections between internal and external stakeholders which help shape the ethos and practice of training and development in an organization. What is less evident when described in this manner is the messy, unfolding nature of events that look more rational and coherent in retrospect than they did at the time.

Key points

Strategic training and development:

- *can be conceived as different things by different organizations, sometimes as an ad hoc activity, sometimes as a response to a complex and changing environment, sometimes even as a strategic device for changing that environment.*
- *will be defined differently by the various stakeholders within an organization. Whether these respective agendas and rationales for training and development are primarily functional, political, legitimatory, symbolic or defensive (Lees, 1992) will determine the design, meaning and outputs sought for any particular training activity.*
- *can be rarely be divorced, therefore, from the wider competitive and cultural*

context of the organization. The prevailing coalition will be especially influential upon the perceived value of, and funding for, training in an organization.

● is likely to be part of an evolutionary process of organization change, with all the false starts, political repercussions, cultural mismatches and backlashes, and fluctuating financial constraints that this implies.

● requires perceptive diagnosis of training need, and 'delivery' (whatever form this might take) by people and methods that connote credibility and relevance to personal and business need.

● is bound up with, rather than separate from, other aspects of human resource strategies that this book covers: structure, culture, manpower planning, recruitment, reward and assessment strategies. Indeed, it could be argued that the skills, knowledge and attitudes engendered by a firm's training and development activities is pivotal to its human resource strategy; for on these depend the appropriateness and efficacy of personal competency, without which no strategy – however elegantly fashioned and meticulously planned – can succeed.

Discussion Questions

1 Which factors, external to an organization, are most influential in determining its training policy and provision?
2 What are some of the reasons that organizations invest in management training? What assumptions lie behind these reasons about how people learn, and what they should learn?
3 Explain why training is a political activity.
4 Why is it unreliable to gauge the effectiveness of an organization's training strategy only by reference to training courses attended?
5 How important is the role of line managers in the effective implementation of training and development strategies?
6 It has been asserted that training and development form the cornerstone of human resource strategy. Can such a view be sustained?

REFERENCES

Ashton, D., Easterby-Smith, M. and Irvine, C. (1975) *Management Development: Theory and Practice*. Bradford, MCB.

Beardwell, I. and Holden, L. (1994) *Human Resource Management: A Contemporary Perspective*. London, Pitman Publishing.

Beer, M., Spector, B., Lawrence, P. R., Mills, D. Q. and Walton, R. (1984) *Managing Human Assets: The Ground Breaking Harvard Business School Program*. London, Macmillan.

Boam, R. and Sparrow, P. (1992) *Designing and Achieving Competency*. Maidenhead, McGraw-Hill.

Bognanno, M. (1990) Facilitating cultural change by identifying the new competencies required and formulating a strategy to develop such competencies. *Conference on Identifying and Applying Competencies within your Organization*, 6 Nov., IIR Ltd., London.

Bognanno, M. (1992) Linking executive competences to a cultural competency model. *Conference on the Latest Developments in Identifying, Measuring and Applying Competences*, 28-9 Jan., IIR Ltd., London.

Bourgeois, L. and Brodwin, D. (1984) Strategic implementation: Five approaches to an elusive phenomenon. *Strategic Management Journal*, 5, pp. 241–64.

Bournois, F. (1992) France. In Brewster, C., Hegewisch, A., Holden, L. and Lockhart, T. (eds), *The European Human Resource Management Guide*. London, Academic Press.

Brewster, C., Hegewisch, A., Holden, L. and Lockhart, T. (eds) (1992), *The European Human Resource Management Guide*. London, Academic Press.

Brooks, I. and Bate, P. (1994) The problems of effecting change within the British Civil Service: A cultural perspective. *British Journal of Management*, 5, 177–90.

Brown, H., Peccei, R., Sandberg, S. and Welchman, R. (1989) Management training and development: In search of an integrated approach. *Journal of General Management*, 15, no. 1, pp. 69–82.

Burgoyne, J. (1988) Management development for the individual and the organization. *Personnel Management*, 20, no. 6, pp. 20–4.

Carnall, C. (1990) *Managing Change*. London, Routledge.

Coulson-Thomas, C. (1990) Development directors. *European Management Journal*, 8, no. 4, pp. 488–99.

Dore, R. and Sako, M. (1989) *How the Japanese Learn to Work*. London, Routledge.

Evans, P. and Doz, Y. (1989) The dualistic organization. In Evans, Doz and Laurent (eds), *Human Resource Management in International Firms*. London, Macmillan.

Everard, B. (1991) The costs and benefits of training. *Training and Development*, Dec., pp. 26–8.

Fox, S. (1989) The politics of evaluating management development. *Management Education and Development*, 20, no. 3, pp. 191–207.

Francis, K. (1992) Using a competency approach to achieve a higher business performance and the acceleration of change in personnel practices: A line manager's story. *Conference on the Latest Developments in Identifying, Measuring and Applying Competences*, 28–9 Jan., IIR Ltd., London.

Garavan, T. (1991) Strategic human resource development. *Journal of European Industrial Training*, 15, no. 1, pp. 17–30.

Guest, D. and Peccei, R. (1994) The nature and causes of effective human resource management. *British Journal of Industrial Relations*, 32, no. 2, pp. 219–62.

Guest, D., Peccei, R. and Rosenthal, P. (1992) Management development and career success. In Bradley, K. (ed.), *Human Resource Management: People and Success*. Dartmouth, Aldershot.

Handy, C. (1987) The making of managers: A report on management education, training and development in the US, W. Germany, France, Japan and the UK. National Economic Development Office, London.

Hendry, C. and Pettigrew, A. (1990) Human resource management: An agenda for the 1990s. *The International Journal of Human Resource Management*, 1, no. 1, pp. 17–43.

Hendry, C., Pettigrew, A. and Sparrow, P. (1990) Linking strategic change, competitive performance and human resource management: Results of an empirical study. In Mansfield, R. (ed.), *Frontiers of Management*. London, Routledge.

Hilb, M. (1992) The challenge of management development in Western Europe in the 1990s. *The International Journal of Human Resource Management*, 3, no. 3, pp. 575–83.

Holden, L. (1992) Does strategic training policy exist? Some evidence from ten European countries. *Personnel Review*, 21, no. 1, pp. 12–23.

Iles, P. and Mabey, C. (1993) Managerial career development programmes: Effectiveness, availability and acceptability. *British Journal of Management*, 4, no. 2, pp. 103–18.

Iles, P. and Robertson, I. (1989) The impact of personnel selection techniques on candidates. In Herriot, P. et al. (eds), *Handbook of Assessment in Organizations*. Chichester, John Wiley.

Iles, P., Robertson, I. and Rout, U. (1990) Assessment based development centres. *Journal of Managerial Psychology*, 4, no. 3, pp. 11–16.

Keep, E. (1989) Corporate training strategies: The vital component? In Storey, J. (ed.), *New Perspectives on Human Resource Management*. London, Routledge.

Kerr, S. (1989) AC or DC? The experience of development centres. Paper presented to the British Psychological Society annual conference, Windermere, Jan.

Kuhn, T. S. (1970) *The Structure of Scientific Revolutions* (2nd edn). Chicago, University of Chicago Press.

Lane, C. (1989) New technology and changes in work organizations. In Lane, C. (ed.), *Management and Labour in Europe*. Aldershot, Edward Elgan, pp. 163–95.

Lauermann (1992) British Airways in Europe. *European Management Journal*, 10, no. 1, pp. 85–6.

Lees, S. (1992) Ten faces of management development. *Management Education and Development*, 23, no. 2, pp. 89–105.

Legge, K. (1984) *The Evaluation of Planned Organizational Change*. London, Academic Press.

Legge, K. (1989) Human resource management: A critical analysis. In Storey, J. (ed.), *New Perspectives in Human Resource Management*. London, Routledge, pp. 19–40.

Mabey, C. and Iles, P. (1993) The strategic integration of assessment and development practices. *Human Resource Management Journal*, 3, no. 4, pp. 16–34.

Mabey, C. and Iles, P. (1994) Career development practices in the UK: A participant perspective. In Mabey, C. and Iles, P. (eds), *Managing Learning*. London, Routledge.

Mangham, I. and Silver, D. (1986) Management training: Context and practice. School of Management, University of Bath, ESRC/DTI Report.

Mintzberg, H. (1988) Crafting strategy. *McKinsey Quarterly*, summer, pp. 71–89.

Mumford, A. (1993) *Management Development – Strategies for Action*. London, IPM.

Mumford, A., Robinson, G. and Stradling, D. (1987) Developing directors: The learning processes. London, MSC report.

Naulleau, G. and Harper, J. (1993) A comparison of British and French management cultures: Some implications for management development in each country. *Management Education and Development*, 24, no. 1, pp. 14–25.

Ogbonna, E. and Wilkinson, B. (1990) Corporate strategy and corporate culture: The view from the checkout. *Personnel Review*, 19, no. 4, pp. 9–15.

Olivas, L. (1988) Designing and conducting training needs analysis: Putting the cart before the horse. *Journal of Management Development*, 2, no. 3, pp. 19–41.

Parkinson, S. (1990) Management development's strategic role. *Journal of General Management*, 16, no. 2 pp. 63–75.

Pettigrew, A., Hendry, C. and Sparrow, P. (1988) The role of vocational education and training in employers' skills supply strategies. Sheffield, Training Agency report in conjunction with Coopers and Lybrand.

Poole, M. and Mansfield, R. (1992) Managers' attitudes to human resource management: Rhetoric and reality. In Blyton, P. and Turnbull, P. (eds), *Reassessing Human Resource Management*. London, Sage.

Preston, D. (1993) Learning the organization: Confusions and contradictions for new managers. *Human Resource Management Journal*, 4, no. 1, pp. 24–33.

Probert, P. (1992) Using a competency model to streamline, restructure, recruit and build a new company culture with the aim of competitive advantage. *Conference on the Latest Developments in Identifying, Measuring and Applying Competences*, 28–9 Jan., IIR Ltd., London.

Purcell, J. (1989) The impact of corporate strategies on human resource management. In Storey, J. (ed.), *New Perspectives on Human Resource Management*. London, Routledge.

Quinn, J. B., Mills, D. and Friesen, B. (1992) The learning organization. *European Management Journal*, 10, no. 2, pp. 146–56.

Reed, M. and Anthony, P. (1992) Professionalising management and managing professionalisation: British management in the 1980s. *Journal of Management Studies*, 29, no. 5 (Sept.), pp. 591–613.

Rose, R. and Wignanek, G. (1991) *Training without Trainers? How Germany avoids Britain's Supply Side Bottleneck*. Anglo-German Foundation.

Salaman, G. and Butler, J. (1990) Why managers won't learn. *Management Education and Development*, 21, no. 3, pp. 183–91.

Schuler, R. (1992) Strategic HRM: Linking the people with the strategic needs of the business. *Organizational Dynamics*, summer, pp. 18–32.

Shackleton, V. (1992) Using a competency approach in a business change setting. In Boam, R. and Sparrow, P. (eds), *Designing and Achieving Competency: A*

Competency-based Approach to Managing People and Organizations. London, McGraw-Hill.

Shepherd, D. (1991) personal communication, Shepherd Associates, London.

Smith, B. and Verran, M. (1992) Business-oriented human resource development. *Conference on the Latest Developments in Identifying, Measuring and Applying Competences*, 28–9 Jan., IIR Ltd., London.

Smith, M. (1992) Utility and human resource management. Supplementary Readings 2, *B884 Human Resource Strategies*, Milton Keynes, Open University.

Sparrow, P. and Bognanno, M. (1993) Competency requirement forecasting: Issues for selection and assessment. *International Journal of Selection and Assessment*, 1, no. 1, pp. 50–8.

Sparrow, P. and Pettigrew, A. (1987) Britain's training problems: The search for a strategic human resources management approach. *Human Resource Manager*, 26, no. 1, pp. 109–27.

Sparrow, P. and Pettigrew, A. (1988) Contrasting HRM responses in the changing world of computing. *Personnel Management*, Feb., pp. 40–5.

Storey, J. (1989) Management development: A literature review and implication for future research. *Personnel Review*, 18, no. 6, pp. 3–19.

Storey, J. (1992) *Developments in the Management of Human Resources*. Oxford, Blackwell.

Storey, J. and Sisson, K. (1993) *Managing Human Resources and Industrial Relations*. Buckingham, Open University Press.

Tayeb, M. (1993) English culture and business organizations. In Hickson, D. (ed.), *Management in Western Europe: Society, Culture and Organization in Twelve Nations*. Berlin, DeGruyter.

Tichy, N., Fombrun, C. and Devanna, M. (1982) Strategic human resource management. *Sloan Management Review*, 23, no. 2, winter.

Tyson, S. (1990) Training civil servants into managers. *Money and Management*, spring, pp. 27–30.

Vickerstaff, S. A. (1991) The management of training in the smaller firm: Paper presented to the British Academy of Management Annual Conference, Sept.

Warr, P. (1992) *Training for Managers*. A report for the Institute of Managers, sponsored by the Economics and Social Research Council, MRC/ESRC Social and Applied Psychology Unit, Sheffield

Whipp, R., Rosenfeld, R. and Pettigrew, A. (1988) Understanding strategic change processes: Some preliminary British findings. In Pettigrew, A. (ed.), *The Management of Strategic Change*. Oxford, Blackwell, pp. 14–55.

Wills, S. (1993) MCI and the competency movement: The case so far. *Journal of European Industrial Training*, 17, no. 1, pp. 9–11.

4 Performance Management

This chapter was contributed by Greg Clark.

Learning Objectives

- *to define performance management, and say how it relates to business strategy.*
- *to model performance management as a cycle consisting of five elements: setting objectives, measuring outcomes, feeding back results, rewarding performance, and amending objectives and activities.*
- *to understand and be able to describe the theoretical frameworks which underpin performance management.*
- *to identify and assess the issues and problems which theory highlights for the design and implementation of performance management.*
- *to assess the results of empirical tests of performance management, using performance-related pay as a vehicle for exploring these results.*
- *to critically evaluate the concept of performance management, and its application.*
- *to determine what factors to consider in assessing whether performance management can or should be introduced into your organization.*

Introduction

Essential to the notion of the *strategic* management of human resources is the requirement that the process of managing people is not an end in itself, but explicitly related to the wider goals of the organization. That is to say, strategic HRM must be a means to achieve strategy. Immediately this differentiates strategic HRM from functional human resource management, or personnel management, which is a more separable, self-referential administration of personnel issues in the organization.

The integration of human resource management and strategy implied by strategic HRM places policies and processes into a system whereby outcomes cannot be assessed without reference to a set of objectives and criteria supplied by other parts of the organization. The management of human resources therefore finds itself being judged on its contribution to wider goals, and, faced with this scrutiny, must develop its own procedures to report on its record. More generally it must provide a framework for internally auditing the means by which it delivers contributions to strategic goals, with a view to continuously improving them. *Performance management* is a means of addressing these requirements.

Performance management refers to a set of techniques and procedures which share the common features of:

- providing information on the contribution of human resources to the strategic objectives of the organization;
- forming a framework of techniques to secure maximum achievement of objectives for given inputs; and
- providing a means of inspecting the functioning of the process links which deliver performance against objectives.

It should be seen immediately that *performance measurement* is based on a particular set of assumptions and hypotheses about the nature of management and its feasibility. Performance management rests on an essentially rationalist, directive view of the organization. A number of implicit assumptions are made, of which the first is that strategy can be expressed in terms of objectives clear enough to be used in framing other policies of the organization; in this case HR policy. The second assumption is that the outcomes of HR processes can be expressed in ways which allow an assessment to be made of whether they are contributing to the achievement of strategic objectives. A third assumption is that HR processes can be analysed as a set of interlinking cause-and-effect sequences whose links can be identified. A fourth assumption is made which is that the chain can be 'managed', in the sense that corrective action can be designed and implemented to repair poorly performing parts of the chain, this being carried out by people designated as 'managers' of the system.

Overview

This chapter examines the concept of performance management as a process which managers of human resources may adopt to assist them in their ability to contribute to wider strategic objectives. Having defined performance management, and introduced the idea of a Performance Management Cycle, we argue that the essential features of performance management systems draw on two theories of social psychology: goal-setting theory and expectancy theory. Each theory highlights some key issues concerning the design, feasibility and desirability of performance management which practitioners must address if they are to succeed in their aims. The chapter makes a critical assessment of the underlying assumptions of performance management systems, and suggests that the models may not have the universal validity which their proponents claim for them since they ignore important contextual factors.

By looking in detail at one specific example of a performance management system, performance-related pay, we demonstrate that empirical evidence supports the observations we make. The lesson for managers is that only following careful design and diagnosis can introducing a system of performance management be expected to produce the outcomes which it promises.

A schematic model of performance management

There is no single, universally accepted model of performance management in use. Rather, the management literature advances a number of separate contributions which fall under the umbrella term 'performance management' because they typically contain and *link* a common set of elements. These can be expressed as a 'performance measurement cycle' consisting of five elements:

1 setting performance objectives;
2 measuring outcomes;
3 feedback of results;
4 rewards linked to outcomes;
5 amendments to objectives and activities.

The Performance Management Cycle is depicted in figure 4.1.

Performance management, as a cycle consisting of these elements, can be both a descriptive and a prescriptive device. Some writers use performance management as a convenient framework in which to analyse different aspects of strategic HR. Others argue that by distilling out the essential elements of the performance management process the cycle represents a model of how the process *should* be conducted by organizations wishing to take a rational and strategic approach to managing human resources.

The *level* at which a performance management system operates will vary according to how the organization chooses to apply the model, or the level at which the commentator analyses the process. That is to say that there is nothing in the model to indicate that the elements apply to the management of individual employees, or to groups and teams, or to divisions or strategic business units, or to the organization as a whole: in principle, the framework can be applied to any and all of these.

As a framework, the Performance Management Cycle refers to types of policies and systems – objective setting, measurement, rewards, etc. – which must be linked if they are to constitute a practising system of performance management. The Cycle does not specify in detail what form these individual policies take. As we shall see, it is possible to operate a system of performance management in which people's performance is measured using automatically generated sales figures, or by individual annual appraisal interviews. Each approach will give rise to different problems of implementation, and may yield different results, but both are consistent with the model of performance management summarized in figure 4.1.

Sketches of human resource management policies at two organizations, the Scottish Development Agency and the National Westminster Bank, offer a taste of different applications of performance management. (See boxes 4.1 and 4.2.)

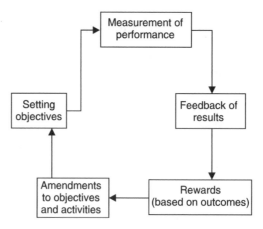

Figure 4.1   The peformance management cycle

Box 4.1   Target-based scheme: Scottish Development Agency

The performance measurement and appraisal scheme includes a system in which between three and six 'principal accountabilities' are identified for each job. These are the major, standing job functions or purposes. At each appraisal, one or more 'goals' are agreed for each accountability target to be achieved during the next period. Each goal is given a percentage weighting, so that achievement of all goals would result in an overall score of 100 per cent. An 'achievement profile' is produced, in which actual achievement is scored against each goal. The total score is used to decide the performance payment. (Source: Bowey et al., 1992.)

Box 4.2   Rewarding performance at National Westminster Bank

In common with other companies in this sector, NatWest has sought to change a culture rewarding predictability, security, long service and loyalty through a slow but steady incremental pay structure into a more dynamic and entrepreneurial one. It has attempted to enhance high performance by recognizing it financially through modifications to its salary structure and its performance appraisal and incremental systems. It has also introduced incentive-based annual bonus schemes related to key targets and incentive-based longer cycle bonus schemes. The aim was to enable all managers to improve their income through performance improvement and to focus attention on key areas of activity. Profit sharing as a percentage of basic annual salary continued, whilst senior managers gained access to an executive share option scheme designed to focus on long-term strategic goals. All of these changes were seen as contributing to 'management by leadership' rather than 'management by control', creating greater understanding of short and long-term strategic goals and focusing managers' attention on goals relating to corporate, divisional-unit and individual objectives. It also aimed to provide general rewards more clearly linked to personal performance and achievement. For the lowest four grades, the level of general increase applied to the published salary ranges continued to be negotiated with the Staff Association and the relevant trade union. (Source: Goodswen, 1988.)

Performance Management: Underlying Theory

Performance management is not new, despite the fact that the use of the term has grown popular recently. Managers have always devised ways, formally or otherwise, to set tasks, see that they are carried out well, and make modifications designed to secure further improvements. Models of performance management may seem to be '*an apparently obvious invention*' (as Jevons (1883) described performance-related pay, one type of performance management system), but nevertheless are built on well-developed theoretical foundations. Or rather it may be fairer to say, since the economist Alfred Marshall described the theoretical case for performance-related pay as 'a formalization of existing practice', that a substantial body of theory has grown up around models of performance management in use. All too often, however, the theory is forgotten in favour of searches for instant solutions to empirical problems. By contrast, referring to underlying theory provides a solid base for understanding and criticizing applications of performance measurement.

The essence of performance management is establishing a framework in which performance by individuals can be directed, monitored, motivated and refined; and whereby the links in the cycle can be audited. Unsurprisingly, given this, the principal theoretical foundation of performance management is social psychology, with its detailed consideration of the ways in which people are motivated to perform. Two theories are particularly pertinent to discussions of performance management: goal-setting theory (e.g. Locke et al., 1981), and expectancy theory (Vroom, 1964).

Goal-setting theory

Goal-setting theory was established by Edwin Locke in a paper published in 1968, in which he argued that goals pursued by employees can play an important role in motivating superior performance. In following these goals people examine the consequences of their behaviour. If they surmise that their goals will not be achieved by their current behaviour, they will eirther modify their behaviour, or choose more realizable goals.

We have already seen in this text that an aim of strategic HRM involves integrating the wider objectives of the organization with the behaviour of its employees. Accordingly, if managers can intervene to establish the organization's goals (or translations of them for the group or individual) as being worthwhile for employees to accept, they can harness a source of motivation to perform, and direct it to securing strategic outcomes.

Subsequent empirical research into goal-setting (cf. Mento et al., 1987) has specified more precisely the conditions neccessary for organizational goals to be motivating to employees; these are that:

- goals should be specific, rather than vague or excessively general;
- goals should be demanding, but also attainable;
- feedback of performance information should be made;
- goals need to be accepted by employees as desirable.

Goal-setting theory has been subject to a great deal of theoretical and empirical scrutiny since it was first advanced. The resulting body of evidence now provides a set of rigorously tested principles which offer clear guidance to designers of performance management systems. Later in this chapter we will be applying each of these lessons to performance management.

Expectancy theory

A book published by Victor Vroom in 1964, *Work and Motivation*, stimulated a flurry of research interest in *expectancy theory* as a framework for understanding motivation at work. Expectancy theory hypothesizes that it is the anticipated satisfaction of valued goals which causes individuals to adjust their behaviour in a way which is most likely to lead to their attaining them.

In fact, while the popularity of expectancy theory is relatively recent, it draws on a tradition which can be traced back to the early Utilitarians. Mill and Bentham described an ethical system in which people determined their actions by a conscious calculation of the consequences which they expected the actions to bring about. In this century psychologists such as Tolman

(1932) and Lewin (1938), as advocates of theories of performance by people which held that performance is governed by expectations concerning future events, turned a normative theory of how people *should* base their actions, into a positive theory of how people *do* behave.

The most immediate precursors of expectancy theory were Georgopoulos et al. (1957), with their 'path-goal' approach to productive performance at work. The path-goal hypothesis stated that 'if a worker sees high productivity as a path leading to the attainment of one or more of his personal goals, he will tend to be a high producer. Conversely, if he sees low productivity as a path to the achievement of his goals, he will tend to be a low producer' (p. 346).

Expectancy theory has been developed from Vroom's early specifications to be expressed very clearly (e.g. Galbraith and Cummings, 1967) as a combination of three factors:

- the person's own assessment of whether performing in a certain way will result in a measurable result. This factor is labelled the *expectancy*.
- the perceived likelihood that such a result will lead to attaining a given reward. This factor is known as *instrumentality*.
- the person's assessment of the likely satisfaction, or *valence*, associated with the reward.

These factors can be expressed in diagramatic form as in figure 4.2.

In practice, if a person sees it as being clear that performing in a certain way will bring about a reward which he values, then he is more likely to attempt to perform in that way than if the relationship between his effort and measured performance, or measured performance and rewards, is slight or uncertain. Although subject to a great deal of empirical investigation and theoretical scrutiny, the expectancy theory approach to the motivation of performance has remained essentially of the form described.

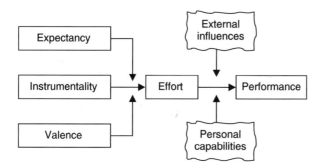

Figure 4.2 A simple expectancy model

Like goal-setting theory, expectancy theory highlights some of the key design principles which practitioners face in establishing systems of performance management.

Designing Performance Management Systems: Lessons from Theory

We have seen that both expectancy theory and goal-setting theory underpin the concept of a performance management system. In this section we will draw on the contributions of each of these models to add depth and complexity to the schematic model of performance management advanced at the beginning of this chapter.

Figure 4.3 summarizes a number of core issues common, in varying degrees, to both expectancy theory and goal-setting theory. They represent the key factors which must be addressed in designing a system of performance management. We review the contribution of theory to each of these issues in turn.

Setting goals

As an instrument of strategic human resource management, a system of performance management is predicated on the need to take the wider, strategic goals of the organization, and translate them into goals for smaller groups and individuals.

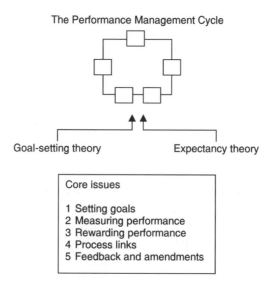

Figure 4.3 Performance management: lessons from theory

Tests of both goal-setting theory and expectancy theory have demonstrated the importance of specifying few, relatively concrete goals. Yet in practice, designing a performance management system which is in keeping with these principles may prove problematical, for three reasons: the organization may be unable to identify and articulate clear strategic objectives; objectives may be more diverse and numerous than are consistent with theory; and the strategic goals of the organization may be inherently unstable.

Identifying clear strategic objectives for itself is a precondition for an organization to be able to translate them into performance goals. You may be familiar, from studying business strategy (e.g. Mintzberg, 1992), with the view that many organizations acquire and follow strategies not as a result of a conscious, rational planning process, but rather that strategies 'emerge' in response to time and events. Further, the organization may have a number of objectives at any one time, some of which may be potentially contradictory or competing (for example, a commitment to investing in people, at the same time as a need to 'downsize'). If the organization is unable to set out explicitly its strategy (which is defined by Johnson and Scholes (1984) as summarizing its objectives and goals), it is unlikely to be able to carry out the next step from this, which is to identify particular dimensions of performance which are most likely to achieve its strategic goals.

Another potential problem is the exhortation of both expectancy and goal-setting models to choose a limited number of performance dimensions to measure and reward. People in organizations, whatever the terms of their written contract, can be said to have a 'psychological contract' with their employer, which is a rich and nuanced collection of shared understandings built up over time. Often to choose and emphasize a limited number of performance dimensions is to fail to appreciate the subtlety of organizational life, and to risk shattering subtle structures of tacit but critical employee commitment by substituting a simplistic set of objectives. It carries the danger that if the system does 'work', in the sense that people focus on those elements of performance which have been selected and highlighted by the organization, the results may be not at all desirable: a pre-existing pride in skill and work may be replaced by a contractual focus on the rules. The real-life example given in box 4.3 illustrates this point.

Box 4.3   When performance targets backfire

A performance management system was introduced into a major continental European telecommunications utility in 1993. An overall corporate strategic objective of improved productivity was set, and cascaded down the organization. For the directory assistance division this objective was translated into a goal of reducing the time spent by operators in dealing with each enquiry. Performance against the goal was measured by a system-generated measure of the average length of call.

Managers scrutinizing the early results of the system found that the average length of each call had declined markedly, but operators seemed still to be continuously busy: apparently improved productivity did not seem to be translated into spare capacity. Closer investigation revealed that operators felt that the pressure to keep calls short conflicted with what they saw as an important personal desire to establish a rapport with callers, which they felt could not be done under time pressure. It turned out that operators had discovered that they could reduce the average time per call by immediately disconnecting one call in three, while continuing to spend the usual length of time in smalltalk with the remainder of their callers.

A third problem concerns timing. Identifying desirable aspects of individual performance which will be measured and rewarded may be possible in an organization which enjoys a relatively stable internal and external environment, but where greater turbulence is experienced it is possible that objectives and hence performance dimensions targeted today may be inapplicable tomorrow. In the early, rapid-growth phase of the UK telephone company Mercury Communications, for example (Bradley, 1992), interviews with staff suggested that objectives set for them were typically overtaken by events within weeks, making any attempt to base a system of performance management on these objectives doomed to failure. Such a problem need not be fatal, but companies must be careful to diagnose the appropriateness of the *time interval* within which their objectives are set.

Measuring performance

Assuming the organization has been able to identify which dimensions of performance it will choose to include in a performance management system, it faces another set of issues concerning how the dimensions will be measured. Goal-setting theory stresses the importance of feeding back information on performance, if objectives set are to result in improvements in performance. Expectancy theory requires performance to be measured in order to make the forward link into rewards.

Some strategic goals, such as increasing sales in a certain country, have implicit in them a measure of performance, but others − for example, contributing to customer satisfaction − may not have an obvious single measure associated with them: there may be several alternative measures, or it may be difficult to think of any means of satisfactorily measuring performance on that dimension.

In practice choosing objectives and setting performance measures is often linked, although not necessarily desirably. Fowler (1990) has suggested that performance dimensions are sometimes chosen not because they are most valued by the organization, but because they are the most easily measured.

Objective measures

Most organizations will use at least some numerical indicators of their performance to assess whether they are achieving the goals which they have set for themselves. For example, many organizations will have financial health as one of their objectives, explicit or otherwise, and so monitor their financial performance regularly, and are quite likely to cascade this objective down through the organization. In doing so they may monitor financial performance against budget for groups and individuals. Moreover, organizations typically generate, or can access, a whole range of quantified data such as sales figures, output, productivity, absenteeism. Two types of problem can arise in choosing quantitative measures in a system of performance management. The first concerns their sufficiency, and the second their quality.

A performance management system which has genuinely distilled from its wider strategy dimensions of performance to be applied to groups and individuals, may find that some of the dimensions are not measured by existing indicators, and these may not be available from the current management information system. It is possible, for example, that increasing customer satisfaction is identified as an outcome to be rewarded and encouraged, but that no adequate measure exists to report this. In this case the organization must do one of two things: either remove the objective from the set which a performance management system will concentrate on, or develop a means to measure the dimension. Doing the former may in practice be quite common, but would undermine the rigour of the performance management system. Designing a new measure will involve the organization in a process of development and testing which must precede any attempt to introduce performance management.

The second problem which must be addressed with quantitative measures is that of their quality. Although so-called 'objective' measures often have an aura of robustness surrounding them, a closer analysis reveals that they may be rather more arbitrary than supposed (cf. Walsh, 1992). Profitability would seem to be a tried and tested performance measure, for example, yet financial managers or accountants will confirm that profits are highly subject to decisions made by managers on how to treat costs and revenues, and when paper gains should be released onto the profit and loss account. In general the quality of an objective measure will depend on the extent to which it meets five conditions. These are that it should be:

1 free from 'noise' (influence by outside factors not relevant);
2 unable to be manipulated by insiders;
3 straightforward to understand;
4 inexpensive to collect;
5 relevant, in the sense of reporting on the dimension of performance desired.

To the extent that these conditions are not met, a performance management system will include flaws which make it depart from the expectancy theory ideal.

Subjective measures

Performance management does not require that the measures which it employs are objective instruments. Many aspects of performance identified for inclusion in a performance management system may, if they are to be measured at all, rely not on objectively observable results, but on the *subjective* judgement of other people. Although objective measures have traditionally enjoyed a higher status, it is clear that many instances of so-called hard data, such as accounting information, are actually much more mutable than is commonly supposed. On the other hand, if procedures to make subjective assessments of performance are well designed, and thoroughly audited, their outcomes may be a more valid and accurate reflection of reality than many objective measures.

Subjective measures of performance are made all the time in organizations. Most people will have a clear, and for that matter complex, picture of the ability and performance of a colleague with whom they work closely. This view will rely only in part on formal results being seen, but may not be less accurate for that. Promotions, for example, (a possible element of a performance management system) are often made on the basis of subjective assessments of a person's performance and suitability for a new job. The challenge for a performance management system is that its procedures should be *auditable*, so that it can be verified that subjective measures are being used effectively. This tends to result in a move to formalize the process of subjective performance measurement. The most common way in which this is carried out is via a system of appraisal.

Appraisal systems can take many forms, from annual verbal discussions between an employee and his superior, to systems which may include written reviews from peers and subordinates, as well as superiors. The common characteristic of each, however, is that on a regular basis a subjective assessment of an employee's performance is recorded. Appraisal systems give rise to a number of issues of theory and practice, which should be considered by managers seeking to design and implement a performance management system.

Some question the extent to which subjective appraisals can ever be an adequate means of assessing employees' performance. One school of thought emphasizes the social processes which underlie performance appraisals. It argues that because ratings are given by people to other people it is impossible to disentangle the social influences which are present: do the appraiser and appraisee enjoy a social rapport? Do non-relevant aspects of the appraisee influence the perception which the appraiser has of his performance? An example of this latter point is US research (e.g. Kraiger and Ford, 1985) which demonstrates that employees receive significantly higher ratings from appraisers of their own race. Other studies have indicated that female success at traditionally male tasks is often ascribed to luck, ease of the task, or 'connections' rather than to superior performance. More generally, appraisers may feel socially uncomfortable about giving appraisal ratings which may be relatively poor. The reaction to this may be to cluster ratings artificially around the mean, or to give way to a general 'rating creep' by awarding more marks above a suggested mean than below.

The social need for this may be very tangible. Barkdoll (1989) has described a phenomenon which he calls the *Lake Wobegon Effect*, after the short stories written by the American author Garrison Keillor. Keillor ends each reading of his stories with a description of Lake Wobegon: 'Where all the women are strong, all the men are good looking, and all the children are above average.' Surveys suggest that Keillor's observation is grounded in fact. Surveys show repeatedly that the average person considers himself to be better than average. For example, professional and managerial employees at General Electric (GE) were asked to rank themselves against other GE employees in similar jobs. The average self-rating was at the 77th percentile. This shows that a system which did overcome the rating-creep problem is not without its own difficulties. Informing people that in your judgement their performance was at the 50th percentile, when they nurture a view of themselves as being excellent performers, may lead to interpersonal difficulties which appraisers are reluctant to expose themselves to.

Another perspective on appraisal comes from the analysis of power. Far from being a neutral excercise in seeking out the truth, appraisal may be a highly political process, with the parties involved pursuing their own power stratagems through it. For example, appraisal may represent an ideal vehicle for a boss to consolidate his or her power over a subordinate by presenting an interpretation of performance consistent with a stance which he or she is trying to adopt.

One type of solution which has been applied to overcome these problems with appraisal is to expand the number of appraisers who contribute to the subjective assessment of an employee. This would tend to even out any 'rater bias' in response that was related to particular appraisers, though of course it would not address a problem of group bias against racial or gender groups, for example. Increasing the number of contributors to an appraisal might also dilute the social pressure on the appraiser, resulting in allocating too high ratings. Another solution to this specific problem, which has been used by some organizations, is to 'force' appraisals to be non-neutral by specifying, for example, that a certain proportion of top grades must be allocated as well as a certain proportion of low grades. This can also be done statistically by forcing a certain desired distribution of ratings onto the actual ratings given by appraisers. (See box 4.4.)

Box 4.4 Incorporating peer reviews in appraisals

Performance management at the investment bank JP Morgan has at its heart an unusual appraisal system. Each employee of the rank of 'officer' (a term which covers the majority of employees) is required to ask up to five colleagues who have worked with him or her during the past year to submit confidential appraisals of his/her performance. In addition, anyone else in the company is entitled to submit an unsolicited appraisal on any other individual they have worked with, and may be positive, negative or a mixture both. Such unsolicited appraisals cannot be given anonymously: the person co-ordinating the assessment has the right to discuss their views further with them, but the identity of the unsolicited appraiser is not revealed to the subject of the appraisal. The manager of the appraisee's department collates the feedback, and summarizes it in a document which also contributes his or her own assessment. This document is discussed with the employee, and forms the basis of a performance ranking on which promotions, pay rises and bonuses will be made.

The solutions to the problems of bias in subjective appraisals can be one cause, however, of another problem frequently encountered by organizations making use of an appraisal system. This is that the process of appraisal becomes bureaucratic and unwieldy. This can lead to it consuming undesired resources in the organization and being seen as an administrative nuisance, and consequently not being taken seriously by either appraisers or appraisees. More fundamentally, the practical implications of this aspect of performance management, in terms of bureaucracy and formalism, may

be in direct opposition to other moves in the organization towards delegation, empowerment, teamwork and devolution of previously centralized
policies.

Rewarding performance

A system of performance management will not succeed in bringing about
high performance against objectives unless employees consciously act in
ways seen as being most likely to achieve the objectives. Expectancy theory
and goal-setting theory both emphasize the importance of ensuring that
employees make this decision, but each takes a different route in describing
what causes this to be made. Expectancy theory specifies the need to tie
performance outcomes to *rewards* which are valued by employees. Goal-
setting theory lays stress on the need for acceptance by employees of the
goals *per se*, so that motivation is more intrinsically based.

At one level, expectancy theory is almost tautological. It seems to suggest
that people will perform in order to attain outcomes which they value,
without specifying what it is which people value. This shortcoming has
roots in the principles of hedonism, on which utilitarianism, and ultimately
expectancy theory, are based. In claiming that all human actions are motivated by the desire to seek pleasure and avoid pain, the philosopher Hobbes
proposed, in effect, a theory of psychological hedonism but failed to specify
what *constitutes* pleasure and pain. If expectancy theory is to be applied
usefully it requires a complementary theory of *what* motivates people; for
the designer of a performance management system this carries the clear
implication that a judgement must be made of what rewards will be valued
by employees.

The concept of valence in expectancy theory establishes the notion that
successful performance will only result to the extent that rewards on offer
are valued by employees. There exists a myriad of rewards which firms can
offer employees, of which money is just one. Others include power, autonomy, praise, status and fringe benefits. A choice must be made by companies as to what rewards are to be granted in response to performance, and
the choice must reflect the importance of that reward to individuals, as well
as what the organization can feasibly offer. Rewards which can be offered
can be thought of as *intrinsic* or *extrinsic*. Intrinsic rewards arise from within
the system itself. For example, the sense of achievement of meeting performance targets may be reward enough for some employees to cause them
to strive for certain performance outcomes. Extrinsic rewards are added
separately to the system and may be pecuniary (e.g. a cash bonus) or
non-pecuniary (e.g. time off from work).

Pay is one possible means of rewarding employees in a system of performance management. Although performance-related pay is widespread,

it should not be assumed that performance management is necessarily driven by money. From its early days, psychological research (e.g. Brayfield and Crockett, 1955) has argued consistently that pay is variable in its attractiveness to employees. In this regard, goal-setting theory is a useful complement to expectancy theory for designers of performance management systems. This is because goal-setting theory places particular emphasis on the *intrinsic* motivation associated with achieving performance goals which have been set.

The problem for practitioners is twofold. First, how to find out which goals or rewards will be valued by employees. A solution to this would seem to be prior research among employees to discover their preferences. A second problem arises from individual differences. Within an organization, different employees may have markedly different preferences for rewards, or views regarding which goals are valuable. While the ideal would be to tailor these to meet the preferences of individual employees, in practice this is likely to introduce excessive complexity into a performance management system already subject to the risk of being overly bureaucratic. As a result companies should recognize they will be constrained to offer a 'second best' system.

All this assumes that, while preferences between people may vary, they are constant within a given person. That is to say, a person who values pay, or autonomy, highly will do so consistently, other factors being equal. There is, however, a *marginal valence problem*. This problem is that the value (or valence) of a particular reward is likely to be subject to diminishing marginal returns, as is the case for most other valued goods and services. The value which a person places on autonomy, say, depends in part on how much autonomy he or she has currently. As more autonomy is granted, the value placed on further increases in autonomy is likely to fall (and may even become negative). Equally, goals which are committed to on one occasion, may be less motivating when repeated time after time. This theory, as well as being consistent with microeconomic models of consumer preferences, ties in with classic psychological models such as those of Maslow (1954), whose 'hierarchy of needs' included the implication that once certain needs were satisfied they would no longer act at motivators to behaviour. For managers designing a system of performance management the marginal valence problem means that it is not sufficient to choose and incorporate rewards, or goals, which are *currently* valued by employees. If the system is to be ongoing, both must be reviewed regularly to assess whether they continue to be highly valued by employees, and if not, they should be replaced with others.

This makes the point very clearly that a system of performance management may not be designed and left unchanged during its period of operation, but must be the subject of continuous review. It is entirely possible that a well-designed but static performance management system may be undermined by its own success: in a situation in which praise and internal recognition are a reward for performance, successful performance may make employees accustomed to such attention, with the effect that the prospect of it becomes no longer regarded as a sufficient reward for further improvements in performance. Similarly, if employees are persuaded to commit to a target improvement in customer service, achieving targets this year may reduce the importance of the objective next year, so that commitment will not be repeated at the same level.

Process links

Expectancy theory and goal-setting theory make it clear that for a performance management system to succeed in securing high performance, it is not sufficient to get the content issues discussed above right. Attention must be paid to the linkages within the system: in other words *how* the system works.

Expectancy theory in particular maintains that it is of crucial importance that employees perceive a close link between their efforts and what is measured as the chosen dimensions of performance. It is equally important that they see strong ties between performance as measured and the rewards which may result. As a psychological theory, expectancy theory is concerned with employees' *perceptions* of these linkages, not whether they actually exist as perceived. However, most organizations expect to have continuing relationships with their employees, so it would be an unusual tactic to attempt to deceive employees as to the real linkages between effort and measured performance, and measured performance and rewards. In practice, therefore, the lesson from expectancy theory is the need to ensure that strong linkages are actually in place if the system as a whole is to operate effectively.

Goal-setting theory takes a different emphasis, which makes it not entirely commensurable with expectancy theory. Empirical tests of goal-setting theory have established that if they are to bring about high performance, goals should be demanding, but not unattainable. To this extent the theory shares expectancy theory's concern with the design of the links between objectives and the ability to attain them. However, whereas expectancy theory predicts that performance objectives which are easily met will, providing that they are closely associated with a valued reward, prompt high performance, goal-setting theory contends that an easily met objective will fail to produce motivation to perform.

Two principal process links are to be found in models of performance management, the link between effort and measured performance, and the link between performance and rewards. We consider each of these links in turn.

Linking effort and measured performance

Expectancy theory carries the clear implication that if a system is to promote effort leading to superior performance, people must feel confident that by adjusting their behaviour they will be able to affect the performance measures which have been established. Ensuring that this is the case will involve both design work and communication by the organization.

It is not automatically the case that an individual will be able to affect a given performance measure. Two reasons account for this. The first, as the expectancy model in figure 4.2 shows, is that individual effort and application are unlikely to be exclusive determinants of performance on a given dimension. The tools, either in the sense of physical equipment, or in the sense of skills and abilities, which someone is equipped with will play an important role in determining outcomes. In some cases the organization, rather than an individual employee, will have the ability to provide the neccessary tools for the job. In this case it is important that a performance management system in which improving performance depends on the use of new skills or equipment ensures that these are available when needed. If this is not ensured, the employee will justifiably feel a reduced ability to influence the performance measures and, expectancy theory predicts, will not engage in an attempt to improve performance.

It could also be the case that achieving performance standards which have been set is beyond the personal capabilities of the employee. Try as she might, a person may simply never have the interpersonal skills required, say, to meet an assesment criterion of being seen as a departmental leader by her colleagues. So what is included in a performance measurement system must be based on an understanding of the capabilities which the workforce has, and individuals within it: targets and objectives which are over-demanding in the light of these are likely to result in a perception that the performance criteria are unachievable, neutralizing any attempt to improve performance.

Another way in which people may feel that they are unable, through their own efforts, to influence performance measures significantly has to do with the size of groups whose performance is measured. An important debate in the economics literature (e.g. Jensen and Meckling, 1979; Cable and FitzRoy, 1980; Alchian and Demsetz, 1972) concerns the question of 'shirking' or 'free-riding' by individuals in groups. This is the idea that if it is the performance of the whole team which is measured, and which determines rewards, then any individual worker can choose to work less hard than his colleagues, to 'take it easy', confident in the knowledge that he will benefit anyway from his team-mates' effort. But of course if everyone in the team thinks in a similar way, then no one will work hard, with the result that the performance of the whole team will be poor. The expectancy theory interpretation of the problem is that any individual will see his own efforts as having sufficiently little individual effect on performance to justify supplying much.

Some writers (e.g. Alchian and Demsetz, 1972) conclude that this problem is fatal for attempts to design team-based performance management systems. Others (e.g. Kanter, 1989) suggest that the problem can be resolved internally by the social processes within groups and teams. Members of a team will be able to keep an eye on how well their colleagues are working, and exert 'peer pressure' on them not to let their performance fall, thereby letting the side down. It is easy to imagine such an atmosphere prevailing in a sports team, for example. Kanter reports that in a group-based performance management system at the Lincoln Electric Company in the USA, 'peer pressure can be so high that the first two years of employment are called "purgatory"' (p. 264).

The issue raises important questions for the design of performance measurement systems. In many circumstances it may be infeasible to separate out the contribution to performance of individual members of a group or team, and so it is that the performance of the group as a whole is measured as part of the system. In other cases it might be administratively more straightforward to measure team performance. Either way, this may be a weak link in the performance management cycle.

Expectancy theory emphasizes the role of the link between effort and measured performance as *perceived* by the employee. To accept the argument that the organization is not so much a rational set of clear structures and policies as a socially determined environment is to allow the possibility that people's perceptions may not be objective pictures of actuality. People may be convinced that their efforts will not be noticed, even if the designers of a system of performance management have in fact addressed the potential problems with the links between effort and performance. It may therefore be necessary for a communcations policy to be used to reinforce the message of the design of the system if perceptions are to be accurate. The type of communications policy that may prove effective could vary: in some organizations only seeing a performance management system piloted may be sufficient to persuade doubters of its validity.

Linking measured performance and rewards

Expectancy theory used as a framework for analysing performance management systems must also draw attention to the links which an employee perceives between measured performance and rewards, if the system is to succeed in encouraging maximum performance. As in the case of the links between effort and measured performance, it is the *perception* of the link which will determine the success of the system, although in an ongoing system the most important determinant of this is likely to be the objective mechanisms in place.

There are two broad ways in which the measured performance–reward contingency can be structured: a formula-based determination, or a more informally determined approach. The advantage of the former is that it provides an objective basis for encouraging the perception that rewards are linked to performance, but suffers the drawback of inflexibility. A less rigidly determined contingency allows for a variety of unforeseen factors which may have affected performance (either positively or negatively) to be taken into account, but runs the risk of appearing arbitrary or political, thereby weakening the degree to which employees consider that rewards reflect actual performance.

Some organizations operating performance management systems, especially those which use financial rewards rather than intrinsic factors as motivators, specify precisely in advance the relationship which will prevail between achieved levels of measured performance and the rewards which they will trigger. This may be in the form of a policy which states, for example, that each grade above the average in an appraisal will earn the individual a bonus of £250. Another form of this approach is to pay out to employees a proportion of the value of something allied to the stated performance objectives, such as increased sales. Gainsharing, a performance management system popular in the United States in recent years (cf. McKersie, 1986), pays out to employees a predetermined proportion of labour cost savings achieved during a specified period. The principal problem with such a mechanistic approach to linking performance and rewards stems from the problem of 'noise'. Performance measures even in a well-designed system may be unable to avoid being subject to the influence of factors other than employees' personal endeavours. External economic conditions, unforeseen incidents and other 'random' variations may still affect measures such as sales or production performance. At a time when these noise elements turn out to have been especially significant in determining measured performance, a closely defined system may distribute rewards unfairly. For example, if an unexpected currency appreciation has severely affected export sales, it may be unfair to penalize a salesforce which did relatively better than the competition, but whose rewards were tied to sales volume. Equally there are companies who reward their executives through bonuses related to their share price, who have found themselves paying out more than they intended following a general rise in the stockmarket, or after takeover interest in the company, unrelated to superior performance, has caused an increase in the share price. To some extent these problems could be solved by better design of measures (using share price *relative* to comparable companies, for example, or sales *relative* to those of competitors), but in practice it may be impossible to specify the whole range of possible contingencies in a performance measure without breaching the important principle that simplicity of design is desirable for the system to be able to be understood.

Box 4.5   Direct Line: A case of excessive PRP?

The question of how the precise relationship between performance and rewards should be specified is a perennial and intractable one. The case of Direct Line, the motor insurer subsidiary of the Royal Bank of Scotland, illustrates the dilemma. Peter Wood founded the Direct Line insurance company in 1985. As a new entrant to a UK insurance market dominated by large, household-name insurance groups, it was uncertain whether Direct Line's strategy of offering low-cost motor insurance by telephone would result in a viable business. Peter Wood sold his stake in the company to the Royal Bank of Scotland in 1988, agreeing to stay on to manage the business. In exchange for his shareholding, Wood negotiated an incentive pay package with RBS which would reward him through a fixed formula tied to the growth of assets of the insurance business.

As it turned out, Direct Line proved a phenomenal success, far exceeding expectations of its performance. Much of the success is certainly attributable to Wood, both for conceiving the strategy, and for proving a shrewd manager of the business. Direct Line's profits reached £50.2 million in the year ending 1993, and by 1994 the company had become Britain's biggest motor insurer. Peter Wood's performance-related pay skyrocketed in line with the success. Wood earned £1.6 million in 1991, £6 million in 1992, and £18.2 million in the year to September 1993.

The Royal Bank of Scotland and Peter Wood became embarrassed by the remuneration figures, which were the subject of increasing public attention. In November 1993 the Royal Bank bought itself out of its contractual obligation by making a one-off payment to the Direct Line chief of £24 million.

The question which was exercising public opinion is unresolved today: is it appropriate for performance which is significantly better than envisaged to trigger rewards which are significantly more generous than envisaged?

However, links between performance and rewards which are not tied to a specific formula may avoid difficulties, such as those mentioned above. Rather than know precisely how much, in terms of reward, a given level of performance might bring, managers may be granted discretion over a certain sum or other pool (e.g. number of days off) which they can allocate to staff on the basis of performance against agreed objectives. For a large organization, this may be the only practical way to run a performance management system: it is likely to be difficult and complex enough to cascade the organization's strategic objectives down to the level of individuals' objectives, without having to specify in detail what the consequences of an individual attaining his or her goals will be. The obvious downside to this greater flexibility, however, is that it may weaken the *perceived* link between measured performance and rewards, and so undermine the system of performance measurement. The extent to which this does occur will be closely related to the level of trust within the organization, and experience of the system in practice. In a context of antagonistic relations within the company, the suspicion that the managers of the system could entice high performance through the promise of rewards which never materialize to the extent envisaged may be enough to prevent that performance from occurring in the first place.

Feedback and amendments

Two aspects of feedback and amendment are relevant to the design of systems of performance management: the feedback and discussion of individuals' performance, to assist them in continuous improvement; and the review of the functioning of the system as a whole.

Goal-setting theory places great emphasis on the need for the feedback of information on performance if employees are to be motivated to perform well, and most applications of the theory go further to specify the need for coaching on how performance can be improved. This reflects the role of performance management as a *communications process*, serving a number of information-flow functions, from establishing strategic objectives in the minds of employees, to offering advice on how performance can be improved. It is obviously the case that, whatever the motivation of a person to perform, if they genuinely cannot see how their behaviour should be altered, then they will be unable to achieve any performance improvements. Performance management, and specifically the appraisal process, should therefore provide a platform for practical advice on ways in which behaviour should be changed to contribute to the organization's strategic objectives. In a study of 120 UK managers, Iles and Mabey (1993) found 'assigned mentors' and 'career reviews with superiors' among the most popular and well-received career development tools, for the very reason that they gave individuals the opportunity to test and discuss career aspirations with someone within the power nexus of the organization.

The difficulty with this aspect of the performance management approach is that it brings together two aspects of communication between which there may be a tension. When an appraisal process determines rewards, expectancy theory itself would predict that employee behaviour within the process will be directed instrumentally towards securing the rewards on offer. This may conflict with the openness and candour needed for a sensitive discussion of ways to improve performance. For example, employees may feel the need to present a façade of confidence and competence to their appraiser which masks difficulties which they are experiencing, and which could possibly be addressed if brought to the attention of the organization. Moreover, from a strategic point of view, the process could encourage a 'groupthink' by which employees feel the need to express commitment to the strategic objectives of the organization (since it is performance against these which is rewarded), with the result that no critical appraisal of the objectives themselves is made, or at least expressed. This carries the great risk that strategies which are proving unworkable, or damaging, persist without amendment and handicap the organization.

The second element of feedback and review concerns evaluation of the performance management process itself. Whereas we have characterized performance management as a cycle, expectancy theory is more often presented as a linear chain, without an internal feedback mechanism. To adapt the analysis of expectancy theory to the particular application of performance management we therefore need to build in a reflexivity into the process.

There are three reasons why continuous review of the operation of performance management needs to be conducted. First, the need for such reflexivity is fundamental to the strategic role of performance management. In the first section of this chapter we described one of the purposes of performance management as being to provide a framework for internally auditing the means by which the organization delivers wider strategic goals, with a view to continuously improving them. Secondly, as we have already pointed out, strategic goals themselves may be far from fixed, but rather constantly evolving. This means that it is essential that performance management systems are geared to meet current strategic objectives, rather than ones which have become out of date. Finally, the discussion in this chapter has underlined the fact that designing and implementing a system of performance management is fraught with complexity on a number of dimensions. As a result, it will be a rare organization which achieves the perfect system of performance

Table 4.1 Feedback loops in performance management

Step	Review questions	Modifications
1 Identifying objectives	Are organizational objectives still appropriate? Are they adequately translated to group or individual level?	Update objectives Amend cascade of objectives
2 Choosing measures	To what extent were measures • noise free? • objective? • simple to understand? • inexpensive to collect? • relevant to objectives?	Design and specify different sets of measures
3 Defining links between effort and measured performance	Is training adequate for objectives to be met? Is equipment adequate for objectives to be met? Is support adequate for objectives to be met? (including time available) Are persons' capabilities adequate for objectives to be met? Does team size encourage perception of weak link between effort and performance? Do employees perceive link between effort and measured performance?	Provide appropriate training if justified Provide appropriate equipment if justified Reconfigure support (time allocation, assistance, organization) Consider substitution of person *or* less demanding objectives Redesign link between measures and rewards Design and implement communications strategy
4 Selecting rewards	Are rewards valued by employees?	Specify different rewards
5 Defining links between performance and rewards	Do employees perceive link between performance and rewards? Are extraneous factors affecting performance or rewards?	Design and implement communications strategy Redesign link between measures and rewards

management for its purposes from the outset. The likelihood is that some unknown contingencies will reveal themselves only in application, so that the system must be capable of reforming itself to take account of lessons from practice.

Table 4.1 summarizes the elements of continuous scrutiny to which a performance management system should be subject. Performing the tasks implied will not be a mechanical process, but will require investigative, diagnostic and design skills on the part of those responsible for the system.

Methodological Criticisms

Above we argued that the performance management approach rests on a set of assumptions concerning the possibility of managing organizations in a certain way which could be regarded as *rationalist*. Expectancy theory, and to some extent goal-setting theory, are themselves founded on an assumption that people – in this case managers (the designers and operators of performance management systems) and employees (the people to whom they are applied) – think in a way which is optimizing, calculative and individualistic. This set of assumptions has been labelled variously *rational economic man* (Hollis and Nell, 1975), *neo-classical rationality* (Etzioni, 1988), or simply *rationality* (Leibenstein, 1976).

These assumptions are rarely made explicit, still less criticized, with the result that often little thought is given to questions such as whether they are correct at all times, and in all circumstances. Yet a growing body of theory and evidence is suggesting that human decision-making does not approximate to that assumed under this conception of rationality at all times and in all places. Mitchell (1980), for example, notes that the essential question is shifting from *does expectancy theory work?* to *where does it work?*

The universalist view of expectancy theory and performance management ignores the contextual factors which determine whether people think in the way which is assumed. Where they do not, there is no reason to suppose that introducing a performance management system will have beneficial effects on performance. These contextual factors refer to differences between people which may derive from their nationality, their organization, the type of work they are engaged in, and a whole host of individually determined factors.

Take the question of national setting, for example. For many years researchers (such as Tonnies, 1922) have identified important and consistent differences in the *values* of different national cultures. Hofstede (1980) has argued that the value of individualism forms an axis by which countries can be categorized: in the United States a strongly individualistic value system suggests that policies which rely on enlightened self-interest may succeed, whereas in Sweden, whose dominant value system emphasizes more collective interests, such policies may fail. Etzioni (1975) found that individualism went hand in hand with a *calculative* decision-making process. Since this is an assumption implicit within expectancy theory, the success of policies such as performance-related pay which are based on this way of thinking will be contingent on an appropriate national setting. It is significant that while performance-related pay is widespread in the United States, it is much less common in continental Europe. Yet this is too often ignored by those who peddle prescriptions: as Hofstede notes, 'the silent assumption of universal validity of culturally restricted findings is frequent. The empirical basis for American management theories is American organizations, and we should not assume without proof that they apply elsewhere' (1980, p. 373).

It is not only nations which have values, governing ways of thinking and behaving, which may not be consistent with that assumed by expectancy theory and performance management. Particular organizations have their own traditions and cultures which may or may not be consistent with the successful use of performance management systems. Companies with an entrenched culture of collective bargaining may find that the introduction of a performance-related pay system militates against the way employees think about their performance, and so prove unsuccessful (see, for example, chapter 8 of this book). At the very least, policies should diagnose at what level performance management should be applied: in an organization with a strong teamwork culture, individual incentives may be resisted as incompatible (witness the hostile reaction to the attempt to introduce an individualized performance management system into the UK police force in 1993). Equally, group bonuses applied to a salesforce may violate passionately held attachment to individual autonomy.

The importance of contextual factors, such as culture, in the success of performance management systems highlights a potential hidden agenda behind some organizations' adoption of the approach. Clark (1995) has argued that while performance-related pay is often claimed to be introduced in order to incentivate improved performance, it is sometimes chosen by managers wishing to instigate *cultural change* rather than to achieve the vaunted improvements in individual performance. This may not be a misplaced strategy: Hofstede (1980) argues that changing first the behaviour of individuals, such as by forcing them to take part in a performance-related pay system, is one of the most effective ways of changing value systems, which are in turn (Schein, 1984) a principal component of organizational culture. As we saw in chapter 2 (particularly figures 2.2 and 2.3 on the trajectory of change), if cultural change is the real objective of introducing performance management systems, their success cannot be gauged on whether the systems improve individuals' performance (because they are quite likely to depress it initially if introduced into an 'inappropriate' context), but must be judged on whether they ultimately bring about changes in attitudes and values.

The Case of Performance-related Pay

Because performance management refers to the integration of HR policies into a system which is measurable, auditable, improvable and links into wider organizational objectives, the number of possible types of performance management systems is as many as the number of different policies which can be linked together to form such a system. This means that assessing the benefits of performance management in a rigorous way is especially problematical. In order to provide an empirical assessment of the theoretical principles discussed above, we will proceed by reference to one possible organizational vehicle for a performance management system which has gained in popularity in recent years: performance-related pay.

Performance-related pay is a means by which organizations attempt to achieve a set of goals by communicating performance objectives to employees, monitoring the achievement of these objectives, and rewarding successful achievements to the end of shaping behaviours to be consistent with those thought to be conducive to the attainment of the organization's wider objectives. As such, performance-related pay is both an application of the performance management approach, and offers an analogy for it.

Increasing incidence of performance-related pay

Performance-related pay is not new, whatever its recent popularity. Forms of performance-related pay, such as share-cropping, in which agricultural labourers receive a fraction of the harvest as payment for their work, have operated for as long as anthropologists are able to report. Performance-related pay today refers to a whole raft of schemes, ranging from piece rates to profit-related pay, and including individual-merit pay and group bonuses, which share the common feature of providing an explicit link between the income of employees and their performance at work.

Since the late 1970s there has been a steady growth in the number of organizations, especially in Britain and the United States, who practise, or claim to practise, systems of performance-related pay. Heneman (1992) reports that surveys show that over 80 per cent of US companies explicitly link the pay of at least some of their employees with their individual performance. The US government's Committee on Performance Appraisal for Merit Pay (Milkovitch and Wigdor, 1991) put this figure at between 94 and 95 per cent. Incidence is higher among large companies than in small organizations, and significantly higher in the private sector than in the public sector, but in all sectors it has increased since the mid-1970s. In Britain, fewer firms practise PRP, but Gallie and White (1992), in a survey of 3,855 UK employees, nevertheless found that 27 per cent received some form of PRP, with team or group bonuses being more common than individual incentives.

Despite its growing importance, empirical testing of the detailed theoretical aspects of PRP, including those discussed for performance management more generally above, has been patchy. In particular, the overwhelming proportion of studies which have been carried out have taken place in American organizations, with a smaller number applied to the British context, and fewer still in a continental European setting. To some extent this reflects what we identified above as an assumed universalism of application of the underlying models, which leads researchers not to regard the restricted testing ground as being noteworthy. Whatever the reason, the culturally restricted test base should be borne in mind when considering ramifications of the evidence discussed below for European practitioners.

Empirical tests of performance-related pay: An overview

There have been various reviews of the empirical literature which have attempted to answer the question, do performance-related pay schemes produce higher performance? Each has presented a set of conclusions which includes some examples of failure in this objective, but they tend to conform to the view that the overall direction of its effects is towards enhanced performance provided the design factors identified above are met (cf. Dyer and Schwab, 1982; Ilgen, 1990). Milkovich and Wigdor (1991) summarize the empirical research as showing that when the necessary expectancy theory conditions are met, between 9 and 16 per cent of the variance in individual performance can be explained by differences in incentives. The same authors find that evidence concerning group performance-related pay tends to be of a case-study design, making overall quantification of the effects of group schemes on performance problematical. However, as with individual PRP schemes, the actual design features of the schemes appeared to be the principal discriminators between enhanced and other performance. (See also the section on 'pay determination' in chapter 5.) Studies show consistently that organizations which manage to base performance-related pay systems on meaningful goals, robust performance measures, significant rewards, and well-provided links between performance and rewards, operate systems which are most likely to result in enhanced performance. In the rest of this section, we supply some empirical background to each of the 'core issues' which we identified for the design of performance management systems in the 'Designing Performance Management Systems' section above.

Setting goals

We saw that goal-setting theory lays particular stress on the need to base performance management systems on a limited number of specific goals, rather than on a larger number of vaguer objectives. Empirical tests of performance-related pay support this design emphasis. The British employment survey (Gallie and White, 1992) reported that 70 per cent of employees covered by performance appraisals involving targets said that the process influenced how they work, compared with 24 per cent where the system did not involve target setting. In an unusually rigorous case study which examined the introduction of performance-related pay in the UK Inland Revenue, two authors from the London School of Economics (Marsden and Richardson, 1992) surveyed 2,423 employees (reflecting a 60 per cent response rate) and searched for reasons why the system apparently failed to enhance performance: 77 per cent of reviewing officers reported no sustained performance increase by their staff. One reason they advanced as a possible explanation was the fact that the performance evaluation system had not succeeded in setting a clear set of performance goals: only 27 per cent of Inland Revenue employees said that the system had led to work targets being set more clearly.

In an extensive survey of performance management techniques in 3,052 US companies, the Wyatt Company (Wyatt, 1989) found that 84 per cent of companies whose system of performance management was effective (defined as meeting its objectives) specified written performance goals as part of it, compared with only 39 per cent among those companies whose system was judged to have been ineffective. Having reviewed the experience of the private sector, the US government Committee on Performance Appraisal recommended that federal policy for performance-related pay in the civil service must 'communicate performance goals that employees understand and consider "doable" ' (Milkovich and Wigdor, 1991, p. 5).

Measuring performance

In his review of the empirical literature, Heneman (1992) acknowledges that the studies establish the adequacy of measures of performance as a crucial determinant of the success of systems of performance-related pay.

He comments: 'there seems to be much stronger support for this view than for other contentions regarding aspects of merit pay' (1992, p. 103). Earlier we saw the problems with objective measurement which distorted performance in the European telephone company directory assistance division. This evidence is typical of a long history of case studies which show the problems which have been associated with literal adherence to specified performance measures.

Subjective measures, usually based on appraisal, have their own problems. Miceli and Near (1988) found that pay-for-performance perceptions were highest when appraisers followed formal standards of assessment. Pearce and Perry (1983) argued that one of the chief causes of a failure of the PRP scheme in the public sector in the US was the use of a flawed system of performance appraisal. Evidence from an attitude survey conducted among federal employees by the US Office of Personnel Management seems to support this interpretation: only 51 per cent of 14,500 respondents agreed with the statement that *my performance rating presents a fair and accurate picture of my actual job performance* (Milkovich and Wigdor, 1991).

One of the criticisms of performance appraisal as an element of performance management was that assessments would tend to reflect social and political influences rather than any objective notion of performance, even if this existed. Longenecker et al. (1987) report a series of interviews with executives in which people admit the manipulation of appraisals to secure politically desirable outcomes. Similarly, Bjerke et al. (1987) showed that raters tended to give appraisals which were thought to be instrumental in obtaining outcomes which they desired, rather than giving true assessments of their subordinates' performance.

Measurement problems are another possible source of failure of the UK Inland Revenue PRP system. Under the system employees were awarded one of five performance grades: 35 per cent of employees felt that favouritism rather than performance was determining the award, and fully 74 per cent of those surveyed felt that staff were frequently denied the grade corresponding to their performance, because of a perceived quota system for each grade (Marsden and Richardson, 1992).

Rewarding performance

We have already made the point that goal-setting theory emphasizes intrinsic rewards stemming from achieving performance goals as securing employee commitment to performance. Performance-related pay is, of course, predicated upon money as a motivator, and hence expectancy theory has been the principal framework used to analyse the motivational effects in the specific case of PRP. Expectancy theory highlights the requirement for rewards to be positively valent if performance-related pay is to lead to enhanced performance. This means that not only should pay be valued by employees, but that it should be available in amounts perceived as significant. Several empirical tests of the effects of performance-related pay have pointed to a failure to observe this latter requirement as a factor which distinguishes unsuccessful schemes from those which succeed in bringing about performance improvements.

Heneman (1992) refers to the need for pay contingent on performance to be consistent with a 'just noticeable difference' – the minimum pay increase required for employees to adjust their behaviour toward achieving it. Field tests show that what constitutes a 'just noticeable difference' varies considerably between individuals, and supports the theoretical notion of a 'marginal valence' problem. For instance Heneman reports that 'a smaller increase is needed to create a "just noticeable difference" for those with lower pay levels' (1992, p. 150).

Empirical studies suggest that the average proportion of pay linked to performance tends to be low. The Gallie and White survey in the UK revealed that only 31 per cent of employees receiving incentive pay in 1992 had a variable element of over 10 per cent of their total annual earnings, while 38 per cent received an average of less than 5 per cent of their remuneration as performance related. In the Marsden and Richardson Inland Revenue study the majority of individual pay awards tended to be small: between 2 per cent and 4 per cent of total pay over two years. The authors suggest that the size of these awards is consistent with those revealed by surveys of private companies in France in recent years. The size of these awards is only important in so far as they are perceived to be inadequate by employees. There is some evidence that this is indeed the case: only 17 per cent of the Inland Revenue respondents declared that the size of the prospective financial reward was sufficient to make them change their behaviour.

This evidence is supported by other empirical studies. In the US Civil Service the Performance Management and Recognition System, which was introduced in 1984, 50 per cent of employees surveyed during the system's first year of operation said the size of rewards on offer was inadequate (Milkovich and Wigdor, 1991). Pritchard and Curts (1973) reported results of laboratory experiments which demonstrated that pay incentives only increased performance when the financial rewards were high.

Less research evidence is available to assess the other aspect of the valence of pay: whether pay is valued as a motivator. Like the designers of performance-related pay systems, most researchers seem to take it for granted that more pay is a desired goal, and proceed directly to the question of how much should be included. Yet there is some evidence which supports the idea that the attractiveness of pay is not standard across all individuals but varies widely. For example, Perry and Porter (1982) review evidence which shows that public sector employees value financial rewards less highly than do their counterparts in the private sector. This may go some way to explain the more equivocal record of performance-related pay in the public sector than in private companies.

Process links

The links between effort, performance and rewards are at the heart of the expectancy-theoretic approach to performance management. Applied to performance-related pay, the hypotheses which result are very clear: PRP systems will fail to bring about enhanced performance to the extent that employees do not perceive strong links between their own effort and measured performance, and between measured performance and pay. Empirical studies of PRP systems in practice have generally supported these hypotheses.

In explaining the lack of success of the 1981 US Merit Pay System, the Committee on Performance Appraisal for Merit Pay found that 'its clearest shortcoming was its failure to establish a demonstrable relationship between pay and performance' (Milkovich and Wigdor, 1991, p. 27). Under the system employees suspected that non-performance factors were influencing their ratings, and hence their pay, and that these ratings were arbitrarily modified. The committee found that employees in most government agencies saw no greater prospect of their performance being rewarded under the Merit Pay System than before the system existed. The committee reports that the subsequent replacement of the system with the Performance Management and Recognition System saw an increase in the perceptions of employees that pay and performance were linked increase from 17 to 36 per cent. While this low level is still likely to be lower than expectancy theory would require for a PRP system to be effective, it is not out of line with private-sector experience. The 3,000-company Wyatt survey found that only 28 per cent of employees perceived a link between their pay and job performance. In the UK, Gallie and White's survey of employees revealed that only 37 per cent of those covered by a performance-related pay system felt that pay rises were given to employees who performed well.

Failure to manage the linkages in the performance-related pay system was also advanced as an explanation for the low level of performance motivation produced by the Inland Revenue scheme. Although 81 per cent of respondents felt that they were capable of producing performance which would merit one of the top two performance ratings (suggesting that the linkage between effort and individual performance was sound), 45 per cent thought that even if they performed at this level they doubted that they would be allocated the appropriate grade. This result clearly indicates a perception that efforts would not affect *measured* performance.

That so many performance-related pay systems have failed to convince employees of a strong link between performance and rewards underlines the fact that a performance management system which is well designed and well implemented is not something which is easily achieved.

Feedback and amendments

Goal-setting theory lays particular stress on feeding back the results of performance if a performance management system is to achieve the organization's strategic objectives. Indeed, for many organizations the principal focus of a performance management system is the opportunity it gives for individual performance coaching, and ultimately career development.

Empirical research tends to support the hypothesis that an effective system of feedback and coaching is a neccessary condition for the achievement of objectives. Some studies suggest, however, that in performance-related pay systems linking performance feedback and coaching with the allocation of rewards exacerbates the political and social difficulties which surround appraisal. This impairs both the perception of links between performance and rewards, and the quality of information provided during an appraisal.

Organizations with failing performance management systems often have poor feedback and coaching mechanisms within the system. In the large-scale US Civil Service Merit Pay System, discussed previously, which was ultimately scrapped, only 23 per cent of 14,500 respondents to a government survey felt that their last performance appraisal helped them to improve their performance (Milkovich and Wigdor, 1991). Successful use of appraisal and feedback, on the other hand, is associated with successful performance management systems. Landy et al. (1982) review a range of studies which show that a genuine system of feedback can raise productivity by up to 30 per cent.

Ensuring that a feedback and coaching system works is a matter of careful design and implementation. The authors of the UK Inland Revenue study felt that the way in which pay had been 'bolted on' to a performance appraisal system in that organization had undermined the useful operation of performance feedback and review. They argued that performance reviews should be separated into two distinct components: a free-standing feedback and coaching session, where information could flow candidly, and a more formal appraisal to determine pay (Marsden and Richardson, 1992). This could, of course, produce its own problems, in particular perhaps reducing the perception of the degree to which pay was tied to performance. Providing feedback in a way which is constructive, and supports improved performance next time may not be something that comes intuitively to many managers. The Wyatt survey of performance management revealed that among companies practising successful performance management systems, 78 per cent had provided training in providing feedback, compared with only 53 per cent in companies whose systems had proved ineffective. Another factor which influences whether a feedback system works well is the trust which exists between appraiser and appraisee. Ilgen et al. (1979) summarized the empirical evidence as establishing that trust and appraiser expertise were essential for performance feedback systems to work.

The other dimension of feedback and review which we argued (above) was neccessary was a continuous reappraisal of the design and components of any system of performance management being practised. Research into performance-related pay systems bear this out. Reviewing the body of empirical tests of merit pay, Heneman (1992) found that evaluating the performance of incentive schemes was a characteristic which distinguished the operators of successful schemes from those which failed in their objectives. In fact, the author concludes that 'the major conclusion from this review of empirical studies . . . is that organizations should evaluate the results of their own merit pay plans' (1992, p. 259). Despite this, what evidence exists tends to suggest that most companies fail to engage in such an exercise in reflexivity, relying instead on an implicit assumption that once designed and implemented, their performance management system will produce the effects intended. The American Bureau of National Affairs, for example, found that only 6 per cent of organizations in their regular pay survey conducted any formal assessment of their performance-related pay systems (Milkovich and Wigdor, 1991). This is ironic given that one of the purposes of operating a system of performance management is to tie into wider strategic objectives, which by their nature are subject to evolution and revision.

Conclusions and Summary

Performance management is an approach to managing human resources which is designed to tie HR policies securely into a framework of achieving the strategic goals of the business. To do so it advocates the formation of a system for managing human resources which generates personal goals from wider strategic objectives, provides information on the extent to which contributions are being made to these objectives, and supplies a means of auditing the process links which deliver the contributions. Rather than comprising a blueprint set of policies, performance management is an approach which can be implemented through a variety of linked policies, including objective-setting, performance appraisal and performance-related pay.

The performance management approach draws on a number of theoretical models, of which expectancy theory and goal-setting theory are the most prominent. Applying the models to performance management highlights a set of critical factors which the designers and practitioners of performance management systems must address. These are associated with the feasibility of setting goals, measuring performance, rewarding performance, the design of the process links within the system, and procedures for feedback and amendment. What emerges is a complexity of issues which a precipitous move to implement a performance management system may overlook. Empirical studies, including those applied to performance-related pay, tend to confirm the importance of getting these factors right. In many cases organizations fail to do so, with the result that the effect of performance management systems on performance has not been strong in practice, and is sometimes negative.

The performance management approach can be criticized for relying on a model of management which is more rational than is achievable in practice. In particular, prescriptions are often couched in universalist terms, which take no account of the contextual factors which play a large part in determining success. The contextual factors include cross-cultural differences between nations, as well as different corporate environments and traditions.

In addition, by contrast with the social systems which link people in the organization, performance management may imply a relatively simplistic model by which to achieve enhanced performance in line with strategic objectives. It carries the danger that it may substitute a crude set of mechanisms for a subtle psychological contract linking the organization and its employees.

The overwhelming lesson from theory and practice is that the complex, and sometimes contradictory, set of issues which performance management comprises require a critical approach to the design of systems. A performance management system, if it is to succeed, must reflect an appreciation of the particular characteristics of the organization, and have included within it a strong element of continuous review. An off-the-shelf approach to choosing a performance management system is highly unlikely to achieve its aim of contributing to the achievement of strategic objectives.

Key points

- *Performance management has become a popular vehicle for attempts to integrate the management of human resources with the organization's wider strategy.*
- *Performance management refers to an approach, rather than a particular package of policies. The approach involves linking five policy elements: setting objectives, measuring performance, feeding back results, setting rewards, and amending objectives and activities.*
- *Performance management is based on a rationalist conception of the organization and management, which may not reflect the subtlety, complexity and ambiguity of the actual world in which managers operate. In particular it has little to say about the social processes and power systems in which it will operate.*
- *Principles of goal-setting theory and expectancy theory underpin the performance management approach. They offer a set of lessons for the design and implementation of performance management systems.*
- *A host of crucial issues of design and implementation mean that operating a performance management system is a complex endeavour, requiring rigorous prior and ongoing analysis.*
- *Empirical studies confirm that performance management systems are successful in improving performance only where fundamental design principles are followed.*
- *The underlying assumptions of performance measurement tend to be universalist: they do not consider the importance of context. Yet the values of countries, organizations and people may depart from what is assumed, making models of performance management limited in their application.*

Discussion Questions

1 Which human resource policies does performance management potentially cover?
2 In what ways do modern performance management approaches draw upon traditional theories of social psychology? What assumptions do such models make, and are these justifiable?
3 What are the benefits and drawbacks associated with performance-related pay?
4 What are some of the contextual factors which might interfere with the more universalistic performance management systems?

REFERENCES

Alchian, A. A. and Demsetz, H. (1972) Production, information cost and economic organization. *American Economic Review*, 62, p. 777.

Barkdoll, G. (1989) letter, *Public Administration Review*, 49, p. 295.

Bjerke, D. Cleveland, J., Morrison, R. and Wilson, W. (1987) *Officer Fitness Report Evaluation Study*. Washington, DC, Navy Research and Development Center.

Bowey, A., Fowler, A. and Iles, P. (1992). Reward management. Unit 10, *B884 Human Resource Strategies*, Milton Keynes, Open University Business School, p. 119.

Bradley, K. (1992) *Phone Wars*. London, Business Books.

Brayfield, A. H. and Crockett, W. H. (1955) Employee attitudes and performance. *Psychological Bulletin*, 52, pp. 396–424.

Cable, J. and FitzRoy, F. (1980) Production efficiency, incentives and employee participation: Some preliminary results for West Germany. *Kyklos*, 33, pp. 100–21.

Clark, G. (1995) *Performance Related Pay in the Public Sector*. London, Social Market Foundation.

Dyer, L. and Schwab, D. (1982) Personnel/human resource management research. In Kochan, T., Mitchell, D. and Dyer, L. (eds), *Industrial Relations Research in the 1970s*. Madison, Wis., Industrial Relations Research Association.

Etzioni, A. (1975) *A Comparative Analysis of Complex Organizations*. New York, Free Press.

Etzioni, A. (1988) *The Moral Dimension*. New York, Free Press.

Fowler, A. (1990) Performance management: The MBO of the 1990s. *Personnel Management*, 22, pp. 75–80.

Galbraith, J. and Cummings, L. L. (1967) An empirical investigation of the motivational determination of task performance. *Organizational Behaviour and Human Performance*, 2, pp. 237–57.

Gallie, D. and White, M. (1992) *Employee Commitment and the Skills Revolution*. London, Policy Studies Institute.

Georgopoulos, B. S., Mahoney, G. M. and Jones, N. W. (1957) A path–goal approach to productivity. *Journal of Applied Psychology*, 41, pp. 345–53.

Goodswen, M. (1988) Retention and reward of the high achiever. *Personnel Management*, Oct., pp. 61–4.

Heneman, R. L. (1992) *Merit Pay: Linking Pay Increases to Performance Ratings*. Reading, Mass., Addison-Wesley.

Hofstede, G. (1980) *Culture's Consequences*. Beverly Hills, Sage.

Hollis M. and Nell, E. J. (1975) *Rational Economic Man: A Philosophical Critique of Neo-classical Economics*. London, Cambridge University Press.

Iles, P. A. and Mabey, C. (1993) Managerial career development programmes: Effectiveness, availability and acceptability. *British Journal of Management*, 4, pp. 103–18.

Ilgen, D. (1990) *Pay for Performance: Motivational Issues*. Washington, DC, National Research Council.

Ilgen, D., Fisher, C. and Taylor, S. (1979) Consequences of individual feedback on behavior in organizations. *Journal of Applied Psychology*, 64, pp. 347–71.

Jensen, M. C. and Meckling, W. H. (1979) Rights and production functions: An application to labour-managed firms and co-determination. *Journal of Business*, 52, 469–506.

Jevons, W. S. (1883) *Methods of Social Reform*. London, Macmillan.

Johnson, G. and Scholes, K. (1984) *Exploring Corporate Strategy*. London, Prentice Hall.

Kanter, R. M. (1989) *When Giants Learn to Dance*. London, Unwin.

Kraiger, K. and Ford, J. (1985) A meta-analysis of rat race effects in performance ratings. *Journal of Applied Psychology*, 70, pp. 56–65.

Landy, F., Farr, J. and Jacobs, R. (1982) Utility concepts in performance measurement. *Organizational Behaviour and Human Performance*, 30, pp. 15–40.

Leibenstein, H. (1966) Allocative efficiency versus x efficiency. *American Economic Review*, 56, pp. 392–413.

Leibenstein, H. (1976) *Beyond Economic Man*. Cambridge, Mass., Harvard University Press.

Lewin, K. (1938) *Conceptual Representation*. Durham, NC, Duke University Press.

Locke, E. A., Shaw, K. N., Saari, L. M. and Latham, G. P. (1981) Goal setting and task performance 1969–1980. *Psychological Bulletin*, 90, pp. 125–52.

Longenecker, C., Sims, H. and Gioia, D. (1987) Behind the mask: The politics of employee appraisal. *Academy of Management Executive*, 1, pp.183–93.

McKersie, R. B. (1986) The promise of gain-sharing. *ILR Report*, fall, pp. 7–11.

Marsden, D. and Richardson, R. (1992) *Motivation and Performance Related Pay in the Public Sector: A Case Study of the Inland Revenue*. London, LSE Centre for Economic Performance Discussion Paper no. 75.

Marshall, A. (1906) *Principles of Economics*. London, Macmillan.

Maslow, A. H. (1954) *Motivation and Personality*. New York, Harper.

Mento, A. J., Steel, R. P. and Karren, R. J. (1987) A meta-analytic study of task performance: 1966–1984. *Organizational Behaviour and Human Decision Processes*, 39, pp. 52–83.

Miceli, M. P. and Near, J. P. (1988) Correlates of satisfaction with pay level and pay system in pay for performance plans. Paper presented to National Academy of Management, Anaheim, Calif.

Milkovich, G. T. and Wigdor, A. K. (eds) (1991) *Pay for Performance*. Washington, DC, National Academy of Sciences.

Mintzberg, H. (1992) Five Ps for strategy. In Mintzberg, H. and Quinn, J., *The Strategy Process*. Englewood Cliffs, NJ, Prentice-Hall.

Mitchell, T. R. (1980) Motivation: New directions for theory research and practice. *Academy of Management Review*, 7, pp. 80–8.

Pearce, J. L. and Perry, J. L. (1983) Federal merit pay: A longitudinal analysis. *Public Administration Review*, 43, pp. 315–25.

Perry, J. and Porter, L. (1982) Factors affecting the context for motivation in public organizations. *Academy of Management Review*, 7, pp. 89–98.

Pritchard, R. and Curts, M. (1973) The influence of goal setting and financial incentives on task performance. *Organizational Behaviour and Human Performance*, 10, pp. 175–83.

Schein, E. (1984) Coming to a new awareness of organizational culture. *Sloan Management Review*, winter, pp. 3–16.

Tolman, E. C. (1932) *Purposive Behaviour in Animals and Men*. New York, Century.

Tonnies, F. (1922) Gemeinschaft and Gesellschaft. Berlin, Curtins.

Vroom, V. (1964) *Work and Motivation*. New York, Wiley.

Walsh, E. (1992) Management accounting and the measurement of business performance: some dilemmas. In Bradley K. (ed.), *Human Resource Management: People and Performance*. Aldershot, Dartmouth.

Wyatt (1989) Getting your hands round performance management. *The Wyatt Communicator*, 4th quarter, pp. 4–18.

5 Industrial and Work-place Relations

This chapter was contributed by Ed Rose.

Learning Objectives

- *explain the nature of the contradictions between human resource (HR) and industrial relations (IR) strategies at work-place level and beyond.*
- *describe the emergence of the 'new' IR.*
- *explain the nature of IR/HRM within both unionized and non-unionized organizations.*
- *identify the major IR/HRM issues relating to both public- and private-sector organizations.*
- *discuss the impact of human resource strategies upon IR at the work place.*

Introduction

It is the intention in this chapter to examine critically the interplay between industrial relations (IR) and human resource management (HRM).

The main theme which underlies this chapter is based on the assumption that there are many contradictions both in theory and in practice between HRM and IR at work-place level and beyond.

The *central* contradiction concerns the very essence of the nature of HRM and IR. IR has been traditionally concerned with *collective representation* of employees. This means that through the process of *collective bargaining*, employee representatives (usually shop stewards/convenors and/or full-time union officials) negotiate with employer representatives over a range of *substantive* issues (such as pay, working conditions, and working arrangements) and *procedural* arrangements (such as disciplinary, disputes and redundancy procedures). Trade unions by their very nature are concerned with protecting the interests of the sellers of labour (the employees), and with securing the highest price for that labour. Employers (the buyers of labour), on the other hand, wish to buy labour at the lowest cost to themselves. There is, therefore, a *conflict of interest* between employees and their representatives, and employers and their representatives. The conflict is ever present and needs to be continually regulated through the process of collective bargaining.

HRM emphasizes, amongst other things, the *commitment* of the individual employee to the employer's organization. The main contradiction referred to above is between the *individualism* of the HRM approach to the employment relationship and the *collectivism* of the IR approach to that relationship.

More recently, however, for reasons which will be considered later, there have been some attempts to incorporate certain aspects of IR within HRM (researchers disagree about the extent of this development), and this has given rise to speculation about the emergence of a contemporary form of IR called 'The New Industrial Relations' (Millward, 1994).

The remainder of this introductory section will be concerned with identifying the relevant components of IR and exploring the main problem areas and issues which impact upon HRM/HRS within the employment relationship.

Industrial relations defined

IR has been defined as 'a particular set of phenomena associated with regulating the human activity of employment' (Salamon, 1992, p. 29). A more detailed definition is offered by Rollinson (1993, p. 4) as follows:

> The study of the relationship between an organization and its employees. This covers the full range of collective and individual interactions and communications between employers and employees, and also the processes by which they adjust to the needs and wants of each other.

Four important characteristics of IR implicit within the definitions provided above are now highlighted:

The *first* characteristic concerns *focus*. IR is composed of a number of contrasting disciplines and perspectives but there is, nevertheless, a degree of consensus about what is being examined within the British context. Baine and Clegg (1974), for example, state that IR is 'the study of the rules governing employment and the ways in which the rules are changed, interpreted and administered'. The rule-making process, which includes collective bargaining, is enacted within institutions and organizations such as trade unions, management and employers' associations, the state and its agencies. Hence the primary focus of IR resides 'in the institutions taking part in rule-making, the processes of interaction between the parties and the rules that result' (Rollinson, 1993).

The *second* characteristic concerns the *level of analysis*. IR traditionally concerns itself with wider socio-economic and political variables such as social class, property ownership, political ideologies and economic policies, and the extent to which these impact upon the organization of work. For example, Marxist perspectives (now largely in abeyance), place particular emphasis upon the nature of the capitalist political economy in attempting to explain manifest and latent IR conflicts (Hyman, 1975). A major assumption here is that IR conflicts are endemic and inevitable, and mirror conflicts of class within the wider society. By way of contrast, the 'systems' perspective of IR (Dunlop, 1957) emphasizes consensus rather than conflict and the extent to which the main parties to IR (state, trade unions, employers and their associations) reconcile conflicts and generate consensus via the rule-making/collective bargaining process.

A *third* characteristic of IR is the emphasis upon *the role of trade unions* both within and outside the organization of work. Within the organization, unions are the main vehicle for presenting collective issues concerning pay, working conditions, etc. Outside the work organization, trade unions, collectively represented by the Trade Union Congress (TUC), act as a political and economic pressure group by attempting to influence government policy.

Finally, IR unsurprisingly assumes differences and conflicts of interests between employees (the sellers of labour) and employers (the buyers of labour), and stresses the rule-making or collective bargaining process as a means of resolving these conflicts. Rule-making is normally a collective process involving representatives of employees and employers, the outcome of which is the *collective agreement*. Collective bargaining operates at work-place or unit level, at organization or company level and at industry level, and may involve more than one union (multi-union bargaining) or more than one employer (multi-employer bargaining).

Figure 5.1 summarizes the system of IR both internal and external to the organization together with the processes characterizing it.

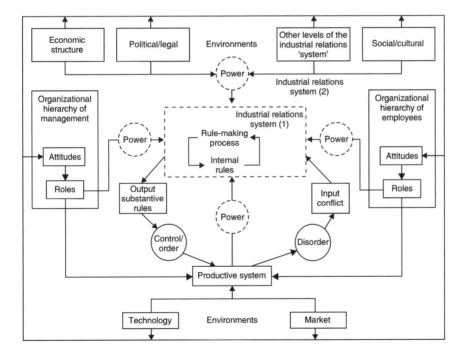

Figure 5.1 The system of industrial relations
Source: Salamon, 1992, p. 47.

Industrial relations and HRM

The central issue with which this chapter concerns itself relates to the extent to which HRM are either compatible with, or opposed to, IR at work-place, organizational and strategic levels. Below we will attempt to establish the background to the debate and identify some of the contradictions and arguments within it.

The background to the debate

HRM and related developments are well documented (Storey, 1992; Storey and Sisson, 1993; Salaman et al., 1992; Oliver and Wilkinson, 1992). HRM emerged in Britain during the mid-1980s after originating in the United States, and could be described as 'the Americanised version of "Japanese" methods' (Storey, 1992). Its development has been somewhat haphazard and eclectic, there being no single, consistent approach to HRM in most organizations which have, by their own admission, adopted such practices. The main reason for this, as Storey goes on to argue, is that HRM is subject to different interpretations both theoretically/strategically, and operationally. For example, HRM is often taken to be synonymous with personnel management; a label change is often considered sufficient, but this merely masks the same old practices and policies. Many organizations go further and attempt to integrate the various personnel management techniques (including elements of IR) in a systematic way. Guest (1989) identifies the former as a weak version of HRM, and the latter as a stronger interpretation which has a philosophical underpinning, setting it apart from Taylorism/Fordism, on the one hand, and from pluralistic conventions of IR orthodoxy on the other. In essence, the 'strong' approach involves interventions at strategic level within an organization in order to foster employee commitment and 'resourcefulness', where these interventions are designed to utilize labour resources to the full and are integrated within an overall business/corporate strategy. As Sisson (1993) states, invoking Kanter (1988), it means 'doing more with less'.

According to Storey (1992), very few organizations fully co-ordinated their IR within an HRM strategy. Storey conducted his research within 15 unionized organizations, two of which are in the public sector. The research does not claim to be representative of either the public or private sectors as a whole, and conclusions derived from the research may therefore be valid only for larger unionized organizations with relatively sophisticated HR policies and strategies. Nevertheless, Storey's findings, while unrepresentative of non-union and smaller organizations, indicated for his organizational sample at least, that:

> While the old-style industrial relations was disavowed, or even scorned, there
> was hardly an instance where anything approaching a 'strategic' stance

towards unions and industrial relations could be readily discerned as having taken its place.

(p. 259)

Moreover, IR is often regarded as low priority and almost irrelevant to serving the needs of the market, and subordinate to new or recently introduced methods of dealing with the human resource. HRM initiatives have tended, at least initially, to focus on managerial grades with only a piecemeal and haphazard extension of these initiatives to the remainder of the workforce. Edwards et al. (1992) reinforce the argument by stating that:

> There is little evidence that British firms have developed a strategic approach to industrial relations.
>
> (p. 60)

This assertion would appear to be valid for both unionized and non-unionized organizations (Storey and Sisson, 1993; McLoughlin and Gourlay, 1994). Edwards et al. cite as examples, poor training records, adoption and then abandonment of 'fads' such as quality circles, and little interest shown by employers in co-ordinating pay bargaining 'so that the system of wage determination remained anarchic' (1992, p. 60).

As a consequence of major changes affecting IR during the 1980s (which are dealt with later in this chapter), the (albeit unsystematic) HRM onslaught, itself symptomatic of employers gaining the upper hand in IR, has had a fragmenting effect on both internal and external labour markets. For example, HRM raises the spectre of 'individualization' of IR through the inception of performance-related pay, individual appraisals, the steady erosion of collective bargaining involving decentralization of bargaining structures and the supplanting of collective regulation by other means such as direct communication structures and employee involvement practices which de-emphasize union representation.

A further example is the 'Japanization' effect, which provides opportunity and greater scope for HRM interventions to take place. Many HRM practices are often the functional equivalents of practices found in major Japanese corporations. Oliver and Wilkinson (1992) argue that where firms in their sample analysis had some sort of HRM input, emphasizing, for example, a high value on product and service quality, a customer- or market-driven ethos, and rigorous measurement of individual and unit performance, then 'a capacity for flexibility, innovation and continuous improvement is frequently found alongside these attributes' (p. 176).

Finally, the continued bifurcation of the labour market has resulted in the emergence and growth of a 'peripheral' workforce with little job security and employment protection and, in the public sector, the ongoing process of compulsory competitive tendering (CCT) has led to a further deterioration in conditions of service and reductions in wages for the vast majority of affected employees. A study of the effects of CCT in the NHS (Milne, 1987) found that CCT resulted in compulsory redundancies, while Ascher (1987) noted a similar trend within local authority cleansing services. CCT has affected pay in two ways, leading firstly to major changes in bonus schemes, and secondly to a 're-orientation of hours worked by individual employees, more specifically a reduction in holiday and overtime and an increased use of part-time workers' (Marsh, 1992, p. 232).

The ER/IR relationship with HRM is therefore an uneasy one. This unease manifests itself both strategically and operationally. It is difficult to marry traditional or orthodox IR with HRM since IR has a mainly collective orientation while HRM's concerns in its 'hard' and 'soft' aspects are largely individualistic. To be sure, the 'individualist' components of IR such as disciplinary matters, grievance and redundancy procedures, and rules governing unfair dismissals and harassment, can often be relatively easily integrated, but the incorporation within HRM remains partial and potentially conflictual, as box 5.1 exemplifies.

Box 5.1 Does 'hard' and 'soft' HRM breed confrontation?

'It is easy to see that the hard faces of HRM will often place it in confrontation with trade unions – especially in those settings where unions still retain some strength. For example, London Underground's wide-ranging plan consists of a package of measures which include staff reductions, salary status for all employees, the abolition of premium pay for weekend working, a reduction in the number of separate grades of staff from 400 to 70, and the replacement of promotion based on seniority to one based on assessed merit. A central plank in its attempted reform of working practices is the tackling of 'split shifts' where drivers work the morning and evening rush hours, take the middle part of the day off but are paid for 12 hours. At the time of writing, the Rail, Maritime and Transportation Union (RMT) is planning an indefinite strike in response to a breakdown in negotiations on this package.

But even the 'soft' aspects – increased communication with employees, team participation techniques, harmonisation of terms and conditions, appraisal and reward – can lead to difficulties between management and unions. The basic reason for this is that whether hard or soft aspects are being activated, HRM in broad terms represents, or is seen as, a departure from the 'joint procedure' formula. To this extent, Guest's (1989) summation would seem to be correct: HRM and trade unionism are incompatible.

But under competitive conditions some sort of *modus vivendi* between industrial relations and HRM (between collectivism and individualism) would appear to be necessary. In some situations managers may choose to take the route of trying to dispense with the unions and thus clear the way for human resource management methods without the need for compromise. Certain greenfield site start-ups and certain NHS Trusts have taken this path. But in the latter cases there are examples where the reality of continuing union membership and the lack of trust emanating from management's refusal to recognise trade unions has eventually led to a decision to recognise the union - albeit on terms relatively more favourable to management than hitherto.

The implication is that in the larger number of cases in the British context some degree of *balance* between individualism and collectivism will have to be struck. This will clearly involve compromises on both sides. The precise nature of that balance and the way it can be managed is currently something of an open question. This issue is at the cutting edge of contemporary practice in the management of human resources and industrial relations.' (Storey and Sisson, 1993, pp. 17–18.)

Contradictions and complementarities

The interface between HRM and IR is problematic. What is at issue here is the *impact* of HRM upon intra-organizational IR and the internal labour market. The overall message of human resource policy is clear enough, as Beaumont (1991b) states:

> The key messages in the HRM literature are a strategic focus, the need for HRM policies and practices to be consistent with the nature of overall business strategy, the need for individual components of a HRM package to mutually reinforce each other and be consistent with corporate culture; teamwork, flexibility, individual employee involvement and commitment are the leading watchwords of this approach.
>
> (p. 300)

However, the impact of HRM upon IR will vary along a range of criteria, the most significant being, within the British context, *the presence or absence of unionization*.

Within *unionized* organizations, the generalized union response as espoused by the TUC, according to Beaumont, is that HRM developments have the potential to individualize IR by rupturing the collective bargaining process with a view to the eventual substitution of union presence in some organizations. Nevertheless, notwithstanding this broad framework response, individual unions have developed their own varied strategies for dealing with HRM/HRS. The EEPTU, for example, has positively endorsed HRM developments, particularly within the greenfield site single-union context. With regard to quality circles, for example, Beaumont cites the EEPTU General Secretary as follows:

> I have no hesitation in advising trade unions to explore with their managements and with their fellow workers how forming such (quality) circles can bring benefits to them as individuals as well as to their organisations. Such involvement would improve personal satisfaction and pride in the job as well as boosting our national performance at the level where a real remedy to our problems lies – in the plant and in the company.
>
> (1991b, p. 306)

On the other hand, the TGWU is still critical of HRM developments as encapsulated in the following statement by its General Secretary:

> We wish to make it clear that the union does not advocate or promote participation in these new-style management techniques.
>
> (Beaumont 1991b, p. 306)

The variety of union responses to HRM and the 'new employment practices' (NEPs) associated with it is noted by Marchington (1994, p. 13), who states:

> British trade unions have responded in different ways to this [HRM] movement, ranging from defensive opposition through traditional negotiations to strategic engagement with HRM. To a large extent the union reaction depends upon their historical relationship with managements and their perception of what managers are seeking from the introduction of NEPs.

A further contribution to the debate (Bacon and Storey, 1994, p. 3) argues that:

> The new emphasis upon the individual employees in management strategies suggests that any notion of a standardised group of workers pursuing similar interests has become increasingly difficult to sustain.

Bacon and Storey (1994) also argue that there has been a 'drift' in union responses and strategies towards both individualism and collectivism, but essentially unions have moved towards an 'individualist' agenda in reflecting the wishes of union members while the 'collectivism' increasingly being adopted by unions is one of closer institutional partnership (where possible) with employers. This latter development is reflected in the growth of the 'New Industrial Relations' considered below.

Within *non-unionized* organizations the relationship between IR and HRM is rather less clear-cut. A growing number of private-sector establishments, particularly those set up since 1980, are non-union (Millward et al., 1992).

Compared with those that are unionized, non-union establishments provide fewer rights and benefits to employees, fewer opportunities to give or receive information, and less scope for employees to voice either constructive suggestions or dissent. Consequently, there is a higher level of absence, labour turnover and dismissal than in comparable unionized plants (Millward, 1994).

Guest and Hoque (1994) identify four possible types of non-union establishment based on (a) whether or not they have a human resource strategy, and (b) the nature of HRM policy and practice. This typology is shown in box 5.2.

Box 5.2 Types of non-union establishment

1   Establishments having a clear HRM strategy using optimistic and positive HRM practices which represent the 'good' face of non-unionism with *high-involvement management* and *high commitment.*
2   Establishments having a clear strategy but making little use of HRM practices and which provide a minimum level of workers' rights. The strategy is geared towards depriving workers of many of their traditional rights including a voice of any sort. They represent the *'ugly'* face of non-unionism and are *efficiency driven.*
3   Establishments which do not have a clear HRM strategy but have adopted many innovative-type HRM practices by stumbling upon them, by copying others or by following 'fads'. This type of establishment may be described as the *'lucky'* face of non-unionism.
4   Establishments having no HRM strategy and low uptake of HRM practices. This reflects poor management in which human resource issues have not been properly considered, and which represent the *'bad'* face of non-unionism. (Source: Guest and Hoque, 1994, p. 2.)

Guest and Hoque's research is part of a larger study of HRM in greenfield sites and examines data from 1,000 new establishments mainly set up since 1980 and which are UK, American, Japanese and German owned. The conclusions of this survey are now summarized.

The first conclusion is that contrary to expectations, the UK-owned establishments claim to be in the vanguard of HRM. At the other extreme, the Germans are least enthusiastic.

The second conclusion concerns differences in the range of outcomes across non-union establishment types. The *good* establishments consistently report the best results for HRM, employee relations and performance outcomes. In contrast, the *bad* establishments consistently report the poorest outcomes. The *ugly* reveal a mixed pattern with some positive outcomes but have distinct problems with IR. Some staff appear to dislike this strategy and vote with their feet, and the researchers state:

> In this respect our results complement those obtained by Millward (1994) who found the greatest number of non-union establishments falling into what we have termed the *bad* or *ugly* categories in his larger WIRS 3 sample.
>
> (p. 13)

The final conclusion is that 'the results demonstrate that HRM/HRS pays off. The *good* with their full utilisation strategy reflected in the extensive use of HRM practices report better results on the three sets of outcomes' (HRM, employee relations, performance). The *bad* report the worst outcomes. Therefore in new, non-union establishments 'HRM is a feasible and sensible strategy to pursue'.

Guest and Hoque's findings would also appear to be consistent with those of McLoughlin and Gourlay (1992, 1994) who examined the extent of non-unionism and IR in the high-technology sector in south-east England. Essentially they argue that:

> Our findings do not lend support to the idea that HRM policies are the exclusive, most predominant, form of management approach to employee relations. Rather, a range of approaches manifested in different management styles have been identified which appear to be related to, but not determined by, both labour and product units as well as factors such as size and age of establishment. . . . The new approach stresses the importance of allowing for the co-existence of individual and collective approaches in the regulation of different aspects of the employment relationship. Thus management styles will also vary according to the degree of 'strategic integration' with overall business policies.
>
> (McLoughlin and Gourlay, 1992, p. 690)

The remainder of the chapter will examine the issues raised in these introductory sections in greater detail. We shall consider the alleged 'retreat' of traditional IR, and the emergence of the 'new' IR within the context of HRM. This section also identifies the external factors which arguably have had a significant impact upon IR and the employment relationship during the 1980s and 1990s. Whether these developments have given rise to a 'sea change' in IR and subsequent incorporation of much of this area into HRM is still open to debate, but the weight of empirical evidence to date appears to confirm the 'incorporation' hypothesis, at least partially. Then we shall consider the two examples of *pay determination* and *trade union exclusion and union de-recognition* in assessing the extent to which these traditional IR processes have been subsumed within organizations' human resource strategies. The final section looks at the relationship between HRM and more specifically HRS and IR.

Is There a 'New' Industrial Relations?

The retreat of traditional industrial relations

Britain's changing pattern of IR has been well documented and analysed thanks to the detailed and comprehensive research data accumulated by the three Workplace Industrial Relations Surveys (Daniel and Millward, 1983; Millward and Stevens, 1986; Millward et al., 1992). The retreat of traditional IR during the 1980s has been accompanied by a concomitant growth of the 'new' IR. Using the Workplace Industrial Relations Survey (WIRS) database, Millward (1994) provides an accurate picture of traditional IR's retreat, as summarized below.

1 From 1984–90 within the trading sector of the economy, the decline in collective representation of employees by recognized trade unions was 'stark and incontrovertible' (Millward, 1994, p. 119). Within the survey the number of work places with recognized unions fell from 52 to 40 per cent during the period.

2 De-recognition of trade unions accounted for a significant part of this decline. Almost 20 per cent of work places that reported recognized unions in 1984 had no recognized unions in 1990. There was no 'half-way house' from full to partial recognition. 'When managements withdrew trade union recognition they did so comprehensively' (ibid., p. 119).

3 Much of the continuing recognition of unions could be explained by a desire of senior management to maintain existing centralized arrangements for the determination of pay. 'Only if union support dwindled substantially across entire companies or enterprises does it seem likely that wholesale de-recognition would become a likely prospect' (ibid., p. 120).

4 Another major reason for decline in union recognition is the changing population of work places. The significant development here lies in the substantially lower likelihood of newer establishments recognizing unions – around 30 per cent of newer work places did so compared with 40 per cent of all work places in 1990. The explanation for this, according to Millward, 'appeared to be the removal of statutory support for union recognition and the decline in the presumption by managements and the state in favour of collective bargaining between trade unions and employers' (ibid., p. 120).

5   Finally, Millward notes that the rate of turnover among establishments
     was higher in the 1980s than in previous years. 'New establishments
     were being created at a faster rate which, with their lower rate of
     recognition, accentuated the decline in the overall extent of recognition'
     (ibid., p. 121).

What, then, is the 'new' industrial relations?

The 'new industrial relations' embraces *three* distinct patterns of IR arrangements which distinguish it from the patterns of the past. These are now
considered in turn.

The 'Japanese model'

This is exemplified by the Toshiba Consumer Products factory set up in
Plymouth in 1981. (See box 5.3)

Box 5.3   The Toshiba package

Sole bargaining rights for a single trade union.
A 'no-strike' agreement with binding 'final offer' arbitration as a last
resort in disputes of interest.
A broadly based forum for consultation and employee participation.
'Single status' conditions of employment.
Complete freedom on the part of management to organize work.
(Trevor, 1988, pp. 221–42.)

The proliferation of single union representation and agreements within
'greenfield' sites since the early 1980s is not a uniquely Japanese-inspired
phenomenon. Many trade unions such as the TGWU and the EETPU, in
the face of declining membership, have, with varying degrees of enthusiasm, encouraged such developments. The claimed advantages of a single
union are that bargaining and consultation are simplified, that disputes are
less likely and that introducing flexible working arrangements is made
easier. According to Bevan (1987, p. 9):

> The fact that agreements are single union, at a stroke, removes many of the
> potential obstacles to flexibility. Inter-union demarcation lines are a thing of
> the past and flexibility depends on nothing more than receiving the necessary
> training to carry out the task required.

Table 5.1 provides two measures of union presence in trading-sector work
places; the presence of a single union, where there are members present,

Table 5.1 Measures of union presence

Sector	Any union member (%)	A single union (%)
All industry and commerce	51	27
All manufacturing	58	29
Metals and mineral products	77	51
Chemicals and manufactured fibres	66	26
Metal goods	61	29
Mechanical engineering	73	27
Electrical and instrument engineering	40	22
Vehicles and transport equipment	52	24
Food, drink and tobacco	51	17
Textiles	76	45
Leather, footwear and clothing	43	33
Timber and furniture, paper and printing	63	28
Rubber, plastics and other manufacturing	32	23
All services	48	27
Energy and water	96	6
Construction	57	46
Wholesale distribution	40	31
Retail distribution	46	40
Hotels, catering, repairs	13	9
Transport	75	35
Posts and telecommunications	99	1
Banking, finance, insurance	88	47
Business services	16	15
Other services	47	28

Source: Millward, 1994, p. 41.

and the presence of any union members among all establishments in the sector.

The second characteristic of these 'new-style' agreements concerns the 'no-strike' clause with dispute resolution in the last resort through pendulum arbitration. Although by the end of 1987, some 28 companies in Britain were known to have strike-free agreements (Oliver and Wilkinson, 1992), Millward (1994) found that these deals were extremely rare in British industry and states:

> A mere 1 percent of workplaces with recognised trade unions had pendulum arbitration and in workplaces with a sole union agreement the figure was less than half of 1 percent. In fact, pendulum arbitration was somewhat more common in multi-union workplaces. It was therefore by no means a distinctive element of 'new style agreements', as much of the literature has portrayed. Nor was it especially a feature of younger workplaces or of the industries, regions and trade unions in which the well-documented 'single union deals' have occurred. We concluded that pendulum arbitration was a rare practice, probably not increasing dramatically in its incidence and

probably of longer standing than the single union deals of the mid to late 1980s. As a distinctive development in British industrial relations, pendulum arbitration has yet to reach the point of take off.

(Millward, 1994, pp. 123–4)

A third element of the new IR is the company advisory board or company council. These boards are often regarded as necessary to provide further stability and predictability in IR. The boards comprise elected representatives who are not necessarily shop stewards or trade union members and are chosen by non-union as well as unionized employees, providing a forum for negotiations on pay and conditions where traditional demarcations between consultation and negotiation are eliminated. Companies adopting this system often experience conflicts of interest as a result of the shift of responsibilities from shop stewards to the boards. In relation to Nissan's deal with the AEU, for example, Crowther and Garrahan (1988, p. 56) claim that:

> it allows virtually no independent role for shop stewards, and whilst it appears that the company does not intend to actively obstruct union activities, the mechanisms for representation are highly supportive of non-union participation.

An argument in support of the company board is, that as a consultative mechanism, it disseminates company information on important matters that UK companies have tended to keep secret – but even this concession is dependent on the goodwill of management.

According to the WIRS analysis conducted by Millward (1994), company boards are neither as popular nor as frequent as is often assumed. A mere 17 per cent of work places having a single union agreement bothered to set up boards, and this was little different from single union work places *without* an agreement and from work places without any recognized unions.

A further characteristic feature of the new IR concerns single status employment conditions. Based on examining differences between manual and non-manual employees, Millward found that only around one in eight work places had equality of employment conditions. In this respect:

> workplaces with sole union agreements were no different from the generality of workplaces in this respect.

(Millward, 1994, p. 125)

A final element of the new IR within the single union representation context concerns the freedom of management to organize work at the establishment in any way it thought fit. Millward (1994) found that:

> management flexibility . . . was widespread. Nearly three quarters of workplaces with recognised trade unions were reported to have complete management flexibility. It was hardly something unique to workplaces with 'single

union deals'. In fact, workplaces with sole union agreements were no more and no less likely to have management flexibility. They simply reflected the common reality of the widespread lack of union influence upon issues of work organisation. Management flexibility was more widespread in younger workplaces and . . . in those with lower levels of union membership. When we looked at single union workplaces . . . it appeared that sole union agreements were associated with less management flexibility, not more as the stereotype of the 'single union deal' had suggested.

(p. 124)

Management/worker flexibility is therefore far more widespread and diffuse within British industry and certainly not confined to single union contexts. It is, perhaps, the single most important factor which characterizes and distinguishes the new IR, and is as common in multi-union, as in single union organizations, in British-owned, as in foreign-owned companies.

The content of flexibility agreements vary around a common core as exemplified in the abstracts from the Komatsu–AEU, and the Hitachi–EEPU agreements (box 5.4).

Box 5.4   Flexibility deals in Komatsu and Hitachi

'In *Komatsu* there is complete flexibility and mobility of employees; changes in processes and practices will be introduced to increase competitiveness and . . . these will improve productivity and affect manning levels. To achieve such change, employees will work as required by the company and participate in the training of themselves or other employees as required. Manning levels will be determined by the company using appropriate industrial engineering and manpower planning techniques.

In *Hitachi*, all company members will agree the complete flexibility of jobs and duties . . . When necessary to fit the needs of the business, all company members may be required to perform whatever jobs and duties are within their capability. The company accepts its responsibility to train, retrain and develop company members to broaden their skills, grow their potential and meet the needs of rapid technological change. The company also accepts that in the instances where more competitive manning levels can be achieved by agreed flexibility, . . . manning levels will be achieved without compulsory redundancy.' (Oliver and Wilkinson, 1992, pp. 293–4.)

More established companies with established unions and agreements have greater problems in introducing such arrangements, and although the UK motor industry has made considerable progress in implementing Japanese-style manufacturing techniques, it has not so readily changed its industrial relations. One notable exception to this is Rover, which recently introduced its 'New Deal' in a multi-union, multi-site context (Rose and Woolley, 1992). Box 5.5 outlines some of the main elements of Rover's New Deal.

Box 5.5   The 'New Deal' at Rover

Following Guest's 'stronger' version of HRM, it would appear that Rover has adapted this distinctive approach to ER management which incorporates the following principles:

1   Strategic interventions designed to elicit commitment and to develop 'resourceful' employees.
2   Strategic interventions designed to secure full utilization of labour resources.
3   Both interventions (1) and (2) above to be integrated within the business strategy.

The outcome of this strategic approach to HRM was the 'New Deal' which is summarized below:

1   Rover will be a single-status Company. We are all employees and the only distinction is the contribution we make. All remaining distinctions between 'staff and hourly-paid' status will be ended.
2   Continuous improvement will be a requirement for everyone – the Company must continually improve its performance and competitive position through the elimination of waste, increased levels of efficiency and reduced levels of manpower – 'working smarter rather than harder'.
3   Employees will be expected to be flexible subject to their ability to do the job, after training if necessary, and subject to safe working practices being observed.
4   There will be maximum devolution of authority and account-ability to the employees actually doing the job. Teams will be responsible for quality of work, routine maintenance, process improvements, cost reduction, work allocation, job rotation, training of each other, material control.

> 5   It is our intention to establish a single grade structure for all our people.
>
> 6   Productivity bonus schemes will be progressively phased out.
>
> 7   Employees who want to work for Rover will be able to stay with Rover.
>
> 8   Constant open and honest two-way communications with employees throughout the Company will be the norm. The process of daily, weekly, monthly and annual employee briefings will be strengthened.
>
> 9   All of us will be expected to participate in Discussion Groups, Quality Action Teams, Suggestion Schemes, and all other activities to continuously improve processes and Company performance.
>
> 10   Employees will continue to have the opportunity to be represented by the recognized Trades Unions.
>
> 11   Consultation with representatives of recognized Trades Unions will be enhanced to ensure maximum understanding of Company performance, competitive practices and standards, product and Company plans and all areas of activity affecting the Company and its employees. (Source: Rover Document.)

The 'New Deal' arrangements at Rover represented the culmination of its 'Total Quality Initiative' (TQI) which began in 1987. After initial resistance from the shop floor, a survey of managers and convenors (Rose and Woolley, 1992) revealed a general endorsement of TQI. The 'New Deal' built upon the TQI and was the result of extensive consultation and negotiation between management and senior convenors. While HRM assumptions and the 'Japanization' elements are important constituents of the 'New Deal' policy, the company's multi-union structure remains intact and collective IR, despite moves towards 'single-table' bargaining, has not been eroded. Rover's improved performance during recent years, together with the relative absence of industrial disputes, would appear to vindicate this policy. The 'New Deal' also represents a further stage of the organizational cultural change process and an unfolding HRS which emphasizes co-operation rather than conflict, and which contrasts starkly with the conflict-ridden years of Rover's past.

Union avoidance and de-recognition

The second component of the 'new' IR concerns the complete and continuing avoidance of trade union involvement. Millward (1994) states:

> Union avoidance at new workplaces was far less controversial and thus attracted much less public attention. In many private sector industries, par-

ticularly those dominated by small independent firms, the absence of trade unions has always been the common pattern. But as yet we do not know whether union avoidance has become a more common feature of newer workplaces or if the processes of maturation that sometimes led to unionisation have been attenuated.

(p. 2)

There is growing evidence that trade union de-recognition has intensified and support for trade unions has weakened amongst employees in unionized organizations. This issue will be considered in greater detail below in the section on strategy.

The challenge of human resource management

While the developments identified so far in this section help to establish what the 'new' IR is, it should be emphasized that in the absence of HRM, the benefits of these developments to employers and employees, particularly in relation to single union representation, single status, flexibility and employee involvement will be less likely to be fully realized. It is, therefore, crucially important to emphasize and acknowledge that the 'new' IR should ideally be part and parcel of an organization's established HRM framework, and that those organizations such as the 'good' in Guest and Hoque's (1994) typology (referred to earlier) are the ones most likely to be successful.

The totality of the relationship between HRM and IR has been considered above. As far as the 'new,' IR is concerned, however, it is necessary briefly to consider the impact of HRM within both unionized and nonunionized contexts, again using the analysis of WIRS data. A summary of the main WIRS findings is provided in box 5.6.

Box 5.6 Summary of WIRS findings

1 Multiple channels of communication more likely to be used in unionized work places.
2 Non-union work places are characterized by authoritarian and hierarchical management practice.
3 Non-unionized workers had few opportunities to influence their working lives.
4 Workers in unionized companies received more information about their conditions of work than employees in non-union companies.
5 'Financial participation' was as common in unionized as non-unionized firms.
6 The most anti-union employers were least likely to offer financial participation schemes.

> 7 Single status was found as frequently in unionized as in non-union companies.
>
> 8 The most anti-union employers were least likely to offer single status.
>
> 9 Unionized employers were more likely to collect information on the general composition of their workforce and pursue equal opportunities policies.

Additional analysis undertaken by Millward and presented by Monks (1994) reinforces the conclusion that *there is no necessary correlation between HRM and anti-unionism.* Furthermore, Monks states (p. 43):

> The more anti-union the employer the less likely it is that HRM techniques will be used. But it should be noted that relatively few employers were implementing the HRM agenda in a systematic way. WIRS revealed a 'pick and mix' approach to the HRM menu, with one or two items being selected without any consideration of the wider implications for the company.

There is, to be sure, a wide gap between the rhetoric of HRM 'speak' and the reality of the work place. While at strategic level HRM is often espoused in accommodatory terms, emphasizing the treatment of employees as 'assets', fostering a broadly based communications system, and involving employees in the organization and planning of work, the work-place experience of employees, and in particular, unionized employees sometimes suggests otherwise. According to the latter perspective, HRM is associated with union de-recognition and a systematic attempt to undermine the union role, and to some extent the WIRS survey and analysis confirms this view. However, there is one significant caveat to be made here which concerns company size and HRM. A large proportion of companies within the *Financial Times* top 50 recognize trade unions and implement at least some 'IR friendly' HRM policies focusing upon information, consultation and employee involvement. Conversely, going down the size scale, the *smaller* the company, the more likely it is to be union free, and where there is a union presence, the more hostile the employer is to that presence.

Notwithstanding the evidence – and most certainly more empirical evidence is required – the unavoidable conclusion is that within both unionized companies, and more especially non-unionized companies, employers have, at best, been only partially successful in developing a positive HRM agenda. The reason for this may lie in the absence of a formal statement of strategy (Hunter and MacInnes, 1994) owing to short-term financial pressures on British managers which prevent them from implementing long-term strategies to develop employee skills and attributes (Sisson, 1993). This issue is explored further below.

Factors influencing the emergence of the 'new' industrial relations

The coming of the 'new' IR has coincided with significant changes in the structure of the British economy. These changes are not only specific to Britain, but are also part of a general transformation of Western economies. Many of these economic changes, together with associated changes in the social structure have clearly affected the nature of IR and HRM. Lash and Urry (1987) have identified several elements which typify the recent transition of capitalism and these are paraphrased in box 5.7. (The HR implications of points 1 and 4 are explored further in chapter 8.)

Box 5.7 The transition of capitalism

1 There is a continuing trend towards globalization of markets and an increase in the scale of operations of large, transnational organizations on the one hand, and a lessening concentration of capital in national internal markets on the other. For Britain and western countries generally this implies a continuing erosion of the traditional manufacturing and extractive industrial base, with well-documented IR consequences such as the decline in union membership and density together with the consequent erosion of trade union power bases.

2 The fragmentation and eclipse of 'class' politics and hence of the (now passé) notion of 'working class solidarity'. In an industrial relations sense this means the increasing 'individualization' of industrial conflict and its counterpart, the individualization of managerial strategies of employee relations (Storey, 1992; Storey and Sisson, 1993).

3 A rapid decline in the manual 'core' working class as economies are de-industrialized. This has been a particularly significant ongoing trend during the 1980s, and has two consequences: first, the emergence of a permanently unemployed and increasingly unemployable underclass; and second, the condemnation of employed labour to an industrial diaspora of low-paid, under- or non-unionized and casualized work.

4 The uncritical adoption of capitalism by Third World countries which become primary producers, and the consequent 'servicization' of First World economies. In Britain the manufacture of

goods is now secondary to the manufacture of services and is reflected in the restructuring of the workforce and the employment relationship. Where pockets of manufacturing remain, manufacturing processes depend upon flexible labour which is increasingly feminized, casualized and subcontracted. Labour-intensive activities are exported to world market factories in the Third World, and to a much lesser extent to rural (greenfield) sites in the the First World. (Source: Lash and Urry, 1987.)

The background factors in box 5.7 play a crucially important part in assisting our understanding of IR change. There are, however, factors specific to the British context which have also facilitated the process. The 1980s in Britain witnessed the erosion of multi-employer representation in collective bargaining and a reduced role for employers' associations; a decline in collective bargaining as fewer work places recognized trade unions, and a reduction in the number of employees affected by collective bargaining. Another development during the 1980s was the continuing trend towards decentralization of pay determination. Evans et al. (1992), for example, argue that labour market deregulation was accompanied by a move towards decentralization of pay bargaining and pay structures within both public and private sectors, whereby employers considered more closely than hitherto the conditions operating within local labour markets, while existing national comparability claims were increasingly ignored.

Undoubtedly, the changing population of work places and employment restructuring during the 1980s provided a further impetus towards the devolution of bargaining structures and processes, but more importantly, and especially within those areas of the private sector where trade union organization was particularly sparse, terms and conditions of work for an increasing number of employees were more likely to be determined unilaterally by employers. Within the public sector, privatization and deregulation programmes have:

> increased employment fragmentation and casualisation [while] competitive tendering forced many workgroups to accept real and relative pay cuts and more intensive work routines in order to remain viable in the face of low wage competition from private sector firms.
>
> (Evans et al., 1992, p. 581)

Another important IR feature of the 1980s and 1990s was a succession of legislation summarized in box 5.8.

Box 5.8   Summary of employment legislation

1980 Employment Act

1 Definition of lawful picketing restricted to own place of work and picket lines restricted to six people; right to take secondary action restricted.
2 Eighty per cent support in a ballot needed to legalize a closed shop; funds offered for union ballots later taken up by many unions.
3 Repeal of statutory recognition procedure; restriction on unfair dismissal and maternity rights.

1982 Employment Act

1 Further restrictions on industrial action with definitions of what constitutes a trade dispute; employers can obtain injunctions against unions and sue for damages.
2 Compensation for dismissal because of closed shop.
3 Union-only clauses in commercial contracts removed.

1984 Trade Union Act

Executive elections to be held every five years by secret ballot; political fund ballots every ten years; secret ballots before industrial action.

1986 Public Order Act

Criminal offence in relation to picketing introduced.

1988 Employment Act

1 Unions to compensate members disciplined for not complying with majority decisions; members allowed to seek injunction if no pre-strike ballot held.
2 Union finances to be open to inspection; unions prevented from paying the fines of officials or members.
3 Action to preserve post-entry closed shop made unlawful.
4 Further restrictions on industrial action and election ballots.
5 Independent scrutiny of unions by specially appointed commissioner.

1989 Employment Act

1 Removal of restrictions on the work of women and young workers.
2 Exemption of small employer from providing details of disciplinary procedures.
3 Time off with pay for union duties restricted.

4 Redundancy rebates abolished.

5 Written reasons for dismissal now require two years' service.

1990 Employment Act

All secondary action now unlawful; unions liable for wildcat action induced by any official unless written repudiation using statutory form of words sent to all members; selective dismissal of strikers taking unofficial action possible. Unlawful to refuse to employ non-union members.

1992 Trade Union and Labour Relations (Consolidation) Act

Brings together all collective employment rights, including trade union finances, elections, dismissal and time off.

1993 Trade Union Reform and Employment Rights Act

1 Individuals can seek injunctions against unlawful action; seven days' notice needed for ballots and industrial action.

2 Allows identification of people involved in a strike ballot.

3 Written consent for check-off required every three years.

4 Financial records, including salaries, to be made available.

5 Independent scrutiny of strike ballots; all strike ballots to be made postal.

6 Higher penalties against unions failing to keep proper accounts.

7 Abolition of wages councils.

Apart from the 1971 Industrial Relations Act, this legislation represents the first systematic attempt to impose a legal framework upon IR. The legislation as a whole has resulted in a progressive diminution of *collective* employee rights which included the removal of statutory underpinning for trade union recognition and undermining of the closed shop (McKendrick, 1988), and the relaxation of immunities in the event of dismissals during the course of industrial action (Ewing, 1991). The purposes for which industrial action could be taken were narrowed; detailed provisions for pre-strike ballots were introduced and restrictions imposed on unions' ability to organize sympathetic and secondary action (Carty, 1991). Failure to comply could result in employer-initiated injunctions and court proceedings, and probably sequestration of union funds.

At the same time, *individual* employment laws were deregulated by, for example, removing statutory and administrative protections of terms and conditions of employment, the abolition of wages councils, repeal of Truck

Acts and the removal of statutory restrictions on the employment of women and young people.

Labour market deregulation proceeded apace, not only as a result of removal of statutory restrictions, but also by government determination to encourage the move towards decentralization of pay bargaining (already referred to) and the projected dismantling of national collective bargaining machinery in the public sector.

Implications of these developments for IR issues

In concluding this section dealing with the emergence of the 'new' IR and the characteristic developments associated with it, the following points concerning their impact upon IR issues should be emphasized.

1   In organizations where HRM is well established and demonstrates high levels of management involvement and employee commitment, then it is more likely that elements of the 'new' IR will be incorporated into HRM and be operated relatively successfully. Within unionized contexts, it has already been established that individual unions are modifying their approaches on both individualistic and collectivist dimensions (Bacon and Storey, 1994). Within non-unionized contexts, most UK organizations do not have well-developed HRM, but within the sample enterprises which Guest and Hoque (1994) examined, there was a sizeable minority of UK greenfield site operations which did, and whose industrial relations were largely integrated within HRM. The deficiency of HRM may also be explained by reference to factors other than the absence (or presence) of the collective union voice.

2   In so far as collective bargaining is concerned, the evidence of the 1980s and 1990s indicates that, according to Brown (1993, p. 195):

> the coverage of collective bargaining has contracted substantially, that the scope of bargaining has narrowed, that the depth of union involvement has diminished and that organisational security offered to unions by employers has deteriorated.

Moreover, Millward et al. (1992) also demonstrate how much worse off are those employees who do not enjoy the protection of collective bargaining in terms of pay, health and safety, labour turnover, contractual security, compulsory redundancy, grievance procedures, consultation, communication and employee representation. Therefore the erosion of collective bargaining as a result of union substitution practices and/or marginalizing the bargaining process has indeed resulted in a deterioration of conditions associated with the employment relationship.

3   The issue as to whether the 'new' IR has or has not had an impact upon organizational performance has been part of a long-running debate in labour economics. The accumulated evidence summarized by Rose and Woolley (1992) suggests that far from hindering productivity and competition, high levels of unionization actually encourage it, particularly when associated with well-developed HRS as within the Rover context. The assumption, therefore, that by encouraging the 'free play' of market forces and by discouraging union involvement and representation this can somehow result in a more highly competitive and performing organization, is seriously flawed. The new, and often de-unionized labour market, where it has emerged, has in general terms not supported improved organizational competitiveness. We may, therefore, endorse Metcalf's (1993, p. 282) conclusions concerning his analysis of IR and economic performance:

> the market solution to industrial relations difficulties has singularly failed to improve macro-economic performance. Just as Donovan failed to 'solve' our wage-setting system, so has the market: surely it is possible to devise a better system of industrial relations and collective bargaining than one that requires three million unemployed to get wage inflation under control?

4   Finally, the impact of the 'new' IR upon the public sector has been far more limited than within the private sector. This view must, however, be qualified by acknowledging, as Bach and Winchester (1994) do, that by the end of the 1980s:

(a) The privatization of public corporations removed entire groups of employees from the public sector.
(b) The introduction of compulsory competitive tendering for many ancillary public services resulted in substantial job losses, a downward pressure on wages and benefits, and more intensive patterns of work.
(c) The introduction of controls over public expenditure affected traditional 'comparability' arguments in pay negotiations and replaced this with 'ability to pay' arguments in face of strict cash limits.

Despite these developments, Bach and Winchester argue that Conservative governments achieved only limited success in encouraging decentralised IR and pay determination on the public services, even though national agreements became more flexible. They go on to conclude that:

> advocates of decentralised market-sensitive pay determination will be disappointed to find no evidence that the government intends to withdraw from the active and inconsistent involvement in public sector pay determination that has characterised its predecessors' policies for the last thirty years.
>
> (Bach and Winchester, 1994, p. 280)

The changes, the reasons behind them and impact of them upon IR referred to in this section, have helped to create a new climate in which IR operates. They have undoubtedly encouraged managements to take HR initiatives and adopt HR strategies geared towards improving employee productivity and commitment and fostering a more harmonious and co-operative employee oriented organizational culture. However, the HRM rhetoric, as stated earlier, belies the reality in many instances. This must be a cause for concern to all parties to the employment relationship, and as Storey and Sisson (1993, p. 50) state:

> In the light of the rhetoric one would expect to find impressive evidence of an upturn in the amount of training and development, in the utilisation of appropriate performance management techniques, in the integration of human resource practices and business strategy, and not least in the economic performance outcomes of British industry. However, . . . Britain still has a long way to go. Senior managers are either not practising what they espouse or they are installing new initiatives in an incompetent and ineffective way.

The next section considers two IR examples which demonstrate some mismatch between reality and rhetoric.

Pay Determination and Union Exclusion

Pay determination

Considered here are both collective pay determination and individual pay determination.

Collective pay determination (CPD)

CPD is subsumed under and cannot be divorced from the process of collective bargaining and the end result, the collective agreement. It is a process associated with unionized organizations, and as levels of unionization decline throughout the economy so does the importance of CPD. However, while there is no necessary correlation between the decline of CPD and the rise of HRM, alternative methods of pay determination – such as performance-related pay – more commonly linked with HRM, exist in those organizations which have experienced an erosion of CPD. The decline in CPD is necessarily related to established and ongoing trends in the collective bargaining process which are summarized in table 5.2.

The most salient feature concerning table 5.2 is the predominance of multi-employer-level pay bargaining in the public sector for both manual and non-manual categories, with coverage of the latter declining slightly by 1990. Single-employer-level pay bargaining was the most prominent

Table 5.2 Most important bargaining level for most recent pay increase in manufacturing, private services and public services, 1984 and 1990

	Manual employees (%)		Non-manual employees (%)	
	1984	*1990*	*1984*	*1990*
Manufacturing				
multi-employer	41	37	20	33
single employer	21	19	36	24
enterprise	38	44	44	43
Private services				
multi-employer	56	35	38	20
single employer	33	52	52	76
enterprise	11	13	10	4
Public sector				
multi-employer	81	81	86	84
single employer	18	18	13	16
enterprise	1	1	1	–

Source: Millward et al. (1992).

feature within private sector services by 1990, but the importance of this level of bargaining declined in private manufacturing to be replaced by enterprise-level pay bargaining for manual employees.

The decline in multi-employer pay bargaining in the private sector is part of a long-term trend towards decentralization of pay determination (CBI, 1988). Towers (1992) identifies a number of factors explaining the trend towards decentralization, which include:

Trade union weakness;
Corporate decentralization preceding decentralized bargaining;
The growth of performance-related pay;
The pressures for employers to link worker productivity with appropriate pay increase.

Palmer (1990) argues that the move towards pay decentralization has also been greatly influenced by the need to recruit, motivate and retain employees of the right calibre to ensure business success. Furthermore, employers desire the freedom not only to determine pay rates and increases locally but also to introduce new pay strategies including profit-sharing, merit pay and pay bonuses more in line with their own business strategies. The growth in the number of large multi-divisional organizations – where arguably HR strategies are most coherent – has, according to Storey and Sisson (1993), meant the adoption of profit and cost centre management with consequent devolution of responsibility for pay determination to local management. Within this scenario, pay and conditions need to be related to the profitability, performance and skills of employees and local labour market conditions. It should, however, be emphasized that notwithstanding the discernible trend towards decentralization/devolution of pay bargaining, many organizations (car manufacturers, banks and retailers, for example) prefer multi-establishment (or company-wide) pay determination, and there are still some industries (clothing, construction and printing, for example) which maintain multi-employer (or industry-wide) bargaining.

The devolution of CPD raises problems related to the extent to which local managers have, or even desire the *responsibility* and freedom to pay what increases they think fit. Millward et al. (1992) reveal what might at first glance be the contradictory finding that within a decentralized context, there was a greater propensity for senior corporate managers to be involved in establishment industrial relations matters, including CPD. Storey and Sisson (1993, pp. 212–13) suggest that despite the contradiction:

> It is perfectly sensible, however: senior managers are trying to get the best and avoid the worst of both worlds. One important consideration is what might be described as the 'limited horizons' problem. It is all very well, in other words, making local managers 'operationally' responsible. They cannot, however, be expected to have the thinking that is going to be required. It is not very efficient to do so either – the organisation is not getting the benefits of the synergies of the large organisation. Simply bringing local managers together to discuss and debate the issues can be enormously beneficial in saving time and in arriving at solutions to common problems.

If decentralization of CPD is to work efficiently in serving the best interests of the organization and its employees, then some strategic thinking in HR/IR is required which identifies the necessary terms and conditions together with the formalization of responsibilities to be shared and allocated centrally and locally. The evidence of such thinking is extremely sparse, and therefore the conclusion appears unavoidable that much of the decentralization/devolution of CPD represents a *tactical* response on the part of many employers to the weakened position of unionized labour.

Individual pay determination

The most conspicuous and widespread example of Individual Pay Determination (IPD) is Individual Performance Related Pay (IPRP). The introduction of IPRP has been one of the more significant changes in employers' approaches to pay and HRM in recent years, and there is no doubt that HRM has provided a greater impetus to the inception and wider use of IPRP. As we saw in chapter 4, the assumptions on which IPRP are based are hardly novel. Mihal (1983) suggests three relevant premises:

1   That individual differences in performance can be accurately measured and communicated.

2 That pay differences can be related to performance differences and will be perceived as being related.
3 That individuals will increase their effort to gain more rewards, resulting in increased performance.

These premises are themselves underpinned by expectancy theory (Vroom, 1964; Porter and Lawler, 1968). The current interest in IPRP coincides with both the development of HRM and the emergence of the 'new' IR with their greater emphasis upon the individualization of the employment relationship. Proponents of HRM identify reward systems as one of its major policy areas, and as Thompson (1992, p. 3) states:

> The growth of HRM as a managerial strategy does appear to be correlated (in intuitive terms) with the wider uptake of individualised payment systems.

Two benchmark surveys undertaken by Thompson for the Institute of Manpower Studies in 1992 and 1993 cover 20 organizations in the public and private sectors, and examine the employer experience (1992) and employee experience (1993) of IPRP. The major conclusions of these surveys are summarized in box 5.9.

Box 5.9 Conclusions of the IMS surveys on IPRP

The Employer Survey

1 In terms of context issues, the report finds that organisational restructuring (in terms of relationship to produce markets and levels of decision making) can often be seen as an important, but not necessarily planned pre-requisite for the introduction of IPRP. A coherent and communicated pay philosophy also appeared to be an important context for the successful introduction of IPRP but few employers appeared to have one.
2 Coverage of IPRP varied, with some employers limiting it to professional and managerial staff and others extending it to lower-level employees.
3 Although most schemes were introduced in unionized environments, the scale and nature of union involvement differed widely. At one extreme was the use of IPRP as part of a de-recognition process, whilst at the other, unions were involved at the outset in design and implementation of the scheme.
4 IPRP schemes require devolution of responsibility to line managers. This may create problems similar to those consequent upon the introduction of devolved collective pay determination.

5 Some organizations experienced problems of integrating IPRP with HRM policies and existing payment systems. For example, IPRP created tensions between the short-term bottom-line needs of the organization and longer-term development needs of the individual.

The Employee Survey

1 IPRP does not serve to motivate (even those with high performance ratings) and may do more to demotivate employees.
2 There was little evidence to suggest that IPRP could help to retain high performers and no evidence to point to poor performers seeking to leave the organizations.
3 Employees are negative or broadly neutral on its impact on organizational culture even in schemes that had been in operation for three or more years.
4 Employees are unclear as to whether IPRP rewards fairly although high performers are likely to perceive it to be more fair than low-rated employees.
5 There is a risk that IPRP may contribute to a downward spiral of demotivation for the bulk of employees and this draws into question the real costs and benefits of such pay systems.
6 The poor skills of line managers may, in the short term, contribute to staff turnover and lower morale. In the long run IPRP may serve to highlight to an even greater extent the failures of UK management, and prompt employers and policy makers to invest in management training and development. Such action, rather than the introduction of IPRP, is more likely to yield productivity growth in the future. Paradoxically, the failure of IPRP may serve to hasten this investment. (Source: Thompson, 1992, 1993.)

Thompson's surveys and others such as Kessler (1993) and Marsden and Richardson (1994) reveal widespread problems concerning the inception and operation of IPRP, but of greater concern is that IPRP:

> would seem to contradict or sit uneasily with a number of other policies and objectives which managers profess to be pursuing.
>
> (Storey and Sisson, 1993, p. 141)

For example, there is a contradiction between IPRP and the prevailing ethos of teamworking in many organizations; concentrating upon individual performance goals can subvert team spirit. Therefore, by rewarding some individuals and not others, and through the individualization of work effort, the well-being and cohesion of the work group/team, section, department or organization may be undermined. This apparent contradiction could be resolved, and some organizations have done this by incorporating factors such as 'contribution to teamworking' in their appraisal criteria (Kinnie and Lowe, 1990). If IPRP is *not* part of an ordered, rational and systematic approach to remuneration, then:

> It is difficult to escape the conclusion . . . that IPRP is being introduced for largely ideological reasons . . . It is no accident that some of the most publicised IPRP schemes have been in some of the newly privatised public utilities . . . and perhaps most important, there is the focus upon the individual; the implication at the very least, is that trade unions and collective bargaining will play a lesser role in pay determination. Indeed in some well-publicised cases, for example, management grades in British Rail and British Telecom, the introduction of IPRP has been directly associated with the withdrawal of collective bargaining rights over pay.
>
> (Storey and Sisson, 1993; p. 143)

Union exclusion and de-recognition

The extent of union exclusion and de-recognition is dependent upon two factors:

1 Government policy and legislation;
2 The overall decline of trade unions in the UK.

According to Smith and Morton (1994) successive Conservative governments have been committed to union exclusion policies including reducing the role of unions in the labour market and within the employment relationship itself. These policies are based on the well-known 'free-market' assumptions where:

> market and contractual relations between individuals are regarded as the most efficient mechanism for the allocation of resources, and hence institutions [and] rules and practices which hinder this process are appropriate targets for statutory intervention.
>
> (Smith and Morton, 1994, p. 6)

The state sector and unions representing employees within it have borne the brunt of these policies, largely because of the monopoly provision of services within that sector and also because of the perceived strength of union representation which allegedly results in inefficiencies and inflated pay levels. The rhetoric of the 'market' has pervaded the state and private sectors with its notions of 'customer care', 'total quality' and 'enterprise', and which belies nothing less than a rejuvenated unitary view which subordinates employees to market forces and is revealed where, for example, PRP has been introduced.

Government IR legislation, as previously commented upon in this chapter, has systematically restricted and regulated unions in their collective roles and has provided further impetus for employers to consider abandoning collective bargaining altogether and establishing 'individual' relationships with employees.

The second important factor is the overall decline of trade unions in the UK. Between 1980 and 1991 overall union membership declined progressively from a high in 1980 of around 12 million to little over 8 million in 1991. By 1994 membership declined further to nearer 7 million. The WIRS (1992) indicates that total union density (the proportion of employees who are union members) fell from 58 per cent to 48 per cent during 1984–90, and employees covered by collective bargaining declined from 71 per cent to 54 per cent during the same period. Another survey (Marginson et al. 1993) reveals a decline in union recognition and the scope of collective bargaining over the five years up to 1993.

Union exclusion in the state sector

The examples of the Civil Service and the National Health Service are considered below. (The information is taken and adapted from Smith and Morton, 1994.)

> Under the 'Next Steps' programme, there are now 76 separate agencies employing 216,370 workers (over 50 per cent of the total workforce), and the formation of another 29 agencies has been announced. In addition, two government departments – Customs and Excise, and the Inland Revenue – have been reorganised into decentralised units, making a total of 297,550 civil servants at present working within the framework of the 'Next Steps' programme. Compulsory competitive tendering of 25 per cent of all posts is going ahead and private contractors will not be required to comply with equal opportunities policies or to continue with union recognition. The likely impact of these changes will be redundancies, casualisation of work and pay cuts.
>
> Government policy is to devolve collective bargaining to subordinate units whilst at the same time seeking to dilute its relevance to individuals through the introduction of IPRP. The Treasury has decided to withdraw from the 66-year-old arbitration agreement with the civil service unions, and the 1992 collective agreements ended automatic payment of annual increments and introduced PRP supplements. Management now has wide discretion to vary pay and conditions. Agencies with more than 2,000 staff have been invited to take responsibility for pay bargaining since April 1994.
>
> Within the NHS 150 new trusts were established from 1 April 1993, making a total of 306 which embraced 70 per cent of all NHS employees. The remainder of the NHS is expected to follow. Each trust constitutes a separate

employer but the political sensitivity of the NHS has hindered any attempt to introduce 'innovative' pay systems, and to date only one additional trust (making three in all) has refused union recognition. The principal thrust of policy at present appears to be an incremental lowering of unit costs through the intensification of capital utilisation and new work practices. However, 'market testing' is well established in the NHS; for example as a result of the contracting out of cleaning and domestic services, costs fell by 29 per cent during 1985–1990. Inevitably, much of this was due to reduced pay and inferior conditions.

The same trends identified by Smith and Morton may be discerned within other state sector services. To be sure, the extent of union exclusion within this sector is not as great as in the private sector, but it does appear to be on the increase for reasons already referred to.

Union exclusion in the private sector

Within this sector, union exclusion is far more widespread, as the following summary points culled from two major surveys suggest.

1   Union recognition within greenfield sites is relatively uncommon. The survey by Millward et al. (1992) revealed that work places less than ten years old recognized unions in 23 per cent of cases, while 52 per cent of work places that were more than 20 years old recognized unions. This finding is supported by the Warwick survey (Marginson et al., 1993) where, of the 80 per cent of companies which reported at least one new site, 59 per cent had not agreed to union representation of the largest group of employees.
2   The survey by Marginson et al. revealed that of the 69 per cent of companies which recognized unions within their existing establishments, 60 per cent have reduced the role of trade unions in collective bargaining. The reduced role of unions in collective bargaining has been accompanied by the decentralization and devolution of bargaining (especially collective pay determination), again confirmed by the WIRS and Marginson surveys. Smith and Morton (1994, p. 8) state: 'This shift amounts to a major assertion of the power of capital over the pay-effort bargain and a commensurate exclusion of unions.'
3   There has been a decline in union organization with the virtual ending of the closed shop, together with a significant decline in the number of union representatives at the work place.
4   The incidence of union de-recognition is patchy but increasing. The proportion of work places with recognized unions in private manufacturing fell by nearly a third, and this tendency is also found in printing and publishing during the period 1984–90. During the same period union recognition fell by 10 per cent in private services and in particular within hotels and catering, transport and business services.

The oil sector is also in a prominent position in the de-recognition league with BP (Baglan Bay), Esso (Fawley), Mobil (Coryton and Birkenhead) and Shell (Haven and Stanlow) being the most important examples. Smith and Morton starkly conclude (1994, p. 12): 'The new industrial relations is characterised by employer-regulated organisation-employment systems, utilising cost minimisation policies devoid of any systematic human resource management content with reduced union input.'

A recent Cadbury–Schweppes management document leaked to the TGWU would seem to confirm the trend (box 5.10).

Box 5.10   'Union unwraps Cadbury's secret strategy'

'Over the years Cadbury has won the respect of trade unions and workforce as well as peers who rate it seventh most admired company. But this reputation only increased the damaging impact of an internal management document on "manufacturing human resource strategy". The strategy embraces many of the elements of present-day HR: the emphasis on communication and feedback, training and development, "performance-focused culture" backed up by reward for skills and competences, and employee involvement.

However, for the union a different and more sinister slant is put on *all* these programmes by the final part of the strategy which calls for the union to be "marginalised by greater focus on direct communication and consultation, but without an overt statement to this effect". It speaks of "the likelihood of downsizing" and adds: "For those groups where the trade union has already been de-recognised . . . it is important that they are not exploited by the company as this would lead to pressure for renewed trade union involvement".

The union (TGWU) describes the approach as "fundamentally dishonest", and Cadbury workers are reported to have instructed shop stewards to halt co-operation with such key parts of the people strategy as Quality Improvement Teams and NVQ skills programmes . . . Far from being willing to be innovative and creative on the company's behalf, the Cadbury unions are explicitly advising members to "take care about giving ideas to management", since it could lead to job cuts, and to refuse co-operation with attempts to individualise pay.

Now there is no reason why union membership should be incompatible with individual development – see Rover for example. But this implies a recognition and negotiation of different, legitimate interests which Cadbury's HR mangers were not prepared to admit. The final irony is that because of the leak it is now out of the hands of the professionals and in the court of top management and the trade unions – which is where the HR project came in in the first place.' (Source: *The Observer*, Dec. 1994.)

The developments identified in this section indicate a substantial move towards 'individualistic' employer initiatives within the employment relationship. At the same time there has been a move away from, or even an abandonment of, exclusive 'collectivist' aspects such as extended collective bargaining, jointly agreed procedures, and communications via trade union channels. In non-unionized organizations, employer 'individualism' proceeds apace, often without any coherent HR strategy to back it up. In unionized organizations where 'collectivist' aspects have been eroded there is an uneasy accommodation between 'individualism' and 'collectivism'. The task for all organizational participants is to devise a human resource strategy where both systems mutually reinforce each other and which achieves the goals of individuals and their representative agencies.

Strategic Management of Industrial Relations

A central assumption of HRM is that it requires a more *strategic* orientation to the management of employees than do traditional personnel management or industrial relations models (Beer et al., 1985; Armstrong, 1992). It is not the intention here to describe at length the various models of strategic HRM, as these are discussed fully in chapter 1, but in order to assess the implications of these models for IR, we nevertheless need to identify their main elements. Two sets of models are commonly identified; the first may be labelled 'Best Practice' and the second 'Contingency'. These two model sets correspond with the typology developed in chapter 1, where they are identified as 'closed' and 'open' respectively.

'Best-practice' models

Beer et al. (1985), and Kochan et al. (1986) are concerned with influences upon HRM policy choices exerted by stakeholders and by 'situational' factors. Appropriate decisions made on this basis will result in beneficial HR outcomes. An IR oriented variation has been developed by Kochan et al. Their basic argument is that IR practices and outcomes are the result of environmental forces interacting with the strategic choices and values of managers, union leaders, employees, etc. Strategic choice, therefore, determines the type of IR system that emerges at the three main levels of strategic decision-making, collective bargaining and day-to-day work-place activities.

Kochan et al. use this framework to track the fundamental changes in American IR over a 50-year period. This enables them to identify the current and prevailing IR orthodoxy, which they label as the 'new industrial-relations' model. This model largely displaces the traditional conflict-oriented model, and emphasizes the involvement of unions at business strategy levels. Unlike the situation in the UK, union involvement means nothing less than 'union engagement' by senior union personnel in strategic business decisions. These decisions concern new investment, new technology, workforce adjustment strategies and new forms of work organization. In order to facilitate this new level of involvement, new attitudes involving a high degree of attitudinal restructuring were required by both unions and management. It is important to note that these shifts in union–management co-operation go far beyond what has happened in the UK and required 'a blending of traditional representation and newer participatory processes along with perhaps additional, more individualised forms of voice and representation' (Kochan et al., 1986, p. 225).

Contingency models of strategic HRM

These models assume that policy choices vary according to changing business conditions. Kochan and Barocci (1985), for example, argue that the type of HRM strategies and priorities an organization selects are contingent upon the life-cycle stage of an organization. Fombrun et al. (1984) posit a contingency model which is concerned with identifying particular strategies and structures, and with linking these to appropriate HR policy choices concerning selection, appraisal, rewards and employee development. A further refinement to the contingency approach is made by Schuler and Jackson (1987) whose model builds upon Porter's (1985) 'competitive advantage' paradigm. Essentially, Schuler and Jackson identify three sets of *strategic options* (innovation, quality enhancement and cost reduction), each of which give rise to associated 'employee role behaviours'. HRM policy choices are required to foster and maintain these behaviour patterns.

The British context: Peaceful coexistence or open warfare?

The strategy models considered above are, however, problematic in their implementation, particularly within the British context where research has indicated an almost endemic *absence* of strategy in British HR/IR together with a failure to incorporate HR/IR within existing business strategies. Storey and Sisson (1993), moreover, challenge the assumptions upon which both best-practice and contingency theorists build their cases.

Assumption one: 'That HR/IR managers have easy access to a business strategy'

This assumption is largely invalid, at least in an operational sense, since access to such a strategy requires HR/IR managers to have a range of knowledge of the practical implications of the exercise of numerous strategic choices within non-HR/IR areas. Moreover, the reality of strategy formulation and planning is rarely as neat as some of the models suggest. Too often, short-term or even day-to-day considerations impinge upon that process: effectively, the process is deconstructed and atomized, making it difficult for HR/IR managers to respond meaningfully in a strategic sense. There is also, as Storey and Sisson suggest, little evidence that, in normative terms, the 'grand' strategy is better than having no strategy at all. In practice the assumed link between HR policies (however sophisticated) and elements of grand strategy is, at least, tenuous. Indeed, in the British context 'pick and mix' and 'firefighting' may still be the HR/IR operational order of the day. Storey and Sisson quote Marginson et al. (1988) in support of this latter assertion:

> it is difficult to escape the conclusion that, although the great majority of our respondents claim that their organizations have an overall policy or approach to the management of employees, with the exception of a number of companies which are overseas owned, or financially centralized, or operating in the service sectors, it would be wrong to set very much store by this . . . the general weight of evidence would seem to confirm that most UK owned enterprises remain pragmatic or opportunist in their approach.
>
> (p. 120)

Assumption two: 'That managers have a genuine free choice of strategic stance'

This assumption is too naïve and raises the philosophical notion of 'free will' and 'determinism'. In practice, organizations and their participants – including the most senior managers – operate within a set of circumscribed constraints as any student who has studied the political, economic and social environment of organizations will readily acknowledge. The absence of such choice goes a long way to explain the tenuous link between corporate and HR/IR strategy (where such a strategy exists).

Are HR and IR strategies truly incompatible?

It is likely that the 'new' industrial relations – as outlined earlier in this chapter – which places greater emphasis upon 'individualist' aspects of the employment relationship together with a correspondingly lower priority to collective and conflictual aspects will be more congruent with HRS provided the latter genuinely reconciles the aims of greater employee commitment, investment in long-term training and development and security of employment with a 'pluralist' orientation towards employee representation and all that this entails. However, should employers continue to espouse contradictory values clothed in the rhetoric of HRS (for example by reiterating the importance of 'quality' and 'customer care' while at the same time precariously cutting costs and 'casualizing' the workforce), then the prospects of any reconciliation between the two seem rather poor. This is, of course, particularly true of the British context where HRS is still regarded by some as an ideological movement whose aim is to disaggregate labour and marginalize trade unions.

Guest's (1989) approach to this problem is to argue that there is indeed a basic incompatibility between unitarist HRS and the pluralist traditions of British IR, particularly within multi-union 'brownfield' sites. It may seem obvious to argue that a fundamental prerequisite for compatibility/incompatibility is that within an organizational context the two systems should be extant. Where HRS is well developed – and within the British context this is still a relatively rare phenomenon – perhaps on the lines suggested by the contingency theories considered above (e.g. Kochan et al., 1986), then IR may well be incorporated within the human resource strategy. Arguably, therefore, compatibility will depend upon the extent to which IR is included as a major component of an organization's HRS. Where, however, the HRS is imposed arbitrarily within a unionized organization and where little thought is given to the IR consequences then the two systems will be in conflict with each other and even mutually exclude each other. In the UK, the problem of incompatibility arises as a consequence of the latter scenario where both senior managers on the one hand, and senior convenors on the other, fear encroachment upon each other's prerogatives. Senior managers may also perceive themselves as having the upper hand, will take advantage of the weakened position trade unions are in nationally, to further weaken them in the work place. The 'softening up' process which includes introducing individualized forms of pay determination thereby diluting collective bargaining, and excluding unions from other forms of decision-making, is seen as a necessary condition for the implementation of 'full-blown' HRS.

There can be little doubt that incorporation of the 'best' elements of an organization's IR system into its HRS is the way forward. Given the paucity of such human resource strategies and the piecemeal way HRM policies have been introduced within British organizations, the task remains daunting. The combined IR/HR strategy (which should contain elements of the 'new' industrial relations examined earlier in this chapter) must, according to Storey and Sisson (1993) satisfy three criteria:

The first of these is that business strategy must be capable of being translated into operational action plans. Second, it must be made absolutely clear to whom the responsibility for developing the strategy actually belongs: does it rest, for example, at corporate headquarters, the divisional office, or at each business unit? Third, some decision has to be taken about the overall thrust of the approach – will it, for example, aspire to match up to one of the 'best practice' models or will it reflect in contingency fashion, the particular needs of the organisation.

(p. 79)

Unless these problems and issues are taken seriously by British managers, then the prospect for a successfully operationalized IR/HRM strategy remain slim indeed.

Conclusion

This chapter has sought to identify and examine the interplay between IR as related to the British context, and HRM/HRS. The interplay between the two must be seen against the backdrop of the decline of collective IR in the UK and the emergence of a 'new' IR which may be more compatible with a strategic approach to HRM.

The decline of collective IR

The past 15 years have witnessed underlying social, economic and political changes encompassing a shift towards free-market economics. The period is characterized by episodic recession and continuing high unemployment and a movement towards 'individualistic' attitudes and values. We have argued that these and other factors have had a significant impact upon IR, and arguably changes in government policy towards the labour market together with the IR legislation have been the most important developments in terms of eroding 'trade union monopoly power' (McIlroy, 1991), removing state support for collective bargaining, depoliticizing trade unions, restricting the opportunity for trade unions to organize and engage in industrial action, and denying union access (via the TUC) to government policy-making.

At work-place level the decline in collective IR is reflected in the decline in trade union membership since 1980, together with an increase in the proportion of establishments with no union representation. Obviously the structural factors referred to earlier in this chapter are important explanations of this trend, but additionally, the individual-choice factor is also highly significant, as McLoughlin and Gourlay (1994) suggest:

individuals still in employment were now resigning from trade union membership or simply choosing not to join in the first place, possibly because of more individualistic attitudes and/or the legal removal of institutional constraints which hitherto forced them to join.

(p. 13)

Another development discussed in this chapter is the growth of union derecognition (or decline in recognition), together with the reluctance of both existing non-union work places and newly formed establishments to provide recognition in recent years.

A further manifestation of the decline in collectivism concerns the coverage and structure of collective bargaining itself. The example of the decline in collective pay determination and the associated strong emergence of individual forms of pay determination such as IPRP were examined. In general terms, while the fracturing of collective bargaining has gained momentum, what is more problematic is whether these changes 'can be seen unambiguously as deliberate steps on the way to complete de-unionisation' (McLoughlin and Gourlay, 1994).

The rise of the 'new' IR and HRM/HRS

The debate concerning the efficient utilization of HRM within both unionized and non-unionized contexts was also considered. Elements of the 'new' IR were identified and examined and consideration given again to union and non-union work places and to differences within the private and public sectors. In so far as the 'new' IR encompasses 'new style' agreements, flexibility agreements and other new employment practices such as employee involvement, TQM, teamworking and empowerment, then it could be argued that the 'new' IR is more compatible with HR strategies than 'traditional' IR. The evidence for this is still relatively sparse and should be related, amongst other things, to IR outcomes such as wage levels, productivity and investment in new technology.

Moreover, there appears to be some convergence between a modified collectivist approach as evidence by the 'new' IR and and HR strategy which is more 'pluralist' in orientation, and which can develop in the context of a well-established trade union presence. Strategic HRM is still relatively undeveloped in non-union environments, and where it exists a variety of approaches tend to be adopted.

We end on a cautionary note. Pemberton and Herriot (1994) argue that there is growing evidence of some faltering of the HRS project. They add:

Far from being right-sized and right-skilled to meet increasing competition, surviving workforces are showing signs of mutiny.

Pemberton and Herriot cite British Telecom and Cadbury–Schweppes as organizations whose remaining employees express anger concerning increased job insecurity, distrust about employers' motives and loss of pride in working for their companies. There can be little confidence that those who remain will wish to deliver what the organization requires, particularly within what some employees perceive as a 'culture of fear' which is undermining the effective implementation of business changes because of a focus on short-term results. They go on to state:

> The willingness to improve customer care through building long-term relationships is likely to be undermined by the [employee's] desire to get out the minute an alternative job opportunity arises. The exhortation to grow with the job and embrace multi-skilling is being undermined by a desire to get even; digging in and resisting overtly or covertly the organisation's agenda.

While this may be a rather pessimistic scenario, it does suggest that as far as some organizations are concerned, playing 'hard-ball' has not produced the business results expected, or sold the case for HRS. In these organizations, the 'new' IR remains elusive and illusory.

Key Points

- *Industrial relations in Britain has undergone a substantial transformation over the past two decades, and this brings into focus the issues concerning collectivism and individualism and their compatibility with HRM.*
- *The emergence of the 'new' industrial relations, which is part of the transformation process, is the result of various economic, political, technological and social factors, and is concerned with redefining the employment relationship in the light of new employment practices.*
- *As aggregate union membership declines, the strong emergence of non-unionized organizations becomes an important phenomenon for analysis, particularly in relation to HRS.*
- *Industrial relations changes and the advent of HRS have an increasingly significant impact within the public sector.*

Discussion questions

1 Discuss the impact of economic and other factors upon IR and HRM.

2   Consider the likely HRM strategies which managers could adopt within a non-unionized context.
3   To what extent is there a future for 'collectivist' industrial relations?

REFERENCES

Armstrong, M. (1992) *Human Resource Management: Strategy and Action*. London, Kogan-Page.

Ascher, K. (1987) *The Politics of Privatisation: Contracting Out Public Services*. London, Macmillan.

Bach, S. and Winchester, D. (1994) Opting out of pay devolution? The prospects for local pay bargaining in UK public services. *British Journal of Industrial Relations*, 32, no. 2, pp. 263–82.

Bacon, N. and Storey, J. (1993): Individualisation of employment relationship and the implications for trade unions. *Employee Relations*, 15, no. 1, pp. 5–17.

Bacon, N. and Storey, J. (1994) Individualism, collectivism and the changing role of trade unions. Paper given to Labour Process Conference, Mar. 1994, Aston University, UK.

Beaumont, P. B. (1991a) *Change in Industrial Relations*. London, Routledge.

Beaumont, P. B. (1991b) Trade unions and HRM. *Industrial Relations Journal*, 23, no. 4, pp. 300–8.

Baine, G. S. and Clegg, H. A. (1974) A strategy for industrial relations research in Great Britain. *British Journal of Industrial Relations*, 12, pp. 91–113.

Beer, M., Spector, B., Lawrence, P. R., Mills, D. and Walton, R. (1985) *Managing Human Assets*. New York, The Free Press.

Bevan, W. (1987) Creating a 'no strike' environment: The trade union view. Paper to Confederation of British Industry Conference, London.

Brown, W. (1993) The contraction of collective bargaining in Britain. *British Journal of Industrial Relations*, 31, no. 2, pp. 189–200.

Carty, H. (1991) The Employment Act 1990: Still fighting the industrial cold war. *Industrial Law Journal*, 20, no. 1.

Confederation of British Industry (1988) *The Structure and Processes of Pay Determination in the Private Sector, 1979–1986*. London, CBI.

Crowther, S. and Garrahan, P. (1988) Invitation to Sunderland: Corporate power and the local economy. *Industrial Relations Journal*, 19, pp. 51–9.

Daniel, W. W. and Millward, N. (1983) *Workforce Industrial Relations in Britain*. Aldershot, Gower.

Dunlop, J. T. (1957): *Industrial Relations Systems*. New York, Holt.

Edwards, P., Hall, M. and Hyman, R. (1992) Great Britain. In Ferner, A. and Hyman, R. (eds), *Industrial Relations in the New Europe*. Oxford, Blackwell.

Evans, S., Ewing, K. and Nolan, P. (1992) Industrial relations in the British economy in the 1990s: Mrs Thatcher's legacy. *Journal of Management Studies*, 29, pp. 571–89.

Ewing, K. D. (1991) *The Right to Strike*. Oxford, Clarendon.

Fombrun, C. J., Titchy, M. and Devanna, M. A. (1984) Linking competitive strategies with human resource management practices. *Academy of Management Executive*, 1, pp. 209–13.

Guest, D. (1989) Human resource management: Its implications for trade unions and industrial relations. In Storey, J. (ed.), *New Perspectives in Human Resource Management*. London, Routledge.

Guest, D. and Hoque, K. (1994) The good, the bad and the ugly: Employment relations in new non-union workplaces. *Human Resource Management Journal*, 5, no. 1, pp. 1–14.

Hunter, C. and MacInnes, J. (1994) Employees and labour flexibility: The evidence from case studies. *Employment Gazette*, June 1994.

Hyman, R. (1974) *Industrial Relations, a Marxist Introduction*. London, Macmillan.

Kanter, M. (1988) *When Giants Learn to Dance*. London, Unwin.

Kessler, I. (1993) Performance pay. In Sisson, K. (ed.), *Personnel Management in Britain*. Oxford, Blackwell.

Kinnie, N. and Lowe, D. (1990) Performance-related pay on the shop floor. *Personnel Management*, Nov., pp. 45–9.

Kochan, T. A. and Barocci, T. (eds) (1985). *Human Resource Management and Industrial Relations*. Boston, Little Brown.

Kochan, T. A., Katz, H. C. and McKersie, R. B. (1986) *The Transformation of American Industrial Relations*. New York, Basic Books.

Lash, S. and Urry, J. (1987) *The End of Organized Capitalism*. Cambridge, Polity Press.

McIlroy, J. (1991) *The Permanent Revolution? Conservative Law and the Trade Unions*. Nottingham, Spokesman.

McKendrick, E. (1988) The rights of trade union members: Part 1 of The Employment Act, 1988, *Industrial Law Journal*, 17, p. 141.

McLoughlin, I. and Gourlay, S. (1992) Enterprise without unions: The management of employee relations in non-union firms. *Journal of Management Studies*, 29, pp. 669–91.

McLoughlin, I. and Gourlay, S. (1994) *Enterprise without Unions: Industrial Relations in the Non-union Firm*. Buckingham, Open University Press.

Marchington, M. (1995) Fairy tales and magic wands. *Employee Relations*, (forthcoming).

Marginson, P., Armstrong, P., Edwards, P. and Purcell, J. (1993) *The Control of Industrial Relations in Large Corporations*. Warwick papers in industrial relations, University of Warwick, UK.

Marginson, P., Edwards, P., Martin, R. et al. (1988) *Beyond the Workplace: Managing Industrial Relations in Multi-establishment Enterprises*. Oxford, Blackwell.

Marsden, D. and Richardson, R. (1994) Performing for pay? The effects of merit pay on motivation in a public service. *British Journal of Industrial Relations*, 32, no. 2, pp. 243–61.

Marsh, D. (1992) *The New Politics of British Trade Unionism: Union Power and the Thatcher Legacy*. London, Macmillan.

Metcalf, D. (1993) Industrial relations and economic performance. *British Journal of Industrial Relations*, 31, no. 2, pp. 255–83.

Mihal, W. L. (1983): More research is needed: Goals may motivate better. *Personnel Administrator*, 28, pp. 61–7.

Millward, N. (1994) *The New Industrial Relations*. London, Policy Studies Institute.

Millward, N., Smart, D., Stevens, M. and Hawes, W. R. (1992) *Workplace Industrial Relations in Transition*. Aldershot, Dartmouth Publishing.

Millward, N. and Stevens, M. (1986) *British Workplace Industrial Relations, 1980–1984*. Aldershot, Gower.

Milne, R. (1987) Competitive tendering in the NHS: An economic analysis of the early implementation of HC (83). *Public Administration*, 65, no. 2, pp. 154–60.

Monks, J. (1994) The union response to HRM; Fraud or opportunity? *Personnel Management*, Sept., pp. 42–7.

Oliver, N. and Wilkinson, B. (1992) *The Japanisation of British Industry*. Oxford, Blackwell.

Palmer, S. (1990) *Determining Pay: A Guide to the Issues*. London, IPM.

Pemberton, C. and Herriot, P. (1994) Inhumane resources. *Observer*, 4 Dec.

Porter, L. W. and Lawler, E. E. (1968) *Management Attitudes and Performance*. Homewood, Ill, Irwin.

Porter, M. (1980) *Competitive Advantage: Creating and Sustaining Superior Performance*. New York, Free Press.

Rollinson, D. (1993) *Understanding Employee Relations*. Wokingham, Addison-Wesley.

Rose, E. and Woolley, E. (1992) Shifting sands? Trade unions and productivity at Rover Cars. *Industrial Relations Journal*, 23, pp. 257–67.

Salaman, G., Cameron, S., Hamblin, H., Iles, P., Mabey, C. and Thompson, K. (1992) *Human Resource Strategies*. London, Sage.

Salamon, M. (1992) *Industrial Relations: Theory and Practice*. London, Prentice Hall.

Schuler, R. S. and Jackson, S. (1987) Linking competitive strategies with human resource management practices. *Academy of Management Executive*, 1, pp. 209–13.

Sisson, K. (1993) In search of HRM. *British Journal of Industrial Relations*, 31, pp. 201–10.

Smith, P. and Morton, G. (1994) Union exclusion, the next steps. *Industrial Relations Journal*, 25, pp. 3–14.

Storey, J. (1992) *Developments in Human Resource Management*. Oxford, Blackwell.

Storey, J. and Sisson, K. (1993) *Managing Human Resources and Industrial Relations*. Buckingham, Open University Press.

Thompson, M. (1992) *Pay and Performance: The Employer Experience*. IMS Report, no. 218, IMS, Sussex, UK.

Thompson, M. (1993) *Pay and Performance: The Employee Experience*. IMS Report, no. 258, IMS, Sussex, UK.

Towers, B. (1992) *Issues in People Management no. 2: Choosing Bargaining Levels – UK Experience and Implications*. London, Institute of Personnel Management.

Trevor, M. (1988) Toshiba's new British company: Competitiveness through innovation. Unpublished paper, University of Cardiff, Wales.

Vroom, V. (1964) Work and motivation. New York, John Wiley.

6 Culture, Organizational Performance and HRS

Learning Objectives

- *to be fully aware of the variety of ways – some of them fundamentally conflicting – in which the concept of culture has been used in analysis of organization.*
- *to recognize the implications, assumptions, strengths and weaknesses of these approaches.*
- *to recognize the nature, origins and limitations of the corporate-culture approach associated with the writings of Peters, Deal and Kennedy, and others.*
- *to be able to identify the key dimensions of organizational cultures.*
- *to be alert to the possibility that the corporate-culture approach may have major ideological elements.*
- *yet also to recognize that despite the difficulties associated with the concept and with the corporate-culture approach there is still good reason for us to be concerned with the nature and role of organizational cultures.*

Introduction

This chapter explores four interrelated issues:

1   The *role* of culture in organizational analysis;
2   The claimed *role* of organizational cultures in determining levels of organizational performance;
3   The *nature* and components of organizational cultures – i.e. how can they be defined and measured?
4   The *possibility of change* of organizational cultures; for *if* they can be changed, *how* can they be changed?

One of the most striking and pervasive claims of the HRS movement is that an organization's culture is the key to its performance, and that these cultures can be manipulated to ensure that employees are enthusiastic, committed, compliant. This chapter focuses on these attempts to identify and manipulate organizational cultures – an approach which is here termed the corporate culture approach to organizational cultures.

However, we shall see that this approach is one of a number of ways in which the concept of culture has been applied to organizations; and because of its importance it is given considerable attention here. Much of this attention is critical, and much of the criticism stems from the simplistic way in which this approach defines culture, and organizations, and from the distorted, ideological nature of these analyses. However, despite many misgivings about the validity of this approach to organizational cultures, and its promises, the chapter concludes with some tentative suggestions for a definition of culture and an approach to cultural change that are defensible and useful, if relatively unambitious.

The concept of culture (and the argument that culture is at the heart of organizational performance and effectiveness) is one of the key ideas of HRS thinking. HRM models and approaches place the management of culture at the heart of the HRM model and as the central responsibility of modern managers (Legge, 1989). It is one of the reasons for the strength and appeal of much HRS thinking (for, as will be discussed later in this chapter, one of the qualities of the organizational culture literature is that it has a particular, and powerful, appeal, especially to managers and consultants). But the emphasis on culture is for many writers also one of the major weaknesses of the HRS approach. Few elements of HRS thinking and consultancy have attracted so much excitement and so much criticism.

The Role of Culture in Organizational Analysis

Box 6.1   Organizational performance and corporate cultures

Wickens, in his analysis of Nissan UK, takes time out to discuss the orientations of other companies. He describes the situation at Pratt and Whitney, USA. The traditional culture of the company is described as product-orientated, where quality was achieved through monitoring and inspection; people were regarded as an expendable resource, management was basically control, and communications were one-way. This situation has now changed; now the 'value-system' (i.e. culture) has changed to one where the 'customer is the centre of the universe, quality is built in and people are regarded as the single most important part of the organisation and its only appreciable asset' (Wickens, 1987, p. 183). Wickens adds that in Pratt and Whitney 'The purpose of management is to facilitate and thus recognise that the largest single repository of ideas is the workforce', so 'two way communication' is of paramount importance (p. 183).

Deal and Kennedy (1982) describe the corporate culture of The Tandem Corporation, and assess its implications. They attribute (albeit guardedly – 'Only time will tell whether Tandem can maintain its pattern of high performance' (p. 8)) the success of Tandem to its strong culture. This has a number of elements: a widely shared philosophy, which stresses its commitment to the importance of people. This value is 'broadcast by T shirts, bulletin boards and word of mouth' (p. 10). Another element is the remarkable lack of formal structures, roles and rules, which are replaced, argue Deal and Kennedy, by their far more effective functional equivalent: unwritten rules and shared understandings. Interestingly the authors note: 'Tandem seems to maintain a balance between autonomy and control without relying heavily on centralised or formalised procedures, or rigid status hierarchies' (p. 11). Another feature of the culture is the emphasis on the heroic status of the company's CEO. These values are supported by and transmitted through a series of social events and activities: 'These provide opportunities for employees to develop a spirit of oneness and symbolise that Tandem cares about employees' (p. 12). The authors conclude: 'Tandem is a unique company. And much of its success appears as intimately tied to its culture as to its product and its market place position. The company has explicit values and beliefs which its employees share. It has heroes. It has storytellers and stories. It has rituals and ceremonies on key occasions. Tandem seems to have a strong culture which creates a bond between the company and the employees, and inspires levels of productivity unlike most other corporations.' (Deal and Kennedy, 1982 p. 12.)

Reference to the two brief cases in box 6.1 shows many of the common themes of recent writings on corporate culture: it is these themes which will constitute the essence of this chapter.

Since the beginning of the industrial period, and certainly the development of factories on a large scale, employers have always faced a crucial dilemma: on the one hand they had to have tight control over what their staff did and how they did it – to ensure that time wasn't wasted, the materials weren't misused or stolen, to ensure quality, etc. On the other hand they relied, to varying degrees but always to some degree, on the goodwill, creative good sense, responsibility, etc. of the workforce. No factory can be run by rules; no set of rules entirely catches all that is required of the employees.

But efforts to achieve control, because they were frequently oppressive, intrusive, unpleasant, demanding, dominating, risked damage to workers' commitment on which their good will and common sense were dependent. It is possible to argue that the history of the changing philosophies of management, organization and work-design systems is nothing more than the history of different management efforts to 'solve' this dilemma. And the final dilemma, arguably, is this: that any solution actually sets up a new problem – or rather an old problem in new form or degree. Ultimately all solutions fail.

It seems, however, as if their depressing dilemma might finally have been solved; it seems that by developing strong corporate cultures managers can finally have it both ways: tight control (no need now for rules or role) and high levels of commitment and enthusiasm. These are ambitious claims; no wonder managers take them so seriously. Maybe we should take them seriously too . . .

There has certainly been a level of interest in corporate cultures in recent years. One commentator notes: 'The concept of culture has been linked increasingly with the study of organization' (Smirich, 1983, p. 339). Even in 1980 *Business Week* ran a cover story entitled 'Corporate culture: The hard way to change values that spell success or failure'. The reason for this high level of interest, of course, is that a number of commentators have argued a direct and positive connection between the nature and strength of organizational cultures and levels of organizational performance and effectiveness.

Interest in organizational cultures, however, comes from two rather different directions, with rather different implications. Not all who write about organizational cultures are primarily concerned with issues of performance. On the one hand there are academics and researchers who 'welcomed the topic of culture as a long overdue source of "fresh air"', an antidote to sterile number crunching focused on easily measured variables'. On the other hand there are those with a more practical agenda who 'were attracted by the seductive promises of culture as a key to improved morale, loyalty, harmony, productivity and – ultimately – profitability' (Frost et al., 1991, p. 7).

Overall the appeal of culture in corporate analysis stems from the high level of concern among managers and consultants (and some scholars) with the importance of employee commitment for corporate performance. Interest in the excellent performance of Japanese corporations has led to a prevalent view, in managerial circles, that this is the result of Japanese workers' deeply-held shared values and beliefs. Concern for the poor performance of Western corporations, and interest in improving it, also lies behind the popularity of the subject.

Practitioner and academic approaches to corporate cultures

The culture literature is not homogeneous: it consists of a literature which at one extreme is consultancy-based, popular, rather bland and prescriptive, aimed at managers; and at the other end more theoretical, descriptive studies aimed at scholars. These different literatures, or usages of the concept 'culture', differ in other ways too: they are discussed below. A number of writers have distinguished these two approaches.

1   Barley et al. call these differences 'practitioner' and 'academic' approaches. Interestingly, these authors note that over time the research focus of both groups, initially very different, began to converge markedly. By 1984, both groups were researching more or less the same issues: the economic values of controlling culture, the scope and role of rationality, and the integrative value of culture (Barley et al., 1988).

However, not only has the concept of organizational culture been defined in a number of very different – even opposed – ways, it has also been used in different ways, in different content areas, to do different sorts of things.

Barley et al. note how early interest in culture arose from two separate sources. On the one hand were those management authors who argued that an emphasis on rational strategies, formal structures and systems led to an underestimation of the role of values, symbols and beliefs in engaging loyalty and influencing behaviour. These authors argued that rational strategies had a limited effect on performance and productivity, and that the manipulation of values, norms, symbols and beliefs was a powerful but under-used source of managerial advantage.

On the other hand, but at very much the same time, a group of academic researchers began to conceptualize organizations in terms of structures of meaning – focusing on how people at work construct and negotiate the sense of their and others' behaviour in terms of values, myths, norms and beliefs. As Barley et al. note, this second approach was essentially an alternative paradigm with which to study organizations: 'thus while the first group turned to culture as a way of improving organisational effectiveness, the second saw in culture the basis for paradigmatic revolution' (Barley et al., 1988, p. 32).

Our focus in this chapter is primarily on the first approach, because of the importance of its claims, and its central role in HRS writings.

2   Knights and Willmott (1987) develop a similar classification: they argue that interest in the concept divides into 'practitioner-oriented' literature and literature which 'is heralded as a new direction in organisational analysis involving a movement away from quantification, prediction and structure toward studies of organisation that are more qualitative, appreciative, and processual' (Knights and Willmott, 1987, p. 40).

3   Sackmann also distinguishes academic from practitioner applications and notes that the first is concerned with understanding, the second control and prediction. She also notes the role of what she calls the cultural anthropologists' tradition, which refers to the academic area where the concept was originally developed. This is only relevant to

organizational applications in that this original sense of the term supplies a degree of rigour and of conceptual clarity which are largely missing from organizational applications. One of the main weaknesses of managerialist and consultancy applications ('practitioner') is that they fail to acknowledge the complexity of the concept and some of the fundamental criticisms, from within anthropology, to which their definition and usage of culture is vulnerable (Sackmann, 1991). For example, to return to the cases presented earlier, Deal and Kennedy, in their description of the culture of Tandem seem, wittingly or unwittingly, to be trying to portray the culture of Tandem as if it were a mini-society, as if this culture was essentially the same as that of a society, or a tribe. Employees 'share values . . . heroes, stories, storytellers, rituals and ceremonies, strong bonds . . . unwritten rules'. We probably accept the power of culture in societies, especially small stable societies; we know that members of such societies can be moved to great levels of commitment, heroism, shame and sacrifice by such values. But can organizational cultures really be compared to societal cultures? Is a flag the same as a corporate T-shirt? And is the role of culture, in a societal, tribal or corporate context, necessarily consensus building, commitment generating, 'positive' in its implications? And who, of course, will define what positive means?

4   Smirich (1983), in a classification of the culture literature, also distinguishes practitioner and academic applications of culture, although she explores and develops the distinction more fully. She suggests five ways in which the concept of culture has been applied. These five applications derive from different ways of seeing organizations and culture, focus on different objectives and carry different assumptions. They are worth our attention because aspects of these applications are apparent in the way those concerned with manipulating corporate cultures approach their subject and their work – even if they don't know it.

Essentially the first two ways of using the concept are concerned with the identification and analysis of cultural variables that are related to variations in organizational performance, and so, broadly, fall within the 'practitioner' school, although work within these areas can vary considerably in its thoroughness and scholarship. The other three approaches ('academic') are concerned not with efficiency or performance, but with understanding what organizations are, and how they work. Her classification is useful for its thoroughness and also because she includes cross-cultural studies.

These five areas are:

Cross-cultural or comparative management;
Corporate culture;
Organizational cognition;
Organizational symbolism;
Unconscious process and organization.

Cross-cultural or comparative management

This approach is concerned with identifying and analysing culturally based variations in management practice and organizational process across countries. Such research is of obvious importance given, for example, the high level of interest in understanding the *Japanese* basis of Japanese economic performance. Broadly speaking this tradition of research defines culture as an independent variable which develops within the organization as a consequence of the organization's location within a host society. The cultural values, distinctive to the host society, are revealed in the behaviours of organizational members. This type of research seeks to map and classify differences in cultural variables and relate these countries.

Child has revived and synthesized this literature very usefully (Child, 1981). He notes that this use of culture has three objectives: to identify the extent to which organizational characteristics vary in relation to their location within different countries; secondly, to isolate the national attributes associated with such differences; and thirdly, if there are national differences, to explain how organizations are coloured by national differences. He notes that research to date shows that some organizational characteristics, particularly employees' attitudes and interpersonal styles, do vary between countries. Take for example the work of Hofstede (1980), who on the basis of an enormous survey of 160,000 employees of IBM argued that there are four discrete dimensions of culture: power distance (extent to which people accept the unequal distribution of power), uncertainty avoidance (the extent to which people dislike ambiguity and uncertainty), individualism (the extent to which people are oriented towards the well-being of themselves/families as against an orientation towards a wider social grouping) and masculinity (the extent to which material forms of success are prized over values such as caring and nurturing. On the basis of his research he argues that countries differ significantly in their 'score' on these dimensions.

In a later work Hofstede illustrates how these dimensions can be used to illustrate organizational cultures and practices. He argues, for example, that two dimensions, power distance and uncertainty, can be combined to form a matrix within which organizations can be located. Organizations low on power distance and low on uncertainty avoidance prefer a lack of overriding hierarchy, and a flexible approach to rules, while organizations with low power distance but high on uncertainty avoidance expect actions to comply with and to be directed by, rules and procedures.

However, in reviewing work on cultural differences, Child argues that there has been little thorough or persuasive work that explains why these attributes are intrinsic to the development of the host societies, or how they influence organizations within these societies. A major source of the problems in the use of national culture as an explanatory variable stems from the way in which the frequently ill-defined concept of culture is simply used to account for identified differences in organizational behaviour or values. It is used as a rather indiscriminate, general explanation to account for differences otherwise unaccounted for. Studies of cross-national differences 'have managed to identify variations in organizational or member characteristic associated with nationality, but have ascribed these to culture without locating it in a relevant social context. Culture has thus been treated as a residual factor' (Child, 1981, p. 306).

While he is aware of the weaknesses of this cross-cultural approach to analyses of organizations, Child is unwilling entirely to reject this approach. This is largely because his review of two other explanations for differences in organizational structures and functioning (these are known as arguments from contingency and from capitalism) suggests that neither of these is wholly satisfactory either. Child therefore seeks to rescue culturalist explanations. This involves a number of elements:

1　While noting the large number of definitions of culture, he emphasizes that the essence of culture is its concern with the normative and the relationship between norms and values and action. If, he argues, citizens of one country hold values in common, then these will presumably influence how they behave in a specified context and in an observable manner.

2　Child then uses a framework for the classification of the elements of cultures. Like many other commentators he uses Kluckhohn and Strodtbeck's (1961) model of value dimensions. We shall discuss this model below.

3　He argues that studies of cultural differences must be able to avoid the common danger of 'simply inferring culture as a national phenomenon from virtually any contrasts which arise from a comparison of organizations located in different countries. Even if such contrasts are unambiguously national in scope, they could possibly be due to other non-cultural phenomena such as national wealth, level of industrialisation or even climate' (Child, 1981, p. 328). This point is very important, for many authors have accounted for national differences in organizational structure and functioning by references not to values *per se,* but to differences in the pattern of industrialization or modernization, or to the institutional structures of societies, the underlying character of the economic system.

Child concludes his analysis by suggesting that despite the problems with the term 'culture' in cross-national analyses, it is worth retaining as long as culture is (a) treated rigorously, and (b) regarded as just one of a number of interrelated relevant variables.

Corporate culture

This application is particularly important for this chapter since it represents the major way in which the concept of culture is employed within the HRS literature. This is the approach that is apparent in the two short cases quoted earlier (box 6.1). Within this tradition culture is seen as an *attribute* of organization – something that organizations *have*. In general this application employs a systems approach to organizations, seeing them as collections of interrelated variables, the interrelationships between which determine the nature of organizational process and effectiveness. Traditionally the key variables identified by such an approach would be the 'hard' variables of structure, technology, etc., but recently 'soft' subjective variables such as culture have been emphasized.

The key argument of this application of culture is simply that the culture of an organization contributes to its performance. This argument, central to HRS writing, will be discussed more fully – and criticized more thoroughly – below.

Culture as a 'root metaphor'

Both the earlier two applications of the concept of culture to organizations see organizations as organism-like entities existing within environments which supply pressures for action and adjustment. In both cases attention is focused on the patterns of relationships within or between organizations and their environments. Smirich notes that both approaches share the assumption that 'The desired outcomes of research into these patterns are statements of contingent relationships that will have applicability for those trying to manage organizations. Underlying the interests in comparative management and corporate culture is the search for predictable means for organizational control and improved means for organizational management' (Smirich, 1983, p. 347).

We shall return to this prescriptive element of the culture literature within HRS in due course.

Thus both applications treated so far, in regarding organizations as organisms, see culture as an attribute of, or an element of, these organisms – something the organization *has*. However, an alternative view is to see organizations *as* cultures. In this sense organizations are seen *as if they were* cultures, a metaphor which stresses the subjective, conscious, expressive and symbolic aspects of organizations rather than seeing organizations in instrumental, material terms. Within this metaphor the focus of research activity is not performance in the sense of efficiency, effectiveness, competitiveness or output, but performance as continuous theatre, as the management of and construction of meaning.

This approach to organizational culture – seeing it as something the organization *is* – differs fundamentally from the earlier approach (something an organisation *has*) not only in its approach but also in its objectives. Here the focus is not on improving performance, supporting management, or strengthening (while disguising) management control, but on understanding organizational action in the terms in which participants themselves understand it.

This 'culture as metaphor' approach to organizational analysis has produced three constituent schools of research:

In one approach culture is defined in terms of the structuring of cognitive processes within organizations. This approach regards organizational cultures as a structure of ways of understanding and knowing the world, of rules that govern cognition. Such an approach, potentially of enormous value in analysing and revealing the taken-for-granted assumptions and convictions that lie behind organizational members' decisions and relationships, focuses on the structures of shared meanings, frameworks and recipes that determine members' analysis and perceptions.

Another variant is when the focus is on culture as systems of shared symbols within organizations. Here researchers seek to analyse – to 'read' – the meaning of members' action, and how members themselves read others' behaviour and learn to construct their own and to display their mastery of the informal, symbolic systems.

Finally, a third form of the metaphor approach to the use of the concept of culture is when organizational cultures are seen as the expression of psychological processes and needs.

We see then that there is general agreement that applications of the notion of culture to organization take two forms: one practitioner-focused, concerned with issues of efficiency and performance, the other more academic and concerned with issues of understanding and analysis. This in itself is not necessarily surprising or terribly important; what makes it highly important in this case is the suggestion, voiced by many writers, that the practitioners' analysis (and the prescriptions and promises built on these analyses) has overlooked some of the complexities of the concept of culture and of organization in its eagerness to discover or pass on their seductive promises. If cultures can be changed it is a lot harder, and a lot less certain in its outcome, than the enthusiasts recognize, or admit.

The Role of Culture in Organizational Performance

The reason for so much recent managerial interest in corporate cultures is, very obviously, because of the claim that culture plays a major part in determining organizational performance. If it was not for the power and appeal of this claim there would be little need to discuss organizational cultures. There would also be little interest in writing about and researching organizational culture. And yet there is enormous interest. Stablein and Nord (1985, p. 22) note: 'Probably never before in organisational studies has an innovative area been given so much attention so rapidly.'

Fundamental therefore to any consideration of organizational cultures from the corporate-culture approach at least, is the argument that such cultures matter greatly because they affect organizational performance. More specifically, the argument of the corporate-culture school is:

- That organizations have cultures.
- That they become more effective when they develop the right 'strong' cultures (which needs careful definition).
- That these cultures create consensus and unity and motivate staff.
- That cultures have an effect on corporate performance.
- That when necessary, cultures can be – and should be – changed.
- That it is the responsibility of senior managers to change them.

The corporate-culture approach presumes that organizational cultures can be assessed, managed, constructed and manipulated in the pursuit of enhanced organizational effectiveness. Employees' norms, beliefs and values can (and when necessary should) be changed so that they contribute the appropriate behaviour, commit themselves to the organization, support management and strategy. This prevalent view holds that the norms and values shared by members of the organization create consensus, induce unity and when appropriate generate appropriate behaviour. Cultures integrate the organization (Meek, 1982).

The corporate-culture approach contains some assertions about the positive role of corporate cultures: 'Organisational culture is considered "the managerial formula for success" (Jaggi, 1985) that determines an organization's success or failure' (*Business Week*, 1983). Managers are promised a 'culture of productivity' (Akin and Hopelian, 1986) if they understand the elements that all cultures of productivity have in common. The 'right' culture may 'reap a return on investment that averages nearly twice as high as those firms with less efficient cultures' (Denison, 1984). 'Sustained competitive advantage' (Barney, 1986) is expected from the 'right' culture, which is also characterized as 'strong' (Bleicher, 1983, p. 495), 'rich' (Deal and Kennedy, 1982, p. 14), 'healthy, blooming' (Ulrich, 1984, p. 313), 'consistent' (Hinterhuber, 1986) and 'participatory' (Denison, 1984, p. 7; see Sackmann, 1991, p. 119).

This argument is probably most associated with (and certainly well developed in) the writings of Tom Peters and the 'excellence' approach which he represents and articulates. Peters and Waterman (1982) argue that in 'excellent' companies employees are committed to their organization and to its goals, and that this is a firmer basis for achieving competitive excellence than the traditional determinants of behaviour – structures, procedures and rules. This argument is nicely caught in the summary of one commentator: 'There is a growing international consensus that, for the western countries, economic renaissance is dependent upon the cultural transformation of large scale business and, in particular, on the extent to which decaying bureaucracies can be replaced with dynamic, organic cultures' (Sadler, 1988, p. 127).

This view is not restricted to Peters. Deal and Kennedy, for example, argue that:

> Since organisation values can powerfully influence what people actually do, we think that values ought to be a matter of great concern to managers. In fact, shaping and enhancing values can become the most important job a manager can do. In our work and study we have found that successful companies place a great deal of emphasis on values. In general, these companies shared three characteristics:
>
> - They stand for something – that is, they have a clear and explicit philosophy about how they aim to conduct their business.
> - Management pays a great deal of attention to shaping and fine-tuning these values to conform to the economic and business environment of the company and to communicating them to the organisation.
> - These values are known and shared by all the people who work for the company – from the lowliest production worker right through to the ranks of senior management.
>
> (Deal and Kennedy, 1982, p. 22)

Notice how 'strong' cultures are here regarded entirely positively. Deal and Kennedy argue, for example: 'Strong culture companies . . . communicate exactly how they want their people to behave. They spell out standards of acceptable decorum – so people who visit or work in any of their places of business can know what to expect. They call attention to the way in which procedures – for example, strategic planning and budgeting – are to be carried out. The fault if the procedures fail is substantive not just a failure to follow prescribed process. . . . In strong culture companies nothing is too trivial . . . These companies take pride in the way they do things and work hard to make sure that the way is right' (Deal and Kennedy, 1982, pp. 59–60).

If organizational cultures have consequences for employees' behaviour and attitudes, then the manipulation of such cultures and the symbols of which they consist becomes a primary tasks for managers – possibly the primary task: 'If organisations are systems of shared meanings and beliefs, and if they are organised through the development of shared paradigms, then clearly one important administrative activity is the development of such understandings within the organisation' (Pfeffer, 1981, p. 21). Pfeffer identifies openly and clearly the potential benefit of such action for commitment and consensus: 'Symbolic action may serve to motivate individuals within the organisation and to mobilise persons . . . to take action . . . Symbolic actions may serve to mollify groups that are dissatisfied with the organisation, thereby ensuring their continued support of the organisation and the lessening of opposition and conflict' (Pfeffer, 1981, pp. 34–5; see also Deal and Kennedy, 1982, and Kilmann et al., 1986).

Many managerialist writers on organizational cultures see the management of cultures and symbols as the prime task of management. Peters, for example, argues: 'symbols are the very stuff of management behaviour. Executives, after all, do not synthesise chemicals or operate fork lift trucks; they deal in symbols' (Peters, 1978, p. 10).

The Nature and Components of Organizational Cultures

Within the organizational culture field issues of definition assume centre stage. If we are to assess the claims of the corporate-culture advocates, we must know what they mean by culture and what assumptions they are making about the nature and origins of culture. The analysis of organizational culture is a focus of an enormous amount of activity, research/academic work and consultancy. We have seen already that there are significant differences in the way in which the culture concept is applied and the usages to which it is put.

It is therefore no surprise to find that the concept itself is defined in very different ways. Much of the confusion and conflict between writings (and recommendations) on corporate culture stem from fundamental differences in how culture is defined. And these differences are related directly to equally fundamental differences in assumptions about how organizations work. 'Organisational culture researchers do not agree about what culture is or why it should be studied. They do not study the same phenomena. They do not approach the phenomena they do study from the same theoretical, epistemological, or methodological points of view' (Frost et al., 1991, p. 7).

Definitions

Our focus within this chapter is mainly on the managerialist, consultancy approach to organizational cultures – corporate culture. Therefore in this section we will focus particularly but not exclusively on definitions of culture from within the corporate-culture tradition. However, other definitions will also be mentioned, mainly in order to highlight and counterpoint the consultancy definitions.

Definitions of culture within the corporate culture approach have a number of features.

First, the definitions are highly functionalistic, normative, prescriptive and instrumental. Cultures are defined in terms of their impact on performance and are regarded in terms of their positive contribution. For example, Kilmann et al. remark: 'A culture has a positive impact on an organisation when it points behaviour in the right direction . . . Alternatively a culture has negative impact when it points behaviour in the wrong direction' (1986, p. 4; quoted in Alvesson, 1989, p. 125). Another contributor to this managerialist tradition displays unashamedly a managerialist perspective: 'Good cultures are characterised by norms and values supportive of excellence, teamwork, profitability, honesty, a customer service orientation, pride in one's work, and commitment to the organisation. Most of all, they are supportive of adaptability – the capacity to thrive over the long run despite new competition, new regulations, new technological developments, and the strains of growth' (Baker, 1980, p. 10; quoted in Alvesson, 1989, p. 125).

Many of these definitions are overtly functionalist in the sense that they argue that existing cultures persist because they play a positive role in the maintenance and effectiveness of the organization: they have a survival role. Schein represents this view very clearly. According to him, 'Culture is:

1　a pattern of shared basic assumptions,
2　invented, discovered or developed by a given group,
3　as it learns to cope with its problems of external adaptation and internal integration,
4　that has worked well enough to be considered valid and therefore,
5　is taught to new members of the group as the
6　correct way to perceive, think and feel in relation to those problems.' (Drawn from Schein, 1992, p. 237.)

Secondly, these definitions of culture commonly refer to the *integrative* role of culture: 'Culture . . . refers to a shared system of values, norms and symbols. The term culture conveys an entire image, *an integrated set of dimensions/characteristics and the whole behind the parts*' (Louis, 1981, quoted in Alvesson, 1987, p. 4; our emphasis).

They also insist that cultures are *shared* by members of the organization. 'Shared meaning, shared understanding, and shared sense-making are all different ways of describing culture. In talking about culture we are really talking about a process of reality construction that allows people to see and understand particular events, actions, objects, utterances, or situations in distinctive ways' (Morgan, 1986, quoted in Alvesson, 1987, p. 5).

Thirdly, these definitions argue that cultures consist of values, beliefs and cognitive assumptions.

However, a different and contrasting approach is offered by Pettigrew's interesting definition of culture (1979, p. 574). His definition differs in that it does not assume that the values in question are shared by all members of an organization (which is empirically highly unlikely anyway). He focuses not on the organization but on the group. He notes that when people work together they develop a sense of what they are doing and why, of how they should relate to each: in short, a system of meanings. But he does not assume that cultures are necessarily positive, or integrating, or shared. 'Culture is the system of such publicly and collectively accepted meanings operating for a given group at a given time.' Pettigrew sensibly objects to the assumption that cultures are unitary, consensual and consistent. He prefers to argue that culture is a source of a family of concepts, all of which have their use: symbol, language, ideology, ritual, belief.

Differences underlying these differences

A number of writers have attempted to categorize and organize the heterogeneous definitions of cultures into categories. The basis for these classifications is usually the purpose that is seen to lie behind the definitions, and these purposes are often categorized in terms very similar to those discussed earlier – of whether the definition is intended to aid managerial objectives, academic understanding, or radical critique of organizations.

Frost et al. (1991) argue that it is possible to organize the different definitions of culture under three headings: integration, fragmentation and differentiation. The integration perspective sees cultures as consistent and consensual; the differentiation perspective stresses inconsistency, variation between, even conflict between subcultures. And finally, the fragmentation perspective sees cultures as ambiguous, fluctuating, inconsistent, unclear.

Obviously the integration perspectives represents the classic consultancy approach of Peters, Deal and Kennedy, etc. It asserts that a strong or desirable culture is characterized by consistency, organization-wide consensus and clarity, and that these result in commitment and improved performance.

Other authors (Stablein and Nord, 1985) have used the work of Habermas to classify approaches to organizational cultures. Habermas's distinction between three types of cognitive interest in a subject is useful. Three such approaches are distinguished: the technical, the practical and the emancipatory. Habermas describes these as: 'information that expands our power of technical control; interpretations that make possible the orientation of action within common traditions; and analyses that free consciousness from its dependence on hypostatized powers' (Habermas, 1971, p. 313; quoted in Stablein and Nord, 1985, p. 14).

The first is aimed at achieving control over the subject; the second seeks to achieve understanding; the third focuses on the achievement of liberation that removes compulsion and reveals power and compulsion. While the first two approaches clearly work to sustain existing relationships and institutions and to legitimate them, the third critiques and questions such patterns. Very clearly, the majority of analyses of organizational cultures fall into the first category: they attempt to harness and direct the power of culture to further the manipulation and control of workers in pursuit of managerial purposes. Certainly the corporate culture approach fits in this category. (This is not to suggest that such efforts are successful. This will be discussed later in this chapter.)

The Ideology of Culture

This section will focus directly on those usages of culture which assert a direct link between cultures and performance – the approaches described by Smirich as the 'corporate-culture' approach, as discussed above.

For some writers this view of culture is flawed, inadequate, unrealistic and ultimately ideological. It is more interesting as a *reflection* of management ideology and culture than it is as an *analysis* of such culture. This critique is important because it clearly claims that the assertions and promises of the corporate culture approach are deeply flawed. The critique usually consists of three separate elements: culture as ideology, conceptual limitations and empirical failings. These criticisms will be briefly outlined below. They will be more fully developed throughout the remainder of the chapter.

Culture as ideology

The corporate-culture approach to culture has been criticized for having major *ideological* elements: it is ideological, purposive and bland because its function is to support management goals, and the aspects of organization associated with these goals.

We must note that these criticisms do not apply to all applications of culture to organizations. Alvesson recognizes that the ideological aspect of culture writings does not apply to the 'culture as metaphor school': he quotes with approval Smirich's comment that 'When culture is a root metaphor, the researcher's attention shifts from concerns about what organisations accomplish and how they may accomplish it more efficiently to how is organisation accomplished and what does it mean to be organised' (Smirich, 1983, p. 353).

Alvesson argues that the corporate-culture approach to organizational culture serves ideological purposes, in a number of ways.

First, these writings are clearly committed to the enhancement of management control by new means, and committed to managerial goals. They focus on the value of controlling organizational cultures and the benefits of so doing. 'The key assumption of authors writing on culture and symbolism proceeding from a technical cognitive interest, is that knowledge about the functioning of symbols and how intentionally to change and control significant symbols in organisations, provides potential means for the management and manipulation of symbols. Symbols are . . . viewed as aspects of organisations possessing the potential to be exploited and subordinated to the intentions of . . . top managers' (Alvesson, 1991, p. 216).

Secondly, these writings are partial and discriminating in the aspects of management culture on which they choose to focus. To some extent this stems from the tendency with these definitions of culture to view it as something shared by the members of the community. The focus on consensus, with its implication of mutuality, obstructs the role of power in underpinning existing organizational structures, and the ways they work. As Knights and Willmott have noted, one of the curious features of the consultancy approach to organizational cultures is that despite the claim to be concerned with structures of values and beliefs, the actual focus is remarkably limited: for such analysis does not usually attend to 'the role of symbols and the expression of culture in the reproduction of labour processes through which the fundamentally exploitative character of production relations, involving the pumping out of surplus from employees, is routinely secured as it is concealed' (Knights and Willmott, 1987, p. 43).

The same point is made by Alvesson (1989) who argues that the concept culture is excessively focused on instrumental preoccupations and values within the organization, while at the same time being insufficiently concerned with exploring (or even acknowledging) core aspects of Western managerial culture which might (a) be inimical or damaging to consensus and cultural unity, and (b) might undermine employee commitment and obedience – i.e. such values as hierarchy, control, instrumental values, racism, and so on.

Thirdly, these approaches are directly concerned with the pursuit of management objectives while presenting themselves as exercises in neutral, academic/scientific research. They support attempts to control the work-force while claiming that their interests are purely neutral and academic. They claim to represent objective scientific analyses of the way the world is – or organizations are. But in fact they represent the way managers see the world, and the interests they pursue. Alvesson notes: 'The questions for-mulated and answered, the perspective taken, the sectional interests sup-ported etc. are grounded in a world view, a set of beliefs and values, which indicate that the top managers of corporations and other organisations are a highly important group, whose actions are normally supposed to support the social good . . . managerial actions . . . are worthy of support and it is the duty of management writers to provide it' (Alvesson, 1991, p. 217).

The focus on 'culture change', for example, is often an attempt to impose a consensual, unitarist conception of the organization on all employees, and thus to gain their commitment. Organizational attempts to achieve homo-geneous, unitary cultures contrast, and possibly conflict, with a view of the organization as an arena of conflicting and different groups and value systems. The rhetoric is denied by reality. Even Wickens, an enthusiast for the corporate-culture approach, acknowledges that 'We spend vast amounts of time talking and negotiating about employee involvement and very little time actually involving employees. As with many of these ideas – the flavour of the month that will be our managerial salvation – we construct an edifice which simply invites opposition' (Wickens, 1987, p. 85).

Conceptual limitations

Although the concept culture is obviously borrowed from cultural anthro-pology, those who have used it in analyses of organizations have drawn selectively from available definitions of culture and have failed to note or address the assumptions underlying the definitions they have employed, or criticisms of these assumptions. Definitions of culture in the corporate-cul-tures approach have made a series of basic assumptions about the nature and role of cultures which are unsustainable.

Meek, for example, notes that corporate applications and definitions of the concept 'culture' borrow heavily from a particular tradition within anthropology and sociology – structural functionalism. The problem with this is that structural functionalist approaches to culture have been roundly criticized, yet these criticisms, which apply equally to corporate applica-tions, have been conveniently overlooked by recent culture writers. A key assertion of the structural-functionalist approach is that 'social order is created and maintained through individuals internalising dominant social norms and values, for its treatment of people holding alternative norms and values as being socially deviant, and for its assumption that the parts of a society exist in a natural state of equilibrium, functioning effectively so as to maintain the effectiveness of the total social structure' (Meek, 1982, p. 195). Within the corporate-culture literature, therefore, this approach argues that cultures are a unifying force; that they reflect the collective will of the organization; that they are consistent with, or derive from, the wishes of senior management; that deviants must be dealt with. As a result of the borrowing of structural-functional assumptions, managerialist approaches to corporate culture tend to ignore inherent systemic conflicts within the organization, ignore structures of power and interest, ignore structures of hierarchy and inequality, and ignore difference and differentiation of groups and of cultures (Meek, 1982, p. 195).

Knights and Willmott (1987) note, as have other authors – see for example Anthony (1994) – that recent research on organizational culture of the corporate-culture variety has tended to remove the study of organizations from the relations of power and conflict that coexist around cultures. The material and political contexts within which organizational cultures develop and with which they engage, are ignored by many studies of organizational cultures. This removal of culture from conflict follows, as Meek notes, the functionalist approach of these views of organizational culture. As a result, culture is viewed 'as a product of consensus rather than as the precarious outcome of continuous processes of contestation and struggle' (Knights and Willmott, 1987, p. 41).

Empirical problems

There are two closely interrelated problems here, both of which follow closely the conceptual issues explored above: that organizational cultures are not necessarily (or even usually) homogeneous and unitary but are differentiated; and that therefore not all employees are equally committed to a single organizational culture.

For example, organizations may be (or have) a number of different, even competing cultures. Pfeffer suggests that organizational subunits may have their distinctive ideologies and structures of meaning. These may compete with other, or more dominant cultures within the same organization (Pfeffer, 1981). And Alvesson has suggested that it is probably more sensible to focus on organizational cultures not as systems of shared values and norms (see above) but as 'a common understanding among individuals about what they are expected to do and say, how to behave, mastery of the subtleties of their existence, which presupposes a certain cultural competence . . . Culture might thus, at least in rational bureaucratic organisations . . . be seen as a common instrumental set of attitudes towards the activities and the setting people are engaged in' (Alvesson, 1987, p. 10).

This may not be a very rich conceptualization of culture; but it may be a realistic one, and one that gets round some of the obvious flaws of the conceptualizations that promise too much but deliver less.

These different cultures may not simply differ, they may conflict. Different groups may hold views which directly oppose other sets of beliefs, and associated practices. These differences may occur on a vertical or a horizontal axis – between groups arranged hierarchically, or between regional, divisional, functional groups.

Organizations are usually the sites for considerable conflict, and one of the axes on which these conflicts occur is structured differences in values. Culture can reflect conflict, can be used within conflict, can be a source of conflict.

Components of Culture

If organizational cultures are important, and if variations in organizational cultures have implications for different levels of organizational performance (a viewpoint which some writers argue), then it becomes important to be able to describe these differences, and to identify the key differences. How do cultures differ? The consultancy literature is awash with various classifications, many of which involve categorizing organizations into simplistic, over-general, monolithic cultural types. However, there are some points that can be made reasonably safely.

First, one aspect of cultures noted by many writers is that they consist of a variety of elements which themselves can be seen as occurring on different levels: symbols, myths, ideologies and rituals. Symbols provide meaning and evoke emotions. Languages are collections of symbols. Cultures also consist of knowledge and assumption – cognitive systems, models and frameworks that structure what members know, and how they think, reason, argue, decide (Meek, 1982; Pettigrew, 1979).

Schein, like other commentators, differentiates a number of levels of organizational cultures. The first level is visible artefacts which consist of technology, art and visible and audible behaviour. The second level – values – focuses on why people behave as they do, and the nature and role of values in determining employees' action. This level is debatable, overt, espoused values. Underlying values are basic assumptions – the third level – which consists of the five dimensions derived from Kluckhohn and Strodtbeck. These, Schein argues, are 'typically unconscious but . . . actually determine how group members perceive, think and feel . . . taken-for-granted assumptions are so powerful because they are less debatable and confrontable' (Schein, 1992, p. 239). These assumptions are 'typically unconscious but . . . actually determine how group members perceive, think and feel' (Schein, 1992, p. 239).

Pettigrew has also noted the different levels of culture, and argued also that 'At the deepest level, culture is . . . the complex set of values, beliefs, and assumptions that define the ways in which a firm conducts its business. Such core beliefs and assumptions are, of course manifested in the structures, systems, symbols, myths and patterns of reward inside the organisation' (Pettigrew, 1990, p. 266). There are two interesting implications to this: first, note that Pettigrew sees such elements as structures and systems as at least partially cultural in the sense that they arise out of, and reflect, basic cultural values; secondly, if culture occurs on a number of levels, attempts to change culture will presumably be more effective (and less significant) at the more superficial levels.

Many more thoughtful commentators recommend or use the same basic framework. Child (1981), for example, recommends a return to a framework for cultural analysis developed by Kluckhohn and Strodtbeck (1961). This lists five key human dilemmas to which there is a limited range of 'answers'. Within a given society a dominant value system will be apparent (Child, 1981, p. 325). All five values/orientations are potentially applicable to organizational structures and behaviour. In table 6.1 Child describes the five variables and suggests some ways in which particular positions of the five variables could relate to organizational issues.

A broadly similar approach has been adopted by both Bate (1992) and Schein (1992). Both use frameworks derived from the work of Kluckhohn and Strodtbeck (1961). But these authors have other features in common. Both suggest that cultures are 'solutions' to, or overviews on, a limited number of basic issues or problems. However, these authors differ fundamentally in their assessment of the adequacy of these solutions.

Also, many writers accept the possibility of a relationship between an organization's culture and the behaviour of its employees and therefore, ultimately, the performance of the organization. But this relationship is (a) attenuated and complex, and (b) is not necessarily positive or negative.

We have, for example, noted Schein's definition of culture earlier in this chapter. Remember that Schein argues that the constituent assumptions of a culture exist in order to 'cope' with the organization's problems of external adaptation and internal integration. He argues that 'Cultural elements are defined as learned solutions to problems' (Schein, 1992, p. 243). He distinguishes five external problems (see table 6.2), and six internal problems (see table 6.3).

There is obviously considerable overlap between these lists and the list of cultural dimensions in Child's table quoted earlier. But note that Schein sees culture as supplying positive, constructive, efficiency-enhancing 'solutions' to these problems, whereas Child and the authors from whom

Table 6.1 Examples of relationships postulated between cultural value orientations and organizational characteristics

Value orientation (> = stronger than, or preferred)	General organizational characteristics	Examples of specific practices
1 Human nature: good > evil	Emphasis on subordinate autonomy and intrinsic motivation	Subordinate goal-setting: job enrichment
2 Man to nature: mastery > subjugation	Policies of innovation, and of developing individual expertise	Support for venture management; positive exercise of strategic choice including active negotiation of boundary conditions with external groups
3 Time orientation: future > past	Strategic emphasis and long-term planning; formal schemes for thorough organizational socialization and career planning	MBO approach rather than budgetary control; use of manpower planning and assessment centres
4 Orientation toward activity: being > doing	Human relations philosophy; emphasis on interpersonal sensitivity; interest in social as well as economic and technological criteria in work organization	Management style high on consideration relative to initiating structure; organizational morale and climate included in performance monitoring
5 Relationships: individual > hierarchical	Minimization of hierarchy; emphasis on delegation and participation; control through assessment of achievement rather than through insistence on conformity to rules	Amenities and fringe benefits not differentiated by status; employees deal directly with members of public (where relevant) without referral upwards

Source: Child, 1981, p. 327.

Table 6.2 Problems of external adaptation and survival

Strategy	Developing consensus on the *primary task, core mission, or manifest and latent functions of the group.*
Goals	Developing consensus on *goals,* such goals being the concrete reflection of the core mission.
Means for accomplishing goals	Developing consensus on the *means to be used* in accomplishing the goals – for example, division of labour, organization structure, reward system, and so forth.
Measuring performance	Developing consensus on the *criteria to be used in measuring how well the group is doing against its goals and targets* – for example, information and control systems.
Correction	Developing consensus on *remedial or repair strategies* as needed when the group is not accomplishing its goals.

Source: Schein, 1992, p. 245.

he derives his classification simply note that these dimensions supply the key bases on which cultures *vary*; they say nothing about the *implications* of these variations.

However, although Schein is in general highly optimistic about the impact of cultural solutions for organizational effectiveness, he reveals some awareness of the possibility of complexity when drawing out the implications of these cultural solutions for organizational performance. He writes, 'It is very important to recognise that cultural strength may or may not be correlated with effectiveness. Though some writers have argued that strength is desirable, it is clear to me that the relationship is far more complex.'

Nevertheless, the general drift of Schein's analysis is clear: cultures supply solutions to problems groups face. Cultures are 'learned solutions' to problems. He offers what is essentially a form of social Darwinism to explain this. When faced with problems groups try out various situations until it finds one that works. This is used and becomes habitual and, ultimately, cultural. Similarly with the attempts to avoid anxiety-creating situations. Again, successful responses become normal and ultimately normative. As Meek has noted of this sort of writing, it assumes a biological metaphor and defines the organization as an organism which ultimately offers metaphysical explanation for organizational structures and processes (Meek, 1982).

The work of Paul Bate is important in two respects: for his classification of the component elements of cultures, and for his analysis of the impact of cultures on performance. With respect to the first, he defines the issues covered by organizational cultures in terms of six key dimensions (Bate,

Table 6.3   Problems of internal integration

Language	*Common language and conceptual categories*. If members cannot communicate with and understand each other, a group is impossible by definition.
Boundaries	Consensus on *group boundaries and criteria for inclusion and exclusion*. One of the most important areas of culture is the shared consensus on who is in, who is out, and by what criteria one determines membership.
Power and status	Consensus on *criteria for the allocation of power and status*. Every organization must work out its pecking order and its rules for how one gets, maintains and loses power. This area of consensus is crucial in helping members manage their own feelings of aggression.
Intimacy	Consensus on *criteria for intimacy, friendship, and love*. Every organization must work out its rules of the game for peer relationships, for relationships between the sexes, and for the manner in which openness and intimacy are to be handled in the context of managing the organization's tasks.
Rewards and punishments	Consensus on *criteria for allocation of rewards and punishments*. Every group must know what its heroic and sinful behaviours are; what gets rewarded with property, status and power; and what gets punished through the withdrawal of rewards and, ultimately, excommunication.
Ideology	Consensus on *ideology and 'religion'*. Every organization, like every society, faces unexplainable events that must be given meaning so that members can respond to them and avoid the anxiety of dealing with the unexplainable and uncontrollable.

Source: Schein, 1992, p. 246.

1992, p. 230). His dimensions do not replicate all of the dimensions listed by Child, but are a development of Kluckhohn's fifth variable: how do people relate to each other? Bate develops and expands this into six constituent elements, described in table 6.4.

Bate's classification is of importance. It is broadly consistent with other useful work which focuses on the ways in which organizational cultures provide norms and values that impact on the nature of interpersonal relationships of various sorts (see Child, 1981).

But Bate's second contribution lies in his view of the impact of cultures (measured according to his dimensions) on performance. Unlike Schein he does not argue that culturally supported patterns of behaviour are necessarily solutions to anything. He does not assume that cultural solutions or viewpoints are necessarily positive, or that they contribute to success. In fact they may contribute to failure.

In his study, Bate argues that the culture of the organization he studied was high on unemotionality, depersonalization, subordination, isolationism and antipathy, and medium on conservatism. The consequence of this profile was significant. He argues that 'culture can affect the type and quality of interpersonal relationships, which in turn affect the approach

Table 6.4 Organization issues with cultural responses

Basic organization issues	Cultural responses
1 How emotionally bound up do people become with others in the work setting? (Affective orientation)	Unemotionality
2 How far do people attribute responsibility for personal problems to others, or to the system? (Animate–inanimate orientation to causality)	Depersonalization
3 How do people respond to differences in position, role, power and responsibility? (Hierarchical orientation)	Subordination
4 How far are people willing to embark with others on new ventures? (Change orientation)	Conservatism
5 How far do people choose to work alone or with and through others? (Individualist–collectivist orientation)	Isolationism
6 How do people in different interest groups relate to each other? (Unitary–Pluralistic orientation)	Antipathy

Source: Bate, 1992, p. 232.

to joint problem-solving processes. . . . certain shared cultural meanings . . . define what are acceptable, natural, desirable and effective ways of relating and acting' (Bate, 1992, p. 228).

But the nature of this impact in the case studied by Bate was negative. It produced a strong sense of futility, pessimism, helplessness, withdrawal, alienation. The situation is one of 'socialized helplessness' where people know it is no use trying to achieve change, and therefore create a self-fulfilling prophecy whereby the resulting organizational inertia and lack of change confirm the cultural assumptions.

Bate's point surely fits better with our own experience than does Schein's optimism. One of the striking features of current organizational change is that organizations are currently trying desperately to change the ways their members think, act, relate, work. The historic 'normal' is no longer adequate. Yesterday's recipes are not suitable for today's problems. The evidence is all around us that organizational cultures are as likely to obstruct (at the very least) as they are to facilitate organizational effectiveness. Bate's work, and one's own experience, suggest that the bland optimism of the managerialist perspective – that strong cultures produce consensus, commitment and productivity – is theoretically naïve and empirically inaccurate.

Other writers have contributed to the debate about the components of organizational cultures by suggesting that some writers on organizational culture may show a preference for some aspects (or levels, in Schein's terms) rather than others. Specifically it has been suggested that some approaches to organizational culture actually reveal the very cultures they study, and that they therefore take for granted some key elements in the culture.

For example, Alvesson has noted (1989) that the corporate culture approach to organizational cultures displays a paradox. While very clearly focusing on the importance of managing cultures for success it actually ignores key and pervasive elements in many corporate cultures. This may be because: 'The tendency to view culture primarily as a "resource" or "instrument" to be exploited and manipulated by dominating groups means that attention is concentrated on the manageable dimensions, while the deeper layers of culture and the cultural context of organizations and managerial actions are taken for granted not only by corporate members but also by researchers' (Alvesson, 1989, p. 128). By the 'deeper layers' Alvesson is referring to the fundamental features of Western organizations, such as 'efficiency, rationalisation, productivity, glorification of advanced technology, exploitation of nature, control, hierarchy, unequal distribution of rewards, dominance of typical male values, glorification of leadership, etc.' He notes dryly: 'For some reason these aspects are not perceived or at least not interpreted as part of organisational and business culture in the vast majority of current writings on the topic' (Alvesson, 1989, p. 128).

In other words, the consultancy approach to organizational cultures, whatever its other deficiencies and partialities, is guilty of an advanced myopia. When insisting that it classifies and describes 'the way we do things around here', it conveniently ignores absolutely fundamental assumptions about organizational practice which could well be the basis for conflict, division, difference. Western managerial culture, it seems, is so 'taken-for-granted' by culture writers that they either don't notice it, or take it as given. This approach to organizational cultures in effect focuses only on what may be performance-related aspects of culture, but ignores other systemic elements which may be seriously counter-productive to the achievement of commitment, loyalty, etc. Alvesson in fact would prefer to shift the focus of enquiry from culture to ideology – while recognizing that the concept 'culture' usefully focuses on a very wide spread of variables and behaviour – 'a complex totality of connections' (Alvesson, 1987, p. 14) – he advocates attention to organizational ideologies. This approach avoids many of the weaknesses identified above and has the merit of drawing attention to differences between ideologies, and to their location in, and relationship between, groups.

The Possibility of Organizational Culture Change

Central to any consideration of organizational cultures is the suggestion that it is possible and fruitful to change these cultures from less performance-enhancing types to positive, performance-enhancing cultures (however these are defined). However, *can* cultures be changed? *How* can cultures be changed? These issues are fundamental.

Many contributors to this debate argue strongly that cultures cannot be changed, at least not fundamentally. Meek, for example, argues against the view that 'there exists in a real and tangible sense a collective organisational culture that can be created, measured and manipulated in order to enhance organisational effectiveness' (Meek, 1982, p. 192). Meek notes that cultures are not created; they emerge through social interactions over a long period. Leaders do not create cultures; on the contrary, leaders reflect the cultures within which they occur.

Similarly, Alvesson remarks: 'when the concept is defined in a theoretically precise way based on anthropological thought, the practical relevance and value of the concept is rather small. It is barely possible to create, or even affect culture in the former meaning. Here it signifies an historically emerged, persistent pattern of beliefs, values and attitudes to social reality, deeply ingrained in consciousness' (Alvesson, 1990, p. 41).

Part of the difference between those writers who are sceptical about the possibility of culture change and those who insist on its possibility clearly stems from the different ways in which they define, approach and use the concept corporate culture. But the disagreement is probably also partly a disagreement about what would constitute evidence of culture change. As we shall see, some authors concede that culture-change programmes have an impact but insist that it is at the behavioural not the normative level. They argue that culture-change programmes may achieve acquiescence but not commitment.

Can cultures be changed?

Any discussion of whether or not cultures can be changed must identify which aspects or levels of culture are being discussed. It is clearly much more difficult to change the beliefs and assumptions of employees than to change what Pettigrew calls the manifestations of culture.

However, even Meek is prepared to agree that while culture as a whole cannot be changed, and the optimistic recommendations of the corporate-culture approach are flawed because of their denial of conflict, differentiation and power, organizational cultures are not static and they do change over time. And while insisting on the variety and complexity of cultures, and their role in internal conflicts she does accept that 'management does have more direct control than other organisational members over certain aspects of corporate cultures, such as control over logos and officially stated missions and ethos' (Meek, 1982, p. 201).

Just the same, the ways in which managers may try to influence some aspects of corporate cultures is, she notes, relatively unstudied and not well understood. There is a great deal more prescription than description. The work of Pettigrew, discussed below, is useful in this respect. But to argue that it is important to assess how management may intervene in organizational cultures, and with what consequences, is very different from blandly assuming that the primary role of management is to create and manage the organizational culture, or assuming that management efforts to manage culture will succeed.

Ogbonna (1992) usefully reviews the literature on the management of culture. He raises the possibility that strategies to change organizational cultures 'are simply extending . . . behavioural strategies' (Ogbonna, 1992, p. 74). That is, at best they change behaviour but not underlying values. They create compliance but not commitment. They achieve what Ogbonna and Wilkinson call 'resigned behavioural compliance' (Ogbonna and Wilkinson, 1988).

Certainly, from what has been said earlier in this chapter about the different levels of culture, it would clearly be extremely difficult to surface, far less to change, deep-seated, taken-for-granted assumptions and frameworks. And ironically this is revealed by much of the corporate culture literature itself, which clearly fails to address its own assumptions about management, organization, hierarchy, etc.

With regard to attempts to manage the more accessible levels of culture, Ogbonna focuses attention on two key issues: the claimed role of leaders, and the role of communications. Of course many people have commented on the crucial importance of the organization's leader in culture-change projects. But Ogbonna notes that employees' values are as much determined by their membership of subgroups; that leaders frequently do not articulate, communicate and personally themselves model the new values; they do not have the power, or the inclination to project the new values but become absorbed by the original culture. Sackmann (1991), too, sees the naïve assertions about the role (and possibility) of leaders managing culture change as a source of serious problems.

Sackmann notes, for example, that cultures are influenced by members, not just by leaders, and remarks that this also suggests that cultures are unlikely to be stable and homogeneous. But the more fundamental point is about the possibility of managing cultures at all. The idea of managing cultures is based, she notes, in a metaphor from rational-mechanistic systems where instructions or directions have a direct and determined impact on what is desired – as in driving a car or switching on a lighting system. But cultures are more complex, and less amenable. Although of course cultures are obviously therefore likely to change constantly, it will be very difficult to change them in a desired direction because of their very nature. She describes how efforts to change and manage organizational cultures ran into trouble precisely because cultures are not amenable to direct management, they are highly complex, are reflexive, with multiple reciprocal relationships. Cultures are not simple systems. For one thing, cultures determine how efforts to change culture are understood and reacted to.

Communications also are frequently stressed in culture-change programmes. Again Ogbonna notes that communications are actually extremely difficult to manage. As we saw in chapter 2, employees often hear information transmitted by management in terms of the cultural values they already hold. Communication success in culture change assumes the very consensus and commitment it is trying to achieve.

In practice, culture-change programmes experience these and other difficulties. A common problem is that the message being transmitted actually contradicts the experiences of the employees. We will encounter this in chapter 9 of this volume where some contradictions around the concept 'integration' are discussed. A good illustration of the ways the values exhorted in cultural change programmes might clash with experienced reality is the tension between the 'hard' and 'soft' sense of HR – that employees may be told they are the organization's most valued resource, and soon afterwards find themselves in a redundancy programme. Or they may be exposed to various forms of participative management styles, teamwork, cellular working, etc., and simultaneously exposed to aggressive anti-union policies. Indeed, there may be contradictions within a single policy: work intensification within job enlargement, for example. Ogbonna noted other contradictions in the organization he studied: for example, between a focus on high trust and commitment, and the installation of surveillance equipment. (See also chapter 5.)

Another possible contradiction lies at the heart of culture-change programmes. Attempts to manipulate organizational cultures are effectively attempts to mobilize new, less overt and more covert forms of organizational control. As such, in themselves they reflect the power resources of those who design the interventions. So managerial attempts to achieve consensus and commitment through culture actually reveal the inequality and differentiation of power and interests within the organization which the culture-change programme may well be designed to deny.

Does this mean that the final message on the management of culture is entirely bleak; that it is impossible? One answer to this focuses on the approach to and definition of cultures. We must remember that answers to this will ultimately depend on the way in which culture is defined, and indeed on how organizations themselves are conceptualized. The definition of culture is a highly practical question: it impacts on whether or not you believe cultures can be changed. An approach to corporate cultures which is based on a foundation of a flawed conception of cultures themselves will itself be flawed. For this reason, in the final section an approach to cultures which avoids the difficulties discussed but offers some (limited) insights into cultures and how they change (and possibly how they can be changed) is necessary.

But at a more practical level, there are some suggestions that are useful and well-founded.

Probably the most important is to reject the bland promises of the prescriptive literature and to recognize that any programme of culture change is going to be long and hard. It is also important to recognize the actual nature of such cultures, as frequently stated throughout this chapter; and to recognize the different levels on which cultures occur, that cultures will not be homogeneous, that there will not be total consensus, that cultures may conflict, that they may be negative as well as positive in their implications for performance, etc.

In this chapter we have noted the difficulties in changing cultures. It is now time to turn to the work of a researcher who has studied and worked with programmes of culture change and who has devised a sensible list of recommendations based on actual practice. It is worth quoting in full. Pettigrew distinguishes 'outer' from 'inner' context. Outer context refers to the social, economic, political and competitive environment in which the firm operates. Inner context refers to organizational context – the 'structure, corporate culture and political context within the firm through which ideas for change have to proceed' (Pettigrew, 1990, p. 267). Note that in his analysis Pettigrew clearly outlines the complexity and arduousness of any attempt to change cultures; and he also notes that such efforts are more likely to affect the surface levels of culture than the core assumptions.

Pettigrew argues that the following factors are important in facilitating changes in organizational cultures:

1 A receptive outer context, together with managerial skill in mobilizing that context in order to create an overall climate for change to occur.
2 Leadership behaviour either from individuals recently brought into the organization from outside, or from individuals who have been pushing for change from a powerful internal position for some time. Most of the cases of change reveal a very clear and consistent drive from the top.

3   The existence of inarticulate and imprecise visions from the agents of change at the very top.

4   The use of discrepant action by key figures in the new guard in order to raise the level of tension in the organization for change.

5   Using deviants and heretics, both external and internal to the organization, in order to say the unsayable and think the unthinkable. External and internal consultants are regularly used for this purpose.

6   Releasing avenues and energy for change by moving people and portfolios.

7   Creating new meetings and other arenas where problems can be articulated and shared and energy focused around the need for change.

8   Altering the management process at the very top. A key aspect of this seems to be the need to change top management processes from being highly divisive in character to being much more coherent and cohesive.

9   Reinforcing any embryonic cultural shifts through closely matched structural changes, then strengthening such cultural and structural changes through the public use of organization's reward systems.

10 Finding and using 'role models' who can through their own public behaviour display key aspects of the new culture. The identification of people who can 'walk and talk' seems to be a key aspect of making concrete and public the desired cultural changes. These role models of the new era also help the continuing reinforcement of change.

11 Carrying the message deep into the organization through the use of training and development strategies.

12 Transmitting the new beliefs and behaviour down into the organization by revamping employee communication mechanisms.

13 Finally, there is the old-fashioned but critical need for persistence and patience. (All points from Pettigrew, 1990, pp. 271–2.)

Pettigrew continues: 'All of the studies of strategic change we are looking at emphasise the complexity and difficulty of effecting such change, even where the change is eventually triggered by major environmental disturbances. Persistence and patience is critically important at the difficult stage of breaking down the core beliefs of the old guard, getting new problems sensed and articulated in the organization, developing a sense of concern that these problems are worthy of analytical and political attention, and then articulating the new order often through highly inarticulate and impressive visions of the future' (Pettigrew, 1990, pp. 271–2).

Conclusion

Organizations are structures of symbols and meaning. Even talking about or researching organizations is symbolic, and life within organizations cannot occur without the symbols and myths that make it meaningful and possible. Therefore we must of course focus on the 'cultural' aspects of organization. Yet while such a (hermeneutic) project is necessary and desirable we have argued in this chapter that much corporate-culture literature is flawed and inadequate – a fad. So why is there so much interest? If definitions of cultures are complex and differentiated; if culture is applied in such different ways, if consensus and unity are rare, if culture occurs at different levels and, most important of all, if cultures are complex and difficult to change, then why has so much effort been spent on studying organizational cultures?

On one level, of course, the appeal is obvious: the corporate-culture approach promises to support management control by winning the hearts and minds of employees (Willmott, 1993, p. 516). But its appeal lies deeper than this.

We have noted that the rise of interest in corporate cultures should be seen in terms of two processes: the gradual historic emergence of a conviction of the importance of 'soft' aspects of organizational structure and process in contrast to rational systems and structures; and the increasingly persuasive argument that the manipulation of organizational cultures offers a solution to the increasingly obvious limitations of traditional, oppressive forms of control. We have also noted the powerful appeal of culturalist writings and prescriptions. How can we account for this appeal? There is something to explain here, because although the appeal of the corporate literature may lie in its promises it is important to recognize that there is little evidence that these promises have been fulfilled. The appeal of the literature lies in the nature of the message and the promise. Somehow these strike a chord with managers.

A number of authors have tried to answer this question. Guest draws connections between elements of the culture literature and some basic themes in the American Dream. And this attempt to identify resonances and affinities with the culture literature and other bodies of values currently powerful within the society has proved a fruitful line of analysis (Guest, 1990; du Gay and Salaman, 1992). Elsewhere Guest (1992) refers to the fact that books such as *In Search of Excellence* are not only about the importance of values and feelings in organizations, they also cleverly tap into, and appeal to, the values and feelings of their manager readers. He quotes the analysis of Conrad to the effect that 'the appeal of a book like *Passion for*

Excellence lies in its mythos, its capacity to transport readers symbolically from a world of everyday experience to a mythical realm' (Conrad, 1985).

The dream that these books promise to realize has long been a dream of managers; their aspiration has always been to be able to manage staff without their knowing or resenting this control, to get workers to accept managerial goals, authority and decisions so that they don't need managing, or controlling; in fact so that they see the organization and their work as the managers see it. The corporate-culture approach offers to managers the seductive promise that they can, in Wilmott's terms, 'colonise the affective domain . . . [by] promoting employee commitment to a monolithic structure of feeling and thought' (Willmott, 1993, p. 517). One of the distinctive features of this approach is that it claims that it is possible to achieve a situation where employees want on their own what managers want them to do. Control would be built-in; employees could safely be autonomous because they would 'own' responsibility for doing, to high standards, what they are required to do. Employees could be 'free' because they could be relied on to do what the organization wants them to do. This is the offer. No wonder the culture literature is powerful and popular.

Alvesson (1990) supports this interpretation of the appeal of the literature. He notes the importance of the business context, of the obvious economic malaise in the West in the reception accorded the corporate-culture approach, but stresses also the attractions of what he describes ironically as 'the product' (organization culture theory): 'the organization culture theory is often presented in a way that makes it appear to be of crucial importance for understanding what is going on in organizations and how get to control of it. The broad area of relevance and application of culture in organisations, concepts that are mystical and phantasy-provoking, are important features of this type of knowledge' (Alvesson, 1990, p. 46). He also notes that a major attraction of this material is its promise to allow managers to manage the meanings and values of employees and thus to enable managers access to powerful but internalized sources of control and commitment.

We have earlier noted some of the problems with the use of the concept culture in organizational analysis – particularly those usages within the consultancy/practitioner approach. However, the weaknesses of this application should not imply that the concept should be abandoned altogether. Certainly this particular approach is seriously flawed – which means that we must consider why it continues to attract so much attention. But in other applications the concept is potentially very interesting and exciting. For the concept to be rescued from the hands of the consultancy writers it is necessary to attend to and address the weaknesses identified earlier (i.e. the consensual, unitary conception of cultures); to acknowledge and attend to the nature and role of power and conflict within organizations as the context of organizational cultures; to recognize the ideological role of cultures (or the ideological components of cultures); and to widen the concept to include aspects of organizational culture that many writers prefer to regard as so 'normal', natural and given that they transcend cultural analysis.

One implication of this viewpoint is that the consultancy approach – 'corporate culture' – to management culture as described earlier can now be seen less as an analysis of existing organizational cultures and more as an element of management's attempts to construct organizational cultures – to gain worker commitment through the management of meaning. 'Once it was deemed sufficient to redesign the organization so as to make it fit human capacity and understanding: now it is better to redesign human understanding to fit the organisation's purpose' (Keenoy and Anthony, 1992, p. 239).

We have earlier argued that, despite the claims of the consultancy approach that culture is used to explore 'the way we do things around here', such analyses in fact studiously ignore certain key elements of organizational structure and process – the nature and role of power, of conflicts, or exploitation of difference. Some of the basic assumptions and taken-for-granted 'realities' of organization are left unquestioned and un-analysed by cultural analyses. The very purposes of culture-change programmes themselves are left unexplored and undiscussed, except in the bland terms of the proposed culture of consensus and commitment. MacIntyre makes the important point that management itself is not a neutral or objectively rational process: 'managers . . . conceive of them-selves as morally neutral characters whose skills enable them to devise the most efficient means of achieving whatever end is proposed. . . . Nonetheless there are strong grounds for rejecting the claim that effective-ness is a morally neutral value. . . . I am suggesting that "managerial effectiveness" functions much as Carnap and Ayer supposed "God" to function. It is the name of a fictitious, but believed-in reality, appeal to which disguises certain other realities; interpretations of managerial effec-tiveness in the same way lack the appropriate kind of rational justification' (MacIntyre, 1981, pp. 71–3; quoted in Carter and Jackson, 1987, pp. 66–7).

Certainly if the concept of organizational culture is to be used to its full potential and avoid the sectional and flawed definition criticized above, it must be deployed in a manner which moves beyond a focus on those dimensions which, if manipulated, could support managerial efforts to achieve control, and instead focus the 'overall cultural characteristics of organisations [which] are not taken for granted in a way that allows for the exclusive concentration on performance-related norms and behaviour patterns' (Alvesson, 1989, p. 129).

Frequently studies of organizational culture reveal these cultures less in their analyses than in their (hidden) assumptions: they themselves reflect the key features of the managerialist culture by their focus on performance, their concern with commitment, their lack of interest in divisive, exploitative, hierarchical aspects of organization – all of which, from a managerial point of view, are 'natural', neutral and necessary. In this respect the corporate-culture approach shares many of the assumptions of earlier organizational analysis which accepted the inevitability and rationality of organizational structures (Salaman, 1981).

The problems with the corporate-culture approach stem from largely unexplored and implicit theoretical assumptions about organizations and how they work, on which the approach depends. This is frequently derived from an unreflexive systems theory – an approach which looks at the organization from the point of senior management; which explains internal organizational patterns in terms of their contribution to the survival of the organization within its environment. As Silverman (1970) remarked in an early and important critique of systems theory, such an approach is defective and would be better replaced by an approach which looked at organizations in terms of the purposes of their members and of their capacities to impose these ends on others. In order to do this, it is necessary to understand the subjective purposes of each actor, or group of actors. And this, of course, means that the analysis of cultures within organizations is crucial to an understanding of structure and process, because such cultures inform members' actions. But the approach to cultural analysis must recognize the diversity of meanings, the variations in interests, the potential conflict between groups, and not wish these away with the bland descriptions of a consensus with which they try to create the very situation they fallaciously describe.

This point has interesting implications for the consultancy approach to corporate culture discussed at length, and critiqued, in this chapter. It may well be that the interesting and useful application of culture of organizations lies less in the pursuit of prescriptive (and probably abortive) interventions aimed to achieve commitment, acquiescence and obedience within the workforce, and more in attempts to uncover some of the deep, and typically undiscussed assumptions on which organizations and management rest. Carter and Jackson, for example, have argued that a valuable application of the culture approach ('root metaphor' or hermeneutic approach in terms of earlier classification) is to explore the cultural assumptions underlying management's model of the world, organizations and management: 'Management's model of the world it manages is not fact, but a particular myth . . . When management for example claims to pursue efficiency, this means efficiency in one sense, among many possible senses' (Carter and Jackson, 1987, p. 79). The value of the culture approach may lie not in its claimed contribution to organizational effectiveness but in its use in exposing and analysing the assumptions and truth claims of managerial discourse.

But such an approach may not totally rule out any concern to change organizational cultures, though it will severely limit these efforts and make them demanding and difficult. Sackmann's work is useful here. Noting the gap between academic (culture as metaphor) and practitioner applications she proposes an approach which uses a definition of culture that avoids the weaknesses of the practitioner approach discussed earlier, but does so in a form that addresses issues in the management of culture. She describes this approach as seeing organizational culture as a dynamic construct. She hopes this approach will combine the pragmatic side of the practitioner perspective (corporate-culture approach) with the rigour and honesty of the metaphor of organizations as cultures approach. She notes that the culture as metaphor approach is not interested in application, but her model of culture in this hybrid approach avoids the weaknesses of the corporate-culture approach discussed above, while at the same time promising less, and insisting on the complexity and arduousness of any attempt to change cultures at any level. 'The problems associated with the variable perspective [corporate-culture approach] are overcome since the underlying assumptions are different and closer to the metaphor perspective. Organisations are seen as evolving, dynamic, complex systems with inconsistencies and paradoxes, and several cultural groupings or meaning systems. Within this perspective, the management of culture can only take the form of a culture-aware management that tries to create, interpret, negotiate, and communicate meanings in conscious efforts. The result of these efforts, however, cannot be determined in advance . . . A culture-aware management is aware of the existing meaning systems within the organization, its cultural strengths and weaknesses. These are consciously cared for, or deliberately neglected' (Sackmann, 1991, p. 138). However, she notes the difficulty of becoming culture-aware management, and its rarity. This takes us back, of course, to the arguments of Carter and Jackson, and others above: that most writings about corporate culture take for granted the same values and assumptions that are embedded in the cultures they study, and therefore fail to notice or address them.

Key points

- *Many recent writers – academics and consultants – have argued seductively that the key to improved organizational performance and the answer to managers' old dilemma of how to attract the commitment and energy of employees, is to understand and manipulate the culture of the organization.*
- *This argument – which is most appealing to managers – is extremely important in its implications; but there is no point and no advantage in confusing the way*

> *we would like things to be with the way they actually are: we need to examine very carefully and very thoroughly the basis, inherent assumptions, and potential limitations of this approach. Does the 'corporate-culture' approach to organizational analysis bear closer scrutiny and rigorous testing?*
>
> - *One important key point is just how differently writers define culture, and what fundamental assumptions they make about organizational cultures. These definitions and approaches require careful analysis, for some definitions carry some very dubious and insecure assumptions.*
> - *Part of the weakness of the corporate-culture approach stems from its very qualities that appeal to managers – this approach relates closely to managers' view of the world and the organization. Possibly part of its appeal therefore is that this approach owes more to management ideology than it does to analytic rigour. This possibility needs investigation.*
> - *If organizational cultures are important then we need a sensible and well-founded basis by which to distinguish the basic dimensions of cultures. Such a system exists and has been much used, and is discussed in this chapter.*
> - *Finally, if cultures can be changed it is necessary to think thoroughly and carefully about the ways in which they can be changed.*

Discussion Questions

1 Discuss and contrast some of the main ways in which the concept of organizational culture has been used in analyses of organizations.
2 Assess the strengths and weaknesses of the 'corporate-culture' approach to organizational cultures.
3 In what senses could the 'corporate-culture' approach be described as essentially a form of management ideology?
4 What are the key dimensions of culture and how could they be applied in an organization you know well?
5 If cultures can be changed what does this require in terms of the way culture is defined, the various levels of culture and the necessary mechanisms of change?

REFERENCES

Akin, G. and Hopelian, D. (1986) Finding the culture of productivity. *Organisational Dynamics*, 15, pp. 19–32.
Alvesson, M. (1987) Organisations, culture and ideology. *International Studies of Management and Organisation*, 17, no. 3, pp. 4–18.

Alvesson, M. (1989) The cultural perspective on organisations: Instrumental values and basic features of culture. *Scandinavian Journal of Management*, 5, no. 2, pp. 123–36.

Alvesson, M. (1990) On the popularity of organisational culture. *Acta Sociologica*, 33, no. 1, pp. 31–49.

Alvesson, M. (1991) Organisational symbolism and ideology. *Journal of Management Studies*, 28, no. 3, pp. 207–25.

Anthony, P. (1994) *Managing Culture.* Milton Keynes, Open University Press.

Baker, E. (1980) Managing organisational culture. *Management Review*, June, pp. 8–13.

Barley, S., Meyer, G. and Gash, D. (1988) Cultures of culture: Academics, practitioners and the pragmatics of normative control. *Administrative Science Quarterly*, 33, no. 1, pp. 24–60.

Barney, J. B. (1986) Organisational culture: Can it be a sustained source of competitive advantage? *Academy of Management Review*, 11, no. 3, pp. 656–65.

Bate, P. (1992) The impact of organisational culture on approaches to organisational problem-solving. In Salaman, G. et al. (eds), *Human Resource Strategies*. London, Sage, pp. 219–34.

Bleicher, K. (1983) Organisationskulturen und Fuhrungsphilosophien in Bettewerb. *Zeitschrift fur Betriebswirtschaftliche Forschung*, 35, pp. 135–46.

Business Week (1983) The hard-to-change values that spell success or failure. 25 Oct., pp. 148–59.

Carter, P. and Jackson, N. (1987) Management myth and metatheory. *Organisational Culture and Ideology*, special issue of *International Studies of Management and Organisation*, 17, no. 3, pp. 64–90.

Child, J. (1981) Culture, contingency and capitalism in the cross-national study of organizations. In Cummings, L. L. and Staw, B. (eds), *Research in Organizational Behavior*. Greenwich, Conn., JAI Press.

Conrad, C. (1985) Review of *A Passion for Excellence*, *Administrative Science Quarterly*, 30, no. 3, pp. 426–8.

Deal, T. and Kennedy, A. (1982) *Corporate Cultures*. Harmondsworth, Penguin Books.

Denison, D. R. (1984) Bringing corporate culture to the bottom line. *Organisational Dynamics*, 12, pp. 5–22.

du Gay, P. and Salaman, G. (1992) The culture of the customer. *Journal of Management Studies*, 29, no. 5, pp. 45–61.

Frost, P., Moore, L., Louis, M. R., Lundberg, C. and Martin, J. (1991) Introduction. In Frost, P., et al. (eds), *Reframing Organizational Culture*. Newbury Park, Calif., Sage, pp. 7–10.

Guest, D. (1990) Human resource management and the American dream. *Journal of Management Studies*, 27, no. 4, pp. 377–97.

Guest, D. (1992) Right enough to be dangerously wrong. In Salaman, G. et al. (eds), *Human Resource Strategies*. London, Sage, pp. 1–19.

Habermas, J. (1971) *Knowledge and Human Interests*. Boston, Beacon Press.

Hinterhuber, H. H. (1986) Strategie, Innovation und Unternehmenskultur. *Blick durch die Wirtschaft*, 20, no. 10.

Hofstede, G. (1980) *Culture's Consequences*. London, Sage.

Jaggi, D. (1985) Corporate Identity als Unternehmerische Erfolgsformel. Paper presented at the Second WEMAR – Tagung.

Keenoy, T. and Anthony, P. (1992) HRM: Metaphor, meaning and morality. In Blyton, P. and Turnbull, P. (eds), *Reassessing Human Resource Management*. London, Sage, pp. 233–55.

Kieser, A. (1987) Zur Funktion von Werten, Mythen, Ritualen und Symbolen. *Working Paper, Institut fur Allgemeine Betriebswirtschaftslehre und Organisation*, University of Mannheim.

Kilmann, R., Saxton, M. and Serpa, R. (1986) Five key issues in understanding and changing culture. In Kilmann, R., Saxton, M. and Serpa, R. et al. (eds), *Gaining Control of the Corporate Culture*. San Francisco, Jossey-Bass, pp. 1–16.

Kluckhohn, F. R. and Strodtbeck, F. L. (1961) *Variations in Value Orientations*. New York, Row, Peterson.

Knights, D. and Willmott, H. (1987) Organisational culture as a management strategy. *International Studies of Management and Organisation*, 17, no. 3.

Legge, K. (1989) HRM: A critical analysis. In Storey, J. (ed.), *New Perspectives on Human Resource Management*. London, Routledge.

Louis, M. R. (1981) A cultural perspective on organisations. *Human Systems Management*, 2, pp. 246–58.

MacIntyre, A. (1981) *After Virtue*. London, Duckworth.

Meek, V. L. (1982) Organisational culture: Origins and weaknesses. In Salaman, G. et al. (eds), *Human Resource Strategies*. London, Sage, pp. 192–212.

Morgan, G. (1986) *Images of Organization*. Beverly Hills, Calif., Sage.

Ogbonna, E. (1992) Organisational culture and human resource management: Dilemmas and contradictions. In Blyton, P. and Turnbull, P. (eds), *Reassessing Human Resource Management*. London, Sage, pp. 74–96.

Ogbonna, E. and Wilkinson, B. (1988) Corporate strategy and corporate culture: The management of change in the UK supermarket industry. *Personnel Review*, 18, no. 6, pp. 10–14.

Peters, T. (1978) Symbols, patterns and settings. *Organisational Dynamics*, 9, no. 2, pp. 3–23.

Peters, T. and Austin, N. (1985) *A Passion For Excellence*. New York, Random House.

Peters, T. and Waterman, R. (1982) *In Search of Excellence*. New York, Harper and Row.

Pettigrew, A. (1979) On studying organisational cultures. *Administrative Science Quarterly*, Dec., pp. 570–81.

Pettigrew, A. (1990) Is corporate culture manageable? In Wilson, D. and Rosenfeld, R. (eds), *Managing Organisations*. pp. 267–72.

Pfeffer, J. (1981) Management as symbolic action. In Cummings, L. L. and Staw, B. M. (eds), *Research in Organizational Behaviour*. Greenwich, Conn., JAI Press.

Sackmann, Sonja (1991) Managing organisational culture: Dreams and possibilities. In Anderson, J. (ed.), *Communication Yearbook*, 13. Newbury Park, Calif., Sage Publications, pp. 114–48.

Sadler, P. (1988) *Managerial Leadership in the Post-industrial Society*. Aldershot, Gower.

Salaman, G. (1981) Towards a sociology of organizational structure. In Zey-Ferrell, M. and Aiken, M. (eds), *Complex Organizations, Critical Perspectives*. Glenview, Ill., Scott Foresman, pp. 22–46.

Schein, E. (1992) Coming to a new awareness of organisational culture. In Salaman, G., et al. (eds), *Human Resource Strategies*. London, Sage, pp. 237–53.

Silverman, D. (1970) *The Theory of Organisations*. London, Heinemann.

Smirich, L. (1983) Concepts of culture and organisational analysis. *Administrative Science Quarterly*, 28, pp. 339–58.

Stablein, R. and Nord, W. (1985) Practical and emancipatory interests in organisational symbolism. *Journal of Management*, 11, no. 2, pp. 13–28.

Ulrich, P. (1984) Systemsteuerung und Kulturentwicklung. *Die Unternehmung*, 38, pp. 303–25.

Wickens, P. (1987) *The Road to Nissan*. Basingstoke, Macmillan.

Willmott, H. (1993) Strength is ignorance; slavery is freedom: Managing culture in modern organisations. *Journal of Management Studies*. 30, no. 4, pp. 515–52.

7 Learning Organizations

Learning Objectives

- *to appreciate the importance of learning for the commercial viability of organizations in the 1990s and beyond.*
- *to differentiate the learning organization from an organization that learns.*
- *to understand the conditions most conducive to adult learning.*
- *to apply the principles of effective individual learning to the design of an organization's training and development activities.*
- *to identify the processes by which individual learning can enhance organizational performance.*

Introduction

The idea of 'the learning organization' has flourished in recent years as one way of summing up the sorts of organizational qualities called for and valued in today's changing environment. Senior management are recognizing that the way an organization learns is a key – possibly the determining – index to the way it innovates and remains a profitable enterprise: 'the rate at which individuals and organizations learn may become the only sustainable competitive advantage, especially in knowledge-intensive industries' (Stata, 1989, p. 64). Competitive advantage will accrue, it is argued, to organizations which develop human resource policies that promote continuous learning, teamwork, participation and flexibility (Dertouzos, et al., 1989). Much recent management literature and thinking stresses such values as flexibility and responsiveness, constant adaptation and change. 'The learning organization' is often a piece of shorthand for referring to an organization which tries to make a working reality of such desirable attributes. But beyond that, what does it mean in practice? According to Mills and Friesen (1992): 'Just as firms were required to create a particular business model (a combination of organisation structure, management practices and internal support systems) to utilise mass production techniques, so will they need to build a business model to effectively encourage learning and utilise the outputs of innovation in their operations' (1992, p. 147). What might such 'business models' look like and what prescriptions should an organization follow if it is to turn itself into a learning organization? This brings us to the central conundrum of the learning organization: if management can be learned, can *learning be managed*? How can we relax control over the learning process while at the same time channelling the benefits from it? (Jones and Hendry, 1994). Swieringa and Wierdsma (1992) are insistent that: 'one has to be prescriptive on the meta-level in order to keep the organization a learning one, especially where the handling of learning principles is concerned' (1992, p. 77). They go on to contrast the effort required to sustain learning with the incipient temptation to sink into the calm and security of the prescriptive organization, and because of this they advise that the desire to remain a learning organization should be non-negotiable. Is this a management paradox or a fatal internal contradiction in the concept of the learning organization? In this chapter we assemble some of the evidence to suggest that the notion of the learning organization is not only meaningful and definable, but also attainable. We also note, however, some of the pitfalls along the way and some of the presumptions that are currently obscuring the pursuit of an ethos where energized individuals and innovative organization processes work in creative tension together.

Organizational Learning and the Learning Organization

Organizational learning

Economists tend to view learning in terms of quantifiable improvements and some business writers equate learning with sustaining competitive edge or innovative efficiency. However, the concern of organization theorists and psychologists is to go beyond this to examine the process of learning as well as its outcomes, *how* things are learnt as well as what is learnt. It is usually assumed that learning generally has positive consequences, that organizations have the capacity to learn collectively and that such learning occurs at different speeds and levels within firms. For instance, R & D contracts with partners, joint ventures, strategic alliances, benchmarking successful competitors, tapping into professional/institutional networks, learning from customers and users, hiring key individuals, reverse engineering, exporting and investing abroad, are all sources of direct and vicarious learning. But it is employees within organizations rather than organizations themselves that learn. Dodgson notes that 'individuals are the primary learning entity in firms, and it is individuals which create organizational forms that enables learning in ways which facilitate organizational transformation' (1993, pp. 377–8). It is here that human resource strategies can play an important role by creating the structures and culture that will purposefully facilitate progress beyond mere adaptive, natural learning to develop and co-ordinate 'generative' (Senge, 1990) organizational learning necessitated by rapidly changing and conflicting circumstances. For instance, Schein (1985) regards culture as the basic assumptions and beliefs that are shared by members of an organization, which operate unconsciously and constitute '*Learned* responses to a group's problems of *survival* in its external environment and its problems of *internal integration*' (1985, p. 6). According to Hedberg (1981) such collective cultural learning actually becomes independent of individuals: 'organizations do not have brains, but they have cognitive systems and memories . . . Members come and go, and leadership changes, but organizations' memories preserve certain behaviours, mental maps, norms and values over time' (1981, p. 3). We might ask how such 'memories' come to be built up and what, in practical terms, a cognitive system looks like. At least three aspects of an organization's structural capability are relevant here: its 'knowledge base' which refers to how a firm acquires, articulates and enhances the unique knowledge which it controls; its 'firm-specific competencies', namely the mechanisms it employs to accumulate and dissipate distinctive skills and capabilities; and thirdly its 'routines' for using the skills and knowledge it possesses in an effective and competitive manners. The latter will include both its formal rules, procedures, technologies and strategies as well as its less formal – and sometimes contradictory – informal structure of beliefs, frameworks, paradigms, codes and cultures (Levitt and March, 1988). However, as Dodgson (1993) points out, such approaches tend to underestimate the complexity and problems involved in learning and assume uniformity in learning capabilities within firms; they also take too little account of the importance of individual human agency. It is, after all, individuals who choose to build up a particular knowledge base or adopt a given routine, albeit influenced by the socializing context of the organization concerned. Furthermore, individual learning theory tells us that learning can be conflictual (new knowledge and its exploitation may undermine the 'status quo'), conservative (it may alternatively serve to sustain existing outmoded structures) and/or unreliable (learning is shaped by new ideas often adopted more for their topicality, availability or political convenience than for their intrinsic worth).

Argyris and Schon (1978; 1981) have drawn attention to how individual learning in organizations can be harnessed positively to produce collective learning. Drawing upon the work of Bateson (1972) they describe the value of moving beyond 'single-loop' learning where errors are detected and corrected – which is effective for day-to-day operational matters but may lead to a rigid, unquestioning culture – to double-loop learning which challenges and examines these taken-for-granted internalized assumptions and results in a deeper level of collective knowledge and understanding, and a reassessment of values. The cyclical and mechanistic nature of such feedback loops is called into question, however, by research on organizational capabilities by Pettigrew and Whipp (1991). They found that the way organizations learnt was in fact a highly intricate and complex process, with vital skills and knowledge often being acquired in hidden and unnoticed ways: 'In general terms the research shows that it is insufficient for companies to regard the creation of knowledge and judgements of their external competitive world as simply a technical exercise. Rather the need is for organizations to become open learning systems. In other words, the assessment of the competitive environment does not remain the preserve of a single function nor the sole responsibility of one senior manager. Nor does it occur via isolated acts. Instead strategy creation is seen as emerging from the way a company, at various levels, acquires, interprets and processes information about the environment' (Pettigrew and Whipp, 1991, p. 30). This is illustrated in box 7.1.

Box 7.1   From IR to HR – the role of learning

'Our . . . concern is with the formidable difficulties which have to be overcome in making the transition at firm level from a conventional IR/personnel orientation to an HRM philosophy. Securing that transition begs enormous questions of both managerial thinking and practice . . . Nor in terms of competition should that transition become an end in itself. The results of this study go beyond the majority of the HRM literature in one major respect: it identifies the role of knowledge as paramount in the way an HRM approach can help create competitive advantage. That knowledge has both technical and social components. What becomes critical is the extent to which a company's knowledge base matches changing competitive conditions through learning. Learning here is seen as not just the acquisition of new knowledge. It also relates to how those within a firm collectively change their values and shared mental models of their company and markets (shown graphically in Kleinwort Benson). Indeed, it is the ability to shed out-moded knowledge, techniques and beliefs, as well as to learn and deploy new ones, which enables firms to carry out given strategies. To do so faster than one's competitors is likely to become one of the cardinal determinants of competitive strength in the 1990s.' (Pettigrew and Whipp, 1991, p. 238.)

According to Jones and Hendry (1994) all the approaches discussed above (even the more sophisticated analysis of Pettigrew and Whipp) characterize organizational learning rather than the learning organization. This is because the learning under discussion is invariably framed within the current purposes of the organization. Thus, links are drawn between training, development and wider human resource management and company performance and competitiveness. Even learning on the job and self-development, apparently enfranchising for the individuals concerned, is described as learning *harnessed primarily for organisational ends*. So for example, in their critique of Total Quality Programmes, Kerfoot and Knights (1994) note some inherent and inadvertent contradictions:

> However, while at this level quality management reflects a concern to collapse or 'flatten' organizational hierarchies, it is also a motive force in their reconstitution and retrenchment. This occurs through processes or claims to empower workers. Suffice to say here that work empowerment and autonomy under quality programmes is heavily circumscribed by the demands for continuous improvement and error free standardization of products. Through a range of what are themselves perhaps bureaucratic procedures for identifying obstacles to efficient production and quality service, norms of quality are established and internalised. Partly out of a fear of the consequences of non-conformance and partly because of reward incentives, these procedures generate the kind of self-discipline that 'secures as it obscures' (Burawoy, 1979) hierarchical forms, thus giving a renewed legitimacy to the authority of bureaucratic structures.
>
> (Kerfoot and Knights, 1994, p. 8)

So long as the assumption remains that learning is essentially to support organizational structures and prescribe how people should behave within them; so long as organizational capability refers exclusively to the 'sum total of the organization working in unison' without reference to 'expanding and building on that which remains undeveloped' (Jones and Hendry, 1994, p. 155), then the point of the learning organization concept is being missed. Indeed descriptions which purport to profile the characteristics of a learning organization may – for these reasons – confuse rather than clarify the concept (see box 7.2).

Box 7.2 A learning organization profile – but on whose terms?

'A learning organization that is functioning well has several elements in place:

- A clear picture of how the organization should operate; employees at all levels understand the importance of both learning and doing.
- Rewards that encourage people to follow these norms. Employees are encouraged and rewarded for asking questions and challenging ways of work, with ideas coming from anywhere. Systems exist that encourage entrepreneurial behaviour.
- Performance reviews and career development that look at both what you do and what you have learned; organizations offer compensation systems that support the stated values and bonuses and incentives that are balanced between current performance, innovation, courage and risk.

- Feedback systems that guarantee ongoing information, not only about what has been done but about what has been learned that affects future actions. Improvement is valued as much as results. Personal feedback on performance, both positive and negative, is given frequently, up, down and sideways in the organization.
- Information systems that are designed and managed to support this balance between performing and doing. Information on "lessons" as well as on results should be widely available.
- Training and education programs that are designed to support the change strategies and the values held by top management. If learning is a priority, educational programmes should be designed to maximize the balance between learning and doing.
- A communication strategy and programme that keeps learning in the forefront of everyone's consciousness.
- A strategic planning process that is thought of as a learning as well as a doing process. More often strategic planning is regarded solely as a way of producing plans to fit the planning cycle. It can, in addition, be a most powerful lever for helping key people to learn, to change their mind-sets, and to develop a future focus.
- Strategic objectives that are defined to include the learning that must take place in order to achieve them.' (Beckhard and Pritchard, 1992, pp. 22, 23.)

While the elements elaborated in box 7.2 refer to the encouragement of taking risks, giving feedback and learning lessons – the 'softer', consensual side of human resource management – the manifest message behind each of these mechanisms or 'levers' is to 'support the change strategies and the values held by top management'. Clearly, for many in the organization, subscribing to and helping to further such values would not coincide with their own interests, and in such circumstances, learning would be equally untenable.

The learning organization

So, if what we have so far discussed misses the point of what the learning organization constitutes, what is it and what aspects of learning does the learning organization concept distinctively represent? Probably the most influential spokesperson in the US for replacing 'old models' of learning is Peter Senge.

In his book *The Fifth Discipline: The Art and Practice of the Learning Organization* (1990) he takes a refreshing look at the new roles and skills required of leaders in organizations and the 'new' tools at their disposal, drawing for inspiration upon seminal work on personal and corporate learning (e.g. Argyris and Schon, 1978; Mintzberg and Waters, 1985). For instance, the need for systemic diagnosis as against event-driven reactivity, the provocative conception of leader as servant, the need to recognize, challenge and defuse defensive routines that inhibit learning, and the return to simple skills like active listening ('balancing inquiry and advocacy'), avoiding premature conclusions ('seeing leaps of abstraction') and discerning the gap between 'exposed theory and theory in use'. In particular, he notes that learning:

1   Can serve a variety of purposes and take a variety of forms. *Adaptive* learning is concerned with developing the understanding and capacity to cope with new situations. It entails reflecting on and analysing what one has done in the past with a view to improving and making amendments to meet specific new needs and demands. 'What did I do?' 'What aspects went well?' 'What could have gone better?' 'How can we solve this problem?' *Generative* learning is concerned with developing new ways of looking at the world – and one's work and organization in particular. It is directed towards the future and involves speculation, creating possibilities and options, redefining one's performance. 'What might we do?' 'What is the problem?' 'What possible ways could we approach it?' 'What would happen and what would it look like if . . . ?' (See box 7.3.)

2   Can result from the creative tension between developing a shared vision and making a fuller analysis of current realities and practices. This is a standard tenet of the organization development approach to change interventions (see chapter 2: Managing Change).

3   Should involve attention to contexts and processes as well as tasks and outcomes. As *designers*, managers can facilitate learning and development, not simply by acting as charismatic leaders or competent role models, but by changing the circumstances which influence and shape their own and their staff's performance – the governing values, the policies and strategies and so forth. Effective learning involves the creation of a sense of shared ownership; the nurturing of strategic thinking is as valuable as the dissemination of the right or correct strategy.

4   Should involve developing insightful views of current practice and realities. As *teachers* managers need to foster and support the capacity to identify and critically evaluate their own 'mental models' – i.e. the underlying repertoire of beliefs, assumptions, values and theories they possess about how the world works. This helps to distinguish espoused theory from theory in use, enabling people to have the confidence and ability to think analytically and self-critically, identifying

interrelationships, systems and processes rather than discrete events, probing behind surface symptoms and immediate causes. All this assists the process of learning.

> ## Box 7.3 Learning at Chaparral Steel: The ups and downs
>
> 'In a learning environment, progress has to be everyone's business – not just that of a few specialists. One of the greatest advantages of this attitude, as a maintenance foreman points out, is that "ideas come from just about everybody. The operators working on the equipment have a lot of input because they see the exact problems when they happen." Moreover, potential improvements are immediately enacted with no wait for management approval or standardization of "best practices." If it works, it is the *de facto* standard. If it improves performance, everyone will imitate it. "Whoever can come up with an idea on how to fix it, from the millwrights or myself right on up to the top, . . . does it right then," explains a foreman. At Chaparral, there is no formal requirement, as at some Japanese companies, for a certain number of improvement suggestions from each employee. Everyone is involved in some process improvement projects, and, as the foreman explains, "We are all out here to make it run. Probably 90 per cent of the problems never even make it to the morning meetings (held among everyone on the shift to discuss problems). They are fixed in the field."
>
> The downside to this intrapreneurial attitude is that although managers see the goals, no one has the authority to tell another employee *how* to accomplish a task. Process engineers and supervisors who know a better procedure often have difficulty convincing operators on the line – much less their peers. "You can't tell them how to do it," Administration Vice-President Dennis Beach admits somewhat ruefully, "and they don't do it the way you would." The engineers concur. They are not called upon enough, in their opinions. However, the benefits from general ownership of all problems are that it is not possible to "pass the buck" and no one expects a steady-state manufacturing process – ever.' (From Leonard-Barton, 1992, pp. 26, 27.)

It should be noted that Senge's view of organizations is primarily an optimistic one. His creative tension principle tends to assume that individual employees will be motivated by a given organizational vision once it has been clearly articulated and the current reality has been accurately portrayed. And his statement that 'negative visions carry a subtle message of powerlessness' may be true, but possibly neglects the incipient plurality of many organizations today in which powerless people cannot (or find it difficult to) create positive visions! (Mabey and Iles, 1994)

The most frequently cited definition of the learning organization in the European literature is that of Pedler et al. (1991, p. 1): 'The Learning Company is an organization which facilitates the learning of all of its members *and* continuously transforms itself.'

There are some important notions captured within this description – the authors refer to it as a 'dream' rather than a definition. First, there are aspects of the way the organization operates that actively facilitate and encourage individual learning: that is, it is insufficient for all members to have a self-development or learning orientation, for the organization to be a Learning Organization. This is partly why they prefer the term 'company' to organization, because its convivial connotation suggests people engaged in a joint enterprise. Second, the emphasis is upon 'all members' of the organization. It is insufficient to be focused on selected groups, at whatever level of the organization. The notion is that individuals learn together in a collective 'system', where the learning of one individual, or subgroup, is likely to have knock-on effects on the learning of another. Where the organization attempts to restrict this transfer of learning, it is unlikely to be acting in the spirit of the Learning Organization.

Third, the definition implies that the organization is undergoing a process of continuous change and adaptation; and focusing upon learning about the change process itself, while at the same time enabling individuals' learning. Fourth, it seems clear from this description that the organization does *not* have all the 'right answers' in terms of how to direct individuals' learning. At times it is likely that individual learning initiatives will provide the leading edge of organization change; while at other times a major breakthrough at the organization systems level of understanding will cause a 'reframing' of individual learning projects and approaches. Finally, there is no single success formula – each organization needs to discover its own learning pathways.

As Pedler et al. (1991) emphasize, the evolution of the learning organization concept is long and varied and its precise form is yet to be (and perhaps will never be) defined. Drawing upon the literature on learning, organizations, training and development, and management of quality they propose 11 dimensions which characterize a learning organization (see figure 7.1).

The enabling *structures* represent the central pivot of the learning organization since they are designed to create opportunities for business and individual development. For instance, rules and procedures are frequently reviewed and changed if necessary; appraisals are geared to

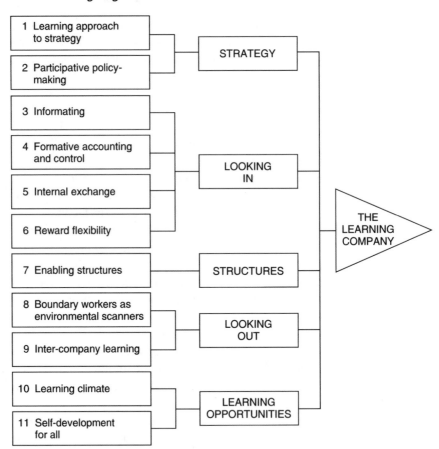

Figure 7.1 The learning company 'blueprint'
Source: Pedler, Burgoyne and Boydell, 1991, p. 25.

learning and development rather than to reward and punishment. The two clusters above 'structures' are mirrored by the two below. *Strategy* consists of (1) a learning approach whereby company policy and strategy formation, together with implementation, evaluation and improvement are consciously structured as a learning process enabling continuous improvement through flexibility; and (2) participative policy-making which involves all stake-holders (including customers, suppliers and owners) in the strategy-forming processes with a commitment to air and work through conflicts. *Looking in* covers three dimensions: (3) informating, which means Information Technologies are used to inform and empower people, encouraging wide access to information and more 'open' systems; (4) formative accounting and control, comprising systems that are structured to assist learning and add value, encouraging individuals and units to act as small businesses and to think about who their customers are; and (5) internal exchange between units and departments as suppliers and customers of each other, encouraging wide sharing of expectations and information, negotiations, contracting and providing feedback on goods/services received; fostering an environment of collaboration rather than competition. The *looking out* cluster embraces: (8) boundary workers as environmental scanners, asking for, respecting and using the experiences of all members who interact with external customers to feedback information on customer needs, and (9) tutor-company learning whereby neutrally advantageous learning activities are initiated, such as joint-trading, sharing in investment and job-exchanges. Finally, *learning opportunities* imply the fostering of (10) a learning climate, a general attitude of continuous improvement, the positive valuing of difference (age, gender, colour and so on), learning lessons from mistakes, and (11) self-development for all, whereby facilities and resources are made available to all members, employees at all levels and external stakeholders. While many of these 'learning organization' nostrums smack of common sense, there are few examples of organizations consistently practising such principles. Perhaps the greatest value of the learning organization debate is the attention it has focused on three areas of learning.

First the emphasis on 'regenerative or transformational' learning begs the question of what an organization is being transformed into and why. Examples of organizations becoming 'learning laboratories' combined with, at a more mundane level, flatter and more open structures, may well create tensions within organizations which result in employees asking searching questions of a social, ethical, moral and personal kind, related to the purpose of work and the nature of society more generally – a theme, incidentally, that has underpinned the self-development work of Pedler et al. (1991) for almost a decade. In the past, the work place has been a major focus for social and personal development, and for fulfilling a wide range of needs through personal interaction. As old values and ways of doing things disappear, new activities challenge such deep-rooted assumptions and organizational structures, and create what people will at first perceive as a disruptive tension.

> The idea of 'disruptive tension' provides the bridge between the developmental and mechanical description of the learning organization on the one hand, and the more philosophical definition provided by Pedler et al. (1988) on the other.
>
> (Jones and Hendry, 1994, p. 156)

Secondly, previous discussion of organizational learning has tended to concentrate on formalized and prescriptive development and training needs, generic sets of competencies and the adoption of universalistic assessment, whereas the learning organization switches attention to the *process* of learning, the individuality of learning styles and creating the right environment for experiential learning to occur.

Thirdly, the debate has prompted the realization that learning is as much acquired through emotion, attitudes, communication and habit mediated through imitation of role models, the forging of meaningful relationships, experience and memory, and developing a sense of self and values. Jones and Hendry (1994) contrast this 'soft learning' with the hard, pragmatic formal training typically undertaken by organizations. Whereas 'soft learning is often unintended, indirect, not controlled by the organization . . . it is at the heart of what the organization stands for while providing added value in adult learning' (1994, p. 160).

In short, the difference between the two concepts seems to be that organizational learning is a descriptive or heuristic device to explain and quantify learning activities and events, and as such, can be subsumed under the wider concept of the learning organization which refers to the less tangible but real philosophical purpose and direction of an organization and its staff. However, as we come to delineate the pathways such learning organizations might take and, particularly in the context of this book, seek to map out the HRS ramifications of such a 'direction', further imponderables arise. Why is it that so many activities under the broad organizational label of training and development patently do not lead to learning – either at an individual or institutional level? Is collective learning more than the sum of individual learning, and if so how and at what point do the two connect and synergize? If learning truly is open and unprescribed, whose needs are being met – who is to determine whether learning is acceptable or unacceptable, helpful or unhelpful? Can and should learning be managed? Is the ultimate custodian and benefactor of new skills, knowledge and attitudes the organization or the individual? As Jones and Hendry note, 'The paradox and dilemma for organizations is how to relax their control over the learning process while channelling the benefits from it' (1994, p. 160). If the benefits of learning *can* be established – and this is a moot point given the unorganized and hidden nature of much insightful experience – can lessons from one organizational context be passed onto another? And if they cannot, what is the value of studying learning organizations? Finally, if it is natural, spontaneous and habitual, why are individuals and organizations so successful at blocking and inhibiting learning?

At first glance, the learning organization appears to be both a timely (Pedler et al., 1991, ch. 2) and attractive (e.g. Drucker, 1992; Senge, 1990) estuary of many promising streams of thought and reflective action that have been sporadically evident through recent decades (organization development, action learning, self-development, pursuing excellence, total quality and continuous improvement amongst others). On closer scrutiny the structural and behavioural manifestations of the concept, even at the metaphorical level, are more elusive and – at times – self-contradictory. In the remainder of this chapter we seek to address some of the problematic issues prompted by the pursuit of the learning organization.

How Do Individuals Learn in Organizations?

In chapter 3, 'Training and Development Strategies', we noted that the trigger for training activity was invariably some awareness of a skills performance gap, which was then addressed in a purposeful and developmental way by the organization. However, the assumption that training and development delivered is equivalent to personal and corporate learning gained is obviously misplaced. In this section we determine what conditions make for a successful learning event or experience. Successful for the individual in that they develop their competence in a given area, and successful for the organization in that this newly won expertise is then effectively deployed to achieve business objectives.

The goals of learning

Over the years many people have endeavoured to categorize learning into different levels in order better to understand the way people assimilate new information and ideas, and the connection between this and changed behaviour and attitudes (e.g. Bloom, 1956; Bateson, 1972). One method of categorization for managers, at least, that has obtained popular currency (Burgoyne and Stuart, 1976) is to break down learning into three classes:

Basic data and information representing those facts which appertain to the specific work environment and relevant professional knowledge understanding. This would include training in such things as industrial legislation, production processes and sources of finance.

Situation-specific skills and response tendencies including the skills associated with sensitivity to events (perceptiveness, data-getting skills) include the following: analytical, problem-solving, decisions/judgement-making skills; social skills and abilities (leadership, influencing communicating, using and responding to leadership); emotional resilience and proactivity – the inclination to respond purposefully to events.

Qualities for self-development including creativity, mental agility, balanced learning habits and self-knowledge.

Rather than seeing these skills and qualities as discrete areas of learning, they can be depicted as three non-hierarchical circles, each of which intersects the other two at some point, indicating that overlap exists between all categories, as shown in figure 7.2. The degree of overlap depends on

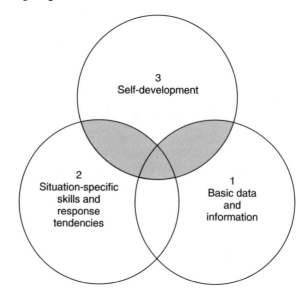

Figure 7.2   The three-circle categorization of learning

specific situations. For instance, a junior manager may be learning to use a new accounting software package for a particular data analysis job; the learning curve is steep in terms of assimilating the numerous computer instructions (circle 1) and his/her keyboard and data interpretation skills may also be quickly enhanced (circle 2). However, because time is short, interfacing the completed analysis with the corporate and external data-bases is left to an analyst, thus limiting the possibilities for self-development (circle 3). If the manager had been led a step further, learning how to access, interrogate and file data from the central network, this would have opened up an infinitely greater range of self-development opportu-nities for the future and the potential for creative learning would have been increased. Likewise, the model should be viewed as dynamic, with the qualities of circle 3, for example, being continually achieved in our daily lives and permeating the qualities of the other two circles. When designing training and development activities it is essential to know which qualities – or mix of qualities – are being sought in order to choose the appropriate learning methods and approaches.

The openness of learning

Alongside the goals of learning we also need to consider the degree of learner autonomy, a subject which has been a major area for researchers in individual learning (e.g. Simpson, 1980; Schon, 1983; Knowles, 1984).

The various philosophies of education and learning might usefully be depicted along a continuum. At one extreme there is a body of knowledge to be taught: practice is deduced from theory and then applied with an emphasis on formal learning methods. In human resource development terms this would result in fairly *instrumental* learning processes; subject matter will be covered in a predetermined syllabus where duration of study and quantity of earnings are important outputs. Tutors are seen as teachers and experts, they will set and mark/give feedback on assignments, and success or completion of the training is often signified by formal qualifications or membership of an elite.

At the other extreme there are what might be called *experiential* learning contexts which are based on the view that an individual's talent, ideas and views are to be drawn out, since knowledge evolves as we learn more about ourselves and the unbounded world we inhabit. This would lead an organization to arrange its training and development activities such that they are much more 'open-ended' and informal, with tutors acting as facilitators to help the learners discover their talents and realize their potential in order to achieve their own learning goals. This discussion about philosophy is an important one because from such presuppositions flow very different conceptions of how learning is deemed to occur, what learning system is appropriate to address given training objectives and in what role the trainer, tutor or mentor should be cast. The messages are pertinent to business schools and in-house training departments alike.

In the field of training and development, the notion of closed and open learning has been a particular focus, which can be likened to Handy's instrumental and experimental philosophies of education (Handy, 1974). Thus closed and instrumental processes are likely to be concerned with the subjects covered in a predetermined syllabus where duration of study and amount of learning are seen as important and the tutor is seen as the teacher and expert. The open or experiential processes, on the other hand, are more likely to be concerned with the learner as an individual who is allowed to choose personal learning goals, with the tutor acting as a facilitator to help the learner perfect his/her own skills and talents in order to achieve them.

So openness correlates with learner autonomy: that is, the freedom of choice exercised by learners over the content of what they want to learn and the process by which they wish to learn it, within the process implemented by the tutor. The graph in figure 7.3 shows the amount of autonomy given to the learner for determining the process (the way the training activities are organized) on the vertical axis, and the amount of autonomy given to the learner for determining the content (the precepts, principles, skills covered) on the horizontal axis. Such a representation is useful when evaluating the most appropriate training methods for the trainees and the subject matter in question.

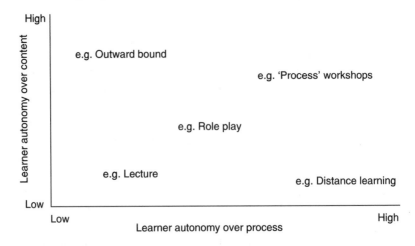

Figure 7.3 Locating training methods against learner autonomy

In the bottom left corner we would place methods like lecture, and any kind of programmed-learning case studies which allow relatively little or no learner autonomy over either content or process. For example, the learner attends a lecture the content of which is transmitted in the way the lecturer chooses, following a curriculum with set readings, and so on. Even a case study, which may appear less constrained, usually conforms to a predetermined pattern of exploration, analysis and 'discovery'. One of the features of well-designed programmed-learning techniques is the increased discretion they give to the learner. But there is a limited number of pathways through a given programme, so that while autonomy is greater than with a lecture, it can still be prescriptive.

Around the middle of the graph we would include such diverse activities as role play, management simulations and business games, projects and small-group work, which provide relatively more learner autonomy in terms of both content and process. For instance, during a role play learners have some choice in the way they portray the given role (content) but do so within a perspective normally set by the rules (process), sometimes behaviour modelled by the tutor or on a video. However, it is possible to use experiential behaviour modelling, thus allowing the learner some autonomy over the process as well as the content.

In the top right corner would appear such methods as encounter groups, counselling and unstructured process workshops, which traditionally have the highest levels of learner autonomy both in terms of content and process. At this level it is usual for the learner(s) to identify the content they wish to work on themselves. The process is facilitated by the tutor, although in such a way as to avoid constraining the learners;

this encourages them to use and/or experiment with processes that feel right for them at that particular time. An example here might be an assertiveness training course where, following tuition and tutor-controlled role play, learners are given the freedom and space to experiment with different behaviours without inhibition. Even here, of course, environmental parameters are still imposed by the 'staff', although the learner always has the ultimate recourse of exercising autonomy by leaving the learning event via the nearest door or window!

These three groups of methods align themselves with the three circles of learning discussed earlier and shown in figure 7.2; the first group with the circle associated with basic data and information, the second with situation-specific skills and response tendencies and the third with self-development. Less easy to categorize are such methods as 'outward bound' and secondments. In cases where the nature of learning is relatively predictable but the way in which an individual goes about it may be idiosyncratic, these would be located at the top left corner. As the content of learning becomes more open-ended, however, so these approaches would move towards the top right.

Designing effective learning

By way of summary we can now set out the different variables we have discussed, each of which has a significant bearing on the structuring of learning activities in organizations along a horizontal continuum (see figure 7.4). The left-hand pole represents the instrumental approach, which also corresponds with low learner autonomy over both content and process and a relatively closed strategy of training delivery. At the opposite extreme, which we term 'experiential', learning is open, with learners exercising free choice over the way they develop.

We started with a consideration of the goals of *learning* and the qualities being sought in a given learner target group. Figure 7.4 rearranges the three intersecting circles along this bipolar continuum. It shows that when addressing basic information and data-handling, the educational process is likely to be highly controlled with little learner flexibility, although it *is* possible to introduce greater discretion and openness of learning, as with a self-paced distance teaching approach. Conversely, when attempting to facilitate self-development, the most congruent process would be one that allows a greater amount of learner autonomy in an open learning environment. An example here would be a voluntary organization working in child care, which arranges self-development for its staff in order to empower them so that they, in turn, can facilitate the development of their clients – the children. This is not to say that self-development objectives could not be met in a more constrained learning environment with an instrumental

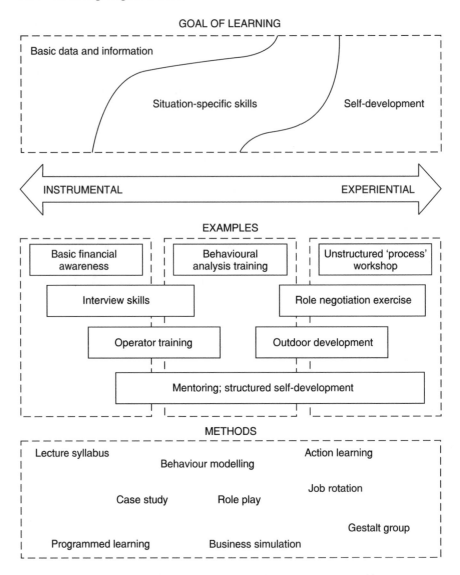

Figure 7.4   Matching the processes of learning to the goals of learning

approach, but it is far less likely. Sandwiched between these two training processes is specific skills training where a middle range of learning processes are appropriate, with decreasing trainer/tutor control towards the right-hand pole. Immediately beneath the three stages of learning contained in the box we have given some training/learning activities *examples*. The third layer of the figure depicts a number of learning methods or *processes* ranging across the continuum.

In reality, most training activities combine two or more types of learning. Training staff in appraisal or interviewing skills will require tutor input on the organization's HRM procedures, as well as the legal and equal opportunities dimensions of the interview process; but it would be hard to imagine such a course not including practical skill sessions with observations and feedback. Hence this training would straddle the first two types in the box. Likewise, supervised self-development, perhaps under the watchful eye of an informal mentor, could well encompass all three types of learning, although its natural 'home' would be the 'high autonomy' end of the continuum, since the individual is the primary driver of the process. Interestingly, if an individual is assigned a mentor by the organization (rather than finding his/her own) it is likely that the emphasis of learning activities will shift to the left.

The three layers have been depicted together in figure 7.4 in order to show how all training and development activities are based on certain implicit principles of learning (see Burgoyne, 1977):

1 Lectures and syllabus-based programmes including most case study approaches assume people learn by organizing, sequencing and relating new information to existing bodies of knowledge. They are appropriate methods for *information transfer* but little else.
2 Programmed learning, as employed by computer-based training, language laboratories and other rote learning based on the premise of *conditioning*: sufficient practice, feedback and reinforcement will change the habitual behaviour of learners.
3 Behaviour modelling and most role play learning processes aim to skill trainees in certain predetermined learnable attributes. The learning premise here is one of *trait modification*.
4 Business simulations rely on learning via *trial, error and feedback*. The learners operate in a designed environment where they learn to cope with relationships which result from their own real interactions, rather than those built into the 'game' by the designer.
5 Action learning and outdoor development programmes switch attention from the learners' behaviour to their *'cognition map'* of the world: the conscious or unconscious knowledge which steers their action. Through shared experience, reflection and insight are encouraged via heightened self-awareness and reinterpreting experiences in new ways.
6 Relatively unstructured activities like encounter groups are based on *experiential learning* theory, involving the total person (feelings, motives and emotions as well as cognition and behaviours): the principles of learning are autonomy and accommodation, and the removal of barriers to allow the natural growth process.

Understanding these derivations is important in matching the appropriate training/learning process to the learning goals being addressed. It is all too easy for a human resource specialist to pick a prepackaged course on, say, project management in the hope that it will help middle managers work more collaboratively on matrix-managed jobs. While the package may impart some excellent planning techniques and even give limited scope for learning and practising team leadership and problem-solving skills, the sponsor may be disappointed to find following the training, that representatives of different departments still do not co-operate despite being on the same project teams. There may be many reasons for this: scarcity of resources, jealously guarded expertise, ignorance of each others' potential contribution, cultural stereotypes, and more. It is clear that even if these other organizational factors are supportive (this is a big assumption!) real cross-functional collaboration will only come about when *attitudes* are changed. Methods rooted in behavioural approaches are not intended to – and are unlikely to – change people's predispositions towards others. It would take developmental activities involving sustained interaction with ample room for reflection, revision of perspectives and further experimentation derived from cognitive or experiential learning to shift attitudes in any significant manner; this could take a very long time.

Nevertheless, techniques which persistently encourage new ways of working in trainees may – through repetition and positive feedback – condition them to think differently also. In other words, repeated actions (particularly when public and freely chosen) may lead to attitude formation. This brings us back to a recurrent theme in this text as to whether staff adopt new attitudes genuinely or expediently as a result of structural, cultural – or in this case – training interventions (Ogbonna, 1994; Mabey and Mallory, 1995). It is not always easy to tell. The important point for training specialists and individuals developing themselves is that, having ascertained development needs, they then select learning activities and methods that are capable of delivering against the objectives chosen.

The discussion so far tends to take for granted that individual development needs can be – and typically are – addressed by the organization setting up some kind of training programme or learning activity for the individuals concerned. At one level this assumption is fine because although a great deal of on-the-job coaching and unstructured personal development does take place on a daily basis in all organizations, it is the case that these learning opportunities are rarely exploited to the full because they remain random, unreviewed and invariably dislocated from wider strategic HRM polices and plans (Mumford et al., 1987). At another level it is problematic because it assumes individual learning takes place to exclusively serve the current purposes of the organization, which by definition remains in control of the learning processes that have been 'constructed'.

This is an agenda issue. If learning, like management, is an active, purposive activity then it faces all the moral and ethical issues raised by the taking of responsibility for purposive action (Burgoyne, 1994, p. 43). In other words, no matter how well matched the goals, methods and educational principles of a given training activity, unless the participant subscribes to its value, timing and personal pertinence, learning is unlikely to ensue. This leads us to consider learning and its outcomes from a less paternalistic view.

Motivation to learn

Kolb, one of the most influential figures in the field, has defined learning as the process whereby knowledge is created through the transformation of experience (Kolb, 1984). The basis of his theory is the experiential learning cycle which suggests that though we may encounter a rich array of experiences in our work and private lives, we often learn poorly or only partially from such stimuli due to inadequate review and thought about how we might approach a similar situation in the future. In other words, most people probably get as far as reflecting on a specific learning opportunity but no further. Some will pursue the learning by looking for new theoretical frameworks with the intention of doing things differently in the future. However, the model suggests that only by translating these intentions into experimental behaviour does real learning take place.

Drawing on the broad experience of adult education and training, Rogers (1986) suggests that, irrespective of wider questions and choices arising from different theories of learning, an awareness of the following general characteristics of adult learners can provide a well-grounded focus to the facilitation of learning in organizations:

First, to be effective, any programme of learning needs to coincide with the processes of maturation, self-fulfilment, perspective and self-determination of the individual learner. All those involved in the process of learning need to affirm that common adulthood in their relationships. Contrary to some assumptions, adults have not stopped growing and developing. The pace and direction of learning and change may vary from individual to individual, but all are actively engaged in a dynamic process of change. Effective learning needs to relate to that process.

Second, everyone brings a range of experience, knowledge and emotional investment to the learning they are embarking on. To be effective, learning has to relate to and build on what adults bring to their learning. Conversely and equally importantly, even when adults are engaged in learning wholly new abilities, devaluing or ignoring what they bring to their learning undermines and rejects their whole identity, not just particular experiences and values.

Third, learning is not simply the satisfaction of needs. It also involves an acknowledgement of the goals, intentions, motivations and aspirations – however diverse, contradictory or confused – that inform someone's decision to learn. The meaning and significance of their learning is shaped by those intentions.

Fourth, on the basis of past experience, adults bring to their learning expectations about both the way in which learning occurs and their own capabilities to learn. Effective learning has to take account of people's initial expectations of the learning process and an individual's sense of the limits and possibilities of what they are capable of achieving.

Fifth, whatever the circumstances or occasion of learning, all adults come to their learning from a complete social environment. They bring to their learning demands and needs which arise from the full range of their relationships – parents, friends, neighbours and so forth as well as working colleagues. Specific learning tasks and programmes are set against the demands and concerns of that wider background.

Sixth, all adults have already developed, implicitly if not consciously, their own particular ways of pursuing and coping with the demands of their learning and development. To be effective new learning needs to build on their preferred learning styles and patterns.

Rogers also offers some more detailed suggestions about the ways in which individual self-directed learning takes place as part of general growth and development. On this basis, he proposes four common features of the way in which most adults pursue a discrete 'learning episode' (see box 7.4).

Box 7.4 Four features of adult 'learning episodes'

1 *They are usually episodic in character, not continuous.* Learning tends to occur in short, intense bursts, absorbing the attention and ending once the purpose has been achieved. Even within programmes of long-term and sustained self-development there are more intensive, short-term episodes of learning directed towards the achievement of certain immediate goals.

2 *The goal that is set is usually some concrete task, some immediate problem that seems important.* Individual learning episodes are usually aimed at the solution of specific problems. This has wide implications. On the whole we do not approach the learning situation academically – i.e. moving deliberately from general theory to applications. In specified instances, we tend not draw on compartmentalized knowledge. Learning is undertaken in the process of doing the

task, of meeting the demands of the situation – rather than as the preliminary steps to practice.

3   *Adults tend to adopt a particular range of learning styles and strategies.* As well as the more general learning styles preferred by individual adults they tend to employ the following strategies for learning: analogical thinking (existing knowledge and experience); trial and error; the creation of general patterns and meaningful wholes to make sense of new material; minimal reliance on memory or rote learning; use of practical demonstration and imitation.

4   *In specific episodes, there is relatively little interest in overall principle.* Efforts are centred on the achievement of the immediate and particular, not the long-term and the general. Once the specific goal has been attained, the episode is closed though the knowledge and skills acquired are stored away for future use. (Adapted from Rogers, 1986, pp pp. 68–71.)

The value of such an analysis of the naturally occurring learning episode lies not in its overall, theoretical cogency but in its practical implications for those responsible for designing and supporting more explicit programmes and processes of learning. Such programmes and processes in organizations are more likely to be effective if they build on the routine ways in which individual adults learn.

Is Collective Learning More Than the Sum of Individual Learning?

In the discussion about individual learning in the section above, there is a tendency for such learning processes to focus on 'hard' as against 'soft' learning and on natural, adaptive as against regenerative or transformational learning (Jones and Hendry, 1994). In other words, most of the learning activities have the potential for contributing to organizational learning but – with the possible exception of those on the far right of figure 7.4 – they still fall short of characterizing a learning organization.

The critical distinction between the two seems to be the extent to which individual learning activities feed and integrate with broader and deeper learning processes in the organization; breadth being associated with the scope of learning transfer and depth being concerned with levels of learning (e.g. being prepared to question the processes of learning themselves). Here we consider some of the hindrances to learning and its transfer and some of the ways these hindrances might be overcome.

Blocks to learning

Not all blocks to learning concern preferred style and not all hindrances to learning transfer can be attributed to the individual. Take the case of off-the-job training courses. An employee's previous learning experience may well have been the latter stages of formal education or attendance on a less than satisfactory training event elsewhere, and this will probably conjure up unhelpful memories. 'Unlearning' may need to take place – emotional and educational – before new learning can commence; in other words, successful development may be as much about the learning environment as the individual's learning style. Note the equivalence here with Lewin's (1951) model of organizational unfreezing which is seen as a necessary precursor to cultural change. This initial willingness to learn will also be influenced by the diagnosis and selection process leading up to the training event: whether the individual's manager is involved in, and supportive of, the training activity; whether personal learning needs have been identified; and so on.

Equally important is the reinforcement of new concepts, skills and attitudes in the work place *after* the training event or learning activities; again, the trainee's line manager plays a key role here in debriefing and overseeing any implementation plans. The less uncoupled the work place and off-the-job training activities the better – which is why on-the-job learning has many inherent advantages. At a wider level, unless the prevailing value system from which the course participant comes actively supports and rewards the new skills and behaviours being acquired, little personal learning is likely to be sustained or consolidated. For example, a 'skills workshop' may stimulate an increased awareness of customer requirements and may cultivate the accompanying listening and problem-solving skills. The trainee returns to his/her work place eager and equipped, only to find that divisional performance targets specify an increased number of queries and complaints to be handled in a given time period. An organizational constraint which not only dampens but actually discourages the application of the newly acquired skills!

However, a far more subtle and potent source of learning disruption comes from the social context of learning itself. Learning usually implies change and work organizations are particularly adept at obstructing individuals' learning when major change is required: ' "Natural" learning processes within organizations seem to engage managers not only in analysing technical data and problems but also in efforts to avoid addressing fundamental issues and questions which may distress, embarrass or threaten themselves or others' (Butler, 1992, p. 40). When new knowledge and new ideas are regarded as dangerous, disloyal or troublesome within the organization, managers learn not to learn, to avoid real issues and moreover to skilfully cover up that they are doing so (see box 7.5). They become guilty of skilled incompetence (Argyris, 1987, p. 8), clever at 'not learning what they "must" learn (in order to make real change and progress) and almost certainly unaware of their own responsibility for the resulting maintenance of status quo' (Butler, 1992, p. 40).

Box 7.5   Organizational defensive routines

'One of the most powerful ways people deal with potential embarrassment is to create organizational defensive routines. I define these as any action or policy that prevents human beings from experiencing negative surprises, embarrassment, or threat, and simultaneously prevents the organization from reducing or eliminating the causes of the surprises, embarrassment, and threat. Organizational defensive routines are anti-learning and overprotective.

These defensive routines are organizational in the sense that individuals with different personalities behave in the same way; and people leave and new ones come into the organization, yet the defensive routines remain intact.

Now to the example: Built into genuine decentralization is the age-old tug between autonomy and control. Subordinates want to be left alone while their superiors want no surprises. The subordinates push for autonomy, asserting that by letting them alone, top management will show its trust. They want management to trust them at a distance. The superiors, on the other hand, wanting no surprises, use information systems as controls. The subordinates see the control device as confirming mistrust.

Many executives I observed deal with this dilemma by acting in a way that they believe will lead to productive consequences. They send mixed messages. They keep communicating, "We mean it – you are running the show." The division heads concur that the message is credible up to the point that a very important issue is at stake and they want to prove their mettle; then headquarters begins to interfere. In the eyes of top management, they intervene precisely when they can be of most help, that is, when the issue "requires a corporate perspective".

Designing and sending an intentionally ambiguous message and having it look as if this is not the case requires skill. The sender has to follow four rules about designing and delivering mixed messages:

1   Design a message that is ambiguous and clearly so; that is imprecise and precisely so.

For example, "Be innovative and take risks, but be careful about upsetting others" is a message that says in effect, "Don't get into trouble." But the designer is careful not to specify exactly what will and will not upset others. The ambiguity and imprecision are necessary to cover the designer. It is also necessary because it is difficult for the designer to be precise ahead of time.

The ambiguity and imprecision, on the other hand, are clearly and precisely understood by the receiver. Indeed, a request for more precision would likely be interpreted as a sign of immaturity or inexperience. Moreoover, the receivers may some day want to use the imprecision and ambiguity to their advantage.

2   Act as if the message is not inconsistent.

When individuals communicate mixed messages, they usually do it spontaneously and with no sign that the message is mixed. Indeed, if they did appear to be hesitant because of the mixedness in the message, that could be seen as a weakness.

3   Make the ambiguity and inconsistency in the message undiscussable.

It is rare indeed for an executive to design and state a mixed message and then ask "Do you find my message inconsistent and ambiguous?" The message is made undiscussable by the very natural way it is carried out and by the absence of any inquiry.

4   Make the undiscussability of the undiscussable also undiscussable.' (Argyris, 1987, pp. 6, 7.)

Connecting the levels of learning

Individual learning is a necessary but not a sufficient condition for organizational learning. As we have seen above, individuals do not always learn that which is genuinely helpful for organizational progress and organizations do not automatically learn when individuals within it have learned something; there has to be a mutual behavioural change. There has to be an enhancement of collective competence among the members of an organization if organizational learning is to mean anything at all. This, in turn, usually means that the learning – at whatever level – is conscious, that there is a collective and explicit review and possible rejection and renewal of the way things are done.

Following Argyris and Schon (1981), Swieringa and Wierdsma (1992) differentiate three levels of collective learning. Single-loop learning occurs when changes are made to existing 'rules', or the way they are interpreted. This does not necessarily equate with single, easy and trouble-free learning, but it is concerned with improving *how* things are done rather than questioning the underlying purpose.

Double-loop learning Swieringa and Wierdsma equate to learning at a higher level of right, questioning *why* things are done. It is called for when external signals indicate that mere adjustment of the 'rules' is inadequate, or internal signals suggest there is confusion or conflict over the organization's 'rules'. Occasionally – indeed rarely – triple-loop learning occurs when the essential principles on which the organization is founded come under discussion: for instance, the company's place in the market, its role as an enterprise, its cultural identity.

Again such learning poses 'why' questions, but this time at the level of collective will and being. Organizational responses to similar circumstances will look very different depending on which level the learning is taking place (see table 7.1)

Swieringa and Wiersdma maintain that many organizations do not progress beyond single-loop learning because managers are fearful of putting basic principles up for discussion. Too often organizations turn to third parties to manage radical transitions instead of mobilizing internal knowledge and expertise; or they start up new learning processes before previous ones have reached the point of concrete and visible behavioural change.

The role of catalysts

This still leaves the question of how the different levels or loops of learning connect. For Garratt (1987; 1990) the vital link between level one and level two is the 'business brain' of the enterprise, not the directors but the people who straddle the domains of strategy and operations, who need to be effective at educating upwards as well as translating new vision and direction into operational reality. Pedler et al. (1991) see the learning company as a number of energy flows (figure 7.5). On the vertical axis there are two crucial 'connections' which are mutually beneficial: 'Individual purpose comes about through shared identity, which, in turn, fires our collective purpose. Equally, collective purpose gives meaning to our lives and our place in the company' (1991, p. 31). On the horizontal axis, there presumably is nothing to stop individual ideas and action to feed each other in a manner which is entirely discrete from the policy – operation loops. What begins to distinguish the learning company, however, is where inner searching and visioning leads to organizational policy, realized in collective operations and expressed through the learning and development of individual members. The authors point out that it is entirely possible for the organization to get stuck in one of the four cycles: perhaps all operations with little policy development, or a great deal of searching which does not

Table 7.1   Examples of collective learning and organization change

Single-loop learning	Double-loop learning	Triple-loop learning
• An insurance company is confronted with complaints from agents about co-ordination and communication difficulties. A quality action is instigated, computer programs are improved, policies are checked three times instead of twice and consultations between inspectors and head office are intensified.	• The insurance company begins to wonder whether perhaps different marketing strategies (such as segmentation) should be considered, and to what extent the complaints might have been caused by collective attitudes among the staff.	• The insurance company begins to wonder whether it ought really to operate with agents at all, whether or not it wishes to give itself a high profile as a market leader and whether it is primarily an insurance company or an institutional investor.
• The atmosphere has sunk below zero in a personnel department; other departments have begun to complain bitterly. Two of the suspected instigators have been dismissed, other members of staff take two two-day periods off to talk the matter through and develop new rules of behaviour.	• The personnel department begins a discussion about how personnel matters could be investigated in a professional way.	• The personnel department begins discussions with the Board on whether a controlling or a supporting staff department should be developed.
• A college of higher education witnesses a gradual decline in applications from new students. It is decided to intensify publicity, to produce a new prospectus, to hold open days and to mount extra-mural activities.	• The college begins to wonder about the curriculum it offers, and the atmosphere at the college.	• Teachers in the college develop a plan to transfer, within five years, from a discipline-based to a problem-based method of education.
• The work of the head of an employers' association is subjected to more and more criticism. He is sent on courses by the management, division of responsibilities between him and his staff is adjusted, and the frequency of reporting is increased, etc.	• Members of the employers' association begin to discuss the structure of the association and the distribution of responsibilities of the office.	• The employers' association calls together its members to consider in a strategic orientation round of talks the mission and goals of the association for the 1990s.

Table 7.1   (Cont'd)

Single-loop learning	Double-loop learning	Triple-loop learning
• An energy company decides to implement a series of major radical investment projects over the coming five years. The management team proposes a plan with details of the consequences of the investments for the functions and responsibilities of operators, supervisors and maintenance teams.	• The management team of the energy company decides to run the project with a matrix structure, with as much involvement as possible from the processing and maintenance departments, in order to ease the transition of the new organization and give personnel the opportunity to learn on the job.	• The energy company, in consultation with the works council, decides not to adopt the blueprint model which would involve considerable opposition and political manipulation, but to opt for a programme of gradual development.
• In one year, complaints in a small technical services company double. After an investigation, improvements are implemented in transport routes, schemes of work, telephone messages, etc.	• When complaints in the technical service company remain at an undesirably high level, discussion of working methods is introduced into this previously very autocratically managed company.	• Two years later, the founder-director of the service company decides to step down and give his son a chance to introduce a new style of leadership into the company.

Source: Adapted from Swieringa and Wierdsma, 1992.

realize the company's full potential. In these circumstances 'the effective intervention is one which helps the organization move out of the impasse which is holding it in unconscious patterns of repetitive behaviour' (Critchley and Casey, 1989, p. 8).

Many organizations have – in recent years – spawned a host of special project teams, cross-functional clusters, quality improvement groups and the like for the specific purpose of preventing this 'stuckness' and stimulating this interchange. However, Hawkins (1991) notes that there needs to be a structure for these strategy groups to dialogue and co-create the new organization together, and some kind of overarching vision to cohere their diverse endeavours. 'The greatest danger lies not in the lack of integration within the operational learning or strategic learning loops, but in the lack of the "business brain" that integrates the two cycles. Without this linkage, the most likely outcome is that there will be single-loop learning within both domains' (1991, p. 176).

The other possibility, of course, is that the top team won't listen to or 'hear' the messages coming from elsewhere in the organization, so reducing the value of generated and collected information (Garratt, 1990) or filtering

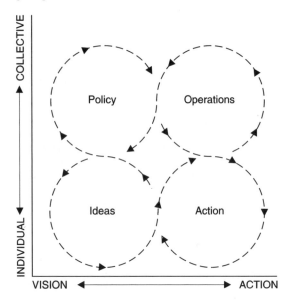

Figure 7.5 The energy-flow model
Source : Pedler, Burgoyne and Boydell, 1991, p. 32.

out its key, provocative insights (Argyris, 1987). As Torbert (1994, p. 68) points out, 'only double-loop feedback adjusted for local coloring and developmental timing specific to this unique occasion' is likely to accomplish the impact and spur the level of learning desired.

The role of leaders

Who or what creates the link between double-loop learning, which helps to move an organization from efficiency thinking to effectiveness thinking, and triple-loop learning which generates the capacity to address the fundamental question: effective for what, or to what end? For Hawkins (1991), the answer is to have at least some key members in the organization who can 'act like "salt to the soup" to draw out the awareness of the deeper purpose which contains and informs the strategic thinking and the operational realities' (1991, p. 183). They should be capable of recognizing the mindsets that are locking the organization into dysfunctional patterns of behaviour and be able to lead an exploration of new purpose and core values, remembering that 'real learning only begins when the leaders of the company change not what they preach, but what they do. When in Argyris's terms, there is a change not just in "espoused theory" but in "theory in action"' (1991, p. 183). While formal leaders do not necessarily equate with opinion leaders, they do nevertheless carry a special responsibility, especially during periods of disruptive organizational change. (See box 7.6.)

Box 7.6 Radical change at Billiton, Royal Dutch Shell

'The basis upon which an organization acts, adapts and implements changes is coming to interact more and more closely with personal values. As all employees play a more vital part in the organization's life so their learning – conscious and unconscious, explicit and implicit – becomes of greater consequence; and as learning in itself becomes more valued in organizations, and therefore more visible as an activity, questions about organizational purpose become more urgent and necessary to address.

A successful example of radical change occurred in the central office of Billiton International metals in The Hague. Billiton is the metals industry division of the Royal Dutch Shell Group. After seven years of fundamental over-supply in the metals market the company, with a turnover at the time of around $1.5bn, had accumulated losses of $750m. The parent company was considering disposal as an option when a new President was appointed in 1986. He advised that the business had to be put in better shape, even to sell it. Every operation in Billiton, world-wide, was reviewed "to determine what businesses we were in and why we were in them". A survival plan resulted, whereby product-oriented divisions were to be scrapped in favour of four core business segments. The management organization needed to be changed from a typical metals industry structure, heavily centralized to permit significant authority and responsibility to be transferred into the operating companies. Consequently, the role of central office had to change from command and control to a dual role which was very different, being more subtle and complex. The roles embraced first monitoring and auditing on behalf of the shareholder (Shell); and second provision of advice to operating companies on request, and at market competitive rates. The radical change in attitude required could be described as being from "we're in charge" to "no one owes us a living". The change in role also required a reduction by half of staff numbers in central office, with some transferring to the operating companies and some taking redundancy, mainly on a voluntary basis.

In review, the management team, which has retained the same personnel throughout the period, have by their own open admission significantly changed the way they individually and collectively behave in business over this period of time. Every member of the central office has attested to a significant rethinking of who they are, where they are leading people, and how this related with the business.

> Most say that the process of radical change, and the ultimate survival of the business, was significantly affected by the close attention to vision, direction and strategy, alongside the implications for the values, expectations and assumptions of each person involved.'
> (Benjamin and Mabey, 1993, pp. 181–6.)

The role of teams

So far, we have been primarily considering how individuals can catalyse the learning of larger systems, but as Marsick (1994) reminds us: 'Managers can involve social units in collective learning – aggregates of people who are united by the pursuit of common concerns. Most obviously this may involve teams, but at the wider organizational levels, vertical or horizontal business networks, multinational business divisions, or customer–supplier partnerships may be involved' (1994, p. 16). The team can be a key to the learning organization because it provides minimum critical mass for the cross-fertilizing of ideas and for setting learning norms for itself (Senge, 1990). A team can also achieve what none of the individuals within can do alone; with the right dynamic, a collection of ordinary individuals can achieve extraordinary feats. But the converse can also occur: a team can fail to achieve what any of its members could easily accomplish. For 'working groups' and 'pseudo-teams' this is not untypical (Katzenbach and Smith, 1993), even when they are comprised of individually 'bright' members (Belbin, 1993). This is because how a group learns is not exactly the same as how individuals learn: new skills and sensitivities are required. Collective competence is to a large degree determined by the interactional competence of individuals. When applied to the running of learning events for groups of staff from a given organization, this results in two further paradoxes:

(1) 'Participants of an organizational course must individually unlearn what they have learned together as a collective. In an organizational course collectively developed rules, insights and principles will be subjected to discussion. It is this collective agreement on what is permitted and what is obligatory which dictates the knowledge and understanding, the courage, the will and the ability of a collective. In an organizational course it is precisely this collective agreement that is the subject under discussion, and with it the ability and knowledge of each individual.

(2) 'An organization which seeks to change its collective behaviour must be ready to discuss what has determined its collective behaviour. This is a paradox which becomes more awkward the higher the level of learning involved. With triple-loop learning, at the level of principles, the paradox implies that you should discuss what it has been agreed not to discuss' (Swieringa and Wierdsma, 1992, pp. 125–6).

So it is possible to identify linkages that integrate learning at individual level through groups and teams to learning at the organizational level. However, while the processes and dynamics that connect individual and group learning are relatively easy to observe, these become more elusive as the scale and the complexity of the social unit grow, and certainly examples of triple-loop organizational learning are few and far between. Perhaps we should follow Marsick (1994) in interpreting 'organizational learning as subsystem learning that occurs across functional lines and takes place on a relatively large scale, for example, a business unit' (p. 16), rather than confining the definition to wholesale organization transformation.

Can a Learning Organization be Created?

Our analysis of learning organizations so far has shown that pursuing the concept in terms of specific structures and cultures, normative models of good practice or grandiose schemes for sweeping change is probably less helpful than identifying the sorts of processes and values found in organizations that are adopting a learning-based approach to their management and development. This means focusing not on what learning organizations do, but on how they do it. It means considering what is appropriate and feasible for an individual manager or team; recognizing what issues and choices are associated with being a learning organization. There is no 'right model' of a learning organization.

The hallmarks of a learning organization

Developing a learning organization is not a matter of adopting formulae and procedures used elsewhere, because such 'copying' inevitably runs contrary to the processes of learning and change. For all its elusivenesss, the learning organization is more than a metaphor or an ideal type, it is attainable and has a recognizable and distinctive 'feel'. The experience of working in such an environment is well captured by Dale (1993). For her a learning organization:

- will work to create values, practices and procedures in which 'learning' and 'working' are synonymous throughout the organization.
- is inextricably bound up with organizational change and will seek to move beyond the learning associated with 'first-order change' – learning to improve current performance and do the same things differently and more effectively – to the learning associated with 'second-order change' – learning how to learn and develop the capacity to continuously generate new ideas and insights in order to do different things.

- will involve the discomfort of living with the uncertainties and ambiguities associated with iterative processes of change. It also involves acknowledging the risk associated with dynamic conservatism and consensus and working through – rather than just overcoming – the positive value of the conflicts arising from multiple agendas and diverging perceptions. (See box 7.7.)
- will require its managers to redefine their own roles and responsibilities. Rather than being essentially isolated individuals, they are members of a professional community of co-learners.
- will provide a safe environment for the risks and openness required for reflective practice in which questioning and self-doubt are as important as certainty and control.

Box 7.7 Top Teams: A European Study

A survey of several thousand top executives in seven European countries (Ireland, Spain, France, Germany, Austria, UK and Sweden) sought to establish which competences – if any – among 'top management teams' influenced organizational performance. They measured this by asking senior managers to rate such things as satisfaction, stress, confidence, ability to meet challenges and structural issues, and ease of managing long-term issues. Six competence areas were found to have a significantly positive bearing on these indices:

- having good interpersonal relationships with understanding of each other's values and management style.
- being able to discuss issues openly without arousing undue sensitivity or tension.
- having a high level of trust in each other.
- being approachable, and willing to receive feedback and criticism, implying the ability to give and receive feedback in an impersonal and objective manner.
- having sufficient discipline and cohesion to implement decisions upon which they agreed, without the need to follow up decisions very closely.
- having the capacity to discuss and understand both long- and short-term issues.

The researchers conclude that 'there is concrete evidence that the quality of interaction within the top management team can either enhance or damage business', and they add that management development should put emphasis on 'examining interpersonal relationships, management styles, attitudes and values, openness, trust and communication within the team'. (From Alderson, 1993.)

Many of the issues and choices raised by the idea of the learning organization relate to broad questions of structure and culture. Individual managers can often feel relatively powerless to do anything about such aspects of their organization. The sorts of changes required to support learning throughout an organization appear to lie beyond the scope and influence of any individual. If real progress is to be made in the area of learning, therefore, it is important to identify the enabling structures, cultures and systems which are needed at organizational and individual levels.

With this goal in mind, Jones and Hendry (1992) have developed a five-phase model of learning in organizations (see figure 7.6). The lower three circles in this figure represent initial phases of individual/organizational learning – not necessarily in sequence, though it is likely that there is a progression from left to right, with the possibility of getting stuck at an early stage. The Foundation phase concerns basic skills development and equipping learners with the habits and enthusiasm to learn more. An organization, in one way or another, must take responsibility for ensuring that these basic 'social survival skills' are acquired, as well as developing HRD strategies to motivate and build confidence for further learning. Jones and Hendry refer to this as a learning organization in embryonic state. The Formation phase encourages and develops skills for self-learning and self-development: here the individual learner begins to learn about the organization as a whole, its meaning and purpose and their own place within it. The challenge here is for the organization to make available opportunities

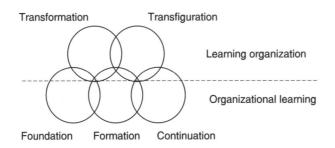

Figure 7.6 Five development phases of the learning organization
Source: Adapted from Jones and Hendry, 1992, p. 32.

and resources for training and development as the learner makes demands for new learning.

In the Continuation phase the learner and the organization are becoming more independent, innovatory, self-motivated and confident. HRD systems need to be sensitive to the differential pace of learning both on and off the job, and include counselling in skill development and a range of support measures for stressed, turned-off and plateaued individuals.

The two upper phases are evidence of a transition from organizational learning to the learning organization. Transformation is concerned with making a complete change in the form, appearance and character of the organization. This will involve change in structures and systems through the influence of technology, social change, and global factors; experimentation with alternative and more flexible work practices; and adapting to newly emerging social and human values, by actively implementing HRM policies and strategies which are not discriminatory in terms of race, sex, religion or disability. Attention is paid to how business is acquired and how its assets managed, so that corruption does not occur. It develops strategies which actively support community initiatives for the enhancement of people at large. The social and ethical dimension underpins all organizational activity, with an emphasis on corporate responsibility; and learning focuses on managing personal change and self-assessment.

Finally comes the Transfiguration phase of the learning organization, where the language description becomes noticeably less concrete and more idealistic (see box 7.8).

Box 7.8 The Transfiguration phase of the learning organization

Concerned with:

- transformation plus elevation leading to idealization.
- people coming first and a concern for society's general welfare and betterment.
- asking crucial questions about why the organization exists in the forms that it does.
- the organization representing a way of life to be cherished because of its values.
- the organization developing to accommodate and understand global cultures, tolerance, integration, and co-operation.

Kinds of activities:

- non-prescriptive because no organization yet exists.

- activities will be different from one organization to another.
- learning is at the centre of activities providing further insight and new skills.
- lack of concern with learning linked to sequential training and credentials.
- an emphasis on learning and organizational development which equalizes people's chances rather than monopolizing them and their distribution by means of certificates and diplomas.
- recognition of casual/experiential learning.
- skill learning by matching 'the right' teacher or circumstances at the right time.
- the organization instructing and controlling itself by means of total involvement in the community, and driven by its own understanding of its future needs.
- an emphasis on people developing as individuals and without fear or favour, doing what they want to do rather than what someone else deems to be appropriate.

Measures of achievement:

- is continuous and about internal organizational learning and development.
- the organization is judged by the extent to which the people which make it up control and teach the organization how to learn, rather than vice versa.
- the organization engages in activities which enable it to get glimpses that it can be 'much more' than it is.
- formal appraisals do not exist.
- each organization is more like an amoeba, able to change shape to suit its environment and to react to the pressures of external demands.
- formal training/learning is no longer institutionalized, it flows naturally and progressively.
- there is a concern for the physical environment and a concern that what is produced harms no one in any shape or form. (Adapted from Jones and Hendry, 1992, pp. 30–1.)

The five-phase depiction of individual/organizational learning – and the authors are careful to point out the dangers of deterministic modelling – highlights a number of issues. First, it suggests (no more) that organizations can develop in a progressive manner towards becoming learning organizations. Second, it poses the possibility that 'an organization, which establishes itself as a learning organization from the very beginning, can transform and transfigure itself without all the trappings of traditional structures and systems' (Jones and Hendry, 1992, p. 33). It also allows for discrete parts of an organization to develop and change at different rates and times. Third, a fairly detailed picture of the practical implications of each of the first three phases can be discerned; for instance, the activities described can readily be subdivided into those which are structural, cultural and HRD issues, each with their own set of implied HR policy initiatives to be hammered out idiosyncratically by a given organization. However, this is less true of the transformation and transfiguration phases, which are necessarily less determinate and less tangible while still giving an experiential flavour of what it might be like to work in such an organization (see box 7.8). Jones and Hendry (1992) quote Illich in this regard: 'Learning is the human activity which least needs manipulating by others. Most learning is not the result of instruction. It is rather the result of unhampered participation in a meaningful setting' (Illich, 1971, p. 39). We now explore how such 'meaningful settings' might be constructed, looking first at organizational structure, and then at culture.

Restructuring to promote learning

The learning organization refers not just to desired actions, but also to ways of designing organizations in order to produce these actions. So achieving the 'learning organization' necessitates structural and cultural change – often radical, uncomfortable change.

Rewards, roles and responsibilities

People must be rewarded and revered not just for achieving the obvious measures of performance, as was discussed in detail in chapter 4, but also for their ability to help others. The practices and values which are necessary for learning must be encouraged – for example openness, questioning, confrontation. Too often, rather than facilitating learning, organization structures inhibit it, or its constituent elements and stages – for example by denial, deference and defensiveness and discouraging debate and discussion (Argyris, 1987).

   If this is the case, the organic type of organization would probably be more conducive to learning than that structured in a mechanistic fashion (Burns and Stalker, 1961), because, if it generates innovation, it does so by encouraging learning. If staff have to rely more on their own understanding of client or market needs, and less on compliance with rules, they must be learning.

   An example of how hierarchical structures can obstruct learning is given by Roberts (1992):

Potential problems of learning are often . . . compounded by the routine processes of operational control. Hierarchies typically reinforce the values of conformity; to contradict a superior can be seen as a challenge to their authority, and it can seem wiser and safer to discount one's own experience and defer. This is just one of the ways in which vital knowledge is censored out of the organization. In times of rapid change these processes are often intensified, with insecurity serving to heighten individual and group defensiveness, thereby further restricting the flow of information within the company. If at this stage the hierarchy is used to impose an ill-informed strategic change, then one has created a recipe for disaster.

(p. 19)

Achieving a learning organization, then, requires activity on a wide range of fronts. It demands serious, far-reaching and probably uncomfortable commitments and changes from senior managers, penetrating to the very basis of the organization (for example, the way the Board define their role, and their relationship with the rest of the organization). The necessary structural changes require new work arrangements, a thorough break with traditional managerial elitism, sincere efforts to attract the commitment of the workforce, genuine reliance on worker initiative and creativity, and consequent reduction in managers' traditional conception of their 'right to manage' (which often means the right to make decisions in ways which are unaccountable and undiscussable). As long as the desire to become a learning organization remains at the level of exhortation via team briefings and quality circles (useful as these may be), and as long as residual patterns and structures of power, privilege and secrecy persist, which reflect differences of interest and commitment between senior management and the rest of the organization, the learning organization will not develop. This is well illustrated in box 7.9, which summarizes some of the key findings of research conducted into the health of quality circles in the UK.

Box 7.9 Why quality circles failed but TQM might succeed

The dominant impression, conveyed by companies with and without circles alike, was of fragility. Every programme needed constant stimulus to keep it alive . . . all the evidence points to the widespread failure of circles to become institutionalised. The rhetoric of the early days of the boom, that circles would become a normal way of doing business, was hollow. Circles never really took hold in the great majority of these firms, remaining both experimental and marginal throughout their lives . . .

The evidence . . . shows that top management did not take an active role in improvement, that responsibility for quality was not joined with the requisite authority, that middle managers were excluded by the dual structure, and that the issue of cultural change was only partly addressed. The ultimate absurdity was to train rank-and-file employees to use modern techniques of quality management while their managers remained largely in ignorance of these. Quality circles were in any case not, on their own, the appropriate vehicles to realise the objectives that senior management had for them. The bulk of quality improvement issues and all the really important ones are beyond the competence of circles, because they transcend the workplace or exceed the authority of workers and foremen, and poor management is the prime cause of lack of competitiveness. Outside the framework of TQM, circles continually run up against the problem that organisations are not structured to respond to bottom-up initiatives and that all levels of management fail to understand the nature of the improvement process, with the result that, even in the limited area where circles have competence, managers may obstruct improvement.

Under TQM, middle managers in each company reported that they had become more involved in quality management than before. The integration of the improvement process into the existing organisation and as part of normal working practices meant that managers could now direct their subordinates to work on specific issues and approve initiatives from below. In every case, improvement activity was seen as more focused, coherent and relevant, less time consuming, and delivering quicker and more substantial benefits, in comparison with circles and other schemes. In the British office automation company where TQM was introduced alongside circles, these continued to operate as before but managers could now assign all employees including circle members to quality improvement groups and corrective action teams. Indeed, quality circles achieved a new lease of life, and, far from withering away as they were doing prior to TQM, new circles were formed and their numbers grew, although they were few in number in comparison with the other group activities. Managers found circles easier to live with under TQM and dualism was less of an issue. The addition of managerially directed groups allowed them to meet their own immediate improvement objectives; the broader understanding they now had of quality improvement made them more appreciative of the value of voluntary commitment to quality; and they suggested that circle activities themselves were now more tightly focused on issues relevant to the quality of objectives of the company. (Sources: Hill, 1991, pp. 551, 556, 559.)

Teams and teamworking

A related approach to the achieving of synergistic learning in organizations is to extend autonomy through teamworking and to devolve decision-making to non-hierarchical work groups. In general terms, what characterizes this approach is the fact that the wider employing organization specifies the required outcomes from different teams and the resources at their disposal; within that framework, teams have varying degrees of freedom to determine for themselves how to allocate tasks and responsibilities. In some ways, a production environment lends itself readily to such an approach to teamworking, but the practice is being explored across all industries and sectors at the present time. The process of decentralization within many departments of both central and local government and the creation of 'internal markets' and systems of contracting within former state bureaucracies are all rooted in such an approach to team learning and individual 'empowerment'.

'Releasing' leadership and learning in this way clearly opens up quite radically new ways of learning and working for all staff – and significantly reshapes the role of managers. Notwithstanding the rhetoric of what is potentially achievable in these ways, greater team autonomy and self-direction also has drawbacks.

For instance, in his assessment of 'teamworking' in the context of job design Marchington (1992) notes that it can lead to a more stressful factory environment when adopted as a managerial technique to intensify the work process and stretch the production system as far as it will go. It can also lead to reduction in the number of management levels, with supervisory jobs being particularly at risk, thus undermining work-place union solidarity. Naturally, such patent disparities in rewards and security, perceived or real, will militate against learning for many in the work place. Even *within* a team, despite an appearance of equality, team members can be frustrated by others who use their seniority to dominate others, by lack of access to information or resources and by group dynamics or covert political conflicts which inhibit contribution (Kanter, 1994).

Cultivating a learning culture

A learning culture is easy to experience but hard to describe. Cultures are significant because they define and encourage established skills, habits and taken-for-granted ways of thinking and behaving. That is why it is often difficult to address culture directly and effectively (see chapter 5). What the outsider sees as an organizational culture, employees simply regard as obvious and almost unconscious ways of acting. Within the range of activities and actions an organizational culture identifies, rewards and recommends, staff will develop skills and habitual practices: things they do and learn to do well. Cultures thus have implications for the skills and activities that are valued within an organization. Within one engineering company, for example, the predominant and heavy emphasis on fact, on hard, scientific and mechanical principles and laws, was related to cultural values of certainty, clarity, precision, being certain and being right. These in turn made it hard for engineers as managers to handle performance-focused discussions with staff in terms of the learning cycle (Kolb, 1984) referred to earlier. For within such discussions, when competently handled, the manager will behave in a way which encourages the other person (through open questioning) to consider data, to think, to analyse; and will help that person through all stages of the learning cycle, not just impose his or her views and suggestions. Yet the organizational culture discouraged open questioning ('Asking questions like this suggests you don't know the answers – managers should always know the answers!') and encouraged a rapid move on the learning cycle from data to action, because of the manager's own strongly held and culturally-valued certainties and experiences. The qualities that get engineers to management positions are thus inappropriate for these positions if management continues to exhibit these cultural norms.

A way of considering the organizational factors which impinge upon the development of learning in a particular work setting is to ask: What kinds of factors are operating which militate against change? What beliefs, habits, actions are perceived as good and what are seen as unacceptable? How is learning achieved, performance analysed, reviewed and reported? How are problems solved? Resistance to learning is often encountered from those who may have most to lose from, or feel most threatened by, intended changes – namely, senior management. Paul Bate, in his analysis of what impeded and finally foiled British Rail's (BR) attempt to introduce the Advanced Passenger Train (APT), suggests the reasons were not only technological, but also related to inappropriate and inflexible human resource strategies – with senior managers being among the most obstructive by imposing limits on innovation:

> the more radical change endeavours, like the APT, were 'paralysed' by BR's organization culture – to be more specific, by its senior management culture. Structural and attitudinal problems were certainly encountered during the study, but many of these were found to be symptoms of the cultural problems affecting the senior management process at the time. The management

culture was putting a straitjacket on innovation, restricting its growth and development. In Kanter's terms it was offering an extremely thin topsoil for the nourishment and growth of the APT project, laying down a whole set of inflexible norms governing what was acceptable and unacceptable, thinkable and unthinkable, possible and impossible in the organization situation.

(Bate, 1990, p. 7)

This is an example of how organizational defence routines are both anti-learning and over-protective (Argyris, 1987). Such patterns of behaviour become so embedded in the culture that they are rarely questioned, and so entwined in the unequal distribution of power that they are rarely challenged. The resultant unproductive cycle *can* be broken as follows: senior managers can be fed with information that they need, rather than what they want to hear. This is initially risky and counter-cultural but may help to challenge any entrenched ideas they might hold; it promotes open testing of ideas and hence people become less cynical and defensive, and more willing to provide accurate information. In turn, the senior managers become less anxious about being out of touch and respond by granting even more discretion to their subordinates.

Conclusion

Pettigrew and Whipp (1991), in a study of the ability of a number of British firms to 'manage' strategic change and to 'assess the outcome for competitive performance', conclude that a common pattern emerges from the ways the firms handled strategic and operational change, and that there was an observable difference between the ways higher performing firms and their less successful counterparts manage change. They identify five key variables: environmental assessment, leading change, linking strategic and operational change, seeing human resources as assets and liabilities, and achieving coherence. All of these are essentially processes and qualities by which organizations learn.

The ability of an organization to understand the environment, for example, is related to the capacity of members of the organization to gather and act on pertinent data:

The starting point in the process of competition derives from the understanding a firm develops of its environment. In general terms the research shows that it is insufficient for companies to regard the creation of knowledge and judgements of their external competitive world as simply a technical exercise. Rather the need is for organizations to become open learning systems. In other words, the assessment of the competitive environment does not remain the preserve of a single function nor the sole responsibility of one senior manager. Nor does it occur via isolated acts. Instead strategy creation is seen as emerging from the way a company, at various levels, acquires, interprets and processes information about its environment

(Pettigrew and Whipp, 1991, p. 135)

It could well be argued that the achievement of all five of Pettigrew and Whipp's conditions requires what might be called a problem-solving approach. They all require the generation of good quality data, good analysis, open discussion, and so on. Indeed, the authors argue precisely this point in their summary:

> The ability of a company to learn should be under regular scrutiny. In other words, the ability of the organization to reconstruct and adapt its knowledge base (made up of skills, structure and values) should be a key task for managers. They should also be able to apply the 'unlearning' test. In other words, is the organization capable of mounting the creative destruction necessary to breaking down outmoded attitudes and practices, while at the same time building up new, more appropriate competencies. If in the wake of globalization, marketing, financial and manufacturing techniques become ever more capable of imitation, then their competitive advantage is correspondingly diminished . . . in this sort of world the ability to learn faster than competitors may be the sustainable advantage.
>
> (1991, p. 135)

Despite the undeniable logic of such assertions, based as they are, upon empirical observations of what differentiates successful from less successful companies, why is it that so few organizations achieve this kind of learning ethos? This chapter has revealed a number of obstacles that impede good intent. At an individual level we have seen that even where careful consideration has been given to the construction of learning activities the performance outcomes are not always as predicted or promised. Even where personal learning is achieved there are many reasons why the wider work place may not benefit, or indeed want to benefit. Where there are huge disparities in rewards and security, conditional access to positions of power, structural inequalities in the development of careers and inherently different perceptions of organizational goals and priorities, learning is bound to be hampered by careerism, anxiety, stress, deference and unresolved conflict. Even where such 'interference' to learning is minimal, mechanisms need to be in place which link individual to collective learning.

Problems here include reluctance to pass on counter-cultural messages, failure to capture and learn from the lessons of past experience, defensiveness of decision-makers to 'fresh' information and ideas or – conversely – the exploitation of such for partisan ends.

Clearly the process of organizational learning calls for extensive changes in structure, mind-set and outlook at all levels. Moving in the sorts of directions outlined above and overcoming the considerable attitudinal and historical barriers to learning discussed earlier cannot be seen as a one-off project. Furthermore, to move from being an organization that learns to a 'learning organization' refers not just to desired actions, but also to ways of designing or changing organizations in order to produce these actions, while allowing for the multiple, and often conflicting, learning agendas of those within the organization.

If a 'learning organization' is one which successfully facilitates the learning of all its members and continuously transforms itself, then human resource development strategy becomes central to business policy and to the development of structures and cultures which encourage learning throughout the organization. Learning becomes a core part of all operations rather than peripheral and intermittent activity under the custodianship of the training department or HR unit.

We have seen that there is no single model of a learning organization. Organizations which are moving from first-order change/learning to second-order change/learning are characterized more by *how* they do things, than *what* they do. Managing within a learning organization is not easy or comfortable. It entails living with change and uncertainty as a constant; being prepared to question; and acknowledging the value of positive conflict and diversity. Individual managers within an organization can work most effectively if they adopt the 'learning company philosophy' in which they approach their work and staff development responsibilities as a community of professionals with a common purpose, rather than as isolated careerist individuals. However, alongside such common purposes, especially if they constitute organizationally inspired 'programmes' designed to empower and increase autonomy, is the ever-present danger that existing patterns of labour fragmentation and control can actually be intensified rather than relaxed. The result may be learning, but highly circumscribed learning.

The prevailing culture and its receptivity to learning is perhaps the most critical factor of all. Theories of organizational change argue that change occurs when certain preconditions are in place. These are: a recognized problem; a shared diagnosis of the issues involved; a determination to face and resolve them; and an understanding of various courses of action and their implications; and finally, the power to act.

Bate (1992) notes that, even when these conditions are in place, change still does not always occur. So why are situations allowed to persist when they are accepted by the parties themselves as problematic and undesirable? Bate suggests that

The culture, once established, prescribes for its creators and inheritors certain ways of believing, thinking and acting which in some circumstances can prevent meaningful interaction and induce a situation of 'learned helplessness' – that is, a psychological state in which people are unable to conceptualise their problems in such a way as to be able to resolve them. In short, attempts at problem-solving may become culture-bound.

(1992, p. 214)

It falls to each organization to determine the best pathways in overcoming dysfunctional, uncreative ways of working and to find the necessary mechanisms by which individual learning can be synergized collectively and channelled for the benefit of all staff in the organization.

Key points

- *All organizations are learning, most of the time. The question is, to what extent is this learning repetitive, and unconscious, or co-ordinated and channelled in a synergistic and progressive manner?*
- *Even when organizations are adopting reflexive learning processes, interpreting new data intelligently, discerning the lessons from past mistakes, experimenting with new ways of working, such activities are invariably designed to support organizational structures and prescribe how people should behave in them.*
- *The learning organization is a term that has been used to characterize an enterprise where learning is open-ended, takes place at all levels and is self-questioning. Here there is an energizing interplay between individual ideals and action, and company policy and collective operations.*
- *So far, the literature has been more successful at describing the learning organization and how it might be experienced, than providing examples of it happening; although by definition, there is no blueprint that can be transposed from one organization to another.*
- *However, there are approaches that will facilitate a more productive learning ethos in a given company. These concern the way individual learning can be connected to organizational learning; the way defensive routines can be challenged and unlearning can be achieved; the way training and development activities are designed and the way learning can be cultivated through revised cultural norms and structural reconfiguration of the organization.*

Discussion Questions

1 What is the difference between organizational learning and the learning organization?

2 How might the purposes and the processes of training/learning activities be matched?
3 Why does effective learning at an individual level often not translate into effective learning for the organization?
4 What are some of the difficulties associated with 'creating' a learning organization?

REFERENCES

Alderson, S. (1993) Reframing management competence: Focusing on the top management team. *Personnel Review*, 22, no. 6, pp. 53–62.

Argyris, C. (1987) The leadership dilemma: Skilled incompetence. *Business and Economic Review*, 1, pp. 4–11.

Argyris, C. and Schon, D. (1978) *Organizational Learning: A Theory–Action Perspective*. Reading, Mass., Addison-Wesley.

Argyris, C. and Schon, D. (1981) *Organizational Learning*. Reading, Mass., Addison-Wesley.

Bate, P. (1990). The cultural paralysis of innovation. Paper presented to the 7th International Conference on Organization, Symbolism and Corporate Culture, Saarbrucken, June.

Bate, P. (1992) The impact of organizational culture on approaches to problem-solving. In Salaman, G. et al. (eds), *Human Resource Strategies*. London, Sage.

Bateson, G. (1972) *Steps Toward an Ecology of Mind*. New York, Ballantyne.

Beckhard, R. and Pritchard, W. (1992) *Changing the Essence: The Art of Creating and Leading Fundamental Change in Organizations*. San Francisco, Jossey-Bass.

Belbin, M. (1993) *Team Roles at Work*. Oxford, Butterworth-Heinemann.

Benjamin, G. and Mabey, C. (1993) Facilitating radical change. In Mabey, C. and Mayon-White, B. (eds), *Managing Change*. London, Chapman.

Bloom, B. S. (1956) *Taxonomy of Educational Objectives*, vol. I. New York, McKaye.

Burawoy, M. (1979) *Manufacturing Consent*. Chicago, University of Chicago Press.

Burgoyne, J. (1977) Management learning developments. *BACIE Journal*, 31, no. 9, pp. 158–60.

Burgoyne, J. (1994) Managing by learning. *Management Learning*, 25, no. 1, pp. 35–56.

Burgoyne, J. and Stuart, R. (1976) The nature, use and acquisition of managerial skills and other attributes. *Personnel Review*, 15, no. 4.

Burns, T. and Stalker, S. (1961) *The Management of Innovation*. London, Tavistock.

Butler, J. (1992) Learning skills for strategic change. *Journal of Strategic Change*, 1, pp. 39–50.

Critchley, B. and Casey, D. (1989) Organizations get stuck too. *Leadership and Organizational Development Journal*, 10, no. 4, pp. 3–12.

Dale, M. (1993) *Developing Management Skills*. London, Kogan Page.

Dertouzos, M., Lester, R. and Solow, R. (1989) *Made in America: Regaining the Competitive Edge*. Cambridge, Mass., MIT Press.

Dodgson, M. (1993) Organizational learning: A review of some literatures. *Organization Studies*, 14, no. 3, pp. 375–94.

Drucker, P. F. (1992) The new society of organizations. *Harvard Business Review*, 70, no. 5, pp. 95–104.

Garratt, R. (1987) *The Learning Organization*. London, Fontana.

Garratt, R. (1990) *Creating a Learning Organization*. Cambridge, Director Books.

Handy, C. (1974) The contrasting philosophies of management education. Paper presented at the Annual Conference of the European Foundation for Management Development, Turin, May.

Hawkins, P. (1991) The spiritual dimension of the learning organization. *Management Education and Development*, 22, no. 3, pp. 166–81.

Hedberg, B. (1981) How organizations learn and unlearn. In Nystrom, P. and Starbuck, W. (eds), *Handbook of Organizational Design*, vol. 1. Oxford, Oxford University Press, pp. 3–27.

Hill, S. (1991) Why quality circles failed but Total Quality Management might succeed. *British Journal of Industrial Relations*, 29, no. 4, pp. 541–68.

Illich, I. D. (1971) *Deschooling Society*. London, Calder and Boyars.

Jones, A. M. and Hendry, C. (1992) *The Learning Organization: A Review of Literature and Practice*. London, HRD Partnership.

Jones, A. M. and Hendry, C. (1994) The learning organization: Adult learning and organizational transformation. *British Journal of Management*, 5, pp. 153–62.

Kanter, R. M. (1994) Dilemmas of teamwork. In Mabey, C. and Iles, P. A. (eds), *Managing Learning*. London, Routledge.

Katzenbach, J. and Smith, D. (1993) *The Wisdom of Teams*. Cambridge, Mass., Harvard Business School Press.

Kerfoot, D. and Knights, D. (1994) Empowering the quality worker? The seduction and contradiction of the Total Quality phenomenon. In Wilkinson, A. and Willmott, H. (eds), *Quality and the Labour Process*. London, Routledge.

Knowles, M. S. (1984) *The Adult Learner: A Neglected Species* (3rd edn). Houston, Gulf.

Knowles, M. S. (1984) *Andragogy in Action*. San Francisco, Jossey-Bass.

Kolb, D. (1984) *Experimental Learning*. Englewood Cliffs, NJ, Prentice-Hall.

Leonard-Barton, D. (1992) The factory as a learning laboratory. *Sloan Management Review*, fall, pp. 23–37.

Levitt, B. and March, J. (1988) Organizational learning. *Annual Review of Sociology*, 14, pp. 319–40.

Lewin, K. (1951) *Field Theory in Social Science*. New York, Harper & Row.

Mabey, C. and Iles, P. A. (eds) (1994) *Managing Learning*. London, Routledge.

Mabey, C. and Mallory, G. (1995) Structure and culture change in two UK organizations: A comparison of assumptions, approaches and outcomes. *Human Resource Management Journal*, 5, no. 2, pp. 28–45.

Marchington, M. (1992) *Managing the Team*. Oxford, Blackwell.

Marsick, V. J. (1994) Trends in managerial reinvention: Creating a learning map. *Managerial Learning*, 25, no. 1, pp. 11–34.

Mills, D. Q. and Friesen, B. (1992) The learning organization. *European Management Journal*, 10, no. 2, pp. 146–62.

Mintzberg, H. N. and Waters, A. (1985) Strategies deliberate and emergent. *Strategic Management Journal*, 6, pp. 257–72.

Mumford, A., Robinson, G. and Stradling, D. (1987) Developing directors: *The Learning Processes*. London, Manpower Service Commission.

Ogbonna, E. (1994) Integrating strategy, culture and human resource management: Dilemmas and contradictions. In Blyton, P. and Turnbull, P. (eds), *Reassessing Human Resource Management*. London, Sage.

Pedler, M., Boydell, T. and Burgoyne, J. (1988) Learning company project: A report on work undertaken Oct. 1987 to Apr. 1988. Sheffield, The Training Agency.

Pedler, M., Burgoyne, J. and Boydell, T. (1991) *The Learning Company*. London, McGraw Hill.

Pettigrew, A. and Whipp, R. (1991) *Managing Change for Competitive Success*. Oxford, Blackwell.

Roberts, J. (1992) Human resource strategies and the management of change. *B884 Human Resource Strategies*, Supplementary Readings 1, pp. 18–38, Open University, Milton Keynes.

Rogers, A. (1986) *Teaching Adults*. Milton Keynes, Open University Press.

Salancik, G. R. (1977) Commitment and control of organizational behaviour and beliefs. In Staw, B. and Salancik, G. R. (eds), *New Directions in Organizational Behavior*. Chicago, St Clair Press.

Schein, E. (1985) *Organizational Culture and Leadership*. San Francisco, Jossey-Bass.

Schon, D. A. (1983) *The Reflective Practitioner: How Professionals Think in Action*. London, Temple Smith.

Senge, P. (1990) *The Fifth Discipline: The Art and Practice of the Learning Organization*. London, Century Business/Doubleday.

Simpson, E. L. (1980) Adult learning theory: A state of the art. In Lasker, H., Moore, J. and Simpson, E. L. (eds), *Adult Development and Approaches to Learning*. Washington DC, National Institute of Education.

Stata, R. (1989) Organizational learning – the key to management innovation. *Sloan Management Review*, spring, pp. 63–74.

Swieringa, G. and Wierdsma, A. (1992) *Becoming a Learning Organization*. Reading, Mass., Addison-Wesley.

Torbert, W. R. (1994) Managerial learning, organizational learning: A potentially powerful redundancy. *Management Learning*, 25, no. 1, pp. 57–70.

8 International HRM

This chapter was contributed by Paul Iles.

Learning Objectives

At the end of the chapter the reader will be able to:

- *appreciate the importance of analysing international human resource strategies at the global, industry, regional/national and enterprise levels.*
- *critically analyse the modernization and the new international division of labour theories at the global level.*
- *evaluate the adequacy of both perspectives in the light of the evidence drawn from the textiles, electronics and software industries.*
- *describe the relevance of differences in national business systems and regional and national cultures for international HRS.*
- *critically evaluate the evidence for a distinctively 'European' model of HRM.*
- *identify differences between domestic and international human resource strategies.*
- *appreciate the significance of differences in continental origin, administrative heritage, managerial orientations, life-cycle phase and corporate strategy for international HRS.*
- *evaluate the significance of different types of organizational configuration in international enterprise.*
- *evaluate the significance of geographical dispersion and cultural diversity for HR policies in the areas of international recruitment and selection, training and development, performance management and the management of international diversity.*

Introduction

Most treatments of international human resource management (IHRM), especially those from the USA, restrict themselves to the problems that multinational companies (MNCs) and other transnational organizations have had in recruiting, selecting, training, appraising and rewarding expatriates. More recently they have begun to include staffing issues associated with joint ventures and other forms of transnational strategic alliances. Both foci of interest appear to be driven by practical problems that seem uniquely American: the apparently high and costly 'failure rate' experienced by American expatriates in comparison with their European and Japanese equivalents, and an apparent belief that their companies have been somehow deskilled and 'hollowed out' when entering alliances with Japanese, Korean and Taiwanese firms in particular.

In contrast, European treatments of IHRM have examined issues of strategic control and co-ordination of the largest multi-national corporations and the contribution that HRM can play; focused at a regional level on what appears to be a European model of HRM as compared to a North American or Japanese model; and explored differences between countries or clusters of countries within Europe in terms of HRM practices and their links with national culture and with national legal, political and social institutions.

Both the North American and European treatments appear to be driven by particular political and economic agendas. In the case of the European approach, the perspectives adopted appear to be influenced by the developing nature of European integration and especially the creation of the Single European Market. The concern is partly to enhance the competitiveness of European industry in relation to its continental rivals; partly to explore what makes (or should make) Europe distinctive in terms of economic and social policy; and partly to map out existing intra-European differences either as possible brakes or barriers to European integration and the harmonization of employment policies or as possible 'building blocks' with which to construct a distinctively European model of HRM.

Our concerns in this chapter are somewhat different. At one level we wish to broaden our analysis of HRS beyond the rather limited definitions of HRM used in existing American and European accounts. At another level we wish both to introduce a wider global perspective by including the Asia-Pacific region, in addition to Japan, within our focus. We also wish to place our analysis of IHRS within a broader examination of the globalization process; in particular, we look at changes within the international division of labour and its relation to some of the broader HRS themes treated elsewhere in the book (flexibility, Fordism, integration, open vs. closed models of HRM, etc.). In locating our analysis within the context of global developments we are making an important point usually overlooked by conventional treatments of 'International HRS' – that is, that a global perspective reveals a number of critically important patterns concerning the nature and role of the international division of labour, and decisions about the location of production, which have a fundamental significance for all the organization's employees and consumers, yet which are frequently not regarded as essentially HRS-type decisions. In this sense, much HRS literature is guilty of socially structured silences on issues which would seem, *prima facie*, to be unquestionably HRS matters; where to locate organizational activities, and who is recruited. For decisions about where to locate production or service activity in order to exploit cheap or congenial or un-unionized labour, or decisions to recruit labour from external sources, are clearly highly significant HRS decisions.

Consequently this chapter will be organized around an exploration of IHRS at four analytical levels:

- the global level, especially in terms of the international division of labour.
- the industry level, exploring the globalization process in selected industries.
- the regional/national level, examining the differences between European, Japanese and North American approaches to HRS and exploring some of the differences in HR practice between countries or clusters of countries.
- the enterprise level, exploring how HRS has been or can be used at the firm or organization level to contribute to competitive advantage.

The major focus of our analysis of IHRS will be at the enterprise level; however, viewing the other three levels as constituting and contributing to the complexity and diversity of the environment faced by the international enterprise allows us to bring out what is distinctive about *international* HRS, and why it matters.

HRS at the Global Level

Globalization as a process has interested not only management theorists and practitioners but also sociologists seeking to go beyond their discipline's equation of the 'social' with the nation state. Advances in technology, transport and communication in particular have contributed to a 'shrinking world' where inter-organizational relationships now transcend national or regional boundaries so that 'events, decisions and activities in one part of the world can come to have significant consequences for individuals and communities in quite distant parts of the globe' (McGrew, 1992, pp. 65–6). The jobs and conditions of Scottish electronics workers in Dundee, for example, may be more dependent on decisions taken in the USA than by local Timex management. This sense of global interconnectedness is well brought out by Hall (1992, p. 299), who uses the term globalization to refer to 'those processes operating on a global scale which cut across national boundaries, integrating and connecting communities and organizations in new space–time combinations, making the world in reality and experience more interconnected'.

Hall's reference to space and time reflects a particular focus of the work by Giddens (1990; 1992) on modernity and its consequences. Regarding globalization as one of its most visible outcomes, he emphasizes the separation and compression of time and space, arguing that: 'in the current era global processes impinge upon the most local and personal aspects of social life; conversely, individual actions and localized social interaction contribute to globally ordered systems' (1992, p. 1). Such a perspective also applies to organizational life and to HRS. Although it may be true – as we shall shortly discuss – that from the beginning capitalism had a global reach, it is undoubtedly the case that the scope and pace of global integration has greatly increased in recent years, and that the multinational or transnational company is one of the major agents of such globalization processes. Production, trade, finance and employment are increasingly organized on a transnational basis, making it less and less defensible to think of purely domestic or national economies, organizations or strategies, including HR strategies.

Yet whilst global integration is increasingly a major theme in strategic management, it is also the case that 'globalizing influences do not work exclusively towards integration; globalization also divides, marginalizes and excludes' (Hall, 1992, p. 1). We shall explore this dimension of globalization not only through an analysis of the need for HRS to be 'local' and 'responsive' as well as 'global' and 'integrated', but also through a discussion of the 'power geometry' of glocalization and the rise of the new international division of labour. The internationalizing of production in particular is a central feature of globalization. This interplay between the global and the local – what Sony refers to as glocalism or global localization – is a key theme of this chapter. As Hall notes: 'globalization (in the form of flexible specialization and "niche" marketing) actually exploits local differentiation' (1992, p. 304).

Modernization theory, development and globalization

Modernization theory, as the term is used in the sociology of development, proposes that social and economic development in what is usually termed the 'Third World' (or developing/less developed countries, or increasingly the 'South'), can occur through the application of Western capitalist methods. With its roots in structural functionalism and conventional distinctions between 'traditional' and 'modern' societies, it asserts the need for Southern countries to modernize their political, social and economic institutions along similar lines (such as an emphasis on enterprise, achievement, rationality and progress) to the Industrial Revolutions in the West. Modernization theory has had significant influence on Western development policies and such transnational organizations as the World Bank and the International Monetary Fund.

Dependency theory, global capitalism and the classical international division of labour

Dependency theory, which originated in attempts to understand the nature and process of third world development, and particularly the relationship between the third world and Western capitalism, clearly has different concerns from the conventional HRS literature – and rather different theoretical perspectives. Nevertheless, it raises important questions about, and offers useful insights into, the nature of international HRS. Dependency theory views the relationship between the West and the third world in terms of relations of power and exploitation. An obvious corollary therefore is that organizations' decisions *vis-à-vis* the third world, whether they concern location decisions, or recruitment or investment decisions, could also be seen in this light.

Originating in Latin America, dependency theory in contrast views the third world as a subsidiary and dependent part of Western capitalism as it spread throughout the globe in the period of Western colonial expansion. Accordingly, the capitalist system is less an engine of third world development than a brake on its development. In the work of Wallerstein (1974; 1984), there was an ambitious attempt to analyse the development of a single 'capitalist world economy' centred on Northern Europe from the sixteenth century until the rise of the United States in the twentieth century. Wallerstein points out that capitalism 'was from the beginning an affair of the world economy and not of nation states . . . capital has never allowed its aspirations to be determined by national boundaries' (1974, p. 19). He also emphasizes the unequal structure of capitalism's global scope, viewing the capitalist world economy as divided into *core* (Japan, North America and western Europe), *semi-peripheral* (southern Europe and eastern Europe) and *peripheral* (the third world) regions. Such terminology is reminiscent of earlier analyses of the division of labour at the level of the domestic economy (e.g. core versus peripheral workers, primary and secondary labour markets) and reminds us that globalization, whatever the modernization theorists might say, is a process that is unevenly distributed both between different sections of the population within nations, and between regions and nations.

Massey (1991) refers to this as globalization's 'power geometry' because different social groups and different individuals may find themselves in positions of influence over the globalization process (for instance senior managers of multi-national companies), whereas others are on the receiving end, especially those residing in the South. As Sklair (1991, p. 6) puts it: 'the global system is marked by a very great asymmetry. The most important economic, political and cultural-ideological goods that circle around the globe tend to be owned or controlled by small groups in a relatively small number of countries.'

The best way to conceive of this asymmetry has been a matter of some debate. Frank's (1966) analysis of 'under-development', conflating global spatial-economic relationships with classical Marxist social class relationships, and Amin's (1974) analysis of accumulation on a global scale and the exploitation of peripheral economies by metropolitan ones have been criticized by more orthodox Marxists. For instance, Laclau (1971) and Warren

(1980) object to the notion that Europe was capitalist at the time of colonial expansion and point to relative neglect of internal class relationships within 'peripheral countries' in much of dependency theory. It might be also argued that such analyses are as economistic, evolutionary and deterministic as modernization theory, and equally Eurocentric in asserting the need for peripheral societies to pass through the classical Marxist 'stages' of feudalism and capitalism toward socialism.

The valuable point of such analyses for our purposes is not only that they draw attention to the inequalities present in the often bland assertions of 'globalization', but that they also highlight the 'international division of labour'. Traditionally, this took the form of Europe and North America (and later Japan) becoming the manufacturers of finished products and the third world simultaneously acting as an exporter of raw materials and cash-crop agricultural products, and an importer of relatively high-priced Western products in a process of unequal exchange. We shall refer to this as the classical international division of labour.

The new international division of labour

The development of flexible production technologies in particular has facilitated a process of decentralization of production and the de-domiciling of capital, with multi-national companies moving parts of their production process outside the home countries, especially to the 'newly industrializing countries' of the Asia-Pacific region. The pursuit of low-cost, disciplined and less-organized labour to work in routinized, labour intensive production has often been ascribed to the multi-nationals' search for low-cost competitive advantage and crisis conditions in the *core* countries. Just as advanced technology and 'sweatshops' may coexist in an advanced metropolis like London or New York, 'Fordist' and 'Tayloristic' practices in Indonesia may coexist within the same company alongside 'post-Fordist' practices in Germany. Jameson (1991) describes: 'the global reconstruction of production and the introduction of radically new technologies – that have flung workers in archaic factories out of work, displaced new kinds of industry to unexpected parts of the world, and recruited workforces different from the traditional ones in a variety of features, from gender to skill and nationality' (1991, p. 319). For Fröbel et al. (1980, p. 12): 'the old or classical international division of labour is now open for replacement . . . developing countries have increasingly become sites for manufacturing – producing manufactured goods which are competitive in the world market . . . this means that any company almost irrespective of its size which wishes to survive is now forced to initiate a transnational reorganization of production.' This relocation of deskilled and routinized jobs seems particularly characteristic of the garment and electronics sectors, explored further in the next section. The West German garment and textile industries, for example, have used North African subsidiaries, working under Taylorist rather than Fordist conditions. Since employment is seen as essentially unskilled, technology transfer is minimal, and there are few links between such enclaves and the rest of the economy. Hence the new international division of labour is seen as deepening historical under-development, not as reversing it.

In this version of the international division of labour, the world market for manufacturing (services were not included in the original thesis) is becoming fragmented and production located wherever the most profitable combination of capital and labour can be obtained. For example, women and migrant labour are commonly employed in the metropolises to perform many of the less desirable, less rewarded and dirtier jobs of advanced industrial economies, whether Mexicans in the USA, Moroccans in France, Indonesians in the Netherlands or Turks in Germany (the lines of migration often following old colonial, imperial networks). Braham (1992) refers to the way in which British firms in the 1980s often subcontracted production to the inner city, with secondary-sector firms making heavy use of minority ethnic labour as well as relocating production overseas. Women workers are often preferred by multi-national companies, being seen not only as cheaper but also as subordinated by their domestic role and beliefs about their 'suitability' for routine, fragmented and repetitive work. Pearson (1988; 1994), referring to the dominant image of nimble-fingered young women working in a South-east Asian electronics factory, points out that female productivity in such conditions is often higher than male productivity. However, she also challenges an undifferentiated view of women's work in the new international division of labour, noting that location decisions are not just about lowest costs but also about other incentives.

In one sense the new international division of labour goes hand in hand with a new sexual division of labour, notably in manufacturing, but also in services, agriculture and the informal sector. Bangladeshi women, for instance, seemed to have flocked to work in the clothing industry, but this may be due to a lack of other options. As Elson (1994, p. 205) puts it: 'while jobs in the clothing factories improve the terms on which young women are able to negotiate the social relations that subordinate them, the structures of gender inequality are not thereby dissolved.'

Hoogvelt (1987) points out that whereas the third world in general has made significant advances in terms of structural transformation and the contribution of manufacturing output to gross domestic product (GDP), the process has been uneven, rendering the relevance of the term 'Third World' questionable (even more so now, given the collapse of the Second World). At one extreme, eight newly industrialized countries are now virtually comparable with the First World, whereas in almost 50 countries industrialization has hardly begun. At the same time, de-industrialization, especially in terms of employment but also in terms of output relative to GDP, has been steadily occurring in the *core* countries. Whilst the third world's share of exports has grown rapidly, this has been extremely sporadic, suggesting that the original thesis as it stands is too sweeping.

A further criticism of the new international division of labour (NIDL) thesis is that it exaggerates the scale of relocation to third world sites. Another is that multi-national companies may relocate not simply in pursuit of cheap labour, but also to establish market position. Reducing direct labour costs is only one route to competitive advantage; increasing labour productivity through, for example, technical innovation or flexible specialization is another. Pearson (1994) argues that relocation is limited and concentrated in a narrow range of goods in specified countries and regions, particularly textiles and garments from East Asia and Latin America and electronics components/assembly of consumer electronics goods from South-east Asia. There has also been an erosion in some sectors of the comparative advantage of relocation, due to computerization and automation, and neo-protectionist measures to restrict imports from the developing world in particular industries have contributed to relocation back to the North.

Having analysed the trends and implications of these shifting patterns of employment at the level of the global system as a whole, we now turn our attention to the industry level, exploring three sectors in particular, two of which (textiles/clothing and electronics) played an important part in the original NIDL thesis. The software industry, which is emerging as important in the 1990s, played no part in the original thesis, but illustrates some emerging trends.

International HRS at the Industry Level

As we have seen, most theorists of the 'new international division of labour' have seized on manufacturing industry as the key exemplar. In fact, service industries too are locating aspects of their activities overseas in areas of cheap skilled labour. Insurance companies, for example, have their claims administration located in India or the Far East. But we must also note that the internationalization of labour does not necessarily require cross-boundary location. Within Western national boundaries, the existence of migrant labour allows the development of a segmented labour market whereby some workers – women, ethnic minorities, migrants – tend to be employed on employment terms that are markedly inferior to those of traditional, skilled workers. Developments under recent conservative governments have encouraged the use, and size, of this 'flexible' cadre of workers. Employers' strategic (i.e. cost-cutting) use of this 'secondary' labour market also reveals a localized international dimension. Many firms in 'core' countries have responded to intensifying international competition through a range of measures, many of which have been discussed in earlier chapters, including closures, rationalizations, mergers and acquisitions, restructuring of relationships with suppliers and contractors, and the introduction of post-Fordist (or neo-Fordist) flexible working practices. They have also shifted production to low-cost areas overseas and engaged in a variety of transnational strategic alliances. This restructuring of employment relationships on a global scale is not normally considered an HR strategy; our argument in this chapter is that it needs to be considered as such. The NIDL thesis is an over-simplification of what is actually happening in the 1990s, even in the industries often cited to illustrate its dynamics.

Globalized production in the textile industry

Globalization is not a new phenomenon in the textile industry; as Elson (1994, p. 189) puts it, 'the production, distribution and consumption of textiles and clothing has epitomised the uneven development of the world economy since the very beginning of industrial capitalism in the eighteenth century, when the high quality, handicraft-based Indian textile industry was destroyed by the output of Lancashire's mills. In its turn, Lancashire gave way to the United States, Germany and Japan, while today South Korea, Taiwan, Hong Kong and, latterly, China challenge the older established locations.'

Nor are flexibility or subcontracting strategies recent innovations. Nation states have always attempted to regulate the global development and patterns of labour utilization in the textile industry. Since the 1970s, the proportion of global production in the South has grown from around 18 per cent in 1975 to over 31 per cent in 1993 (Elson, 1994), and not just in the low-tech areas. Despite restrictive measures like the Multi-Fibre Arrangement, an increasing share of global exports has also come from the South, especially from a few East Asian countries. In contrast to the NIDL thesis, off-shore assembly by Northern MNCs for re-export to the North is not a feature of fibre and fabric production; nor is foreign direct investment (FDI), except by Japanese companies, an important dynamic. Networks or 'commodity chains' of small and medium-sized firms, including developing-country firms owned by citizens of such countries, are much more characteristic. Western MNCs have played little role, for example, in the South Korean and Bangladeshi industries, although Japanese companies have been active. The state in many East Asian nations has often sought to stimulate production and export activities through export processing zones, subsidies and other measures.

As the leading role of textile companies in the industrialization of South Korea, for example, has declined under lower-cost competition from China and Indonesia, South Korean companies have looked for locations in countries like Bangladesh. Although jobs have been shed on a massive scale in the North, this is not just the result of job transfer to the South, but also due to growth in productivity and changes in demand. In general, wages and conditions in the South seem better in larger, export-oriented factories and in MNCs than in local firms. Given that the North does retain its leading role in new technology, the South continues to feel pressures to invest in new technologies and in training.

Box 8.1 shows the experience of one British textile MNC, Tootal. Its development shows the limitations of the NIDL thesis in its focus on low-cost assembly as the driving force behind the globalization of production.

Box 8.1   The internationalization of Tootal

One of the three leading British textile/clothing MNCs, Tootal's drive to internationalization and its reduction of its British labour force seems to owe more to a desire to access East Asian markets than a search for cheap labour. Offering design, technical, marketing and financial expertise to a variety of Southern partners, it attempted to reposition itself as a service company. Production factories in Asia were rarely wholly-owned export platforms for the UK market, although integrated into its global sourcing network. Cloth imported into the UK was printed with batik designs and re-exported to West Africa as 'traditional costume'. In the 1980s, the over-valuation of sterling reduced its competitiveness and left it vulnerable to takeover from Coats Viyella. (Source: Elson, 1994.)

Regional division of labour in the electronics industry

The electronics industry is second only to garments and textiles as a source of manufacturing employment in the South. Southern states have seen it as an attractive, capital and knowledge intensive industry, able to deliver higher value-added and faster economic growth. Its ability to stimulate demand for engineers and scientists, specialized supplies, components and services, and fuel pressures for investment in education and training have also made it attractive (Henderson, 1994). However, the realization of this potential has been largely limited to the Asian and Latin American 'new industrial countries' (NICs), and only Korea and Taiwan compete directly with the dominant core industries, leaving most of the others foreign-owned and at the labour intensive, low value-added end of the spectrum. As Henderson (1994, p. 263) puts it, 'the largely US and, more recently, Japanese companies responsible for FDI developed a global production system which, until the late 1970s, was perhaps the supreme example of an industry organised according to the principles of the new international division of labour thesis'. Control, R & D, and capital and technology-intensive parts of the production process remained firmly in the North.

However, 'by the mid to late 1980s, the international division of labour as represented by semi-conductor production had already been trans-formed' (Henderson, 1994, p. 263). There had been extensive investment in high-skill, high-technology processes in Singapore and Hong Kong in particular; the Singapore government forced up labour costs in a successful attempt to encourage MNCs to emphasize high-technology operations, with both countries emerging as regional headquarters. The more peripheral Asian economies then became subject to a secondary layer of control and dependency from Hong Kong and Singapore, creating a regionally segmented division of labour as the peripheral economies became increasingly integrated into the production systems of the Asian NICs. The whole region became subject to substantial FDI by Japanese companies driven not just by the search for lower labour costs, but by the demands for localized production to serve just-in-time systems.

A particular feature of note is that the electronics industry in the Latin American and Asian NICs owes much of its origin and development to *state* industrial policy, in contrast to many of the free-market/organizational autonomy arguments often associated with HRS. Linkages with the local economy, the upgrading of personnel and genuine technology transfer have been mainly limited to Singapore, Korea and Taiwan (which are also among the most egalitarian of NICs). However, changing market conditions, declining demand in the North, the need for technological upgrading and the dependent nature of many production systems on Original Equipment Manufacture all pose problems for the continued development of the NICs. (See box 8.2.)

In general, it seems as if the NIDL is giving way to commodity chains and inter-firm relationships where peripheral economies are becoming subject to the technical and managerial control of intermediary economies like Taiwan and Korea, as well as core economies like Japan. FDI from the North to the South, except for that going to the Asian and Latin American NICs and near NICs, and China, has collapsed, making it unlikely that other Southern countries can create viable electronics industries.

The original NIDL thesis focused on static technologies and standardized mass production. Fears of job transfers to the South have, however, recently been voiced even in the software industry, as highly skilled but low-paid employees in India, China and Eastern Europe can now communicate with Western mainframe computers directly by satellite.

> # Box 8.2   IT operations migrating South?
>
> The entry of the previously closed Indian, Chinese and Eastern European economies into the global capitalist system, the return of US-trained software graduates, and a well-educated labour force (often female) prepared to work for relatively low wages has stimulated the electronics industry in the South. Lufthansa and Swissair, for example, have outsourced all or part of their IT operations to India through subsidiaries or contract partners, whilst BA has established a satellite ticket reservation processing facility in Delhi. Other companies have established joint ventures, whilst some Indian software houses have exported directly to the North. However, growth areas like 'object-oriented' systems and the selling of 'total solutions' remain in Western hands. (Source: Crabb, 1995.)

IHRS in a borderless world?

The NIDL thesis, with its vision of footloose multi-nationals with no specific ties, constantly on the move to close down unnecessary locations and continually seeking new investment opportunities in search of lower labour costs, is curiously paralleled by authors more clearly located in the 'modernization' camp, who trumpet the 'globalization of markets' and propose that international business is becoming increasingly 'borderless' and international corporations increasingly 'placeless'.

For example, Levitt (1983) has argued that all markets are becoming global and that the globalization of operations is becoming a requirement for all companies. Whilst 'internationalization' is seen as referring to the geographical dispersal of operations across national boundaries, 'globalization' is seen as a qualitatively different process, involving the *functional integration* of such internationally dispersed operations. For example, Reilly and Campbell (1990, p. 7) define globalization as:

> The integration of business activities across geographical and organisational boundaries. It is the freedom to conceive, design, buy, produce, distribute and sell products and services in a manner which offers maximum benefit to the firm without regard to the consequences for individual geographic locations or organisational units . . . the global firm is not constrained by

national boundaries as it searches for ideas, talent, capital and other resources required for its success. In short, the global firm operates with few – if any – self-imposed geographical or organisational constraints on where or how it conducts its business operations.

For Levitt (1983), technological change and the 'proletarianization' of communications, transport and travel have caused consumer tastes across the world to converge. This has required companies to develop globally standardized products that are advanced, reliable, functional and low-priced, and able to deliver what *everyone* is said to want – the alleviation of life's burdens and the expansion of discretionary time and spending power. The global corporation will increasingly operate 'as if the entire world (or major regions of it) were a single entity; it sells the same things in the same way everywhere' (Levitt, 1983, pp. 92–3).

This reference to 'major regions' already introduces one qualification to the argument – Levitt is primarily concerned with what Ohmae (1985) refers to as the 'Triad' of North America, Europe and Asia-Pacific. Ohmae (1989) also stresses the key role of information in creating a 'borderless world', although he also acknowledges the continued importance of distinctive national tastes and cultures. For Ohmae (1989, p. 94), talking about the global firm, 'Country of origin does not matter. Location of headquarters does not matter. The products for which you are responsible and the company you serve have become denationalised.' Reich (1991), US Secretary of Labor at the time of writing, has also asserted that, in the future, there will be no more 'national' corporations. For routine production workers, there will be a constant shifting of jobs to ever-lower-paying locations – just as the NIDL theorists predicted! Routine personal service workers will also find their wages depressed. However, knowledge workers will gain, finding a larger and larger market for their services. The importance of education, training, skill and high technology will continue to grow, making IHRS of even greater significance.

In the 1970s, modernization theorists locked horns with dependency theorists over whether capitalism had developed or could develop the South; yet both remained imprisoned within similar technological/teleological, deterministic, evolutionary and Eurocentric frameworks, allowing little space for diversity. In the 1990s, new international division of labour theorists spar with globalization theorists about the benefits of the emerging stateless, placeless, footloose multi-national constantly driven to reduce its labour costs. Perhaps similar charges could be levelled at the arguments put by both sides in the 1990s?

For it is clear that the kind of global, geocentric, standardized low-cost strategy championed by Levitt (1983) is only one possible global strategy. Many transnational companies have adopted other successful HR strategies, focusing on innovation, differentiation or quality; have focused on regions through 'regiocentric' strategies; and focused on different domestic markets, through polycentric or multi-domestic strategies. Adopting a 'global perspective' does not mean always adopting a product-driven, standardized strategy; customer needs and interests remain diverse, even within nations, and indeed, as Hall (1992) has pointed out, globalization may also stimulate differentiation and the creation of diverse identities (e.g. companies in Cataluña now have to advertise in Catalan as well as in Spanish). It does not seem to be the case that price rather than variety or quality of service is becoming increasingly important, and flexible specialization appears to be undermining the advantages of standardization in many instances. For example, the standardized, low-cost approach of Zanussi, highly successful up to the 1970s, was undermined within Europe by niche operators and firms operating more diverse, multi-domestic strategies, leaving Zanussi to be acquired by Electrolux. The bases of global competition are dynamic – some markets may well be truly global, others may well be local, others regional. In a later section, we will explore the role of HRS in supporting such differentiated corporate strategies.

In rebuttal of Ohmae (1989) and Reich (1991), all firms, including MNCs, remain embedded in particular national and cultural milieux and carry with them features of their parent-country environment, as well as taking on some of the characteristics of their host-country environment. MNCs continue to have most of their assets located in particular states, continue to look to particular countries for legal and diplomatic protection, continue to be at least potentially taxable on global earnings in particular nations, and continue to employ parent-company nationals, both in senior positions at headquarters (usually in the home country), and to run foreign subsidiaries. MNCs, in this sense, are little different from national corporations with international operations, embedded in a home base (Dicken, 1992). This requires us to abandon the wilder claims of the globalization/new international division of labour theorists, and recognize that places – i.e. nation states – still matter, and will continue to matter. As we saw earlier, nation states have engaged in a series of protectionist measures, like tariffs, quotas, transnational agreements like the MFA and GATT, and intervene to support foreign investment through tax incentives, subsidies, infrastructure developments, export processing and employment legislation. The state has played a key role in developing the textile industries of Korea, Taiwan and Hong Kong, and the electronics industries of Singapore and Brazil. We have also shown how a *regional* division of labour is emerging, pointing to the growing importance of regional trade groupings such as the European Union. This requires us to consider international HRS not solely at the global and industry levels, but also at the national and regional levels. We will begin by exploring the role of the state in setting the context for HRS and then briefly explore the role of regional groupings and blocs. Both analyses confirm the importance of geographical dispersion and cultural diversity to our conception of IHRS.

International HRS at Regional and National Levels

The role of the state in IHRS

As we saw above, the state can play a major role in setting the context for HRS. A particular focus in the 1990s has been the growing acceptance in the North that it must avoid pricing itself out of world markets and pay particular attention to labour costs (an emphasis common to many of the globalization and 'new international division of labour' arguments). As table 8.1 shows, differences in labour costs in the manufacturing sector are very considerable, even within Europe, but differ even more when other countries are taken into consideration. Of course these figures disguise differences within each country – especially the different terms, conditions, wage rates, training, career possibilities etc., of 'primary' and 'secondary' labour categories. While remaining within a single country employers can strategically exploit significant differences in wage rates and employment conditions by decisions on the location of activities, or the employment conditions to prevail.

Clearly, high wages do not necessarily imply high unit labour costs, or low wages low unit labour costs. The efficiency with which labour is utilized – itself a function of HRS – can be much more important, and social

Table 8.1 Contribution of labour to manufacturing costs – a cross-country comparison 1991 (average US$ per hour)

Country	Pay for time worker	Holiday pay and bonuses	Non-wage labour costs (A)	Total labour costs (B)	(A) as a per cent of (B)
EC average	9.92	2.95	4.08	16.95	24.1
Germany	12.67	4.63	4.87	22.17	22.0
Italy	8.66	3.04	5.48	17.18	31.9
France	8.34	2.56	4.36	15.26	28.6
UK	9.88	1.60	1.94	13.42	14.5
Spain	9.03		3.62	12.65	28.6
Non-EC countries					
US	11.33	1.00	3.12	15.45	20.2
Japan	8.38	4.14	1.89	14.41	13.1
Asian countries	3.82		0.38	4.21	9.0

welfare costs can also affect overall costs considerably. Governments, how-ever, do seek to influence wage costs, inflation rates and internal relativities, as well as the external value of the currency against others so as to affect relative labour costs. Governments also seek to influence non-wage costs, such as welfare benefits, and to influence tax rates. Legal regulations are often seen by companies as adding to their costs – an argument made strongly by the UK government (and some UK companies) in relation to the 'social costs' perceived as inherent in much European legislation con-cerned with employee protection (e.g. equal opportunity, health and safety, hiring and firing regulations). Governments also seek to use education and training to create a more productive labour force, although even here there are competing calls, and some governments (such as the British govern-ment) have sought to push much of the cost onto individuals or private companies, not all of whom have fully taken up this responsibility, as chapter 3 ('Training and Development Strategies') showed. Education and training not only enhance skills, but also affect discipline and motiva-tion, allowing a high-wage country like Germany, with a highly skilled and educated labour force, to successfully compete with countries offering much lower wages.

The role of regional trade groupings in IHRS

For Ohmae (1989), successful globalization requires that companies com-pete in the three regions (or Triad) of North America, Europe and Asia-Pacific. In recent years, the North American Free Trade Association (NAFTA) has been ratified in Canada, the USA and Mexico, whilst the Asia-Pacific Economic Council has emerged as a looser association, centred on Japan. Neither, as yet, has gone as far down the road to both economic and political integration as the European Union, but HR policies and practices are increasingly likely to be influenced by such emerging trade blocs. The development of the Single European Market in particular means that the 'domestic market' for national firms no longer stops at national borders. Wage levels, jobs, inflation rates and interest rates are increasingly influenced by pan-European decisions, and HRS is no longer able to address purely local or national issues. In addition, European social policy, as embodied in the Treaty of Rome, and amended by the Single European Act of 1986, is having an increasing impact on a range of HRM issues by creating principles which fall within the jurisdiction of the European Court of Justice and which domestic legislation in a whole range of areas needs to take into account (see box 8.3). Such issues include the right to freedom of movement, to equal treatment, to employee participation, and to equal pay and benefits.

Box 8.3 Implications of the European Social Charter

The Social Charter, a developing framework initiated in 1988 and ratified as the Social Chapter in 1991 at the Maastricht Council, is also becoming increasingly important to HRS. The British government has, so far, expressed an opt-out on the grounds that its implementation would endanger competitiveness and the free operation of the market. Though not legally binding, the implementing directives that will be developed from it will have legal force. These principles cover such areas as equal treatment, free movement, working conditions, social protection, freedom of association and collective bargaining, vocational training, equal opportunity, health and safety, the protection of young children, young people and the elderly and the disabled, and the right to information, consultation and participation. Under the Delors presidency, the Commission has pursued the idea of 'l'espace sociale' to accompany the 'economic space' created by the Single Market, in part to avoid 'social dumping', where companies move jobs within the EU from the richer North, with its high social costs, to the poorer South, with lower social costs (critics and NIDL theorists, of course, would point out that such companies could transfer jobs out of Europe altogether). Large multinational companies in Europe will need to set up European Works Councils for information and consultation by 1996. Despite the UK opt-out, European legislation is having an increasing impact on British employment practices. An Institute of Directors survey reported that 80 per cent of UK multi-nationals were preparing to set one up (Bassett, 1995). Over 300 UK companies may be affected – more than in any other European country.

Within the UK, the pursuit of harmonization and the role of European law has become embroiled in wider arguments about a common currency and defence policy and eventual political integration. Some have argued that the UK government has deliberately sought to lower labour costs to attract Japanese and Korean inward investment, although there may be other reasons why such investment has continued to flow (e.g. the English language infrastructure, market position). Similar arguments have occurred within NAFTA over whether US jobs would be exported to Mexico or whether wages would converge closer to the Mexican level rather than the US level. It is clear that, even if the 'strong' version of the NIDL thesis and the placelessness and footlooseness of MNCs is rejected, MNCs will continue to assess alternative investment opportunities within the various regional blocs, and that unit labour costs will be a major consideration. Other factors, however, will come into play, such as cultural factors and the kind of HRM systems in existence in the various blocs and the nation states that make them up, and it is to these aspects of comparative HRM that we now turn.

Culture and IHRS at regional and national levels

Traditional questions raised in connection with the relationship between culture and international HRM include (e.g. Kidger, 1991):

- Are HRM practices culture bound or culture free?
- Can we introduce a successful HRM practice from one national setting to another?
- Are policies and practices universally applicable or must they be adapted to fit the local culture?
- Are national and corporate culture potentially antagonistic forces in the MNC?
- What are the implications of this for developing a global workforce?
- Should an international company pursue different strategies in different countries or follow global strategies?

The major analyses of cultural differences between managers from different parts of the world have generally surveyed attitudes using questionnaires. On the basis of a massive survey of IBM employees, Hofstede (1980) found statistically significant differences between national groups of managers on four discrete dimensions: Power Distance, Uncertainty Avoidance, Individualism–Collectivism and Masculinity–Femininity. Managers from the same society were, of course, not uniform in their views, but tended to be more similar than managers in other societies. However, the common conflation of nation and culture is inexact – not only can countries be clustered into regional groups (e.g. within Western Europe a Nordic, Germanic, Anglo-Saxon and Latin group), but regions within countries can show considerable cultural differences (e.g. between French-speaking Wallonia/Walloons and Dutch-speaking Flanders in Belgium). Later studies by Hofstede and Bond (e.g. Hofstede and Bond, 1988), perhaps following the logic of their own position to its conclusion, have argued that such dimensions did not fully capture the dynamics of East Asia. Using Asian scholars, they developed a scale termed 'Confucian Dynamism' (forward looking, persevering, thrifty, long-term, work and family oriented, etc.). This scale seemed, in particular, to distinguish such societies, although it was also applicable to other countries (e.g. the UK appeared very short-term compared to the Netherlands). It is, of course, tempting to argue that such a value-orientation is associated with the recent economic success of those East Asian countries historically influenced by Confucian thought.

Other approaches in this area have also used attitude survey methods. For example, Laurent (1983; 1986) compared the attitudes of different groups of managers to organizational authority structure and success, finding that whereas German managers emphasized technical expertise and knowledge, French managers emphasized identification as high potentials and political connections. British managers emphasized self-presentation, negotiation and communication. Trompenaars (1993) has used a 57 item questionnaire given to managers in around 50 countries and followed it up with workshops presenting managers and others with a series of scenarios or dilemmas. He has identified six dimensions on which cultures differ:

- universalism vs. particularism
- individualism vs. collectivism
- affectivity vs. affective neutrality
- specificity vs. diffuseness
- achievement vs. ascription
- internality vs. externality

These dimensions are curiously reminiscent of the variables held to distinguish 'modern' from 'traditional' societies, as emphasized by the modernization theorists discussed above.

Hofstede (1980) has also shown that it is possible to 'cluster' countries together on the basis of similarities and differences in their scores on the four dimensions. Within Europe, there emerges a Germanic group, characterized by high masculinity and low power distance; a Scandinavian group, including the Netherlands, characterized by low masculinity and low power distance; an Anglo-Saxon group, characterized by high individualism and masculinity and low power distance and uncertainty avoidance; and a Latin group, showing high uncertainty avoidance and high power distance.

As we have seen in chapter 5, however, the use of 'culture' in this sense (and particularly its association with the generating of organizational commitment) is problematic. In an MNC, for example, local employees may adjust their behaviour to head-office 'corporate culture' requirements at a superficial level, whilst deeper-rooted societal cultural values may affect the meaning given to actions. In this sense corporate culture may be merely complied with rather than internalized. This suggests that one of the challenges for international HRS is to solve 'a multidimensional puzzle located at the crossroad of national and organisational cultures' (Laurent, 1986). One suggestion is to develop policies which are not uniform and universal, but can accommodate multiple value systems, cultural diversity and different interests. This challenge for IHRS of responding to cultural diversity is taken up later in this chapter. One key implication is that underlying cultural beliefs about relationships to nature and to others may affect the acceptability and effectiveness of HRM practices, such as recruitment and selection, performance management and socialization. However, culture is only one of the elements that constitute a national or regional 'business system' and it is to such a comparative analysis of business systems that we now turn.

Comparative business systems and IHRS

Originally, most theories of international business focused on the *country* level, and sought to explain why countries traded with each other. Mercantilist views, emphasizing the need for trade surpluses, gave way in the eighteenth century to theories of absolute and comparative advantage in production, generating an international division of labour. 'Factor endowments' like land, labour and capital were held to be particularly significant. However, the rise of the 'third world multi-national' and the recognition that trade does not occur on a fair and equal basis have cast doubt on such 'traditional' explanations of foreign trade. Despite the assertions of Ohmae (1989) and Reich (1991), recent 'orthodox' theories have recognized the importance of 'place'. Porter (1990), in his analysis of the 'competitiveness of nations', has argued that national competitiveness and firm competitiveness are interlinked, and that the determinants of national advantage form a 'diamond' or playing field. The home market (such as the existence of internationally competitive suppliers and related industries) has great significance for international business – close, collaborative and competitive relationships with suppliers and domestic rivals, such as those in the Italian footwear and fashion industries or Japanese automobile industries, can stimulate innovation and enterprise. This suggests that *domestic* HRS can act as a level or springboard for *international* HRS (e.g. Hendry, 1993), a contention given further weight by Porter's (1990) suggestion that one of the major 'factor conditions' in the diamond of national advantage is the presence of skilled labour, knowledge, resources and infrastructures. These, which have clear relationships with HRS, are influenced by cultural characteristics.

HRS at the company level in an international enterprise is influenced both by the parent- or home-country context from which it originated and the host-country context in which it operates. We therefore need, in order to make sense of the complexity and diversity of the environment in which international enterprises operate, to develop a framework for analysing the HRM systems of nations and regions. Begin (1992, p. 380) defines HRM systems as 'all HRM structures, processes, policies and policy effects at the societal and organisational levels of a particular country that comprise the operation of internal and external labour markets'. Particular constellations of institutional components may mould domestic businesses and their HR strategies. Whitley's (1992, p. 6) analysis of comparative business systems sees these as 'particular arrangements of hierarchy–market relations which have become institutionalised and relatively successful in particular contexts'. The three broad components, shown in figure 8.1, are the nature of the firm; market organization; and authoritative co-ordination and control systems.

For Whitley (1992, p. 6), 'these differences can be seen as alternative responses to three fundamental issues. First, how are economic activities and resources to be co-ordinated and controlled? Second, how are market connections between authoritatively co-ordinated economic activities in firms to be organized? Third, how are activities and skills within firms to be organised and directed through authority relations?' The coherence and stability of such institutions and their dissimilarity across nation states is seen to determine the extent to which business systems are distinctive, integrated and nationally differentiated. We need to focus more closely on national and regional differences in HRM practice as one key element in the analysis of comparative business systems.

Comparative HR practices: Convergence or divergence?

Some general empirical studies of comparative HRM practices and policies demonstrate the existence of regional 'clusters' sharing HRM systems in common and marked off, to some extent, from other regional clusters. Moss-Kanter (1991), for example, presents a global survey of management practices and expectations drawn from 1,200 managers. This distinguishes 'cultural allies' such as the US, UK and Australia from 'cultural islands' such as Korea and Japan, which represent unique HR systems. She also found a 'north European' cluster of Germany and the Nordic countries and a 'Latin' cluster of southern European countries and Latin America.

Another study re-analysing IBM–Towers Perrin data drawn from a global survey of CEOs and HR directors in 12 countries found a similar pattern, but also revealed some interesting differences. Using cluster analysis on 15 dimensions of HR practice and policy, Sparrow et al. (1994) identified several regional clusters and also several 'islands'. In one cluster they placed an Anglo-Saxon group of Australia, the US and Canada with Germany and Italy; in another, the Latin American countries (but not Italy); in another and on its own, France; in another, Japan; and in another, Korea. In some ways, their results support culturalist explanations such as Hofstede (1983) and Trompenaars (1993) – the Anglo-Saxon countries

---

1 The nature of the firm

- The degree to which private managerial hierarchies co-ordinate economic activities.

- The degree of managerial discretion from owners.

- Specialization of managerial capabilities and activities within authority hierarchies.

- The degree to which growth is discontinuous and involves radical changes in skills and activities.

- The extent to which risks are managed through mutual dependence with business partners and employees.

---

2 Market organization

- The extent of long-term co-operative relations between firms within and between sectors.

- The significance of intermediaries in the co-ordination of market transaction.

- Stability, integration and scope of business groups.

- Dependence of co-operative relations on personal ties and trust.

---

3 Authoritative co-ordination and control systems

- Integration and interdependence of economic activities.

- Impersonality of authority and subordination relations.

- Task, skill and role specialization and individualization.

- Differentiation of authority roles and expertise.

- Decentralization of operational control and level of work-group autonomy.

- Distance and superiority of managers.

- Extent of employer–employee commitment and organization-based employment system.

Figure 8.1   The components of comparative business systems
Source: Whitley, 1992.

tended to emphasize empowerment, equality, diversity and flexibility; France and Korea were less interested in these dimensions of HRS and more interested in centralization and hierarchy; Latin America was less interested in flexibility and more interested in managing outflows.

As the authors themselves note, their study methodology has limitations in sampling only large organizations judged internationally competitive and in assuming that the items had the same meaning for all the respondents. Sparrow et al. (1994) reported that respondents in all countries rated all

HRM items higher for the year 2000 than they did in 1991, the year they completed the survey. This suggests that HRM was becoming increasingly important to strategy. Firms in all clusters were placing increasing emphasis on empowerment, diversity and equality, as well as on other dimensions, suggesting some 'convergence' of HRM policy.

Convergence versus divergence

This theme of 'convergence or divergence' has also been taken up by authors with a particular interest in European HRM. In part, this focus is driven by the apparently essentially American origin and nature of the classic HRM model (e.g. Guest, 1992). This raises the question of whether such a model, with its individualistic, task-oriented view of human 'resources' to be 'managed', is applicable to Europe. In part, this is a view driven by a concern, often stemming from the European Commission itself, to strengthen and improve the competitive position of 'Europe' (in practice, the European Union). Some studies have sought to identify whether a distinctive 'European model' of HRM exists or is emerging (see box 8.4).

Box 8.4   A European model of HRM?

Clearly influenced by developments over the 'Social Chapter or Social Charter', Thurley (1990) and Thurley and Wirdenius (1991), identify four principles they regard as essential building blocks for a 'European model', distinct from both the American and Japanese models of HRM:

- dialogue between social partners;
- multicultural organizations;
- participation in decision-making;
- continuous learning.

This stress on a supposedly distinctive European 'social market' model, with its emphasis on social partnership and social responsibilities (and fears over its vulnerability to intensifying global competition), is also reflected in the studies based on interviews with 51 chief executives and others from 40 major European multinationals associated with the European Round Table of Industrialists and ESC Lyon (Bloom et al., 1994). This project identified the following characteristics of an emerging 'European management model':

- a focus on managing international diversity;
- an emphasis on social responsibility;

- an orientation towards people;
- a stress on internal and external negotiation between stakeholders and partners;
- less reliance on formal systems;
- a product orientation;
- management between the US and Japanese extremes, especially over time frames and the relationship between the individual and the collective.

Not only does this model (box 8.4) represent something of an idealized 'wish list', it also obscures much of the diversity within Europe, even the geographically and culturally limited Europe under study. The interviewees themselves showed some ambivalence towards the UK, recognizing that in some respects its model of HRM seems closer to the USA or lay perhaps mid-way between 'Europe' and 'North America'. This transatlantic/mid-Atlantic perception of the UK has probably been reinforced by the experience of the long years of Conservative rule, with their idolization of the market, the dominance of the City and shareholders to the exclusion of other stakeholders, and the emphasis given to deregulation and the diminished role of the state and trade unions in economic strategy.

As we have seen, Moss-Kanter (1991) distinguished an Anglo-Saxon, a Northern and a Latin model, whilst Sparrow et al. (1994) differentiated France from Italy in their approaches to HRM. In fact, of course, Bloom, Calori, and de Woot (1994) are sensitive to internal diversity within Europe, but still see a 'European model' emerging at a certain level of abstraction. On the basis of their interviews, they first distinguish the UK from the rest of Europe, and then 'the North' from 'the South'. The 'South', seen as presenting more state intervention, protectionism, hierarchy and intuitive/chaotic management, is differentiated between France and the other Mediterranean countries. The North, seen as presenting less state intervention, more liberalism, more participation and more organization, is differentiated into the Nordic/Scandinavian countries (more relationship oriented, more egalitarian and more people oriented), the Germanic countries and the Benelux countries. The small countries are seen as exhibiting diverse cultural influences (the Dutch from the British, the Belgians from the French and all from the Germans) and as having a generally 'more international' outlook.

The German model is of particular interest because it has often been taken to be *the* paradigm European model of HRM (e.g. Thurow, 1992). This is in part a reflection of the size and economic power of Germany within Europe, in part a reflection of its apparent economic success, and in part because its model offers a clear contrast to the American model of HRM. Albert (1991), for example, differentiates 'capitalisme Anglo-Saxon' from 'capitalisme Rhénan' – Rhenish capitalism is seen as closer to the Japanese model in some respects, with a common focus on organized competition rather than liberalism, a stakeholder rather than a shareholder orientation, a long-term orientation, a strong emphasis on high investment and stable capital structures, a high status given to production, a high sense of community and loyalty to the firm, and low geographical and inter-firm mobility of personnel.

However, just as Anglo-Saxon management in the UK differs from the US, German HRM, of course, differs from Japanese. Its stress on individuals and on specialisms differentiates it from the Japanese emphasis on teams and generalists, and the German social market economy and its relationships with trade unions find no parallels in Japan.

Box 8.5   National models of HRM: The case of Germany

This Germanic model of HRM, with its strong links between banks and industry, its balance between the state and the regions, its well-developed systems of training and development, its system of co-determination and workers' representatives on the board, its collective orientation, its long-term orientation and its in-house career systems, has been most fully analysed by Lawrence (1994). He stresses its formal (but not bureaucratic or authoritarian) management style, as manifested in titles, names, dress codes and reliance on official documents, regulations and committees (whereas Hofstede, 1983, found Germans to score quite highly on uncertainty avoidance, they scored only modestly on power distance – no more than the UK). He also emphasizes the crucial and distinctive role of education and training in the German system – the abundance of graduates and managers with doctorates, the emphasis on engineering, the paucity of MBAs, the emphasis on in-company, specific, technical training, the under-emphasis on 'managerial' training, and the stress on 'Technik' (engineering knowledge and craft skills) as both a means and an end, with a corresponding de-emphasis on marketing and finance compared to the USA and UK. Lawrence also draws attention to the social market economy, the role of *industrial* trade unions, the way wages are typically negotiated between the relevant trade union and employers' associations on an industry-wide basis and on a region (Land) by region basis, according to a well-understood timetable of Lander and industries. He also crucially points to the role of the industrial democracy or co-determination system. Employee participation operates at three levels: representatives on the supervisory board, a labour director on the executive committee, and elected representatives on the works council. This whole system is legally based and of long-standing, and appears well accepted by employers. The works councils in particular have played a key role since 1952, having the legal power to decide on many practical issues such as working hours, holidays, breaks, canteen prices, appointments and transfers. Its economics committee has the right to receive information on the company's economic position.

In general, this German model of HRM (box 8.5), with its procedural, legalistic and regulatory overtones, contrasts sharply with the Anglo-American model of HRS described in chapter 1. In particular, the functional personnel specialist plays a very different, more reactive, more technical and less strategic role. The role is seen in much more legal terms, with the traditional qualification being a doctorate in law and the main role being to address the Labour Courts designed to settle labour disputes.

Such a model of HRM is a salutary reminder that the Anglo-American model of HRS, with its focus on employee autonomy, deregulation, mobility and enterprise-level strategies in terms of pay, recruitment and training is not the only path to economic success; nor does it seem, if we add Japan to Germany, that the economic prizes in recent years have gone to those countries valuing risk-taking and uncertainty or emphasizing free markets and an absence of state intervention. However, whilst both Albert (1991) and Lawrence (1994) are keen to stress their admiration for the German model and attribute German economic success to it, they also acknowledge downsides and limitations. Lawrence (1994, p. 148), whilst claiming that 'this single-minded brand of management is one of the key factors in the success of post war reconstruction as well as in the sustained economic performance of West Germany', also points out that 'German management has been relatively insular and self-sufficient (and a little bit self-satisfied as well)'. Its high labour costs and relative downplaying of marketing may not help it in the future, whilst its technical, function-based system of management development and relative lack of interest in international management development or in globalizing its managerial labour force may not equip it to deal with the complexity and diversity of globalization.

However, Lane (1992) argues that the German system is internally consistent, integrated and stable with mutually supporting elements, in contrast to the British system, which is much looser. Recent ideologies of employee involvement and commitment in the UK are still fragile and unsupported by more prevalent contractually oriented institutional arrangements.

Many studies have been content to interview a few selected multi-national CEOs (e.g. Bloom et al. 1993) or survey large company CEOs and HR directors on a limited range of topics (e.g. Sparrow et al., 1994) or conduct more historical/cultural studies based on secondary sources (e.g. Albert, 1991).

In contrast, the Price-Waterhouse–Cranfield study of HR practices across Europe has surveyed 14 countries and by 1995 had analysed 16,000 questionnaires (e.g. Brewster, 1994). Brewster and his colleagues have also been interested in the notion of a 'European model' of HRM, drawing attention to the lack of employer and managerial autonomy in many European countries, in contrast to the assumptions behind the US model of 'strategic HRM'. The embeddedness of European organizations within cultural and legal limitations and within district patterns of owner-ship by the state, families and banking and finance systems has also been noted. In addition, trade union involvement is seen as a further distinctive factor. All of these factors restrict organizational autonomy, make hiring and firing more difficult, restrict employee mobility, and give a greater role to the social partners, in particular the trade unions, than is typical of the US model of HRM. Collective bargaining at the national or regional level, greater state intervention, more comprehensive welfare systems and stron-ger links between educational experiences and career success also seem to characterize a European model. Brewster (1994, pp. 328–9) argues that a European model of HRM is required because current trends in Europe 'do not fit comfortably with the original US concepts of HRM . . . what is happening in Europe is that there is a move towards the HRM concept but one which, within a clearly established external environment, accepts the duality of people management. Thus, objectives include both organisa-tional requirements and a concern for people; the focus on both costs and benefits means fitting organisational policies to external cultures and con-straints; union and non-union channels are utilised; the relationship with line managers at all levels is interactive rather than driven by either spe-cialists or the line.' This view of what is happening reinforces the need for an 'open' rather than 'closed' approach to HRS, and also demonstrates how European developments in HRS embrace both 'hard' and 'soft' approaches, to use the terminology developed in chapter 1. The approach is seen to be 'open' in the sense that it accepts and recognizes different degrees of managerial independence, different ways of working with trade unions, different roles for government and different routes to enhanced economic performance.

Towards a common European HRM practice?

What are these trends in European HRM practice? Brewster (1994) concentrates on five topics: pay and benefits; flexible working; equal opportunity; training; and employee relations - all key issues addressed in this text. His broad conclusion is that with regard to pay, flexibility and training, the US model fits, whereas with regard to trade union recognition and communications, it does not. Let us consider each of these areas in turn, and then address an area not considered by Brewster (1994): recruitment, assessment and selection practices.

With regard to pay, trends in this area (discussed in chapters 4 and 5 of this book) include the increasing decentralization of pay bargaining in both highly centralized systems, such as most Nordic systems, and in more decentralized systems, such as the UK and France, although national industry bargaining for manual workers remains common in much of UK industry.

Within the Nordic countries, commitment to multi-employer bargaining with trade unions remains high, with some shift to the industry level; less change is evident in Germany, where binding collective agreements remain in place. However, in general, variable pay, merit pay and performance-related pay initiatives have spread across Europe. These kinds of initiatives seem least common in Scandinavia, with Denmark, the UK and the southern European companies making most use of them. Profit sharing and share options seem less widespread. Brewster (1994, p. 315) argues that 'in spite of some common trends towards more variable pay and pay decentralisation, national and cultural differences remain strong'. In a similar vein, flexible working practices (defined here as atypical work patterns or contracts, a rather narrow definition) have become much more widespread, leaving Brewster (1994, p. 319) to conclude that 'all of the results . . . suggest that organisations across Europe are moving towards greater flexibility, even if they are starting from different positions'.

However, practice around equal opportunity is much more divergent, with, for example, childcare facilities in France and Scandinavia being much more widespread and women participating in the labour force much more actively than in Greece or Spain. However, substantial vertical and occupational segregation based on gender is a feature of all European countries. With the exception of the UK and the Netherlands, the issue of racial discrimination has been much less of a concern than gender discrimination.

Again, training provision varies considerably between European countries, although there has been a general increase at all levels and especially for managerial staff. With the exception of France, where the law requires companies to spend at least 1.2 per cent of their pay bill on training, many organizations are unable to assess how much is spent on training. Relationships with trade unions remain a key issue for most European organizations, with union membership varying from 90 per cent in Norway to around 12 per cent in France. Grahl and Teague (1991) argue that in general, employee relations has moved from a Fordist trajectory to either one of competitive flexibility (the UK) or constructive flexibility (Germany and Scandinavia).

Table 8.2 shows some of the similarities and differences between countries in terms of HR practice revealed by the Price-Waterhouse–Cranfield survey. One interesting dimension shown in table 8.2, and of interest to the general themes of the book, is the extent of 'HR integration' across Europe (in this instance, measured by such factors as having a written HR strategy and having the head of HR on the Main Board). The most integrated countries were France, Sweden and Norway; the least were Germany and Italy. Once again, the position of Germany shows that HRM integration, often asserted as a key plank of any HR strategy, is not necessarily associated with economic success.

Another dimension brought out in the Cranfield studies in addition to 'integration' is that of devolution or 'devolvement', associated with decentralization and the sharing of HRM responsibility with line managers. Brewster and Larsen (1993) have plotted different countries against these two dimensions to generate an integration/devolvement matrix. The typical Swedish or Swiss organization is seen as exhibiting high levels of both integration and devolvement. These 'pivotal' types, with an orientation to facilitation and internal consulting by personnel managers, differ from the 'wild west' organizations found in Denmark and the Netherlands, where low integration and high devolvement leave line managers with considerable power and autonomy, running the risk of incoherence and inconsistency. German, British and Italian organizations typically score low on both dimensions, with their 'professional mechanic' personnel managers exercising specialist but limited (and strategically isolated) skills. Finally, the typical Norwegian, French or Spanish organization contains 'guarded strategists', highly integrated with senior managers but showing low levels of devolvement to the line.

Such an analysis is interesting, but perhaps obscures as much as it reveals. As we have seen, the German model of HRM differs substantially from the typical British model, yet both are classified as 'professional mechanics'. The specialist expertise of personnel managers is exercised quite differently in the two business systems.

Before we leave the analysis of comparative HRM, let us look at an area less fully explored by the Price-Waterhouse–Cranfield project – that of recruitment, selection and assessment practices. It is clear from many studies (see table 8.3) that in all countries studied, interviews, application

Table 8.2 Organizational dimensions of HRM by country (percentages)

	CH	D	DK	E	F	FN	I	IR	N	NL	P	S	UK
1. Head of Human Resources Function on Main Board	58	30	49	73	84	61	18	44	71	42	46	84	49
2. Written HR strategy	58	18	72	37	34	52	33	41	71	44	34	73	50
3. At leat one-third of managers trained in performance appraisal	69	34	19	31	47	42	45	43	64	51	32	77	71
4. Information on financial performance given to manual employees	38	44	54	9	42	83	24	36	66	40	18	68	49
5. Change in union influence over previous three years (increase–decrease)	+5	+14	–23	+19	–33	–6	–30	–13	+16	+11	–	–18	–50
6. Proportion spending more than 2% of annual wage bill on training	37	43	25	23	80	36	24	40	36	40	39	60	26
7. Increase in line manager responsibility for training over last three years	–	13	39	53	55	51	–	43	56	50	18	67	46

Notes: Country coding: CH – Switzerland; D – Germany; DK – Denmark; E – Spain; F – France; FN – Finland; I – Italy; IR – Ireland; N – Norway; NL – Netherlands; P – Portugal; S – Sweden; UK – Britain.
Sources: Brewster, C. and Hegwisch, A. (eds) (1994) *Policy and Practice in European Human Resource Management – The Price-Waterhouse–Cranfield Survey*. London, Routledge.

forms/CVs and references are the most widely used methods, yet these are often regarded as amongst the least valid predictors of job performance. However, some interesting differences persist (see box 8.6).

Box 8.6 Differences in selection practice across Europe

Shackleton and Newell (1994, p. 91) argue that 'harmonisation of selection practice in Europe is a long way off. Habit, tradition and culture determine the choice of selection method.' Belgian practice shows divisions between its Flemish and French-speaking regions, for example, especially in the use of graphology. This is a technique far more commonly used in France than in the Netherlands or the UK, where it is generally regarded as no better than astrology. The British seem wedded to the equally unreliable reference; Italian organizations seem least likely to use any other selection method than the interview; German organizations seem less convinced of the value of psycho-metric tests, and less likely to see the value of test training or training in giving feedback than British ones; French organizations seem less likely to use panel interviews and more likely to use a series of one-to-one interviews with progressively more senior line managers.

What such surveys, including the Price-Waterhouse–Cranfield survey, often fail to explore are the *reasons* for such observed national and regional differences. Not only are such surveys typically limited to large organiza-tions and frequently display a low response rate, it is often unclear whether the terms used carry a common meaning for respondents. The term 'psychometric test' or 'assessment centre', for example, may mean very different things to respondents, who may not be in a position anyway to know what goes on in their organization at grass-roots levels. Brewster et al. (1994) note that respondents interpreted identical questions within specific cultural and legal contexts; for example, 'flexible working' in the UK and Germany was interpreted in terms of the participation of women in the labour force, whereas in France it was seen in terms of general changes in lifestyle. It is tempting to invoke *post hoc* cultural, historical or institutional factors to 'explain' certain findings (for example, perhaps the professionalization of psychologists in the UK and the Netherlands 'explains' the greater use of psychometric tests and assessment centres; perhaps the French use of serial interviews is related to their higher uncer-tainty avoidance and power distance indices than is characteristic of Britain; perhaps the wide range of methods used in Belgium is also related to their

Table 8.3 Summary of comparative frequencies of use of assessment methods in seven countries

Assessment method	Greece	UK	France	Australia	Germany	Netherlands	USA
Interviews	High	High	High	High	High	High	High
CV/Application form		High	High	High	High	High	High
Ability and personality tests	Low	High	High	Moderate	Moderate	High	High
Assessment centres		High	Low	Low	Moderate	Low	Moderate
Biodata		Low	Low	Low	Low		Low
References	High	High	High	High	High	High	High
Personal contacts	High						
Simulations		Moderate	Moderate	Moderate	Very low		Moderate
Graphology		Low	High			Low	

Notes: Low = used in less than 10% of assessments approximately; Moderate = used in 10–50% of assessments approximately; High = used in more than 50% of assessments approximately.
Source: Nyfield, 1993.

culturally expressed need to reduce uncertainty), but such hypotheses are rarely tested for at the time, and *reasons* for using particular techniques are rarely probed.

One reason for considering comparative differences in business systems, culture and HR practices across nations and regions is that such differences contribute to the diversity and complexity of the global environment faced by international enterprises attempting to co-ordinate their activities across different locations and environments. It is the role of IHRS at this enterprise level that we turn in the next section.

International HRS at the Enterprise Level

This section will explore ways in which organizations are using human resource strategies to create more strategically coherent, competitive international enterprises, using cases drawn from Asian, US and in particular European organizations in the light of changes in the international business environment.

It is frequently asserted that the increasingly global nature of business activities has placed new demands on organizational and managerial performance and has called for new responses. International assignments, for example, are being increasingly used not only for staffing, control and representational purposes, but as vehicles to develop managers' skills and knowledge and as ways of enhancing organizational learning and capabilities. More managers are now involved in managing transnational joint ventures, mergers and acquisitions, and are operating in increasingly diverse environments with multi-cultural teams. Senior managers are often called upon to manage geographically and culturally diverse businesses, balancing the demands of global integration and centralization with those of local sensitivity and responsiveness. The geographical dispersion of operating units and the multi-cultural nature of international enterprise are often seen as posing new challenges for IHRS, including:

- How to ensure that organizational structures and systems enhance global effectiveness and enable organizations to achieve both global integration and local responsiveness.
- How to foster organizational cultures which value diversity and difference whilst simultaneously creating a sense of unified mission and acting as the 'corporate glue'.
- How to install effective personnel systems that attract, place, retain and develop managers and other key employees with the knowledge, skills and attitudes required to perform effectively in a global business environment.

This section will develop a framework for analysing international HR strategies, outlining the policy options and choices available in developing appropriate IHRS strategies in international enterprise.

In order to develop such a framework, we will need to go beyond our earlier description of the external environment facing international enterprises as characterized by complexity, diversity and geographic dispersion.

Strategy, structure and IHRS in a global environment

One helpful framework for analysing the global environment faced by international enterprises is provided by Bartlett and Ghoshal (1989). They see the early phase of MNC activity, primarily dominated by European MNCs, as 'multi-national'. Since this term is also often used to describe any kind of transnational corporation, we shall follow Harzing and van Ruysseveldt (1995) and use the term 'multi-domestic', since up to the end of the Second World War MNCs emphasized foreign production for local domestic markets with decentralized decision-making and local autonomy. With a decline in protectionist policies, a reduction in tariff barriers and improved transportation, communication and logistics, American MNCs in particular entered international markets and initiated significant foreign direct investment. In this 'international' phase, as high-tech products produced in the US became more standardized, they were exported and then produced overseas. As the product became completely standardized, economies of scale and mass production made low-cost production in less-developed countries possible, giving rise to the 'new international division of labour' analysed above.

Japanese companies in particular began to move beyond this phase in the 1970s as declining communication and transport barriers, new technologies and a greater homogenization of consumer tastes rendered centralized, standardized production and exporting activities profitable. This Bartlett and Ghoshal (1989) term the 'global' era, and it describes the kind of environment Levitt's (1983) globalization thesis was designed to address.

However, the rise of trade barriers, increased national regulation and the growth of flexible technologies in the 1980s have reinforced the importance of local responsiveness, stimulating not the reappearance of 'multi-domestic' environments, since the world-wide innovation and global efficiency demands of the international and global eras remain important, but the rise of what is termed the 'transnational' era (Bartlett and Ghoshal, 1989; Harzing and van Ruysseveldt, 1995).

If we move from the global level to the industry level, we can see links between the competitive environments faced by MNCs and the demands of particular industries. Some industries remain multi-domestic (e.g. branded packaged goods, like detergents and food) – international strategy here essentially consists of a set of independent domestic strategies, and cultural, social and other national differences remain powerful influences. European companies are important players in this industry.

Other industries have become global, with standardized needs and efficiencies of scale putting an emphasis on centralization and integration. The global industry does not consist of separate domestic industries, as the competitive position of the company in one country is linked to its position in other countries. The consumer electronics industry explored above is the classic example, dominated by Japanese and other Asian corporations.

In international industries, the ability to transfer knowledge and technology evolved in the home market to foreign affiliates is the key to success, as in telecommunications switching. It is a competence which has been particularly well developed by US companies. In the developing transnational industries, companies need to respond to the complex and often contradictory demands of characteristics of the other three types of industry – the global efficiency demanded by global industries, the national responsiveness demanded by multi-domestic industries and the rapid transfer of learning, knowledge and innovation demanded by international industries (Bartlett and Ghoshal, 1989).

This brief excursion into the realms of international competitive strategy has several implications for IHRS, particularly for organizational structure. First, we will note its relationship to the continental origin of the leading MNCs, as this seems to have influenced their 'administrative heritage' (Bartlett and Ghoshal, 1992).

People and structure in IHRS

The driving organizational perspectives or bases that shape the distribution of power, influence and control in international enterprise are primarily function, product and geography. These three bases may compete with, conflict with or complement each other. Japanese multi-nationals like Nissan and Hitachi have typically divided their global operations along functional lines (e.g. production, marketing) and can be said to be functionally driven. American multi-nationals have tended to stress a product perspective, whereas European multi-nationals such as Shell, ICI and BP have tended to be area driven or geographically driven. Only in the last few years have such organizations moved towards a more product-driven strategy (Humes, 1993).

Some multi-nationals have sought to combine or mix approaches, creating a variety of 'hybrids', perhaps with some parts of the corporation stressing one approach and other parts another (e.g. Exxon). Other companies, like Philips, have developed 'matrix' or 'tilted matrix' approaches, attempting to balance product and geography, often in transition to a product-driven strategy. Other companies, especially American ones like P & G, have tended to continue to use an international division to manage their overseas operations, whilst their domestic operations remain product driven.

On all three major 'Triad' continents, international enterprises have tended to place greater stress on either product perspectives (e.g. Bayer, Philips, BP, ICI) or area perspectives (e.g. Sony). According to Humes (1993), Japanese multi-nationals have typically combined functional perspectives with a managerial emphasis on shared values; American multi-nationals a product emphasis with a focus on structures and systems; and European multi-nationals an emphasis on area alongside the use of staffing practices to bring about co-ordination and control. However, multi-nationals from all three continents have attempted to utilize all three sets of dynamics in recent years.

Each of the phases discussed in the previous sub-section has tended to be associated with MNCs from different continents. The typical American multi-national company, for example, has tended to rely on an international division to co-ordinate all its international activities, often managed by a senior executive group at headquarters. Such a form tends to rely on formal structures and control systems, to adopt an ethnocentric orientation and to use PCNs (parent country nationals) for control and co-ordination purposes. European multi-nationals, in contrast, have taken a different path, often moving directly from a classic '*mother–daughter*' structure characteristic of the multi-domestic phase, to a divisionalized global structure employing transcontinental product or area divisions and polycentric staffing, without adopting the transitional stage of the international division. Japanese multi-nationals have tended to rely on trading companies to manage their international activities, with only slow movements towards other phases of internationalization and with the adoption of basically an 'ethnocentric' orientation. However, by the 1990s there has been some convergence among the leading multi-nationals from all three continents towards reliance of global operating divisions and towards the adoption of a geocentric or transnational perspective (Humes, 1993).

The increasingly complex international environment encountered by an MNC may push it towards global integration, whereas host government pressure and the need for responsiveness to local markets and cultures may push it towards local responsiveness. To address this dilemma, international companies have often sought to go beyond a divisional structure towards other structures, such as mixed, matrix and network structures.

However, matrix forms in many international organizations have proved hard to manage, due to dual reporting leading to conflict and confusion, a proliferation of channels leading to log-jams, overlapping responsibilities producing a loss of accountability and battles over turf, and barriers of distance, language, time and culture combining to make conflict very difficult to resolve.

According to Bartlett and Ghoshal (1989) the most successful international organizations are now less likely to be searching for an ideal structure and more likely to be attempting to develop managerial abilities to operate 'a matrix in the mind', putting the emphasis on finding and developing managers with good interpersonal skills and tolerance of ambiguity. Whilst European multi-nationals, with their strong local presence, have tended to maximize responsiveness, Japanese organizations with their global-scale efficiencies have focused on global integration. Other organizations (often American) like GE or P & G have seemed very good at facilitating innovation. However, the challenge facing international organizations in the future may be to *simultaneously* build multiple strategic competencies. As Bartlett and Ghoshal (1989, p. 16) put it, 'to compete effectively, a company had to develop global competitiveness, multinational flexibility and world-wide learning capability *simultaneously*'. This requirement is seen as stimulating a new organizational model, the transnational, able to build on the advantages of the other organizational forms.

Bartlett and Ghoshal (1989, p. 61) use the term integrated network to emphasize 'the very significant flow of components, products, resources, people, and information that must be managed in the transnational. Beyond the rationalisation of physical facilities, the company must integrate tasks and perspectives; rich and complex communication linkages, work interdependencies, and formal and informal systems are the true hallmark of the transnational.'

Such an orientation seems more characteristic of multi-nationals with roots in smaller European countries like Sweden (e.g. Electrolux, Ericsson), Switzerland (e.g. Nestlé) and to some extent Holland (e.g. Philips, Unilever) than of American, British or Japanese multi-nationals, perhaps because such countries experienced an earlier and greater need to move beyond very limited national boundaries, as we have seen above. Box 8.7 shows one such example.

Box 8.7   Coaching from the HQ touchline

Electrolux, for example, makes over 80 per cent of its sales abroad and whilst in some respects it has sought to maintain a centralized approach with its global 'white goods' strategies and use of common components world-wide, in other respects it has sought to push central functions out to the subsidiaries, with headquarters acting as coach and co-ordinator. National units have global responsibility for developing and manufacturing specific products: for example Italy for washing machines, the UK for microwaves. Multi-disciplinary task forces are drawn from different units to facilitate design and development. (Source: Barham and Oates, 1991.)

Where the analysis of Bartlett and Ghoshal (1989) is helpful is in pointing to the differentiated nature of MNC strategies and their links on the one hand to particular eras and industries and on the other to organizational structure and HRM policies. In contrast to the globalization thesis of Levitt (1983) and the assertions of the NIDL thesis, MNCs do not just pursue globally integrated strategies of efficiency, low-cost production and standardization, though such strategies did appear to have predominated in certain eras (the 1970s), certain industries (electronics) and amongst certain corporations (especially Japanese ones). Some MNCs may pursue multi-domestic strategies emphasizing national responsiveness, and especially European MNCs operations in the packaged goods sector. Other MNCs may pursue international strategies emphasizing the transfer of learning, especially US companies in high-tech industries. Other MNCs from all three parts of the Triad recognize that they face simultaneous demands for local differentiation and global efficiency and world-wide innovation, and attempt to pursue 'transnational strategies'. These are especially important given the rapid changes experienced by different industries – for example, the use of synthetics and washing machines has put the emphasis on standardization in the multi-domestic detergents industry; political pressures for local production, trade barriers and renewed differences in customer taste have made responsiveness more important in the global consumer electronics industry; and whilst deregulation and new technology have placed greater importance on global efficiency in the 'international' telecommunications industry, government recognition of its strategic importance has also emphasized the importance of local responsiveness (Bartlett and Ghoshal, 1989). It is also worth emphasizing that this analysis is at a high level of generality; different units, locations, tasks and functions may have considerable room for choice within these broad parameters.

Another valuable implication of the Bartlett and Ghoshal (1989) framework is its rejection of the notion that there should be a 'fit' between strategy and structure in favour of the recognition of organizational and strategic flexibility in the face of dynamic, complex environments. This ties in with our earlier analysis of the notion of integration and our emphasis on 'open' rather than 'closed' conceptions of HRS. Similar considerations apply to IHRS, and one of the benefits of the Bartlett and Ghoshal (1989) framework is that it points to the importance of management processes as the key to the successful implementation of strategy. However, the

authors themselves, being corporate strategists, do not follow their argument through in detail to a consideration of human resource strategies. To
do so requires us to pay closer attention to another model of IHRS, one
that focuses on managerial choice and management orientations to international enterprise, and to the ways in which HR strategies at the functional level may differ in international, as opposed to domestic, enterprise.

The importance of managerial orientation to IHRS

Successful implementation of international HRM is often seen as requiring
a shift in managerial orientations or 'mind-sets'. For example, Laurent
(1986) argues that a truly international conception of HRS requires explicit
recognition that:

- particular ways of managing human resources reflect particular values
  and assumptions;
- these ways are different, not universally superior or inferior;
- foreign subsidiaries and affiliates may have different ways of managing
  people, perhaps more effective locally;
- such differences need to be accepted and discussed so as to make them
  usable as resources and assets;
- more creative and effective ways of managing people can be developed
  as a result of cross-cultural learning.

If an organization or its senior management has a weak global orientation,
the importance and distinctiveness of international enterprise may be
under-emphasized or ignored. But as Bartlett and Ghoshal (1989) state,
even companies that were not seeking to expand abroad were confronted
by the emerging challenges as the forces of internationalization reached out
to embrace them. Companies may adopt a *parochial* stance, ignoring what is
happening elsewhere. Or they may adopt an *ethnocentric* stance, believing
that 'their way is better' and that domestic HRM practices are easily
transferable to operations in other countries, despite the evidence of substantial cultural differences and difference in business systems reviewed
above.

One of the most influential approaches to international HRM emphasizing the importance of managerial orientations is that of Perlmutter (1969).
He distinguishes between four basic orientations to international enterprise:
the ethnocentric, the polycentric, the geocentric, and the regiocentric.

An ethnocentric attitude is associated with the view that home-country
managers, management style and appraisal criteria are superior to the host
country, implying that only parent country nationals (PCNs) are suitable for
senior management at home and abroad. A polycentric attitude is associated with the recognition that national differences and the need for local

responsiveness demand the use of local managers (HCNs), or host country nationals in host countries, but home-country managers remain dominant in headquarters. A regiocentric orientation also recognizes the importance of national and cultural differences, but perceives these as most important at the regional level. So a US company may adopt a 'Eurocentric' strategy within the EU, seeing European managers as suitable for movement anywhere within the EU but seeing Asian affiliates as best run by Asian managers (HCNs) whilst using American expatriate PCNs to run affiliates in Africa. In contrast a geocentric attitude is associated with a global view, with managers drawn from any region of the world and appointed to positions at headquarters or subsidiaries regardless of nationality.

Many European companies, for example, in order to maximize local responsiveness, have attempted to staff local operations with HCNs rather than with expatriates. Such staff are deemed to know their own cultures, work ethics and markets best (a polycentric strategy). Local subsidiaries often may then operate almost independently, the major controls being financial (e.g. Unilever and Lever Brothers in the USA). However, locals may then find that they are barred from executive positions at headquarters because of their perceived 'over-local' perspective! The local responsiveness emphasized in the polycentric orientation may push organizations towards decentralized structures, giving maximum autonomy, flexibility, and independence to local enterprises. The global perspective of the geocentric orientation may simultaneously call for greater centralization, co-ordination and integration.

One way of building on these orientations is to link them to our previous analysis of organizational configurations and global eras. The ethnocentric orientation, for example, seems to be particularly characteristic of domestic companies and export oriented companies as well as those displaying a 'global' strategy. The polycentric orientation seems particularly characteristic of the classic multi-domestic/multi-national strategy, whereas 'international' companies may be more inclined to display regiocentric orientations. The geocentric orientation seems particularly characteristic of the transnational company.

If we extend Perlmutter's (1969) analysis of managerial orientations to the analysis of HR strategies, we can develop a framework which can guide the choice of recruitment and selection, training and development, performance management and other HR strategies in an international context. Before we do this, we need to consider two other useful approaches to IHRS, the 'stages' approach of Adler (1991), and the 'dual logics' of Evans and Lorange (1989).

Our discussion of the structural options open to MNCs is helped by analysing the 'two logics' facing international enterprise presented by Evans and Lorange (1989). We have already characterized the environment faced by MNCs as both more complex and more diverse than that faced by domestic organizations, primarily due to geographical dispersion and cultural diversity. Evans and Lorange (1989, p. 144) ask themselves 'how can a corporation operating in different product markets and diverse social-cultural environments effectively establish human resource policies?', and propose two logics that shape IHRS: a product-market logic related to the product life-cycle (thus introducing the notion of phase or stage) and a social-cultural logic related to the diverse legal, social, political and cultural environments faced by MNCs and the cultural diversity of their workforces. How MNCs respond to the question of diversity can be analysed in terms of Perlmutter's (1969) 'managerial orientations', or the 'administrative heritage' of the organization (Bartlett and Ghoshal, 1989). By this term the authors are referring to the dominant management styles, values, patterns, assets and capabilities built up over generations (and themselves related to imperial origins, as we have seen). These two related dimensions mediate the response of the organization to the strategic pressures it faces, affecting how it structures itself, according to such criteria as: whether to emphasize the global or the local, whether to pursue decentralization or centralization, whether to focus on differentiation or on integration, and whether to emphasize cultural logic or product logic (this list is taken from a much longer list of 'dualities' presented by Evans and Doz (1989)). These design choices in turn are related to the bases of co-ordination and control selected by the organization, as to whether to structure by area, product or function, or whether to use some kind of matrix structure employing two or more dimensions, or whether to use an international division to co-ordinate and control international activities. Finally, such choices influence the kind of configuration adopted, to use the terminology of Bartlett and Ghoshal (1989).

Stage approaches to IHRS

A particularly useful framework for understanding the process of engaging in international HRS is presented by Adler (1991). This approach is based on a 'stage' or 'evolutionary' approach to internationalization, proposing that firms typically pass through several phases of organizational development as they internationalize, such as moving from exporting to establishing a sales subsidiary to establishing foreign production to creating an international division. What Adler tries to do is relate these evolutionary stages to HR policies and emphases, and it is this feature of her model that will be developed here. She argues that organizations have typically moved in their international activities through four phases or stages – from purely *domestic* organizations to what she calls *'international'* (or multi-domestic) organizations, and then from international organizations to *multi-national* organizations. She identifies a fourth, emerging phase of development in international enterprise – the *'global'* organization. Each of these phases is characterized by differences in orientation, strategy, technology and product or service. Each phase is also characterized by the increasing importance of international enterprise to their overall business activities. Table 8.4 shows how this 'stage' perspective may be applied to the issues of how to manage people in international enterprise. Unfortunately Adler (1991) uses the terms differently to Bartlett and Ghoshal (1989), causing some confusion. The 'domestic' organization is typically characterized by a centralized structure and a focus on functional divisions. The 'international' organization on the other hand typically operates with a more decentralized structure and tends to concentrate its activities in an international division. 'International' affairs may then be isolated from the mainstream of business, which is seen as primarily 'domestic' in focus. Consequently there may be little interchange or communication between the international division and the rest of the business, whether of ideas, people or practices, and little mutual learning or development.

The multi-national organization attempts to move beyond this, perhaps by decentralizing and creating multi-national business lines. As it evolves, it may increasingly enter into global alliances, and attempt to exercise a variety of measures such as the creating and communication of a common, though shared, mission, the development of a shared sense of purpose and corporate culture, the use of management development practices to create a cadre of 'corporate resources', and the use of financial controls.

Of particular interest to IHRS is that the issue of *culture* is seen as assuming increasing importance at each stage of internationalization. Using the Perlmutter (1969) framework, it can be seen that the domestic organization typically assumes an 'ethnocentric' perspective to HRS. Cultural sensitivity is regarded as of little importance, and the organization assumes there is only 'one way' (or at least 'one best way') to manage and organize. The international organization is held to take a more regiocentric perspective. Cultural sensitivity therefore becomes of critical importance, especially in managing employees of different backgrounds and dealing with clients, customers and suppliers of varying cultural backgrounds. It may seek to prioritize responsiveness and sensitivity to local labour and product markets.

Paradoxically, the *multi-national* organization in Adler's analysis places somewhat less importance on culture, recognizing its importance primarily in dealing with its own employees and managers. Its focus is primarily on 'one least cost way'. The *global* organization, on the other hand, is regarded as taking a more fully developed geocentric or multi-centric perspective towards its operations. For it, culture becomes of critical importance, whether dealing with employees, executives, customers or suppliers, as it is held to take the view that there are simultaneously 'many good ways' to manage and organize.

Adler's framework is clearly open to the criticism that it is somewhat deterministic, implying that it is best to locate oneself on the right-hand side of table 8.4. Of most value to our analysis of IHRS is the attempt to identify the specific HR implications of different stages of internationalization. The advantage of Adler's analysis is that it tries to bring together the 'product-market' and 'social-cultural' logics identified by Evans and Lorange (1989), linking the product life-cycle emphases of Vernon (1969) and Bartlett and Ghoshal's (1989) concern with strategy and structure to issues of culture and HRM. Table 8.4 shows this framework, much modified to give greater emphasis to HRS issues.

Organizations at the *domestic* or export stage may only require low-level global training, mainly emphasizing the local culture of the export target and its consumer values and behaviour and the interpersonal skills necessary to negotiate, sell and market to that culture. There is a need to carry out some training of HCNs, mainly in helping them understand home-country products and policies. At the *international* stage more extensive training is needed, with more emphasis on technology transfer, stress management and local business practices and law. At the *multi-national* stage, the emphasis now shifts to two-way technology transfer, corporate values, and international strategy and more emphasis is placed on the training of HCNs in both technical and cultural issues. The *global* stage requires more rigorous, extensive training of HCNs and of all employees, including senior executives, in such areas as global operations, global strategy, multiple cultural values, and socialization into the corporate culture. Managing international diversity thus becomes of critical importance.

Shortly we will use the framework presented in table 8.4 to briefly review strategies in four HR policy areas of great significance to IHRS: recruitment and selection, training and development, performance management and managing international diversity. But first we need to note a few caveats (in addition to the suggestion that we should not read such a table in an overly deterministic, evolutionary way, nor read it as suggesting that HR strategies can somehow be 'read off' for each phase in an overly prescriptive way). The first caveat is that the Perlmutter and Bartlett and Ghoshal phases do not perfectly match or lock in to Adler's phase model; note that we have collapsed Bartlett and Ghoshal's multi-domestic and international phases (with their very different orientations to responsiveness and learning) into one phase equivalent to Adler's 'international' phase. Also note that not all analysts see the 'geocentric' strategy as most effective in all cases – some prefer a 'regiocentric' strategy, with a regional strategy seen as a stepping stone to more effective international competition. As Morrison et al. (1991, p. 24)

Table 8.4 Globalization and IHRS

	Phase One	Phase Two	Phase Three	Phase Four
Adler 1991	Domestic	International	Multi-national	Global
Bartlett & Ghoshal 1989	Domestic	Multi-national	Global	Transnational
Permutter 1969	Ethnocentric	Polycentric	Regiocentric	Geocentric
Strategy and structure:	Export	Foreign direct investment, technology transfer	International sourcing, production, marketing	Global strategic advantage
	Product/function centralized	Decentralized/co-ordinated federation, international division	Centralized hub, multi-national business lines	Integrated network, alliances
Importance of cultural diversity:	'Marginal; one-way/one best way'	Important, esp. customers, clients, suppliers; 'many good ways'	Moderate, for managers and employees; 'one least-cost way'	Critically important for all staff; 'many good ways simultaneously'
Recruitment and selection:				
expatriates	Very few	Many	Some, esp. top performers	Many, all levels
purpose	Reward	Fill position, complete project, transfer technology	Control, complete project career development	Co-ordination, integration, career and organization development
career impact	Neutral, negative	Negative, except locally	Important	Essential
repatriation	Difficult	Very difficult	Less difficult	Easy
origins of executives	Home country PCNs	Home country PCNs and token TCNs	Home country PCNs and token TCNs, HCNs	HCNs, PCNs and TCNs
career track	Domestic	Domestic	Token international	Global
identification	Home country HQ	Host country	Home and host	Global
Training and development				
extent	Little	Limited	More extensive	High, continuous
rigour	Low	Moderate	High	High
target	Few	Expatriates, few HCNs	Expatriates, some HCNs	

Table 8.4 (Cont'd)

	Phase One	Phase Two	Phase Three	Phase Four
skills	Technical, managerial	Plus cultural adaptation	Plus cultural diversity	Plus cultural synergy
content	Local cultural awareness	Plus interpersonal skills, technology transfer	Plus two-way transfer, global strategy	Plus global systems, multiple values
communications	Little	Little	One-way	Two-way, all ways
Performance management:				
criteria	Corporate HQ	Local subsidiary	Corporate HQ	Global, universalized and local
motivation	Financial	Financial, adventure	Challenge, opportunity	Challenge, opportunity, advancement
reward package	Compensation	Compensation	Global	Global

Notes: HCN= host country national; PCN= parent country national; TCN= third country national.

put it, 'under a regional strategy, companies extend home and country loyalties to the entire region. Regional Managers are given the opportunity to solve regional challenges regionally.'

For example, Hilb (1992) argues that a 'Eurocentric' HR strategy is the most appropriate response for a European company. Such a strategy can exploit European-wide human resources instead of concentrating only on PCNs or HCNs, a consequence of following an ethnocentric or polycentric HR strategy, and can help identify subsidiary employees with corporate pan-European strategies.

In addition it can help create a pan-European company culture able to derive benefit from the advantages of all the specific national cultures in which the company operates, and offer career opportunities across a more integrated Europe by avoiding some of the staffing, communication and motivation problems inherent in a geocentric policy. However, some disadvantages of such a regiocentric policy are that it neglects human resources outside Europe, can close off career paths outside Europe and career paths for non-European TCNs, and its focus on Europe may neglect other markets of great importance, especially in the Asia-Pacific region.

Figure 8.2 shows why Hilb (1992) feels that the advantages of a Eurocentric policy outweigh the disadvantages, and why such a policy is seen as capturing both local and global advantages more successfully than its rivals.

If we look at BP's evolution over the last 50 years (box 8.8) we can see that though there appears to be some relationship to the phases outlined in table 8.4 (e.g. the move from ethnocentric to polycentric to regiocentric orientations, the move from international to multi-national to transnational strategies), the 'fit' is by no means perfect. For example, BP in the 1980s re-centralized and re-emphasized an ethnocentric orientation, and it has

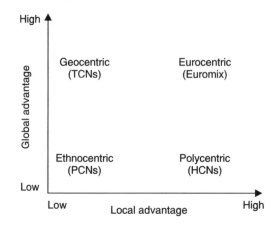

Figure 8.2 Stages of European HRD
Source: Adapted from Hilb, 1992, p. 580.

Table 8.5 Shifts in strategy, structure and HRS at BP

Era	Structure	Orientation	Aims	Focus
1940–73	Integrated	Ethnocentric (international)	Skill transfer	Expatriate terms and conditions
1973–80	Conglomerate; matrix	Polycentric multi-national	Skill transfer	Expatriate terms and conditions
1980–90	Centralized	Ethnocentric	Common corporate culture	Expatriate career management
1990–	Horizontal; network	Regiocentric/ geocentric (global?)	Learning 2-way; transfers; teams	Expatriate career management; team culture

Source: Hendry, 1993, p. 87.

stopped short of utilizing a fully 'geocentric' model in favour of more 'regiocentric' models. In the 1990s, re-centralization again appeared to be on the agenda. This example shows how international enterprises can move backwards and forwards along the path suggested in table 8.4. Table 8.5 shows some of these shifts, described in box 8.8.

Box 8.8 Keeping career shifts well-oiled at BP

BP is the UK's largest company in terms of sales, responding to increasing complexity and diversity by developing a changing portfolio of products and markets and revamping its HR strategies. Like Exxon, it has always tended towards greater centralization than Shell, and has moved away from its 'imperial' sphere of influence in the Middle East. Between World War 2 and the oil crisis of 1973, it primarily emphasized integration and strong central control of overseas plants and businesses through an 'ethnocentric' HR strategy focused on transferring skills through a large cadre of primarily British career expatriates on long-term assignments. Expatriate terms and conditions were a major HR focus. After the rise in oil prices due to the actions of OPEC, BP used its oil revenues to open up reserves in Alaska and the North Sea and to diversify through acquisition into chemicals, animal feeds and coal. In this 'conglomerate' phase, a more 'polycentric' HR strategy was followed with a continuing focus on skill transfer and expatriate terms and conditions. A strong matrix organization focused around 11 business streams and 70 national affiliates was developed to manage this complexity.

However, this structure seemed not to facilitate decentralization, but to increase complexity. In the 1980s, following privatization, BP re-focused on its core oil business, acquiring both Britoil and Standard Oil of Ohio to provide marketing expertise and Alaskan outlets. This more centralized phase both increased the number of employees and brought in superior skills and expertise in some areas. A renewed 'ethnocentric' HR strategy attempted to integrate these businesses within an overall BP culture, using short-term expatriate assignments by senior managers, marketing and technical staff to exercise greater control from London. Career management therefore became a major issue for IHRS. However, with the growth of non-oil businesses as alternative sources of power and influence (e.g. nutrition in the Netherlands), BP in the 1990s has begun to pursue a more regiocentric philosophy, with moves towards a 'global' or 'transnational' strategy. This has manifested itself in the use of two-way secondments, a more fluid, less British, less geographically focused expatriate cadre, and the encouragement of career management, teamwork and organizational learning. Such a focus requires not direction by a centralized personnel function but more fluid negotiation between individuals, businesses and functions, managed primarily through regional structures. Training and development activities are used to foster teamworking and an awareness of cultural diversity, whilst INSEAD and Harvard are increasingly used for top management education instead of British universities. However, 1992 witnessed the departure of the chairman, a growing awareness of over-indebtedness, scrutiny of such under-performing businesses as chemicals and nutrients, and greater emphasis on cost-cutting, redundancies, disposals and central controls. (Source: Hendry, 1993)

The HRS Implications of Internationalization

The analysis in the last section presented a framework for analysing the environment, industry, strategy, structure and HRS options associated with international enterprise. It suggested that organizations in a multi-domestic industry should follow a multi-domestic strategy and adopt a multi-domestic/multi-national structure, and that similar principles should apply for international, global and transnational industries (Harzing and van Ruysseveldt, 1995). The HRS options associated with such a framework are perhaps best represented by using the integration/responsiveness matrix presented by Prahalad and Doz (1987), allied to the Perlmutter (1969) framework. Figure 8.3 shows the framework with the vertical axis representing the level of global integration or central co-ordination and the horizontal axis representing the level of national responsiveness or differentiation. Note that these two dimensions attempt to capture the importance of both cultural diversity and geographical dispersion previously cited as key dimensions of the complexity and diversity of international environments. As we have also stressed, our 'open' model of IHRS allows corporations to select a strategy and structure that does not 'fit' its industry exactly, perhaps in accordance with internal capabilities or as part of a move to transform its industry characteristics (Hamel and Prahalad, 1995).

As we have noted throughout this chapter, different emphases may be appropriate for different situations, businesses, functions and industries. For example, packaged goods may put a greater emphasis on responsiveness than chemicals, the sales function may focus more on responsiveness than R & D, product policy may be more conducive to global integration than promotion or distribution (Bartlett and Ghoshal, 1989). So we do not intend that figure 8.3 is used in a deterministic 'matching process' – it merely suggests ideal types. It does seem, however, as though certain organizational configurations have historically been associated with certain HRS orientations, mix of employees and continent of origin. Figure 8.3 also does not fully capture the position of the 'international' company, though this company has some degree of concern with both national responsiveness and global integration, its major emphasis being on world-wide learning and innovation, a dimension not captured in the model presented in figure 8.3.

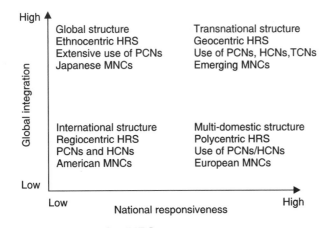

Figure 8.3 A framework for IHRS
Source: Adapted from Harzing and van Ruysseveldt, 1995, p. 47.

We now need to look briefly at four functional areas important in IHRS, namely:

- managing international diversity and multi-cultural teams;
- recruitment and selection;
- training and development;
- performance management.

Figure 8.4 shows how these four policy areas can be seen as part of an IHRS 'cycle', each contributing to more effective international perform-ance and learning at both the individual and organizational levels of ana-lysis. These areas are treated extensively in most textbooks of international HRM (e.g. Torrington, 1994; Hendry, 1993; Dowling et al., 1994). Since our focus is on the strategic aspects, our discussion will be briefer. We will begin with an area highlighted earlier in our discussion on the regional and national level of analysis, and also highlighted in table 8.4: the relevance of cultural diversity and the need to manage it successfully.

Managing international diversity

In a previous section we saw that international enterprise is characterized by geographic dispersion, greater complexity and cultural diversity. Much attention has been given to the need for MNCs to be 'locally responsive', but the issue of cultural diversity goes much wider than this.

The workforce of all organizations is growing even more culturally diverse. In many countries extensive migration has meant that workforces

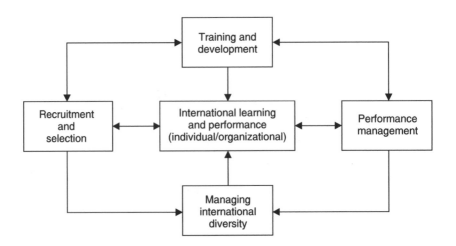

Figure 8.4 The international HRS cycle

often consist of people from a variety of ethnic, racial and cultural backgrounds. Internationalization has stimulated the exchange and transfer of human resources across borders and across continents. Managing this multi-cultural workforce poses a number of new challenges for HRS. Many organizations have sought to incorporate cultural diversity into their products and services in order to meet diverse customer needs and to recruit, retain and motivate a culturally diverse workforce.

A particular focus of interest in this area has been to develop multi-cultural teams which can use their diversity as a resource so as to achieve synergy (seen as a characteristic of the transnational/global organization in table 8.4). For example, some European-based multi-nationals like Exxon have begun to introduce diversity training as part of their attempts to manage international diversity, as box 8.9 shows.

Box 8.9 Diversity Training at Exxon Chemicals, Europe

Exxon Chemicals, part of the Exxon Corporation, has 'valuing diversity' in terms of culture and nationality as one of its core values. Given the changing demographics of its workforce and its belief that enhancing the effectiveness of diverse teams could be a source of competitive advantage, it conducted a pan-European employee attitude survey to serve as the basis for action. Employees felt that Exxon was mono-cultural, stressed conformity, tended to label and stereotype on the basis of gender and nationality, was male dominated, and US-dominated. These characteristics were felt to limit the job satisfaction and contribution of women and minority nationalities in particular, resulting in problems of communication and demotivation. Recommendations emerging included strengthening minority recruitment and career goals, removing artificial barriers and introducing more flexible contracts and conditions. Existing training was reviewed to reflect diversity issues, and experiential, outdoor development focused on awareness training for top management ('Quest') and middle managers ('Choices'). A multi-national group with multi-lingual faculty worked on team-building and outdoor-development activities focused on such issues as leadership, diversity, teamwork and partnership. A personal action plan and a team project based on course members and 'back home' teams followed this programme. (Source: Phillips, 1992.)

The management of multicultural teams is likely to be of growing importance to international enterprises. These include not only teams that may be formed to work on specific projects like technology transfer, strategic alliances, joint ventures and headquarters–subsidiary relations or cross-unit integration, but also global cross-functional and task teams to work on issues of product development and service delivery. Indeed, some claim that 'the central operating mode for a *global* enterprise is the creation, organization and management of multicultural teams-groups that represent diversity in functional capabilities, experience levels and cultural backgrounds . . . effective, efficient multicultural teams are the key to future global competitiveness' (Rhinesmith, 1993, pp. 106–7).

Many organizations, especially *parochial* and *ethnocentric* ones, have attempted either to ignore or suppress the cultural differences presented by multi-cultural teams. It is true that, initially at least, such teams may present difficulties of communication, comfort and comprehension, perhaps leading to tension, conflict and confusion. However, if actively managed, cultural differences can be an asset and a resource, especially where the organization needs to devise new ideas, entertain new perspectives and expand on existing plans. Diversity in teams can lead to greater flexibility and openness and the avoidance of 'group think' (e.g. Janis, 1977) whereby homogenous, cohesive teams come to suppress new or challenging ideas through self-censorship or through self-appointed 'mindguards' labelling any challenge as disloyalty or treachery. If cultural differences are recognized, valued and used to the organization's advantage, then greater synergy can result. But for this is to be realized, team-members will need to display both cultural self-awareness and cross-cultural awareness, as we shall see in the next section.

Adler (1991) suggests that culturally diverse groups can perform either extremely well or extremely poorly. She also suggests that diversity may well be an asset in the creative, divergent-thinking phase of a task, but a source of friction and misunderstanding in the convergent-thinking, decision-making phases. It may, because of the potential for tension, misunderstanding and friction, be less of an asset in routine performance tasks (e.g. implementing strategy and evaluating options, as opposed to developing new products or services). If the potential synergies available from cultural diversity are to be realized, then members will need to be interculturally competent. They will need not only to understand their differences, but also continue to communicate effectively across these differences through empathy, negotiation and the ability to create a shared reality through collective participation, the open resolution of conflicts and the ability to use cultural differences as a resource. For instance, cultural diversity at all levels of an international organization

can lead to greater understanding of diverse markets and customer preferences, as well as greater understanding of employee and supplier
values, aspirations and preferences. It may also result in more culturally
aligned human resource practices especially in the areas of leadership
style, communications, training, appraisal and recruitment. This implies
that *intercultural competence* should be a selection criterion in the recruitment
and section policy area, which we explore next.

International recruitment and selection

In most accounts of IHRM, the issue of international recruitment and
selection is seen primarily as an issue of *expatriate* selection. However, internationalization affects many other types of role. Bartlett and Ghoshal
(1992), for example, identify four types of international manager, each of
which requires a different mix of competencies:

1 *Business managers* or product-division managers, 'strategists plus archi-
   tects plus co-ordinators'.
2 *Country managers*, 'sensors plus builders plus contributors', conveying to
   others the importance of collecting and evaluating information and
   responding to local sensitivities.
3 *Functional managers*, 'scanners plus cross-pollinators plus champions',
   extremely important for organizational learning in scanning globally for
   specialized information and promoting the transfer of best practice and
   information between different parts of the organization.
4 *Corporate managers*, 'leaders plus talent scouts plus developers', who play
   the initial role of co-ordinators and developers of new talent.

However, such a full range of roles applies only to the few fully developed
'transnationals', and only focuses on top managers. International responsibilities, skills and mind-sets need to be developed much deeper into the
organization and at other managerial levels.

This point can be illustrated by reference to table 8.4, which shows that
different international strategies require different kinds of manager and
different requirements for cultural sensitivity. In phase one the *domestic*
ethnocentric organization, little in the way of international experience or
orientation is valued. In the phase two *international* organization, cultural
diversity and an international orientation becomes very important for a
variety of functional managers – sales representatives, technical experts
and managing directors amongst others.

Box 8.10 Diversity in recruitment practice in L'Oréal

L'Oréal, having diversified into publishing and television, sees the need for a broadly educated management group with flexibility, technical expertise, and interpersonal skills. It has consciously sought to recruit from different disciplines and sources and to expand its recruitment base beyond France in order to reflect a wider mix of nationalities and cultures. The most important recruitment criterion is willingness to work in a team, with the recruitment decision made with participation from all levels of the organization. Personal skills and ability to live within the L'Oréal culture are emphasized; recruitment policies are not dictated from above or written down. Most cadres are recruited young, with experienced people only rarely brought in. (Source: Sadler, 1994.)

When organizations do attempt to recruit across borders, they may find that the selection systems they use are ineffective, as we discussed above. National differences within Europe, for example, may put barriers in the way of harmonizing recruitment practices and developing pan-European recruitment policies. British graduates may find it insulting to be told that they have been rejected by a French company over their handwriting. French graduates from prestigious *grandes écoles* may find it equally insulting to be put through a battery of psychometric tests and group exercises in an assessment centre ('Haven't I proved my intellectual ability already?'). An Italian graduate may find both practices equally bizarre ('Why don't they just look at my record and ask me about it at interview?').

If we move from graduate recruitment to the recruitment of more experienced managers, it appears shortages of such managers are hampering the globalization efforts of many British and Irish companies in particular (Scullion, 1992; 1994). The failure to recruit, retain and develop host country nationals (HCNs) already noted is of course one factor worsening such a situation. Such firms often appear to lack knowledge of local labour markets, show ignorance of the local education, training and qualifications system, ignore language and cultural problems, and attempt to export 'domestic' recruitment practices to foreign countries. One response to the shortage of international managers has been to use *external* recruitment more often to fill international management positions. Broadening recruitment activities to include a more internationally diverse pool in which to fish, especially in developing 'Euromanagers', is also, as we have seen, a step many firms have taken. However, restrictions on international mobility remain, and the pace of internationalization may outstrip the supply of appropriate international managers. One area is the *reward package* offered, an especially acute problem for British firms in particular. Another is the growing *resistance to international mobility* exhibited by many managers, stemming from a variety of sources. These include perceived political and security instability, a concern with the home economy in a recession and its impact on 're-entry', an unwillingness to disrupt children's education, a concern with 'quality of life' issues and dual-career family issues in particular and the increasing reluctance of partners to leave their own job or career. In the face of such recruitment difficulties, it seems bizarre of many European MNCs to rarely consider *women* for international positions (though American financial services companies in particular are increasingly using women in these roles). There is some concern that women may not be politically, socially or culturally acceptable in many countries where women in management in particular are a rarity. However, it seems that women expatriate managers in Japan, for example, are perceived and treated more like foreign expatriate managers than like Japanese women. MNCs operating in Japan may well find Japanese women a highly educated, but relatively under-employed, recruitment source who may well prefer to work in a European or North American environment than in the more restrictive, male-dominated environments of much of corporate Japan (Adler and Izraeli, 1994).

Many organizations have engaged in more international recruitment, selection, development and career-planning activities in the 1980s and 1990s (for example: Brewster, 1991; Scullion, 1992). Some have attempted to manage local skills and labour shortages, others have tried to meet the staffing needs of foreign subsidiaries or joint ventures. For others, it is important to ensure national representation in the host country for political or status reasons, whilst to control the activities of foreign subsidiaries is often cited as a major reason for using expatriates. More recently, companies have sought to use international assignments to develop high potential individuals by giving them experience of a 'bigger' job and/or giving them international experience, and to assess and test potential through such assignments. As table 8.4 shows, a further motive behind international assignments is to develop the organization by encouraging the learning and sharing of new perspectives and the fostering of organizational learning.

Traditionally, many multi-nationals as well as governments and aid agencies have used *career expatriates* to meet staffing needs, ensure national representation and exercise control. This is true of organizations displaying an ethnocentric orientation, i.e. one not trusting local expertise and wishing to retain control from the home country. However, such a strategy is now less common. Political problems, the resentments and frustrations of local employees, the need to be more locally responsive and the expense and decline in the numbers of such career expatriates for a variety of reasons, including dual-career family pressures, have all contributed to other strategies being adopted.

International training and development

As the above discussions and the review of multi-cultural team-building suggest, intercultural competence is often seen as a necessary attribute in developing an international manager or other employee. What might we mean by this term?

A review of Danish practice by Gertsen (1991) argues that what she calls 'inter-cultural competence' consists of three dimensions: not only 'affective competence', but also 'behaviour' (or communicative) competence (the ability to communicate effectively both verbally and non-verbally with HCNs) and 'cognitive competence'. By this she is referring to the ability of successful managers to be 'cognitively complex', not using crude stereotypes or narrow categorizations but dividing up the world in more subtle ways. This capacity seems to echo Ratiu's (1983) research on the ways in which successful international managers use tentative, provisional 'private stereotypes' rather than using the fixed, inflexible 'public stereotypes' typical of the less successful international managers.

The development of the global or transnational organization requires senior managers who are not only internationally mobile but who 'in their minds can also travel across boundaries by understanding the international implications of their work' (Barham and Antal, 1994). How can such competencies best be developed? Many more organizations now seek to use international assignments for individual and organizational development, often with the assistance of a centralized human resource function which can plan and track the career of staff on a global basis. For example, Unilever's top Special Committee tracks as many as two hundred managers moving through developmental assignments all over the world as an essential part of its succession planning procedures. However, not all companies may adopt this formal, centralized solution. Electrolux, for example, prefers more informal dialogues between managers and units. Grand Metropolitan's subsidiary company IDV has instituted a 'cadre' programme which sends young high-potential managers on international assignments where they can experience the full range of activities within a function, gain early experience of responsibility and prepare for senior positions in the home country (Barham and Oates, 1991). Other organizations have broadened their use of international assignments to include technical staff, senior managers and mid-career or 'plateaued' managers.

Some organizations, such as Shell, have sought to include specific inter-cultural training workshops for new graduates. Others, such as GE or Unilever, have sought to internationalize all courses. A common aim has been to include a mix of nationalities as trainers and participants. Training is often held in different countries alongside international action learning programmes to facilitate both formal and informal interaction. For example, Philips has developed a programme whereby teams of young, high-potential managers work in multi-national teams on real problems outside their area of expertise. Such programmes are integrated with the appraisal of performance and potential, and also make use of human resource data-banks for succession planning, allowing the board to co-ordinate, track and monitor international development (Van Houten, 1989).

A particular focus in this area has been the training and development of expatriates, especially in terms of pre-departure training. However, the strategic use of training and development is less common at other stages of the 'international career development cycle' (figure 8.5), which is surprising, since the culture shock of repatriation is often as great or greater than expatriation, since both the expatriate and the job to be filled (if there is one) will have changed, mentors and colleagues will have moved on, and strategic priorities will have shifted. Some Japanese companies seem to make more extensive use of training and development and in particular better use of repatriates, as box 8.11 shows.

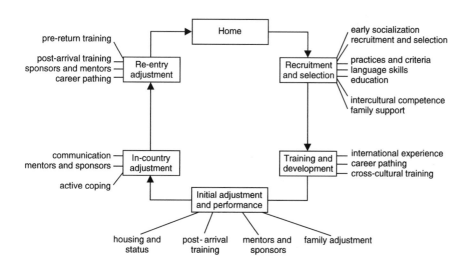

Figure 8.5   The international assignment career cycle
Source: Black et al., 1992; Adler, 1991.

Box 8.11   International HRD in NEC Japan

NEC is one of the world's largest manufacturing companies, with around 25,000 non-Japanese employees out of a total workforce of roughly 100,000. Its guiding vision is 'C and C', the convergence of computers and communications. It has evolved sophisticated HRD systems to 'internationalize' its personnel and, like many Japanese companies, sees continuous learning and education, especially English language learning and on-the-job training, as keys to its success. In 1974, it began an international education programme and began to abolish distinctions between domestic and international careers for promotion decisions, so as to encourage international assignments. Employees are rigorously appraised for their suitability for overseas assignments, so as to match people with opportunities. The overall aim is to develop 'global business people' who are technically competent, skilled at communication and adaptable. Ten development programmes target a wide range of staff, providing business, area and orientation knowledge and skills. Distance-learning is used for overseas staff, including HCNs, whilst returnee programmes are used to reintegrate repatriates. Repatriates' experiences are used to generate case studies for the cross-cultural training of future expatriates. Secondments overseas are used to internationalize perspectives and HCNs are trained both locally and in Japan. All HRD initiatives have a strategic focus, seeking to reach all employees, and overseas careers are positioned as attractive career moves. (Source: Holden, 1994.)

However, much 'training' is restricted to rather limited orientation sessions and cultural briefings, often imparted via lectures, handouts or case studies and supplemented by further reading. The analysis of intercultural competence (e.g. Gertsen, 1991) noted that cognitive awareness and understanding, whilst important, are not the only important attributes of a successful international manager or expatriate. Black et al. (1992) suggest that the more novel the international assignment is, the more extensive interaction with HCNs will be, and the more culturally distant or culturally tough the host country will be from the home country. For example, take an individualistic, low power distance, task-oriented, tolerant of uncertainty Anglo-Saxon manager taking up an assignment in a collectivist, high power distance, relationship-oriented, uncertainty-avoiding Asian culture, to use the Hofstede (1980) framework. In such cases training and development need to be 'rigorous' and extensive, although the authors do not fully define rigour, except in terms of social learning theory. However, it is likely to be the case that intercultural competence in general, and competence in dealing with novel jobs involving extensive interaction with 'culturally distant' locals in particular, is best developed through more 'experiential' methods. Figure 8.6 develops and applies the framework introduced in

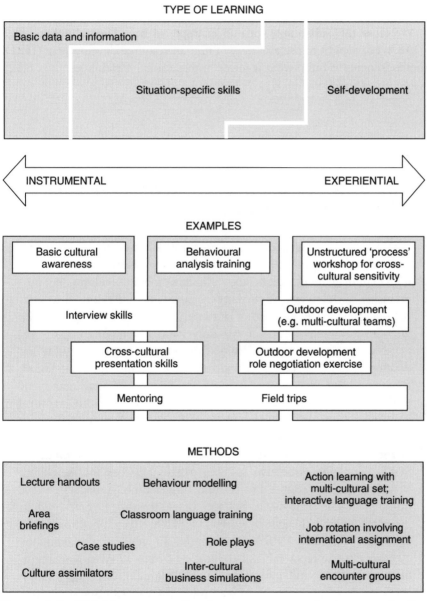

Figure 8.6 Matching cross-cultural programmes and processes to the qualities being developed in diversity training

chapter 7 ('Learning Organizations'). This suggests that self-development, especially awareness of oneself, one's culture and how it impacts on one's beliefs, values and behaviour – an essential part of intercultural competence – is best developed through more experiential methods such as cross-cultural sensitivity workshops, outdoor development with multi-cultural teams, field trips, action learning with a multi-cultural set, job rotation involving international assignments, and multi-cultural team-building exercises.

We close this subsection with an example of how Deutsche Aerospace (DASA) has sought to use a variety of human resource development (HRD) methodologies to build what it terms 'transnational capabilities' (box 8.12).

Box 8.12 Building transnational capabilities in Deutsche Aerospace AG.

DASA sees cross-cultural HRD as a 'core skill' and has developed a variety of development programmes, learning alliances and transnational management, team and organizational development programmes to develop it. A corporate unit of Daimler-Benz, with wide-ranging aerospace and other interests, it has participated in an intercultural research project with universities and other companies to develop expertise in intercultural training and consultancy. It has developed a range of initiatives, including an international board, recruiting and developing high-potential international managers, exchange programmes, conferences, meetings, specific cultural awareness and intercultural skills training, and preparation for international assignments. Specialist staff are educated at the European Consortium for Advanced Training in Aeronautics. Systems integrators receive training in the Network for Aerospace Management in Europe. Project and Programme Managers receive training at the European School for Aeronautical Sales, whilst potential general managers receive an MBA education through the European Executive MBA Consortium. In general, the company eschews generic cross-cultural training in favour of tying learning to business strategy and integrating it into planned, ongoing business activities using a cross-cultural team of facilitators working in a cross-cultural learning environment. (Source: Sattelberger, 1994.)

International performance management

Here, we extend the earlier analysis of performance management (see chapter 4) to consider some issues raised by the management of performance in an international context. We will focus on the *differences* and the *options* available in designing suitable international performance management strategies.

Performance appraisal

Successful performance in international assignments requires not only technical competence, but also (as we have seen) cross-cultural skills, interpersonal skills, empathy, sensitivity and adaptability. These factors might therefore be incorporated into performance evaluation systems at a strategic level. Differences in international roles demand different criteria and a different mix of head-office and subsidiary inputs. Operational criteria are likely to be of particular relevance to technical experts, strategic criteria to senior managers and subsidiary chief executives. Such criteria are likely to include adherence to *long-term* plans and goals, recognizing the complexity and flexibility involved in these areas. The overall performance of the subsidiary and the evaluations of (for example) the regional general manager (e.g. Europe, Asia-Pacific) may be used to help ensure comparability and relative objectivity in promotion or transfer decisions.

However, appraisal in such contexts is affected by a number of factors, including separation by time and distance, differing levels of market maturity, problems in collecting comparable, relevant statistics, environmental volatility and the desired mix between global and unit performance (Dowling et al., 1994). In addition, expatriate performance is clearly affected by the national environment and its potential for facilitating successful performance. Jobs which demand a considerable degree of interaction with HCNs, perhaps particularly with government officials, are likely to be more dependent on social, interpersonal and cultural skills than more technical jobs. Jobs which differ in content and novelty from jobs previously held are also likely to be more demanding.

The framework for IHRS, shown in figure 8.3, can help to devise policy options in this particular area because the international enterprise's *general approach* will also affect who sets what performance standards for whom. For example, *ethnocentric* enterprises are likely to use PCN and HQ standards, whilst *polycentric* enterprises are more likely to use local and HCN standards. As the business matures and changes its focus (e.g. from technology transfer to global performance), the priority and weighting given to various criteria are also likely to change. The accounting and financial strategies adopted by the international enterprise will also affect the meaningfulness of using financial data as appraisal criteria.

Some MNCs such as ICI are beginning to incorporate environmental performance (in the 'green' sense) into their appraisal and reward systems, whilst some US MNCs in particular (e.g. Digital, Avon) incorporate the achievement of equal opportunity, diversity and positive action goals into managerial evaluations. Others use behaviour or process-oriented criteria (*how* things are done) instead of results-oriented criteria (*what* is achieved) or use them to complement such criteria (a hybrid or mixed approach). For example, concern over corrupt practices, perhaps embodied in specific legislation such as the US Foreign Corrupt Practices Act, may direct attention to the process used in obtaining results, not merely whether goals and targets are met. The issue of who conducts the appraisal and how much weight they carry – whether it be the subsidiary CEO, the immediate supervisor, the home country manager, the HRM function – is also managed differently by different companies (Dowling et al., 1994).

Other issues arise in appraisal, such as the cultural acceptability of appraisal itself in group oriented or collectivist countries like Japan, where *indirect* criticism and a focus on team or company performance seem to be emphasized. It is notable that many Japanese owned or influenced manufacturing plants pursuing quality enhancement strategies use more process, long-term and team-based criteria. Many western MNCs, attempting to introduce more team-based structures have also experimented with team appraisal and upward appraisal (where the boss's performance is appraised by direct reports). Such US inspired 360 degree feedback systems may not be acceptable in high 'power distance' cultures such as many Asian countries (or even France!). Some degree of cultural sensitivity will therefore be required, as well as consultation with HCNs about local suitability. Other organizations are attempting to use a flexible 'competency architecture' to co-ordinate recruitment, selection, assessment, appraisal, development and reward activities, and broadly defined behaviour criteria may help comparability and give managers a common performance language. One example is Pepsi-Cola International (PCI) (see box 8.13).

Box 8.13 Performance feedback in Pepsi-Cola International

PCI has devised a common appraisal system designed to enhance individual performance whilst achieving administrative consistency. Factors associated with high performance in diverse markets and nations were identified so as to generate a common performance vocabulary. The dimensions emerging were: handling business complexity, results orientation, leadership, executive excellence,

organizational savvy, composure under pressure, maturity, technical knowledge, positive people skills, effective communication and
impact. Each dimension might be interpreted flexibly in different
environments, but with the same overall goal of generating
results. A five-step feedback mechanism is used to drive high
performance and balance cultural diversity and global
co-ordination: Instant feedback, coaching, accountability-based
appraisals, development feedback, and human resource planning.
How instant feedback is given is of less importance than *that* it is
given; successful delivery requires cross-cultural adjustment.
(Source: Schuler et al., 1993.)

Managing rewards

Reward management in an international context requires that organizations are familiar with a range of issues not normally considered in a
domestic context. One set of issues concerns industrial or employee relations; others include foreign-country legal and employment practices, inflation, currency fluctuations, and the application of particular allowances in
particular countries. The reason for the importance of these issues is that
expatriates are usually costly employees – a main reason for US companies
in particular to reduce their number and rely increasingly on HCNs. As
with reward management generally, international reward management
needs to serve a variety of objectives. These include supporting overall
corporate strategy, contributing to cost-effectiveness, attracting, retaining
and motivating needed employees, facilitating employee transfers and
ensuring perceived equity among employees.

Clearly there may well be tensions and conflicts between these various
objectives. Using Perlmutter's (1969) framework, different policy options,
especially for PCNs, can be determined:

home-based policies linking base salaries to the salary structure of the
relevant home country: an ethnocentric strategy.
host-based policies linking salaries to that of the host country but with
significant international supplements (such as cost of living and
adjustments, housing, schooling and other allowances) related to home-
country salary structures: a polycentric strategy.
region-based policies to reward expatriates in their home regions (e.g.
Europe) at lower levels than in distance regions (e.g. the Gulf).

Companies typically differ in the kinds of reward systems they install, such
as the reward mix (cash versus non-cash elements) and the basis of reward
(seniority versus individual performance versus group or unit or company

performance). An obvious difference arises in relation to the 'company car' – much more common at all levels of management in Britain (usually exquisitely tied to hierarchical position!) than in most of mainland Europe or the United States. Box 8.14 shows some of the differences encountered in an Anglo-French joint venture, and some of the organizational responses.

> ## Box 8.14   Ferranti-Thomson Sonar Systems: IHRS in an Anglo-French joint venture
>
> In 1990, the large French-based multinational Thomson, the world's largest non-American electronics company, bought a 50 per cent stake in the sonar systems division of Ferranti Computer Systems Ltd., based in Stockport, UK. Initially, all employees were ex-Ferranti, and the strong Ferranti culture persisted. Cultural differences encountered were a greater French requirement for detailed, written information within a formal hierarchical framework, a greater French preference for unstructured agendas, and a French preference for making important decisions outside formal meetings. Despite the official company language, tuition is provided at Stockport and bilingual secretaries and other staff are now preferred. The prospect of international experience is seen as an important factor in recruitment, and awareness of the European and global picture has become more important. The Thomson international training programme of residentials, conventions and seminars is now available to Ferranti, though few personnel exchanges had occurred by 1994, partly due to the problems of security in the defence industry. Payment structures, pensions and salaries have continued to be determined locally. British managers had noticed that their French counterparts had fewer company cars, but generally higher salaries. (Source: Moran, 1994.)

In general, most analysts argue that a company's performance management strategy should be aligned with its overall corporate strategy. Companies stressing technology transfer and short-term assignments, for example (e.g. hi-tech companies) may wish to use reward systems to encourage easy expatriation and rapid reintegration to the domestic reward structure. Companies using longer-term assignments (e.g. banks) may wish to encourage inter-country mobility and teamworking, so may wish to discourage nationality discrimination and use some kind of 'international' reward structure. Finally, a company with an articulated global strategy and a desire to build up an international management team with a global orientation may place greater emphasis on international experience in appraisal, reward and career development, and use its reward structure to attract people oriented to such a career and to facilitate international transfers (Dowling et al., 1994).

Conclusions

The field of international HRS is relatively immature. Based on the little that has currently been written on the subject and drawing upon ideas and models from related fields, this chapter has identified some of the key human resource strategies and choices open to organizations who are attempting to bolster their international and global presence. Supplemented by observations of several case-study organizations, we have discovered a mixture of structural, cultural and HRD initiatives being used to heighten understanding of national diversity, to facilitate operating across international boundaries, to optimize the advantages of employing an increasingly multi-cultural workforce, and to create transitions into a more global marketplace. Much of the evidence is as yet normative and uncritical, but what there is suggests that some organizations are achieving success in these areas, although – as noted – the effort and investment to support international human resource strategic change is high and not without continuing instances of cultural insensitivity. The chapter also illustrates some important lessons concerning managing diversity: for example, intercultural experiential workshops and sensitivity training may prove particularly powerful means of creating positive working relationships and customer perceptions.

Inevitably, many questions still remain. For instance, research on 'domestic diversity' demonstrates that valuing minorities helps them achieve better job satisfaction, job involvement, career achievement and lower turnover due to greater cultural value congruence. However, are such findings applicable to internationally diverse organizations? The evidence in this chapter suggests this is the case for attracting and retaining staff, enhancing creativity and problem-solving, and responding to customer needs through developing new products and services, but more work is needed to test such linkages between the HR approaches and performance outcomes.

Key points

- *The literature on International HRM is often restricted to the analysis of expatriate recruitment and selection, training and development, and appraisal and reward. Occasionally, it also embraces the HRM problems of strategic alliances and of the very largest MNCs. Our focus is broader and more analytic, including analyses at the global, sectoral, regional, national and enterprise levels, and embracing structural and cultural issues.*

- *At the global level, earlier debates over modernization and dependency seem to be reflected in the current analysis of globalization and the new international division of labour. Whilst acknowledging the increasing integration and interconnectedness of organizational life resulting from globalization, we reject the more sweeping claims of both camps (the increasing standardization and convergence of markets, the impact of the restless, placeless MNC searching for lowest-cost labour) in favour of a more nuanced, regionally-focused approach more attentive to diversity, both of national and regional cultures and business systems, and of corporate strategies.*

- *At the industry level, we pay particular attention to the textile/clothing, electronics and software industries, and especially to the Asia-Pacific region. The emergence of a regional division of labour is noted.*

- *At the regional/national level, we pay particular attention to diversity in terms of business systems, and national and regional cultures, noting the implications of geographic dispersion and cultural diversity for IHRS. Of particular interest for European HRM is the issue of whether, given the diversity of European practice in the areas of recruitment and selection, training and development, employee relations, equal opportunity, flexible working practices and performance management reviewed in the chapter, a 'European model' of HRM, distinct from the Japanese and American models, can be said to be emerging, or whether there is a fundamental split between an 'Anglo-Saxon' model closer to the USA and a 'Rhenish' model centred on Germany and closer to Japan. The implications of such models for IHRS are discussed.*

- *At the enterprise level, we discuss the differences between international and domestic HRM in terms of scope, country and employee national origin and develop a framework for IHRS based on cultural diversity, managerial orientations and product life cycle. This framework is then applied to four functional HRM areas (managing international diversity, recruitment and selection, training and development and performance management) in the light of the diversity and complexity of the environment faced by international enterprises, the structure and configuration adopted, and the need to react both to local responsiveness and to global integration pressures.*

Discussion Questions

1 How different is IHRS from domestic HRS?
2 How relevant are the modernization, dependency, globalization and new international division of labour theses to an understanding of IHRS?
3 What is the significance for IHRS of national and cultural differences and differences in national business systems?
4 Is a 'European' model of HRM emerging, and what is its significance for HR practice at the enterprise level?
5 How are international managers best recruited, selected, trained, developed, appraised and rewarded?
6 How useful are stage or phase models to IHRS?

REFERENCES

Acuff, F. (1984) *International and Domestic Human Resources Functions: Innovations In International Compensation.* New York, Organization Resources Counsellors, pp. 3–5.

Adler, N. J. (1991) *International Dimensions of Organizational Behavior.* Boston, Kent Publishers.

Adler, N. J. and Ghader, F. (1989) International business research for the twenty-first century: Canada's new research agenda. In Rogosan, A. (ed.), *Research in Global Strategic Management: A Canadian Perspective.* Greenwich: JAI Press.

Adler, N. J. and Izraeli, O. N. (eds) (1994) *Competitive Frontiers: Women Managers in a Global Economy.* Oxford, Blackwell.

Albert, M. (1991) *Capitalisme contre capitalisme.* Paris, Seuil.

Amin, S. (1974) *Accumulation on a World Scale.* New York, Monthly Review Press.

Amin, S. (1976) *Uneven Development.* Brighton, Harvester Press.

Barham, K. and Antal, A. B. (1994) Competencies for the pan-European manager. In Kirkbride, P. S. (ed.), *Human Resource Management in Europe: Perspectives for the 1990s.* London, Routledge.

Barham, K. and Devine, M. (1990) *The Quest for the International Manager: A Survey of Global Human Resource Strategies.* London, Ashridge Management Guide/ Economist Intelligence Unit.

Barham, K. and Oates, D. (1991) *Developing the International Manager.* London, Business Books.

Bartlett, C. A. and Ghoshal, S. (1989) *Managing Across Borders.* London, Hutchinson.

Bartlett, C. A. and Ghoshal, S. (1990) Matrix management: Not a structure, a frame of mind. *Harvard Business Review,* July–Aug. 1990, pp. 138–45.

Barlett, C. A. and Ghoshal, S. (1992) What is a global manager?. *Harvard Business Review,* 70, no. 5, pp. 124–32.

Bassett, P. (1995) No escape from the works councils. *The Times*, 2 March, p. 32.

Begin, J. P. (1992) Comparative human resource management (HRM): A systems perspective. *International Journal of Human Resource Management*, 3, no. 3, pp. 379–95.

Berger, M. and Watts, P. (1992) Management development in Europe. *Journal of European Industrial Training*. 16, no. 6, pp. 13–21. Reprinted in Mabey, C. and Iles, P. A. (eds) (1994) *Managing Learning*. Milton Keynes, Open University.

Black, J. S., Gregerson, H. B. and Mendenhall, M. (1992) *Global Assignment*. San Francisco, Jossey Bass.

Black, J. and Mendenhall, M. (1990) Cross-cultural training effectiveness: A review and theoretical framework for future research. *Academy of Management Review*, 15, no. 1, pp. 113–36.

Bloom, H., Calori, R. and de Woot, P. (1994) *Euromanagement: A New Style for the Global Market*. ERT/ESC, Lyon, Kogan-Page.

Braham, P. (1992) The division of labour and occupational change. In Allen, J., Braham, P. and Lewis, P., *Political and Economic Forms of Modernity*. Cambridge, Polity Press.

Brewster, C. (1991) *The Management of Expatriates*. London, Kogan Page.

Brewster, C. (1993) Developing a 'European' model of human resource management. *International Journal of Human Resource Management*, 4, no. 4, Dec., pp. 765–84.

Brewster, C. (1993) European human resource management: Reflection of, or challenge to, the American concept. In Kirkbridge, P. (ed.), *Human Resource Management in the New Europe of the 1990s*. London, Routledge.

Brewster, C. (1994) The integration of human resource management and corporate strategy. In Brewster, C. and Hegewisch, A., *Policy and Practice in European Human Resource Management*. London, Routledge.

Brewster, C. (1995) HRM: The European dimension. In Storey, J. (ed.), *Human Resource Management: A Critical Text*. London, Routledge, pp. 309–32.

Brewster, C., Hegewisch, A. and Mayne, L. (1994) Trends in European HRM: Signs of convergence. In Kirkbridge, P. (ed.), *Human Resource Management in Europe*. London, Routledge.

Brewster, C. and Larsen, H. H. (1993) Human resource management in Europe: Evidence from ten countries. *International Journal of Human Resource Management*, 3, no. 3, pp. 409–34.

Clark, T. (1993) Selection methods used by executive search consultancies in four European countries: A survey and critique. *International Journal of Selection and Assessment*, 1, no. 1, pp. 41–9.

Cox, T. (1993) *Cultural Diversity in Organisations: Theory, Research and Practice*. San Francisco, Berrett Kochler.

Crabb, S. (1995) Jobs for all in the global market? *People Management*, 26 Jan., pp. 22–7.

Derr, C. B. and Oddou, G. (1991) Are US multinationals adequately preparing future American leaders for global competition? *International Journal of Human Resource Management*, 2, no. 2, pp. 227–44.

Derr, C. B. and Oddou, G. (1993) Internationalizing managers: Speeding up the process. *Europe Management Journal*, 11, no. 4, pp. 435–42.

Dicken, P. (1992) *Global Shift: The Internationalisation of Economic Activity*. London, Chapman.

Dicken, P. (1995) Geography in The Open University. *B890 International Enterprise*, MBA, The Open University, Milton Keynes.

Dowling, P. J., Schuler, R. S. and Welch, D. (1994) *International Dimensions of Human Resource Management*. Belmont, Calif., Wadsworth.

Doz, Y. L. and Prahalad, C. K. (1986) Controlled variety: A challenge for human resource management in the MNC. *Human Resource Management*, 25, 1, pp. 55–71.

Doz, Y. L. and Prahalad, C. K. (1991) Managing DMNCs: A search for a new paradigm. *Strategic Management Journal*, 12, pp. 145–64.

Dunlop, J. (1958) *Industrial Relations Systems*. Carbondale: Southern Illinois University Press.

Elson, D. (1994) Capitalism and development in global perspective. In Sklair, L. (ed.), *Capitalism and Development*. London, Routledge, pp. 165–88.

Evans, P. and Doz, Y. (1989) The dualistic organization. In Evans, P., Doz, Y. and Laurent, A. (eds), *Human Resource Management in International Firms*. London, Macmillan.

Evans, P., Doz, Y. and Laurent, A. (eds) (1989), *Human Resource Management in International Firms*. London, Macmillan.

Evans, P., Lank, E. and Farquhar, A. (1989) Managing human resources in the international firm: Lessons from practice. In Evans, P., Doz, Y. and Laurent, A. (eds), *Human Resource Management in International Firms: Change, Globalization, Innovation*. London, Macmillan, pp. 113–43.

Evans, P. and Lorange, P. (1989) The two logics behind human resource management. In Evans, P., Doz, Y. and Laurent, A. S. (eds), *Human Resource Management in International Firms: Change, Globalization, Innovation*. London, Macmillan, pp. 144–61.

Frank, A. G. (1966) The development of underdevelopment. *Monthly Review*, 18, no. 4, pp. 23–8.

Frank, A. G. (1971) *Capitalism and Underdevelopment in Latin America*. London, Penguin.

Franke, R. H., Mufstede, G. and Bond, M. (1991) Cultural roots of economic performance: A research note. *Strategic Management Journal*, 12, summer, pp. 165–74.

Fröbel, F., Heinrichs, J. and Kreye, O. (1980) *The New International Division of Labour*. Cambridge, Cambridge University Press.

Gertsen, M. C. (1991) Intercultural competence and expatriates. *International Journal of Human Resource Management*, 1, no. 3, pp. 341–62.

Giddens, A. (1990) *The Consequences of Modernity*. Cambridge, Polity Press.

Giddens, A. (ed.) (1992) *Human Societies: A Reader*. Cambridge, Polity Press.

Goodstein, L. and Burke, W. (1991) Creating successful organization change. In Mabey, C. and Mayon-White, W. (eds), *Managing Change*. London, Paul Chapman Publishing.

Grahl, J. and Teague, P. (1991) European level collective bargaining: A new phase? *Relations Industrielles*, 46, no. 1.

Guest, D. (1989) Human resource management: Its implications for industrial relations and trade unions. In Storey, J. (ed.), *New Perspectives on Human Resource Management*. London, Routledge.

Guest, D. (1990) Human resource management and the American dream. *Journal of Management Studies*, 27, no. 4, pp. 377–97.

Guest, D. (1992) Right enough to be dangerously wrong: An analysis of the 'In Search of Excellence' phenomenon. In Salaman, G. et al. (eds), *Human Resource Strategies*. London, Sage.

Hailey, J. (1994) Localising the multinational: Limitations and problems. In Segal-Horn, S. (ed.), *The Challenge of International Business*. London, Kogan-Page, pp. 110–26.

Hall, S. (1992) The question of cultural identity. In Hall, S., Held, D. and McGrew, A. (eds), *Modernity and its Future*. Cambridge, Open University/Polity Press, pp. 273–326.

Hall, S., Held, D. and McGrew, A. (eds.) (1992) *Modernity and its Future*. Cambridge, Polity Press.

Hambrick, D. C., Davison, S. C., Snell, S. A. and Snow, C. C. (1993) When groups consist of multiple nationalities: Toward a new understanding of the implications. Paper presented to the Academy of Management Conference, Houston, Tex., Aug.

Hamel, G. (1991) Competition for competence and inter-partner learning within international strategic alliances. *Strategic Management Journal*, 12, pp. 83–103.

Hamel, G. and Prahalad, K. K. (1989) Strategic intent. *Harvard Business Review*, 89, no. 3, pp. 63–76.

Hamel, G. and Prahalad, C. K. (1994) *Competing for the Future: Breakthrough Strategies for Seizing Control of your Industry and Creating the Markets of Tomorrow*. Boston, Harvard Business School Press.

Harzing, A. W. and van Ruysseveldt (1995) *International Human Resource Management*. University Heerlen, Sage.

Hawthorne, P., Tung, S. and Kirk, P. (1990) Creating the culturally sensitive Hong Kong bank manager. *EMD Journal*, 4, pp. 14–17.

Henderson, J. (1994) Electronics industries and the developing world: Uneven contribution and uncertain prospects. In Sklair, L. (ed.), *Capitalism and Development*. London, Routledge, pp. 252–88.

Hendry, C. (1993) *Human Resource Strategies for International Growth*. London, Routledge.

Hilb, M. (1992) The challenge of management development in Western Europe in the 1990s. *International Journal of Human Resource Management*, 3, no. 3, pp. 575–84.

Hofstede, G. (1980) *Culture's Consequences: International Differences in Work-related Values*. Beverly Hills, Sage (reprinted 1984).

Hofstede, G. (1983) The cultural relativity of organizational practices and theories. *Journal of International Business Studies*, 14, no. 1, pp. 75–89.

Hofstede, G. (1991) *Cultures and Organizations: Softwares of the Mind*. London, McGraw-Hill.

Hofstede, G. (1993) Cultural constraints in management theories. *Academy of Management Executive*, 7, no. 1, pp. 81–91.

Hofstede, G. and Bond, M. (1988) The Confucius connection: From cultural roots to economic growth. *Organizational Dynamics*, 16, no. 4, pp. 4–21.

Holden, L. (1991) European trends in training and development. *International Journal of Human Resource Management*, 2, no. 2, pp. 113–31.

Holden, L. (1994) NEC: International HRM with vision. In Torrington, D. (ed.), *International Human Resource Management: Think Globally, Act Locally*. Hemel Hempstead, Prentice-Hall, pp. 122–42.

Hoogvelt, A. (1987) The new international division of labour. In Bush, R., Johnston, G. and Contes, D. (eds), *The World Order: Socialist Perspectives*. Cambridge, Polity Press.

Humes, S. (1993) *Managing the Multinational: Confronting the Global–Local Dilemma*, Hemel Hempstead: Prentice Hall.

Iles, P. A. (1994) Diversity in selection and assessment practice: Context, culture and congruence. *International Journal of Selection and Assessment*, 2, no. 2, pp. 111–14.

Iles, P. A. and Mabey, C. (1994) Developing global capabilities through management and organization development strategies. Paper presented to British Academy of Management Conference, Lancaster University, Sept. 1994.

Jackson, S. E. and associates (1992) *Diversity in the Workplace: Human Resource Initiatives*. New York, Guildford Press.

Jacques, E. (1990) In praise of hierarchy. *Harvard Business Review*, Jan.–Feb., 90, no. 1, pp. 127–33.

Jameson, F. (1991) *Postmodernism, or, the Cultural Logic of Late Capitalism*. London, Verso Press.

Janis, I. (1977) *Groupthink*. Boston, Houghton Mifflin.

Keenan, A. (1992) Graduate recruitment and the Single European Market. *European Management Journal*, 10, no. 4, pp. 485–93.

Kidger, P. (1991) The emergence of international human resource management. *International Journal of Human Resource Management*, 2, no. 2, pp. 149–63.

Kobrin, S. J. (1988) Expatriate reduction and strategic control in American multinational corporations. *Human Resource Management*, 27, no. 1, pp. 63–75.

Laclau, E. (1971) Feudalism and capitalism in Latin America. *New Left Review*, 64 (May–June), pp. 19–38.

Lane, C. (1989) *Management and Labour in Europe*. Aldershot, Edward Elgar.

Lane, C. (1992) European business systems: Britain and Germany compared. In Whitley, R. (ed.), *European Business Systems: Firms and Markets in their National Contexts*. London, Sage.

Lauermann, E. (1992) British Airways in Europe: A human resources viewpoint of development. *European Management Journal*, 10, no. 1, pp. 85–6.

Laurent, A. (1983) The cultural diversity of Western conceptions of management. *International Studies of Management and Organization*, 13, no. 102, pp. 5–96.

Laurent, A. (1986) The cross-cultural puzzle of international human resource management. *Human Resource Management*, 25, no. 1, pp. 91–102.

Lawrence, P. (1993) Management development in Europe: A study in cultural contrast. *Human Resource Management Journal*, 3, no. 1, pp. 11–23.

Lessem, R. and Neubauer, F. (1994) *European Management Systems: Towards Unity out of Cultural Diversity*. London, McGraw-Hill.

Levitt, T. (1983) The globalization of markets. *Harvard Business Review*, May–June, pp. 92–102.

McGrew, A. (1992) A global society? In Hall, S., Held, D. and McGrew, A. (eds), *Modernity and its Future*. Cambridge, Polity Press.

Marshall, C. (1993) Interview in *Business Life*, Sept. (supplement on Global Partners).

Maruca, R. F. (1994) The right way to go global: An interview with Whirlpool CEO, David Whitwam. *Harvard Business Review*, March–April, pp. 135–45.

Massey, D. (1991) A global sense of place. *Marxism Today*, June.

Mendenhall, M., Dunbar, E. and Oddou, G. (1987) Expatriate selection, training and career-pathing: A review and critique. *Human Resource Management*, 26, no. 3, pp. 331–45.

Moran A. P. (1994) Ferranti-Thomson Sonar Systems: An Anglo-French venture in hi-tech collaboration. In Torrington, D. (ed.), *International Human Resource Management: Think Globally, Act Locally*. New York, Prentice-Hall, pp. 111–21.

Morgan, P. U. (1986) International human resource management: Fact or fiction. *Personnel Administrator*, 21, no. 9, pp. 43–7.

Morrison, A. J., Ricks, P. A. and Roth, K. (1991) Globalization versus regionalization: Which way for the multinational? *Organizational Dynamics*, winter, pp. 17–29.

Moss-Kanter, R. (1991) Transcending business boundaries: 12,000 world managers view change. *Harvard Business Review*, 69, no. 3, pp. 151–64.

Neale, R. and Mindel, R. (1992) Rigging up multicultural teamworking. *Personnel Management*, Jan., pp. 36–9.

Nyfield, G. (1993) Assessing the international manager. Paper presented to Personnel Decisions, University of Minnesota International Assessment Conference, Minneapolis, Oct.

Odenwald, S. (1993) *Global Training*. Homewood, Ill., ASTD/Irwin.

Ohmae, K. (1985) *Triad Power: The Coming Shape of Global Competition*. New York, Free Press.

Ohmae, K. (1989) The global logic of strategic alliances. *Harvard Business Review*, March–April, pp. 143–55.

Ohmae, K. (1990) *The Borderless World*. New York, Harper Business.

Pearson, R. (1988) Female workers in the first and third worlds: The 'Greening' of women's labour. In Pahl, R. E. (ed.), *On Work: Historical, Comparative and Theoretical Approaches*. Oxford: Blackwell.

Pearson, R. (1994) Gender relations, capitalism and third world industrialization. In Sklair, L. (ed.), *Capitalism and Development*. London, Routledge, pp. 339–58.

Pedler, M., Burgoyne, M. and Boydell, T. (1991) *Towards the Learning Company*. London, Van Nostrand.

Perlmutter, H. V. (1969) The tortuous evolution of the multinational corporation. *Columbia Journal of World Business*, Jan.–Feb., 4, no. 1, pp. 9–18.

Phillips, N. (1992) *Managing International Teams*. London, *Financial Times*, Pitman.

Porter, M. E. (1980) *Competitive Strategy*. New York, Free Press.

Porter, M. E. (1990) *The Competitive Advantage of Nations*. London, Macmillan.

Prahalad, C. K. and Doz, Y. (1987) *The Multinational Mission*. New York, Free Press.

Pucik, V. (1994) Introduction; Globalization and human resource management. In Pucik, V., Tichy, N. and Barnett, C. K. (eds), *Globalizing Management*. New York, John Wiley, pp. 1–11 and 61–84.

Ratiu, I. (1983) Thinking internationally: A comparison of how international executives learn. *International Studies of Management and Organization*, 13, nos. 1–2, pp. 139–50.

Regan, M. (1994) Developing the middle manager for globalization: The case of Electrolux. In Kirkbridge, P. (ed.), *Human Resource Management in Europe*. London, Routledge.

Reich, R. (1991) Who is them? *Harvard Business Review*, 68, no. 1, pp. 53–64.

Reilly, R. and Campbell, B. (1990) quoted in Barnett, C. (1990) The Michigan global agenda: Research and teaching in the 1990s. *Human Resource Management*, 29, no. 1, pp. 5–26.

Rhinesmith, S. M. (1993) *A Manager's Guide to Globalisation*. Homewood, Ill., ASTD Irwin.

Robertson, I. T. and Makin, P. J. (1986) Management selection in Britain: A survey and critique. *Journal of Occupational Psychology*, 59, no. 1, pp. 45–57.

Ronen, S. (1989) Training the international assignee. In Goldstein, I. (ed.), *Training and Development*. San Francisco, Jossey-Bass.

Sadler, P. (1994) *Managing Talent*. London, *Financial Times*, Pitman.

Sattelberger, T. (1994) Building transnational capabilities. Presentation to American Society for Training and Development International Conference, Anaheim, Calif., May.

Schneider, S. (1988) National vs corporate culture: Implications for Human Resource Management. *Human Resource Management*, 27, no. 2, pp. 231–46.

Schuler, R. S., Dowling, P. J. and de Cieri, H. (1993) An integrative framework of strategic international human resource management. *International Journal of Human Resource Management*, 4, no. 4, Dec., pp. 717–64.

Scullion, H. (1992) Attracting management globetrotters. *Personnel Management*, Jan., pp. 28–34.

Scullion, H. (1994) Strategic recruitment and development of the 'international manager': Some European considerations. *Human Resource Management Journal*, 3, no. 1, pp. 57–69.

Shackleton, V. and Newell, S. (1991) Management selection: A comparative survey of methods used in top British and French companies. *Journal of Occupational Psychology*, 64, no. 1, pp. 23–36.

Shackleton, V. and Newell, S. (1994) European Management selection methods: A comparison and critique into market. *International Journal of Selectional Assessment*, 2, no. 2, pp. 91–102.

Shackleton, V. and Newell, S. (eds) (1994) Special issue of *International Journal of Selection and Assessment*, 2, no. 2.

Sklair, L. (1991) *Sociology of the Global system*. London, Harvester; and Baltimore, Johns Hopkins University Press.

Sklair, L. (ed.) (1994) *Capitalism and Development*. London, Routledge.

Sklair, L. (1994) Capitalism and development in global perspective. In Sklair (1994).

Snow, C., Snell, C., Canney Dansan, S. and Hanbruck, D. (1993) Developing transnational teams in global network organizations. Executive Summary, ICEDR report, Nov.

Sparrow, P. and Bognanno, M. (1993) Competency requirement forecasting: Issues for international selection and assessment. *International Journal of Selection and Assessment*, 1, no. 1, pp. 50–8.

Sparrow, P. and Hiltrop, J. M. (1994) *European Human Resource Management in Transition*. Hemel Hempstead, Prentice Hall.

Sparrow, P., Schuler, R. S. and Jackson, S. E. (1994) Convergence or divergence: Human resource practices and policies for competitive advantage worldwide. *International Journal of Human Resource Management*, 5, no. 2.

Teague, P. (1993) Towards social Europe? Industrial relations after 1992. *International Journal of Human Resource Management*, 4, no. 2, May, pp. 349–76.

Teague, P. (1994) EC social policy and European Human Resource Management. In Brewster, C. and Hegewisch, A. (eds), *Policy and Practice in European Human Resource Management*. London, Routledge.

Thurley, K. (1990) Towards a European approach to personnel management. *Personnel Management*, 22, no. 9, pp. 54–7.

Thurley, K. and Wirdenius, H. (1989) *Towards European Management*. London, Pitman.

Thurley, K. and Wirdenius, H. (1991) Will management become 'European'? Strategic choices for organizations. *European Management Journal*, 9, no. 2, pp. 127–34.

Thurow, L. (1992) *Head to Head*. London, Nicholas Brealey.

Tichy, N. M. (1994) Global development. In Pucik, V., Tichy, N. M. and Barrett, C. K. (eds), *Globalizing Management*. New York, John Wiley, pp. 206–26.

Tichy, N. M., Brimm, N. I., Charan, R. and Takeuchi, H. (1994) Leadership development as a lever for global transformation. In Pucik, V., Tichy, N. M., and Barnett, C. K. (eds), *Globalizing Management*. New York: John Wiley, pp. 47–60.

Torrington, D. (1994) *International Human Resource Management; Think Globally, Act Locally*. Hemel Hempstead, Prentice Hall.

Towers Perrin (1992) *Priorities for Gaining Competitive Advantage: A Worldwide Human Resource Study*. London, Towers Perrin.

Trompenaars, F. (1993) *Riding the Waves of Culture*. London, Nicholas Brealey.

Tung, R. L. (1982) Selection and training procedures of UK, European and Japanese multinationals. *California Management Review*, 25, no. 1, pp. 57–71.

Tung, R. L. (1988) Career issues in international assignments. *Academy of Management Executive*, 11, no. 3, pp. 241–8.

Van Duk, J. (1990) Transnational management in an evolving European context. *European Management Journal*, 8, Dec., pp. 474–9.

Van Houten, G. (1989) The implications of globalism: New management realities at Philips. In Evans, P. et al. (eds), *Human Resource Management in International Firms: Change, Globalization, Innovation*. London, Macmillan, pp. 101–12.

Vernon, R. G. (1966) International investment and international training in the product cycle. *Quarterly Journal of Economics*, May, pp. 190–207.

Walker, B. (1991) Valuing differences. In Smith, M. A. and Johnson, S. J. (eds), *Valuing Differences in the Workplace*. University of Minnesota/American Society for Training and Development. Reprinted in Mabey, C. and Iles, P. A. (1994) *Managing Learning*, Open University, Milton Keynes.

Wallerstein, I. (1974) *The Capitalist World Economy*. Cambridge, Cambridge University Press.

Wallerstein, I. (1984) *The Politics of World Economy: The States, The Movements and the Civilisations*. Cambridge, Cambridge University Press.

Warren, B. (1980) *Imperialism: Pioneer of Capitalism*. London, Verso.

Watson, W., Kumor, K. and Michaelson, L. (1993) Cultural diversity's impact on interaction process and performance: Comparing homogenous and diverse task groups. *Academy of Management Journal*, 36, pp. 590–602.

Whitley, R. D. (ed.) (1992) *European Business Systems: Firms and Markets in their National Contexts*. London, Sage.

Wierdsma, M. F. and Bantel, K. A. (1992) Top management team demographies and corporate strategic change. *Academy of Management Journal*, 35, no. 1, pp. 91–121.

Willis, S. and Barham, K. (1994) Being an international manager. *European Management Journal*, 12, no. 1, pp. 49–58.

9 HRS – Some Key Difficulties

Learning Objectives

- *be aware of the complexities and contradictions that underlie much HRS prescription and thinking.*
- *be aware of the limitations – and strengths – of HRS recommendations and thinking.*
- *recognize the key ways in which the core concept of HRS – various types of integration – may be problematic in reality.*
- *understand how the processes of decision-making underlying the design and implementation of HRS projects may be less rational and successful in reality than they appear in many HRS writings.*
- *be alert to the possibility that HRS is as important as a powerful management rhetoric as it is as a guide to practice.*
- *be able to come to your own, informed and balanced assessment of the value of HRS.*

Introduction

The appealing and attractive simplicity of the HRS approach to organizational change, which focuses and legitimates change programmes, masks a number of problems and complexities.

For example:

1   Do the current nostrums of HRS actually work? And indeed, what does 'work' mean in this connection? If and when HRS does support the achievement of organizational strategies is this because HRS is essentially an approach to the effective management of cost cutting and decline, or because it is an approach which enables the full development and harnessing of the human potential of the organization? Are HRS organizations lean and fit, or anorexic and debilitated?

2   Do the classic prescriptions of HRS models (see chapter 7) fit together and support each other? Let's take a common HR strategy – reducing inventories and installing 'just-in-time methods'. While these initiatives are intended to achieve reduced lead times and improved quality, they could also lead to a clash of priorities. If assemblies were not available in time (and many assemblies come from outside), time would be wasted. In order to ensure that a buffer of stocks existed, inventories might creep up again. So quality and reduced lead times could clash.

Or we might consider new styles of management with enhanced local autonomy which could clash with the need to achieve policies that operate throughout the company as a whole or across the site. New styles of management could clash with less delegated structures that survive with the result that practices and culture could differ. Local arrangements between management and staff could be vulnerable to company-wide developments stemming from financial exigencies, or difficulties with trade unions at national level.

3 Is HRS more significant as an ideology of change than as a set of change principles? Is HRS essentially a way of legitimating and disguising programmes of change, which, by using the language of strategic focus, of restructuring, staff commitment, empowerment and 'ownership', and by claiming the value of 'human resources' all in the name of environmentally driven change, actually serve to justify and direct programmes of change whose main purpose is increased control over labour while reducing its cost? Is HRS 'a meta-narrative: an image intensifier which presents us with a set of idealised action imperatives'? (Keenoy and Anthony, 1992, p. 240)

One element of this is the insistence in much HRS language, of the key role of 'the market'. Not only is internal change now explained by and attributed to developments in the market (and the role of HRS is to ensure that internal organizational developments 'fit' the strategy that this market requires), but within the organization itself, relations between organizational sub-units are reconceptualized and structured as if they too were market relations. The market rules. Chandler's (1977) dictum that the development of the large-scale modern enterprise depended upon the development of an administrative component which was able to co-ordinate internally the activities of numerous business units and functions – the 'visible hand of management' replacing the invisible hand of market forces – is now entirely upturned. But for how long? (See Hales, 1994.)

Is HRS concerned with substantial restructuring of the *status quo* to ensure that the organization allows and enables employees to commit themselves, to contribute to the establishment of organizational goals, to contribute to decision-making; or is it essentially concerned with repackaging, the manipulation of the symbols of consensus and commitment?

4 Similarly, and even more seriously, the ways in which business units' business 'performance' is measured may have serious negative consequences for the organization overall. Treating each section of an organization 'as if' it were a separate business may be short-sighted and counterproductive. Defining internal organizational relationships as if they were market transactions may generate internal divisions and short-sightedness, and discourage investment and co-operation.

For example, the use of financial contribution may well encourage unhelpful behaviours – principally, by discouraging long-term planning, by encouraging conservatism and risk avoidance. Use of financial returns to control profit centres may also encourage managers to achieve results by lack of investment and reduced technological innovation. It has been argued with respect to the decline of manufacturing in the USA that: 'Analysts of manufacturing decline almost unanimously pinpoint the rise to prominence of [financial] calculations as the immediate cause of the sharp decline in expenditure on new process technologies, facilities and research and development' (Higgins and Clegg, 1988, p. 80). Solutions to one problem can breed new problems; solutions that may seem right because they resonate with current values and convictions may still have limitations, and all suggested solutions need thorough and sceptical assessment.

This chapter will address these issues: *can* HRS 'work'? *Does* it work? Is it based on naïve and simplistic notions of what organizations are, and how they work? The main focus of the chapter, which will be pursued through the constituent sections, is the nature and feasibility of HRS-style integration. Integration is the core idea behind HRS. If there are difficulties, even contradictions, surrounding the possibility and practicality of achieving integration, these will severely limit the possibility of HRS itself.

The chapter begins with some remarks about the concept integration and its centrality within HRS, and notes some difficulties surrounding the concept. Then the role of politics and conflict in HRS – and in achieving integration – are discussed. The subsequent sections deal with: some limitations to the assumptions of managerial decision-making within models of HRS, which seriously undermine the possibility of achieving integration; the role of political factors in HRS decision-making; the observation that HRS often assumes an excessively rational view of decision-making; and questions as to whether HRS is actually happening in practice. Finally, we offer an overview of some radical critiques of the gap between rhetoric and reality in HRS.

Integration in HRS

The fundamental feature of HRS, as a set of ideas, is that the design of human resource structures and systems, and indeed 'human resources' themselves – employees – are integrated into, and support, the organization's strategy. Everything must support competitive advantage or other strategy-based measures of organizational performance.

> The main dimensions of HRM [involve] the goal of integration (i.e. if human resources can be integrated into strategic plans, if human resource policies cohere, if line managers have internalised the importance of human resources and this is reflected in their behaviour and if employees identify

with the company, then the company's strategic plans are likely to be more successfully implemented), the goal of employee commitment, the goal of flexibility/adaptability (i.e. organic structures, functional flexibility), the goal of quality (i.e. quality of staff, performance, standards and public image).

(Guest, 1987, quoted in Legge, 1988, p. 24)

Integration is the core idea of HRS. It takes four main forms within HRS writing.

1   Reference to the definitions of HRS in chapter 1 shows the centrality of this core idea: that HRS is integrated with, or supports, or fits, the organization's strategy. For example, Beer and Spector (1985) remark: 'a business enterprise has an external strategy . . . It also needs an internal strategy: a strategy for how its internal resources are to be developed, deployed, motivated and controlled . . . the external and internal strategies must be linked' (pp. 5–6, quoted in Beaumont, 1993, p. 23). Or, businesses 'need to establish a close, two-way relationship between business strategy . . . and HRM planning' (Beaumont, 1993, p. 4). This 'fit' between business and HR strategies is *vertical* integration.

2   Also critical is the idea that the various elements of HRS (personnel systems of various sorts, structures, cultures) 'fit' together; that is, that they mutually support each other to generate appropriate behaviour. 'The very idea of an internal (HRS) strategy implies that there is consistency among all the specific tactics or activities that affect human resources. Hence the need for practices to be guided by conscious policy choices to increase the likelihood that practices will reinforce each other and will be consistent over time' (Beer and Spector, 1985, p. 6). This is *horizontal* integration.

3   But there is more to the centrality of integration than these two forms, fundamental though they are. There is also a third type of integration – that of the individual into the organization – 'high levels of individual employee and work group participation in task-related decisions' (Beaumont, 1993, p. 27). As Sewell and Wilkinson (1993) have noted, one of the central claims of the HRS literature is that it is possible – and profitable – with HRS practices, to close the gap between the interests of the organization and the employees. This is done through each and every dimension of the HRS approach: selection, induction, training, reward, job design, culture change, etc. Furthermore, the achievement of this 'fit' of employee and organization ensures the valuable pay-off of a congruence between organizational and employee values and goals.

4   A fourth and final key form of integration is the integration of the various departments, disciplines and groups within the organization into one unified system. 'The American models of HRM . . . assume a unitary

frame of reference: that "there is a long-run coincidence of interests between all the various stakeholders of the organization"' (Beer and Spector, 1985, p. 283; Legge, 1988, p. 25). This is either seriously naïve or deliberately manipulative. While HRS proponents may *wish* that organizations were consensual and unitarist, and even try to achieve this through policies which reduce the power of unions and engage with employees on an individualistic basis, many of the policies which stem from HRS initiatives display very clearly the potential opposition of interests between senior managers and other employees. This is discussed in chapter 5.

In the rest of this chapter some problems surrounding the achievement of integration are considered.

Integration: The Impossible Dream?

An important starting point for an analysis is the distinction noted earlier in chapter 1 between two types of definition of HRS – one 'open', stressing the need for integration of HRS and strategy but not specifying the nature of any particular HRS programme, the other, 'closed', specifying that a particular combination of HRS elements: flexibility, participation, commitment, etc. (We shall leave, for the moment, the question of whether these goals are actually characteristic of contemporary HRS-type organizational change – see below.)

These two views offer incompatible conceptions of integration. HRS cannot simultaneously be open to choice but also insist on just one set of answers in every case.

There is an obvious inconsistency arising from two opposed notions of integration: 'at the surface level the value of integration that it [HRS] promotes contains a logical contradiction, given the dual usage of the concept of "integration". "Integration" appears to have two meanings: integration or "fit" with business strategy and the integration or complementarity and consistency of "mutuality" employment policies aimed at generating employee commitment, flexibility, quality, and the like. . . . The problem is that while "fit" with strategy would argue a contingent design of HRM policy, internal consistency (at least within the "soft" human resource values associated with "mutuality") would argue an absolutist approach to the design of employment policy' (Legge, 1988, p. 29).

Thus it is impossible to argue on the one hand, that different types of business or organizational strategies should be (or are) associated with ('integrated with', or 'fit') different patterns of HRS activity, and also to argue that whatever the business strategy, one set of HRS policies will *always* be best. It must be at least possible that some business policies, for example a low-cost strategy, will dictate HRS policies that 'fail to emphasise commitment, flexibility and quality' (Legge, 1988, p. 30).

A similar distinction has been stressed by Bartlett and Ghoshal (1992) and Galbraith and Kazajian (1986), who identify a basic problem in the HRS literature – the idea that as organizations sought and achieved structural 'fit' they actually disabled themselves for the complex and inherently changeable environment. In other words, any HRS 'fit' would soon become inappropriate – as new circumstances require new strategies and new arrangements. The solution to this takes the form of an emphasis on the flexible, or learning organization – a type (or state) of organization where the key characteristic is not the fit of HRS and strategy, but the capacity of the senior managers to scan the environment, analyse data, think creatively, design and implement change – and then change it all before it is complete. This approach to HRS stresses 'organisational and strategic flexibility rather than structural fit. To build the most viable strategic process, [these] models shift towards considering the management process that will make strategic decisions work. . . . The role of management must therefore be to create an internally consistent and balanced design' (Paauwe and Dewe, 1995, p. 57).

This point is developed in chapter 7 on the learning organization. It is supported by, for example, the research of Pettigrew and Whipp. However, this focus on the role of management in designing and implementing constant processes of change is not specific to this approach: management plays a similar, if less emphasized role in all HRS models. For this reason, the nature of and limitations to management thinking and decision-making constitute a major theme of this chapter. For it is clearly important that we consider what factors might facilitate or obstruct the capacity of managements to behave in the way required.

Another major flaw in the HRS emphasis on integration focuses on another contradiction that surrounds the 'soft human resource values associated with "mutuality": commitment, flexibility and quality'. Storey has usefully noted that the term HRS allows two interpretations, and that in fact both readings are apparent within the logics of HRS programmes of change. On the one hand HRS can be viewed in terms of the priority and value of treating 'human resources' as valued assets to be developed, cherished, whose commitment, creativity are crucial. This is the 'soft' sense of HRS: 'which treats labour as a valued asset rather than a variable cost and which accordingly counsels investment in the labour resource through training and development and through measures designed to attract and retain a committed workforce' (Storey, 1989, p. 8). And there is no question that within the rhetoric of HRS there is enormous focus on the nature and importance of an approach to staff and to organization which 'empowers', liberates, develops the individual employee in order to develop and engage employees' commitment and creativity and energy.

On the other hand, HRS also allows an alternative view which stresses the importance of identifying and implementing whatever HR strategy is appropriate for the chosen business strategy (which might well include 'downsizing' or cost cutting). More than this, the very notion of HRS allows for, even encourages, a conception of organization and of employees as resources to be exploited like any other organizational resource. Some have seen this as a 'tension' – between HRS as a way of ensuring and justifying (or even disguising) attempts to maximize economic returns from 'human resources' by the efficient and consistent use of these resources – reducing numbers, cutting costs; and HRS as a way of releasing resourcefulness.

What is at issue here is not simply managerial honesty or opportunism, important as these are. There are obviously going to be occasions when overt espousal of the 'soft' sense of HRS is hypocritical or dishonest – mere PR. But there may also be cases when the commitment is real, but is overtaken by events. One writer, after reviewing the literature on the take-up of HRS in practice, reports: 'The picture these studies present reveals a contradiction between the rhetoric of the "soft" HRM model and the realities of the "hard" model, and of tensions between the values embedded in the "soft" model' (Legge, 1994, p. 45). She goes on to note that quality management techniques, with their emphasis on surveillance, could undermine employee commitment; the introduction of teams may not aid empowerment, but management control through peer pressure (p. 46).

There is also a basic ambiguity in the notion of allying HRS initiatives to market and strategic exigencies, when these may require measures which do not comply with, may even directly oppose, the welfare-humanist principles of some common conceptions of HRS. In the 'open' view of HRS, strategy and the environment may require a highly instrumental approach to 'human resources'. This view 'emphasises the quantitative, calculative and business strategic aspects of managing the head counts resource in as "rational" a way as for any other economic factor. By contrast, the "soft" version traces its roots to the human-relations school; it emphasises communication, motivation and leadership' (Storey, 1989, p. 8). However, in practice, the 'hard' approach to HRS-type organizational changes is a very common one. In practice, whatever the good intentions of those who espouse or disseminate the 'soft, welfare-humanist' conception of HRS, they are likely to be overwhelmed by the exigencies of financial performance measures and requirements. For example, it is likely that as Miller (1986) and Legge (1988) have noted, there is no reason to believe or expect that senior managers will respond to external competitive pressures, or the dictates of corporate head-office expectations of sub-unit contribution, by measures designed to generate employee commitment rather than by cutting costs, reducing head count, and other measures which treat labour as a variable cost rather than as a resource to be cherished and developed.

Under these conditions of competitive pressure many organizations may find it hard to pursue in practice the goals of classic HRS: 'matching HRM policies to business strategy calls for minimising labour costs, rather than treating employees as a resource whose value may be enhanced, in terms of Guest's model, by increasing their commitment, functional flexibility and quality' (Legge, 1988, p. 32).

There are, as noted, two main conceptions of integration in the HRS literature: 'vertical' integration of HRS into the corporate strategy and 'horizontal' integration of the various aspects of HRS. Concerning the first, it has been noted that if an organization is made up of a number of diverse businesses, then logically, at least according to the 'open' conception of HRS, different businesses within a conglomerate might sensibly wish to pursue different HR strategies. However, while this may certainly affect the degree of corporate-wide HRS integration, arguably it would not affect the integrity of HRS integration at the business unit level. It has also been noted that some of the classic prescriptions of the HRS literature (closed model) might produce effects very different from those that are desired. For example, there may be a conflict between strong organizational cultures and employees' capacity to respond flexibly and quickly. Strong cultures can be conservative, limiting responses that fall outside of, or challenge, the shared core assumptions of the culture (Legge, 1988, p. 36).

On a more prescriptive level, it has also been noted by Lengnick-Hall and Lengnick-Hall (1988) that much HRS literature assumes a uni-directional model of vertical integration – the designing of human resource structures to fit strategies. They note: 'rarely are human resources seen as a strategic capacity from which competitive choices should be derived' (1988, p. 456). They argue for a multi-directional approach to both strategy and HR strategy – whereby both develop interactively: strategy should be developed in terms of HR capability, and HR strategies should be developed in terms of business strategies and their implementation requirements.

Overall, however, the main difficulties with 'vertical' integration arise from the possible *naïveté* of conceptions of strategy formulation which overestimate the clarity and rationality of this process (for if there is no coherent or unified strategy, then no HR strategy can be integrated with business strategy); and from the nature of assumptions about relations between groups within organizations and between individuals and organizations that are fundamental to the achievement of vertical integration. These issues will be considered below. We shall argue that the strength of HRS as a movement, and as a body of 'theory' and rhetoric, arises in part from its suppression of ugly and difficult organizational realities in the purveying of a rosy conception of possibilities which is problematic not simply because it is unrealistic, but precisely because it attempts to redefine reality whilst simultaneously denying and reproducing it.

There are also problems in achieving 'horizontal' integration. These difficulties arise with the 'closed' approach to HRS – i.e. that approach which advocates a precise 'package' of HRS measures. Simply, is it empirically likely that these measures are internally consistent? Keenoy has usefully mapped some major inconsistencies. He has noted that the individualistic focus of many of the 'packaged' prescriptions of the closed model to encourage staff are internally incompatible. They simultaneously encourage staff 'to compete with each other through the use of individual contracts, performance related pay and individual performance appraisal and to take individual responsibility for budgets, while at the same time being expected to become team players through quality circles, team briefing and communication cascades. The imperatives of marginal cost must co-exist with the insistence on quality and customer care. Managers are exhorted to minimise unit and variable costs while at the same time being expected to develop and create loyalty and commitment from their valued human resources' (Keenoy, 1990, p. 379).

Organizational Decision-making and Organizational Politics

The HRS literature ignores two key issues. These are: 'the inherent features of the employment relationship which structures employer–employee relations and . . . [the] impact of organisational structures on behaviour. Both require reference to power-relations and the institutionalisation of socio-economic conflict. . . . differential competing interests are an inevitable feature of any social institution characterised by the division of labour and a hierarchy of authority' (Keenoy, 1990, pp. 380–1).

This issue is highly relevant to an analysis of integration within HRS. Chapter 1 argued the importance and value of an HRS approach: matching human resources and behaviour to organizational objectives. That chapter also identified a number of developments which *could be* evidence of HRS. But if the achievement of integration is central to the achievement of HRS, and if the processes of matching HRS to business strategy (and furthermore, the processes of decision-making that lead to the development of organizational strategy) are themselves influenced by politically inspired decision-making, and by systemic and inherent irrationality, then integration is unlikely, and so is the achievement of HRS.

Furthermore, if the integration of employees into the organization (commitment, involvement) is central to HRS, and if the co-operation and agreement of different groups (consensus) is also critical, then the existence of political or sectarian issues will gravely threaten these forms of individual and group integration.

Does the HRS literature assume a naïve, apolitical, consensual conception of organizational decision-making and of organizational life? It is important to distinguish between the realities of organizational conflicts and politics and the neat, consensual but unrealistic models purveyed in the literature. If this book is to be of practical value we must engage with the real, if muddled, world of actuality. Lorenz's accounts of the process of decision-making at BP (see chapter 1) hint strongly at such messy realities: struggles between 'regional barons' or between them and the centre; individuals opposing or embracing change for reasons connected with their vigorous, but possibly sectarian view of what was valuable and necessary to BP (and conceivably to them); individuals, we are told, behaved in ways which were aggressive to others such that a senior manager had to 'read the riot act'.

In reality organizational decision-making is characterized by conflict, opposition, careerism, negotiation, compromise. But usually these do not appear in blatant form: they are likely to appear in the form of arguments that deny their very existence and which lay claim to consensual, harmonious values and principles – for example, about what is best for the company – and in claims about key organizational values. But underlying the rhetoric are struggles for resources, jobs and power; struggles about what the organization should be like and about individuals' roles in it. These political, sectional elements have an impact on decision-making.

Thus we find a crucial, if paradoxical, aspect of HRS decision-making and implementation. Organization structures within which HRS decisions are made, which include decisions about future structures and systems, are themselves structures of power and interests. This will affect the nature of decisions about HRS. In other words, existing power structures will affect future (or planned) HRS structures.

This has been neatly expressed by Poole:

> Human resource policy choices are not taken in a vacuum. On the contrary, they depend on the strategic managerial group being sufficiently powerful to ensure that particular policy choices are taken along lines which are consistent with an overarching strategy, and are also reflected in actual practices within the firm itself. Power is also relevant for understanding the relationship between human resource policy choices and situational factors (the power of the various stakeholders being important here). Furthermore, it is especially consequential so far as the implementation of human resource

policies and choices within the actual company is concerned. Thus, in organizations with plural power centres, implementation is problematic, frequently circumscribed and often subject to detailed negotiation with diverse interest groups. Moreover, to the extent that one of the key elements of human resource management (i.e. employee influence) is developed to its full potential, the more likely it is that diverse values will impact upon (and ultimately shape) human resource policy choices themselves.

(Poole, 1990, p. 8)

This political dimension of HRS has a number of implications.

First, the HRS approach itself frequently carries fundamental assumptions about the possibility and role of conflict and politics within organizations. These assumptions concern the possibility of achieving the 'integration' of the organization – the achievement of consensus, co-operation and commitment among a divided and differentiated workforce.

Secondly, it means that the implementation of human resource strategies and choices is dependent on the successful overwhelming of political fissures and forces. Those responsible for HRS must consider carefully – strategically – how they are going to design, prepare, launch and implement their chosen package in order to build support, undermine resistance, persuade, and win over the resisters and the sceptical. The implementation of any HRS programme must take cognizance of internal political structures and interests, and must recognize that any organizational change affects established interests and values (see chapter 2); but, more fundamentally, the processes of strategic design themselves will be significantly influenced by the existence of political structures and interests within the organization. Existing HR structures will influence the ways in which senior managers design new HR strategies.

HRS and the unitarist conception of organizational structure and functioning

Organizations are structures of power: they only exist and survive because their members can be relied on to comply with orders. They are also arenas of conflict: 'there are recurrent struggles over the question of whose purposes, or interests, work [production] is to serve – the owner, the manager, the producer, the consumer? . . . there are [also] struggles over how work is to be organised – autocratically, bureaucratically, democratically?' (Alvesson and Willmott, 1992, p. 6). Organizations are also systems for the highly unequal distribution of rewards and resources (including, of course, power itself, but also many others: pay, security, fringe benefits, job discretion, etc.). 'Organisations and environments should be conceived as arenas. Within these arenas differentially valued resources are competed for by differentially powerful agencies, exercising differential control of these resources, in complex games with indeterminate rules which each agency seeks to exploit to its advantage' (Clegg, 1990, p. 85). It is because of variations in the distribution of power and resources that the possibility of conflict arises along lines of perceived differences of interest and control (typically on lines of subordination/super-ordination). One major line of horizontal fracture (but by no means the only one) along which such conflict commonly occurs is between shop-floor staff and management, and it is this sort of conflict which is expressed by, and underlies, structures of employee representation and organization: trade unions.

There are constant struggles within organizations over issues such as the direction in which the organization should move, the interests it should serve, how work is to be organized, which group or section should suffer, or benefit. These struggles do not necessarily take explicit or obvious form. Nor need they be institutionalized in organized, or organizational, form. But they exist. Analyses of organization – or suggestions for organizational structuring – that ignore such realities are misleading. Organizations systematically produce conflict (and of course co-operation) as a result of their hierarchical and inegalitarian structures. However, this always remains a possibility, never a certainty. Precisely how, in any particular organization at any historical moment, conflict arises (and it may or may not be expressed in an organized form) remains an empirical matter. Nevertheless, this model of organizational structures and processes has significant implications for a consideration of HRS.

An implication of the political nature of organizations is that HRS and the changes associated with it represents the views and goals of a particular political faction – senior management. That is, that HRS is a form of senior management ideology. The view within HRS thinking and writing of the organization as an organic unity; the insistence that there exist no serious conflicts of interest within the organization (unless externally introduced) – these ideas and values represent the view of one organizational group, and are of benefit to it. HRS values are also highly individualistic – focusing on the importance of employees relating to the organization as individuals rather than members of representative bodies or groups. Much HRS writing clearly adopts such views: that the interests of all members of staff are the same, that the commitment of all staff to organizational (i.e. senior managers') objectives can be achieved; that systematic conflict can be removed, and is a thing of the past; that unions are unnecessary as a form of collective negotiation and can now be replaced by considerations of career and rewards on an individual basis; that all members of the organization are equally powerful. Hales, for example, in an analysis of internal marketing as an approach to HRS, notes the limitations of the view that employees and employers meet equally in the market for labour. Within the organization, employees are not consumers of the employer, and lack the sorts of power normally associated with consumers. 'Therefore when the interests of employees and employers diverge . . . it is not the interests of employees which . . . generally prevail' (Hales, 1994, p. 62).

Not only are these ideas in themselves clearly sectional – i.e. they represent the views and the interests of senior managers; they are also unrealistic. The reality of many HRS changes, and the ways they are imposed on employees, may be surrounded by the rhetoric of HRS but the nature of the impact of these changes on employees will indicate to them the extent to which senior management is really prepared to commit itself.

Most HRS programmes involve management efforts to generate commitment, change culture and attitudes. Such efforts not only assume a unitarist view of the organization (see below), they also try to gain something for nothing: 'management appears to be adopting the vocabulary of commitment without recognising the two-way nature of commitment, and the need to support their call for higher employee commitment through improved job security, high quality terms and conditions of service, and prospects for career advancement' (Blyton and Morris, 1993, p. 128).

HRS has been seen to assume an anti-union stance, and Guest has noted that HRS can threaten unions in three ways: by bypassing them and developing new channels of communication; by implementing management practices which are less likely to require traditional defensive reactions; and, in non-union organizations, by HR policies which are designed to ensure that there is no – or little – need for unions (Guest, 1989, p. 44). See chapter 5, above.

However, although the rhetoric of HRS is either opposed to unions, or assumes (and tries to achieve) their irrelevance, the practice of HRS as noted above, is unlikely to encourage employees to agree with such view of unions. On the other hand, recent events have so weakened the power of unions that employees may well feel that they are unlikely to be able to support resistance to management programmes of change. In fact, as Storey and Sisson have noted, the evidence suggests that HRS programmes of change – or at least some of the elements of HRS change, and the individualistic values associated with them – seem to coexist with more collectivist values and practices: trade union recognition and union relations and bargaining coexist with HRS changes in work design and communication and pay systems (Storey and Sisson, 1993, p. 22)

It remains to be seen how far these assumptions of consensus can survive the pressures of competitive pressure, technological innovation, variations in demand, and other environmental threats. A major source of internal organizational conflict is experiences which are interpreted by staff as indicating a conflict of interest between management and staff, head office and the operating company, etc. Employees' conceptions of the degree of coincidence of their interests and the organization's, their preparedness to commit themselves to the organization, are developed primarily not by the rhetoric of management, not by slogans and logos, but by experience: how they are treated.

The focus on 'culture change', for example, is often an attempt to impose a consensual, unitarist conception of the organization on all employees, and thus to gain their commitment. This is explored in chapter 6.

The HRS focus on seeking to achieve a homogeneous or consensual organizational culture and values is unrealistic in the face of a view of organizations as pluralist entities. As was noted in chapter 6, is it appropriate for the values of the managed to be decided by people other than themselves?

The application of HRS principles, with their assumptions about what relations between categories of staff ought to be like, may well be threatened by the imperatives of external factors which then produce responses which threaten consensus. This point clearly relates to the distinction between 'hard' and 'soft' definitions of HRS noted earlier.

Also, many HRS developments are either intended to have an impact on existing industrial relations systems and patterns, or to take advantage of a period when trade unions are relatively weakened by numerous factors (labour markets, legislation, management initiatives, IT, a particular ideological climate). A concern to redefine industrial relations is particularly apparent in the US HRS literature. The possibility of either intention being achieved is significantly affected by specific historical conditions. By the time this book has been in use for a few years we may well witness changes in the role and power of organized labour. It is therefore unwise to assume that HRS requires or can rely on a consensual organization. It is safer to assume that it needs to achieve a greater degree of compliance and consensus, whilst recognizing that this achievement will always be vulnerable.

Organizational Divisions, Politics and Decision-making

The achievement of integration – and thus of HRS – assumes that managers are able to identify what needs to be done, and are able and willing to implement HR strategies that 'fit' with each other and with the business strategy (and indeed that they are able to develop appropriate business strategies). But are these assumptions about the processes of organizational decision-making realistic and sound? In this section we consider the nature of organizational decision-making, and the role of structured differences of power and interest in influencing management thinking on HRS issues. Organizations do not simply *respond* to clear, unambiguous environmental demands; strategies do not simply emerge; HR strategies have to be actively developed. In all aspects of HRS thinking, and in the achievement of all types of HRS integration, managerial intervention, thinking and rationality are critical.

For example, how the 'environment' is defined and understood and scanned, and how 'responses' are framed and selected are themselves consequences of prior conceptions, ideological convictions, and other limiting assumptions and values. If senior managers and others are now keenly aware that their existing systems, structures, cultures, job-design principles, etc., are inefficient, and even counter-productive, how then were these elements ever introduced and allowed to continue? How was it possible for organizations ostensibly concerned with efficiency to accept systems which were not efficient? Did those who designed or reproduced or worked within bureaucracies appreciate their negative effects? How can we be confident that the decision-making currently in progress towards achieving new systems and structures is any better than the thinking which for years tolerated, even supported, the now much-maligned old methods?

There are a number of possible answers: that managers knew and were indifferent because in some ways the systems suited them, or their departments; that managers were unaware of the deficiencies of earlier forms of organization; that these structures fitted earlier, less competitive times, or that it was too difficult and dangerous to confront such issues.

These possibilities raise the prospect that organizations can be poor at identifying and correcting errors and incompetence when these are produced by structures and systems in which managers responsible for decisions and for evaluating decisions have positions, status, and some considerable investment. Also, if managers may be unaware of the unhelpful implications of the structures and systems in which they work, then ignorance or lack of awareness, not collusion and defensiveness, are significant.

All these possibilities demonstrate the complex relationship between structures and ways of thinking, seeing and deciding. Existing organizational structures both reflect ways of thinking (e.g. bureaucracy and the typical bureaucrat, the isolation of the holders of centralized power) and generate ways of thinking – which will have major implications on the view and possibility of fundamental organizational change. (See the discussion of BP's Chairman in chapter 1.) This raises questions about the complexity of designing structures and systems to produce desired behaviours, and the possibility that such structures, however well designed, might produce unforeseen and undesirable consequences (as the earlier forms, such as bureaucracy, clearly did).

These tendencies are illustrated in the case of ELB, in box 9.1.

Box 9.1 Organizations and environments

ELB is a British company that started life in the early 1900s and early in this century developed its markets in Europe, Africa and the Near East. The 1950s and 1960s saw a huge growth in demand for its products. By mid-1970s it had enjoyed 15 years of uninterrupted growth in sales and profits, had a turnover of over £100m and employed 9,000 people. However, building new factories and developing new products drained considerable amounts of money from the business. Profits peaked in 1977 and in the following two years the company drew heavily on reserves. By 1980 the dividend had to be cut.

The problem was that the company could not learn. It was a victim of its own history of success – the immediate experience of 15 years of uninterrupted growth. Senior managers simply projected the company's past into the future. 'Not to believe in the company's traditional product strengths would have been to deny their experience. Success brings with it a confidence and trust in one's own judgement: a belief perhaps that success flows from one's own wisdom and experience rather than fortuitous changes in the market.' The world brand strategy that emerged explicitly in 1976 (and which contributed significantly to the company's misfortunes) was an affirmation of senior managers' experiences. The company's strengths became weakness: success recipes were applied when they were inappropriate; senior managers deluded themselves into feeling invulnerable; their confidence being based on the company's historic near monopoly in the UK; and their market strength allowed them to export their inefficiencies. Internally the company's performance made senior managers capable of resisting any calls for change. To question policies was seen as questioning the basis of managers' authority. The hierarchy obstructed key processes of environmental scanning, signal recognition, data analysis, identification and assessment of possible new strategies and goals. Hierarchy created silence and deference. Individuals began to believe that the 'system' was beyond change and control; that power was elsewhere; that they individually were not responsible for what many of them could see happening around them. It was always 'them'.

The causes of the company's demise lie not in the changing environment, but in senior managers' unwillingness to scan and understand this environment – in using lessons from the past to study the future. Their strategic myopia stemmed from their corporate isolation. 'It is to the routine effects of the working of the hierarchy one must look to explain how senior managers came to pursue a strategy that went so clearly against the experience of so many junior managers and which carefully excluded consideration of important changes emerging in ELB's market.' (Roberts, 1992, pp. 18–38.)

There is an important issue here: the relationship between organizational structures and organizational decision-making. Differentiated and hierarchic structures are inherently likely to produce decision-making of a politicized (incremental and negotiated) sort, and to encourage defensive, politicized behaviour. Alvesson and Willmott remark: 'managers are obliged to justify their existence by demonstrating their value to the organization as a whole. Yet the demonstration of their value . . . barely conceals their sectional interests . . . in developing or sustaining arrangements that, they anticipate, will secure their position of . . . comparative privilege.' (Alvesson and Willmott, 1992, p. 18).

Organizations have by implication in HRS texts been defined as neutral, rational structures, which can with sufficient knowledge be adjusted by their employees to enable them to do their work more effectively. Not only does this raise questions about what efficient structures would look like, it also raises questions about the relationship between structures and managers' actions and decisions, including their decisions about the structures themselves. The worrying possibility exists that by virtue of their location within organizational structures, managers' decision-making might be affected in ways that reduce its rationality.

This possibility follows from two important aspects of organizational structuring: the vertical differentiation of power and privilege and horizontal differentiation into functional or discipline (or regional) departments and specialisms. The first can generate deference, careerism, arrogance and defensiveness; and the exercise of power and control, particularly when associated with differences in levels of reward, opportunity and privilege (as between management and shop floor) can generate sharply opposed conceptions of interest and hence conflict. Thus the vertical differentiation of organization can result in the development of a variety of conceptions of the nature and objectives of the organization, and to antagonistic internal organizational relations.

The horizontal differentiation into specialist areas and departments breeds politics: differences of perspective, priority and interest. Within structures of power individuals and groups seek to defend and advance their sectional interest by proclaiming that it is in the interests of the organization as a whole and its 'real' objectives. As individual members of organizations compete for scarce rewards, so departments, sections and specialists tend to defend their share of the budget, their resources, their conception of the organization's purpose, and their particular skill and information. One consequence of the inevitable sectionalism of large organizations is that information becomes a useful resource for protecting or advancing sectional interests: and change becomes potentially threatening to some (but attractive to others).

Each service, each division, indeed every sub-unit, becomes a guardian of its own mission, standards and skills; lines of organization become lines of loyalty and secrecy. In industry, the personnel department defends its control of selection and training; accounting, its standards of reporting; production, its schedules of output; sales, its interest in product design and customer service – each restricting information that might advance the competing interests of the others (Wilensky, 1967, p. 48).

One obvious example of this is when, as increasingly happens, organizations are structured in terms of separate profit centres. This has advantages in terms of encouraging on-the-spot responsiveness and commercial and business responsibility; but it clearly also discourages relations and co-operation across the various business units.

When these phenomena result in conflict, manipulation of information, sectionalism, occasional distrust and politicking, the outcome may be a pattern of decision-making which varies considerably from the super-rationalist conception of decision-making that is frequently assumed by much HRS literature – that is, a pattern of decision-making which is emergent as well as deliberate (Mintzberg and Waters, 1989, p. 4), incremental, politicized, negotiated to some degree. Thus decision-making and the strategies it produces can best be seen as the product of the political, cognitive and cultural fabric of the organization. The expectation would be that strategic decisions could be explained better in terms of political processes than analytical procedures; that cognitive maps of managers are better explanations of their perceptions of the environment and their strategic responses than are analysed position statements and evaluative techniques; and that the legitimacy of these cognitive maps is likely to be reinforced through the myths and rituals of the organization (Johnson, 1989, p. 43).

Argyris has analysed the ways in which senior managers' thinking and analysis may be clouded by their location, specifically that it may suffer from defensive routines whereby issues of apparent threat or embarrassment are avoided, and so learning and analysis are also avoided. The way in which managers work together when developing organizational or human resource strategies – in teams – may encourage this tendency towards politically inspired decision-making, which seeks to support analyses and decisions that are felt to be acceptable to existing power groups and to existing cultural and group norms. A moment when this is particularly apparent is in organizational discussions of poor decisions. Such post-mortems offer a marvellous opportunity for organizational and individual learning, but all too often what takes place is a process which Argyris (1986) describes as 'skilled incompetence': being skilled at ensuring the analysis does not embarrass, threaten or even surprise one's colleagues. These techniques, which Argyris labels defensive routines, are organizational and collective.

Newcomers to the organization learn how to avoid learning and how to avoid threatening others. Furthermore, the very fact that this process is occurring becomes in itself something that cannot be talked about without risking disapproval or charges of betrayal.

Argyris describes this common situation as follows. Within an organization it has become clear that a major decision was a mistake. However, 'Questioning the original decision violated a set of nested organisational norms. The first norm was that policies and objectives, especially those that top management espoused, should not be confronted openly. The second norm was that bad news . . . had to be offset by good news . . . These two norms had to be camouflaged . . . When the participants camouflaged the norms, and camouflaged the camouflage, they did so because they knew that to hide information violated organisational policies . . . If they exposed the errors, they would call into question a set of nested norms that were supposed to be kept covert. If they did not expose the errors, they created and/or reinforced processes that inhibited organisational learning' (Argyris and Schon, 1978, p. 3).

The description of 'group think' as analysed and conceptualized by Janis (1972) is also relevant to HRS decision-making and incorporates similar processes to those described by Argyris. Group think refers to the phenomenon where ties of group loyalty, plus deference to senior figures, discourages radical questioning of assumptions, obstructs the critiquing of proposals, encourages the selective use of data to support popular solutions, and results ultimately in the achievement of a sort of collective fantasy where much thought is given to how to install and implement the strategy but far too little to evaluating its quality.

HRS Decision-making: An Over-rationalist Approach?

The achievement of integration of HRS elements, and of HRS and corporate strategy, is central to achievement of HRS. Yet are there organizational limitations on the capacity or willingness of senior members of

organizations to embark on, design and implement, such integrated programmes of HRS change?

Do models of HRS assume a naïve and over-rationalistic view of the
processes of organizational strategic decision-making? Do these models
assume that managers are omniscient, rational, willing and able to pick
up relevant information, process it and act on its analyses? Managers are
not functionaries; they are not cyphers, they will respond actively to perceived environmental challenge or plans for restructuring in terms of their
ideologies, cultures, interests, limitations. The social relations within which
managers live and work will systematically 'foster and sustain very limited
and often distorted forms of communication between different groups
within the organization' (Alversson and Willmott, 1992, p. 7). Existing
structures influence managers' role in and reaction to change.

There are two possible approaches to the possibility of limitations on the
rationality of managers' decision-making, which entail different measures of
rationality. One approach would be to consider the wisdom and rationality
of currently fashionable nostrums and to point out that senior managers
who implemented such fashionable ideas were likely to produce effects they
did not desire simply because they were blinded by, or misled by, current
fashions of organizational restructuring.

How 'rational' are the forms and principles of organizational restructuring that are fundamental to current approaches to HRS change? As noted
earlier in this chapter, this question may lead us to consider the relationships *between* dimensions of these change programmes – between processes
of control, and processes designed to gain commitment, between the focus
on the individual, and on the team. We certainly need to consider the value
and effects of some key HRS principles, for some commentators have
argued that these principles are positively dangerous and damaging; that
they are inherently flawed.

One such is the focus on the use of *Return On Investment* (ROI) as a basis for
the measurement of organizational performance (part of the current strategy of eliminating bureaucratic rules and requirements – liberating,
enabling, empowering – while insisting on the achievement of tightly
defined performance targets). Clegg has argued, building on earlier work
of Hayes and Abernathy, that such measures of performance can encourage
unhelpful long-term behaviour and strategy. For one thing, ROI can be
manipulated to appear more positive simply by reducing the 'Investment'
side of the equation which immediately improves the level of return. 'A
profit-centre manager can achieve quicker, surer and easier results
by delaying replacement of old or worn out equipment, replacing equipment eventually with technologically dated or inferior substitutes, and
skimping on maintenance, research and development and personnel development' (Clegg, 1990, p. 197). Some commentators have argued that the

prominence of such managerial values – and the skills required to enforce them – have produced managers who systematically mismanage: 'They regard plant as an embarrassing constraint on financial manœuvrability and try to buy pre-packaged solutions, commonly on an inappropriate and grandiose scale. But what they do well is more damaging than what they do badly. "Managing by the numbers" collapses time frame: individual businesses have to show quick returns on minimal outlays or be deliberately run down and liquidated as "cash cows"; in conglomerates individual businesses are reduced to bargaining chips, quickly acquired and shed. A "successful" American manager doesn't plant or harvest' (Thurow, 1984, p. 23, quoted in Clegg, 1990, p. 199).

The second approach to HRS irrationality looks not at the nature of HRS values and methods, but at the processes whereby HRS decisions and strategic decisions are made.

Interestingly, while the literature on strategic decision-making addresses the ways in which this decision-making process is likely to be emergent, negotiated, politicized, conceptions of HRS decision-making tend to be much more rationalist and in consequence unrealistic.

Much HRS literature 'assumes a naïve view of organizational decision-making. Not only does it ignore political realities; as we have noted it also ignores how senior managers' understanding, knowledge, analysis and decisions on HRS matters (the challenges of the environment, the need for change, the possibilities for change, etc.) are themselves shaped by the organizational structures, cultures and personnel systems within which the managers exist. It is hardly too much to say that managers' capacity to make HRS decisions (by virtue of their senior location) is often precisely what makes the resultant decisions inadequate. This is not surprising: senior managers have developed within the organization, have absorbed its culture, have risen because of their skills, have positions of seniority and power within the structure. They have a very real interest in the *status quo*. Indeed, the very distinction between structures and cultures and individuals hardly holds. Senior managers have often absorbed and internalized much of the organization. Therefore their thinking on the need for change, and their thinking about what change is needed will be coloured by their membership of the organization that needs to be changed.

Johnson argues the importance not only of differentiating aspects of organizational structure, but of shared values and ways of thinking – what he calls a paradigm, which can be seen to include strong cultural or ideological elements, for it covers not only taken-for-granted knowledge and ways of seeing, knowing and doing things, but also values and moralities: the ways things should be done around here.

This point is of great importance. The key element of organizational change is not any particular direction of change, but achieving the constant capacity to change. And this means that those responsible for change need to be able to break out of the paradigms, the ways of thinking and seeing, of the existing organization. Pettigrew and Whipp, in introducing their study, note that their central aim is to 'link the competitive performance of British firms to their ability to adapt to major changes in their environment' (Pettigrew and Whipp, 1989, p. 26). Similarly Hamel and Prahalad (1989) note that 'An organisation's capacity to improve existing skills and learn new ones is the most defensible competitive advantage of all' (p. 69). Clearly, if the achievement of this capacity is crucial, it is also complex and difficult. A fundamental starting point is the realization that achieving the capacity for organizational learning will probably require unlearning; and this can be painful and worrying, not only because existing skills are frequently almost unconscious, but also because they are cherished and comforting.

Pettigrew and Whipp (1991, p. 290) remark: 'The ability of a company to learn should be under constant scrutiny. In other words, the ability of a company to reconstruct and adapt its knowledge base (made up of skills, structures and values . . .) should be a key test for managers. They should also be able to apply the "unlearning test". In other words, is the organisation capable of mounting the creative destruction necessary to break down outmoded attitudes and practices while at the same time building up new, more appropriate competence?'

Learning new skills and behaviours must start with unlearning old ones, now inappropriate. And just as existing skills and practices can hamper new behaviours, so the achievement of corporate strategies can be obstructed by tried and tested success formulas. Hamel and Prahalad (1989) note that a competitor's commitment to a 'success formula' is possibly its greatest vulnerability, because strategy recipes limit opportunities for competitive innovation (p. 72). They list a number of such common recipes: over-commitment to strategic business units with consequent business-unit de-skilling, over-commitment to the use of financial ratios which can be improved, reductions in stock, investment, etc., rather than growth of revenues (pp. 73–4). This point has also been noted by writers concerned with the nature and implications of corporate cultures. Bate, for example, shows that even when the established 'preconditions' for successful organizational change were in place, change did not occur: 'Something . . . was enmeshing people in their problems in a persistent and repetitive way.' Bate (1992) argues that under certain conditions culturally valued practices and attitudes produce a 'learned helplessness' (Bate, 1992, p. 214). He identifies the issue as follows: 'why were situations allowed to persist when they were accepted by the parties themselves as problematical and undesirable?' His answer: 'the parties were actively colluding in a process which effectively removed all possibility of a resolution to their problems . . . people in organisation evolve in their daily interactions with one another a system of shared perspectives of "collectively held and sanctioned definitions of the situation" which make up the culture of these organisations'. Furthermore, this culture offers to employees ways of thinking, seeing and knowing which prevent rational analysis and understanding.

Is HRS Actually Happening?

'HRM is the repository of good intentions. Management of human resources is the area in which executives realise they ought to be doing more and to which they promise to turn their attention the day after tomorrow' (Guest, 1989, p. 392).

Beaumont has noted that with HRS, prescription is running ahead of practice – or that academic discussion of HRS is in advance of an understanding of what is actually going on. Pettigrew and Whipp (1991) analysed the ability of a number of firms in four sectors of UK industry to manage strategic change to achieve competitive success. Their analysis investigates the relationships between competitive performance and their ability to adapt to major environmental changes. This relationship requires two organizational qualities: the capacity of the organization to identify and understand the competitive situation and the capacity of an organization to mobilize and manage the resources available to support a given response.

Pettigrew and Whipp identify five central factors for managing change successfully:

Environmental assessment: 'it is insufficient for companies to regard the creation of knowledge and judgements of their external competitive world as simply a technical exercise, rather the need is for organisations to become open learning systems' (1991, p. 279).

Leading change: Although the authors point out that no universal rules apply here they stress the importance of building a receptive climate within the organization; establishing the capacity for change; identifying the vision or direction of change, and identifying small incremental stages of change (p. 281).

Linking strategic and operational change: 'The need is to appreciate therefore how intentions are implemented – and hence transformed – over time' (p. 281).

Human resources as assets and liabilities: The first step here is to establish the importance and role of HRS in relation to business strategies. Thereafter the precise details of an HRS programme can be situational and *ad hoc*.

Coherence in the management of change: This describes the 'ability to hold the business together as a totality while simultaneously changing it' (p. 283).

Pettigrew and Whipp do not devote much attention to HRS concomitants of these variables: that is, they do not describe in detail what HRS steps are necessary to achieve them, although in passing they note the role of such things as teamwork. But their analysis is of value, mainly because unlike so much HRS literature it is empirically based, and focused on clear indices of corporate performance. Other researchers (see chapters 1 and 2) have used other classifications of types of corporate strategy in order to try to identify patterns of HRS which may relate to patterns of strategy. Some have used the product life cycle or expansion strategy. Hendry and Pettigrew review a number of these approaches. There is no need to spend long on these research models: they are of potential value when a clear and consistent pattern of relationship between the two aspects of strategy is revealed. However, an individual organization, with an interest in identifying appropriate and matching strategies at the organizational and HRS levels, would rely less on the discovery of such patterns and more on initiating its own process of organizational, strategic and environmental analysis.

But this still leaves the key question: how common are these findings? And how do the prescriptions of the HRS literature relate to actual practice?

There is considerable case-study and general media information available about HRS developments. The BP case (see chapter 1) is one of a number of well-known recent examples of apparent attempts to adjust one or more of the key dimensions of HRS (usually culture) in order to achieve some significant (often fundamental) change in employee behaviour. Within TSB, for example, as in many UK banks, the thrust is to achieve a radical change in staff behaviour and attitudes as the bank moves from a focus on performance, as measured through compliance with bureaucratic procedures and rules, to a focus on business-getting and profit-making.

The research evidence, on the other hand, is somewhat confusing. We have seen throughout this volume that there are a number of widespread changes occurring on a number of fronts. But do these constitute strategic change? And do they have the sort of impact on organizational performance that HRS change is desired to achieve? Guest (1989, p. 51) argues that the changes apparent to achieve flexibility, quality, etc. 'are consistent with moves towards human resource management'. But other commentators are far less sure of this.

Some researchers have concluded on the basis of empirical studies that certainly in the early 1980s, 'By and large British management does not have a strategic approach to the management of people: pragmatism or opportunism continue to be very much the order of the day' (Sisson and Sullivan, 1987, p. 492). Similarly, Ahlstrand and Purcell argue that on the basis of their research into the relationship between corporate strategies and strategies concerning employee relations (a subset of HRS), 'in the formulation of corporate strategies, management and employee relations issues are rarely taken into account unless the effect of a strategic decision has distinct industrial relations and personnel implications, seen for example in major redundancy and plant run down' (Ahlstrand and Purcell, 1988, p. 9).

Secondly, these authors point out that some common corporate developments may themselves have limiting effects on HRS progress. For example, the need to respond to market demands for reduced costs and increased efficiencies, 'makes it more difficult for the enterprise to adopt institutional strategies or management style statements which provide the basis for coherent, corporate-wide standards of employee relations management based on beliefs about the best way to manage people at work. Diversity and decentralisation are encouraged' (Ahlstrand and Purcell, 1988, p. 29). This tendency could be exacerbated by processes of decentralization and delegation which 'push down' responsibility to semi-autonomous business units, exerting strong pressure to cut costs, limit investment, improve margins. These are examples of the contradictions recognized earlier and described by Guest as the conflict between the hard and soft versions of human resource management: one which regards human resources as a cost, the other as an asset to be developed. But development costs money and takes time.

Purcell (1989) directly addresses the relationship that exists between strategy and structures, specifically HRS developments. He identifies different levels of strategic decision-making and attempts to relate these different levels to differences in HRS planning. It starts with what he calls 'first-order strategic decision-making' at the level of decisions about cash generation or cash usage. This analysis is organized in terms of differences in product market life cycle, as classified by the well-known Boston Consulting Group matrix.

He then focuses on 'second-order strategies' which affect the ways the organization is structured and business units are controlled.

This level of strategic decision-making relates closely to the classification by Child (1987) discussed in chapter 1. Purcell uses the classification of types of relationship between head office and business units identified by Goold and Campbell (1986). In this way he seeks to relate HRS developments to high-level developments in business planning. In a sense he is asking: from what we know (or are told) about the higher-level strategic decisions concerning business planning and organizational structuring, is it likely that organizations will develop and maintain human resource strategies? His conclusion is, indeed, gloomy. Essentially, he argues that current pressures on organizations, which frequently lead to stronger financial controls, make it harder 'to develop integrated and meaningful institutional strategies or management style at the corporate level, and – to the degree that short-run rates of return on investment, emphasis on margin improvement, and tight financial controls are imposed on unit managers – harder at the unit level to develop and maintain long-run human resource policies' (Purcell, 1989, p. 90). This should not be interpreted as arguing the impossibility of HRS, but rather the difficulty of achieving it. He suggests that despite the powerful appeal of HRS ideas, ideas which are strongly represented in chairmen's statements in annual reports (see Gowler and Legge, 1986), in reality external pressures make the achievement and maintenance of HRS difficult.

Similarly, Armstrong (1989, p. 156) has noted the dangers of a close and supportive relationship between HR practice and HR practitioners. As Keenoy remarks, 'personnel professionals will increasingly marginalise their independent contribution by subjecting their activities to the value criteria of budgetary planning and control' (Keenoy, 1990, p. 365).

On the other hand there is evidence, as reported by Guest (in Storey, 1989, p. 50) that 'at a significant proportion of foreign-owned green-field sites, management is pursuing some of the central features of HRM. These include flexible working, employee commitment and attention to high quality, which is partly reflected in the investment in careful selection and training.'

Furthermore, we may question whether Guest's findings on the incidence of aspects of HR in practice necessarily represent support for HRS as a whole. There is no doubt that organizational change of various sorts is occurring; there is no doubt that some of these changes are concerned either with classic HRS 'levers' of change (culture, performance-related pay, flexibility, etc.); there is no doubt that some of this change is associated with the rhetoric of HRS, and the claimed values of HRS. But none of this is necessarily to suggest much more than that managers are opportunistically and haphazardly applying some of the change initiatives associated with HRS. It is not in itself confirmation that HRS is occurring. If the test of genuine HRS is that the change programmes are concerned with the welfare-humanist conception of employees – the soft view of HRS – then this is a test that many change programmes simply cannot pass. (See Keenoy 1990 for a useful summary of the articles in Storey, 1989 which support this conclusion.)

Guest himself, as noted earlier, has argued that while HRS consists of four 'policy goals' – high commitment, high quality, flexibility and strategic integration – and has asserted that 'Only when a coherent strategy, directed towards these four policy goals, fully integrated into business strategy and fully sponsored by line management at all levels is applied will the high productivity and related outcomes sought by industry be achieved' (Guest, 1990, p. 378). Clearly with such a demanding set of criteria very few full cases of HRS can be found, particularly when Guest's definition emphasizes a clear and direct causal connection between policy goals and productivity outcomes. Also, by arguing the causal relationship between policy goals and performance, Guest excludes situations where other measures (cost cutting, increased controls) are used to achieve performance.

Another test of the degree to which organizational change programmes are evidence of, or part of, HRS, is the extent to which these initiatives are genuinely strategic. Here again we find that problems arise. There are two issues here, which pull in different directions. On the one hand some approaches (including that of Guest) to HRS would argue that true HRS involves senior managers being committed to, and seeking to implement in HRS terms, an overall approach to staff and organization (e.g. the four policy goals described by Guest). If it appears that HRS decisions are not inspired by this sort of approach, then the initiatives would not be regarded as genuine HRS. The evidence seems to support this conclusion. Armstrong has noted (1989) that decisions about organizational structures and process, and the treatment of employees are as much influenced by accountancy logic as by HRS principles, such that 'the treatment of human resources [becomes an] instrument for the achievement of short run accounting targets' (p. 164.) Similar arguments – that organizational change pro- grammes – in a variety of areas – frequently show a greater concern for cost reduction, increased control, improved surveillance, rather than for increased autonomy and participation, come from Storey's recent collection (1989).

Recent work by researchers at the University of Warwick studied the value underlying programmes of organizational change. They concluded: 'it is difficult to escape the conclusion that, although the great majority of our respondents claim that their organisations have an overall policy or approach to the management of employees, with the exception of a number of companies which are overseas owned, or financially centralised, or oper- ating in the service sectors, it would be wrong to set very much store by this . . . the general weight of evidence would seem to confirm that most UK owned enterprises remain pragmatic or opportunistic in their approach' (Marginson et al., 1988, p. 120; quoted in Storey and Sisson, 1993, p. 71).

Support for this argument can be found in a number of studies. For example, Delbridge and Turnbull (1992) argue that JIT systems and quality control actually represent a significant increase in control, surveillance, and the capacity to identify and 'correct' worker mistakes and performance: 'Quality control is therefore used not simply to improve product quality, but to discipline the workforce. Quality charts in particular are part and parcel of a more extensive system of surveillance and monitoring which is used to ensure compliance' (Delbridge and Turnbull, 1992, p. 65). Indeed these authors go further, and argue that the distinction between 'soft' and 'hard' conceptions of HRS may ultimately be compatible – for many of the key principles of soft HRS may really involve new forms of control: 'teamwork, quality consciousness and flexibility which characterise . . . HRM strategies are in essence the means by which the workforce is controlled, through a mixture of stress, peer pressure, surveillance and accountability' (Delbridge and Turnbull, 1992, p. 68).

Similarly, Blyton and Morris (1993), in a review of flexibility initiatives, conclude that despite the long-term, strategic focus of HRS (in principle), in practice the enthusiasm for flexibility in the UK is largely short-term, cost-driven and *ad hoc*. Furthermore, as they note, the introduction of flexibility, far from being part of a general strategy to maximize employee potential and commitment, is more likely to undermine employee commitment (Blyton and Morris, 1993, p. 127).

On the other hand, if strategy is defined not by reference to a set of core HRS values, but simply by reference to the degree of fit of HRS initiatives to corporate strategy, the result is hardly more impressive. Here the issue is not that certain currently popular organizational changes have been initiated, but that the changes can be seen directly to support the organization's strategy. This is Miller's test: 'We can say that if managements manage their employees in ways which recognise their role in strategy implementation, it is behaving strategically. If, on the other hand, it makes decisions simply in order to avoid trade unions, or better to control employees, it is operating in a fashion which is separate from the business and [is] non-strategic' (Miller, 1986, p. 51; quoted in Storey and Sisson, 1993, p. 67).

This point is supported by Beaumont, who notes that if the key to HRS is the existence of a 'close, two-way relationship between business strategy or planning and HRM strategy or planning', research suggests that such a linkage rarely exists to any sizeable extent or depth across a wide range of organizations (Beaumont, 1993, p. 4).

There is much support for these views of the reality of HRS/strategy linkages, and for the role of non-strategic priorities and opportunism in HRS thinking. Hendry and Pettigrew note that while much HRS literature, especially the Excellence literature, makes a claim for the integrative role of corporate culture, the reality is that HRS initiatives are 'simply pragmatic and/or expedient – "less reflective of a coherent set of management attitudes than it is of the economic environment in which that organization operates"' (Hendry and Pettigrew, 1986, p. 5; quoting Beer et al. 1984).

Some writers have argued that one cause for the limitations of HRS in practice is that it draws too heavily on the values and priorities of senior management, to the exclusion of other organizational groups, and involves an over-rationalistic conception of organizational processes. McKinlay and Starkey (1988) consider HRS developments in three UK companies. Beginning with a useful summary of the background to HRS, the authors point to the growing appreciation of the need for a 'broader change agenda' than that encompassed by the 'highly rationalistic' structural focus of earlier change programmes. A significant part of the authors' argument can thus be seen to confirm the view that the behaviour of employees is a result of more factors than merely structural ones, and, more contentiously, that it may be simpler and easier to manipulate these non-structural factors. Furthermore, the authors maintain that complex, multi-layered organizations (sometimes called bureaucracies) generate 'inertia, slothful and adaptive change, and the chronic attachment to buried assumptions and routine behaviour'. They argue that increasingly change programmes are designed to attack these behaviours and the structures which generate them. Their conclusions are important. Not only do they identify the crucial role in HRS of developments in corporate strategy, but they see that these strategic shifts are those which are best served by a move towards flexibility. But more significant for our concerns here are the authors' comments on the 'non-rational aspects of organisational behaviour dimensions', which they have placed 'at the centre of their analysis of organisational transitions. For innovating organisations responding to the new challenges of industrial dematurity, the key task is to mobilise those intangible social forces which perpetuate organisational inertia' (McKinlay and Starkey, 1988, pp. 56–9). Kochan and Dyer (1992) support the point that 'transformational' change will require more than the enthusiasm and values of top management, but must incorporate the priorities and values of 'stakeholders' to be successful. Guest reports the work of Kochan, Katz and McKersie as not supporting the claim that HRM is now common or normal (Guest, 1989, p. 389).

Thus, apart from doubts about the internal consistency and possibility of HRS (the tension between hard and soft, the possibility of achieving 'integration', the possible conflicts between aspects of HRS, etc.), there is evidence that many of the apparent HRS changes are more to do with increased employee control and a focus on cost control and the 'bottom line', than on initiating a new form of, and approach to, the management of staff. When HRS does occur it is usually in unusual and distinctive organizations. Despite the rhetoric of HRS, the reality is that much HRS-type change is concerned with hard 'utilitarian-instrumentalism' (Keenoy, p. 368) than with 'developmental-humanism', i.e. is hard rather than soft. As the following section will argue, HRS is important for supplying a powerful rhetoric, a rhetoric which facilitates increasing control and management of employees, of structures and of meaning itself. Storey and Sisson argue, for example, that 'there is little evidence of a strategic approach to human resource management being adopted in most organisations' (Storey and Sisson, p. 172; quoted in Keenoy, p. 371). Part of the problem here lies in how HRS is defined – what the nature of HRS is seen to be, and specifically whether the various dimensions of HRS occur together, and indeed are mutually compatible. The research does not show that firms who are introducing HRS-type initiatives are doing so because of a commitment to Pettigrew and Whip's dimensions – to 'developmental-humanism', to the soft values of HRS. On the contrary, Hendry, Pettigrew and Sparrow (1988) conclude: 'the essence of our argument is that those firms which have made developments in their HRM have done so under the pressure of competitive forces'. The conclusion is supported by others: 'Evidence from other studies also supports the view that strategic HRM is primarily directed toward increasing organisational efficiency in the use and productivity of the labour resource in order to compete more effectively' (Keenoy, 1990, p. 377).

However, Storey and Sisson (1993) have noted that even in terms of efficiency there is a 'massive gap' between rhetoric and reality. Despite the enormous public espousal of 'soft' HRS values by senior managers, the evidence on levels of installation of such key elements of HRS as training and development, and the integration of HR practices and business strategy, suggest that 'Britain still has a long way to go . . . Senior managers are either not practising what they espouse or they are installing new initiatives in an incompetent and ineffective way' (Storey and Sisson, 1993, pp. 50–1).

HRS as Rhetoric and Discourse: Its Values and Assumptions

There are major difficulties in the achievement of the types of integration fundamental to HRS. These problems arise from the realities of organizational structures and processes. We have noted that for many commentators, the achievement of HRS is empirically uncertain. Yet this does not mean that HRS is a delusion, is unimportant; far from it. HRS is powerful and important. Yet the importance of HRS is as much in HRS as a body of ideas (with certain consequences) as it is in HRS as a set of practices: 'what is significant about "human resource management" – and the factor that could explain the remarkable level of interest in it – is that it marks a departure from a largely prevailing orthodoxy, it promises an alternative or (more accurately and significantly) a set of alternatives to what might be described as the "Donovan" model' (Storey, 1989, p. 8).

The importance of HRS is greater and wider than the various practices which arguably reflect its operationalization. While there are undoubtedly many changes occurring in organizations that impact on the structure and processes of work and employment, these are less significant as indicators of a new HRS approach to human resources, and more important because of their simultaneous appeal to powerful new values and assumptions and reliance on old forms of power and control.

For some writers it is this combination of new rhetoric and old imperatives – old problems, new solutions – that is most important about HRS.

The radical critique of HRS would see HRS as a powerful and new form of managerial rhetoric, whose power lies not in its impact on performance, but in its capacity to reflect current societal values and political priorities, and to represent managerial conceptions of the organization, and of intra-organizational relationships. It is thus seen as a new form of managerial control – not simply control through managerial practices and organization change and restructuring, but control of the ways in which thinking about, understanding and knowing organizations, and organizational dynamics and purposes – and critically, organizational members – is conducted and framed. Such an approach would argue that the preoccupations of management remain the same as ever – to achieve control, ensure, and increase productivity and profitability, yet at the same time to ensure that as far as possible, employees are willing to do what is required, are compliant, co-operative, creative. This is the essential paradox of management. If HRS offers anything really new, it offers new techniques, and new language and constructions of meaning, with which management approaches this dilemma.

Furthermore, there may well be a connection between changes in work organization which require discretion on the part of workers, and an approach to management, organization, training and culture change. These seek to ensure compliance on the basis not of formal (rigid) rules, but on the basis of 'shared norms of understanding, a common grammar of interpretation . . . the internalisation of the organisation's "goals" or "norms" to ensure that the individual interprets the area of discretion correctly from the organisation's point of view' (Townley, 1989, p. 103).

As Keenoy and Anthony remark: 'to understand the HRM phenomenon in Britain it is necessary to treat it as a cultural construction comprised of a series of metaphors which constitute a "new reality". HRM reflects an attempt to redefine both the meaning of work and the way individual employers relate to their employees' (Keenoy and Anthony, 1992, p. 234). Or as du Gay and Salaman have noted with respect to a key element of HRS thinking – the focus on market forces and relationships, and thus on the value of enterprise: the discourse of enterprise within organizations (and the practices and organizational technologies which are inspired by this focus) is essentially co-terminus with the political-economic-social project of Thatcherism (du Gay and Salaman, 1992, p. 627).

The important point here is not simply that HRS ideas and practices carry 'ideological' implications and priorities, but that these ideas are realized and reproduced through a set of HRS practices occurring at many levels – structures, cultures and personnel practices which display the power and reality of the rhetoric. Thus HRS is at the same time about attempts to change behaviour, and to transform values and norms, and to define this project of behaviour and value-change in terms of the values and principles of HRS, regardless of its appropriateness in fact.

HRS thinking thus argues that it is 'simply' the application of enterprise and market principles ('releasing initiative', 'empowering staff', 'replacing hierarchy by market principles', 'establishing autonomous business units', etc.) to organizations. Thus its own ideology is represented as realism.

Much of the HRS literature displays a dual focus: on changed practices, and on the management of meaning – the assertion of the morality, or moral value of the restructuring principle. Frequently in this book we have referred to studies which have suggested that what changes are apparent may be defined in terms of, and legitimized by reference to, the values and assumptions of HRS. But in fact, they bear little resemblance to the strategic, humanistic values associated with the 'soft' conception of HRS.

The HRS literature in general, and the 'Excellence' literature in particular, is marked by its less than rigorous conceptual clarity and its cavalier use of evidence on which claims are based. But the point is not simply that much HRS literature is conceptually ambiguous, or confused, or that it is ill-based, empirically. The critical point is rather that the rhetorical, symbolic power of the HRS message is important in itself – important in masking, or distorting, undesirable and inconsistent views of reality.

For example, discussions of the flexible firm illustrate how an idea widely promoted by government agencies and frequently offered in management literature as a panacea for the ills of Western capitalism, is significant precisely because it resonates with key current values and is part of a powerful and attractive model of the organization of the future (Pollert, 1988).

Pollert has noted that writings on flexibility and the flexible firm are characterized by 'a consistent style of global prophesying, sweeping generalisation from very limited evidence, economic or technical determinism and an assumption of radical break with the past' (1988, p. 229). Flexibility is frequently seen as a universal panacea for the ills that are associated with bureaucracy. Bureaucracy is regarded as equivalent to rigidity, and is therefore negative; flexibility is associated with responsiveness – to circumstances and to clients, and is therefore virtuous. This view overestimates the negative aspects of bureaucracy and ignores its many strengths (see du Gay, 1994). In other words, the 'flexible firm', as an idea, by combining aspects of organization and strategic response, is particularly attractive to management writers and ideologies.

Furthermore, Pollert argues that part of the appeal of the concept of flexibility is that it resonates with broader, societal and political values and purposes. She notes that part of any explanation of the power of the notion of flexibility during the 1980s certainly must require reference to environmental issues – Japanization, neo-classical economic policies. But these are not sufficient, there is also a need to understand the resonance between the nature and power of the concept of flexibility and an 'ideological level of explanation'. By this she refers to the linkages between flexibility and the theory of industrial society which focuses on the 'universal evolution of technological and economic rationality which led to the convergence of all societies towards "industrial society"', and which she claims assumed considerable power in social, political and social science thinking and writing in the 1980s (Pollert, 1988, p. 8).

She argues persuasively that the attractiveness of the idea – the background to its power and importance – is due less to its empirical existence or success, and more to its association with powerful political and ideological values: 'Its preoccupation with labour flexibility and market recovery swim with the stream of the neo-classical revival; at the same time its concern to find a new solution or "third way" for the future which is neither "Keynesian" nor "monetarist" and its obsession with fragmentation suggest that beneath the surface of certainty and assertiveness lie disorientation and a desperate search for panaceas . . . But its analytical weaknesses do not necessarily mean its downfall. While its political message remains strong, it may well survive into the 1990s' (Pollert, 1988, p. 30).

Pollert's critique of flexibility is extremely useful, for this form and focus of analysis can be applied more widely to the HRS movement as a whole, as well as to its constituent ideas and practices.

For example, the Excellence literature is powerful and influential as a body of ideas rather than simply a set of practices. Like much HRS writing, but to a greater degree, the 'Excellence' literature represents the very process it advocates. It argues the importance of the managerial manipulation of meaning – the management of organizational culture – a focus that Legge has argued is fundamental to HRM: 'Most HRM models emphasise the organisation's culture as the central activity for senior management' (Legge, 1988, p. 26). Yet the 'Excellence' literature itself, like all HRS literature, represents a major attempt to manage meaning – to reflect and manipulate some critical current conceptions of organizations, management and employees.

Whatever the academic assessment of the 'Excellence' literature, it should be taken very seriously indeed; by now it is almost taken for granted, as unquestionably true, as beyond debate. It has become almost sacrosanct.

How do we explain this phenomenon and wherein lies the power of these messages? These issues are explored by David Guest (1992). Guest notes that the appeal of these ideas lies not simply in the elements of the approach but also in its timeliness: 'It is American, optimistic, apparently humanistic and also superficially simple' (Guest, 1992, p. 379). He charts the main elements of the 'Excellence' approach and offers an explanation for the power of these ideas. He critiques it from two standpoints: those analyses which have addressed the empirical validity of the literature and, more significantly, the normative appeal of the literature. As he says, one possibility is that Peters and Waterman are right; another is that whatever its validity, 'managers and other readers believe the message to be correct. In one sense the medium is the message' (Guest, 1992, p. 13). An important reason for the success of the book is the way in which its messages resonate with other, broader, socio-political values and assumptions among managers (see Guest, 1990; and box 2.9).

The same point has been argued with respect to the emphasis on customer relations as a blueprint for internal organizational relations by du Gay and Salaman (1992) who trace the connections between the success of this idea and aspects of political ideology under Thatcher. These authors argue that many programmes of organizational change are centred around the attempt to redefine internal organizational relations and structures *as if* they were market relations – between suppliers and customers. This in turn has significant consequences for the redefinition of key roles, and their constituent competences (and for the identities of those who fill them) (see du Gay et al. 1994). But more importantly for our purposes here, the focus on, and value of, enterprise also demonstrates key resonances with external, socio-economic political values and assumption: Thatcherism – 'the key feature of contemporary political rationalities and technologies of government has been the attempt to establish connections between the self-fulfilling desires of individuals and the achievement of social and economic objectives' (du Gay, 1991, p. 58).

It may well be that ultimately the distinction between rhetoric and reality becomes blurred and meaningless and loses its value. The rhetoric becomes real, and real in its consequences. The power of HRS to redefine management, organization and the employee, and to impose a conception of how managers and employees relate to each other and to the organization (and the customer) as liberated, autonomous, enterprising employees, supplies a conception which is unassailable. This is because of its resonance with, and dependence upon, wider societal/political conceptions of the market and the primacy of market forces and values, and conceptions of the individual. The rhetoric and language wherein HRS is explained and developed and justified, the activities in which it results, are inextricably related to practices and systems which define, develop, reward and empower the individual.

These HRS rhetorics and practices in turn connect not only to the challenges of recession and the increased competitive threat, but also to the constant attempt to devise new strategies, cut costs and improve margins. And in turn these views of managers, workers, and their relationships through structures and cultures, are embodied in expert systems of classification, payment systems, and other technologies, in job design, assessment systems and criteria.

HRS is a system of knowing and understanding the organization, the environment and the individual employee (and crucially the relationships between these three). It is therefore a basis for the redesign of organizations; it supplies assumptions, classification systems, technologies, and ways of talking and thinking about organization and employees, which reflect and support this knowledge, and which are important for their effects on individuals even when the actual patterns of organizational restructuring cannot – as so often – be seen as genuine examples of HRS practice.

One view of this is to see the hidden hand of management, deliberately using the language of HRS to mask its real purposes, and to seek to gain employees' commitment to, or resignation in the face of, programmes of change. Keenoy remarks: 'far from indicating a new era of humane people-orientated employment management, . . . the primary purpose of the rhetoric of HRM might be to provide a legitimatory managerial ideology to facilitate an intensification of work and an increase in the commodification of labour' (Keenoy, 1990, p. 375).

Others would see the emergence of contradictions that have been seen to characterize in some form every attempt to redesign the nature of work and employment: particularly the contradictory need for management to achieve, simultaneously, control over the workforce (a need which is even more important today with JIT, TQM, etc). and the need to develop and attract the commitment and creativity of the workforce. The emergence of these dual but opposed needs may underlie the way HRS is implemented. Legge, for example, notes: 'What evidence we have is of a patchy implementation of practices designed to achieve flexibility, quality and commitment, often constrained by the contradictions inherent in enacting these slippery concepts, and motivated more by the opportunities afforded by high levels of unemployment and the constraints of recession and enhanced competition, than by any long-term strategic considerations' (Legge, 1994, p. 47).

Yet others, however, would stress the role of power in HRS thinking and practice not in its role in serving the functions and interests of senior management but in terms of the overall *government* of the organization. The use of the term government draws attention to the fact that power 'traverses all practices – from the "macro" to the "micro" – through which persons are ruled, mastered, held in check, administered, steered, guided, by means of which they are led by others or have come to direct or regulate their own actions' (Rose, 1990). Power is thus not seen as located simply or only in the actions of senior management; it is present in all knowledge and practice that regulates individuals.

One key idea in the HRS literature is its analysis and treatment of causality and 'responsibility' – of the nature of relationships between key elements or levels of the approach: environment, organization, individual. HRS locates organizational responsibility (for performance, quality, the 'implementation of change', etc.) as the responsibility of liberated, empowered, autonomous individual employees. The responsibility of managers is to ensure that the organizational environment and structure are 'enabling'. Once this is achieved, the employees must rely on his/her competence and, crucially, enterprise, to ensure that individual performance meets the demands of the myriad of customers by whom employees are now surrounded and whom they supply. Thus the metaphor of the market becomes the organizational reality by which employees and their work are judged, and how they judge themselves. It thus 'deflects human responsibility to the hidden hand of the market in the justification of means for ultimate ends' (Keenoy and Anthony, 1992, p. 249). Possibly the most important feature of HRS is not simply the many changes – many of them far-reaching and pervasive – which are taking place in organizations, but the manner in which HRS supplies a new, authoritative theory of how organizations work and how individuals must be managed, rewarded and directed, which, because of its strong links with associated notions of 'excellence', the role of markets and of enterprise, seeks to redefine not just organizations, but individuals. It is this that is the greatest contribution of HRS, and potentially the most ominous.

Conclusion

HRS promises a great deal; its influence on recent and current programmes of organizational restructuring has been enormous. To a major degree HRS supplies the agenda for programmes of organizational change – the introduction of internal markets within the UK National Health Service; the subcontracting and privatizing of public utilities; the delayering and devolving of many previously centralized businesses; the introduction of JIT, TQM, teamworking, PRP and all the other current fashions, many of which have been considered in this volume.

But if it promises much, what does it deliver? We have reason to be wary of fashionable programmes of organizational restructuring; after all, we have been here before, or somewhere very similar: there have been other philosophies of organizational restructuring – Scientific Management, Human Relations, Worker Participation, MBO, OD, etc. The fact that senior managers seem to like HRS, that politicians clearly approve of some of its central elements, does not make it true, or right.

There is therefore a need to consider HRS in terms of its key ideas and assumptions and to assess its feasibility as a body of recommendations and assumptions. This analysis is conducted in this chapter. Such an analysis shows that HRS is characterized by a number of basic problems, limitations and contradictions: it means a variety of different things ('open' versus 'closed', 'hard' versus 'soft'); it makes a set of recommendations which could well conflict; it claims high moral purposes but seems to be vulnerable to short-termism.

Central to HRS is a concern for the integration of structures and strategies and for HR systems with each other. Without these integrations, HRS becomes meaningless. Yet as this and other chapters have shown, achieving these sorts of integration is far from assured. A major reason for this is that HRS depends upon a highly rationalist notion of management decision-making – for the design and implementation of HRS projects depends on the alertness and analysis of senior managers. Can we assume that senior managers will actually determine HRS in this way? In fact this chapter argues that from what we know of how other decisions are made in organizations, and from what we know of the role of existing structures, cultures, mind-sets and politics on managers' thinking, there are serious grounds for questioning managers' decision-making rationality.

But is there evidence that HRS is actually occurring? The evidence is that fundamental change is certainly taking place, but whether or not this constitutes HRS is more questionable. For many writers the picture is less one of organizations becoming more flexible, building employee commitment, putting into practice the commonplace adage that their most precious resource is their staff; and more one of cutting costs, tightening control, delayering, installing quality monitoring systems, reducing inventories, subcontracting peripheral activities.

Yet these activities are presented as if they were genuine HRS, and this coexistence of programmes of organizational change which derive from the 'hard' sense of HRS while accompanied by the rhetoric of 'soft' HRS has caused some commentators to see this situation not as accidental or temporary or a result of overwhelming recessionary pressures, but as central to HRS itself. For these writers HRS becomes a sort of stage-management – a process of magical transformation of actions aimed to cut costs and tighten control, into actions which are strategic and people-focused, and aimed at building commitment. In this view HRS becomes an exercise in the management of meaning, disguising real purposes, claiming the logic of disembodied natural forces ('the environment', 'the market', 'performance', 'the customer', quality, etc.) and thus building the legitimacy of measures which are ultimately no less sectional than the more obviously oppressive measures of earlier generations of managers.

Key points

- *While HRS sounds great in theory – and obviously appeals to many managers and management consultants and writers – it is no help to anyone to gloss over what may be serious inherent problems in this approach. These problems are of various sorts. Some arise from contradictions in the very idea of HRS itself – for example, the conflict between 'open' and 'closed' models or between 'hard' and 'soft' approaches. Others tend to centre around the notion of integration, intrinsic to HRS models, the approach to organizations, and organizational relationships intrinsic in HRS thinking, and the view of management decision-making adopted within HRS models. All these are arguably very simplistic and unrealistic.*

- *Four main kinds of integration are assumed and promoted by HRS thinking, and they are all significant as sources of problems in the achievement of HRS. These types are explored and their implications considered. This is important because if any of these types of integration is impossible or difficult to achieve it will have devastating implications for the possibility of HRS in practice.*

- *Much HRS thinking and prescription assumes a naïve conception of the neutrality, objectivity, analytic competence, open-mindedness and disinterestedness of senior management decision-makers whose responsibility it is to recognize that an HRS decision is necessary, to gather the relevant data and analyse them, and to make a sensible decision. If these assumptions are infirm, the HRS decisions will be flawed. The limitations on managers' decision-making are explored. Perversely, they include the consequences of the prevailing HRS situation, which will limit how managers see the situation and how they react to it.*

- *Given the apparent inherent problems surrounding HRS it becomes all the more important to see to what extent HRS is actually occurring – the empirical test of HRS as distinct from the assessment of HRS conceptually. Here the evidence is ambiguous. Change is certainly occurring; but it is not certain that it is always or even frequently sufficiently strategic, or is more than* ad hoc *opportunism.*

- *For some commentators this gap between HRS theory and empirical reality is not an incidental feature of HRS but is actually central to HRS: HRS is significant more as rhetoric than reality – as a large-scale attempt to manage meaning for managers and employees.*

Discussion Questions

1 Discuss some of the inherent contradictions in, and limitations of, HRS thinking.
2 Why is integration – of various types – central to HRS, and why are these likely to prove difficult to achieve?
3 What are the in-built limitations to the rationality of senior managers' thinking and decision-making on HRS issues?
4 Is HRS happening in practice?
5 Is HRS more rhetoric than reality? And what are the implications of this?

REFERENCES

Abernathy, W., Clark, K. B. and Kantrow, A. M. (1981) The new industrial competition. *Harvard Business Review*, Oct., pp. 69–77.
Ahlstrand, B. and Purcell, J. (1988) Employee relations strategy in the multi-divisional company. *Personnel Review*, 17, no. 3, pp. 3–11.
Alexander, L. D. (1989) Successfully implementing strategic decisions. In Asch, D. and Bowman, C. (eds), *Readings in Strategic Management*. Basingstoke, Macmillan Education, pp. 388–96.
Alvesson, M. and Willmott, H. (1992) Critical theory and management studies: An introduction. In Alvesson, M. and Willmott, H. (eds), *Critical Management Studies*. London, Sage, pp. 1–20.
Argyris, C. (1986) *Change and Defensive Routines*. Boston, Pitman.
Argyris, C. and Schon, D. (1978) *Organizational Learning: A Theory of Action Perspective*. Reading, Mass., Addison-Wesley.
Armstrong, M. (1992) *Human Resource Management: Strategy and Action*. London, Kogan-Page.
Atkinson, J. (1984) Manpower strategies for flexible organisations. *Personnel Management*, Aug., pp. 28–31.
Atkinson, J. (1985) Flexibility: Planning for an uncertain future. *Manpower Policy and Practice*, no. 1, summer.
Atkinson, J. (1986) The flexible workforce: Ostriches or opportunists? *Manpower Policy and Practice*, 1, no. 4, summer.
Atkinson, J. and Gregory, D. (1986) A flexible future: Britain's dual labour force. *Marxism Today*, April.
Bartlett, C. A. and Ghoshal, S. (1992) *Transnational management*. Homewood, Ill., Irwin.
Bate, P. (1992) The Impact of organisational culture on approaches to organisational problem-solving. In Salaman, G. et al. (eds), *Human Resource Strategies*. London, Sage, pp. 219–34.
Beaumont, P. (1993) *Human Resource Management*. London, Sage.

Beer, M. and Spector, B. (1985) *Human Resources Management: A General Manager's Perspective*. New York, Free Press.

Beer, M., Spector, B., Lawrence, P. R., Mills, Q. N. and Walton, R. E. (1984) *Managing Human Assets*. New York, Free Press.

Blyton, P. and Morris, J. (1992) HRM and the limits of flexibility. In Blyton, P. and Turnbull, P. (eds), *Reassessing Human Resource Management*. London, Sage.

Blyton, P. and Turnbull, P. (eds) (1992) *Reassessing Human Resource Management*. London, Sage.

Brewster, C. J., Hegewisch, A., Holden, L. and Lockhart, T. (1990) Trends in human resource management in Europe 1990. Cranfield, Bedfordshire, Price-Waterhouse Cranfield Project working paper.

Chandler, A. D. (1977) *Strategy and Structure*. Cambridge, Mass., MIT Press.

Child, J. (1987) Information technology, organization and response to strategic challenges. *California Management Review*, 30, no. 1, fall, pp. 33–50.

Clegg, S. (1990) *Modern Organisations*. London, Sage.

Delbridge, R. and Turnbull, P. (1992) Human resource maximisation: The management of labour under just-in-time manufacturing systems. In Blyton, T. and Turnbull, P. (eds), *Reassessing Human Resource Management*, pp. 56–73.

du Gay, P. (1991) Enterprise culture and the ideology of excellence. *New Formations*, 13, spring, pp. 45–62.

du Gay, P. (1994) Colossal immodesties and hopeful monsters: Pluralism and organizational conduct. *Organization*, 1, no. 1, 125–48.

du Gay, P., Rees, B. and Salaman, G. (forthcoming) Making up managers. *Journal of Management Studies*.

du Gay, P. and Salaman, G. (1992) The culture of the customer. *Journal of Management Studies*, 29, no. 5, pp. 45–61.

Evans, P. A. L. (1986) The strategic outcomes of human resource management. *Human Resource Management*, 25, no. 1, pp. 149–67.

Galbraith, J. R. and Kazajian, R. K. (1986) Organising to implement strategies of diversity and globalisation. *Human Resource Management*, 25, no. 1, pp. 37–54.

Goold, M. and Campbell, A. (1986) Strategic decision-making: The corporate role. *Vol. 1. Strategic Management Styles*, London Business School, Centre for Business Strategy.

Goold, M. and Campbell, A. (1987) *Strategies and Styles: The Role of the Centre in Managing Diversified Corporations*. Oxford, Blackwell.

Gospel, H. and Littler, C. R. (1983) *Managerial Strategies and Industrial Relations: An Historical and Comparative Study*. London, Heinemann.

Gowler, D. and Legge, K. (1986) Images of employees in company reports – Do company chairmen view their most valuable asset as valuable? *Personnel Review*, 15, no. 5, pp. 9–18.

Guest, D. (1987) Human resource management and industrial relations. *Journal of Management Studies*, 24, no. 5, pp. 503–21.

Guest, D. (1989) Human resource management: Its implications for industrial relations and trade unions. In Storey, J. (ed.), *New Perspectives on Human Resource Management*. London, Routledge, pp. 41–55.

Guest, D. (1992) Right enough to be dangerously wrong. In Salaman, G. et al. (eds), *Human Resource Strategies*. London, Sage, pp. 5–20.

Hales, C. (1994) Internal marketing as an approach to human resource management. *Journal of Management Studies*, 5, no. 1, pp. 50–71.

Hamel, G. and Prahalad, C. K. (1989) Strategic intent. *Harvard Business Review*, May/June, pp. 63–76.

Hayes, R. H. and Abernathy, W. (1980) Managing our way to economic decline. *Harvard Business Review*, 58, no. 4, pp. 67–77.

Hendry, C. and Pettigrew, A. (1986) The practice of strategic human resource management. *Personnel Review*, 15, no. 5, pp. 3–8.

Hendry, C. and Pettigrew, A. (1990) Human resource management: An agenda for the 1990s. *International Journal of Human Resource Management*, 1, no. 1, pp. 17–43.

Hendry, C., Pettigrew, A. and Sparrow, P. (1988) Changing patterns of human resource management. *Personnel Management*, Nov., pp. 37–41.

Higgins, W. and Clegg, S. R. (1988) Enterprise calculation and manufacturing decline. *Organisation Studies*, 9, no. 1, pp. 69–89.

Janis, I. L. (1972) *Victims of Groupthink*. Boston, Houghton Mifflin.

Johnson, G. (1987) *Strategic Change and the Management Process*. Oxford, Blackwell.

Keenoy, T. (1990) HRM: A case of the wolf in sheep's clothing? *Personnel Review*, 19, no. 2, pp. 3–9.

Keenoy, T. and Anthony, P. (1992) HRM: Metaphor, meaning and morality. In Blyton, T. and Turnbull, P. (eds), *Reassessing Human Resource Management*. London, Sage, pp. 233–60.

Kochan, T. and Dyer, L. (1992) Managing transformational change: The role of human resource professionals. Paper for the Conference of the International Relations Association, Sydney.

Legge, K. (1978) *Power, Innovation and Problem-Solving*. New York, McGraw-Hill.

Legge, K. (1988) Personnel management in recession and recovery. *Personnel Review*, 17, no. 2.

Legge, K. (1994) HRM: Rhetoric, reality and hidden agendas. In Storey, J. (ed.), *Human Resource Management: A Critical Text*. London, Routledge, pp. 33–62.

Lengnick-Hall, C. and Lengnick-Hall, M. (1988) Strategic human resources management: A review of the literature and a proposed typology. Academy of Management.

Littler, C. and Salaman, G. (1986) *Class at Work*. London, Batsford.

McKinlay, A. and Starkey, A. (1988) Competitive strategies and organisational change. *Organisation Studies*, 9, no. 4, pp. 555–71.

Marginson, P., Edwards, P. K., Martin, R. J. and Sisson, K. (1988) *Beyond the Workplace: Managing Industrial Relations in the Multi-establishment Enterprise*. Oxford, Blackwell.

Miller, D. (1986) Configurations of strategy and structure: Towards a synthesis. *Strategic Management Journal*, 7, pp. 233–49.

Mintzberg, H. and Waters, J. A. (1989) Of strategies, deliberate and emergent. In Asch, D. and Bowman, C. (eds), *Readings in Strategic Management*. Basingstoke, Macmillan Education, pp. 4–19.

Morris, J. (1974) Developing resourceful managers. In Taylor, B. and Lippitt,   G. L. (eds), *Management Development and Training Handbook*. New York, McGraw-Hill.

Paauwe, J. and Dewe, P. (1995) Organisational structure of multinational corporations. In Harzing, A. W. and Ruysseveldt, J. V. (eds), *International Human Resource Management*. London, Sage, pp. 51–76.

Pettigrew, A. (1985) *The Awakening Giant: Continuity and Change in ICI*. Oxford, Blackwell.

Pettigrew, A. (1988) Introduction: Researching strategic change. In Pettigrew, A. (ed.), *The Management of Strategic Change*. Oxford, Blackwell, pp. 1–14.

Pettigrew, A. and Whipp, R. (1989) *The Management of Strategic Operational Change*, Swindon, ESRC.

Pettigrew, A. and Whipp, R. (1991) *Managing Change for Competitive Success*. Oxford, Blackwell.

Pollert, A. (1988) The flexible firm: Fixation or fact. *Work Employment Society*, 2, no. 3, pp. 281–316.

Poole, M. (1990) Editorial: Human resource management in an international perspective. *International Journal of Human Resource Management*, 1, no. 1, pp. 1–15.

Purcell, J. (1989) The impact of corporate strategy on human resource management. In Storey, J. (ed.), *New Perspectives on Human Resource Management*. London, Routledge, pp. 67–91.

Roberts, J. (1992) Human resource strategies and the management of change. In *B884 Human Resource Strategies, Supplementary Readings Book 1*. Milton Keynes, Open University, pp. 18–38.

Rose, N. (1990) Governing the soul. Paper presented at Conference on the Values of the Enterprise Culture, University of Lancaster, 1989.

Sewell, G. and Wilkinson, B. (1992) Empowerment or emasculation? Shopfloor surveillance in a total quality organisation. In Blyton, P. and Turnbull, P. (eds), *Reassessing Human Resource Management*. London, Sage, pp. 97–115.

Sisson, K. (1989) Personnel management in transition. In Sisson, K. (ed.), *Personnel Management in Britain*. Oxford, Blackwell, pp. 23–54.

Sisson, K. and Sullivan, T. (1987) Management strategy and industrial relations. *Journal of Management Studies*, 24, no. 5.

Storey, J. (1989) Introduction: From personnel management to human resource management. In Storey, J. (ed.), *New Perspectives on Human Resource Management*. London, Routledge, pp. 1–18.

Storey, J. and Sisson, K. (1993) *Managing human resources and industrial relations*. Buckingham, Open University Press.

Thurley, K. and Wood, S. (eds) (1983) *Industrial Relations and Management Strategy*. Cambridge, Cambridge University Press.

Thurow, L. (1984) Revitalizing American industry: Managing in a competitive world economy. *Californian Management Review*, 27, no. 1, pp. 9–40.

Townley, B. (1989) Selection, and appraisal. In Storey, J. (ed.), *New Perspectives on Human Resource Management*. London, Routledge, pp. 92–108.

Wilensky, H. (1967) *Organizational Intelligence*. New York, Basic Books.

Index